NORTH CURRY

A Place in History

ANGELA DIX

PHOTOGRAPHS BY JULIAN COMRIE

SKETCHES BY ANTONIA KEITH-WELSH

First published in Great Britain
by Angela E. Dix
Calmady House
North Curry, Taunton
Somerset TA3 6LG

Designed and Typeset by Brian Dix

Cover illustration based on 1782 Day and Masters Map of Somerset
reproduced by courtesy of Somerset Studies Library

Cover design by Short Run Press Limited

Printed and bound in England by
Short Run Press Limited, Bittern Road, Sowton Industrial Estate,
Exeter, Devon EX2 7LW

British Library Cataloguing in Publication Data
A catalogue record for this book is available from the British Library

ISBN-10 0-9531141-1-2
ISBN-13 978-0-9531141-1-5

We have made every effort to verify the accuracy of material in this book and apologise should there be any errors or omissions.

CONTENTS

Colour plates follow pages 72 and 176

FOREWORD

by

Tom Mayberry

County Heritage Officer
Somerset County Council

It is more than one hundred years since H P Olivey published the first detailed history of North Curry. Olivey's pioneering work remains a key source of reference, but recent research has added greatly to our knowledge of this ancient and very special place.

North Curry is fortunate that in Angela Dix there is a historian with the dedication and skill to retell the story of the manor and parish for the 21st century. Drawing on a wide range of published and unpublished evidence, she provides a lively and authoritative account of North Curry from prehistory to modern times, and sets its development in a national context. She has also gathered some excellent illustrations.

For anyone interested in the history of North Curry, and in the complex processes which went to the making of an important Somerset parish, this will be a book with many riches. It deserves to be widely read and consulted.

INTRODUCTION

I came to live in North Curry in 1994 and being new to Somerset sought to learn about the village, the county and my new surroundings from the local history books that were then available. The books written about North Curry by Hugh Olivey in 1901, Daniel Pring in 1930 and Albion Kirke in 1932 had been concerned mainly with the Parish Church and the influence it had on the village. Important as that is, I saw a need for a detailed and more up-to-date look at the evolution of the parish and set about indulging my passion for local history. The plan for a new North Curry history book was born. The pages that follow are the result of many pleasurable hours spent reading, transcribing, listening to and absorbing absolutely anything that offered an insight into the North Curry of the past.

North Curry is a large village with an extensive parish encompassing the hamlets of Wrantage, Knapp, Lillesdon, Newport and Helland. The parish is situated seven miles east of Taunton, the county town of Somerset, and lies on an elevated spur of land between West Sedgemoor and Curry Moor at the southwest edge of the area known as the Somerset Levels.

A settlement in the location of North Curry definitely existed in Saxon times, when it gave its name to the Hundred, and probably for centuries before. We know that it was a royal manor and belonged to the Crown at the time of King Harold, thus falling into the hands of William the Conqueror in 1066. It was administered by the Crown until it became the property of the Bishop of Bath in 1189. It was later settled on the Canons of Wells Cathedral and administered by the Dean and Chapter of Wells until the 19th century. This led to the Church having a great influence on the lives of the inhabitants of the parish. North Curry boasts a magnificent Parish Church which possibly began as a Saxon Minster and was enlarged into a prominent Christian site as time went by. The community evolved within the framework of English customs, law and order. Life in North Curry reflected a pattern that existed in parishes throughout the land.

This book comprises three parts. Part 1 documents the history of North Curry alongside a broad outline of English history from pre–history to the 20th century with an emphasis on the Wessex side of the country and on historic events which have had an impact on the parish of North Curry. This should provide some context for the reader who is less familiar with national history. Inevitably there are some periods of history where little is known about specific events in North Curry, and in including these periods to provide continuity and completeness I seek my readers' tolerance if they sometimes read several pages without a mention of the parish.

Part 2 looks at the life and traditions of the parish. It explores the origins of the place-names and describes the customs and administration of an evolving community together with details of buildings, families, institutions and infrastructure, drawing on many years of detailed research.

Part 3 examines the parish documents, national censuses and maps that have recorded the lives of North Curry inhabitants, and shows how these sources have evolved over the centuries. This material has proved invaluable throughout my research of this book, and I hope awareness of these records, as well as of more modern sources such as the Internet, will encourage others to share my endless journey of discovery.

During the writing of this book many individuals from both within the village and elsewhere have given me a tremendous amount of invaluable assistance and I have recorded my thanks to them in the Acknowledgements section at the back of this book. I would like particularly to thank Tom Mayberry, County Archivist and County Heritage Officer, Somerset County Council, who has not only written the Foreword, but has also supported my efforts over many years with advice and encouragement.

I have been fortunate to secure the services of Julian Comrie who has spent many hours producing most of the photographic work in this book. Through the viewfinder he has skilfully captured a panoply of buildings, scenes and activities in and around North Curry today, as well as sensitively recording many items from the archives. Antonia Keith-Welsh has created the sketches that so aptly set the scene at the commencement of each chapter. I extend my sincerest thanks to both of them for all of their hard work and dedication.

Finally I would like to thank my daughter Virginia for her expert editing skills and my husband Brian who has provided vital encouragement at times when I thought this work would never be completed. Brian has also helped with the intricate business of editing, formatting, typesetting and moulding the text and graphics into their final shape. His patience and support have ensured that after ten years I have been able to realise my aspirations for this book.

Angela Dix

North Curry
October 2006

PART 1 – NORTH CURRY THROUGH THE AGES

1 - 1

PREHISTORY OF THE ENVIRONS OF NORTH CURRY

The ancient County of Somersetshire, one of the largest in England, covers more than a million acres. It lies between the Bristol Channel and the counties of Devon, Dorset, Wiltshire and Gloucestershire, and can be divided into five regions: (i) Highland Somerset in the west stretching across the moorlands of Exmoor; (ii) the eastern and southern border characterised by fertile green lands; (iii) the uplands and rocky valleys of the Cheddar region rising to a plateau in the north and east; (iv) the coastal plain along the River Severn divided again by higher ground; and finally (v) the Somerset Levels and Moors at the heart of the county, a low flat land of green meadows, watery rhines, peatfields, stubbly willows and grazing cows.

The Somerset Levels and Moors are flanked by rims of hills that today we call the Quantocks to the west, the Mendips to the north and east, and the Blackdowns and North Dorset downlands to the south. These uplands form a horseshoe shape and enclose a basin comprising a low flat landscape of wet moors interrupted by small hills and ridges which form islands surrounded by a pattern of small fields, ditches and rhines. The entire area is intersected by rivers which all flow to the Bristol Channel, with the prominent ridge of rock of the Polden Hills dividing the wetlands in two, King's Sedgemoor and East Sedgemoor to the north, and West Sedgemoor to the south.

These wetlands are among the best examples remaining in the country. In a report from Somerset County Council in 1983 the Somerset Levels and Moors are referred to as the 140,000 acres of the flood plains of the Rivers Axe, Brue, Huntspill, King's Sedgemoor Drain, Parrett and their tributaries. The Levels comprise the five or six-mile-wide coastal clay belt, while the moors are found in the inland river valleys. Each has its own river, separated from the next by clay and limestone ridges.

The rivers Tone, Parrett, Isle, Yeo, Cary, Brue, Axe, Kenn, Banwell and Congresbury Yeo flow across the peat moors, and in places the level of the river beds is nearly equal to that of the surrounding land. A belt of marine clay extends along the coast of the Levels just above sea level and acts as a barrier to the seaward flow of flood water, thus causing flooding on the inland peat moors. As the tide penetrates the river estuaries water accumulates behind the coastal clay belt and today flooding is controlled by tidal doors preventing the tide from flowing inland. However the rivers Parrett and Tone are tidal and at times of excessive rainfall the effect of high tides, exacerbated by natural silting, leads to much flooding of the surrounding land.

Various communities that inhabited the region began drainage of waterlogged areas as a result of enclosure and division of land well before the Domesday Survey of 1085, and by the medieval period much land had been reclaimed for agricultural purposes. Today the water is carefully controlled through pumping, but there are times when the land is flooded with water and the scenery becomes reminiscent of the prehistoric marsh.

Imagine this area as it was before the ice sheets of the Northern Hemisphere began to melt 10,000 years ago. Erosion of the Triassic and Jurassic rocks resulted in the formation of a broad valley with an uneven surface flanked by today's hills. As the ice melted, this valley or basin became flooded, and water drained into the Bristol Channel. Following the end of the Ice Age from about 8300BC, this low-lying area was under sea-water for some 2,000 years, the surface broken and separated by narrow limestone ridges, low hills and occasional small islands of rock or sand. North Curry lies slightly to the east of the centre of a ridge, today known as the Curry Ridge, which extends from West Hatch to Athelney. The small rock and sand islands that projected above the water are known today as Brent Knoll, Glastonbury Tor, Burrow Mump, Puriton, Meare, Sowey, Burtle and the Isle of Wedmore.

With much of the Levels waterlogged, the area became an extensive estuary, with salt marsh and widespread mud flats at the seaward end of the valleys. The drowned valley floor was covered in silt and clay, which built up naturally to form a sea barrier, and the development of sand dunes prevented the salt-water penetrating the inland marshes, stopping tidal flooding. Areas of reed fen grew on the valley floors. The sea gradually receded and by about 4500BC the interior was transformed into a huge swamp with reed-fringed edges and with great expanses of open brackish water.

By 3500BC, as the great reed swamp gradually became shallower through the build-up of peat, parts of the Levels became sufficiently dry and firm to support fenland trees such as birch and alder, and many hill slopes became densely wooded. By 3000BC rivers brought enough inland water to create freshwater conditions in the ponded areas. As rainfall increased, fen trees were drowned, initiating the growth of bog moss which provided a raised freshwater bog environment. Generations of plants that did not rot fell into the semi-stagnant surroundings, building up organic matter which became peat. By AD400 climatic conditions had altered, and although the area was prone to flooding, it was less frequent and the formation of peat ceased.

The Romans constructed sea walls, and in the Middle Ages the monks of Glastonbury developed sea defences and drainage to alleviate flooding. Today the flat landscape shows evidence of man's efforts to control water across the peat moors with elevated riverbanks and a pattern of rhines and ditches. There is a distinct difference between the Levels, with an elevation of about 6 metres above sea level contained in a wide clay belt along the coast, and the peat Moors which are lower than the Levels, being only about 3 metres above sea level.

Man first occupied the area when it became a freshwater swamp. As peat formed and gradually accumulated in the swamps and marshes of the Levels, it engulfed and preserved much material belonging to prehistoric man, and provides extensive evidence of his activity and way of life. Modern peat cutting has exposed this evidence and a wealth of material has been preserved in the form of substantial wooden pathways or trackways linking the islands in the Levels where early man built his campsites. We can build a good picture of the development of human life on the Levels from early times by studying artefacts of wood, as well as stone, discarded flint tools, bronze and pottery, together with the environmental evidence from pollen samples, beetles and seeds.

In prehistoric times Great Britain formed part of a large peninsula which stretched out into the Atlantic from the northern shores of France and Belgium. Animals such as bison, mammoth, lemming and reindeer inhabited this peninsula, and among the remains of these creatures flint hunting tools and weapons made by primitive man are occasionally discovered in the drier regions and on the islands in the area. These hunters and gatherers travelled by foot over the hills and islands seeking refuge and making campsites while searching for wild foods, and clothing themselves with the skins of the wild beasts they hunted.

There is evidence of man living in the caves of Wookey Hole and Cheddar and in rock shelters in gorges and cliff faces that are among the earliest homes of prehistoric man in these islands. Flint tools and hand axes of stone have been found in these caves, together with animal bones that show their craftsmanship, artistic skills and industry. These races are given the name Palaeolithic, or Old Stone Age men or cave men.

From about 10000BC when the ice sheets retreated and Britain became separated from the continent by the English Channel, the Mesolithic or Middle Stone culture was born. A superior race of people developed, and to improve their hunting skills, they knapped flints of a better shape and fitted them into handles of wood and bone. They eventually learned to construct log boats or rafts to move across the expanses of water and reed. They fished and hunted game such as deer, wild pig, wild cattle and wildfowl using spears, bows and arrows, traps and snares, made of flint, wood and plant fibres.

During the early period of raised bog formation, prehistoric man continued to occupy many parts of the Levels, and throughout a long sequence of waterlogging and peat formation anything made of wood and used by man that was caught in the vegetation was quickly buried and remained wet thereafter. We therefore have a wealth of archaeological evidence preserved throughout the area. Finds from this period have included a yew mallet and a yew longbow that might have cast an arrow for 100 metres or more. The hunter-gatherer culture had disappeared by 4000BC.

These people were superseded by settlers from Europe who, with their knowledge of the domestication of animals such as sheep and cattle, and with their understanding of cereal cultivation, selected the best land for their crops and pastures and created farming communities. They brought with them domestic animals such as dogs, oxen, pigs and goats and they created tribal centres. They chose areas such as the Somerset Levels and Moors, where they not only could work the land, but also use the hills and marshlands to hunt and fish and gather wild foods. These people are given the name Neolithic men or New Stone Age men, and by 3000BC they became well established. Surviving artefacts demonstrate their skills in weaving, spinning and pottery and show their expertise in excavation, mining and boat-building. They buried their dead with great care, making a chamber of flat stones in which they placed the body. They then built an elliptical covering of earth and stones creating burial places that are known today as long barrows. During this period man began to build the great stone or megalithic monuments, the best known of which is Stonehenge in Wiltshire.

By 2500BC the Bronze Age of nearly 1,500 years was born. From about 2400BC invaders from Europe, called Beaker Folk, descended on our shores. These people were so called because of the pottery drinking vessels that they buried with their dead. They improved the techniques for flint tool and weapon making, and brought skills in metalworking. They made elaborate pottery, cloth and metal objects for ceremonial uses and adornment which they traded extensively. Many bronze artefacts have been discovered in river valleys across Somerset, and recently a local landscape archaeology group found a Bronze Age flint arrowhead and some flint scrapers on Haskey Moor in North Curry giving evidence of at least a hunter being present here during the Bronze Age (see Plate i).

Immigration continued over the next centuries bringing many new ideas, materials and objects of daily use, and by 700BC iron tools and weapons were first seen in Britain, imported by incomers from Europe. Methods of making iron had been in use since 1000BC at Hatstatt (now a site in Austria) and in La Tene in Switzerland. Iron-working began in Britain in 600BC. Iron ore was much more plentiful than copper and because no complicated alloying was necessary, the techniques of iron-making were relatively simple. By 500BC iron made from the raw material on our shores had begun to replace bronze for everyday tools such as ploughshares, bill-hooks and sickles, leading to a more civilised way of life. The Iron Age had arrived.

We are fairly certain that the Iron Age people settled in areas around North Curry, as a local landscape archaeology group has found a number of pieces of Iron Age pottery among field scatter. In 2002 an archaeological dig, undertaken by county archaeologists in the area of the site of Athelney Abbey, uncovered Saxon artefacts including some scythe blades and some evidence of metalworking. Underneath the site further evidence was found of Iron Age metalworking activity.

During the Iron Age, tribes of warlike Celtic conquerors from Europe infiltrated and eventually destroyed the ancient cultures. These people lived in hill-forts such as Ham Hill and South Cadbury and were in possession of iron and bronze metal weapons. They were able to drive out the older race by their strength, numbers and skills and to take possession of districts where game was most plentiful and agriculture was most productive. They cultivated wastelands, drained fens and felled forests, burying their dead in graves covered with a barrow shaped like a cone or bell. During the 1st century BC Britain was settled by the Belgae, people from France and Belgium who introduced a new type of plough pulled by oxen, as well as crop rotation and sheep farming, which resulted in a more efficient system of agriculture within an organised tribal unit. These Iron Age Celtic Britons remained as inhabitants until the Romans found our shores in 55BC.

From c.3500BC to 300BC numerous wooden platforms and hurdle trackways were constructed by man between the islands of drier land and the hills. These provided access across the wet marshland and fen woodland serving as a means of communication between the tribes and facilitating wider hunting areas. The earliest wooden structure found in the peat on the Levels is the early Neolithic *Sweet Track* named after Mr Ray Sweet, a peat-cutter who discovered it in 1970. An excavation revealed a raised trackway lying low down in a ditch that had provided a raised path across a wet reed swamp between patches of firmer ground that ran from the Polden Hills to Westhay. It comprised a long pole of ash, alder, hazel or elm on the marsh surface with pairs of oblique pegs pushed down into the soft surface to either side of the pole, so they crossed over it. The pegs were set every metre and planks were placed on these 'V' formations. Notches were cut on the underside of the planks to lodge them onto a peg and create a plank walkway above the water. A worked flint axe and numerous flint flakes used to cut reeds and wood have been found during the years of excavation. Environmental studies of the track wood, using tree-ring dating techniques, beetle and plant studies, together with the evaluation of other artefacts, suggest the trackway dates from 3800BC.

Among later Neolithic trackways found was one made of hazel hurdles that virtually floated on the surface of soft ground and was constructed in such a way as to spread the top-bearing load. It was used for a trackway across Walton Heath, near Street, and a preserved panel can be seen at the Somerset County Museum. It dates from around 3500BC. Another trackway was built off an island of firm ground at Westhay to give a hard edge from which other trackways radiated. It comprises a platform of brushwood held in place by stakes, and dates from 3000BC.

In 1835 a farmer cutting a rhine found another trackway, and in 1880, C W Dymond, a Fellow of the Society of Antiquaries, was invited to publish a report on it. It had originally been named *The Abbotts Way* based on a story that it had been built to link a Glastonbury Abbey building at Meare with medieval Burtle Priory. However, the trackway was dated from c.2000BC, pre-dating these buildings by 3,500 years. The structure was a wooden trackway made from split alder trees laid side by side which were laid over a raised bog to form a dry route for one and a half miles between the sand island of Burtle and the rock island of Westhay.

In the centuries after 2500BC the great raised bogs of the Levels continued to develop, and to overwhelm and bury the successive attempts by man to build roadways, footpaths and platforms in the marsh. Other trackways found include *The Eclipse Track* dated to about 1800BC forming a path across 1,000 metres of wet marsh. One across Shapwick Heath dated at 900BC and one on Godney Moor dated at 400BC suggest the present-day craft of hurdle making has existed for 5,000 years in Somerset. Another major trackway dating from 1400BC was discovered in the 1930s. It runs from Meare Heath towards Shapwick over a raised bog for a mile and was constructed of oak.

In the 1890s Arthur Bulleid, a doctor, began a search on the Levels for sites similar to the well-known prehistoric Swiss lake villages. In 1892 he discovered two Iron Age farming settlements at Godney near Glastonbury, and at Meare, dating from about 300BC. He was joined in 1904 by Harold St George Gray, Curator of the Somerset Archaeological and Natural History Society's Museum, and together they excavated the sites and published reports in 1911 and 1917.

The two settlements became known as the Lake Villages of Glastonbury and Meare. The Glastonbury settlement of over three acres was situated between Godney and Glastonbury and was built in an area of open water broken by patches of willow, alder and reeds, occupying an artificial island site which used the felled trees as a foundation. Eighty nine mounds or platforms of clay were found, some having outer rings of post holes suggesting walls, each representing sites of dwellings, stables, workshops, cooking shelters or other domestic structures. A wooden palisade of upright logs of alder, birch and oak enclosed the whole, with a causeway leading out from the village, possibly to a landing stage on the River Brue.

The plan of the site at Glastonbury suggested there were five to seven clusters of round thatched wattle and daub huts with one or two rooms having hearths and clay floors. A population of about 100 in individual family groups was housed in the village with paths and open spaces dividing the separate community buildings. The people of the Glastonbury village worked a farming economy with fields growing wheat, barley, rye and vegetables. Cattle, sheep and oxen were kept and the villagers were skilled workers of wood, stone, clay, bronze, wool and glass.

Artefacts of iron that have been found on the Levels have often suffered corrosion, although over 100 recognisable iron objects were discovered within and around both Lake Villages. These included iron weapons, knives, billhooks and saws, and together with the remains of a furnace and crucibles proved that ironworking was carried out from smelting the ores to hafting and sharpening the finished tools. Artefacts made of materials other than iron were also found, such as flint, suggesting there was a flint industry, and local stone in the form of querns, grinders, polishers and hammerstones, indicating that the inhabitants were involved with milling processes. Bone, horn and antler were used for hammers, bridle bits, handles and modelling tools, beads and needles. Many objects made of bronze, tin and glass were also found, mostly used as items for personal adornment. A large number of potsherds were unearthed, as well as glass beads, lead, tin, bronze items and many weaving combs; although very few intact pottery vessels were found.

The site at Meare was excavated over a period of 48 years from 1908 and consisted of two mounded areas situated north of Meare Island on the edge of a raised bog. It was not surrounded by a palisade, and although clay covered mounds were found similar to those at the Glastonbury site, they were not laid on a foundation, but directly onto the wet boggy ground, and little structural evidence of huts remain. This may suggest that Meare was not a farming settlement but a seasonal one, only usable in the summer because of winter flooding, or the site of an annual trading fair. The site was rich in food debris and personal possessions and many artefacts were found, with much evidence of their use and manufacture indicating a centre of production. Bulleid and Gray dated the foundation of Meare at 250BC and its end at AD50 when rising water engulfed it. With the abandonment of the settlements at Glastonbury and Meare, almost certainly due to declining environmental conditions, the evidence for prehistoric occupation of the uneven landscape of the Levels came to an abrupt end after 4,000 years.

There are 94 archaeological sites in the Parish of North Curry according to *The Historic Environment Record (HER) for the County of Somerset* as listed in Appendix 4. These include probable sites of deserted settlements, farms, and wind and corn mills, together with earthworks, cropmarks and sites where flint tools from the Neolithic and Bronze Age periods have been found. They give clear evidence of early human settlement in the Parish of North Curry.

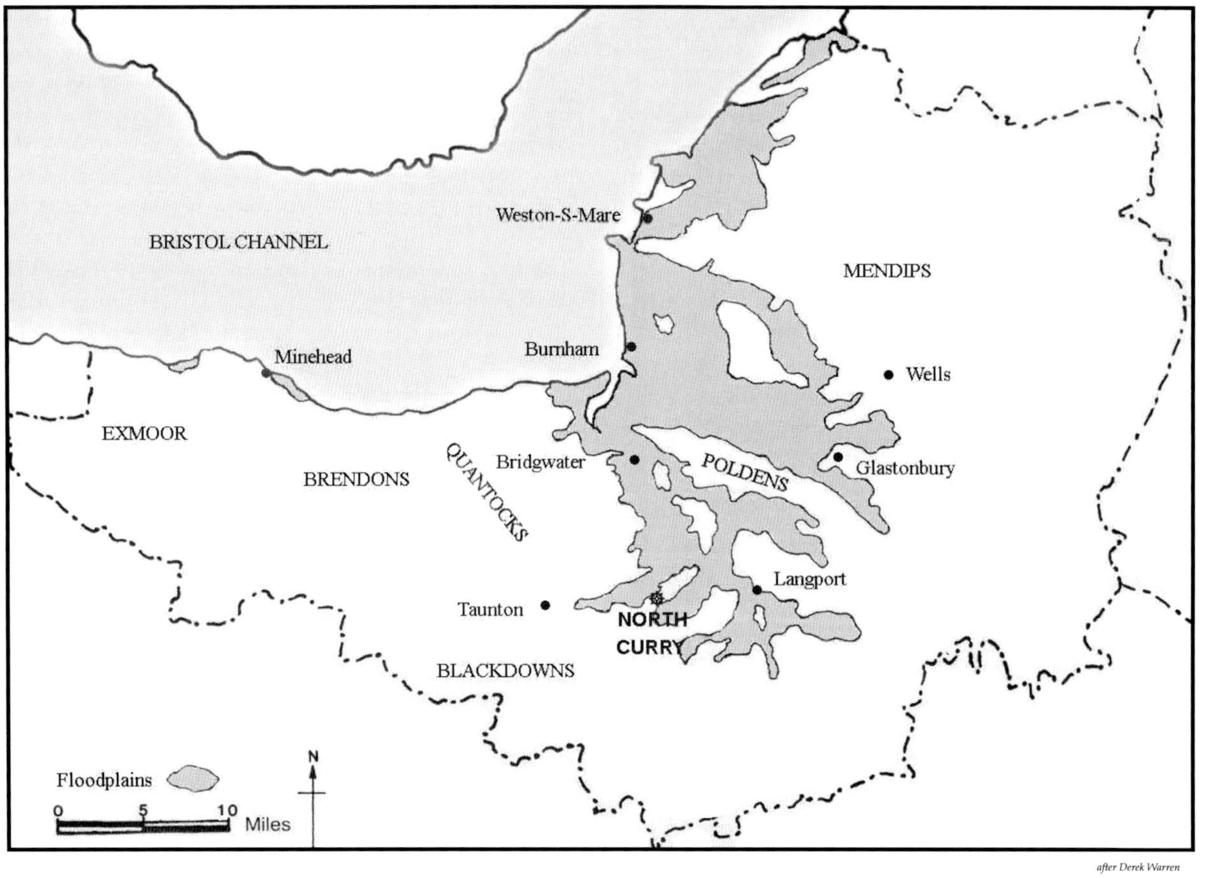

after Derek Warren

FLOODPLAINS OF THE SOMERSET LEVELS

NORTH CURRY TIMELINE – PREHISTORY AND THE ROMANS

Precambrian Age	4,550,000,000BC		Creation of the Earth
		3,500,000,000BC	First life
		250,000,000BC	Dinosaurs and mammals emerge
Lower Paleolithic (Earlier Old Stone Age)	2,000,000-150,000BC	1,000,000BC	First true man *Homo Erectus* migrates through Old World
		700,000BC	Man learns to control and use fire
		200,000BC	Neanderthal man developing into *Homo Sapiens sapiens* emerges in Europe using stone hand axes
Middle Paleolithic Age (Middle Old Stone Age)	150,000-35,000BC	70,000–10,000BC	Last Ice Age
Upper Paleolithic Age (Later Old Stone Age)	35,000-10,000BC	35,000BC	Modern *(Cro-Magnon)* man emerges in Europe using stone, flint and bone tools
		20,000BC	Invention of needle makes sewing possible. Cave painting
Mesolithic Age (Middle Stone Age)	10,000-8,500BC	10,000BC	Bow and arrow invented in Europe
Neolithic Age (New Stone Age)	8,500-2,500BC	8,000BC	Hunter culture emerges using worked flint tools and bone spearheads.
		7,000BC	Cheddar Man
		6,500BC	English Channel formed
		6,000BC	First agriculturists arrived from Europe
		3,800BC	Sweet Track and various tools and artefacts found on Levels
		3,700–2,500BC	Burial of dead in barrows
		3,300–2,670BC	Stone circles with monoliths
		3,300BC	First pottery
		3,000BC	Domestication of animals. Weaving, pottery and boatbuilding
		2,950BC-2,000BC	Stonehenge evolved
Bronze Age	2,500-1,000BC	2,400BC	Beaker Folk migrated from Europe
		2,000BC	Bronze made from copper alloyed with tin in use
			Discovery of flint tools gives evidence of human occupation in North Curry
Iron Age	1,000BC	700BC	Carts and chariots made of wood with metal fittings
		600BC	Iron working began in Britain
		300BC	Glastonbury Lake Village
		250BC	Meare Lake Village
		100BC	First coins struck in Britain
Roman Invasion of Britain	AD43		Roman coins found in Lillesdon in 1748 show Roman activity in area
		AD49	Fosse Way constructed, Moredon could have been a Roman hill fort
		AD122	Hadrian's Wall construction began
		c.AD314	St Curig possibly journeyed from Wales
		AD410	Romans abandoned Britain
		AD450	Legendary King Arthur

Note: Some early dates vary considerably from one source to the next and should not be interpreted precisely

1 - 2

THE ROMAN OCCUPATION AND THE BEGINNINGS OF CHRISTIANITY IN SOMERSET

In 55BC Julius Caesar was the first Roman to send forces to Britain. His numerous attempts at invasion were hindered by storms, which damaged his shipping at the beachheads, and by the defence of the Britons in their war-chariots. The Emperor Claudius undertook the true conquest of Britain in AD43 and Britain continued to be occupied by the Romans until AD410, becoming a province of the Roman Empire.

In southern England the Romans generally found a heavily populated landscape of productive pastures and meadows. However the land in the area now known as Somerset, including the Levels and the higher areas of Exmoor and the Quantocks, was encumbered with forests, moors and marshes. Towns were nothing but huts surrounded by stockaded earthworks in forest clearings, and tribes were occupied in perpetual warfare against each other. The religion of the Britons, which had been adopted by the continental Celts, was Druidism. The Dubunni tribe controlled north Somerset and the Dumnonii tribe occupied the west with an eastern boundary that was probably the River Parrett. South Somerset and the Levels was Durotrigan territory. Because of the adverse environmental conditions and changing sea levels, Roman settlement avoided much of the Somerset Levels and used only existing early British occupation sites on the surrounding uplands, conquering the Britons' hill fortresses at Ham Hill, Cadbury Hill, Solsbury and Dolebury.

The Romans brought many new ideas. They introduced a road system that linked the whole country, and by AD49 the Fosse Way had been constructed as a military road connecting a series of forts. Forts certainly existed at Ilchester and possibly at Shepton Mallet, and they are also believed to have existed beyond the Fosse Way at Ham Hill, South Cadbury, Charterhouse and Wiveliscombe. Two routes across the Levels linked to the Fosse Way, which was an important route that ran along the eastern upland edge of the area between Bath and Ilchester. One was the ridge road along the Polden Hills linking the Roman ports of Combwich and Crandon Bridge. This road also served as a supply route for timber to serve the elaborate house heating systems for the numerous villas the Romans were erecting in stone and brick, some built as near North Curry as Langport, and to serve the many farmsteads and large settlements all over Somerset.

If the theory of the establishment of an Iron Age settlement in North Curry is correct, one could assume that the Romans would also have subsequently occupied it after their invasion. The Romans, intent on building roads and forts quickly to establish their superiority, would probably have found the prominent position of the North Curry Ridge attractive.

The other road across the Levels served large scale industry, which included the mining of silver and lead around Charterhouse on the Mendips and pottery manufacture at Shepton Mallet. The extraction of sea salt near the village of Burtle was also an important industry. There was a Roman camp on Brent Knoll, a spot chosen by them to oversee the comings and goings of the local inhabitants as they went into the depths of the marshes. There is evidence of Romano-British settlement on the drier ground and on the raised coastal clay belt. The Romans possessed drainage skills and it is possible they built the first sea defences and drained the marsh by the coast. The River Parrett was well used as a means of transportation to the sea and many places along the river became ports and staging posts.

For nearly four centuries Roman rule continued in Britain and their regime was generally advantageous; a certain level of peace and justice was established among the people, compelling quarrelling tribes to settle their differences in law courts. The Romans changed the face of the country, building roads, bridges and fords across previously impassable terrain, enabling access between towns throughout the year and easing the movement of military troops to garrison their conquered territory.

The Romans spread themselves over vast areas. Numerous artefacts have been uncovered in Somerset, including coins, pottery and evidence of Roman buildings and pavements. From time to time evidence is uncovered suggesting the Romans may have occupied areas in the present Parish of North Curry. A hoard of Roman coins and other objects have been found. The Roman coins were found under a hedge in a field in Lillesdon (see Plate i).

In 1748 it was recorded in *The Gentleman's Magazine*, Volume xviii, page 405, as follows:

> *At North Curry, near Taunton, Somersetshire, July 12, 1748, there was ploughed up, in a field where a hedge had stood, an urn, in which were contained several silver Roman coins, viz., of Gratianus, Velentiniaunus, Valeus, Theodosius, Honorius, Arcadius, Constantinus, Constans, Julianus, Mag. Maximus, and many other. They are all of the same size, excepting one of Gratianus, with the inscription: D.N. GRATIANUS.P.F.AUG. and, on the reverse, a sort of an angel standing with one of his feet on a globe, with a shield in his hands; in which are these words, VOT.V.MUL.X. and in the round, VICTORIA AUGUSTOPRUM, and in the bottom, S.M.T.R. This piece is three times as large as any of the others, and weighs very near a shilling. There have been found about 150 of the smaller pieces, and the greatest part of them are now in the possession of the Rev. Mr. Woodforde, vicar of North Curry above mentioned.*

In 1906 Woodforde's great granddaughter, Miss Mary Woodforde, donated eight of these Roman silver coins to the Somerset County Museum (formerly Taunton Castle Museum), where they remain today. Whether they had been hidden or lost on their way to pay garrisoned Roman soldiers at a fort or defensive earthwork at nearby Moredon, in North Curry we shall never know.

It has been suggested that a road might have linked the River Axe in Devon to the estuary of the Rivers Tone and Parrett in Somerset. The strategic importance of this route would have required a fort at the western end at Seaton in Devon and another at the eastern end sited on the high ground by the water's edge. A beach of shells was discovered in 1890 during digging operations at the foot of a slope near the site where the house named Moredon stands today, which could well have been the site of the eastern fort or defensive earthwork. It would have afforded a splendid lookout position and the waters of the salt marsh would almost certainly have lapped the bottom of the ridge where North Curry now stands. *Moridunum* is the Romano-British word for fort by the sea (*mor* and *mare* - the sea, and *dun* - camp or fort). The old field-name given to a field just below Moredon was Casters or Castor Mead. This can be translated from the Latin word *castra* meaning a Roman castle fort and *mæd/mede* an Old English word meaning meadow. Therefore Moredon could be termed a fortified place by the sea.

The road that runs along the base of the Moredon ridge with a ditch running adjacent to it is still called The Fosse. A translation of the Romano-British word *fosse* is ditch. A local landscape archaeology group has recently found numerous pieces of pottery dating from the Roman period during fieldwalking activities in fields on a slope below the Moredon site. On the strength of this evidence we are fairly sure that the Romans occupied sites near to the village of North Curry.

The decline of Roman power necessitated the withdrawal of their troops from Britain in about AD410 to defend their Empire elsewhere. Britons were left to defend themselves against attack, not only from Europe across the English Channel and North Sea, but also from the Picts and Scots in the north and from the Irish in the west. Britain reverted to the tribal divisions and petty kingdoms that existed prior to the Roman invasion, engaging once again in fighting each other. The Celtic Britons comprised many races that had come from all over Europe and Asia and their religion was of pagan worship. The gods Woden and Thor were the common gods most of these Celtic Britons worshipped. Whilst Britain was occupied by the Romans, temples and shrines were erected in their settlements to enable individual legionaries to worship their pagan gods. Christianity was frowned upon by the imperial Roman authority in Britain and many Christians were persecuted.

However, there were Christians among the Roman army that occupied Britain and eventually, whether by the influence of these individuals or by missionaries of the Christian faith from other lands, Christianity struck its roots into British soil. In about AD200 Origen the Alexandrian, who was one of the Fathers of the Church, stated that the Christian faith had reached the shores of Britain. Evidence for the Christian presence is sparse, but several accounts confirm the martyrdom at Verulamium of St Alban, a former Roman soldier who perished for sheltering a fugitive priest.

Important clues to this period are to be found in *The Historia Ecclesiastica Gentis Anglorum* by the Venerable Bede (c.AD673-735) sometimes known as *the father of English history* and also in the *Anglo-Saxon Chronicle.* The Edict of the Christian Emperor Constantine in AD313 raised Christianity to be one of the tolerated cults, and in AD391 Theodosius the Great declared it to be the sole religion of the Empire of Rome. The Celtic Church in Britain was thus able to spread the Christian word by using the improved methods of communication left by the Romans. In c.AD400 Ninian converted southern Britain to Christianity, and in AD565 Columba converted many other tribes including the Picts, who had sheltered from the Roman Conquest behind the highlands of Scotland.

In AD314 three British bishops represented the British Church at the Gallic Council of Arles. St David of Menevia, whose memory is preserved at Barton St David, Dubritius of Caerleon, commemorated at Porlock, who crowned the legendary King Arthur, and Cyrig, Bishop of Llanbadarn, whose name is associated with several places in Somerset. Indeed, the name of North Curry is associated with this Celtic saint, and it has been debated over many years that St Curig may have journeyed across the Somerset Levels from Wales in a small boat, establishing a place of worship (see page 76).

During the centuries between the Roman occupation and the Saxon Conquest the Celtic Christian Church was the influence for law and order throughout the district. Many Celtic saints' names are still incorporated into numerous place-names in Somerset. The Reverend D J Pring, Vicar of North Curry in the early-20th century, studied early Christianity in Somerset and concluded that many hills, rivers, localities and settlements of the inhabitants were placed under the protection of these Celtic leaders of religious life. For example, the Brendon Hills are linked to St Brandon and the Quantock Hills to St Crantog or St Cwantog. Pring maintains that St Padernus is the tutelary saint of the River Parrett, and is also associated with the name Petherton, and that the River Culm which rises in Somerset derives its name from St Columba. The River Tone, anciently the Tain, and the ancient marsh of Stanmoor are derived from the Celtic saint St Tangwyn, and many churches are dedicated to other early saints such as St Julian at Wellow, St Vigor at Stratton on the Fosse, St Pancratius at Bagborough, St Romanus at Rumwell, and St Laurentius at Lydeard St Lawrence.

The memory of St Bridgit is preserved in many local place-names such as Highbridge where the first part is derived from the Old English *heah* meaning bright, glorious or noble. Another is Axbridge which Pring maintains represents St Bridgit's oak from the Old English *aec* for oak tree. It was customary for worshippers to gather for worship beneath a sacred tree. Pring maintains that the ancient form of Bristol was *Bridgetstowe*, which was later shortened to *Bristowe*. He quotes from the Place-name Society's vocabulary that *stow* usually denotes *land dedicated to some saint or sacred enclosure*. His theory also is that the harbour with its small community at the mouth of the Parrett River was placed under the tutelage of St Bridgit and became known as Bridgwater.

Later dictionaries of place-names do not agree with Reverend Pring's theories. For example *The Cambridge Dictionary of English Place-names* edited by Victor Watts derives both Bristol and Bridgwater names from bridge crossings not Bridgit. Hence Bristol is allegedly derived from *brycgstowe* or *assembly place by the bridge* from the *Anglo-Saxon Chronicle*, and Bridgwater from *brugie* or *bridge belonging to Walter of Douai* from the *Domesday Survey* (1086).

Glastonbury, which is only 18 miles from North Curry, became a shrine for Celtic Christians and the focus of spiritual life. Legend has ascribed its foundation to Joseph of Arimathæa, and pilgrims to this consecrated place, dedicated to the worship of Christ, came frequently from all over the West Country and further afield. St Patrick, who was a Catholic Christian born before the end of the 4th century and who became known as *The Apostle of Ireland* between AD432 and AD461, was the outstanding figure in the Celtic Church during this period. He was the son of a Christian priest and was given the Roman name Patricius Calpurnius. He was captured by Irish raiders from his father's house in Wales and sold as a slave, but his faith prevailed and he became the evangelist of the Irish people. He returned to England and retired to Glastonbury where he died at the age of 100. A Benedictine Abbey was founded there to honour him.

In AD565 Pope Gregory sent Augustine with 40 monks to preach to the Britons. He was responsible for converting to Christianity the Saxon King Athelbert of Kent, who later became overlord of the whole of southern England. In AD597 Augustine became the first of a long line of Archbishops of Canterbury, firmly establishing the place of the Christian Church in England.

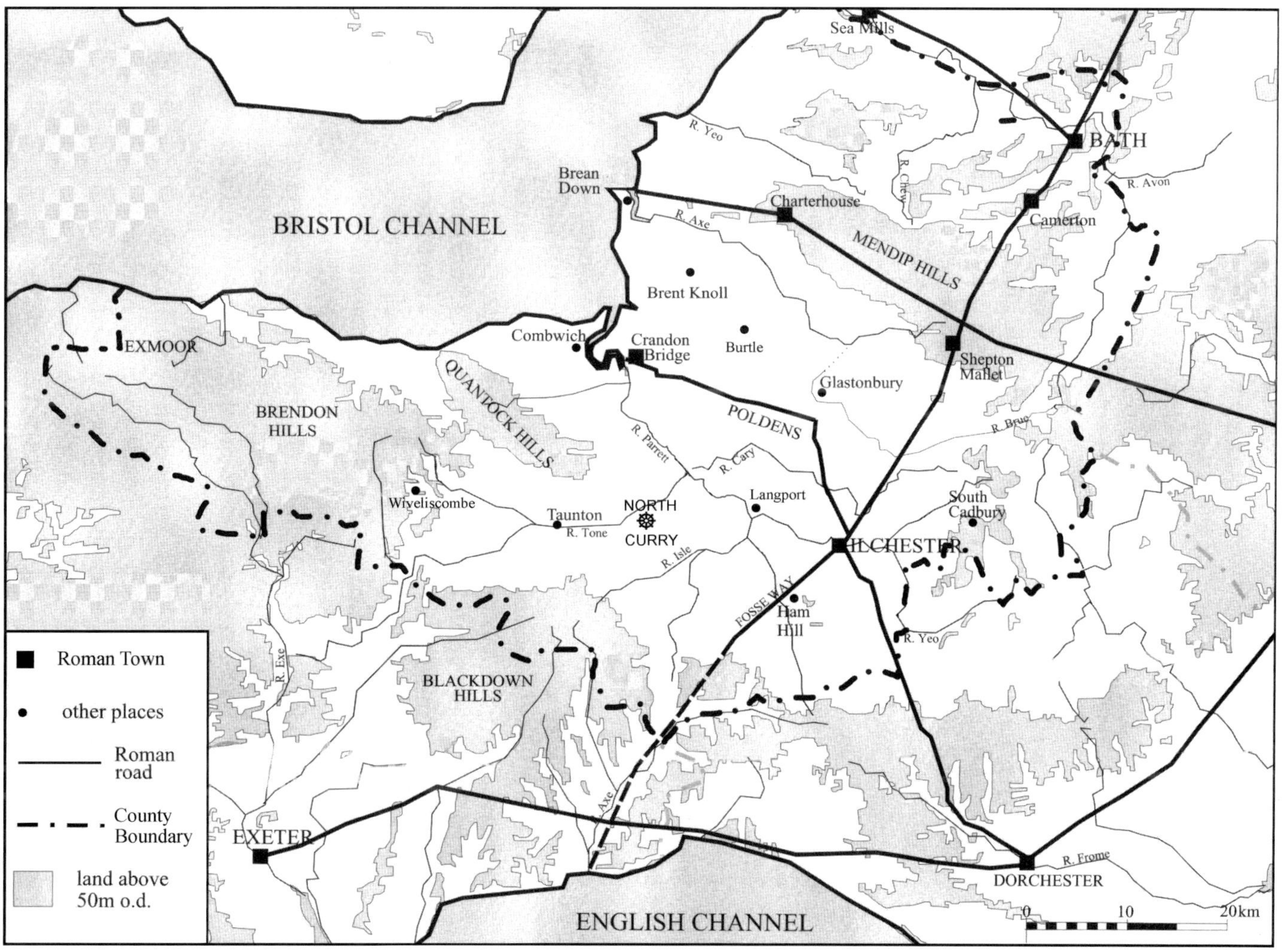

after Peter Leach 2001

SOME PRINCIPAL SITES IN ROMAN SOMERSET

1 - 3

SAXON WESSEX

After the departure of the Roman armies early in the 5th century the south-west peninsula of England remained in the hands of the Britons. Some British families had crossed the channel to the safer lands of Brittany. A governing body settled in the Kingdom of Dumnonia which encompassed Devon, Cornwall and a part of Somerset around Glastonbury, but parts of Somerset including the south suffered decline from Roman standards with towns, roads and villas becoming neglected. Legend takes the place of history in the story of King Arthur, the leader of the British army who, using his Roman-trained cavalry, held off attacks from barbarian invaders. His name is linked to South Cadbury, which is widely claimed to be the Camelot of Arthurian legend, and to Glastonbury Tor, his legendary burial place, which is known as the Isle of Avalon. He was said to have fought to preserve the heritage of Rome in Britain.

In AD495 the West Saxons, a hostile Germanic race opposed to Roman civilisation, landed on the south coast of England. Cerdic (or Cherdic) led this invasion, and proceeded to settle his followers in Dorset, parts of Hampshire and South Somerset. Wessex was ultimately to embrace the modern counties of Somerset, Dorset, Wiltshire, Hampshire and parts of Berkshire. The town of Chard takes its name from Cerdic, as does Chardstock, Charmouth and Charcombe now Chaffcombe. In about AD530 Cerdic founded the royal line of Wessex. During this period until AD700, often termed the Dark Ages, the area became dominated by these invaders, and during the 7th century the Saxons advanced into Somerset, occupying hilltop sites such as South Cadbury and Glastonbury Tor, with Somerset becoming one of the shires of the West Saxon kingdom. The Britons fought and won the battle of *Llongborth*, believed to be Langport, and the Saxons were unable to penetrate any deeper into West Somerset than the line of the River Parrett. The River Parrett has been the limit and boundary of hostile advances in many periods of history.

Other invasions into England continued, not only from the Saxons, but also from Angles, Jutes and Frisians from Germany, Denmark and the Rhine delta of the Netherlands. These savage fair, blue-eyed raiders spread terror and formed a hostile culture wherever they penetrated, attacking, overthrowing, plundering, and stealing from the Britons any treasures that remained in the deserted Roman villas and settlements. Celtic groups consisting of Scots, Manx, Irish, Welsh, Cornish and Bretons all undertook warlike incursions into the area known today as England and much fighting ensued. So began the slow Saxon conquest and the occupation of Somerset.

The West Saxons Cuthwine and Caewlin won victories at Dyrham in Gloucestershire and Old Sarum in Wiltshire in AD552 and penetrated further into Somerset taking possession of the Mendip area. In AD635 Cynegils, King of Wessex, converted to Christianity at Dorchester through the teaching of St Augustine and his followers, and in AD650 his son Cenwealh (Cenwalch) founded the Bishopric of Winchester. This encompassed nearly the whole of Wessex, including Hampshire, Wiltshire and Somerset as far as the River Axe.

Cenwealh, who became the next King of Wessex, won a great victory over the British at Peonna (Penselwood) in AD658 and drove the Britons back into Somerset as far as the River Parrett. Cannington (Centwine's tun), Glastonbury and Eastover (near Bridgwater) all fell into Saxon hands. These victories opened the way through forests and marshes leading to some settlement taking place. However, the west Somerset Levels remained untamed and inhospitable to outsiders. The drainage system of the Levels had ceased by then and the land had become waterlogged, with towns being deserted and Roman sites forgotten.

As the Saxons took over other parts of Somerset they brought in thousands of their own countrymen as settlers. The newcomers were forest folk, who built in wood, not stone, and preferred country sites which they cleared and settled, living in their traditional wooden houses. Britons who had survived the early fighting and were accepted by the Saxons remained in some areas. The West Saxon tribe who settled in the Somerset Levels, the sea-moor settlers or people of the summer pastures known as the *somorsoetas*, gave the name Somerset (*Sumer sæta*) to the whole county. The vicinity of North Curry would probably have been chosen because it provided a safe location with good pastures and meadows. Saxon names such as *stanwegg* now Stoneyhead, *oldweg* or Oldway, *greenweg* or Greenway, and Westfield and Layfield derived from the Saxon word *feld* meaning a flat unwooded land, all indicate an early Saxon presence in the area.

The Saxons preferred village life to that of the town. Families settled in hamlets, preserving their own family existence independently of other families or villages. Sites for homes were selected with an adequate water supply and with meadowland and pasture for their cattle. The clearing of scrub, the felling of trees for domestic buildings and the ploughing of land in the valleys for agriculture provided areas of settlement. Cenwealh retained all the land from Somerton to the River Parrett in his own hands as Crown land. He left the Britons to continue their trade and river traffic on condition of payment of royal dues to himself.

The territory of West Somerset did not become Saxon until King Ine defeated the British King Geraint in AD710. He centred his activities on Somerton and attacked the Britons from the hills of south Somerset descending into the Vale of Taunton. After his victory he founded the town of Taunton and a minster at Wells, and many churches were built in the area with Christian laws being established. His rule provided fair and tolerant treatment of the Christian Britons and the earlier Celtic Christianity survived. He built and dedicated the first Saxon church at Glastonbury in AD704 and after his death a small monastic settlement at Muchelney was established in AD750 as a thanksgiving to Ine's victory over Geraint.

King Ine was responsible for introducing an open field system of co-operative farming for communities. Individuals were allocated equal portions of common pasture and arable land, which they were obliged to fence against stray animals and to cultivate for the good of the whole community. Dues, in the form of payments in kind to the King and court when they journeyed through the area, formed the basis of a tax system, which brought the Britons and Saxons into one people. His laws allowed a social system to evolve with a hierarchical structure affording protection to individuals.

After Ine's death in AD726 Wessex was challenged by other powers and wars continued with other kingdoms. However the greatest threat came from the Vikings, Norsemen from Norway and Denmark, who began infiltrating our shores in AD789, beginning yet another invasion of England. The *Anglo-Saxon Chronicle* records the Danes invading in their thousands, causing devastation by destroying, burning and killing all before them. They used the tidal rivers to penetrate deep into areas of Wessex. The islands of Flat Holm and Steep Holm in the Bristol Channel are identified as bases from which the Danes invaded the Somerset coast in AD877.

In AD871 Alfred, who was only 22 years old, had succeeded to the throne. King Alfred made the Isle of Athelney (*Athelungeig*), known as the *Prince's Island*, the centre of resistance against the Danes. By AD878 the Viking invaders had conquered and overrun most of Wessex leaving Alfred and his army isolated in Athelney. This small area of elevated ground in the marshes near the Rivers Tone and Parrett provided an inaccessible and secure stronghold. Later that year he led his army from Athelney to Selwood where he gathered further men from Somerset, Wiltshire and Hampshire and fought a decisive battle at Edington, 15 miles from the Danish camp at Chippenham. This victory by Alfred against the Danes forced them to agree a peace. The Danish leader Guthrum and 30 others came to meet Alfred peacefully at Aller, near Athelney, where Guthrum was baptised into the Christian faith. A peace treaty was drawn up and signed at Wedmore later in AD878 and the Danes were forced to return north leaving Alfred supreme in the south of the country.

King Alfred, who reigned until AD899, founded a Benedictine Abbey or monastery on the island of Athelney in AD880. This monastery became an important Christian foundation and helped to establish a structured Church organisation with a college of priests spreading the Christian word to the surrounding area. The prominent ridged site of North Curry three miles away would probably have been chosen to establish a small Christian foundation and a small church might have been built. Athelney Abbey was destroyed in 1539 and no traces of it remain above ground, but a small pillar erected in a field in Athelney in 1801 by John Slade, the then owner of the land, marks the site of this monastery.

The following is an account of Athelney from *The Deeds of the Bishops of England (Gesta Pontificum Anglorum)* by William of Malmesbury (1095-1143), translated by David Preest.

> *Athelney is not an island in the sea, but its marshes and spreading stagnant waters make it so inaccessible, that it can only be approached by boat. There is a very large grove of alders there, in which live deer, goats and many beasts of that kind. On the firm ground, which is a bare two acres broad, is the little monastery and the monks' outbuildings. It was built by King Alfred, who once had found a snug hiding place there for a time, when he had been driven out of his lands by the Danes. Soon afterwards he received assurance from St Cuthbert in a dream that he would be restored to his kingdom, and vowed to God that he would build a monastery there. He also built a church. In area it is only small because of the narrowness of the room available, but it was built in a new style. Four posts fixed in the ground, encircled by four apses, support the whole construction. (The style of the church, showing influence of Carolingian France, is an example of Alfred's wide cultural contacts. The community, consisting largely of monks from France after the almost total extinction of English monasteries by the Danes, did not prosper.) The monks there are few in number and poor, but their love of peace and solitude makes them put a high value on their poverty - or make them feel better about it. Their patron is St Aethelwine. As they continually experience his sanctity in the benefits he gives them, they are always praising him and lauding him to the skies. There is a persistent opinion he Aethelwine was the brother of Cenwalh, King of the West Saxons (643-72), and that he increased the greatness of his family by his holy character. Weakness kept him perpetually fettered and imprisoned, but he served God none the less actively. He made a good end, and now he is a ready help in trouble to all who call upon him.*

In the early-15th century a monk of Athelney compiled a cartulary for the abbey, containing copies of charters and other documents which were in the abbey's archives from its beginnings. The cartulary belonged to Sir William Wyndham of Orchard Portman in Somerset, and in 1735 an abbreviated transcript was made of its contents by the anitiquary George Harbin. Sadly the cartulary itself, together with the first part of Harbin's transcript then vanished without trace. Parts two and three survived and a *Calendar* of these was published by the Somerset Record Society in 1899.

However in 1993 the missing first part of Harbin's transcript was found among papers in the Somerset County Record Office in Taunton and contained transcripts of three Anglo-Saxon charters, including a purported foundation charter for the abbey.

Charles Wyndham, son of Sir William Wyndham, moved to Petworth, in Sussex in the late-18th century and it seemed possible the original cartulary might be among his papers, but no evidence appeared in the library catalogues at Petworth. Hopes of finding it there were fading until in June 2001 the archivist looking after the Petworth archives on behalf of the present Lord Egremont, found the original 15th century Athelney cartulary at the back of a dark shelf in the old strong room there. In July 2001 Professor Simon Keynes, head of the Anglo-Saxon, Norse and Celtic department at Cambridge University since 1999, gave a lecture in the church at Stoke St Gregory to commemorate the 200th anniversary of the raising of the Athelney monument. He was able to announce during his lecture the discovery of the long-lost cartulary, which caused great excitement.

The cartulary contains 245 folios written by a single scribe in the early-15th century with some later 15th century additions. The fuller texts of all the documents that are now available for study include the abbey's foundation charter together with a charter of King Edgar dated 962, and show that the monks of Athelney were aware and proud that the history of their abbey stretched back to King Alfred's time in the 9th century.

Alfred was a remarkable scholar and encouraged widespread learning. Evidence suggests his continued presence in the vicinity of Athelney. In 1693 in Newton Park near North Petherton, an Anglo-Saxon jewel, now known as the Alfred Jewel, was discovered (see Plate i). It is about 50 millimetres long and just over 25 millimetres wide with a gold setting holding a quartz crystal, and it depicts a nobleman in coloured enamel carrying two flowers. On its border is the inscription *Aelfred Med Heht Gewyrean - Alfred ordered me to be made*. Study suggests the crystal decoration was a copy of a Roman wall decoration. It is believed its use was as a little pointer or aestal used to follow lines when reading a manuscript. It is now in the Ashmolean Museum in Oxford. King Alfred's was buried in his capital city of Winchester, and is the only English monarch in history to have been known as *the Great*.

Early in the 20th century an ironbound and studded coffer was discovered below the bell pit of the tower in the ringing chamber of the Parish Church of St Peter and St Paul in North Curry. North Curry, being three miles from Athelney, may have been a safe haven for the coffer when Athelney Abbey was destroyed. This coffer is described in detail on page 105.

The 10th century was a period of great reform in the Church, most of the parishes in the country having been established, each with its own place of worship. For the ordinary churches the Saxon system was based on the minster, a central church with a group of resident clergy who served in it, and also in the smaller churches in the villages around, as parish priests. Pitminster, Ilminster, Wells, Bath and Glastonbury were centres of monastic life in Somerset. The whole of Wessex had been within the diocese of Winchester, until in AD705 King Ine divided this area into two. The western part became the seat of a new bishop, Aldhelm of Sherborne. At the time of Edward the Elder in AD909 this diocese was further sub-divided into four bishoprics, one of these being Wells, which included the whole of Somerset. Athelm became the first, and Giso the last, of 14 Saxon Bishops of Wells during a period of 179 years, having their *sees* at Wells, in the Church of St Andrew. These bishops were succeeded in 1088 by John of Tours, a doctor by profession, who decided to transfer the episcopal throne to Bath.

During the two centuries following the reign of Ine the Saxons founded many of the towns and villages in Somerset. At that time the country from the River Parrett to Exmoor, 50 miles long by 20 miles wide, was a continuous forest abounding in game, especially deer. Throughout the Saxon period game, boar flesh and venison formed a major part of the diet. Salt was used to preserve the meat of cattle and sheep, and honey took the place of sugar and was used to make mead. Bread and cakes made of barley and oats, cheese from the milk of sheep and cattle, fish and wildfowl all provided a good, mixed diet. Wool and skins were used for clothing, with the rich being able to buy gold, silver, ivory, silks and gems from travelling merchants.

The country was divided into great earldoms, which included Wessex, Mercia, Northumbria and East Anglia. Surviving charters record the boundaries of these settlement estates, and many of these Saxon shire boundaries coincide with those of our modern parishes. These shires were divided into *hundreds*, and came under the administrative control of the Shire-reeve or Sheriff. The term hundred is thought to have derived from an area of 100 *hides*. The true meaning of the term hide has been the subject of considerable scholarly debate over many years and the explanation which follows is not universally accepted.

A hide or *carucata* was considered to be the amount of land which would support and sustain a peasant family or household and its dependants. The term hide is used throughout the *Domesday Survey* when referring to the measurement of land. It has been frequently interpreted as being a pure measure of land area, and in Somerset was typically regarded as containing 120 'acres', which was not 120 x 4840 square yards, but 120 times the amount of land that a plough team could plough in a single day or the amount of land that a plough team could plough in a year. A *plough* or *caruca* implies a plough team with eight oxen and the plough itself.

However the equivalent rate of 120 acres to the hide was by no means universal, and in practice the hide was an abstract concept representing an area of land which varied greatly from region to region depending on local conditions, and was employed as a unit of tax liability, i.e. effectively the rateable value of land as determined by the government of the day. In North Curry the hide accounted for 170 acres (see page 27), which because of tax-exempt wildernesses and moors, was a lot more than the average of 120 acres in other regions where there might have been mostly good arable land. The word hide from the Old English *hiwisc* has survived locally in the place-name Huish Episcopi.

Within each hundred the maintenance of law and order was placed in the care of small groups of men known as 'tithings' involving ten people who were jointly responsible for the behaviour of individual members. Each man was answerable for the life and conduct of another by a freely given oath or *frankpledge*. A system of fines was introduced for any misdemeanour and, coupled with the severe penances imposed by the Church; day to day life became one of strict social order.

Numerous charters detailing estate boundaries and other written sources exist for the period 700–1066. There were important early Christian foundations at Muchelney, Glastonbury and Wells. From an early period there are likely to have been small villages and fortified sites known as *burhs* or boroughs. The document known as the *Burghal Hidage*, dated AD912, lists boroughs for Somerset at Bath, Watchet, Axbridge, Lyng and Langport. These boroughs were intended as protection against Danish invasions from the sea. Lyng appears to have been a fort while the others were small towns, all fortified by walls. By the late–10th century Lyng appears to have been abandoned. Langport had about 120 acres assigned to it, with a wall and natural boundaries to provide a stronghold in case of attack.

King Alfred's son Edward, known as *Edward the Elder,* succeeded to the throne in AD900. He continued to hold on to the hard won land of Somerset, reconquering northern and eastern lands of the Danelaw. He styled himself *King of the Anglo-Saxons* and with this new royal title he assumed authority over every Englishman in the country, becoming recognised as King not only of Wessex and the south-east but also of East Anglia and Mercia.

A Saxon Charter of AD904 refers to a large royal settlement known as Curig, which has since been identified as North Curry. It states that:

> *Curig (North Curry) in conjunction with land at Stoc (Stoke St Gregory) when Bishop Denewulf cedes certain land to King Eadweard of Wessex and acknowledges his liability to provide the King with attendance, horses and carte when he made his progress to Curig and the King granted the Bishop various liberties to his monastery.*

This subject is explored more fully in Chapter 2-1.

Edward's eldest son, Athelstan, became King in AD925 and by then Somerton had became the chief town and the seat of government in the area. *Longmarket* or Langport became the centre of trade with almost 300 residents, and was granted a licence to mint silver pennies. The penny would buy sufficient wheat to make bread for eight men, fodder for five horses and would also buy a sheep. If a man wanted a smaller coin, he broke the penny into halves or quarters. Trade flourished with markets encouraging smiths, millers, bowyers, furriers, brewers, fishmongers and livestock vendors to sell their wares. In these Anglo-Saxon times each man owed service to, and depended upon, someone of higher status than himself. The peasant looked to his lord for military protection, justice and material help, while in return the lord restricted his freedom and profited from his labour. There developed a system of accepted law and social custom, interpreted by the King's officers, *thegns* or nobles, and religious clerics. Saxon kings were known to have hunted with dogs, hawks and falcons and the moors around North Curry would have afforded rich hunting grounds. The King visited one estate after another, not only for his sport, but to supervise personally the local courts. Each manor was obliged to make their customary payments in kind with enormous feasts, banquets and entertainment being the responsibility of the individual towns and villages.

King Athelstan was the first King to exercise control over all the English. He had extensive political and family connections throughout Europe, and he consolidated the authority of Wessex over other parts of England. Somerset continued to have an important religious influence on the whole country. During the reigns of Kings Edmund, known as *Edmund the Magnificent* (AD939), Eadred (AD946), Eadwig (AD955), and Edgar (AD959), the towns of Cheddar, Somerton, Bath and Glastonbury all had important religious communities or royal palaces. King Edgar's coronation was devised by Dunstan and has been the model of English coronations ever since. Dunstan, born near Glastonbury in AD909, the year when his relative Athelm became the first Bishop of Somerset, became Archbishop of Canterbury in AD960. King Edgar became known as *Edgar the Peaceable* and he was responsible for revising the law of the land (see Chapter 2-2). He died in AD975 and the Crown was worn for only a short time by the young 12-year-old King Edward, named *Edward the Martyr,* who was Edgar's son from his first marriage to Athelfleda. Edward was murdered in AD978, many believed by order of his stepmother, Elfrida, King Edgar's second wife, who wanted the throne for her son Athelred who thus became the next King.

Early in the reign of Athelred II the Danes started to invade the country again. This weak and cowardly King was nicknamed *Athelred the Unready,* and over several years allowed the Danes to overrun the country. Somerset, with the rest of Wessex, once more came under Danish control. Athelred and his second wife Emma, who was the daughter of Richard, Duke of Normandy, fled to France, returning briefly to promise reforms. However he became ill and died in April 1016 at the age of 48, leaving his second son Edmund by his first wife Elgiva to continue the battle against the Danes, until months later he also died, having possibly been murdered. Canute, who was the son of Sweyn, King of Denmark, claimed the English Crown and became King in November 1016. He ruled peaceably, repairing much of the devastation wrought by the Danes. Canute eventually married Emma of Normandy, the widow of Athelred, and they produced a son Harthacanute. Canute died at the age of 40 and after much infighting for the right to the Crown, Harold Harefoot, son of Canute's first marriage to Elfgiva of Northampton, became King Harold I and was crowned in 1037. However he died soon afterwards, possibly as the result of foul play by his successor Harthacanute, Canute's eldest son. In 1040 Harthacanute was crowned King of England, having already been crowned King of Denmark in 1035. In order to defend his kingdom there he raised an excessive tax in England, which caused much rebellion. It is to this period that the legend of Lady Godiva belongs. It is recounted that by riding naked on her horse though the streets of Coventry she persuaded her husband Leofric, Earl of Mercia, to reduce this tax across his domain. King Harthacanute was an unpopular and much hated King. He remained unmarried, and when he died young in 1042 the throne returned to the Saxon line - to Athelred's son, Edward.

Godwin, the powerful Earl of Wessex, who had been instrumental in this king-making process, established large estates in Somerset. The marriage of his daughter Edith to King Edward was intended to consolidate the alliance between the two. He became the power behind the throne and manipulated Edward, who became known as *Edward the Confessor*, because of his weak but kindly religious manner. In 1066 the dying King Edward chose Harold Godwin's son as his heir, and Harold Godwinson became King Harold II the day after the Confessor's death.

There is no conclusive evidence of a settlement in North Curry in these Saxon times; however a Saxon coin of Athelred II (AD978-1016) has been discovered in the churchyard of North Curry Parish Church. This coin, a long cross type penny (1VA Winchester), can be seen in the Somerset County Museum (see Plate i). It is reported that a number of mints in Ilchester and South Cadbury were producing coins during Athelred's reign. It could therefore be assumed there was human activity at a possible settlement site near to the supposed Saxon church in North Curry at that time.

The death of King Edward in January 1066 ended a long line of Saxon kings. He had the oldest pedigree in Europe, being descended from Cerdic, who in AD500 began five centuries of Anglo-Saxon dominance. His memory was to rule English hearts for centuries until people abandoned Edward as the nation's patron saint for the mythical St George. The Anglo-Saxons had conquered the native Celtic-speaking Britons and unified the culture, calling the British lowlands England or *Angla-lond* (Land of the Angles). By the 9th century they called themselves *Angelcynn* or *Angle-kin* and spoke *Englese*, now called Old English, which was the precursor of Modern English.

While Edward was mourned at home, William, who was the bastard son of the Duke of Normandy, made ready for an invasion to claim the throne of England. William believed he had a right to the throne as the nephew of Emma, wife of both Athelred and Canute, and had also unofficially been promised the throne by King Edward.

The Normans were descended from pagan Viking adventurers who had settled in Northern France in AD911, and had evolved into a class of knights and nobles who formed an excellent trained army. William and his Norman army invaded England in September 1066. A bloody battle was fought near Hastings, on the south coast, with King Harold II and his English army. It is said Harold was killed from an arrow through his eye, and William, Duke of Normandy claimed victory. *Edgar Atheling* of the House of Cerdic was elected King by the English but was never crowned, conceding the throne to William who became King of England in December 1066.

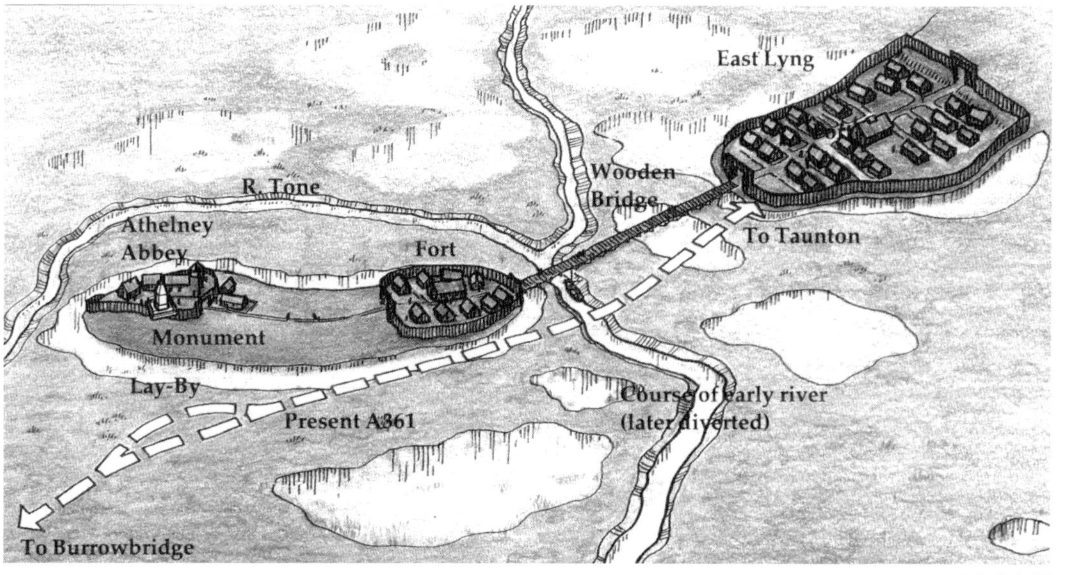

after Ken Fletcher SCC

KING ALFRED'S FORTRESS AT ATHELNEY

REX TEN NORTCVRI HERALD TENVIT

T.R.E. GELDB P.XX.HID:

1 - 4

THE NORMANS AND THE DOMESDAY SURVEY

When William, Duke of Normandy ascended the British throne as William the Conqueror and took possession of all the various estates of England, he reserved the royal demesnes of Edward the Confessor (1042-1066) for his own use. The remainder he distributed to religious foundations and to those whom he favoured. To pay back his loyal supporters William the Conqueror granted the estates of the Anglo-Saxons to his barons, who in turn built their motte and bailey castles on their new manors as powerful symbols of their strength. The leaders and the rank and file of the winning Norman army were the next to benefit from the sharing out of this English land. Of the 180 tenants-in-chief only two were English; of the 1,400 lesser tenants-in-chief only 100 were English; and the 6,000 sub-tenants were mostly English now leasing land which previously they had owned freely.

The Norman Conquest was a brutal and violent takeover which involved the deaths of thousands from war, thousands more from famine and disease and the destruction of villages and towns. When the natives of England did try to resist the Norman advance, which they did in Somerset on the hill of Montacute, the Normans wreaked terrifying revenge by destroying villages and inflicting terrible penalties. The country remained hostile towards the French-speaking Normans for at least 20 years, but gradually as the conquerors integrated into the native society and accepted the English past as their own, Saxon resistance abated.

In many respects the Normans conquered a people more civilised than them. Anglo-Saxon England was Europe's oldest kingdom, and one of the richest. William the Conqueror inherited a unified country with its own coinage, a standardised language and sophisticated systems of government, chancery and law. They inherited the most efficient system of government in Western Europe, which enabled them to accomplish so much so quickly after the invasion.

In 1083-1084 William I revived the *Danegeld* or Army Tax that had been levied since AD991. A survey called the *Gheld Inquest* was made for the purpose of levying a war tax of six shillings on every hide of land. As explained on page 21, the hide was a unit of land measurement of uncertain area used to calculate taxation. The survey contained the earliest records of land tenure and gives the names of the hundreds and parishes into which every county was divided, allowing William to distribute the responsibility of provisioning and maintaining his Norman army among the Saxon landholders according to their previous wealth. The shire and hundred-court system which dealt with law and order and the implementing of fines, already existed in the country. It was organised so that every man should have a lord and was accessible by justice and the taxman. The system provided evidence of how much land the mass of ordinary Englishmen held and the conditions on which they held it. Every village belonged to a hundred whose court met every four weeks, and every hundred to a shire whose court met twice a year. Royal Commissioners took the survey by sworn inquest from a local jury, consisting of a Sheriff, the Lord of each Manor, the Parish Priest, the Reeve of each village and six villagers. This procedure provided a comprehensive framework for the new English feudal structure of landholding in return for allegiance by the people to the King.

In 1086 a more detailed survey of England was commissioned by William I to furnish all manors, all tenants-in-chief and all sub-tenants with a land tax. This was called the *Domesday Survey* and took eight months to complete. This operation instilled such fear in the mainly Anglo-Saxon population that they compared it to the final Day of Judgement which *spared no man, but judged all men indifferently, as the Lord in the great day will do.* The people felt there would be no escape from the answers they gave to the questions in this enquiry, hence the name Domesday. They therefore referred to the resulting written summary as the *Domesday Survey* or *Domesday Book.*

The information was collected at Winchester and copied by one writer into a single volume, the parchment pages showing clear Latin handwriting with red ink markings for the 13,400 individual place-name headings. It was held originally in the King's Treasury at Winchester and was later moved to Westminster where it was kept under lock and three keys in a chest which still survives. It was moved to the Public Record Office in the 19th century.

King William I died in September 1087, and the *Domesday Book* shows signs of having been completed in a hurry. The information from the three eastern counties of Norfolk, Suffolk and Essex was not condensed in the usual way, but was bound together to form a second volume, while that from all the other counties was fitted into volume one. The volume, which covers the survey text of 37 counties, is called *Great Domesday* and the other, which covers only three, but in much greater detail, is called *Little Domesday*. There were two copies made for the south-western counties which included Somerset. The *Exon. Domesday* is one of the early versions of the survey; it is written in Latin - *Exon.* is an abbreviation of the Latin *Exoniensis* (Exeter) - and it contains answers from Somerset, Devon and Cornwall. The other, written in Norman French, is called the *Exchequer Domesday* and is the final version.

The recorded population of Somerset as given in the *Domesday Survey* is 13,764, but the Exeter version gives 13,307. If each person mentioned was the head of a family of four then the estimated population of Somerset was around 70,000.

Many lands in Somerset became the direct property of King William I when he ascended the throne. The most important land was the ancient demesne of the Crown and the land formerly held by Edward the Confessor. This included the 12 manors of Carhampton, Williton, Cannington, North Petherton, South Petherton, Curry Rivel, Frome, Bruton, Somerton, Cheddar, Bedminster and Milbourne. These manors were granted special privileges including the exemption of tax. The royal manors previously held by Earl Harold Godwinson, who became King Harold II, which were forfeited to the Crown on his death, included North Curry, Crewkerne, Congresbury and Dulverton. Other royal estates at Bath, Batheaston, Chewton, Martock, Keynsham and Milverton that had been in the possession of Queen Edith, the wife of Edward the Confessor, also became the property of the King and he became Lord of the Manor of them all. The Church was the other main landowner in Somerset at the time. The principal owners were the Bishop of Wells (Giso of Wells remained Bishop until his death in 1088, being succeeded by John of Tours, who removed his seat or throne to Bath), the Bishop of Winchester and the Abbeys of Bath, Glastonbury, Muchelney and Athelney. Important Saxon nobles held other lands.

At the time of Domesday the population of England was 1.25 million, with the majority of people being *unfree* i.e. being the property of the Lord of the Manor (see Chapter 2–2). Of the rural population who held land on each manor, the 268,984 enumerated in the survey were mostly unnamed. Some 40.6 per cent were *villeins*, 32.4 per cent *bordars* or *cottars* and 10.5 per cent were slaves, with only 13.7 per cent being *freemen*, i.e. men who held land of the Lord of the Manor at a fixed rent. Those who are named in the survey are the members of the ruling class, the nobles, bishops and abbots, and the many ordinary lords of manors who were holding estates in 1086, along with their predecessors who occupied the same positions in 1066. Some 13,418 places are named in the *Domesday Book.*

The *Anglo-Saxon Chronicle* records that in 1085 the King sent men all over England to each shire to find out what land and livestock the King himself owned. They also calculated how much land belonged to his archbishops, bishops, abbots and earls, how much land each man possessed and how much money it was worth, in order to claim a land tax on every hide of land as explained earlier. The survey's function was not to record all the landholdings of the country, but to register all taxable holdings, therefore not all lands or buildings are noted because many, particularly those owned by religious houses, were exempt from taxation.

The following is a translation of the questions posed by the investigators or commissioners making the survey taken from the Record Commission's edition of the *Domesday Book*, London 1816.

> *Inquisitio Eliensis – The Swearing and the Questions*
> *Written here below is an enquiry into lands as the King's barons made it, that is by the oath of the sheriff of the shire and of all the barons and of their Frenchmen of the whole Hundred, of the priest, the reeve, and six villagers of each and every village:*
> *What is the manor called?*
> *Who held it in King Edward's time?*
> *Who holds it now?*
> *How many hides?*
> *How many ploughs in lordship, how many* (belong) *to the men?*
> *How many villagers, how many cottagers, how many slaves?*
> *How many free men, how many sokemen?*
> *How much woodland, how much meadow, how many grazing–lands? How many mills, how many fisheries?*
> *How much has been added or taken away?*
> *How much was it worth altogether and how much now?*
> *How much each free man or sokeman had or has there?*
> *All this in triplicate; that is, in the time of King Edward and when King William gave it and as it is now.*
> *And if more can be had than is had.*

The following is a translation of the entry for North Curry in the *Domesday Survey* taken from the *The Victoria History of the Counties of England – A History of the County of Somerset* – Vol.1 (1906). This translation is a combination of the shorter *Exchequer Domesday* and the fuller *Exon.* text (see Plate x).

> *The King holds NORT CURI*
> *Earl Harold (T.R.E.or Tempore Regis Edwardi) held it, and paid geld for 20 hides.*
> *There is land for 40 ploughs.*
> *Of this there are in demesne 5 hides, where (are) 5 ploughs and 18 serfs and 23 coliberts, and (there are) 100 villeins less 5 and 15 bordars with 30 ploughs and 11 hides.*
> *There are 1 riding–horse and 20 beasts and 20 swine and 100 sheep.*
> *There are 60 acres of meadow, 50 acres of woodland.*
> *Pasture 2 leagues long and 1 league broad.*
> *To this manor belong 5 burgesses in Langporth (Langport) paying 38 pence and 18 serfs and 4 swine–herds and 2 cottars.*
> *The whole manor pays 23 pounds of white silver and when William received as much.*
> *There is a fishery, which does not belong to the feorm and 7 acres of vineyard.*
> *Bishop Maurice holds the church of this manor with 3 hides of same land.*
> *He has 7 villeins and 11 bordars and 2 serfs with 4 ploughs and 18 acres of meadow and 5 acres of pasture and 12 acres of woodland.*
> *It pays 60 shillings.*
> *Of the same land in this manor Ansger Brito holds 1 hide of the Count of Mortain.*
> *It is worth 20 shillings.*

A modern interpretation of the above to correspond with the known land acreages in North Curry at the beginning of the 20th century follows:

> *King William I holds the Manor of North Curry*
> *The Earl of Wessex (later King Harold II), held it before 1066 in King Edward the Confessor's time.*
> *It paid tax for 20 hides.*
> *There is arable land for 40 ploughs or 4,800 acres.*
> *Of this, 5 hides with 5 ploughs or 600 arable acres belong to the Lord of the Manor (the King's demesne) who has 18 slaves and 23 coliberts.*
> *There are 95 villeins and 15 bordars who work 30 ploughs or 3,600 arable acres and have 11 hides.*
> *There is 1 riding horse, 20 cattle, 20 pigs, and 100 sheep.*

There are 60 acres of meadow and 50 acres of woodland, and 2,885 acres of pasture.
There are 5 burgesses based in Langport who belong to North Curry manor who pay 38 pence, with 18 slaves, 4 pigmen and 2 cottars.
The whole manor pays 23 pounds of white silver when King William acquired it.
(240 pennies could be minted from a pound weight of silver).
There is a fishery that pays no tax.
There is a vineyard of 7 acres.
Bishop Maurice (Bishop of London 1085–1107) holds the church in North Curry with 3 hides. He has 7 villeins, 11 bordars and 2 slaves who work 4 ploughs or 480 arable acres and 18 acres of meadow, 5 acres of pasture and 12 acres of woodland.
This area pays 60 shillings in tax.
Ansger the Breton holds 1 hide of land in this manor from the Count of Mortain. It is valued at 20 shillings. (It has been suggested this hide was the land of West Hatch that the King gave as a holding to his half brother, the Count of Mortain, as a reward for his allegiance and he became tenant-in-chief of the land, and sub let it to Ansger.)

There were 4,800 acres of arable, 62 acres of woodland, 78 acres of meadowland and 2,885 acres of pasture, together with a fishery and seven acres of vineyard, which was a considerable area cultivated for that purpose in this country at the time. As stated on page 21, the hide varied greatly from region to region, this depending on the local convention of calculation, local economic conditions and the quality of soil. In Somerset the hide or carucate has been interpreted as being the equivalent to an average of 120 acres, the figure used in the above interpretation. In 1900 the acreage in North Curry was estimated as 11,027 acres but in the *Domesday Survey* it was stated as 7,832 acres (65 hides) which clearly demonstrates the inaccuracy of the 120 acres per hide figure, the correct figure being around 170 acres per hide. This difference is probably accounted for by the wastelands not being measured. However tax was only paid for 20 hides which might suggest that royal lands were allowed discounts on the hidal taxation or hideage. The recorded labouring population entry in the *Domesday Survey* for North Curry was 195 males. If it is supposed each person was the head of a household of four or five people then it would appear that about 1,000 people were living in the Manor of North Curry in 1085.

The following words were used to describe persons, land measurements and terms in the *Domesday Survey* and are explained in the Glossary:

Acre, Bordar, Burgess, Carucate, Chain, Colibert, Cottar, Demesne, Feorm, Franklin, Freeman, Furlong, Hide, Ploughland, Serf, Slave, Sokeman, Thegn, Villein, Virgate.

Written evidence up until this time had given no indication that North Curry had played any significant part in the rich pattern of England's history. However, by the time of the Norman invasion North Curry appears to have been established as an important centre, and, as the *Domesday Survey* indicates, it featured as a prominent place in Somerset. As this Norman manor developed and the feudal community grew, a village evolved to serve the needs of the different levels of society. Earlier the name North Curry or *Nort Chori* was given to the hundred wherein it was placed in Somerset and comprised the parishes of North Curry, Stoke St Gregory, West Hatch, Thornfalcon and Thurlbeer. In the Domesday Survey the manor is described only as embracing North Curry, Stoke St Gregory and West Hatch.

During these times the Normans began to build or rebuild castles, monasteries, cathedrals, churches, halls and manor houses. In the *Domesday Survey* Dunster and Montacute were mentioned in Somerset, but others were soon built to serve as strongholds against attack. The Normans in North Curry chose to erect a church on the ridge site where the Parish Church stands today, and this would have become the focal point of the settlement. The Parish Church of St Peter and St Paul is one of the few churches in Somerset that shows evidence of Norman architecture in the form of round-headed arches. Details of this evidence are explored on page 101.

The *Domesday Survey* entry of Bishop Maurice, a high-ranking Norman government official holding the church in the royal Manor of *Nort Curi*, endorses the hypothesis that North Curry Parish Church was originally a Christian foundation chapel in this royal village. This may have prompted the Normans to allow the church to undergo a certain amount of remodelling from a Saxon to a more substantial Norman stone building.

William II succeeded his father and became known as *William the Red* or *William Rufus.* He inherited an England governed by feudal laws, with dissatisfaction amongst the greater barons who owned properties on both sides of the English Channel. They owed feudal allegiance to two sovereigns, and William witnessed much rebellion from all sides. He was mysteriously shot through the head while hunting in the New Forest, and in 1100 William's brother, youngest of the Conqueror's sons, became King Henry I. The new King Henry was well educated and became known as *Henry Beauclerc* meaning fine scholar, promising the English an improved justice system. This required the Hundred Courts to try offences, rather than the courts of the manors which were presided over by Norman lords.

King Henry I, a good man who was held in great awe, reigned for 35 years, 29 of them in Normandy. In 1100, just before his coronation, he married Matilda, the grand-daughter of Edmund II Ironside, the son of Athelred the Unready. A son William and a daughter Adelaide were born, but in 1120 his son was drowned in the *White Ship* disaster during a voyage across the Channel when the crew were allegedly drunk. A dynastic crisis ensued with no male heir to the throne, although Henry had illegitimately fathered some 20 children. Queen Matilda had died in 1118 and Henry quickly made a marriage of convenience to Adeliza of Louvain, but the marriage was childless. He promised the succession of the Crown to his daughter Adelaide who had adopted the name Matilda on her marriage to Heinrich V, the Emperor of Germany. Heinrich V died and in 1127 she married Geoffrey of

Anjou, but quarrelling ensued between Henry and the Norman barons on the one side and his daughter and her husband on the other. However, when Henry I died in 1135, his nephew Stephen of Blois, a grandson of William the Conqueror, persuaded the Church to make him King. Civil war erupted and Matilda tried to gain the throne and win support from the Church, but Stephen overcame this challenge to his authority. However, in return for life possession of the throne, Stephen was persuaded to adopt Matilda's son Henry as his own son and therefore heir to the throne. Henry's father had been the Count of Anjou, and his emblem had been the *Planta Genesta* or the broom. On the death of King Stephen in 1154, his adopted son Henry was crowned Henry II of England and later became known as *Henry Planta Genesta* or *Henry Plantagenet*.

after E Sprankling

NORMAN DOORWAY TO NORTH CURRY PARISH CHURCH

NORTH CURRY TIMELINE – SAXONS AND NORMANS

West Saxon (Germanic) invasion	495		West Saxon settlement in parts of Somerset
Cerdic	519–54	530	Cerdic founded the royal line of Wessex
Cuthwine, Caewlin	554–611		Further Somerset occupation
Cynigils	611–643	635	Converts to Christianity
Cenwealh	643–672	650	Bishopric of Winchester founded, which encompassed whole of Wessex
Cuthred, Seaxburh, Aescwine, Centwine, Caedwalla	672–688		Further Somerset occupation
Ine	688–726	704	Church at Glastonbury built
		705	Wessex divided into two dioceses – Winchester and Sherborne
		710	Defeat of Geraint and Taunton founded
Athelheard, Cuthred, Sigebert, Cynewulf	726–786	750	Monastic settlement at Muchelney established
Beorhtric	786–802	789	Vikings invade parts of England
Egbert	802–839		Beginnings of a united England
Athelwolf, Athelbald, Athelbert, Athelred I	839–871	854	Saxon Charter granted to *Curig* – North Curry became a royal manor
Alfred the Great	871–899	877	Alfred makes Athelney his base. Vikings invade Somerset coast
		878	Vikings defeated and peace treaty signed at Wedmore
		880	Athelney Abbey founded
			Church possibly built on the site of the Parish Church in North Curry
Edward the Elder (King of the Anglo-Saxons)	899–925	904	Charter refers to royal settlement at *Curig*
		909	Diocese of Sherborne divided. Wells became separate bishopric
Athelstan	925–939		Kingdom of England established
Edmund I, Eadred, Eadwig, Edgar, Edward	939–978		Cheddar, Somerton, Bath and Glastonbury became important centres
		973	Coronation of Edgar devised by Dunstan at Bath Abbey
Athelred II (the Unready)	978–1013		Coin found in North Curry churchyard in 20th century
Sweyn of Denmark	1013–1014		Danes overrun country and Wessex returns to Danish rule
Athelred II (the Unready)	1014–1016		Returns as King to rule conditionally
Edmund II (Ironside)	1016		Canute, son of Sweyn, defeats Edmund
Canute	1016–1035	1017	Marries Emma, widow of Athelred
Harold I (Harefoot)	1035–1040		Regent between 1035 and 1037
Harthecanute	1040–1042		King of Denmark and son of Canute and Emma
Edward (the Confessor)	1042–1066		Son of Athelred II. Last of the Saxon kings
Harold II (Godwinson)	1066		Killed at the Battle of Hastings
William I	1066–1087	1083	Gheld Inquest
			North Curry Parish Church built probably replacing earlier Saxon church
		1086	North Curry appears in the Domesday Book
William II (Rufus)	1087–1100		Suffers mysterious accidental death
Henry I (Beauclerc)	1100–1135		Offences tried in Hundred Courts
Stephen	1135–1141	1136	Robert de Lewes enlarged Wells Cathedral and reinstated Bishop's throne in Wells and Bath
Matilda	1141		Ruled for six months but uncrowned
Stephen	1141–1154		Restored to throne

1 - 5

MIDDLE AGES ONWARD

King Henry II, known as *Henry Plantagenet*, ascended the throne of England in 1154. He had married Eleanor of Aquitaine, recently divorced by Louis VII of France, and ruled not only England, but also all the great provinces of western France. England was living in relative peace with the Saxon population reconciled to Norman rule, and Henry, who was well tutored and fully literate, was eager to see justice done. He sought to reform feudal laws and forced the Church to submit to English Common Law. He developed the *assize* system of trial by jury. The word *assize* derived from the French word for 'a sitting'.

King Henry's changes caused much conflict within the Church of Rome, which believed that the King's religious role was obedience to the Church. The King appointed Thomas Becket, who was Chancellor of the King's household, as Archbishop of Canterbury, hoping that the ambitions of the Church in state affairs would be curbed. However Becket chose to champion the Church against the Crown and an open quarrel ensued. Eventually, in 1170, the King ordered Becket's assassination, but this resulted in martyrdom of the Archbishop and the Church continued to influence the legal system for the next 300 years. As part of the King's penance for the murder of Thomas Becket, he founded in 1178 the first Carthusian monastery in England at Witham Friary near Bruton in East Somerset. To release land for this monastic settlement it was arranged for several hundred inhabitants to be moved to Knapp in North Curry as described on page 77. Over this period there was considerable evolution of the church in North Curry. Details of the church history can be found in Chapter 2–4.

Henry II died in 1189, out of favour with his four sons who had allied themselves to the French King. His eldest son, Richard, succeeded Henry as King, but he only visited England twice in the ten years of his reign. His main occupation and passion was as a fighting soldier in the Crusades to the Holy Lands, and he became known as *Richard Coeur de Lion* or *Richard the Lion Heart*. He thought little about his English kingdom, except as a means of raising money for his crusading expenses. He sold every office of state and made heavy taxation demands on the people. When King Richard I was imprisoned by Leopold of Austria, who handed him over to the Emperor Henry VI in 1194 after the failure of the third crusade, he needed 150,000 marks to pay for his ransom.

In order to raise this money he sold Scotland back to King William of Scotland, and many towns and manors bought charters from him which allowed them to control their own tax and toll collecting. North Curry was one of the manors that he handed over, having until this time been in the hands of the Crown, which had been Lords of the Manor since Saxon times. In November 1189 King Richard I made a short stay at Canterbury before he crossed the English Channel on his way to Jerusalem, and he conferred many privileges and properties on Bishop Reginald de Bohan (also known as Reginald FitzJocelin) of Bath who had accompanied him to the Holy Lands on earlier crusades. Bishop Reginald had gained his favour and thus in 1189 obtained the manor of *Curry* and the land of *Wrentich and Hatch*. In 1190 Reginald settled the manor, by licence from the King, on the canons of the Church of St Andrew, Wells.

The entry in the *Calendar of the Manuscripts of the Dean and Chapter of Wells Liber Albus I* gives the following notes in *Folio 9*:

> *i. Charter of King Richard I giving to the church of St Andrew Wells and Reginald bishop of Bath and his successors in frank almoin his manor, advowson, and hundred of Northcuri, with all liberties. Witnesses: Hugh bishop of Durham, Godfrey bishop of Winchester, Hugh bishop of Chester, Hubert, bishop of Salisbury, Earl Hamelin de Warenn', Earl Robert of Leicester, Earl Richard of Clare, William Mariscallus John his brother, William de Forz, Henry de Longo Campo, Roger de Pratellis, John his brother, William de St John, Geoffrey son of Peter, Ralph son of Godfrey the King's chamber. Iain, Hugh Bard', Robert de Witefeld. Dated Canterbury, 27 November 1189, Richard I, by the hand of the elect of Ely, chancellor.*
> *ii. Order of King Richard I to the men of Northcuri, reciting the above gift, to regard the bishop as their lord. Tested by Hugh bishop of Canterbury, 4 December 1189*
> *iii. Writ of King Richard I to the Sheriff of Somerset and his bailiffs, directing them to deliver seisin of the manor and advowson of Northcuri with appurtenances to the church of St Andrew Wells and Reginald Bishop of Bath and his successors.*
> *Tested by Hugh Bishop of Durham, Canterbury, 26 November 1189*

In 1123 Godfrey Giffard succeeded John de Villula, or John of Tours, as Bishop of Bath. Robert de Lewes, who rebuilt the cathedral at Wells, followed him in 1136. Robert decided to reinstate his Bishop's throne at both Wells Cathedral and Bath Abbey, ensuring election by both Chapters. Robert was succeeded in 1174 by Reginald de Bohan referred to above, and in 1192 by Bishop Savaric FitzGoldwin. He annexed Glastonbury by force and took the title of Bishop of Bath and Glastonbury, dying in 1205. He was followed in 1206 by Bishop Jocelin Troteman de Welles who in 1219 gave up all claims to Glastonbury and styled himself the Bishop of Bath only. However, he was responsible for rebuilding and extending Wells Cathedral with a nave and choir, adding the beautiful west front and founding a grammar school. In 1242 Bishop Jocelin of Bath made a gift of North Curry Manor to the Dean and Chapter of Wells Cathedral and they became Lords of the Manor of North Curry. They continued to administer the Manor in this capacity until 1866. Bishop Jocelin died in 1242 and the monks of Bath elected Roger de Salisbury as his successor. However the Wells Chapter appealed to the Pope who decided in 1244 that Roger should be styled Bishop of Bath and Wells and that the old arrangement of joint election should in future be observed. That title has been borne by the Bishops of Somerset ever since.

Richard I died from a bolt from a crossbow at the age of 42 while seeking treasure in France, and in 1199 his brother John became King. John was the youngest and favourite son of Henry II and Eleanor of Aquitaine, but he created enemies by refusing to take authority seriously, preferring to concentrate on administrative matters in England. France seized Normandy when King John neglected his lands there. By 1204 all that remained of the Duchy of Normandy under English rule was the Channel Islands. King John also upset Pope Innocent III by not accepting the new Archbishop of Canterbury, and the whole country was excommunicated, with the churches remaining closed for six years. John's barons, in order to restrain a despotic and defeated King, drew up a document at Runnymede which became known as the *Magna Carta* or The Great Charter. There were 63 clauses of numerous rights and privileges and legal arrangements, which in 1215 the King guaranteed to observe. Amongst them it decreed that the Church of England should be free to elect its bishops and other officials without interference from the King. It also decreed that the Council of the Realm - later this came to mean Parliament - *must consent to the raising of taxes and that no free man shall be tried for crimes except by his peers and the law of the land.*

King John was known to visit Somerset often, appearing at castles and assizes and making his royal presence felt. North Curry was noted as one of his favourite hunting grounds. During the King's summer visits to North Curry it was customary for one of the tenants to superintend the mowing and haymaking in the *kingesmeade* in white gloves and with a white rod in his hand. The following entry in the *Calendar of the Manuscripts of the Dean and Chapter of Wells Liber Albus II* notes that in 1314 this custom had been handed down as a responsibility to a number of tenants in North Curry after King John's reign.

> *....Thomas de Mere, Robert de la Chaumbre, Roger atte Venne, William Edwyne, William Brygge, Simon de Domerham to come to Kyngesmede wearing white gloves with a white wand as overseer of the mowers and superintend those that toss the hay behind them.*

There are two fields, numbers 1004 and 1005 on the *Tithe Map of North Curry* in *Wrantage Tything*, called King's Meade which measure about ten acres.

King John is also believed to have instituted what was to become known as the *Reeve's Feast*, a custom described in detail in Chapter 2-3. Customs governed the life of everyone, especially in farming, giving each tenant of the manor a defined part to play. North Curry was evidently becoming a thriving centre of activity and was soon to become a market town. In a Wells Charter of 1199 (see Plate xi) King John confirmed the granting in 1189 of the Manor of North Curry to Wells. He is credited with the granting of a market in North Curry by Charter in 1206.

> *Charter of King John confirming grants made by King Richard I and by himself while count of Mortain to the church and canons of St Andrew Wells, of the manor, hundred and church of Northcuri with the land of Hacche* (West Hatch) *and Wrentis* (Wrantage), *and warrenty. Witnesses: Geoffrey, archbishop of York, Roger, bishop of St Andrews, Earl David, William of Arundel, William de Humetis, constable of Normandy, Hugh de Gornay. Dated le Mans, 30 September. 1 John, AD 1199.*
>
> *Charter of King John confirming to the church and canons of St Andrew Wells grants made by King Richard I, and by himself when Count of Mortain, of the manor, hundred, and church of Northcuri with the land of Hacche and Wrentis, and warranty; also granting a market at Northcuri every Wednesday. Witnesses: Hugh Archbishop of Dublin, etc. Dated Bristol, 10 September 1206.*

The following entries in the *Calendar of the Manuscripts of the Dean and Chapter of Wells Liber Albus II Folios 256 and 405* note the changing of the market day from Wednesday to Tuesday and the granting of a fair on the vigil, feast and morrow of the day of the collection of *Peter's Pence* (a tax of a penny for each hearth or house). This became known as the Lammas Fair, and was held on 1st August - Lammas Day - the day on which it was customary to consecrate bread from the first ripe corn of harvest. It was also known as *lambs selling day*, being the day when spring lambs were sold.

> *Also a grant of King Edward I to Bishop Robert, dated 24 December 8 Edward I (1280). With a further grant of a market and fair at Northcory.*
> *Confirmation by King Edward III of former charters of Kings Henry III, John and Richard I, granting markets, etc. at North Cory, and a further grant by King Edward of a market at Northcory every Tuesday, in lieu of the market they previously had, and a fair to last three days every year, namely the vogo; feast and morrow of St Peter.*
> *Given at Wyndesore, October 12, 13 Edward III. (1337)*

It is believed this market and fair in North Curry were held in The Shambles - this word meaning a meat market. In these medieval times life would have centred on the church and square, and on market and fair days all the inhabitants of the manor would bring their livestock and wares, their crafts and their goods for barter. The fair lasted for two days, with the business being carried out on the first day when the sheep and livestock were penned up in The Shambles, labourers were hired and tradesmen's and doctors' accounts settled. The second day was when the inhabitants of North Curry indulged themselves in beer and sweetmeats, had their teeth drawn, watched entertainments by strolling players and musicians and maybe found their future wives. The fair continued to be held on 1st August until 1790 when it was changed according to a printed circular at the time:

> *Whereas North Curry fair has hitherto been held on the first day of August (Lammas Day). This is to give notice that the said fair will in future be held on the First Tuesday in September, for the sale of all sorts of fat and lean cattle, sheep, and horses, and for the encouragement of butchers, horse dealers, and others, the inhabitants will endeavour to get a good show of every kind. Dated 5th day of June 1790.*

The market in North Curry was discontinued in 1841 and the fair soon afterwards, although the residents of the village still enjoyed fair days in the fields below Moredon as described on page 62. In recent times the May Fayre held in Church Road, and the North Curry Flower Show both follow the tradition of these early events.

King John was able to rescind the oath he had sworn to the Pope, but the barons in England despaired and they encouraged the King of France to try to capture the Crown of England. War ensued for a year, but King John died of a fever and the French were eventually defeated. His son Henry was only nine years old when he became King in 1216 and was too young to rule. By 1227, having been protected by Church and state, he declared himself of age and began his rule. Henry III was a devout, but weak King. He married Eleanor of Provence whose relatives were given key offices of state in England, amongst them Boniface of Savoy who was made Archbishop of Canterbury. His brother-in-law, Simon de Montfort, Earl of Leicester, eventually took control and governed England in the name of the King. His position weakened however, and when Henry III died and was buried in his newly rebuilt abbey at Westminster in 1272, Henry's son Edward became King.

King Edward I aimed to make England, Wales and Scotland into one kingdom, Great Britain. The population was then about 3 million in England, which was becoming a land of exporters and importers. Wool to Flanders, corn to Norway and France and fish to the Continent were traded in return for timber, French and Italian wines, ginger, peppers, currants and jewels. Much wool was manufactured into cloth in England, with the number of weavers, fullers and dyers increasing rapidly. Iron, tin, lead, salt and coal provided many with a livelihood. Most people, however, were peasants, with the small band of rich becoming richer.

The King ordered a survey of villages to ascertain who held which land within each hundred. The King's principal advisor was his Chancellor, Robert Burnell, Bishop of Bath and Wells. Taxes were introduced on all moveable property and heavy taxes were levied on wool and hides to fund military campaigns in France and to impede the attempts of Wales and Scotland to gain independence. With the death of the Welsh leader Llewellyn, Wales was subdued and Edward's eldest son, who was born at Caernarfon, was presented to them as the Prince of Wales in 1301.

Scotland stood firm against Edward's plan for unity with England. A marriage planned between Margaret (known as the Maid of Norway) granddaughter and heir of King Alexander III of Scotland, and Edward's son Edward, would have achieved a union of the royal families. However, Margaret died before the marriage could take place and Scotland again began to resist England's interference with its affairs. A battle ensued in 1297 and the English, with the help of their new longbows, defeated the Scots. In 1306 Robert the Bruce was crowned King of Scotland and he continued relentlessly but unsuccessfully to attack the English. King Edward I died in the middle of another conflict, to be succeeded in 1307 by his son Edward II, who was idle and pleasure-loving. The Battle of Bannockburn in 1314 was won decisively by the Scots, partly because of the over-confidence of the English who, under a weak King, were ill-prepared. Edward II was deposed by Parliament, declared unfit to rule and was eventually murdered in 1327. His son Edward III was proclaimed King at the age of 15. Peace with Scotland was concluded in 1328, but there was no union as Edward I had hoped. Most of Edward III's reign was occupied by war with France, to become known as the Hundred Years War, with his greatest victory being at Crecy in 1346.

The Church dominated life in the villages during these times. Its income came mainly from revenues from the parishes, derived from tithes (a contribution of ten per cent of the villagers' produce), and gifts from parishioners. North Curry Parish Church shows much evidence of the new *Decorated Gothic* style of architecture (1272–1377). The church was enlarged and strengthened and by this time the succession of vicars had become established. Between 1200 and 1350 chantries were founded in connection with churches throughout England. Chantries were founded for the singing of the mass, i.e. chanting, from the Latin word *cantare* meaning to sing, and were built in memory of their founder. Six chantries were established in North Curry: one was in the cemetery of North Curry and a second in the vicarage orchard, a third in Stoke St Gregory, a fourth at Lillesdon, another at Stathe and a sixth at Wrantage.

The following entries in the *Calendar of the Manuscripts of the Dean and Chapter of Wells* mention three of these endowments:

> *1246*
> *In order to promote the honour of God and the glorious Virgin Mary, we assign 20 shillings yearly to Richard Treigoz, vicar of North Cury and his successors, for a daily mass in the chapel built and dedicated to the honour of the glorious Virgin in the cemetery of North Cury. This payment to cease if the service ceases.*
> *Wells MSS Liber Albus I Folio 66d*

> *1317 June*
> *The Chantry of St Mary in the chapel at North Cory, with houses and lands appertaining* (possibly on the site of Fosse Cottage) *granted by the dean and chapter to Roger de Molyns the chaplain for life.*
> *Wells MSS Liber Albus I Folio 149d*

> *1355*
> *Indenture between John de Carletone dean and the chapter and Sir John de Troubrigge, vicar of Northcory, to increase the portions of the vicarage and augment the vicarage with certain lands, and give coppice wood annually as an endowment for a chantry in the chapel of Lillesdone. The vicar is to pay one rose annually on the Nativity of S John the Baptist, and shall during the term of his life celebrate or cause to be celebrated a mass every Wednesday and Friday, if a double feast shall not fall upon those days, and if the lord and lady of Lillesdone Hugh de Bello Campo* (Beauchamp) *and Idonea shall be present, for whose good estate and for whose souls the said chantry is established.*
> *Wells MSS Liber Albus II Folio 211*

With the continuing refurbishment of the church in North Curry and the establishment of a market, the village centre would have expanded with housing plots extending along the main routes into the village. The earlier settlement sites with their open field system would have merged with the extended community centred on the village. North Curry has no trace of any large manor house or castle, but more substantial dwellings were being built to replace the simple peasant huts or earlier settlements. During the 12th and 13th centuries timber-framed hall houses with an open hearth in the middle and more substantial stone houses were being built throughout England, but no properties attributed to this period can be found in North Curry. Most people, however, were housed in simple houses with one storey and one room where they ate, slept and kept their livestock. These houses were built using local stones and cob - mud and straw built up in layers - producing thick sloping and rounded walls with a roof of straw thatch, turf or reeds. They only lasted for around 20 or 30 years.

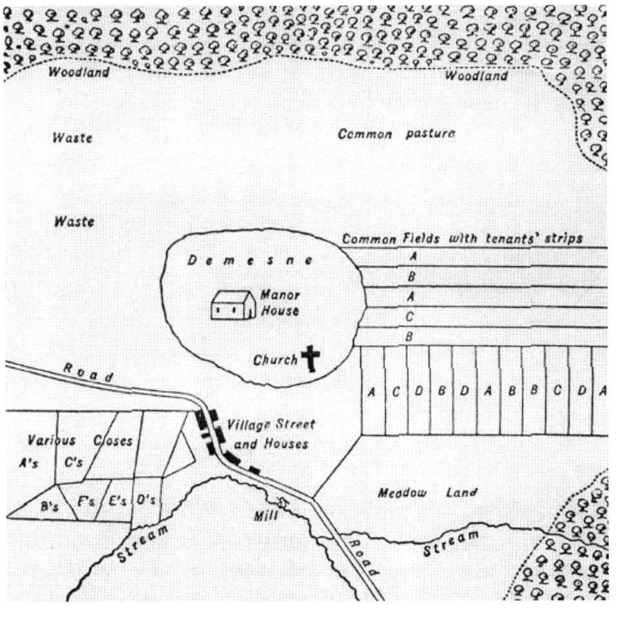

OLD FIELD SYSTEM OF PASTURE AND ARABLE LAND
(A to F are the Tenants)

In these times the arable land of an ordinary village was cultivated in two or three great open fields, each of them stretching over scores or even hundreds of acres. Each of the fields was sub-divided into blocks or *furlongs* and these further divided into individual *strips*. These strips were sometimes called a *selion* from the French word *sillon* meaning furrow. Their length and breadth was dictated partly by the lie of the land and partly by the manœuverability of the plough-teams of eight oxen. The farmers ploughed so that the land was turned inwards to make a central ridge down the middle of the strip, the team going up one side and down the other, turning on the headlands left unploughed at the strip ends. This method of ploughing meant that the soil turned inwards towards the central line, and made the strips stand up in curving ridges, dipping on either side to a furrow or drain to carry away the water, hence the phrase *ridge and furrow ploughing*. There are traces of these ridges and furrows around North Curry today. Instead of the straight lines of today's modern ploughing the old ploughlands lie curving gracefully across the fields like an inverted elongated letter 'S', reproduced again and again. The area resembled a patchwork quilt, with irregular strips or selions lying in various ways to fit the angle of the field with some unploughable patches left uncultivated. Peasant farmers (*villeins and cottars*) who held a number of strips scattered around the fields tenanted each individual strip. The village as a community would agree at regular meetings which crops should be grown in which field and which should be left fallow. Grazing was managed in common *closes*. Woodland was also of great importance for the provision of building and fencing timber. The right to cut and collect wood was strictly monitored and many disputes arose from abuse of these rights. Windmills appeared in the 13th century after the crusading knights had seen them on their travels, and evidence remains in North Curry of at least two, one below Moredon and another on Windmill Hill (see Appendix 4).

As discussed on page 170 litigation took place as early as 1316 between the Dean and Chapter of Wells and other landowners over disputes pertaining to the diversion of the rivers Parrett and Tone to assist their commercial uses. These diversions inevitably caused flooding in agricultural and populated areas and disputes were bitterly contested between the various landowners. Fish weirs were constructed on the River Tone at Ham causing the lands adjacent to them to flood during certain times of the year, and a mill constructed in the Parish of North Curry caused much conflict. In order to provide a head of water to power a waterwheel the course of the river was diverted and gates were erected, which caused hardship for many of the local parishioners.

The Black Death reached England from Europe in 1348 and it is estimated to have claimed the lives of 2-3 million people. This bubonic plague changed the social structure in England due to the resulting scarcity of labour. In North Curry the records name four incumbents of the Parish Church who died from the plague in 1348 and 1349. There is evidence of a deserted village site in fields in the Newport area of North Curry, and this could well have arisen as a consequence of this plague (see page 79).

The poet Geoffrey Chaucer (1340-1400) joined many on pilgrimages to Canterbury to the shrine of St Thomas Becket, and wrote the *Canterbury Tales* during this time, describing people and conditions in England. He helped to establish the English of the south-eastern lowlands as the main language of English literature in place of French and Latin.

Edward III died in 1377 and was succeeded by his grandson Richard, son of Edward *The Black Prince* and Joan of Kent. The name Black Prince was given to Edward for unknown reasons, and he was one of the outstanding English leaders in the Hundred Years War (1337-1453) with France, who died from a form of dysentery a year earlier in 1376. Richard II was only ten years old when he came to the throne and his uncle, John of Gaunt, became Steward of England and ran the Regency for the boy-king. The Peasants' Revolt brought about by the imposition of a Poll Tax in 1380 caused much unrest and compelled France and England to stop fighting for a while. In England nearly all men became free to hire themselves out as labourers for money wages, or to pay money rents as tenants or yeoman farmers. The physical appearance of the countryside changed, with fields and wastes becoming enclosed by hedges, fences and walls. The declining population made arable farming more difficult and more sheep farming was introduced. This brought new prosperity and the resulting wealth was frequently directed to the parish churches. Between 1377 and 1460 the Parish Church in North Curry was the subject of further rebuilding in the fashionable *Perpendicular Gothic* style of architecture.

Richard II, the last Plantagenet King, was impulsive and changeable and offended many noble families. Parliament proclaimed him unfit to rule and deposed him in 1399 and he was mysteriously murdered. Henry Bolingbroke, son of John of Gaunt, became Henry IV, the first King of the House of Lancaster. The Hundred Years War with France continued and he faced war in Scotland and Wales, building up huge debts. He died in 1413 afflicted with leprosy, and the Crown passed to his eldest son Henry. Henry V was a great soldier King who defeated the French at Agincourt in 1415. He married the daughter of the insane French King Charles VI and eventually ruled both France and England. However, Henry V died at the age of 33 leaving his infant son to become Lancastrian King Henry VI in 1422. Joan of Arc was to persuade France to accept the Dauphin Charles as the French King, leading to the end of the dual monarchy and the Hundred Years War with France, which actually lasted for 116 years.

King Henry VI was a pious, kindly and learned man, but unable to keep his barons in order. In 1444 he had married Margaret of Anjou, who many Englishmen hated, and when he suffered an attack of insanity the throne became vulnerable. Henry VI had previously appointed Edmund Beaufort, the Duke of Somerset as his closest advisor, even though he had been responsible for the loss of most of the English lands in France. Somerset was also the sworn enemy of Richard, Duke of York and when Richard was made *Protector of the Realm* in 1454 he banished Somerset to the Tower of London. A year later the King had Somerset released and York dismissed, a battle ensued and Somerset was killed.

With Henry unable to govern effectively, Richard raised an army of Yorkists against Queen Margaret who assumed leadership of the Lancastrians on behalf of the King. This led to a series of civil wars known as The Wars of the Roses, since the Yorkists took a white rose as their badge, whilst the Lancastrians chose a red one. York was the ultimate victor and Richard was declared heir to the throne in 1460, but died soon after in battle at Wakefield. Three weeks later Richard's son, Edward, decisively defeated the forces of Henry VI at Towton, securing his claim to the throne, and becoming King Edward IV in 1461. Henry VI and Margaret of Anjou fled to Scotland, seeking sanctuary with King James III of Scotland. Henry was eventually smuggled out of Scotland only to be captured by English forces and imprisoned in the Tower of London. Struggles for Henry to be reinstated as King followed and for a short time in 1470 he was restored to the throne. However Edward overcame Henry's supporters and Henry was once again imprisoned in the Tower where he was murdered in 1471.

Edward IV became popular amongst his subjects, although his secret marriage to Elizabeth Wydville from a family of Lancastrian sympathisers had sullied his reputation. Richard Neville, Earl of Warwick, who was termed *Warwick the Kingmaker*, was made Chamberlain of England and had plans for the King to marry a French princess in order to secure an alliance with France, but he felt humiliated by the King's marriage. Warwick withdrew his support for Edward and devised an unsuccessful plan to overthrow him so that Edward's brother George could become King.

Edward carried out many reforms that led to better executed offices of the Crown and more effective administration of the law. He exerted considerable diplomacy abroad and negotiated peace with Louis of France. He was a great patron of the arts and encouraged William Caxton, helping to finance the first book printed in England, *The Dictes and Sayenges of the Phylosophers*. He died in 1483 at the age of 41. Edward IV had wished for his 12-year-old son Edward to become his successor, but his uncle Richard, Duke of Gloucester, declared Edward, together with his nine-year-old brother Richard, Duke of York, illegitimate. The two Princes were imprisoned in the Tower of London and were eventually murdered. The Duke of Gloucester declared himself King Richard III and was crowned in 1483.

Richard III's wife was Anne Neville, the daughter of the Earl of Warwick, and widow of Edward, the Prince of Wales and son of Henry VI. Their only child Edward was born in 1476, but died in 1484. Richard III was secure on the throne but had to deal with several rebellions from Henry Stafford, Duke of Buckingham who supported the exiled Henry, Duke of Richmond's claim to the throne. Henry had married Elizabeth of York uniting the Houses of York and Lancaster. Henry and Richard III met at Bosworth in 1485 where a battle took place between the Houses of York and Lancaster. Richard was killed, the last English King to die in battle. England wished to be delivered from the last of the Yorkists and chose Henry, Duke of Richmond, with only a distant connection with the House of Lancaster, to take the Crown. Henry's claim to the throne was derived from his mother's descent from the third marriage of John of Gaunt, Duke of Lancaster. Parliament proclaimed Henry VII as King of England beginning the line of Tudor sovereigns.

1 - 6

TUDOR ENGLAND

When Henry VII came to the English throne in 1485 he was intent on breaking the power of the barons, strengthening the Crown and bringing peace to a population of 4 million people. Most of the leading nobles had been killed fighting in the Wars of the Roses and the introduction of the muzzle-loading cannon meant that the castles of the remaining barons were no longer so impregnable. Henry VII united the houses of Lancaster and York by marrying Elizabeth of York, Edward's IV's daughter, and made a treaty with Spain arranging for his first born son Arthur to marry Katherine of Aragon in 1499. Arthur died a year later, and his brother Henry became betrothed to Katherine. King Henry VII made alliances with Scotland and married his daughter Margaret to James IV of Scotland in 1503. He made treaties with the Netherlands, and restored peace with France. He began building warships as a precursor to the foundation of a Royal Navy by his son, and encouraged English merchants to trade overseas. In 1492 Columbus landed in America and in 1496 Henry financed an expedition, led by the Genoese Sebastian Cabot who lived in Bristol, to the Americas. A replica of Cabot's ship the *Matthew* can be seen in Bristol.

In 1485 Henry VII founded the Yeoman of the Guard, the first permanent military force in England, sporting the emblem of the Tudor Rose, a combination of the white and red roses of Lancaster and York. Weights and measures were standardised and trade flourished. The cloth trade brought much wealth to many areas and spinning and weaving and teazle growing were amongst the main occupations in many villages. Lady Margaret Beaufort, the daughter of John Beaufort, the first Duke of Somerset, was the mother of Henry VII and inherited much land in Somerset. The church in Langport was restored in her honour and bears the emblem of the Beaufort portcullis. Henry VII was able to dispel the claim of the throne of England by Perkin Warbeck who pretended to be the younger of the prince's in the Tower, declaring himself Richard IV. He eventually confessed his imposture at Taunton in 1497 and was executed for treason at Tyburn.

As discussed in detail on page 170 further disputes took place at this time between the Dean and Chapter of Wells and other landowners over the construction of a mill on the River Tone and the resultant flooding.

Henry VII ruled for 24 years, during which time he promoted scholarship, founding King's College, Aberdeen. His mother Margaret Beaufort endowed many colleges in Oxford and Cambridge. A better-educated population began to evolve, helped to a large extent by William Caxton and his successors' work of book printing. Henry began building the Chapel at Westminster Abbey in 1503 as a shrine to Henry VI, only to be buried there himself on his death in 1509. He lies, together with his wife Elizabeth who had died after the birth of his eighth child in 1503, in a tomb with a monument which stands in the middle of Westminster Chapel.

Henry VIII, the third child of Henry VII, succeeded to the throne in 1509 at the age of 18 and immediately married Katherine of Aragon who was 24. He was vain, pleasure loving and a spendthrift, although a devout Catholic, and quite a learned scholar. In 1513 Scotland invaded England, a bloody battle at Flodden Field was fought under the direction of the Earl of Surrey, and the Scots were defeated with King James IV of Scotland dying in battle. The infant son of Henry's sister Margaret became King James V and succeeded to the Scottish throne.

Henry chose among his advisors Thomas Cromwell, Thomas Cranmer and Thomas Wolsey, who he left to run many of the affairs of state while he enjoyed the merry-making and extravagances of monarchy. In 1511 a son, Henry, Prince of Wales was born, but died at the age of two months. Katherine was unable to produce a male heir, only giving birth to a daughter, Mary, in 1516. Henry was tired of his older wife and wanted to marry Anne Boleyn. In 1527 he asked the Pope to annul his marriage because Katherine had previously been married to Arthur, Henry's brother who had died. The Pope refused this request and Henry turned against his Chancellor, Wolsey, who by now was a Catholic cardinal. Wolsey was eventually arrested for high treason and died.

Henry turned to Thomas Cromwell and to Thomas Cranmer, Archbishop of Canterbury, and the Church was prosecuted in the Law Courts and payment of taxes to Rome was stopped. The authority of the Pope was abolished and King Henry VIII was declared supreme head of the Church of England. Henry's marriage to Katherine was declared null and void and Katherine's daughter Mary was declared illegitimate. After this Henry married Anne Boleyn and in 1533 a daughter, Elizabeth was born. Henry, who wanted a son so desperately, accused Anne Boleyn of treasonable adultery and she was beheaded. He then married Jane Seymour, who in 1537 gave birth to a long-awaited son, Edward, but she died soon after giving birth. Other marriages followed to Anne of Cleves, Katherine Howard and Katherine Parr.

Henry, in need of money, again sought the advice of Thomas Cromwell, who had set about destroying all the wealth of the churches. In 1536 Cromwell suggested that more money could be taken from the Church by dissolving the monasteries and acquiring their land. Lands worth £100,000 a year came into the Crown's possession by this means. Former monastic properties were sold to country gentry and people of high nobility, enabling them to create fine estates, and realising a further £1.5 million for the Crown.

The Reformation of the Church by Cromwell required in 1538 that clergy place a new translation of the Bible in English in each church for every man to look at and read. The clergy were required to teach their congregation the Lord's Prayer, the Articles of Faith and the Ten Commandments and also to introduce the English Prayer Book into churches. At this time chantries and free chapels were also confiscated and the chantries in North Curry mentioned in previous chapters were destroyed. A buttress on the front wall at the south-west corner of the house at Lillesdon Court is all that remains of the chapel and chantry dedicated to St Martin for the Lord and Lady of Lillesdon. All images that had become objects of worship rather than aids to devotion were ordered to be destroyed. It is possible that the rood screen in the Parish Church of St Peter and St Paul in North Curry, and the images on the outside of the south porch and the stoup for holy water there could also have been destroyed if they were regarded as Catholic ornaments and idols.

In 1538 Sir Thomas Cromwell ordered that Parish Registers be kept in churches so that all people's baptisms, marriages and burials would be recorded to establish population statistics for poll tax purposes. Chapter 3-1 describes the *Parish Registers* of North Curry.

In 1542 the English again defeated the Scots, this time at the Battle of Solway Moss. James V died leaving the Scottish throne to the infant Mary, later to become Queen of Scots. England also faced invasion from France and the government was nearly bankrupt. Henry had spent all the money from taxes and from the sale of monastery lands. Silver had become more plentiful in the world and Henry had issued more coins with less silver content to the detriment of trade. All prices of goods, services and rents were raised. Small tenants suffered from *enclosure* where profits from enclosed land held by a single farmer were better than profits raised from strip farming in open fields. Sheep farming was more profitable than arable because it used less labour, and the rich grew richer with the peasants suffering hardship. However, Henry was determined to defy the Catholic powers of Europe and when in 1545 a French armada attempted to invade England it was foiled by the Royal Navy, which Henry had created with ships equipped with heavy cannons.

In 1547 Henry VIII died leaving his nine-year-old son to become King Edward VI. Edward was too young to rule and the Duke of Somerset became Protector of the Realm. In order to replenish the impoverished treasury, church furniture and property was again plundered and common land seized, depriving many livelihoods. In 1552 Lord Somerset had many enemies who disagreed with his way of governing and they revolted, leading to his execution for treason. In 1553 Edward died at the age of 15.

An attempt to place Lady Jane Grey on the throne failed after nine days. She was the Protestant great niece of Henry VIII and under his will she had the right of succession to the throne after the deaths of Henry's own children and their heirs. There was overwhelming public support for Mary, daughter of Henry VIII and his first wife Katherine of Aragon. However Edward VI had signed an amendment to his father's will that set aside his sister Mary's claims to the throne and nominated Lady Jane Grey who was proclaimed Queen of England on 10th July 1553. Jane was arrested and imprisoned in the Tower of London on 19th July 1553 and was executed in 1554 having been found guilty of treason. Mary was crowned Queen on 1st October 1553.

Mary was a Catholic and she desired reunion with Rome. Queen Mary I, known as Bloody Mary, married Philip, the Catholic future King of Spain. She tried to reverse the Reformation and re-establish the Catholic Church in England, with the result that many Protestants were executed becoming martyrs to their faith, including Cranmer, Archbishop of Canterbury, who was burned alive. Mary died childless in 1558 and the Crown passed to her Protestant half-sister Elizabeth, daughter of Anne Boleyn.

Elizabeth I restored religious peace. England became Protestant by law and she was declared Supreme Governor of the English Church. Puritan theology was rearing its head and she managed to subdue extreme religious activity from all sides establishing a more settled Anglican Church and using the Book of Common Prayer as the only legal form of service, with everyone required to attend church. However there were many Catholic families keeping their faith with priests disguising themselves and hiding in *Priests' Holes* when at risk of discovery. In 1558 Mary, Queen of Scots, married the King of France, and after he died in 1561 she returned to Scotland, only to seek exile in England when a civil war developed due to feudal and religious conflicts. Her power was diminished, leaving her Protestant son James VI on the throne of Scotland. She was imprisoned in England and eventually executed as a political necessity; as a Catholic she threatened Elizabeth and endangered the English throne.

During the years 1500 to 1700 housing in the land changed dramatically. The need for fortified dwellings such as the cold, dank and draughty castles ceased as violence diminished, and they were replaced with houses designed more for comfort. Many villages changed in appearance, and although there were still many poor living in hovels, larger houses were built for the yeoman and husbandmen who had prospered from the land. Hall houses were built with wooden frames which at first only had earthen floors with one room and a parlour. A ladder was used to reach an upper sleeping area and the hall had a central open fire. This design was to be replaced later with smoke hoods or bays and then with chimneys which helped to conduct the smoke out of the house. Windows of glass replaced shutters and the animals that had shared domestic accommodation were moved outside into outbuildings and byres. The living standards of the people improved. The poor had rough wooden furniture, plain chests for their clothes, wooden platters and spoons, and slept on flock mattresses instead of straw, with a few prized treasures of pewter or exotic pottery. The wealthy slept on carved bedsteads with feather and down mattresses with sheets and bolsters, filling their parlours with carved cupboards, embroidered hangings and quilts, porcelain, silverware and fine clothing. Mats of plaited rush covered the floors and cleanliness improved, although poorer people covered their floors with hay to absorb the scraps of food and general debris. Foreign plants and flowers, medicinal herbs and tobacco were introduced into English gardens, and people bathed in wooden tubs enhanced with scented soap and used perfumes made from flowers and herbs.

Within the Parish of North Curry are many houses whose origins stem from the 15th and 16th centuries. The structural history of these houses is discussed in Chapter 2-5.

It was at this time that Queen Elizabeth made provision for the relief of large numbers of tenants who had been turned out of their smallholdings, unemployed soldiers and labourers. Many hungry, homeless and helpless people roamed the country and, treated as wrongdoers, they were obliged to beg and steal to survive. The Poor Laws of 1572, 1597 and 1601 required every parish to support its own poor, establishing that the state had a duty towards them. Two unpaid officials, the Overseers of the Poor, recruited annually from the inhabitants, were required to raise a poor rate from occupiers of property within the parish, and to spend it on the relief of poverty within their bounds. All poor, old, young, sick and unfortunate were to be fed and cared for; the children were taught a trade and the able-bodied found work of a suitable kind. This work, typically processing raw material such as hemp, wool or flax, was usually carried out in the paupers' homes. The ones who refused were punished and sent to a house of correction and forced to work. There is reference in the *Calendar of the Manuscripts of the Dean and Chapter of Wells* to the building of a prison in North Curry, which is believed to have dealt with these miscreants.

> *1597 July 1*
> *Roger Michel of Fifett, tanner, to have timber to build up the prison at North Curry, and to have a lease of the prison house for 21 years, paying the usual rent and keeping it in repair.*
> *MSS Wells Liber Ruber II Folio 111d*

Those classed as incapable of work could be looked after together in a purpose-built poorhouse, which evidence suggests was situated within the curtilage of Fosse Cottage in North Curry.

England led the world in wool production; although most of England's overseas trade was with continental Europe. Her economy was suffering and there was a great need for trade to be extended towards the New World, which was dominated by the Spanish. The design of shipping improved and fleets of warships using gunfire successfully challenged Portugal and defeated the Spanish Armada in 1588. John Hawkins, who traded in slaves and gold; Humphrey Gilbert, who discovered Newfoundland in 1583; Francis Drake, the first Englishman to sail his ship round the world; and Walter Raleigh were all masters of seamanship. These maritime explorers returned from foreign lands with riches, exotic goods and treasures and enabled England to become established as a leading maritime nation.

In Elizabethan England people were divided into distinct classes and few thought this was unjust. The sovereign was above all ranks of men and immediately below the monarch came the gentlemen class. This included nobles of the realm as well as country squires with small manor houses. The nobles were addressed as *My Lord* but the rest as *Master* (Mr) and written to as *Esquire*. Some gentlemen were immensely rich, well educated and famous, while others were quite poor, crude and hardly able to read. They had in common, however, ownership of land. Many had acquired land at the time of the Dissolution of the Monasteries. Some gentlemen were appointed as Justices of the Peace who were the unpaid magistrates responsible for fixing local wages, collecting the poor rate and appointing the Overseers of the Poor, arranging for highways and bridges to be repaired, for inns to be licensed, and for law-breakers to be brought to justice. Next came merchants, who often sat as Members of Parliament. Below them were the yeoman farmers from the country, both freeholders and prosperous copyholders, and the highly skilled craftsmen who were addressed as *Goodman*. Lastly came the day-labourers together with farmers, whose landholdings were too small to support them unless they worked for wages as well. The diet for the rich was enhanced with new breeds of pig, sheep, goose, hen, pigeon, duck, peacock, swan and turkey. These foods, as well as oysters, eggs, butter, white bread, tarts, jellies and highly spiced sweet puddings and fruits of all kinds were eaten at two mealtimes. Dinner was at 11 or 12 o'clock in the morning and supper at 6 or 7 o'clock in the evening. Ale, cider, perry and mead wine were drunk in copious amounts.

The love of games and sport was to be found everywhere. Quoits, bowls, shooting, archery, wrestling and ball sports were all played after work, on holidays and during organised festivals on special days. People flocked to see cock fighting, bull and bear baiting and large crowds turned out for executions and burnings of criminals and witches. Country sports included deer hunting and hare coursing, and in North Curry hawking and fowling were also pursued. In 1599 in the *Calendar of the Manuscripts of the Dean and Chapter of Wells* notice of a lease of fowling was granted to Hugh Portman as follows:

> *1599 April 2*
> *A lease of all the fowling in the Hundred of North Curry granted to Hugh Portman, for 21 years at a rent of 4d a year, reserving to the Dean and Chapter the right of hawking and fowling there when it shall please any of them to do so.*
> *MSS Wells Liber Ruber II Folio 121*

Art, sculpture, music and poetry was appreciated by many, and William Shakespeare (1564-1616) together with many other dramatists and actors encouraged literacy. Companies of strolling players acted in scenes from history and legend and performed in the open air during the summer months. The Elizabethan custom of the *mumming* play about George and the Dragon took place. Mumming is a type of ancient folk play that combines music, dance and sword fighting in episodes involving the death and revival of certain characters. The players were amateurs and all male and performed their play travelling from house to house. The name derives from a French word meaning 'masked' and the mummings are thought to symbolise the resurrection of the year having been part of spring festivals, although they were eventually performed during the winter months. The tradition still survives in North Curry and can be seen being performed in the centre of the village on Boxing Day when this play attracts and pleases a large audience.

Parliament, especially the House of Commons, played an important part in Tudor government. In 1559 the House of Commons had 462 members and they met every three years for nine weeks in Elizabeth's reign. England was short of money even with the benefit of the plunder Drake had taken from the Spaniards. Although the Queen still ruled overall, Parliament was responsible for the state purse and became more powerful. Elizabeth died in 1603 after a reign of 45 years and her wish for the Crown to go to her Protestant cousin, James VI of Scotland, was fulfilled. Disputes about religion and money were to cause much instability in England and turbulent times lay ahead.

NORTH CURRY TIMELINE – MIDDLE AGES, TUDORS AND STUARTS

Henry II (Plantagenet)	1154–1189	1166	Trial by jury introduced
		1178	Influx of Witham inhabitants to Knapp
Richard I (Lionheart)	1189–1199	1189	King Richard gives Manor of North Curry by Charter to Bishop of Bath and Church of St Andrew in Wells
John	1199–1216	1199	King John confirms 1189 grant of Manor by further Charter, visits North Curry and is purported to have initiated Reeve's Feast
		c.1200	Enlargement of North Curry Parish Church started
		1206	Charter of King John grants market in North Curry
		1215	Magna Carta
Henry III	1216–1272	1234	Richard de Treigoz recorded as first North Curry Vicar
		1242	Manor of North Curry given to Dean and Chapter of Wells Cathedral and they became Lords of the Manor
		1244	Bishop of Bath styled Bishop of Bath and Wells
Edward I (Anjou)	1272–1307	1280	Grant to hold a fair for three days every year in North Curry
		1290	Mappa Mundi made
		c.1296	Lillesdon Court possible site of manor court
		c.1300	North Curry Parish Church completed in Decorated Gothic style
			Windmills in North Curry. Churchwardens appointed
Edward II (Anjou)	1307–1327	1317	Chantry established in North Curry – possibly on site of Fosse Cottage
		1327	North Curry pays Lay Subsidy Tax
Edward II (Anjou)	1327–1377	1355	Chantry established in Lillesdon on site of Lillesdon Court
		1348	Black Death claims the lives of many North Curry inhabitants
		1360	Thoma atte Sloo effigy in church installed
Richard II (Anjou)	1377–1399	1380	Men became free and enclosure of land began with random strip cultivation for individual tenants

NORTH CURRY TIMELINE – MIDDLE AGES, TUDORS AND STUARTS

Henry IV (Lancaster)	1399–1413	c.1400	North Curry Parish Church enlarged in Perpendicular Gothic style
Henry V (Lancaster)	1413–1422		Ruled both France and England
Henry VI (Lancaster)	1422–1461		Wars of the Roses
Edward IV (York)	1461–1470		Ptolemy mapping theories reconstructed and printed
Henry VI (Lancaster)	1470–1471		Restored to throne
Edward IV (York)	1471–1483		Restored to throne
Edward V (York)	1483		Murdered in the Tower of London
Richard III (York)	1483–1485	1485	Battle of Bosworth between York and Lancaster
Henry VII	1485–1509	1502	Chancel in North Curry Parish Church rebuilt
			Perkin Warbeck loses claim to throne
			Lady Margaret Beaufort honoured in Langport
		1507	Mill dispute at Ham between Wells and Bishop of Winchester resolved
Henry VIII	1509–1547	1536	Dissolution of the Monasteries
		1538	Reformation of churches by Cromwell – introduction of English Prayer Book and chantries in North Curry destroyed
		1539	North Curry Parish Register started
			Many timber-framed houses built in North Curry
Edward VI	1547–1553	1552	Poor Law directed parish chests to be provided in churches
Lady Jane Grey	1553		Uncrowned
Mary I (Bloody Mary)	1553–1558		Surveyors of Highways first elected
Elizabeth I	1558–1603	c.1570	Manor Farm off Stoke Road built
		1575	Saxton Map of Somerset published
		1585	First Churchwardens' Account Book for North Curry
		1597	Prison house built in North Curry
		1599	Hawking and fowling pursued in North Curry
		1600	East India Company founded
		1601	Overseers of the Poor nominated
James I	1603–1625		England and Scotland share monarch
Charles I	1625–1649		Residents in North Curry made Protestation Oaths
		1642–1649	English Civil War
Commonwealth	1649–1658	1653	Oliver Cromwell becomes Lord Protector of England
		1650	First nonconformist meeting in North Curry
		1662	Hearth Tax introduced
Commonwealth	1658–1659		Richard Cromwell, son of Oliver, assumes power
Charles II	1660–1685	1685	Many North Curry residents took part in Battle of Sedgemoor
		1685	Duke of Monmouth captured and executed
James II	1685–1688	1685	Many North Curry men hanged or transported for life
Mary II	1689–1694		Mary rules England and Scotland jointly with William III (II of Scotland)
William III	1689–1702	1689	Act of Settlement disallowing Catholics to succeed to the throne of England.
		1696	Window Tax introduced
Anne	1702–1714	1707	Formation of United Kingdom of Great Britain

1 - 7

STUART TIMES

James I, a middle-aged Scotsman, became the first Stuart King of England in 1603. From that time England and Scotland have remained under the same monarch. From 1606 Scots were officially called English citizens. James was the son of Mary, Queen of Scots and her cousin and second husband Henry Stuart, Lord Darnley. In 1589 James I, who was then King James VI of Scotland, had married Anne of Denmark and they had six children. The King's mother had been a Catholic, and as he had been brought up as a Presbyterian the Puritans in England expected favours from him, which he refused. They planned to destroy the Protestant monarchy and install James's young son Charles as King. In 1605 a small group of Roman Catholics of the Jesuit party plotted to blow up the King and the members of both Houses of Parliament with gunpowder and fuses set up by Guy Fawkes. This attempt was foiled when one of the plotters lost his nerve and Guy Fawkes was caught in the act of lighting the fuse. He and members of the conspirator's group were put to death.

The King quarrelled with the Puritans after his bishops disallowed any alterations to church services, but he did allow an improved translation of the Bible, which became known as the Authorised Version or King James's Bible. The Puritans were forced outside the Church and many left the country, later sailing to America.

James I was financially extravagant and by 1608 the Crown debt left by Elizabeth I had increased six-fold. He had to ask Parliament to authorise new taxes and this weakened his authority as King as they were then able to assert conditional powers in areas such as foreign policy. In 1613 the King arranged for his daughter Elizabeth to marry Frederick, the German Protestant, later elected King of Bohemia, and from whom the Hanoverian Kings of England were descended. He also attempted an alliance with Catholic Spain with the suggestion that his son, Charles, marry the Spanish Infanta. This idea failed and war with Spain was declared when James came under pressure to support his son-in-law, Frederick of Bohemia, who had gone to war with Spain's ally, Catholic Austria. Charles married Henrietta Maria of France, a Catholic and sister of Louis XIII, completing an alliance with Spain's great rival France. At this time the sovereign power of the Crown was being questioned by Parliament, the middle classes were unhappy to let the government be ruled by the King, and civil war loomed.

Exploration and piracy of the seas continued and England made a serious effort to establish colonies in other lands. The idea of trading woollen cloth and other English exports for hemp, flax, tobacco, sugar, currants, timber and furs brought not only the prospect of wealth, but also power abroad. English settlers founded Protestant colonies in Ireland, settling on confiscated lands in Ulster. The first settlers on the other side of the Atlantic arrived in Jamestown, Virginia, establishing a profitable export trade in tobacco. The Puritan *Pilgrim Fathers* who sailed in the Mayflower settled the second colony, Plymouth, New England. The third settlement, Bermuda, began after a shipwreck of an expedition intended for the American mainland. On the other side of the world the East India Company set up trading centres and factories in India, and trading posts were also set up in the East Indies and in Newfoundland. The British Empire was built up as a result of this trading. When King James I died in 1625 he was succeeded by his second son, Charles, his first son, Henry Frederick, having died at the age of 18.

Charles I was a great patron of the arts and literature but lacked statesmanship. His marriage to Catholic Henrietta Maria, daughter of King Henry IV of France, and his refusal to dismiss the Duke of Buckingham, who Parliament felt had mishandled foreign policy, caused Parliament to withhold the customs duties on goods brought in from abroad that he had sought to claim for his own use. This led Charles to impose other taxes without parliamentary sanction, and he revived old feudal military tenure taxes with many landowners, including one Oliver Cromwell, having to pay fines to the King. He also revived the tax known as Ship Money, whereby all seaports and inland towns were obliged to provide ships or money for coastal defence.

For the next 11 years, between 1629 and 1640, the King ruled without Parliament. He made peace with France and Spain and installed William Laud, Bishop of London, as Archbishop of Canterbury. Laud attempted to enforce a strongly Presbyterian Scotland to acknowledge and use the English Prayer Book which the Scots thought was the work of the Pope. This caused a national rebellion, which Charles tried to quash without a proper army and without much money. He was unsuccessful and in 1640 he made further attempts to summon Parliament to assist by granting him money in the form of taxes, but they again refused and curtailed the King's power. Charles I was isolated. Parliament had the support of the Scottish army and claimed control of the militia. Many lords and commoners, notably John Pym and John Hampden and his cousin Oliver Cromwell, urged their supporters to choose Puritans as new Members of Parliament. They proposed to bring the Church under the control of Parliament and reform the Prayer Book. Charles gathered around him a bodyguard of unemployed officers and gentlemen's sons who wore their hair long and carried swords and became known as *Royalists* or *Cavaliers*.

The Civil War between the King's supporters, the *Cavaliers*, and supporters of Parliament, the *Roundheads*, was under way. Most of the poorer people in England remained neutral. The middle-class country gentlemen and richer citizens, who wanted the Puritan religion, were on the parliamentary side, seeking to prevent the King from interfering with trade, controlling taxes and influencing foreign policy. On the King's side were his own courtiers and the people who did not want change. The Commanders in Chief were, on the King's side, Prince Rupert, the King's nephew, and on the parliamentary side firstly Lord Manchester and later Oliver Cromwell who introduced the *New Model Army*.

In 1641 and 1642 Parliament arranged a signed protest against the possibility that a future *arbitrary and tyrannical government* should interfere with people's beliefs and practices. All male parishioners over the age of 18 were invited to subscribe to the declaration and make an oath, known as the *Protestation Oath Returns*, which abhorred the designs of priests and Jesuits who were plotting to conspire to subvert the fundamental laws of the kingdom. A number of residents in North Curry, Knapp, Lillesdon and Wrantage made this oath, and it is believed the village as a whole was sympathetic to the Royalist cause. In 1638 the Reverend Sebastian Smith, who was Vicar in North Curry during the Civil War; disappeared, to be found later in 1664 at the Chapter in Wells. In 1661 the Reverend Henry Griffith is mentioned in Weaver's *Somerset Incumbents*, and in 1662 the Reverend George Pierce appears to have been ejected from the ministry of North Curry Parish Church on St Bartholemews's Day 1662, and described as *superstitious, unscrupulous and scandalous*. He subsequently appears in 1669 as a *teacher* of the nonconformist meeting at Fivehead.

Somerset people were mostly Royalists and the county became the scene of several fiercely contested fights. At Wells in 1642 *Cavaliers* lodged in the Bishop's Palace and grounds, where they were surrounded by an overwhelming force of *Roundheads* and forced to retreat towards Cornwall. There they met up with strong Royalist forces and proceeded to win many battles at the beginning of the War and occupy Taunton, Bridgwater and Dunster Castle, driving the enemy to Batheaston and Bath. However, in 1645 a strong parliamentary army, which included Admiral Robert Blake, a native of Bridgwater and Member of Parliament, entered Somerset and drove the Royalists from every town. They were not received well and many people were later fined for their support of the King. Langport was a Royalist town from 1643 to 1645 with a defence along the line of the Parrett and a fortification around Langport Hill. The Royalist commander, Goring, fought a bloody battle and lost to the parliamentarian army under General Cromwell and Sir Thomas Fairfax at the Battle of Langport. Other important battle sites in England were Edgehill where the battle in 1642 was indecisive, Marston Moor in 1644 and Naseby in 1645, where battles resulted in Royalist defeats. By the autumn of 1645 the War was over, with the Royalists defeated and the parliamentarians accepting Charles's surrender. He remained King for a while, but without the existence of Parliament and proper legal practices he was tried for treason, and in 1649 he was beheaded.

The Monarchy, the House of Lords and the Anglican Church were all abolished and England was declared a Republic or Commonwealth. Meanwhile only the Scots and the Irish proclaimed King Charles's eldest son as King Charles II of Great Britain. However, the country was now to be governed by the Commons or *Rump* and a Council of State. Cromwell became Lord Protector of England. Presbyterians were expelled, leaving only independent Puritans in the Commons who had the support of most of the army leaders. All the overseas English colonies accepted the Commonwealth, and in 1651 a Navigation Act was passed laying down that when goods from outside Europe were imported into the Commonwealth or its colonies they must be carried in Commonwealth or colonial ships. This deprived the Dutch of their extensive shipping trade, which in turn led to a state of war with Holland. Admiral Blake secured the blockade of Dutch ports and the Commonwealth was firmly established in power with a strong navy and army. By 1653 Parliament was experiencing constitutional problems with few elected commoners, thus enabling Cromwell to dissolve it, leaving himself as both commander of the army and master of the country. He allowed religious tolerance encouraging Baptists, Presbyterians, Puritans and Quakers to flourish, and accepted, albeit discouragingly, Roman Catholics and members of the Church of England. By the late 1650s there was a nonconformist meeting in North Curry as described in detail in Chapter 2-4.

During the period of the Commonwealth, marriages, baptisms and burials in North Curry seem to have been performed by laymen. Edward Ceeley, Thomas Court and John Pyne are names of such laymen that appear in the parish records.

Oliver Cromwell died in 1658 and was succeeded by his son Richard, who retained power for only a few months. Parliament was returned and the majority agreed to recall Charles II who had been exiled in France and Holland for nine years, inviting him to reclaim his throne in England. He returned in 1660 and the period of Reformation began. Elections for a new Parliament were held and most members supported the Crown and Church. Nonconformist religions were punished and Church of England followers were reinstated with livings and power.

Many of the Crown jewels used at modern coronation ceremonies were made for the coronation of Charles II, for most of the earlier regalia had been broken up after the execution of his father Charles I. Charles II was 30 years old and soon married Princess Catherine of Braganza, daughter of the King of Portugal, but she was unable to provide him with an heir. Charles, known as *The Merry Monarch*, was charming, lazy and passionate and enjoyed a succession of mistresses with whom he fathered 14 children, but he also had courage and a shrewd head for business.

An artistic and scientific revolution was beginning at this time. Works from the Baptist writer John Bunyan (1628–1688), poetry from the Puritan John Milton (1608–1674), drama from the Catholic John Dryden and others all contributed to a greater literary appreciation. Samuel Pepys, secretary to the Navy Board, writing in his diaries from 1660 to 1669, recorded wonderful descriptions of life in Stuart times. He wrote a first-hand account of life in London and described the extravagances of dress, people's habits and eating, and the extremes between the wealthy and poor. Science became the leisure occupation of many gentlemen and many colleges and societies were formed. The College of Surgeons was founded in memory of William Harvey who first described the circulation of blood, and King Charles II was instrumental in the founding of the Royal Society for scientists in 1662. Galileo (1564–1642), followed by Isaac Newton (1642–1727), laid the foundations of scientific discovery by novel applications of mathematics. The microscope was invented, the chemist Robert Boyle (1627–1691) and the astronomer Edmund Halley made remarkable discoveries about the universe, and many other notable academics increased the depth of human knowledge in all scientific areas.

In 1665, after a period of drought, there was a terrible outbreak of bubonic plague, especially severe in London. Almost 100,000 citizens, nearly a quarter of the population, died in London. Fleas that infested black rats, which in turn infected humans, carried the infection, and people of all classes fled to the country, often taking the disease with them. The Great Fire of London, which started in September 1666, followed the plague. It raged for three days before being brought under control by blowing up houses in its path. It destroyed the City of London, between the Tower of London and Temple. It was estimated that 13,000 houses were burnt, leaving many people homeless and businesses at a standstill. Christopher Wren (1632–1723), the great architect of the time, was commissioned to build 51 churches and the Cathedral of St Paul's to replace the 88 churches destroyed, and to construct many other public buildings. After the fire many buildings in the City of London within the city wall were rebuilt in brick, influenced by designs of the architect Inigo Jones.

England had been at war with the Dutch at various times between 1652 and 1674. Peace brought an expanded Empire with the winning of the Dutch colonies of New Jersey and New York. When New York was in Dutch hands it was called New Amsterdam and was re-named by the Duke of York. The Hudson's Bay Company was formed and settlement of the Bahamas, North and South Carolina, Delaware and Pennsylvania followed. Until then 80 per cent of the British population had worked in agriculture. The biggest industry, cloth, was still a cottage industry. The Civil War had demanded great quantities of iron for weapons leading to new methods of wind power to propel pumps for the mining of iron, silver and tin and the development of the use of blast furnaces for smelting. As a result of improvements in extraction methods coal was to replace charcoal for burning bricks, burning soap, making glass, metalworking and casting brass. The wealth generated by overseas trade enabled these industries to develop.

Money in the form of taxes was being paid by all householders throughout the land and in 1674 there were 61 persons in *North Curry Tything*, 12 persons in *Lylsdon Tything*, 20 persons in *Knap Tything* and 29 in *Wrantage Tything* liable for Hearth Taxes (see Chapter 2-2).

King Charles II was allowed only limited powers by Parliament, and although new taxes were introduced to give the King revenue, they did not bring as much as he hoped and the Crown remained short of money. Although he was head of the Church of England, and Parliament was mainly Anglican, he secretly wished to convert to Catholicism. His brother James, Duke of York, had become a Catholic in 1669 and was heir to the throne. When suspicions of popish plots to murder the King arose, Parliament chose to exclude James from the succession and suggested that the Protestant Duke of Monmouth, King Charles II's illegitimate son by Lucy Walter, should succeed him. However, Charles would not betray the succession, and when he died of natural causes in 1685 James II became King of Great Britain and Ireland, the first Catholic monarch since Bloody Mary.

James II reigned for three years. He was first married before he was King to Anne Hyde who gave birth to two daughters, Mary and Anne. These children remained Protestant after he and his wife became Catholics, and Mary went on to marry the Protestant Prince William of Orange, ruler of Holland. James's second wife was Mary of Modena, who in 1688 gave birth to a son James.

Parliament at this time consisted of Tories and Whigs. The Tories were loyal to the King but Whigs chose the Duke of Monmouth as their leader hoping to maintain the Protestant succession. Monmouth was received gladly throughout the West Country and he set sail from Brussels where he had been in exile and landed at Lyme in Dorset in 1685 to start a rebellion to challenge James II to the throne. He was welcomed by large numbers of supporters from Dorset and Somerset, ranging from yeomen to peasant labourers. An army of 7,000, many armed only with pitchforks, underwent a perfunctory training and were given pikes and muskets before marching to Taunton where 40 years before they had fought the Royalists in the Civil War. Taunton was a prosperous place, being the seat of woollen manufacture, and many men from the surrounding villages enlisted, with some from the Parish of North Curry. However the leading Somerset families would not support the Duke, as they knew he could not legally be regarded as the heir to the throne. There was a shortage of horses and supplies and the local forces were ill-equipped to engage the forces of the royal army of James II. However, although the Duke of Monmouth's men lost numerous battles only to re-engage with new recruits along the way, they nearly defeated the royal army at the Battle of Sedgemoor. From a vantage point at the top of Bridgwater's Parish Church, Monmouth observed the enemy in Westonzoyland, surrounded by the swamps and marshes of the moors. He advanced towards the enemy, successfully breaching two rhines, only to be trapped in the third, Bussex Rhine, and be overwhelmed by the royal forces. The Battle of Sedgemoor, the last battle to be fought on English soil, was ended. Monmouth was captured and was executed on Tower Hill.

The Chief Justice, Judge Jeffreys, was sent down to the West County to try the survivors. Some 300 people were hanged, with 900 more transported to the West Indian sugar plantations and sold as slaves. Many were sent in the name of the Queen who received payment of about £12 for each of them. This visit was named the Bloody Assize and many were tried in the Great Hall of Taunton Castle. Hundreds of rebels were hanged, disembowelled and quartered, and displayed in market places along roads and on the greens of villages or in church porches. Several rebels with friends able to pay a sum of gold were allowed to escape and rich people paid a high price for a pardon.

The men of the Parish of North Curry who were called to answer for their involvement with the Duke of Monmouth's army are listed below. Some of those mentioned escaped or went into hiding, and probably lived in fear for the rest of their lives.

ROLLCALL OF THE REBELS

John Bartlett	*of Stoke St Gregory 'in arms, siding and assisting James Scott in the time of the rebellion'*
Nathan Beavis	*of North Curry 'absent, in arms'*
William Blunt	*of North Curry 'absent, in arms'*
Elias Bragg	*of North Curry 'absent'*
William Broadbeare	*of North Curry 'out in the late rebellion and in prison tried at Wells and transported thence for Bridgeman by White on the 'Constant Richard' 31st October to Jamaica'*
Jonas Cheeke	*of Thornfalcon of North Curry 'absent'*
Philip Cheeke	*aged 16, plowman of Thornfalcon of North Curry 'out in the rebellion and in prison; tried at Taunton and transported thence for the Queen on the 'Jamaica Merchant' 9th December to Barbados; sold on 12th March to Edward Hurlston'*
Robert Curry	*of North Curry 'absent'; 'a tenant and holds a cottage, fled, not yet apprehended'*
Robert Dyer	*of North Curry 'absent, in arms, a sergeant'*
Joseph Furze	*of North Curry 'wanting' and in the late Duke of Monmouth's service, dead*
John Gifford	*of Lillesdon, North Curry 'absent'*
Christopher Gillard	*of North Curry 'absent'*
Lawrence Guddridge	*of North Curry 'taking up arms against the King; killed at Sedgemoor or died of wounds'*
William Halesey	*of Lillesdon, North Curry 'absent'*
Nicholas Hebbett	*of North Curry 'absent'*
B Hobart	*of Lillesdon, North Curry 'absent'*
Robert Kewer	*of North Curry killed at Norton St Philip*
Peter Lea, senior	*of North Curry 'wanting from his home and in the late Duke of Monmouth's service'. Killed*
Gabriel Lyddon	*of North Curry, 'taking up arms against the King'*
Gabriel Marks	*of North Curry 'absent, taking up arms against the King'*
John Odsey	*of North Curry 'absent' fled, taking up arms against the King'*
James Osmans	*of North Curry 'taking up arms against the King'*
William Osmans	*of North Curry 'taking up arms against the King'*
Phillipe Osmond	*of North Curry 'in arms against the King'*
George Rooke	*of North Curry 'in arms against the King'*
Thomas Snow	*of North Curry, Thornfalcon, 'absent, in arms, fled'*
Robert Soper	*of Stoke St Gregory, North Curry, killed at Sedgemoor*
Richard Stephens	*of Wrantage, North Curry 'out in the late rebellion and in prison; in Bridgwater prison, tried at Taunton; hanged at Crewkerne'*
Richard Stephens	*of North Curry, 'out in the late rebellion and in prison, tried at Taunton, transported for Booth from Taunton Bridewell via Bristol 24th October on the 'John' to Barbados; sold to John and William Holder. One of these two was a cordwinder'*
Thomas Stone	*of Wrantage, North Curry 'absent, in arms, fled'*
Barnard Thatcher	*of Stoke St Gregory ' in the rebellion and in prison; tried at Taunton for concealing Bovett, hanged at Yeovil'*
Henry Toogood	*of North Curry ' absent'*
Richard Verrier	*of North Curry ' absent, in arms against the King'*
Thomas Verrier	*of North Curry ' absent, in arms against the King'*
William Verrier	*of North Curry, aged 17, carpenter, 'out in the rebellion and in prison, tried at Taunton; transported for the Queen, 9th December on the 'Jamaica Merchant' to Barbados' sold on 12th March to Archibald Johnson.'*
Robert Walter	*of North Curry 'absent, in arms against the King'*
Edward Watts	*of Wrantage, North Curry, 'absent, in arms against the King'*
William Wensley	*of North Curry 'absent in the late Duke of Monmouth's service; killed'*
John Young	*of North Curry 'absent, fled'*

James II proclaimed religious tolerance and appointed Roman Catholics to jobs in the army and government and to public offices of every kind, upsetting both the Whigs and the Tories. With the birth of a son to James II's second wife, England faced the prospect of a whole line of Catholic kings. Parliament sent a message to Prince William of Orange and his wife Mary, the Protestant daughter of James II, to act as regents for James II. William of Orange badly needed the support of England against the French and when James fled to France he agreed that he and Mary should rule jointly. In 1688 he became William III and his wife Mary II. By the Act of Settlement in 1689 it was made illegal for a Catholic to succeed to the Crown of England. In 1701 an Act of Succession was passed, ensuring the retention of a Protestant monarch and barring any member of the royal family who married a Catholic from the royal succession. This rule remains in force today.

Meanwhile James had regained his nerve and Louis of France's friendship and was planning the recovery of his lost kingdom. He landed in Ireland with French troops but was later defeated by William III at the Battle of the Boyne and retreated to France where he died in 1701. Queen Mary II died of smallpox in 1694 and William III in 1702. Anne, who was the second daughter of James II and Anne Hyde, succeeded them. In 1694 a group of Whigs offered to raise £1 million and lend it at eight per cent interest to the government. Subscribers to the loan were given the privilege of forming the first English bank with the right of issuing notes and bills of exchange, and thus the Bank of England was formed.

Queen Anne, the last of the Stuart monarchs, married Prince George of Denmark, but although she became pregnant 18 times they had no surviving child. She ruled with the reliance of the friendship of the Earl of Marlborough and his wife Sarah Churchill whose eldest daughter was married to Sidney Godolphin who became the Queen's Lord Treasurer and managed Parliament. A dispute between France, Austria, Holland and some German states about who should rule Spain led to Britain's involvement in the War of the Spanish Succession. Marlborough led armies to many great victories over the French including Blenheim in 1704, Ramilies in 1706, Oudenarde in 1708 and Malplaquet in 1709, resulting in the British Isles becoming the leading power in Europe. Spain had restored her monarchy agreeing to the Treaty of Utrecht in 1713, and the British had gained Minorca, Gibraltar, Nova Scotia, Hudson Bay and Newfoundland and declared peace with France. In 1707 the Act of Union with England and Scotland became law and linked Scotland with the 1536 union of England and Wales. The result of this union was the uniting of the Parliaments of England and Scotland and the formation of the United Kingdom of Great Britain.

The Great Britain of Queen Anne was still a very sparsely populated country. It is estimated that only 5.5 million people were then living in England and Wales, about 1 million in Scotland and about 1.5 million in Ireland. Most people earned their living from the soil, growing either barley or wheat, and by sheep farming. For the majority the diet consisted of salt-meat, grain and ale, with few vegetables other than turnips, together with poultry, eggs and salted or local river fish. Only the rich ate fresh meat. Agricultural changes were needed to feed an increasing population and new methods of crop rotation were tried. Innovative ways of sowing crops with the help of a seed drill were introduced by Jethro Tull (1674-1741) continuing the Agrarian Revolution. The woollen cloth industry was mainly a domestic occupation, and both linen and silk were being made. Coal was beginning to be mined from deeper shafts and in 1712 Thomas Newcomen, an ironmonger from Dartmouth, produced the first successful steam pump engine, laying the foundation for a revolution in technology and practical science. Iron ore was being smelted by charcoal until Abraham Darby (1677-1717) of Coalbrookdale began to use coke. Other industries developing at this time were shipbuilding, the manufacture of luxury goods such as jewellery, silverware and fine clothes and calico printing.

Foreign trade was conducted by merchants and members of chartered companies, including the East India, Hudson's Bay and Royal African Companies. Transport was by sea around the coasts, since rivers were not deep enough for substantial vessels. Although roads were uncomfortable, the horse with wagons was still the best way of moving goods. London continued as a thriving capital city with the seats of law, parliament and the royal court, and was the centre of the country's manufacturing and commercial life. The port handled foreign trade, and nobility, professionals and merchants had houses in London, but vast numbers of uneducated labourers lived in the utmost squalor and poverty, herded together in cramped living conditions spreading disease and infection. With the introduction of cheap gin, criminal life, unchecked by any police force, was rife.

Jonathan Swift (1667-1745) who published *Gulliver's Travels* in 1719 and Daniel Defoe who published *Robinson Crusoe* also in 1719 were both pioneer journalists producing newspapers and pamphlets. A postal service was introduced and for the wealthier members of society there were many pleasures with music and the arts flourishing. George Frideric Händel (1685-1759) was naturalised British and came to London in 1710, composing many works including his Messiah and Water Music Suite for royal audiences, and many dramatists and playwrights performed in the theatres. These, together with opera at Covent Garden, all provided splendid entertainment and a highly diverse social life for Londoners. Queen Anne paid visits to Bath in Somerset, establishing the town's prosperity as a fashionable centre with renowned architecture. Richard Nash (1674-1761) known as *Beau Nash*, and his son, who later designed the Royal Crescent, were instrumental in building and moulding Bath, with its hot spring baths, into a popular resort. Queen Anne, the last of the Stuarts, died in 1714.

1 - 8

HANOVERIAN RULE AND THE GEORGIAN AGE

Following the Act of Succession of 1701 nobody but a Protestant could become King of England. The late Queen Anne's half-brother, James Edward Stuart, the son of the displaced James II by his second and Roman Catholic marriage, was a candidate or Pretender for the English throne. Those who supported the Pretender, the Scots and most Tories, were called Jacobites after the Latin for the Pretender's name James. However, James refused to renounce his Catholic faith and his support dwindled. George I, the 54-year-old great grandson of James I, and Duke and Elector of Hanover in Germany, was Queen Anne's closest Protestant cousin. Hence, in 1714, he became the new King of England, even though he could speak no English, and the Hanoverian reign of England, Scotland, Wales and Ireland thus began.

The influence of Parliament had grown during the 17th century and regular elections resulted in positions of office being filled by the land-owning classes. Instead of spending their money on embellishing churches, they built their own houses and improved their estates, although a financial scandal called the *South Sea Bubble* led to the ruin of many. Architecture was inspired throughout the country by the traditions of the classical style. Sir John Vanbrugh (d.1726) designed many notable buildings in England, including Castle Howard and Blenheim Palace. William Kent (d.1748) designed Holkham Hall in Norfolk and the Horse Guards Parade in London and Robert Adam (1728-1792) built Syon House in Middlesex. Artificial landscaping of gardens and grounds originated in Britain and Lancelot Brown (1716-1783), known as Capability Brown, became the royal gardener. He set up a practice as a consulting landscape artist and transformed many stately homes of England owned by the high nobility including Blenheim, Hampton Court and Longleat. He also designed the Burton Pynsent column at Curry Rivel and advised on the layout of the Burton Pynsent gardens nearby. The rich were filling their houses with silver and plate and English porcelain produced by the factories of Chelsea, Bow, Derby and Worcester and the Wedgwood potteries at Stoke. The lesser nobility or country gentry favoured such pastimes as hunting, shooting, gambling and drinking. The yeomen of the country areas were content with very few organised pleasures concentrating in pursuits on their land and in their houses. The lesser social orders contented themselves with fishing, bird snaring, hawking, playing football, boxing, cock fighting and horse racing, smoking and drinking.

In 1720 an entry in the *Calendar of the Manuscripts of the Dean and Chapter of Wells Liber Ruber II* states:

> *Lease to Marshall Brydges of Wells, clerk, for 3 lives, of the decoy pool newly made within the manor of North Curry and a little dwelling house newly built thereon and all tame fowl, and all structures buildings, engines, pipes, reed-works and the sole liberty of fishing, fowling and hunting within the said manor. Lessee to pay £2.10s yearly rent and also "fifteen couples of fatt and good fowle, viz. duck, mallard, widgeon and teale, for the use of their audit dinners on the first Munday in December".*

Another entry in the *Calendar of the Manuscripts of the Dean and Chapter of Wells Liber Ruber II* in 1721 describes an encounter with a gentleman who claimed the profits of the fair in North Curry as a result of his purchase of a property:

> *1721 July 21*
> *Ordered that Mr. Collins, who lays claim to the prison house and fair of North Curry shall be wrote to that the Dean and Chapter insists on their right thereto, and that Mr. Collins forthwith produce his title, otherwise that a legal proper method be taken for recovering the same.*

A full enquiry was instituted and the result reported in 1723 as follows:

> *1723 November 14*
> *Whereas a dispute hath arisen between the worshipful Dean and Chapter of the Cathedral Church of Wells and Francis Collins of Wiveliscombe in county Somerset, gent, purchaser from the family of Sandfords who claimed from the family of Aishfords of the remains of the manor of Knapp within the Parish of North Curry touching the exercising the office of bayliffe of the Hundred of North Curry, and the fees and perquisites thereto belonging, and also touching the right and title of the fair and the prison house. Mr. Collins for good consideration releases and quitclaims for himself and his heirs to the Dean and Chapter and their successors all his rights, titles and claims.*

For many years there had been a steady increase in the population of the country and it was becoming clear that farming methods had failed to evolve rapidly enough to serve the resulting increase in food demand. The root of the problem lay in large areas of arable land being cultivated in long, unfenced strips with one third lying fallow every year, and with common animal grazing plots for the poorer people to share in almost every parish.

Some improvement was made by introducing root crops and sowing more productive strains of cereals, and the government tried to address the problem by authorising the conversion of landholding and agricultural practice from open-field farming to compact holdings, each held by a single farmer. Between 1755 and 1815 some 4,000 Acts of Parliament had facilitated a further wave of the system of enclosure for 5.9 million acres of land. Land was reallocated so that each farmer's holding was clustered together rather than being sprinkled randomly in various fields over the village, and this led to changes in the physical appearance of many villages. The General Enclosure Act of 1836 enabled farmers to enclose land without direct reference to Parliament. The bigger landowners had the resources to enclose more land and farm it more effectively. Many poor people suffered when their small farms were joined together to form larger ones, and their common-land grazing plots were enclosed and incorporated into larger holdings. Many of the poorer smaller farmers were forced into the towns to seek work. Straight hedgerows were introduced with the roadways being realigned and straightened by the parliamentary commissioner's surveyors, and waterlogged ground was brought into production by more effective drainage. When reclamation took place in Currymoor, Haymoor and West Sedgemoor during the first half of the 19th century, land was apportioned in return for the upkeep of drains, ditches, embankments and common rights. In 1816 an Enclosure Act was passed to deal with 3,000 acres of land in West Sedgemoor. The Parish of North Curry was apportioned with some 1,330 acres to be shared with Stoke St Gregory and West Hatch. The land was, and often still is, in danger of flooding, and was used originally only for summer pasture.

King George I chose Whigs to form his new government and in 1722 chose Robert Walpole as his chief minister. Peace had been established with France and Spain but domestic conditions in Britain were deteriorating. Excise duties and taxes on spirits were introduced to stop the smuggling and consumption of alcohol, and turnpike toll taxes were levied to improve the sad state of repair of the roads, both making Walpole unpopular.

George I died in 1727 and his son became George II. The new King detested the English but his wife Queen Caroline became an ally of Walpole and did much to persuade the King to accept British ways. She died in 1737. In 1745 another Jacobite rising to seize the throne ended when Prince Charles Edward or *Bonnie Prince Charlie*, the son of James II, was beaten at the Battle of Culloden. King George II was embroiled in seven years of war, first in Austria and then with the French, which dominated his reign and left Britain as the leading world power. The territories of Senegal, Canada, Nova Scotia and Grenada in the West Indies were acquired, and with Robert Clive (1725-1774) gaining provinces in India the government of Britain took control of the East India Company and appointed the first Governor General of India.

This period in English history produced many famous names in the arts and sciences. William Hogarth (1697-1764) the cartoonist and painter drew attention to thought, style and fashion of the time. Adam Smith (1713-1790), the first economist, published his book *The Wealth of Nations*, and Edward Gibbon (1737-1794), historian and author, published the *Decline and Fall of the Roman Empire.* Samuel Johnson (1709-1784) published the first *Dictionary of the English Language*, while writers Thomas Gray (1716-1771), Richard Sheridan (1751-1816) and Oliver Goldsmith ((1730-1774) together with actors David Garrick (1717-1779) and Sarah Siddons (1755-1831) added much to the depth of English literature. Celebrated artists such as Sir Joshua Reynolds (1723-1792) and Thomas Gainsborough (1727-1788), together with Thomas Chippendale (1718-1779), who became famous as a rococo furniture designer, all contributed to an elegance of style in the land. There were improvements in medicine with Guys, St George's and Middlesex hospitals being founded in London between 1720 and 1745, and Edward Jenner (1749-1823) conquering the disease of small-pox using an inoculation of cow-pox.

The start of the Industrial Revolution during the 18th century brought with it the introduction of new processes and improved working practices. Many successful business and professional men sought upward social mobility by buying estates and property and seeking to join the landed gentry. Landless labourers were also eager to earn a wage to keep them fed and clothed. Factories and mills developed making cotton cloth and these provided them with employment. With inventions such as John Kay's flying shuttle (1733), Richard Arkwright's water frame (1769), James Hargreaves' spinning jenny (1770), and Samuel Crompton's spinning mule (1779), machinery was introduced into the spinning and weaving industry, resulting in cheaper and more efficient production. The ironworks started by the Quaker Darby family in Coalbrookdale in Shropshire in the early part of the century flourished and expanded. During the reign of George II, James Brindley built the first true dead-water canal between 1759 and 1761 to transport coal to Manchester, starting the age of canals that helped to advance the Industrial Revolution. The first scheme in Somerset was proposed by a group of Taunton men who invited James Brindley to investigate the possibility of a canal from Weston-Super-Mare to Burrowbridge, then using the River Tone to Taunton, with another canal from Taunton to Exeter. Nothing came of this at that time and it was not until 1825 that the Bridgwater and Taunton Canal opened (see page 173).

In 1760 George II died and his grandson became George III, his son Frederick having died nine years before. George III, having been born in England and brought up as an English gentleman, was conscientious in terms of his religion and duty. He married Charlotte, a German princess, and 15 children were born to her. He ruled over a country of 6.5 million people, who had the greatest possessions in the world, but troubles with trade restrictions in the colonies of North America were beginning. The wars and the gaining of British territories had cost money, and in 1765 the American colonies were asked to pay their share of the expenses of the Empire by means of a Stamp Act and further subsequent tax measures such as the Sugar Act. In 1773 the East India Company was granted a virtual monopoly on the importation of tea. In protest, a group of Boston citizens disguised as Indians boarded a ship and dumped chests of tea into Boston harbour in a protest known as the Boston Tea Party. The so-called Intolerable Acts caused further unrest and in 1775 the colony was declared to be in a state of rebellion. This led to the Declaration of Independence being made on July 4th 1776 and a constitution was drawn up by which the United States of America is still governed today. Fighting continued until the final British withdrawal in 1783.

The granting of a market and fair to North Curry by Royal Charter in medieval times is mentioned on page 32, and further reference was made to this in an article by Nathaniel Spencer in *The Complete English Traveller* of 1771 which states:

> *Near Taunton is North Curry, a small market town situated on the Tone, but has nothing remarkable. It has a weekly market on Tuesdays, and a fair on the 1st August for cattle and toys. The inhabitants are plain, simple, industrious people, seemingly content with their station, and few of them ever leaving their native place. Provisions are in great plenty, the gardens and fields being well cultivated, so that the whole reminded us of those descriptions of the innocence of rural life often mentioned by the poets.*

At the time when, in 1791, the Reverend John Collinson described the area in his book *The History and Antiquities of the County of Somerset*, North Curry had already become a noted ancient parish with a depth of history. An extract is reproduced as follows.

> *The Hundred of North Curry is a parish of large extent, seven miles nearly east from Taunton, and ten south from Bridgwater, including a town of its name, and several tithings and hamlets.*
>
> *The principal part of the town is an irregular street near the church, which stands on an elevated plot, and commands from its tower a finely varied prospect of woody inclosures, and extensive level moors, skirted with a lofty ridge of hills to the east and south. West-Moor, Curry-Moor, and Hay-Moor, are all included within the precincts of the parish; and the inhabitants have right of common on West-Sedgmoor, Stanmoor, Warmoor, and West-Wall, adjoining to the Isle of Athelney, where the commonage is unlimited for all sorts and numbers of cattle throughout the year.*
>
> *The River Tone runs through this parish under a stone bridge of one arch, in its way to Boroughbridge, where it mingles with the Parret.*
>
> *Here was formerly a market on Wednesday long since discontinued, but a fair of ancient standing is still held on the first of August.*
>
> *The tithings and hamlets within this parish are Knap, Lillisdon, Wrantage, Hillend, Newport and Moordon.*

The arts continued to flourish in Britain, with novelists Henry Fielding (d.1754), Samuel Richardson (d.1761), Tobias Smollett (d.1771) and Jane Austen (d.1817) writing many works. The romantic poets Robert Burns (d.1796), John Keats (d.1821), Percy Bysshe Shelley (d.1822), Lord Byron (d.1824), Walter Scott (d.1832), Samuel Taylor Coleridge (d.1834) and William Wordsworth (d.1850), wrote much imaginative poetry. Artists including George Stubbs (1724-1806), J M W Turner (1775-1851), John Constable (1776-1837) and Edwin Landseer (1802-1873) contributed much to the world of painting. The style of Georgian architecture spread to smaller houses in both town and country. As prosperity grew it became fashionable to build houses in red brick and introduce large sash windows with a porch of classical decoration. Two or three houses of this period were built in North Curry, possibly by wool merchants from Taunton using bricks from Bridgwater. The houses of North Curry are discussed in Chapter 2-5.

During these times Captain James Cook (1728-1779), as Captain of the *Endeavour*, made many sea explorations to the Southern Hemisphere, and was credited with finding the cure for scurvy by feeding his sailors with citrus fruit. Cook was killed by islanders in Hawaii, but only after he had staked the British flag on previously unknown areas of the world by his skilful development of charting and marine surveying. In 1764 James Watt (1736-1819) devised an improved form of steam engine, Josiah Wedgwood (1730-1795) was establishing the potteries and John Macadam (1756-1836) macadamised roads, which transformed the countryside by providing better and longer-lasting surfaces and speeding mail coach communication. In 1779 Abraham Darby III built the world's first cast-iron bridge which spanned the River Severn at the Severn Gorge in Shropshire, giving the name Ironbridge to the entire industrial valley which was dubbed the birthplace of the Industrial Revolution. In 1748 Henry Fielding, the chief Justice of the Peace at the time, set up a force to combat crime called the *Bow Street Runners*.

The Whigs had dominated politics in the 18th century and included as Prime Ministers the Duke of Newcastle (1693-1768) and William Pitt (1708-1778). Sir William Pynsent left the estate of Burton, near Curry Rivel, to Pitt, who had sat as MP for Bath between 1757 and 1766. It was here that Pitt erected the Pynsent column designed by Capability Brown as mentioned earlier in this Chapter. The Whig George Grenville (1712-1770), whose estates included Dillington in Somerset, was Prime Minister from 1763-1765, followed by Charles Watson-Wentworth in 1765. William Pitt returned for a second term in 1766, followed by Augustus Fitzroy in 1768. Lord North (1732-1792) became Prime Minister in 1770. Watson-Wentworth returned in 1782, followed by William Petty-Fitzmaurice and William Cavendish in 1783. They were followed later in 1783 by the Tory William Pitt the Younger, who was the youngest British Prime Minister of all time at the age of 24, and under whose guidance Britain recovered her prosperity.

However, in 1789 the Revolution started in France and war became imminent. In 1793 King Louis XVI and his Queen, Marie Antoinette, were put to death and the *Reign of Terror* in France took place under Jacobin Robespierre. He proclaimed *Liberty, Equality, Fraternity* for the French, and Britain was declared as France's enemy. Income tax was implemented by William Pitt the younger in 1798 to pay for weapons and equipment in preparation for the Napoleonic wars (see page 90). Meanwhile, Ireland was eager for independence but differences between the Catholics and Protestants forced Pitt to decide that complete union of Ireland and Ulster with the mainland was the way forward, and in 1800 introduced the Act of Union when Ireland's Parliament was merged with that at Westminster. This was expected to lead to emancipation of Catholics, but King George III did not allow it, and William Pitt resigned in 1801. His successor was Henry Addington who suffered a lack of parliamentary support, and William Pitt the Younger returned to office in 1804 until his death in 1806.

Napoleon Bonaparte was attacking most of Europe and was planning to invade England. However under the leadership of Admiral Horatio Nelson the British Navy of some 300 warships conquered Napoleon's fleet at Trafalgar in 1805. War continued in Europe, but in 1815 Napoleon was finally defeated at Waterloo by the British army led by the Duke of Wellington.

Industrial output had increased, resulting in high employment having been directed towards the war effort with the manufacture of munitions. With Europe's trade isolated and technical innovations in the British cloth industry and iron-works, Britain began to capture many world markets. The population of towns continued to expand assisted by soldiers being released from the army and an influx of country dwellers seeking work. This led to overcrowding, bringing slum conditions, starvation and misery to many parts of the country. Poor relief was increased, income tax abolished, and a Corn Law banning foreign imports introduced. The latter legislation was greatly resented by the poorer section of the British community because it increased the price of bread.

In 1788 King George III showed the first signs of insanity and although at times he seemed to recover, he continued to drift into short bouts of madness until in 1810 permanent insanity overtook him. When he died in 1820, having reigned for 60 years, his son the Prince Regent, who had taken over the powers of the sovereign during the King's illness, became King George IV. King George IV had married Caroline of Brunswick in 1795, but after the birth of their daughter Charlotte they lived apart. The Regency period in Britain saw new styles of clothing, furniture and buildings with gas lighting in fashionable places. Robert Peel organised a police force which was to be the forerunner of to the organised Police Service in London established in 1829 (hence the word *bobby* being used for policeman). There was a great deal of unrest in the industrial areas of Britain with many losing their jobs, and it was feared the government would lose control. The Prime Ministers of the time included Liverpool, Canning and the Duke of Wellington. Reform Acts, designed to allow more people to vote in parliamentary elections, were passed, and moves began towards the establishment of trades unions. Laws had also been passed allowing Roman Catholics to sit in Parliament. King George IV died in 1830.

Princess Charlotte, daughter of George IV, had married Prince Leopold of Saxe-Coburg but died the year after her marriage before her father became King. The brothers of George IV were therefore the next heirs to succeed him. The Duke of York, the second son of George III had died three years before George IV and left no heirs, so William Henry, Duke of Clarence, the third son of George III ascended the throne as William IV in 1830. He married Adelaide of Saxe-Coburg-Meiningen but she was unable to have children. Further Reform Acts, firstly under Prime Minister Charles Grey, the second Earl Grey, and later in 1834 under Prime Minister William Lamb, second Viscount Melbourne, enabled the larger towns to send more members to the House of Commons and more people were allowed to vote. Due to the efforts of William Wilberforce in the reign of George III, an act to abolish slavery in British colonies was passed. A new Poor Law forcing manufacturers and farmers to pay a living wage to labourers was introduced. A Factory Act restricting children's working hours was passed in 1833. However, these regulations were not very well observed due to the lack of paid enforcers. In 1834 the Poor Law Amendment Act was passed which made help to the poor available through the workhouse and only housed those of genuine destitution. Parishes were to be organised into Poor Law Unions under elected boards of guardians, supervised by the Poor Law Commission in London who advised on the construction of new workhouses, which in the words of Edwin Chadwick were *uninviting places of wholesome restraint*. In 1839 15,000 of the nation's parishes had been grouped into 600 Poor Law Unions and 350 new workhouses were built. In 1838 a Union Workhouse was built in Taunton to serve the needs of the surrounding area, which included North Curry.

In 1814 George Stephenson (1781-1848) invented the steam locomotive which ran on iron trackways. Together with his son Robert Stephenson (1803-1859) and Henry Booth he founded the firm Robert Stephenson and Co. which constructed steam-locomotives such as the Rocket. These first served the collieries in Leeds and then in 1825 the Stockton and Darlington Railway was opened for passengers. In 1830 a railway was opened between Manchester and Liverpool. This allowed speedier transportation of raw cotton from Liverpool to the mills in Manchester, with the woven cloth being returned to Liverpool for shipping back to America. Isambard Kingdom Brunel together with other engineers developed a railway system that eventually served the whole of Britain, bringing quick and cheap travel for both passengers and goods. Steamships were also being developed, firstly for river transport and later as iron ocean-going vessels. Overseas trade grew, emigration was made easier and Britain's links with the rest of the world improved. In 1830 the Scottish geologist Charles Lyell (1797-1875) published the *Principles of Geology* which described how he found the fossilised remains of prehistoric animals embedded in geological strata, providing evidence that the earth had evolved, rather than being created in a short time. In 1834 Charles Robert Darwin (1809-1882) sailed in his ship, the *Beagle*, on a voyage to the Galapagos Islands studying plant and animal life, and on his return he established his theory that man had evolved over millions of years. These new concepts changed much scientific thought and lead to the study of genetics which was to influence greatly the medical profession in the ensuing years.

When William IV died in 1837 without an heir, Victoria the daughter of Edward, the Duke of Kent, the fourth son of George III, became Queen.

NORTH CURRY TIMELINE – HANOVERIAN TIMES TO PRESENT DAY

George I	1714–1727	1714	Avenue of elms planted in Parish churchyard
			Conversion of open field farming to individual enclosures
			Start of Agrarian Revolution
George II	1727–1760	1750	Machinery introduced into spinning and weaving industry
		1750–1850	Enclosure Acts resulting in hedged landscape with fields re-distributed
		c.1778	John Wesley reputed to have visited North Curry
George III	1760–1820	1779	Ironbridge founded – birthplace of Industrial Revolution
		c.1780	First surgeon practised in North Curry
		1787	First map of the whole of North Curry published
		1789	French Revolution
		c.1790	Many Georgian houses in North Curry built in this period
		1805	Battle of Trafalgar
		1809	Sunday School founded in North Curry
		1814	George Stepehenson's steam locomotive
		1815	Battle of Waterloo; first New Bridge constructed
George IV	1820–1830	1822	228 families employed in agriculture in North Curry
		1825	North Curry Baptist Chapel built
		1827	Bridgwater and Taunton Canal completed
		1832	North Curry Parish Church first restoration completed
		1833	Methodist Church in North Curry built
William IV	1830–1837	1836	Tithe Commutation Act
Victoria	1837–1901	1837	Organ in North Curry Parish Church installed
			Civil registration of all births, marriages and deaths
		1838	Workhouse built in Taunton
		1840	Tithe Map of North Curry published
		1841	First modern Census of Population taken
		1848	North Curry village school built in 1848
		1853	Durston Station opened
		1866	North Curry property commuted from Dean and Chapter of Wells to Ecclesiastical Commissioners
		1868	Reeve's Feast funds converted to Parish charity
		1875	North Curry Parish Church second restoration started
			Wrantage School built
		1879	Lieutenant Chard awarded Victoria Cross
		1894	First North Curry Parish Council elected; PO opened on present site in North Curry
		1897	Jubilee Monument erected in Queen Square North Curry
Edward VII	1901–1910	1903	Parish Magazine first published
George V	1910–1936	1920	War Memorial erected in North Curry
		1928	Women's Institute in North Curry founded
		1930	Lych-gate of North Curry Parish Church built
		1931	Tacchomo School on site of Long's House established
Edward VIII	1936		
George VI	1936–1952	1941	War damage to Wrantage School
Elizabeth II	1952 – present	1970	North Curry designated Conservation Area
		1980	North Curry Health Centre built
		1981	Village Hall built in Greenway, North Curry
		1987	North Curry V C School moved to Greenway in North Curry
		2001	National Census reports 1,740 people live in 751 households in North Curry (of these 130/56 estd. to be in Durston)

1 - 9

THE VICTORIANS AND 19TH CENTURY LIFE

QUEEN VICTORIA'S REIGN

Queen Victoria ascended the throne of Great Britain in 1837 when she was 18 years old. Her father Edward, Duke of Kent, brother of William IV had been heir to the throne but he had died in 1820. The Queen was christened Alexandrina Victoria because George IV insisted she be named after her godfather, Tsar Alexander I of Russia. Her second name was after her mother who was Princess Victoire, daughter of the Duke of Saxe-Coburg. In 1839 the Queen fell in love with her cousin Albert of Saxe-Coburg-Gotha. They were married in 1840 and had nine children. The first, Victoria, the Princess Royal, who married Frederick III, the future Emperor of Germany, was followed by Edward, Prince of Wales, the future King Edward VII, three more boys and four more girls.

Prince Albert supported many causes to improve social conditions in the land and engaged himself in encouraging trade and industry, his great achievement being the Great Exhibition of 1851 which showed off British industrial prowess. He also acted as the Queen's advisor and private secretary, and in 1857 he was given the title Prince Consort. In 1861, at the age of 42, Prince Albert contracted typhoid and died, causing Queen Victoria great distress and leading to a period of mourning which was to last for many years.

Queen Victoria ruled Britain and the Empire for 64 years, during which time 10 Prime Ministers and 19 governments served her. In the early years of her reign Queen Victoria trusted, and was guided by the Whig, William Lamb, 2nd Viscount Melbourne. Lord Melbourne had become Prime Minister in 1834 and acted as her mentor and father-figure on matters of state when she became Queen. He resigned in 1841 after a vote of no confidence in his weak government and died a year later. The Tories came to power with Sir Robert Peel as the new Prime Minister. Having been a cotton manufacturer in Lancashire, he understood the distress of the poor and became a great social reformer. Queen Victoria respected Peel and he encouraged her to pay state visits overseas. In 1841 he introduced the penny postage stamp which aided communication, and in 1842 he revived Income Tax which was set at seven pence in the pound.

Peel's government was attacked by Chartism, the first political movement of the industrial working class, who wanted their voice heard in Parliament and political equality. Chartism, which had taken its name from a parliamentary bill or *People's Charter* drawn up in 1838 by William Lovett, had aimed at improving the social and economic conditions of the working classes by parliamentary legislation. Its aims were to make Parliament more representative of the whole nation and comprised six points including universal male suffrage, a secret ballot and the payment of Members of Parliament. However, a violent element penetrated the leadership creating confusion, riots and strikes and resulting in the movement being disbanded. Peel was also attacked by the Anti-Corn Law League and in 1846 following the Irish potato famine the Corn Laws were repealed leading to his resignation. He led his supporters into opposition and Peelites and Whigs became united as Liberals. The Anti-Corn Law League was led by Richard Cobden and John Bright who believed that free trade in corn would allow food prices to fall and industry to expand, by making more money available for the purchase of consumer goods, leading to full employment.

In 1832 the first Parliamentary Reform Act was passed conferring the vote on selected propertied adult males and increasing the electorate from 435,000 to 652,000, but still excluding the working class. In 1867 another Reform Act made parliamentary seats available for redistribution. More landholders, ratepayers and skilled workers in new town boroughs were given the vote, resulting in a third of all adult males being eligible to vote, but no women or agricultural labourers being enfranchised. In 1884 voting rights were extended to the countryside to include more occupiers and lodgers paying certain rentals. A short time later more parliamentary seats became available for redistribution, but there were still only 5.6 million electors out of a population of some 36 million in the United Kingdom. It wasn't until after the Representation of the People Acts in 1918, 1928 and 1948 and 1969 that all men and women over the age of 18 were allowed to vote.

Some form of local government had existed for centuries, and much of the work involved had fallen on the Justices of the Peace. With the effects of the Industrial Revolution and the growth of towns, these people had too much to do. In 1832 all householders were allowed, by a clause in the Reform Act, to elect town councillors and choose a mayor. Small towns formed Urban District Councils, while the countryside was divided into areas under Rural District Councils. In 1888 the Local Government Act allowed County Councils to be elected. A similar Act of Parliament in 1894 established Parish Councils for villages.

In 1846 the Whigs were returned to power with Henry Temple, 3rd Viscount Palmerston (1784-1865) as Foreign Secretary, and Queen Victoria became unhappy with his policies, wanting to retain international co-operation between the rulers in Europe. In 1848 revolution again broke out in France, King Louis Philippe was expelled, and a Republic proclaimed with Louis Napoleon Bonaparte, nephew of the earlier Emperor, being installed as President. In 1854 the Crimean War broke out when Britain and France declared war on Russia in support of Turkey. Lord Palmerston became Prime Minister, and due to his efforts victory ensued and Russia was forced to cede territory to Turkey.

The Conservative, Benjamin Disraeli, 1st Earl of Beaconsfield, (1804-1881), and the Liberal, William Ewart Gladstone (1809-1898), were in political opposition from 1868 to 1885, each holding the post of Prime Minister on more than one occasion. Gladstone was responsible for a group of reforms including the reorganisation of the army with new entry and promotional procedures and improved conditions of service. He also stipulated that entry into the Civil Service would be by examination, but he suffered an intolerant relationship with Queen Victoria. Disraeli established a close relationship with the Queen and during his ministry reformed education, savings, public health, housing and factory conditions and in 1868 persuaded Parliament to grant Queen Victoria the title of Empress of India. He acquired shares of £4 million in the Suez Canal and returned from the Congress of Berlin in 1878 proclaiming he had achieved *peace with honour* between Bismarck's Germany, Russia and all of Europe. He died in 1881 as conflicts in the Transvaal in southern Africa were starting between the Boers, who were displaced farmers, and the British. War continued until 1902 when the Boer republics were absorbed into the British Empire.

In 1884 Egypt was rebelling against French and British rule and General Charles Gordon had been sent to help. He was killed by the Arab nationalists and it was not until General Herbert Kitchener's re-conquest in 1898 that peace was restored.

Queen Victoria died on the Isle of Wight at Osborne House in 1901 at the age of 81. Her reign had been an age of progress in the arts and sciences, in literature, in the art of government, and in the comfort and wellbeing of the people. Peace and prosperity had flourished at home, and abroad the boundaries of the Empire had widened and Britain had consolidated her position as the workshop of the world, becoming the leading merchant, freight carrier, shipbuilder, insurance underwriter, banker and creditor. Patriotic fervour had never been higher and people understood the society in which they lived.

Social and Economic Growth

Life in the 19th century was changing rapidly with great progress in agriculture and industry. Economic growth brought about an increase in the number and size of towns and an expansion of the middle classes. More than half the population were regular attendees at church and chapel which encouraged a moralistic outlook on life, with emphasis on hard work and learning and a desire for self-improvement. However, there were many towns with slum areas displaying extreme poverty, portrayed so vividly by Charles Dickens in his novels. Travel was made easier by the railways, which replaced horse-drawn coaches. Road vehicles of all kinds from horse-drawn omnibuses and cabs to carriages and carts served most local needs. The large houses still remained the centres of life in the countryside with improvements in material comforts and the employment of large numbers in domestic service. Only 15 per cent of the cultivated land in England was worked by direct owners, with the remaining 85 per cent being worked by tenants. A third of farmed land in England and Wales was laid out in farms of between 200 and 500 acres.

By 1830 the first stage of the Industrial Revolution was over, resulting in vast numbers of the population employed in industry and commerce. In 1838, in an early speech to the House of Commons, Benjamin Disraeli coined the phrase *Workshop of the World* to describe a country where factories, mines, heavy industry and ports serviced by a good transport system between a number of dynamic industrial centres, combined with inventions and technological advances, had put Britain at the forefront of trade. Britain boasted a thriving successful worldwide commercial system. London had replaced Amsterdam as the world's leading financial centre. Banks, joint-stock companies, venture capital and insurance were in place. A rapidly expanding labour market, free of the serfdom restrictions still current elsewhere in Europe, was waiting to service the new Empire.

By 1851 Britain's industrial growth had already far outstripped many others, and her total exports increased from £71 million in 1850 to nearly £200 million in 1870. Her imports trebled in these years from £100 million to £300 million. The gap between imports and exports was more than bridged by her *invisible exports* in the form of shipping, banking and insurance services. Out of the United Kingdom population of 21 million in 1851, the most significant areas of employment were as follows:

Agriculture	1,790,000
Textiles	1,650,000
Domestic service	1,000,000
Metal, engineering, and shipbuilding	750,000
Quarries and mines	500,000
Machine manufacture	106,000
Railway construction	65,000

Petrol, obtained from oil, eventually replaced steam power for transport purposes, but because the British law restricted the speed of vehicles the Germans Otto, Daimler and Benz led this development. In 1876 Nicolaus Otto constructed the first practical four-stroke internal combustion engine which he built into a motor cycle. In 1885, the mechanical engineer, Karl Benz designed and built the world's first practical automobile to be powered by an internal-combustion engine. In 1885, Gottlieb Daimler (together with his design partner Wilhelm Maybach) took Otto's internal combustion engine a step further and patented what is generally recognized as the prototype of the modern petrol engine using a petrol-injected carburettor, with a vertical cylinder. In 1886, Karl Benz received the first patent for a petrol-fuelled car.

Britain's H Ackroyd-Stuart experimented in the use of heavy oil, later called diesel oil, after the German inventor of the diesel engine, which was used in ships and generating plants, and J B Dunlop invented the pneumatic tyre in 1888. In 1896 the law was changed, permitting cars to travel at a speed of up to 14 miles an hour and a motor industry became established, with Messrs Lanchester, Austin, Rolls, Royce and Morris (later Lord Nuffield) becoming car producers.

By the middle of the 19th century numerous new developments had changed the life of society, and as the century progressed there were many advances in medicine, science and technology. Public health improved during the century, due mainly to more educated, qualified medical practitioners. Between 1818 and 1831 medical schools had been established in Bristol, Manchester, Sheffield and Leeds, following those in London, and interest in the subject was revived at Oxford and Cambridge. At first surgeons were faced with problems of how to relieve pain and how to prevent blood poisoning. Experiments with ether and nitrous oxide lead to painless surgery using anaesthetics, with James Simpson (1811–1870) in Edinburgh using chloroform for the first time in 1847, a practice which gained considerable legitimacy when he used it on Queen Victoria during her pregnancy in 1853.

The crowding of patients into dirty hospital wards resulted in infection spreading easily on the hands of doctors and nurses, leading to blood poisoning. Few practised using antiseptic materials in hospitals. The French scientist Louis Pasteur (1822–1895), working on fermentation and decomposition in connection with brewing and wine-making, discovered that these processes were caused by living organisms or germs, and that these germs came from the air. Joseph Lister (1827–1912), who was professor of surgery at Glasgow and Edinburgh, realised in 1865 that such germs must also be the cause of blood poisoning. He revolutionised surgery by using antiseptics to sterilise hospital equipment and treat wounds. Florence Nightingale (1820–1910) raised the standard of cleanliness in hospitals during her work in the Crimean War and made nursing a regular and respected profession by improving hospital administration. From 1880 a number of the bacteria that caused diseases were isolated and studied, and means of counteracting them discovered. The use of soap and water to secure household and personal cleanliness, new methods of avoiding contamination of food and the pasteurisation of milk all furthered improvement in health. Inoculation and immunisation against tetanus, diphtheria and the rabies virus were subsequently developed.

In 1842 a Commission was set up to report on female and child labour in the mines. It was revealed that children as young as five were employed in underground pits for up to 16 hours a day in darkness and damp. An Act was passed prohibiting the employment of female labour and boys under ten in the mines. In 1843 the government introduced a Factory Bill that restricted young children working in factories and mills to a day of six-and-a-half-hours instead of nine and enabled women to be protected by a 12-hour day. In 1847 all women and young people aged 13 to 18 were restricted to a ten-hour day with all work being undertaken between 6 am and 6 pm.

People's health was also affected by their living conditions in the ever-growing towns and industrial areas that were becoming miserable regions of damp, dilapidation and decay. A German named Friedrich Engels (1820–1895) described the conditions in Manchester in an account entitled *The Condition of the Working Class in England* in 1844 as *grim factories overshadowing dark streets and lanes, the undrained, uncared-for rows of poorly built cottages, the clouds of black smoke, the malodorous river Irwell swirling underneath the narrow bridges*. Besides the lack of sanitation there was much overcrowding, with 15,000 people living in cellars in 1840. In 1842 Edwin Chadwick (1800–1890) published his *Report on the Sanitary Conditions of the Labouring Population* which revealed *the number of deaths from typhus fever was double that of the lives lost by the Allies in the battle of Waterloo.*

Epidemics of cholera in 1832 and 1848 in London and the provinces ravaged the homes of the rich and poor, with the result that Boards of Health were set up by Parliament to address matters of poor water supply and drainage. In 1848 Parliament passed the Public Health Act which led to improved sanitation, housing, water supplies and sewage systems. In 1875 another Public Health Act laid down rules for sanitation which all house owners had to obey. Every local council had to appoint a medical officer of health, a surveyor, and a sanitary inspector, and provide a water supply unless already provided by a private company. The Act stipulated that sewers must be maintained in good condition, the making, paving, cleaning and lighting of the streets must be attended to and scavengers must be employed to collect refuse regularly. Other duties included the supervision of markets and slaughterhouses, with the right to seize and destroy unsound food, and to provide washhouses and public baths and examine the sanitary conditions of workshops. Introduced in 1875, the Sale of Food and Drugs Act did much to stop the sale of injurious and falsely described ingredients.

The development earlier in the century of methods of converting coal into coke, producing coal-gas, had led to domestic gas lighting with gas works being installed nationwide. Sir Humphrey Davy (1788–1829) had discovered new elements and demonstrated the method of electrolysis leading to the discovery of electric lighting using batteries. The physicist Michael Faraday (1791–1867), who was Davy's assistant, had worked on magnetism and electricity and developed the first electrical generator. William Sturgeon (1783–1850), who had discovered the electro-magnet as a means of driving a rotary engine, helped Faraday, and in 1867 their work saw the commercial production of dynamos. Electric lighting was first introduced in Britain eight years later. This development was due to Joseph Swan (1828–1914) in England, and Thomas Edison in America, whose simultaneous discoveries resulted in the electric light bulb. Electricity made an unparalleled contribution to the growth of communications and transport. In 1844 a telegraph line was opened between Paddington and Slough using the Morse Code, a code of dots and dashes, invented by Samuel Morse (1791–1872). This was followed by the teleprinter, by which typewriters sent and received typed messages. In 1851 a cable linked Paris with Dover, followed 14 years later with a cable under the Atlantic, greatly benefiting business communication. In 1876 Alexander Graham Bell (1847–1922), a Scotsman who had emigrated to Canada and then to the United States, patented a magnetic telephone. He launched the Bell Telephone Company in 1877 and invented instruments such as the photophone and gramophone. In 1900, as many as 3,000 people in Britain had a telephone.

In 1881 an electric railway was opened in Berlin and shortly afterwards stretches of track were electrified in England. An underground railway using steam engines had been opened in London in 1863 but it produced unpleasant conditions in the tubes, and in 1890 these engines were replaced with electric locomotives. In Liverpool an overhead electric railway was opened in 1893, and by the end of the century most cities had converted their steam trams to overhead electric wires. In 1884 Charles Parsons (1854–1931) invented the turbine engine enabling electricity to be generated in central power stations, which led to electricity being distributed to mines and factories in the 20th century. In 1897 James Clerk-Maxwell (1831–1879) advanced the theory of the existence of electro-magnetic waves. This prompted the German, Heinrich Hertz, and the Italian, Guglielmo Marconi, to use these waves as a means of radio communication. In 1897 messages were sent for short distances without wires once again using the Morse Code.

In 1856 inventions by Henry Bessemer (1813–1898) and William Siemens (1823–1883) made the production of steel easier and cheaper. Bessemer's converter process and Siemens' open hearth process eliminated carbon and silicon from pig-iron, the first stage in steel manufacture. Britain adopted these methods and the steel industry built up a large export trade. At the Great Exhibition of 1851 Sir Joseph Whitworth displayed his new machine tools for planing, drilling, slotting and shaping, leading to advances in precision engineering. Whitworth and Henry Maudsley (1771–1831), who had previously produced numerous lathe inventions, were pioneers in inventing precision engineering tools to advance Victorian mechanical engineering.

At the beginning of the century the chemist John Dalton (1766–1844) had propounded an atomic theory, enunciated in his *A New System of Chemical Philosophy*. He also invented a symbolic language for his theory and produced tables of the atomic weights of the elements measured relative to hydrogen, which remains central to modern concepts of matter. As the century progressed other scientists investigating the structure of matter were led to the discovery of the enormous energy stored in every atom. In 1897 J J Thomson (1856–1940) discovered the electron, while his pupil, Ernest Rutherford (1871–1937) worked on wireless transmission and the ionisation of gases, beginning a period of advanced scientific research that stretched into the 20th century.

In order to support a large-scale and complex industrial system there was a growing need for education. Revival of public schools and the creation of private schools were demanded by the wealthier members of the population. The old public schools such as Eton, Winchester, Westminster, Shrewsbury, Harrow, Charterhouse and Rugby had fallen into a bad state during the 18th century. Food and accommodation in these schools were poor, the boys were unruly and there was frequent flogging. Early in the 19th century many were reformed following the examples of great headmasters such as Dr Thomas Arnold of Rugby and Samuel Butler of Shrewsbury. To meet the growing demand from the new middle classes, who could now afford to pay for education, many new public schools such as Cheltenham (1841), Marlborough (1842) and Wellington (1859) were founded, and long-established schools such as Sherborne and Repton were expanded. There were also some 800 endowed or private grammar secondary schools that were opened in the 19th century, which were largely boarding institutions drawing pupils from all over the country. Acts of Parliament in 1868 and 1869 were passed to broaden the curriculum of many of the older schools to encompass mathematics, chemistry and physics together with the old subjects of Latin and Greek.

As the population increased more children needed schooling in additional schools in order for England to compete with a skilled continental workforce. Elementary education was seen as essential for all children, and in 1833 a Factory Act required employed children to attend school for two hours a day. The government made a grant of £20,000 a year to the charitable institutions towards the building of more schools. Voluntary church societies had been providing elementary education in some 3,500 schools during the previous 20 years.

However, almost half of the children in the land still went without education. Those that did go to school suffered dark, cramped, dreary and overcrowded classrooms. Lessons were taught without much imagination and many pupils were harshly punished for mistakes as they learnt the three R's i.e. reading, writing and arithmetic. In 1870 W E Forster (1819–1886) introduced an Education Act which required the provision of *state* or *board* schools where there was not a *voluntary* school in existence. Before the end of the century elementary education had become compulsory and free for over five million children, and as new teaching methods and a broader curriculum were introduced the standard of education improved. The foundation of a national state system of elementary and secondary education and education for all was achieved. The history of education is discussed further in Chapter 2-7.

The Victorian age saw extensive new building of public and town halls, clubs, offices for banks and insurance companies, railway stations and churches, with the architecture of the time very often imitating earlier ages. Architects were generous with internal space and paid great attention to façades with elaborate ornamentation. Gothic and Greek styles grew in popularity with Augustus Welsby Pugin (1812–1852) rebuilding the Houses of Parliament in the Gothic style, the original having been accidentally destroyed by fire in 1834, and Sir George Gilbert Scott (1811–1878) restoring many old churches. New domestic houses were also built in these styles with the regency form of architecture giving way to Gothic design, and many were built in this ecclesiastical decorated style displaying pointed arches, stained glass windows and elaborate entrances.

Middle class homes were built of three storeys with a basement for the servants. Furnishings for these houses frequently came from examples of craftsmanship on show at the Great Exhibition of 1851. Iron was used for fireplaces, bedsteads and baths, and rooms were filled with clumsy mahogany furniture. Ornamental pieces of bric-a-brac and large paintings were displayed in rooms lit by oil lamps with heavy drapes, curtains and carpets. However the poor fared badly, particularly in the towns, where they were housed in closely packed rows of houses standing back to back and separated by narrow lanes. Several families often shared one or two rooms, and water was only available for an hour a day from a communal pump in the road. Rents for these families were about a sixth of their weekly wage, and the majority were poorly nourished. It was estimated that 30 per cent of the population of London were below the poverty line and unable to afford food of acceptable calorific value to perform their work. Meat was a rare luxury for the poor, but at the other extreme many upper and middle class Victorian families loaded their tables with huge amounts of food with numerous courses. Isabella Beeton (1836–1865) wrote a cookery book that sold two million copies in ten years.

Clothing was very formal, demanding frock coats and morning dress with top hats for the professional classes and bowler hats for the working man. Ladies' dress was extremely elaborate with layers of starched garments under vast crinolines of silks, and lace. Recreation consisted of trips to the sea or country by train, park visits, lectures, libraries and theatrical entertainment in the towns and, for the working man, drinking in the pubs. The new commercial and professional middle classes left the field sports of hunting, shooting and fishing to the country gentry, and supported team games that they had learnt at school or university. W G Grace (1848-1915) developed the game of cricket which, together with football and rugby became a popular school game. Later these sports employed professional players and gained a spectator following, with many factories and mining communities supporting their own teams. Rowing, croquet, archery and tennis were popular pastimes for the upper classes. The formation of the Amateur Athletic Association in 1866 helped to foster an enthusiastic public attitude to sporting life. Horse-racing also became popular, especially the Grand National steeplechase run at Aintree since 1839.

An expanding literate population brought an increase in demand for newspapers, novels and other literary works. Charles Dickens (1812–1870) published many novels such as *Oliver Twist, Nicholas Nickleby* and *A Christmas Carol*, drawing attention to the social conditions of the time by describing the lives of the poor. Mrs Elizabeth Gaskell (1810–1865) based her novels upon her acquaintance with factory conditions and Charles Kingsley (1819–1875) dealt in some of his published novels with working-class stress during the 1840s. Robert Louis Stevenson (1850–1894) wrote books and stories that appealed to children, with such tales as *Treasure Island* and *Kidnapped.* Rudyard Kipling (1865–1936) wrote of life in India in his *Jungle Books*, and H G Wells (1866–1946) provided early science fiction in his books *The Time Machine* and *The Invisible Man.* The poets Alfred Tennyson (1809–1892) and Robert Browning (1812–1889) both published their works, and William Thackeray wrote *Vanity Fair*, Thomas Babington Macaulay wrote the *History of England* and the Bronte sisters wrote their many novels, all contributing to a great literary foundation in Britain. Newspapers were growing in number and their price was kept down through devoting pages to advertisements. In 1857 *The Daily Telegraph* was launched as the first one penny London morning newspaper. There were many provincial newspapers and the public began to buy specialised publications relating to their work or hobbies.

Music played an important part in Victorian life. Light operas, many composed by Gilbert and Sullivan, philharmonic orchestras, church and factory choirs, and music hall concerts were enjoyed by many. The wealthier families made music in their homes, encouraging their daughters to be proficient in singing or playing a musical instrument.

Art continued to flourish in the Victorian age and British painters followed in the steps of their 18th century predecessors. Art reproductions from many of these such as Constable and Landseer decorated numerous Victorian homes. They were followed by the pre-Raphaelite movement of painters, followers of Holman Hunt and John Everett Millais, which also included Ford Maddox Brown, Dante Gabriel Rossetti, who was also a poet, William Morris and Edward Burne-Jones.

THE BRITISH EMPIRE

In 1783 the independence of the 13 American colonies seemed to spell the end of the British Empire. Britain's overseas territories extended to several West Indian Islands, parts of West Africa, Australia, large parts of India and North America. However, with her bases and supply centres, such as the territories of Malta and Cape Colony, Britain was able to maintain and extend her Empire. Aided by a strong Navy, the British command of the sea remained unchallenged after the Battle of Trafalgar in 1805. Together with the rising rate of emigration after the Battle of Waterloo in 1815, with the settlement of millions of British emigrants, Britain became the greatest imperial power in the world. In 1832 there were more than 100,000 emigrants, and after the potato failure in Ireland in 1846 the average number for the next three years was 150,000. The discovery of gold in California (1849) and in Australia (1851) offered a further encouragement to venture overseas and from 1850 to 1854 annual emigration averaged 325,000.

British North America was the part of the Empire to attract most settlers after the Battle of Waterloo, and between 1815 and 1865 the population rose to 3.5 million. Since 1759, when General James Wolfe captured Quebec and destroyed French power in North America, the region experienced many years of confrontation between the local British government and the population, particularly the French, over language, religion, politics and economics. In 1791 Quebec was divided into two provinces of Upper and Lower Canada, with separate governors appointed by the British government. However, in 1837 continuing nationalistic rivalry between the English and French culminated in rebellion. In 1840 the Reunion Act brought French and Canadians together with a Parliament of two Houses. In 1867 the British North America Act established a Federal government and created the office of Governor General with Canada's establishment as a Dominion. This was a precursor to the later transformation of the British Empire into the British Commonwealth. Canada's economy in the early-19th century was based mainly on fur, fish and timber, whilst later the expansion of the railway network gave access to ports, enabling the export of wheat to world markets. Canadian loyalty to Britain was demonstrated at the end of the century by their sending 8,000 troops to fight the Boer War.

British interest in India had developed from 1600 when the East India Company was founded. The initial intention was to establish a trading network to acquire exotic goods such as spices, precious stones, saltpetre, cottons and silks for the European market. With the disintegration of the Mughal Empire in the 18th century, feuding European rivals engaged in armed conflict. British troops led by Robert Clive, a 25-year-old officer of the East India Company, defeated both French and Indian forces, and as a result the Company's powers were extended beyond their trading posts based in Bombay, Madras and Calcutta.

In 1858 the people of India had rebelled against the rule of the East India Company and felt that the railways, roads, telegraphs and schools that had been imposed on them across the countryside were threatening their ancient society. They had inflicted a terrible massacre on the British at Cawnpore and were quashed by British troops. Eventually an Act of Parliament took away the East India Company's territories and gave them to the Crown, who became advisors and protectors to some 700 states and princes, and India came under the direct sovereignty of Queen Victoria.

British influence in the East during the early-19th century extended both westwards and eastwards from India. Aden became a British protectorate in 1839 when the position of the port on the new Egypt to India steamship route became important as an imperial base. The Burmese gave Britain the entire coast of northern Burma, safeguarding the approaches to India. In 1786 the East India Company had purchased the island of Penang, off the West Coast of the Malay Peninsula, to protect the tea-trading route to China. Later the island of Singapore was purchased to provide a trading base at the foot of the Malay Peninsula, and together with other small states and kingdoms these territories were progressively combined into British colonial protectorates with British administration. In 1839 war broke out with China after the Chinese attacked a British ship, and they forbade all trade with Britain following a dispute about opium trading. Britain captured Canton and other towns, resulting in Shanghai, Canton and other ports opening to European trade. Hong Kong was ceded to Britain in 1842 as part of the terms of peace.

Australia began her history as a penal colony when, stemming from reports brought back by Captain James Cook (1728-1779), Botany Bay in New South Wales was chosen as a suitable location for a settlement for transported convicts. Transportation continued to other areas of Australia until 1868 and, as many of these convicts had been transported for only minor offences and sought permanent residence when their freedom was granted, new townships and roads were built and the country evolved as an emigration destination. The British government passed the Waste Lands Act enabling long, cheap leases on land and by 1870 a million people had settled in Australia or New Zealand. Ex-convicts and settlers merged into one community, mostly engaged in sheep farming, strengthened in the second half of the century by the discovery of gold. Because of the vastness of the country several separate Crown colonies evolved in the 1850s - Victoria, South Australia and Queensland. By 1900 the Australian Commonwealth Act enabled the first Federal Parliament. New Zealand was also raised to the status of a Dominion at the end of the 19th century and her economy, based heavily on the export of lamb, prospered further from 1882 when meat refrigeration became possible.

The West Indies was the wealthiest colonial region, supported by the tropical products of sugar and tobacco that relied on a labour force of slaves from Africa. The work of William Wilberforce (1759-1833) culminated in 1833 in a parliamentary bill to end the trading and transporting of slaves, and in 1838 in the British West Indies 750,000 African slaves became completely free, returning to work as paid labourers on the sugar estates. The planters received several million pounds in compensation for the loss of the slaves. In 1846 free trading of sugar was established, and with the widespread production of beet sugar in Europe, together with large areas of land being taken over as free settlements for former slaves, local fortunes diminished.

However, by 1870 Chinese and Indian immigration helped with the labour shortage in the West Indies and alternative crops such as cocoa, coffee, bananas and cotton led to an economic revival.

South Africa was the other imperial territory that attracted British settlers in the first half of the 19th century. The Dutch Cape Colony had been seized by the British in the war with France in 1795 and was finally ceded to Britain in 1814. Within a population of millions of Africans there were many warring African Bantu tribes known as the Kaffirs, and together with the original Dutch settlers, the Boers, and the British settlers who established a settlement named Albany, there was much confusion. The Boers were becoming dissatisfied with British rule and they left the Cape in 1836 to settle in what became the Orange Free State, Natal and the Transvaal. Diamond discoveries in the late 1860s and the Gold Rush of the late 1880s provided the impetus for British expansion, much of it into Boer-controlled states. The British attempts to tighten control over these Boer territories eventually led to the Boer War of 1899.

With British people emigrating by the thousand to lands that had to be governed and protected, together with the East India Company preserving and administering its territories, and Britain requiring naval vantage points to protect British trading, an extensive British Empire again developed.

North Curry in Victorian Times

Against this background of Victorian prosperity, North Curry was evolving as an increasingly self-sufficient agricultural community. Christopher and John Greenwood writing in *Somersetshire Delineated* in 1822 described North Curry as having 228 families employed in agriculture.

North Curry, together with many other rural villages in England, underwent great change during the 19th century. There was much hardship and poverty for the labouring classes at the beginning of the century. With poor harvests in the 1790s, and the cost of the war with France, grain prices rose to high levels. Many small tenant farmers lost their livelihood when their land was incorporated into larger farms and they were forced to rely on poor relief. By the 1830s there was much discontent and agricultural labourers sought revenge by hayrick burning and machine breaking with the consequence that employers were forced to pay an adequate wage for regular employment.

In 1841 the population of North Curry rose to its highest recorded level and stood at 2,219, probably inflated by the presence of canal construction workers, but by 1901 it had dropped back to 1,525. A detailed review of the development of the North Curry population during the 19th century together with information on occupations and further details gleaned from the National Census and other demographic sources appear in Chapter 3-2.

Although life was harsh by 21st century standards and poverty was quite common, people tended to accept their station in life with equanimity and grasp the small but steady improvements in lifestyle that evolved. In Somerset in 1851 there were 1,873 landed proprietors and 8,438 farmers, with 8,500 farm servants living in, and 37,000 agricultural labourers. The average weekly wage for the agricultural worker in the middle of the 19th century was between eight and ten shillings, with a daily allowance of three pints of cider. At the time of haymaking bonuses could be earned by the whole family, and other tasks such as weeding, potato and turnip picking and bird scaring were allocated to the younger members of the family.

In North Curry the nearby new railway had driven the stage coaches, which had stopped at the Angel Inn in Stoke Road, off the road. Only the local traffic of farm carts, and carriers' wagons, farmers' traps and the carriages of the wealthier people moved along the roads into the village. North Curry was a very independent and self-sufficient place, with the inhabitants having a strong pride in their birthplace with its own traditions and customs. Many of the families had lived in the village for generations and followed a trade handed down from father to son. Mutual tolerance prevailed, with everyone being seen to be of value, contributing in some way to the general life of the rhythmic agricultural community. Farm workers inhabited most of the dwellings in the Parish, and although wages were low, the cost of living was also low. Cottage rents were about one shilling a week, and for this the tenant had a garden in which he grew all his own vegetables. Many farmers also allowed their men extra ground to grow potatoes and other vegetables.

Corn gleaned at harvest time supplemented family food and skimmed milk was bought from the farm dairy at a small cost. Bacon was the principal meat eaten. Ale, cider and home-made fruit or flower wines were the favourite drinks. Basic inexpensive fare consisted of boiling water poured on to lumps of bread and dripping, with a little pork or bacon. Bread was baked once a week in a brick oven heated by bundles of twigs bound together, known as faggots, and the countryside provided mushrooms, berries and nettles that supplemented the families' food. Fuel was mainly wood and cost very little. The biggest item of expenditure was clothing. The village cobbler made and mended shoes, and they were one of the most costly items of the family budget, together with the hats that the milliner made for churchgoing and special occasions. Clothing was mostly sewn or knitted at home and made from materials with lasting qualities. Men wore weather-resisting smocks and corduroy breeches and women wore wool dresses and thick shawls with knitted stockings in winter, and cotton dresses and sunbonnets in summer, with starched white aprons worn over full skirts. For those who could afford it tailors and dressmakers were employed to make the occasional Sunday best clothes for high days and special occasions.

As the century progressed many inhabitants took up new occupations instead of agricultural labouring. Many of these new occupations still supported agriculture, with people being employed servicing the farming society and those employed in it. Work started at an early hour to make optimum use of the daylight, and many were employed from a young age. Transport was improving, resulting in people being employed building roads, railways and canals. A more mechanised society encouraged small cottage industries and service crafts and trades, often with back-breaking demands, and many people were engaged in supporting and serving the needs of a growing population. More housing for all levels of society was demanded, and building trades flourished.

Masons and roof thatchers were employed, as well as carpenters who undertook the making of doors and window frames, and who also made chairs, tables, coffins, gates and fences. There were saddlers who made the collars and harnesses for the local horses, and a variety of leather goods. The blacksmiths and farriers, besides shoeing all the horses in the village, made agricultural implements and ploughs, hooks, hinges and ornamental ironwork. There were wheelwrights who made all the carts and wagons that were needed locally, sending their wooden wheels to the forge where the iron rims were fitted. A carrier took parcels to and from Taunton and Bridgwater and sometimes took passengers in his wagon. There were a number of skilled basket-makers in the village and many, including women and children, were employed cutting, bundling, stripping and boiling the willow sticks or rods, known locally as withies, in readiness for the making of baskets that were used in the home, on the farms and by the many tradespeople. Women practised many crafts in their homes such as glove-making, lacemaking, quilting and making straw plaits for hat manufacturers.

The growing population needed to be fed, clothed, schooled and entertained, and North Curry became a thriving self-supporting centre catering for the needs of this more demanding population. Many inhabitants chanced their luck by seeking work in Taunton and other towns, and a number of North Curry families emigrated to Australia, America and Canada.

Many inhabitants of North Curry were in service to the wealthy families who occupied the larger houses in the village. Moredon, Guyon House, Calmady House, Whatley House, Long's House and Fosse House were among the larger houses employing live-in servants. According to the *Census Return* of 1851 Moredon supported 11 servants - one governess, one cook, three housemaids, one kitchenmaid, one butler, one footman and one coachman, one groom and one gardener. Other workers were employed as labourers to work the estate grounds and land.

Education became available for all children residing in the Parish. The village school in North Curry was built in 1848 providing a standard of education compatible with that of the rest of the country, improving and widening as the century progressed. By the end of the century most children could read, write and calculate, enabling them to integrate into a more sophisticated working environment. Improved medical practice and surgery made for a healthier population. Taunton Hospital was opened in 1812 and patients with serious complaints were transferred there from that date. Dr Robert Kinglake, a forbear of a North Curry resident, who was one of the first physicians there, would have attended them. Schooling and medical practice in North Curry are discussed in greater detail in Chapters 2-6 and 2-7.

The inhabitants of North Curry had little time available for entertainment. Sundays were spent attending church and as most people were members of large families entertainment was provided by visiting or giving hospitality after church services. Harvest time and May Day were times in the year when processions, feasts and dances and other amusements took place, and many looked forward to the annual fair at Bridgwater. Families were entertained by magic lantern shows, readings, recitations, and open-air picnics. Travelling musicians, Morris dancers and the *mummers* would visit occasionally.

Sports such as cricket and football were established as the major outdoor activities, and the children were taken for special outings by the Sunday School, whilst the men and boys enjoyed outings organised by the church and men's societies. The men who enjoyed playing skittles and other pub games frequented the beerhouses and cider houses. The children played marbles or bowled hoops and spun tops, skipped and played hopscotch.

An annual fair or fete, which probably derives from the annual market which had taken place since medieval times in the centre of the village and is described in page 32, was held in the fields below Moredon in Victorian times. Great enjoyment ensued with visiting entertainers mixing with local stallholders providing sweetmeats, ribbons, baubles and other fancy goods and competitions such as bicycle races and milk-drinking contests, tug-of-war and dancing to music provided by the local band.

From early times up to the First World War almost every household in the village of North Curry would have kept chickens, a cow, a few sheep, pigs or geese and perhaps bees to support their families' food stocks, and others would keep livestock on the moor. Frequently these animals escaped their enclosures and any stray cattle or other livestock were put in a *pound* until claimed by their owners and released on payment of a fine. The site of an early pound is in the Fosse near the church gate in what was known as the vicarage orchard, now Manor Lodge. It would appear that this ceased to be the pound around the beginning of the 18th century and a new pound was provided in Moor Lane. The site, still known as The Pound, is now occupied by a pair of contemporary houses.

In the minutes of a vestry meeting held on 25th March 1885 is the first recorded reference to the appointment of a Pound Warden, and later in 1908 two Pound Wardens, Josiah Andrews and Christopher Andrews, were appointed. Their duties were:

> *1. The Pound Wardens to keep the key of the pound in their possession and keep such pound duly locked at all times and on no account to allow any goods, live or dead stock or property of any description to be lodged or placed in such pound, but the pound is to be strictly kept of the purpose only of, impounding straying or trespassing cattle or livestock.*
>
> *2. Persons applying to the Pound Warden for the key to impound stock shall be liable to pay the sum of six pence to the Pound Warden for the use of the pound for such purpose, such sum to be repaid to the impounder by the owner of the impounded stock when same is removed.*
>
> *3. The Pound Warden shall supply food and water to such impounded animals and be entitled to charge the person liable for the fair cost thereof and a reasonable charge for the time and trouble for supplying the same.*
>
> *4. The said sum of six pence for each lot of impounded stock shall be the full remuneration to which the Pound Warden shall be entitled other than is mentioned in Rule 3.*

The pound was about 14 metres square, surrounded by a stone wall about two metres high. It is reported that Mr Andrews, who was the blacksmith, remembered a time when over 300 geese, 22 turkeys and 8 ducks were impounded. A man was required to remain on the wall of the pound continuously for three days and two nights having his food, drink and tobacco brought to him. His duty was to prevent the birds flying out over the top of the pound.

The Post Office in the middle of North Curry was established in 1861 and was one of the earliest to be opened in the country. The first Postmaster, who also acted as the Registrar of Births and Deaths, was John Horsey Nicholls. Letters arrived from Taunton at 7.45 am and left North Curry for dispatch at 6.00 pm. In 1871 the premises were listed as a grocery store with Robert Palmer, a lodger there, employed as the telegraph clerk, and later was the first place in North Curry to be connected with a telephone (see page 122).

On 22nd January 1879 Lieutenant John Rouse Merriott Chard of the Royal Engineers, whose sister was married to Major Barrett of Moredon in North Curry, was awarded the Victoria Cross for his part in the defence of Rorke's Drift in the Zulu War. On his return to England from South Africa he was promoted to the rank of Major and invited to Balmoral to be presented with a gold signet ring by Queen Victoria. Later a great welcome and reception was prepared for him in North Curry when he paid a short visit to his brother in law (see page 148).

In 1887, in celebration of the 50 years of Queen Victoria's reign, an iron lamp-post with an inscription was erected on grass in the middle of the village of North Curry. Two more iron lamp-posts with lanterns lit by oil were also erected, being paid for by the Barrett family of Moredon. By the early–20th century ten more street lamps were erected in the village with lamplighters employed to fill and light the paraffin lamps in the evenings. When electricity came to the village in 1936 there were difficulties in justifying the cost of maintaining the lamps and they disappeared from their sites, never to be replaced, with many of them being sent for scrap iron to support the war effort. A village garden was planted in Queen Square in 1890, later to be adopted by the Parish Council for use by residents of North Curry, becoming known as The Shrubbery.

In 1894 a Parish Council was elected for North Curry. It consisted of nine members who were mainly property owners who had previously served as members of the Church Vestry Meeting which had supported the parish poor. Mr C R Morris was the first chairman and this civil body, now separate from the church, assumed the position of an elected representative group that the population of the Parish could approach on any matter of concern.

In 1897, amidst great national celebrations, Queen Victoria celebrated her Diamond Jubilee. In North Curry a stone memorial was built to commemorate this 60th anniversary of her reign. The monument in the form of a cross, and built with Hamstone with Blue Lias stone steps surrounded with iron railings, since renewed, was designed by the Diocesan Architect, Mr Edmund Buckle. It was built and erected by Mr Charles Trask of Stoke–sub–Hamdon at a cost of £250. The Dutch gables are carved with the Star of India, the royal coat of arms and St George and the Dragon, while the small gables have a thistle, a rose and a shamrock. It is inscribed *Her Most Gracious Majesty Queen Victoria completed the 60th year of her reign on June 20th 1897.* In order to raise money for the cost, subscriptions from village residents were requested. Some 44 residents subscribed, giving sums ranging from one shilling to £80. The sum of £324.7s.5d was raised, and together with the proceeds from an outdoor fete held in the village on Jubilee Day in that year raising £87, enough money was raised to pay for the monument and to provide entertainment for the parishioners of North Curry in celebration. The monument, which has become known as *The Pepper Pot* because of its shape, is situated in the centre of the village where the roads converge. Some claim the location was named Queen Square to commemorate the Jubilee but in fact the name was certainly in use at the time of the 1861 Census, although it then only covered part of the present-day Queen Square.

Queen Victoria would remain on the throne into the 20th century enabling her to become the longest-serving British monarch with a reign of 63 years.

1 - 10

THE FIRST HALF OF THE 20TH CENTURY

The British at the beginning of the 20th century were still Victorians, and Victoria, who had reigned from 1837, was Queen of Great Britain and Ireland and Empress of India. 41 million of her people lived in the British Isles; 32 million of those were English or Welsh, and 9 million Irish or Scots. She also ruled over 300 million people in her Empire, which covered 6 million square miles.

Half of all merchant ships were registered in the United Kingdom and 30 per cent of manufacturing imports abroad came from British factories. The world's bank and trading institutions traded in sterling, and people in Britain were quite prosperous with an average wage of £40 a year. However, most were poorly nourished relying on a cereal diet. Eight out of ten people lived in towns and cities and death rates were high. There was much prejudice in religion, schooling was only compulsory for children under ten and women did not have the right to vote. Dress was very formal, the cinema was in its infancy, and transport by rail with an underground electric rail system in London was well-established, but trams were still horse-drawn and motor cars were a luxury. The three main political parties were the Liberals, the Conservatives or Unionists and the Liberal Unionists, with the Labour Party just being formed but with no representatives yet elected.

Queen Victoria died on 22nd January 1901 and a funeral of much pomp delivered her to Windsor, where she was laid to rest beside the remains of her late husband, Prince Albert. Her son of the House of Saxe-Coburg-Gotha became King Edward VII and Hanoverian rule ceased. He was the eldest son, but the second child of Victoria and Albert and had been born in 1841 becoming the Prince of Wales. He had been baptised Albert Edward but was known as Bertie and during the 60 years he waited to be King he was seen as frivolous, pleasure loving and flirtatious, forming intimate friendships with a number of beautiful women. Although he performed many public duties and travelled on state visits he was deemed unsuited to the responsibilities of monarchy. He had married Princess Alexandra of Denmark in 1863 and through many scandals she remained tolerant and understanding of his love affairs.

In 1906 the Liberals won the general election and there followed a period of social reform with the introduction of old-age pensions and National Insurance promoted by William Beveridge (1879-1963) and David Lloyd George (1863-1945). Winston Churchill (1874-1965) had entered the House of Commons in 1900 by winning the Conservative seat at Oldham, only to change allegiance to the Liberals. He became President of the Board of Trade. King Edward did much to strengthen Britain's friendship with countries in Europe, with visits to Paris, Athens, Oslo, Stockholm and meetings with the Tsar of Russia, winning him the nickname of *Edward the Peacemaker*. However the Germans became increasingly suspicious and accused him of building anti-German coalitions.

The occupations of Britons in 1911 were changing, with fewer than 2.3 million working on the land, and nearly 2 million indoor domestic servants. Their employers included 52,000 clergymen, 27,000 lawyers, 28,000 physicians and surgeons, and 276,000 schoolmasters, professors and lecturers. Drivers on the nation's roads increased from only 703 in 1901 to 48,000 in 1911 and the internal combustion engine was powering motor vehicles and ships. William Morris, later to become Lord Nuffield, developed a cheap two-seater car, donating funds from the profits to charities and good causes. The internal combustion engine gave man the power to fly and in 1908 Louis Bleriot crossed the English Channel. The telephone had been invented by Alexander Graham Bell in 1876 and eventually the Wireless Telegraphy Company was formed with Post Office licences being required to operate wireless equipment. Wireless radio transmission was first achieved by Guglielmo Marconi in 1894 and in 1897 he founded the Marconi Company, establishing the first permanent radio link. By 1901 he had sent the first ship-to-shore message. Radio became more available with the development of the thermionic valve by John Fleming, who was employed by Marconi. The King and Queen devoted much time to the improvement of the health service and the district nurse service was born.

At that time Britain's imports exceeded her exports, the Germans and Americans had become successful commercial rivals, and the countries of the Empire were beginning to seek independence within the Commonwealth. A clash occurred when liberal Lloyd George introduced his People's Budget in 1909, proposing a super tax over and above income tax, a rise in death duties and a tax on land values, and the Conservative majority in the House of Lords threw it out. This culminated in the Lords' powers being curbed by the Parliament Act of 1911.

North Curry was totally self-sufficient at this time, independent of other centres, with all the trades and occupations needed to support and sustain a fairly large population. The 1901 *Census Return* gives the population in North Curry as 1,525 and records a diverse range of households. The gentry, sometimes practising their professions as medical practitioners, lawyers or military and naval officers occupied the more substantial properties. Schoolteachers practised in private educational establishments or at the National School (see Chapter 2-7). The village supported numerous beerhouses and inns, breweries and malthouses, together with mills and slaughterhouses. Improved transport had yet to take the residents of North Curry further afield to service their needs and experience a broader choice of goods. Day-to-day needs were serviced by bakers, butchers, bootmakers, tailors, milliners, dressmakers and glovemakers. Blacksmiths, wheelwrights, coachbuilders, harness makers and saddlers supported horse-based transport and these, together with many other trades and professions, satisfied most people's demands locally.

In North Curry in 1903 the *Parish Magazine* was started by the Reverend Daniel Pring. It was published monthly except for a period during and immediately after the Second World War when it was published quarterly as an economy measure. At the time of writing it is again distributed monthly and contains many items of interest to the whole community of North Curry. The Reverend Pring's early magazines gave details not only of church matters but also his observations on life in the village. Entertainment for both young and old are well documented and the following extracts provide an insight into North Curry life during the reign of King Edward VII.

1903
The Sunday School Christmas tree proved in every way as popular an event as might have been expected. Colonel Keighley, Superintendent of the Upper School, cut off the first present, and many a child's heart was soon gladdened with a pretty toy or useful article of apparel. A capital entertainment was given in the Schoolroom, consisting of animated photographs, with vocal and instrumental music. This was supplied by the North Curry Band and songs were kindly given by Mr. Coates, Miss Coombs and Mr. Smith.

Two or three days skating were enjoyed in the middle week of January. The floods being well up over Haymoor and Curry Moor, their frozen surface afforded a splendid opportunity for safe going; and there was plenty of room for everybody.

The Eleventh Annual Flower Show was held in the Vicarage Grounds but the weather proved unsettled and rainy. The total number of entries was 667. There were eight competitors in the Decorated Dinner Table Class. A new feature this year was A Farm Produce Class. A Steam Circus provided some of the entertainment and The North Curry Band acquitted themselves creditably. Dancing followed in the evening on a rather sodden green.

The North Curry Church Lads Brigade went to Uphill for a week camping with a number of other companies. The Girls Bible Class Outing went to Weston in August. The Choir Boys Treat was to Uphill and Weston in August. The Adult Choir Excursion was to Exeter where they visited the Castle and Cathedral and by train beside the River Exe to Dawlish, returning by train to Durston.

1904
The Annual Choir Supper was given at the Vicarage on January 19th. The party assembled at 7.30, and after supper an adjournment was made to the Parish Rooms, which had been carpeted and arranged for the occasion. Here the rest of the evening was spent in music and singing, Mr. F. Pring's phonograph affording a pleasing variety in the programme. The proceedings were brought to a close by singing "Auld Lang Syne" in orthodox fashion.

1905
The North Curry Glee Club gave their first concert in the Assembly Rooms on April 25th.

1906
Arrangements have been made for a Cinematograph Entertainment to be held as usual at this time of the year in North Curry School. The date fixed is January 10th and some new and very interesting subjects will be presented, including "The King at the Grand National", "A Stag Hunt on Exmoor", "Grand Pantomime of Blue Beard", etc. The prices will be as usual and we trust we may have as crowded a room as on previous occasions.

In July 1904 the internal combustion engine had obviously not arrived in North Curry as the following entry reports a potential disaster saved with the assistance of two types of very basic transportation.

We desire to express our very sincere sympathy with Dr. and Mrs. Fisher on account of the recent alarming fire on their premises. But our chief reflection must be a sense of thankfulness that things were no worse. The credit of this seems to attach first of all to Mrs. Fisher's plucky ride to Moredon on her bicycle to give the alarm. Then to Captain Barrett's speedy appearance on the scene with the Moredon Fire-engine, and to the excellent way in which he managed it. By this means the fire was confined to the stable buildings, and Dr. Fisher's house and the cottages adjacent to the stable on the other side escaped. But does not the incident demonstrate the need of a village organisation, with proper appliances, to cope with fire? The parish should be most grateful for the assistance of the Moredon Fire Brigade but it cannot be expected to do everything!

When the motor car did arrive in May 1906 another unfortunate incident occurred:

On Easter Monday, the North Curry Company of the Church Lads' Brigade under the command of Lieutenant Pring, took part in the field day at Castle Neroche under the command of Major W.H. Speke. The Company undertook some arduous flanking movements, and acquitted themselves well in the manoeuvres. The motor car accident to Dr. Fisher (the Medical Officer of C.L.B.) and Miss Pring somewhat marred the closing stage of the outing, but all are thankful that the consequences were not more serious, and that both the injured occupants of the car continue to make satisfactory progress.

Efforts were made in the village to encourage reading as a pastime but it obviously did not appeal to all.

1907
During the past winter over sixty persons have joined as members of the Parish Lending Library, and upwards of 650 volumes have been taken out. This may be deemed satisfactory so far as it goes, but considering the very low rate of subscription and the character of literature provided, being suitable to all sorts and conditions of readers, it might be supposed that more people would take advantage of the Library than they do. The "One Shilling" for the Season for one volume a week works out to be about a farthing per book, so it would be impossible to make it much cheaper.

1909
Why cannot some of our young men join the Library? We are sure it would be much better for them if they could find a corner at home to enjoy a quiet read, instead of standing by the Post Office corner in the wet! Perhaps it is that the

corner at home is difficult to find; or the effort to read is too laborious. In that case it doesn't say much for our boasted education! But at any rate we would suggest that a Library Book might be preferable to a "Penny Dreadful", for such things are to be seen occasionally.

Efforts to recruit the villagers of North Curry into a non-drinking way of life fell on stony, if not frosty, ground.

1909
A meeting in connection with the Church of England Temperance Society "Forward Movement" was held in the Parish Hall and an address given by the Reverend Prebendary C.W. Bennett. It was a fine night, but exceedingly cold, and the attendance unfortunately was somewhat scanty. At the end Mr. Bennett set off on his bicycle to ride back to Pilton, the other side of Glastonbury, through the frosty moonlight.

In 1910 King Edward VII died after an attack of bronchitis at the age of 68 and his second son Prince George Frederick Ernest Albert became King George V. Prince George's elder brother Albert Victor, Duke of Clarence had died in 1892 whilst engaged to Princess Victoria Mary of Teck, known as *May*, and Queen Victoria encouraged George to take Princess May as his wife. They had travelled widely and fulfilled many royal duties before their reign began and had witnessed Irish republicanism, militant suffragettes, Indian nationalism, the threat of the Imperial German Navy and other crises. King George V and Queen Mary enjoyed a successful, stable and loving royal marriage, complementing each other in their desire to do their duty for Britain. Their children, Prince Edward born in 1894, Prince Albert born in 1895, followed by Princess Mary in 1897 and Princes Henry, George and John were brought up to exacting upper-class standards.

In 1912 the new liner the *Titanic* sank and in 1914 Ernest Shackleton's ship, the *Endurance*, was crushed by ice in the Antarctic. In 1912 Captain Robert Falcon Scott reached the South Pole only to learn that the Norwegian Roald Amundsen had been there a month before. Emily Pankhurst, who had established the Women's Social and Political Union in 1903, continued a campaign of nuisance tactics to press for women's suffrage and in 1913 Emily Davison, another suffragette, died after throwing herself under a horse at the Derby. Education of children was much improved due to the Education Acts, and 60 per cent of 12 to 14-year-olds were now at school. Around 4 million working men were members of trade unions who looked after their interests, but there were 1 million men who were unemployed, although labour exchanges were helping to find them work.

Europe was divided by a number of defensive alliances, and although Britain was not a member of these, naval rivalry and trade competition had alienated her from Germany.

The series of events leading to the Great War or First World War commenced when Austria, having accused Serbia of complicity in the murder of their Emperor Franz Josef, joined with Hungary to declare war on Serbia on 28th July 1914. Kaiser Wilhelm II of Germany supported Austria, and Russia mobilised along the frontiers of Austria and Germany and pledged support of Serbia. France honoured a treaty agreement with Russia, leading Germany to declare war on Russia and France on 1st and 3rd August 1914 respectively.

Germany then invaded Belgium, and because Britain was bound by treaty obligations to uphold Belgium's integrity, Britain declared war on Germany on 4th August 1914. Germany and Austria-Hungary were joined by Turkey and Bulgaria.

Over the next four years many countries became caught up in military conflicts and 10 million troops were killed in action throughout the world, with hundreds of thousands of civilians killed as a result of fighting, disease and deprivation. New weapons such as fighter aircraft, submarines, tanks, machine-guns and mines brought about by technical innovation resulted in new levels of devastation on the battlefields. Thousands of Britain's youngest men died and a whole generation was lost.

In March 1918 the Germans began a series of offensives on the Western Front but failed to break through. Allied counter attacks began on the River Marne and in August a decisive British victory at Amiens convinced the Germans to seek peace. Turkish forces were defeated by General Sir Edmund Allenby in Palestine and together with Austria-Hungary they also sued for armistice.

In North Curry before the War a number of young boys had been encouraged to join the Church Lads Brigade, an organisation that taught them military skills, and when war loomed these boys were amongst the first to enlist. The enthusiasm for the brigade is summed up by an entry in the *Parish Magazine* in January 1905.

A capital Display of Drill was given in the National Schoolroom by Company 2064 of the Church Lads Brigade. The items in the programme included Manual and Firing Exercises, Free Gymnastics and Physical Drill, Bayonet Practice, Dumb-bell Exercises, etc. If it is true that a healthy and well-developed body contains a healthy and well-developed mind, then every lad in the place should make up his mind to become a member, for no one could see the systematic way in which the Lads are drilled without being fully convinced of its efficacy in bringing into healthy use every muscle of the body.

The North Curry War Service List published in 1918 lists 244 men who enlisted and fought from North Curry, of whom 18 were killed in action. 59 of those enlisted had previously been members of the Church Lads Brigade. Three women from the village served in hospitals with the British Red Cross, and most women in the village helped by sewing and making items for hospitals and soldiers, which was reported as follows:

"Ninety pillows have been made and sent to different Military and Naval Hospitals at Mudros, the Dardenelles, and a pillowcase for each pillow. Also a parcel of woollen comforts, including knitted sweaters, socks, mittens, cuffs, and mufflers to the Gallipoli Peninsular; and shirts, night-shirts, pants, hospital-bags, knitted rubbers, milk covers, and tray-cloths to various Depots for distribution."

The children also helped with this war work:

> *Mrs. Berthon writes to say how very pleased she is with the way in which our children in School "have knitted socks for our Tommies at Salonica, and for all the trouble Miss Hann has taken over it." "The children put cigarettes in the toes of their own accord. It was nice of them! Some of the poor people of North Curry have also knitted for me."*

During the war years Charlie Chaplin entertained large audiences in the cinema, and novelists such as Virginia Woolf, Aldous Huxley, John Galsworthy and D H Lawrence were writing books that were widely circulated through public libraries. The Germans shot Nurse Edith Cavell for helping allied soldiers to escape from Belgium to Holland, and Elizabeth Garrett Anderson, the first licensed woman doctor, died. In 1916 male military service became compulsory, leading to women being employed in great numbers in the factories and on the land where the need to grow more food was becoming necessary to feed the nation. Many were released from domestic service to fulfil this need, and life in the large houses changed dramatically as a consequence.

In 1917 Lord Davenport made a request to everyone to eat sparingly and this was reported in the North Curry *Parish Magazine* as follows:

> *Lord Devonport has appealed to the nation for a certain curtailment of the consumption of food. He says that the need for such curtailment is urgent. The situation requires that the heads of families should endeavour to limit themselves and the weekly purchase for each person comprising the household should be: Bread, 4 lbs. (or its equivalent in Flour, 3lbs for breadmaking); Meat, 2½ lbs; Sugar, ¾lb. The nation is placed upon its honour to observe these conditions. Economy is not only a patriotic duty, but also a necessity. Frugality practised at home will ensure a sufficient supply for all, despite any effort of the enemy, and, as hitherto, an unstinted provision for our soldiers and sailors.*

The First World War ended with victory for Britain in 1918 and the country recovered only to witness a period of strikes and protests. By the summer of 1921 there were over 2 million people unemployed, and the wartime coalition government of David Lloyd George's Liberals and Andrew Bonar Law's Conservatives collapsed. The Tories were returned to power and Andrew Bonar Law became Prime Minister, but became ill, resulting in Stanley Baldwin becoming his successor in 1923. In 1918 Fisher's Education Act ensured that all children would stay on at school until 14 years old, but it was not until 1944 that everyone in Britain was entitled to full-time education. Also in 1918, women who were over the age of 30, who were ratepayers or married to a ratepayer, were given the vote, and in addition were allowed to become Members of Parliament. In 1928 the voting age for women was reduced to 21 years in line with men.

A scheme was put forward by the Vicar, the Reverend Daniel Pring soon after the War, to build a Parish War Memorial. It was decided to launch an appeal for at least £500, of which £150 should be devoted to the erection of a memorial cross. This War Memorial was erected in Queen Square at a cost of £150, and dedicated, at a service held on 28th November 1920 and conducted by the Bishop of Taunton, to the glory of God and in memory of those from North Curry who fell in the First World War. *The Glorious Dead* by Colin Trim, published in 2005, gives an account of this memorial and of those who lost their lives in the First World War.

An offer was made by Major A G Barrett to convert a house in the village known as The Grange into a Parish Social Club using the remainder of the appeal money. The Reverend Pring, writing in the *Parish Magazine* in July 1920, stated:

> *A Parish Institute is just what is wanted – a centre of life and social interest to the whole Parish. Here should be reading and writing rooms for both sexes. A place to sit, and smoke, and read. A library, and rooms for games, cards, billiards, etc.; a canteen, where you can get your cup of tea, or other refreshments. Lectures should be given from time to time and other entertainments; instructional, amusing, interesting. Music should not be wanting. It could all be done, if there is the will. We want £500 at least. It ought to be possible to do something more perhaps to cover in the Courtyard at "The Grange" for use as a Picture House.*

However this scheme did not have sufficient support, and the remainder of the money subscribed was used for a brass plaque in the Parish Church inscribed with the names of all those who served, as well as those who fell in the First World War.

In 1920 in Europe Adolf Hitler had become a leading figure in the National Socialist German Workers' Party (NSDAP) and by 1923 he was building a nationalistic Germany. At the same time Joseph Stalin was ruling the Russian people. Also in 1920, the Anglo-Irish Treaty was signed, establishing the Irish Free State as a self-governing dominion within the Commonwealth, later in 1936 to be named Eire. Full independence as a Republic was granted in 1949. The six loyalist Ulster Protestant counties in the north-eastern part of the island wished for self-government within the United Kingdom. They, together with the other three counties of Ulster that were mainly Catholic, became Northern Ireland, with a Parliament in Belfast. This separation of Northern Ireland caused considerable unrest during the ensuing years.

In 1917 the Privy Council proclaimed that from that date the royal family would be called the House of Windsor, divesting itself of all its German styles and titles. In 1923 Lady Elizabeth Bowes-Lyon married King George V's second eldest son, the then Duke of York. Prince Edward, the heir to the throne and nicknamed *David* had begun to irritate and infuriate King George V. He had shown sympathies towards Germany before the War and had grown to love parties, drink and women while at university at Oxford. In 1934 he fell in love with an American divorcee, Wallis Simpson.

The prosperous years of the early 1920s became known as the roaring twenties and were characterised by a lighter side of life emerging with cinemas, dance bands and jazz music sweeping through Britain. Performers such as Charlie Chaplin, Stan Laurel and Oliver Hardy, Harold Lloyd, Douglas Fairbanks and Rudolph Valentino became the first film stars. Technical advances had brought the gramophone to towns and villages. Motor racing and water speed records were broken, and the age of international long-distance air flights was beginning. In 1926 licence fees from the owners of wireless receivers financed the British Broadcasting Company (BBC), and millions of the listening public were better informed and entertained. Eleven national newspapers were circulating in Britain at this time with Lords Northcliffe, Beaverbrook and Thomson the main proprietors.

After a short-lived Labour government with Ramsey Macdonald as Prime Minister in 1924, Stanley Baldwin was returned to power and he called upon the workers to accept lower wages to ease the worsening economic crisis. In 1926 the General Council of the Trades Union Congress organised a General Strike, but it was only to last nine days and workers returned to lower wages and longer hours enduring much poverty. A worldwide economic slump began in 1929 with the Wall Street crash in America, and by 1931 Britain's unemployment figure had reached 3 million.

The mainly rural community of North Curry appears to have been largely unaffected by the political and economic situation in the rest of the country, and many amusements and entertainments were offered to the residents of the Parish. In December 1922 the inaugural meeting of the North Curry Literary and Scientific Society - the forerunner to today's North Curry Society - took place, with membership set at two shillings and sixpence a year. It attracted 51 members and was described at the time as *an institution as may serve to stimulate our interest and increase our knowledge in things about us, particularly matters of local interest, and at the same time afford an opportunity for meetings possessing an element of a pleasant social character.* The first lecture was given by Mr Walter Raymond and was called *Somerset Character, Custom and Dialect.* This was followed in December of that year by a lecture illustrated with lantern slides by limelight by the Reverend F C Jourdain, the Leader of the Oxford University Expedition to Spitzbergen. The following year saw the group visit the museum at Taunton Castle with tea being partaken afterwards at Deller's restaurant in Taunton, and charabanc excursions to such places as Brean Down and Cothelstone were arranged. Typically the cost of a trip to Dunster for the whole group, to include the cost of transport, teas, tips, guide fee and admittance to Cleeve Abbey was £10. Concerts and dances with music provided by the Village Band, together with lectures, whist drives and public meetings, were held in the Assembly Rooms in North Curry. Mr Richard Spearing Morris presented this building to the Parish Council in 1924. A legacy of £500 was left by Mr C W Morris and this allowed for the building to be improved and furnished to seat 250 people. It became known as the Morris Memorial Hall. In the first half of the 20th century a police house was situated in Greenway and a Police Sergeant and Constable were on hand to keep law and order.

The Women's Institute in North Curry came into being in 1928, largely through the initiative of Mrs Violet Cookson, who then became president for 14 years. The inaugural meeting was held in the Morris Memorial Hall with 109 ladies present, and Miss Morris of Gwyon House taught them the song Jerusalem. Miss Coombs, who was the headmistress of Wrantage School, became the treasurer, and sought ways of raising funds. They transferred the venue for their meetings to the Methodist Hall where the hire fee was only three shillings and sixpence rather then twelve shillings and sixpence for the Morris Hall. The Women's Institute continues to thrive in North Curry today.

In 1921 the North Curry Flower Show was revived and Mr Charles Heale's Steam Circus was engaged to provide entertainment. A summer fete which was a successor to the early medieval fair in the The Shambles and the later Victorian fair at Moredon, had been held in the grounds of the vicarage, now called Manor Field off The Fosse, for some years. In 1903 it was reported in the *Parish Magazine* as follows:

> *The Summer Sale and Parish Fete included the following stalls and entertainments. Fancy Work, Plain Work, General Stall, Sweet Stall, The Bran Tub, The Maypole Dance, The Hat Trimming Competition, The Bicycle Gymkhana, and A Motor Car providing rides round the village for those that cared to adventure themselves thereon.*

In July 1905 more sophisticated attractions were on offer:

> *The Fancy Fair took place in glorious weather and raised over £55. Mrs. Barrett opened the Fete and among the many attractions were a Shooting Range managed by Colonel Barrett who lent his range with moving targets, and, at the rate of two-shots a penny, 444 shots were fired. The Milk-Drinking Competition caused much amusement. The successful competitor received a box of Beecham's Pills, and the consolation prize was a baby's comforter.*

The gross takings of the July 1925 fete, described below, amounted to £182.5s.0d:

> *Church Sale and Summer Fete to be held in the Vicarage Grounds. Entrance will be by the Vicarage front gate, and the Sale with its various side-shows will be held in the Paddock, tea being served on the Lawn, where a space will also be reserved for Dancing. The Fete will continue from 3 p.m. to 9.30 p.m. There will be various stalls including a Pound Stall, Bran Pie, Girls' Missionary Stall, Sweet and Cake Stall, Plain Work Stall, Fancy Stall, Produce Stall, "Hidden Treasure", Ladies Sports, Men's Sports, and other Entertainment's.*

In 1929 Ramsey MacDonald's Labour government came to power. The states of the Balkans were brought together under the name of Yugoslavia. The League of Nations, which had been set up after the First World War to prevent antagonistic alliances forming, was failing and Germany, where Hitler became Chancellor, withdrew from it in 1933. India was demanding independence and in the Middle East the Jews who were being forced to emigrate from Russia and Germany were trying to establish a homeland in Palestine. In 1931 Ramsey Macdonald was forced to concede to a coalition government with Liberals and Conservative members in order to cope with economic depression. The population in Britain was about 49 million and falling due to contraception and the hardships that ensued from lack of money. There were more opportunities to spend money on domestic goods such as vacuum cleaners, electric ovens, irons and boilers, and affordable housing with garaging was becoming available to families with fewer children.

From the beginning of the century the medical surgery for the village was housed at Trevarrick House (see page 155), and in the early days of medical practice the doctors would visit their patients using their horses and traps. Later prescriptions for medicines were either delivered by the various men and boys who delivered provisions or were left on the step of the surgery for collection. Most medical complaints requiring surgery were dealt with by the doctor in the village, but a few patients with more serious afflictions were transferred to Taunton Hospital which had opened in 1812. From 1931 a dentist, W G Elsmore, attended in Queen Square between 10.00 am and noon on Thursdays. To assist the doctors in their day-to-day attendance in North Curry there have been a number of notable parish or district nurses. Nurse Peart was appointed in 1915, Nurse Alice Rich from 1922 to 1948, Nurse Lockhart until 1953 followed by Nurse Mills. Nurse Rich delivered most of the babies in North Curry in her day, and she was remembered bicycling around wearing knee high rubber boots to protect against fleas.

In the 1930s public buses were running a return service to Taunton several times a day and Eric Foster ran a taxi-service and the school bus. The *Bijou* cinema adjacent to Lantern Cottage in Moor Lane - accredited with being the smallest cinema in England - provided the village with entertainment on it's doorstep by showing the latest films starring Laurel and Hardy and John Wayne. There were two bank sub-branches in the village at this time. Farming was still the main occupation in North Curry in 1931 and, together with a substantial number of tradesmen and professional people operating to serve the community, the village continued to be self-supporting. The list of tradespeople appearing in the 1931 *Kelly's Trade Directory* for North Curry can be seen in detail in Appendix 3.

In 1935 King George V celebrated his silver jubilee, Communist leader Mao Zedong began his long-march to the safety of northwest China and the Japanese marched into Peking. Stanley Baldwin again became Prime Minister and Britain was enjoying musicals by George Gershwin and jazz from Benny Goodman. John Gielgud, Laurence Olivier and Peggy Ashcroft were on the London stage. Allen Lane, the pioneer of paperback book publishing, produced the first ten Penguin titles.

George V died in 1936 and was succeeded by his eldest son who became King Edward VIII but was never crowned. He declared his intention of marrying the American divorcee Wallis Simpson in a morganatic marriage, whereby she would not become Queen, and any children would have no right to the throne. Stanley Baldwin would not allow this as it was against British law, and on 10th December 1936 King Edward VIII abdicated. The next day his brother, 41-year-old Prince Albert Frederick Arthur George, who had married Lady Elizabeth Bowes-Lyon in 1923, became King George VI. Elizabeth, the elder of his two daughters who was ten years old, became next in line to the throne.

In celebration of the Coronation of King George VI in 1937, Mrs Emma Coate, a resident of North Curry and the oldest woman in England, planted an oak tree in Church Road in her 106th year. She died in 1939 at the age of 108 years. In 1938 Richard Rodham Morris, an estate agent resident in North Curry, married Kathleen Tacchi Stagg, who became a well known peace campaigner. More details of her life can be read on page 154.

King George VI and Queen Elizabeth paid important visits abroad to France, America and Canada during the time that Germany was annexing Austria, occupying the Rhineland and marching into Czechoslovakia. Hitler invaded Poland on 3rd September 1939 and Neville Chamberlain broadcast an announcement to the nation that Britain and France were now at war with Germany - the Second World War had commenced. In April 1940 Germany occupied Denmark and Norway and in May 1940 Winston Churchill became Prime Minister with a coalition government, and Germany invaded the Low Countries. The British Expeditionary Force in Europe was forced back onto the beaches of Dunkirk and 330,000 men were rescued by hundreds of small boats from Britain. In June 1940 France surrendered and in July of that year Britain avoided invasion by the resistance of the Royal Air Force fighter pilots in the Battle of Britain. In June 1941 Germany attacked Russia, and America entered the war in December 1941 when the Japanese bombed Pearl Harbour. By February 1942 the Japanese had occupied most of south-east Asia and Singapore fell with the surrender of 100,000 men. In October 1942 General Montgomery defeated the German General Rommel at El Alamein. In January 1943 the Russians won at Stalingrad and Italy surrendered. In June 1944 the British returned to France with their American allies in the Normandy landings and within a year the British, with the Americans and Russians, converged on Berlin to accept the German surrender. War in Europe ended on 8th May 1945 and celebrations followed Winston Churchill's Victory in Europe broadcast. In 1945 two atomic bombs were dropped on Hiroshima and Nagasaki and in September of that year the Japanese surrendered.

In North Curry, as elsewhere, during the war years signposts were removed, windows blackened and gas masks issued and many men were called up for service in the Army, Navy and Air Force. The ones who stayed behind worked the land and others joined the detachments of Home Guard and Civil Defence Units manning the stop lines and pillboxes scattered around the Parish. 3,900 women and children had been evacuated from London and from other danger areas of the country to Somerset by September 1939. Some came to North Curry and the school was required to absorb the children into its classes. On the night of 28th June 1941 enemy aircraft passed over the Parish and jettisoned a quantity of parachute mines, one of which directly hit Wrantage School. Fortunately no lives were lost that night. Six men from North Curry lost their lives in the Second World War and their names are engraved on the War Memorial and on an oak panel in the Parish Church.

Reports from the *North Curry School Log Books* of the time are as follows:

> *1939 September 1st*
> *School closed for evacuation.*
>
> *September 18th*
> *School re-opened. One room has been given up to evacuees. Gwyon Cottage, adjoining the school has been taken for two other groups. Two classes of local children plus unofficial evacuees are being taught in the large classroom.*
>
> *December 8th*
> *Have been approached by the Matron of the Society of Hope Girls Home, now evacuated to Hunt's End, North Curry, with a request that some twenty of the Home children be admitted to the school. Report of this sent to the Education Officer.*
>
> *December 15th*
> *Miss Peake, County Inspector visited the school and reported that the local school should take ten, and the evacuated school ten of the above mentioned Home children.*
>
> *1940 July 10th*
> *Report on the damage sustained by Wrantage School by enemy action on the night of June 27 and 28. Damage reported to County Council and War Damage Commission. A request sent for using The Hut as a temporary Council School. If compensation obtained resolved to request re-building of school as a Voluntary school.*

Early in the War, food rationing came into force for everyone and the allocations per person declined as war progressed. The size of the ration per person was typically as follows:

Bacon and Ham:	4oz (100g)
Meat:	*To the value of 1s.2d* (6p today). *Sausages were not rationed but difficult to get; offal (liver, kidneys, tripe) was originally un-rationed but sometimes formed part of the meat ration.*
Cheese:	2oz (50g) *sometimes it went up to* 4oz (100g) *and even up to* 8oz (225g).
Margarine:	4oz (100g)
Butter:	2oz (50g)

Milk:	*3 pints* (1,800ml), *occasionally dropping to 2 pints* (1,200ml). *Pregnant women could have an extra pint per day. Household milk (skimmed or dried) was available: 1 packet per four weeks.*
Sugar:	8oz (225g)
Jam:	1lb (450g) *every two months.*
Tea:	2oz (50g).
Eggs:	*1 fresh egg a week if available but often only one every two weeks. Dried eggs 1 packet every four weeks.*
Sweets:	12oz (350g) *every four weeks*

People who had gardens were encouraged to *Dig for Victory* to augment their basic rations with vegetables and fruit. Those living in rural areas were able to get rabbits and game as an addition to their diet, and they could also keep chickens and a pig. Fish was unrationed, as were bread and potatoes. In 1945 more rationing was introduced in order to make more food available for the liberated countries of Europe. Sixty clothing coupons were allocated over a 16-month period. For example, a woollen dress cost eleven coupons, men's shoes seven coupons and two ounces of knitting wool one coupon. Rationing continued for most food until 1954 and for coal until 1958.

In October 1945 the United Nations Organisation was created as a means of bringing the nations of the world together to discuss their differences. In Britain Labour defeated Winston Churchill and the Conservatives and Clement Attlee became the new Prime Minister. Their reforming plans culminated in public ownership and the nationalisation of key industries and sources of supply, and the introduction of a National Health Service, a new National Insurance scheme, and the National Assistance Act. In 1946 Attlee announced that India would become the first part of the British Empire to achieve separate nationhood and independence. However leaders of the Muslim League and representatives of the Hindus rejected Britain's initial proposals. The League wanted a separate Muslim state, which would be to the north of the Hindu territory and be known as Pakistan, a name made up from Punjab, Afghanistan, Kashmir, Sind and Baluchstan. Eventually partition was agreed and the two new states of India and Pakistan, the latter being divided into West and East (becoming Bangladesh in 1971) came into being amidst large scale violence. In 1947 Lord Mountbatten was sent to India as Viceroy to effect a smooth transition from British rule and Indian rule. In 1950 India became a federal republic within the Commonwealth. Burma also became a sovereign state in 1948. The austerity measures introduced immediately after the war eased as exports increased and Britain enjoyed a balance of payments surplus.

In 1947 Princess Elizabeth, the eldest daughter of King George VI and heir to the throne, married Lieutenant Prince Philip Mountbatten, son of Prince Andrew of Greece. Upon his marriage Prince Philip was created Duke of Edinburgh. Prince Charles was born in 1948 and Princess Anne in 1950. In 1952, while the Princess and the

Duke were away on a long tour of the Empire, King George VI died and Queen Elizabeth II began the second Elizabethan reign.

The Coronation of Queen Elizabeth took place on 2nd June 1953, with 20 million Britons watching the procession ceremony on television and a further 12 million listening to the radio broadcasts. In North Curry there was much jubilation on the day and on 3rd June Major Alexander (Alec) Barrett, who was 86 years old, planted an oak tree in Queen Square to mark the occasion. This tree had been grown from an acorn planted on VE Day by Mr Fred Lock. A sports day was held in Mr Jeanes' field, east of Greenway, and there was a fancy dress competition for the children. A tea in the Morris Memorial Hall followed this when 270 children received Coronation mugs and the pensioners of the village received vouchers for five shillings and sixpence. In the evening a huge bonfire was lit in a field on Lillesdon Hill. During Coronation year two bells in the tower of the Parish Church were re-cast and the royal cypher *E II R* was impressed on them.

The nine-member North Curry Parish Council elected at the Annual Parish Meeting continued until 1946 when, by order of the County Council, a 13-member Parish Council was to be elected every four years by secret ballot. The Council in its early days dealt with matters concerning a new water supply scheme, the securing of a public electricity supply and also with the provision of a fire-engine which was eventually rejected. In 1920 they borrowed £500 from the Public Works Loan Board to purchase a five-acre field in Greenway for allotments. This same field went on to provide not only allotments but playing fields and a village hall. In 1969, under the chairmanship of Mrs Rosemary Ryan, a playing field Management Committee was set up. Until that time space for sporting interests in the village was provided informally on fields within the village, but within a few years the Committee provided the Playing Field with a wooden sporting pavilion. This was replaced in 1998 with a new brick building to cater for the needs of footballers and cricketers. It also serves today as a social meeting venue and a playgroup for young children meets there. In 2006 a new Multi Use Games Area (MUGA) was erected on the site using Lottery funding. In 1977 a Village Hall Management Committee independent of the Parish Council was set up. They raised funds which, together with a loan from the Parish Council, were used in 1981 to build a new village hall in succession to the Morris Memorial Hall. In 2006 a derelict stable in the village centre adjacent to Town Farm was refurbished using a government grant to provide a location for a Parish Office and Archive together with two commercial units. These were initially occupied by a coffee shop and a hairdressing salon.

In the last few years new buildings and housing developments have been erected that have changed the shape of the village. The Parish Council of elected members continues to serve the community. It has a sub-committee for planning matters and supports its functions by raising funds from the Parish by precept, which is additional to the Borough Council Tax. The aim of this Parish Council is to preserve, maintain and develop services and facilities that enhance the quality of life for all residents. The Council holds regular monthly meetings that are open to all parishioners who are given a time slot to air views and grievances.

A monthly newsletter is circulated to all parishioners, keeping everyone informed of village events and functions. The *Parish Magazine* published by the Parish Church also keeps subscribers abreast of activities and is used as a tool for advertising local businesses. The village website is proving an invaluable resource for all members of the community to promote and learn of village happenings and businesses, with links to other services. Visitors are given a unique overview of the village by means of an engraved map which has been erected in Queen Square.

A village store, which incorporates the Post Office, continues to thrive in the village centre today and provides a well-appreciated local service as well as being a source of information and contact for everyone. The public houses in the village still provide meeting points and venues for entertainment, with one continuing to support local skittles teams. The churches retain good congregations of worshippers, and provide centres of friendship and comfort. There are numerous village organisations and interest groups that meet regularly. The annual Flower Show provides a platform for competition for gardeners, cooks, artists and photographers and the May Fayre held in Church Road follows a long-held tradition going back to the medieval fair that began in The Shambles and moved firstly to Moredon and later to Manor Field. It embraces sideshows and stallholders selling their wares, and includes visits from Morris dancers and other travelling entertainers. The performance from the *mummers* of their play of ancient origin continues to take place in Queen Square on Boxing Day, rain or shine.

North Curry continues to preserve its essentially rural character and also retains its magnificent church and fine houses, many within the Conservation Area. The village remains surrounded by a mixed landscape of wooded hills, apple orchards, rich arable farmland and swampy Levels. Plant and wildlife abound with the huge RSPB West Sedgemoor Nature Reserve nearby. Curry and Hay Moors, West Sedgemoor and North Curry Meadow (a field of wild orchids) are all designated by English Nature as Sites of Special Scientific Interest (SSSI).

Life in North Curry in the second half of the 20th century and the beginning of the 21st century has continued to progress, influenced by events in the rest of Great Britain that many people in the village today have witnessed and remember. It is not my intention to write further about these modern times, but to leave recording the history that is in the making to those who follow me.

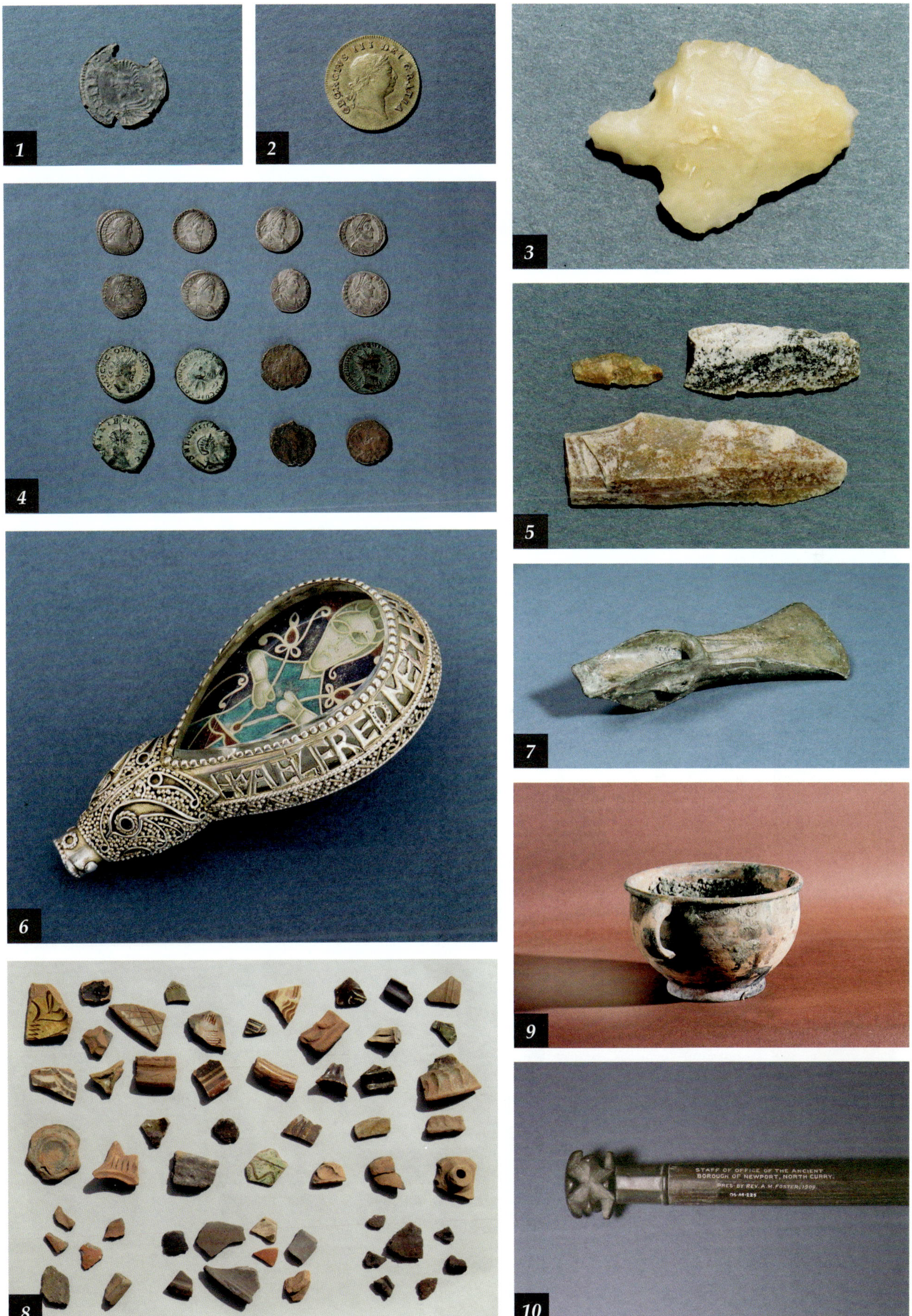

Artefacts found in and around North Curry: **1.** *Athelred II silver long cross type penny,* **2.** *George III gold half-guinea,* **3.** *Early Bronze Age flint arrow head,* **4.** *Roman coins,* **5.** *Early Bronze Age flint blades,* **6.** *The Alfred Jewel (a replica),* **7.** *Bronze Age palstave,* **8.** *Fragments of pottery AD1750–700BC,* **9.** *C18th Donyatt porringer,* **10.** *Newport Borough mace*

North Curry Parish Church**:** ***1.*** *West and south fronts,* ***2.*** *Tower,* ***3.*** *Lych gate,* ***4.*** *Norman doorway,* ***5.*** *West door,* ***6.*** *South porch,* ***7.*** *Belfry doorway,* ***8.*** *Memorial cross,* ***9.*** *North front from moor,* ***10.*** *New graveyard from tower,* ***11.*** *Barrett memorial,* ***12.*** *Weather vane,* ***13.*** *St Peter crossed keys,* ***14.*** *St Paul crossed swords,* ***15.*** *Tombs,* ***16.*** *Chained devil gargoyle*

***North Curry Parish Church*: 1.** *High altar and east window,* **2.** *Carved reredos detail,* **3.** *High altar reredos,* **4.** *West window detail,* **5.** *Bells,* **6.** *Coffer,* **7.** *Lectern,* **8.** *Coffer lock,* **9.** *Thoma atte Sloo effigy,* **10.** *Cadaver tomb detail,* **11.** *Font,* **12.** *Modern altar frontal,* **13.** *Cadaver tomb,* **14.** *Organ pipes,* **15.** *Organ*

In and around North Curry: ***1.*** *Village centre,* ***2.*** *River Tone,* ***3.*** *Willows on flooded Levels,* ***4.*** *North Curry from Moredon Hill,* ***5.*** *Corn stitches,* ***6.*** *A rhine,* ***7.*** *Knapp Bridge,* ***8.*** *Orchid field*

North Curry houses: ***1.*** *The Old Vicarage,* ***2.*** *Calmady House,* ***3.*** *The Rising Sun,* ***4.*** *Oldways,* ***5.*** *Thatchers,* ***6.*** *Manor Farm,* ***7.*** *Fosse End,* ***8.*** *The Manor House,* ***9.*** *Moredon,* ***10.*** *The Old Brewery*

North Curry today: ***1.*** *Methodist Church,* ***2.*** *Showing the way,* ***3.*** *White Hart Inn,* ***4.*** *Baptist Chapel,* ***5.*** *Village Map in Church Road,* ***6.*** *The Bird in Hand,* ***7.*** *Health Centre,* ***8.*** *Victoria Memorial,* ***9.*** *The Canal Inn,* ***10.*** *Post Office and Stores,* ***11.*** *War Memorial,* ***12.*** *Village Hall,* ***13.*** *Community Stable,* ***14.*** *Playing Field and Pavilion,* ***15.*** *Primary School*

Traditional local occupations and customs: **1.** *Traditional farming,* **2.** *Withy boiling,* **3.** *Elver fishing,* **4.** *Flower Show,* **5.** *Morris men,* **6.** *May Fayre,* **7.** *Reeve's Feast re-enactment,* **8.** *Mummers on Boxing Day*

***Bygone North Curry trading establishments**: **1.** Moulds – saddler, Moor Lane, **2.** Angel Inn and Gillard – saddler and harness maker, Stoke Road, **3.** A W May – builder and undertaker, Stoke Road, **4.** Thos. Giblett – draper and grocer (later London House Stores), Queen Square, **5.** Squire - motor engineer, The Pavement, **6.** G H Hutchings & Sons – newsagent, Queen Square, **7.** John Webb – ironmonger, Queen Square, **8.** C Young – grocer, Wrantage*

PART 2 – LIFE AND TRADITIONS OF NORTH CURRY

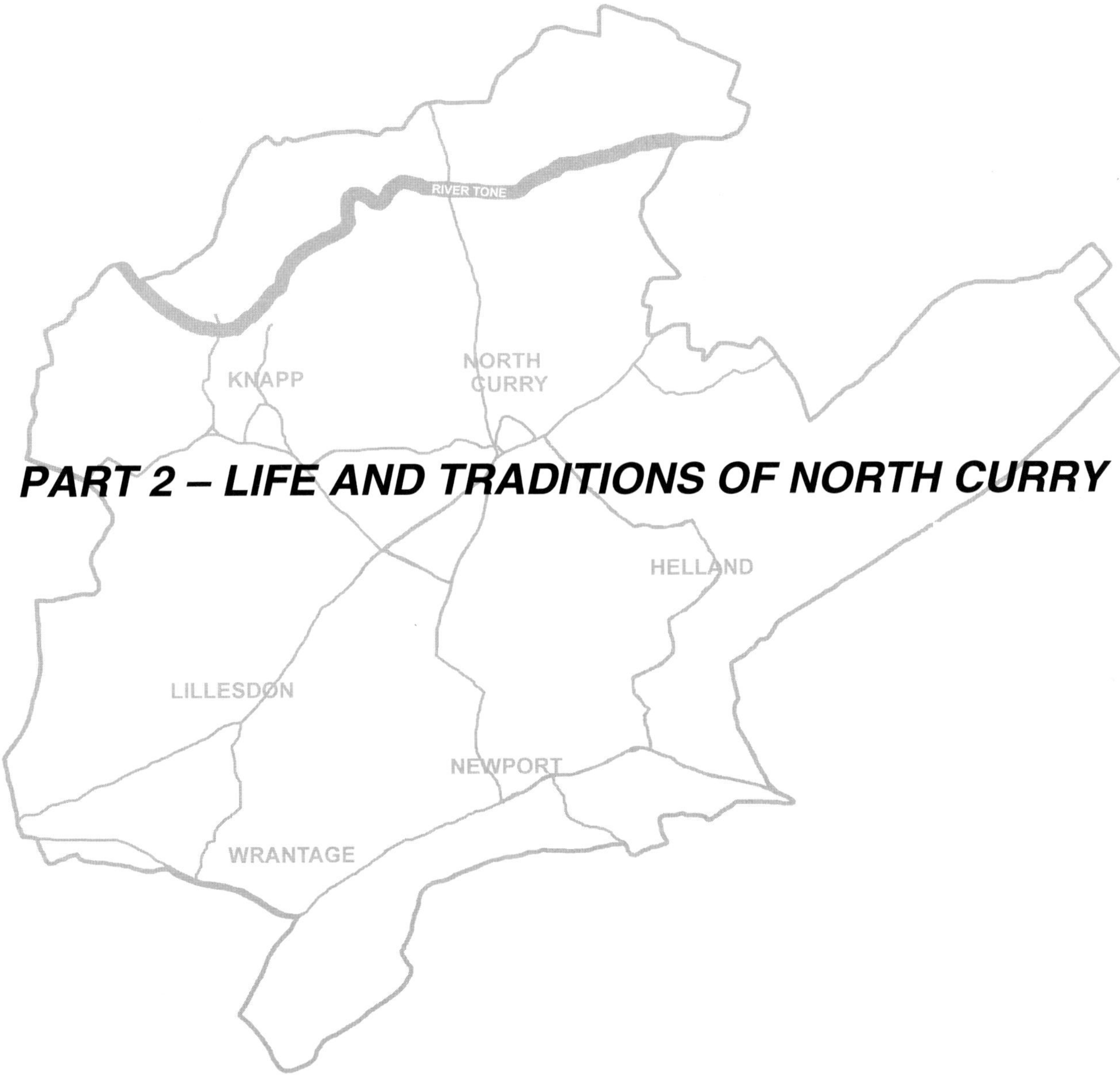

2 - 1

PLACE–NAMES AND PLACES IN THE PARISH

North Curry, Knapp, Lillesdon, Newport and Wrantage are the areas included in the Parish of North Curry today. Before 1846 the tithings and hamlets within the Parish included in the North Curry ecclesiastical district were Knapp, Lillesdon, Wrantage, Helland, Broad Lane, Moredon and the Borough of Newport together with the villages of North Curry, West Hatch and Stoke St Gregory.

NORTH CURRY

It is interesting to understand how the name North Curry became established, and learn how it evolved, as society developed with the need to identify places. The first place–names either applied to local physical geographical features or to human features. The first settlers gave names to the places where they recognised certain physical conditions such as water, marshes, hills or plains. Adjectives were often used to distinguish between different features. By the time of the Roman occupation British place–names were established. They were mostly Celtic in origin and mostly descriptive in character. As time went by these place–names underwent adaptation by other languages. The Romans brought Latin, the Anglo–Saxons brought Saxon or Old English, the Vikings brought Norwegian or Danish and the Normans brought French. However, it is thought that most English place–names contain some Celtic origins.

After the departure of the Romans, and following the West Saxon invasion of England in AD495, Cerdic and his followers settled in Dorset, Hampshire and South Somerset. The royal line of Wessex was founded in AD658. Other conquests in Somerset followed and when King Ine defeated the British King Geraint in AD710, the territory of West Somerset also became Saxon and the whole of Somerset became one of the shires or counties of the West Saxon Kingdom. It seems probable that the large royal settlement known during Saxon times by the name *Curig* was in fact North Curry. Saxon Charters of AD854 and AD904 include the place–name Curig (see page 22).

In the reign of King Edgar (AD959–975) the law of the land was revised and The Hundred Ordinance was introduced whereby shires were divided into hundreds for administrative purposes. The shire of Somerset was divided into two parts, eastern and western, and one of the hundreds in the western division was called the Hundred of Curig using the name of the established royal settlement at that time. As explained on page 21, the hundred was a local territorial unit comprising 100 hides. In 1791 John Collinson described the Hundred in *The History and Antiquities of the County of Somerset:*

> *The Hundred of North Curry is a narrow tract of land, lying between the hundreds of Abdick and Bulston on the south, and Andersfield and part of Somerton on the north. On either side are two large moors, called Stanmoor and West–Sedgmoor, which are a dead flat, extending to the foot of that ridge of hills, which runs from Curry–Rivel westward to Bickenhall. The west, northwest and southwest parts are inclosed, and interspersed with cultivated hills and fruitful vallies. It contains five parishes, of which the principal is North–Curry, whence it derives its name.*

The Hundred of North Curry is described in *A Topographical Description of Somersetshire* by Christopher and John Greenwood in 1822 as being situated in the southern part of the county, east of Taunton, and consisting of five parishes, North Curry, West Hatch, Stoke St Gregory, Thornfalcon and Thurlbeer. The Hundred Ordinance defined the duties of the basic territorial unit of the kingdom. Each hundred was to have a court that assembled every four weeks. The laws were common to the whole nation. All the freemen domiciled within a hundred would meet monthly as a hundred court, which was responsible for solving local disputes, overseeing the peace and punishing crime. Law enforcement was dependent at the most local level on the tithing, a group of ten mutually responsible households.

Cor, later spelt *Cur*, is an ancient British word or Celtic stem of a word signifying an area having patches of elevated land, with a large amount of low land or moor around which was swamp subject to inundation by the sea. The name may therefore signify the land about the marsh. As discussed in Chapter 1–1, all the flat country in the centre of Somerset formed a vast salt marsh. Before the days of rhines and ditches there was no drainage, and the incoming tide spread over all the flat ground and became a huge expanse of mud with occasional patches of marsh grass, reeds and rushes. Islets of higher ground, such as Nythe, Thong, Lyng and Athelney, rose above this vast expanse of water, inaccessible except by boat through brackish water channels. All the early settlements were set of necessity on some hill or ridge rising out of the plain. Haymoor, Currymoor, Sedgemoor, Stanmoor and Saltmoor, the names of the different areas of flat ground use the suffix *moor* that stems from *mere* meaning 'a marsh'.

In 1950 Dr A G Turner ascribes a Celtic origin to the name. He refers to Professor Eilart Ekwall's suggestion in his *Dictionary of Place–names* that *Curry is no doubt the old name of the stream that runs near the places.* He maintains that Curry is similar to Coryton and Cory Brook in Devon and Babcary and Castle Cary in Somerset, in that both are based on English River names. Although no streams of the River Cary can be traced close to North Curry, courses could have been altered when the moors were drained. He also suggests that Curry may be connected with the Cornish *cor* meaning 'limit, border or boundary'. Hence the word may denote the boundary of the flat wet land. Others put forward the theory that Curry consists of two words *cor* meaning a 'stony hill', and *y* or *ig* meaning

Spelling	Date	Source
Curig íe mære	854	Cartularium Saxonicum
Curig	904	Cartularium Saxonicum
Curi	934–9	Cartulary of Muchelney Abbey
æt Curi	1066–88	Codex Diplomaticus aevi Saxonici
Cori, Chori, Couri	1084	Geld Roll
Nortcuri	1086	Domesday Book
Nortchori, Churi, Chori, Curi	1086	Domesday Book Exon
Curiet, Nordcuri	1156	Pipe Rolls
Corilade	1157	Athelney Cartulary
Curi Malet and Curry Revel	1225	Assize Rolls
Chori, Cory, Corye, Corylond, Curi, Currie, Curilade, Cury, Currye, Kury, Norchuri, Norcury, Nordcuri, Nortchory, Northairy, Nortchury, Northcori, Northcory, Northcorylonde, Northcuri, Northcury, North Cury,	1189–1770	Manuscripts of the Dean and Chapter of Wells
Corymore, Corymormede	1262–3	Feet of Fines, Somerset
Byestcory	1327	Lay Subsidy Rolls

Sources: *SANHS Proceedings XCV 115–6 (1950): Notes on Some Somerset Place–names* by A G C Turner
The Concise Oxford Dictionary of English Place–names by Professor Eilert Ekwall

'watery place'. Therefore Curry means a stony hill surrounded by water, or marsh or perhaps just a marsh.

Others have suggested the word Curry is derived from the Celtic word *Cory* that they interpret as roughly meaning 'the end of'. North Curry, Curry Rivel and Curry Mallet are situated on the higher ground of the peninsula known as the Curry Ridge. This could have been considered the end of inhabited territory before the uninhabited stretches of the Somerset Levels and Moors. North Curry is the most northerly of these Curry villages. Curry Rivel is believed to have been named after Richard Revel, a nobleman living at the time of Richard I and Curry Mallet is thought to have been named after William Malet who is said to have been awarded this land after the Norman invasion of 1066. Parts of the Parish of Stoke St Gregory were previously known as East Curry.

Some historians point to the 4th century St Curig, termed *The Blessed* in Welsh Celtic literature, giving his name to this and neighbouring villages as well as to Capel Curig in Caenarvonshire, Newton St Cyres, near Exeter and St Cyres Down in Devonshire. St Curig was the Christian Bishop of Llanbadarn, who attended the Council of Arles in AD314 as a representative of the British Church. Legend suggests that St Curig and his associate St Badoc together with a band of Welsh missionary monks came to evangelise or spread the Christian word in Somerset. They were said to have crossed the Bristol Channel and entered the estuary of the River Parrett, eventually coming inland through the marshes, and landing their boat on the higher ground near what we now know as the Curry Ridge. Today on an area of elevated ground just above the moor is a farm called Lawnmoor Farm with a natural spring nearby called Whitewell. The name Lawnmoor could be a corruption of the Celtic *llan* meaning 'church' and *mere* meaning in Somerset 'marsh', hence signifying the church by the marsh. This could have been where St Curig and St Badoc would have erected a small wattle cell or oratory as a place of worship for their converts to Christianity, and this may have been the forerunner of the later settlement of North Curry. Nearby there is an area of land known as *Badoc's–linch* or, as it has been referred to for generations, *Bradlinch or Badlinch Hollow.*

When Somerset became wholly Christian in Saxon times it is possible, because of the proximity of Athelney, that a small Saxon church built of wood and thatch would have been built on the prominent site where the Parish Church of St Peter and St Paul, North Curry stands today. This could have been replaced with the Norman church that was there a few centuries later, and which became the centre of the settlement of North Curry.

Clearly the name has undergone numerous orthographical or etymological changes in arriving at the spelling North Curry after many years of usage. It is unlikely we will ever be certain of the precise origins. There have, over the centuries, been many different spellings of the name Curry as shown above.

KNAPP

Knapp included the area called Ham from early times and was an important part of the Parish, growing into a fairly large settlement when the River Tone began to be used as a source of communication and power. It is suggested the name Knapp derives from the Old English word *cnæpp* meaning 'top of a hill' or 'hillock'. Other early spellings of the name were *Cnappe* and *Knappe;* both used in the Dean and Chapter of Wells' documents, and *Knap–Fee* in later documents.

The earliest reference in the *Calendar of the Manuscripts of the Dean and Chapter of Wells* is c.1154 as follows:

Charter of Henry II giving to Gilbert de Norfolc 8 librates (four ox gangs or fifty-two acres) of land in Knappe in the King's manor of Northcory (in exchange for his land of Parva Whiteham (Little Witham) *which the King has given to the brethren of Chartosa), to hold of Gilbert Malet on the same terms as he held the land in Whiteham.*
MSS Wells Liber Albus II Folio 81d

Subsequently, as mentioned on page 31, one of the first Carthusian monasteries in England was built at Witham, near Bruton in Somerset. The land chosen for this site was in the possession of the Malet family and it was necessary for the inhabitants to be moved from there so the building could commence. According to the above entry an exchange of land took place with land at Knapp also belonging to the Malets, and several hundred inhabitants were moved 30 miles to be re-settled there. By royal munificence they were given £10 for seed, ten *marks* for clothes and one hundred *crannocks* of corn worth 62s.6d to help them with this transfer. In 1280 a grant was made giving tenements and land in Cnappe to John de Cnappe, Henry le Deye and William Hughet by Walter de Caam, Lord of Knapp. During the years 1280, 1303, 1316, 1319 and 1350 John de Knappe was called on many occasions as a witness at numerous court proceedings.

In 1305 Walter de Cadamo (son and heir of Richard de Cadamo of County Norfolk) sold his lands in Knapp for £200 to Dean John de Godelee of Wells. This transaction is noted in the *Calendar of the Manuscripts of the Dean and Chapter of Wells Liber Albus I Folio 79* in 1306. The tenants who were included in this transfer of land were John de la Knappe, his wife Margery and his son together with 22 others with *messuages* and parcels of land. In 1307 John de Godelee transferred the Manor of Knapp to Hamelin his brother, and in 1314 John de Cnappe is mentioned as a Hundredman and as the King's Bailiff in the Hundred of North Curry. In 1316 John de Cnappe granted to the Dean and Chapter of Wells power to create a watercourse on his land to a new mill from the town of *Hamme* and to make a road to the old *Cnappe* mill. In 1317 a William Colne acknowledged that he had destroyed a watercourse for the Dean and Chapter's new mill and was fined.

By 1324 Hugh de Bello Campo *(Beauchamp)* and his wife Idonea had acquired some lands from John de Knappe. They were promised compensation by the Dean and Chapter if their land became flooded whilst a new watercourse was being made from below the River Tone below *Hamme* to serve a new mill at *Cnappe*. Two new bridges were also built to assist them and their tenants for the carrying of hurdles and the driving of their cattle. In 1351, 1352 and 1355 Thomas de Cnap, possibly the son of John, is mentioned as a witness in numerous manor court proceedings. Later, in the 1787 *Schedule* of the *Survey of the Manor of Knap-Fee* by William White of Wedmore, the mill is described as in a derelict state - *A Wrecked Mill tenanted by Charles Ryall*. The site of the old mill in Knapp is in evidence near the present Knapp Bridge on the River Tone where a rectangular level platform raised some 1.2 to 1.5 metres above the level of the surrounding ground survives. There is also a ditch running nearby that could have been the *leat* serving the mill.

There was a quarry that supplied much of the sandstone that was used in the building of the Parish Church in North Curry and many of the older houses in the Parish, and which also supplied the stone that built Queen's College in Taunton. The remains of this quarry are still in evidence on the land at Snellgroves in Knapp.

In 1787 there were 26 dwellings in the tithing area of Knapp ranging from houses with four acres or more to tiny dwellings of no more than 14 perch. By 1840 the number of dwellings had reached 43. Many of these were very substantial farmhouses reflecting the wealth of the inhabitants in earlier times, and included Lower Knapp Farm (now named Manor Farm), Birds Farm, Knapp Farm, Higher Knapp Farm and Garnsey Farm, with the latter two still farming today. Some of these houses are discussed in Chapter 2-5. During the early-20th century, as well as many farms there was a general store run by Mr and Mrs Lunniss and The Rising Sun Inn which grew into a renowned restaurant, both of which have now ceased trading. There was also the thriving withy yard run by the Derham family which remains in use today.

In Knapp and Ham in 1851 people were engaged in the following occupations:

16 farmers farming from 3 to 280 acres most employing labourers
29 agricultural labourers
10 paupers
3 shoemakers
2 blacksmiths, innkeepers, strawjoiners and retired
1 baker, basketmaker, boatman, carpenter, cordwainer, dressmaker, gardener, harness maker, hay dealer, Relieving Officer and a miller and a coal merchant in Ham.

Knapp today mostly comprises private houses with only a few working farms. The number of houses is almost the same as in 1840, although much rebuilding on demolished house sites and infilling has occurred.

LILLESDON

Lillesdon has been spelt in various ways throughout history including *Lellesdon, Lellisdon, Lillesdone, Lyledon, Lylesden, Lyllesdon, Lyllesden* and *Lyllysdyn*. *Lill* or *Lilla* is possibly the name of a Saxon landowner and if *don* or *dun* means 'hill, down' or 'hill pasture' as Ekwall explains, then Lillesdon is the hill settlement of Lilla. Others have described Lilla as a Saxon leader who invaded the area of Sedgemoor and established stockades on the slightly higher ground. This land may well have been claimed by him by using the Saxon method of cutting a hide into strips and appropriating as much land as these *thongs* would enclose. Listoke or Lilla's stockade could be assumed to have originally been one of these sites, and Thong Island or the area of Thong Farm may well have been another (see page 133).

From the earliest times Lillesdon has been one of the tithings of North Curry. At the time of Edward I (1272–1307) Lillesdon was the land of Baldric of Noneton who held it on behalf of the King. In 1317 Hugh de Bello Campo (*Beauchamp*) was the owner and a chapel was granted to him there. In 1330 John Brodhomre granted a *moeity* (or half) of the Manor of Lillesdon to Richard de Stapledon for life. The other half was probably granted to William de Monte–Cuto *(Montacute)* who was also granted Slough (in Stoke St Gregory). It then passed to the Bonville family and then to the Wyke family of Nynehead. In 1363 John Beauchamp is called Lord of Lillesdone and in 1554 William Lyte is at Lillesdon, followed in 1587 by John Buller the younger, whose family name appears regularly in the *Parish Registers* of North Curry. In 1666 Edward Courte is described as *of Lillesdon* and Edward his son and Alexander his brother followed him. In 1790 John Collins of Hatch Beauchamp, who was Lord of Huntham and Slough, was the owner and in the 19th century the Hon. H P Gore–Langton, who was also owner of Slough Court, took possession. The building called Lillesdon Court is one of the oldest substantial stone buildings in the Parish of North Curry, and it is possible that this was the building where at one time the manorial court for North Curry was held. The extract below is a translation of a *Wells Charter* that was granted at Lillesdon in 1296:

> *1296 Charter 139*
> *Release by Robert le Brun to Thomas de Mere of North Cory and Avice his wife, daughter of Sir Walter de Loveny, and the heirs and assigns of Thomas, of the lands given by Thomas to Robert in North Cory, Mere, and Slou.. Witnesses: Sir Walter de Loveny, knight, Richard de Loveny, Robert Gyan, Geoffrey de la Slow. Dated, Lillesdon, Monday after SS Simon and Jude, 24 Edward I. Round seal: a lion dormant beneath a tree. S... de Ryngesburn.*

Lillesdon Court seems to have been the chief seat of the Beauchamp family. In medieval times chantry chapels were established with endowments of rent or land by persons who wished to receive masses by the local mass–priest for their well–being on earth and their souls after death. Such a chapel was instituted for the Beauchamps at Lillesdon and dedicated to St Martin, and entries in the *Calendar of the Manuscripts of the Dean and Chapter of Wells* report as follows:

> *1317*
> *Settlement of questions that have arisen between the Dean and Chapter and Hugh de Bello Campo and Idonea his wife, about a chantry of three days in the week at S Martin's chapel, in Lillesdon.*
> *MSS Wells Liber Albus II Folio 217*

> *1355*
> *Indenture between John de Carletone dean and the chapter and Sir John de Troubrigge, vicar of Northcory, to increase the portions of the vicarage and augment the vicarage with certain lands, and give coppice wood annually as an endowment for a chantry in the chapel of Lillesdone. The vicar is to pay one rose annually on the Nativity of S John the Baptist, and shall during the term of his life celebrate or cause to be celebrated a mass every Wednesday and Friday, if a double feast shall not fall upon those days, and if the lord and lady of Lillesdone shall be present, for whose good estate and for whose souls the said chantry is established.*
> *MSS Wells Liber Albus II Folio 211*

> *1356*
> *Agreement made between d/c and the lady Idonea de Beauchamp (lady and heir of Lillesdone) to have a chantry in her chapel (St Martin) at Lillesdone.*
> *MSS Wells Liber Albus II Folio 219*

Lillesdon passed out of the Beauchamp family when Alice, who was the daughter and heir of John Beauchamp, married Nicholas Buller. Johan Connock, who married four times and whose second husband was John Buller of Lillesdon, is commemorated by an altar frontal displayed in North Curry Parish Church (see page 104).

The significant houses in Lillesdon today, in addition to Lillesdon Court, include Higher Lillesdon Farm and Hammonds Farm which both continue as working farms. Also Sunny Farm and Spearings, both early houses, Jackless Cross, Lillesdon Green Farm, now the site of a college, and Star Cottages, once an inn.

WRANTAGE

The village of Wrantage lies two miles to the south of North Curry and has developed in a linear fashion on the main road between Taunton and Langport. It is situated on a valley floor, but is sited above the main level of flooding, at a height of about 15 metres O.D. (Ordnance Datum). The remains of part of the Taunton to Chard Canal, which was opened in 1842 and operated until 1866, lie in the village. The canal crossed the main road in Wrantage by means of a stone aqueduct that has since been demolished, and ran south up an *inclined plane*. It then passed through a tunnel, which remains today, and ran for about a mile at a height of about 30 metres O.D. to emerge on the other side of an escarpment near Beercrocombe. The project was never completed, being halted by the emergence of the railways. More details of the canal can be found in Chapter 2–8.

A Saxon origin has been given to the name Wrantage, maybe stemming from *Wrenna's Tich*. Ekwall suggests that *Wrenna* or *Wren* may have been a nickname. *Tiche* or *thecen* are Old English words for 'a homestead', hence *we have the home of a small, wren–like keen and sprightly Saxon warrior.* Ekwall also gives the meaning of *Wraena* as the Old English word for 'stallion', therefore *Wrentich* may mean *a stallion enclosure or stud farm on a large estate.* Wrantage was one of the earliest tithings of the Parish of North Curry and has been recorded in many of the early Wells Cathedral documents. The various spellings of the name in these documents were *Wrentis, Wrentise, Wrentisse, Wrentyssh, Wrentich, Wrentiche. Wrentisford, Wrentiche–ford* and *Wrentiches–ford* were also used, suggesting the place may have been sited upon the stream that runs through the valley. The first mention of the name was in a *Wells Charter* of 1199 when King John included Wrantage in the grant of North Curry to the canons and the Church of St Andrew, Wells as follows:

Charter of King John confirming grants made by King Richard I and by himself while count of Mortain to the church and canons of St Andrew Wells, of the manor, hundred, and church of Northcuri with the land of Hacche and Wrentis, and warranty. Witnesses: Geoffrey, archbishop of York, Roger, bishop of St Andrews, Earl David, William of Arundel, William de Humetis, constable of Normandy, Hugh de Gornay. Dated Le Mans, 30 September, 1 John, AD 1199.
MSS Wells Liber Albus I Folio 9

Many other details of landholding transactions occur throughout the documents from that time, and in 1528 Lord's Wood in Wrantage is mentioned in a Wells document of an account of the Reeve's Feast. A number of Wrantage residents appear in the *Protestation Oath Returns* of 1641, and 29 residents of Wrantage were liable for Hearth Tax in 1674. In 1685 a number of residents of Wrantage were included in the punishment list *Rollcall of the Rebels* after the Battle of Sedgemoor. In 1787 there were 415 landholdings in Wrantage in the *Survey of the Manor of North Curry*. Growth took place in Wrantage c.1840, probably as a result of the building of the Chard Canal. In the 1841 *Census Return* for North Curry the area of Newport and Wrantage had a total of 477 residents with many engaged in stone cutting and in agriculture. In the 1851 *Census Return* Newport and Wrantage, including Crimson Hill, Rock Hill, Old Way and a part of Sedgemoor, had a total of 366 residents, mostly engaged in agriculture. By 1901 the population was 302 residents. Today there are nearly 200 residents.

Planning restrictions were being imposed as far back as the 18th century, and below is an example of the penalty imposed on an inhabitant who attempted to build a house on waste ground without permission of the Dean and Chapter of Wells. The case appears in the proceedings of a Court Leet held on 21st April 1702. *We present William Curry for beginning to build a house in Mare Green in Wrantage Tything beinge on the Lords Wast of the Manor aforesaid, tyme is given him to pull downe the same and lay it level to the green by the twenty-fourth of June next makinge default to fforfitt five pounds.*

There are about 12 houses named as farmhouses in Wrantage, few of which maintain farmland today. The two oldest are Weaver's (16th century), and Oldways (17th century), and these are described in more detail in Chapter 2-5. In 1879 Wrantage School was built by voluntary subscription on land given by the Ecclesiastical Commissioners and conveyed in trust to the Vicar and Churchwardens of North Curry. It operated as a smaller sister school to the National School in North Curry. It was described in *Trade Directories* for North Curry between 1881 and 1902 as a Parochial Mixed School and from 1906 to 1927 as a Public Elementary Mixed School, serving the children of Wrantage and nearby. It suffered structural damage from a German parachute mine in 1942 and closed down a short time later, amalgamating with North Curry School (see Chapter 2-7).

A Methodist Church was built in Wrantage c.1845, but was de-consecrated c.1975, the building being converted to a private house. A forge was situated in the heart of the village serving the needs of local farmers and residents, but was demolished in the 1960s, with a bungalow being erected on the site.

There were three public houses in Wrantage during the 19th and 20th centuries. The Wrantage Inn with a skittle alley was located at the Newport end of the village. The Wheelwright's Arms was at Stoneyhead, and was the site of an early wheelwright. The Canal Inn, which was much frequented at the time of the building of the Chard Canal, still trades today. A story recalls the time when dormitory rooms were used there to house the many stone workers needed in the construction of the canal. There was also a general store and a Post Office situated in the village, but today only Wrantage Seed Mills, suppliers of agricultural goods and animal feeds, remains.

NEWPORT

Various spellings of Newport have been used such as *Nieport, Nyweport* and *Nywport*, and there are a number of theories regarding the origin of the name. The first is that *port* means a 'gate' or 'entrance', and Newport was the new gate to the Manor of North Curry from the road to Wells. The second is that it was a haven or port town on the River Tone, and was mentioned c.1625 when Newport was described as *anciently a Haven Towne*, although today the River Tone flows a mile and a half away. Thirdly, as explained by Ekwall, the Old English word *port* means a 'town' especially one possessing market rights, and with Langport or Long Market with its 10th century roots in close proximity, Newport or *new market* may have been set up soon afterwards. From the earliest periods of written documentation the Parish of North Curry was divided into tithings and the Borough of Newport was one of them. Newport may have been called a borough from the Saxon word *burh* signifying a fortress settlement, later to become a town with *burgage* plots or plots within an ancient borough. Although it was not a borough of any great size, free tenure of burgage plots was granted with certain privileges and officers such as a Bailiff were instituted.

An Archaeological Assessment by Somerset County Council in 2002 states that the new market town of *New-port* was probably established shortly after the time when administration of the Manor of North Curry was transferred to Wells. This was in 1190, and Newport was then considered to be a separate entity from the Parish of North Curry. Field boundaries suggest that the shape of the town was originally in the form of a large rectangle with internal sub-divisions. Today there are remains of earthwork platforms and enclosures, possibly evidence of former structures, which may have included houses, workshops, roads and boundaries, as well as a chapel and manor house.

However, as North Curry flourished the Borough of Newport declined and by the 18th century the layout of the town had disappeared. This may have been due to the failure of market trading, the failure of farming or the Black Death. A map of 1797 shows thin enclosures possibly representing these abandoned house sites running along each side of a central road that may be the remains of burgage plots. An archaeological survey has not as yet been carried out, and the only buildings remaining there today are post-medieval including Newport Manor, Newport Farm, Brook Farm, Newport Cottage and Newport Mill, with most evidence of any known settlement coming from documents of Wells Cathedral. A Toll Gatehouse is referred to on the 1840 *Tithe Schedule* for North Curry and was situated on the road near to the present entrance of the St Giles Kennels. The landowners of the site were the Commissioners of the Taunton Turnpike Road and it is possible this building served for the payment of tolls from early days when Newport was a borough.

The following is a list of tenants of Newport of 1390 taken from the *Calendar of Manuscripts of the Dean and Chapter of Wells*. The tenants hold no more than five acres, and there are references to customs and privileges of the manor.

Rental of Newport
John atte Brygge messuage and arable land (2 acres); rent 2s; suit of the court of Niwport; common on all moors etc. of Northcory. Reversion to his son or other right heir, relief 4s. (two year's rent), and the lord shall have custody and marriage of the heir. No payment due for a daughter's marriage; but notice must be given to the bailiff of Newport borough, and by him to the bailiff of Northcory; no heriot or mortuary, because all tenements in the borough were of the lords' demesne, by livery of Sir Robert Berkele, their steward.
Thomas Hugh, I acre with house, 3 perches of meadow, I acre of wood : rent 2s.3d etc as above.
Alice Britel 1 acre and 1 acre of meadow : rent 2s.
Robert Curteys 1 acre with house, 1 acre of meadow, 1 acre of wood : rent 2s. 6d.
John Faber 2 acres with house, 2 acres of meadow : rent 4s.
Alice Britell 1 acre with house, 1 acre of wood : rent 15d.
Robert Curteys 1 acre. 1 acre meadow, 1 acre wood : rent 2s.3d.
Simon Ury 1 acre with house, 1 acre wood : rent 15d.
John in the Hurne 1 acres with house, rent 3s.
Robert Shire 1 acre with house, 1 acre of wood : rent 15d.
Robert Martyn 1 acre with house, 1 acre of wood : rent 15d.
Stephen the sutor 1 acre with house : rent 12d.
Cristina Borewold and Alice her sister 1 acre with house, 1 acre of meadow, 1 acre of wood : rent 2s.3d.
John atte Hurne 1 acres with house, 1 acres of meadow, 1 acre of wood : rent 4s. 3d.
Philip Bouswayn ½ acre with house, ½ acre of meadow ½ acre of wood : rent 13 ½d.
John Borewold, as the last.
Robert Shire 1 acre with house : rent 12d.
William le Poyer, as the last.
Robert Russell 2 acres with house, 1 acre of meadow, 1 acre of wood: rent 3s.6d.
Robert Curteys 1 acre at Twelfacres, as overland, for the lives of himself and his wife according to the custom of the manor of Northcory : rent 3d.
Alice Britol 2 acres at Twelfacres and 1 acre at la Breche similarly for life : rent 9d.
Robert Curteys similarly 2 acres at Twelfacres and 1 acre at la Breche : rent 9d.
Simon Ury similarly 1 acre at l; la Medheye ; rent 8d. The said Simon similarly 1½ acres in Bouekysheye : rent 18d.
Alice Britell similarly 1½ acres of meadow there : rent 18d.
John Borewold similarly 1 acre at Twelfacres : rent 3d.
The said John similarly 1 piece of land at la Combe : rent 12d.
Philip Bouswayn similarly 1 acre at Twelfacres : rent 3d.
Walter Rouk similarly 1 acre there : rent 3d.
Robert Russell similarly 1 acre there : rent 3d. The said Robert similarly ½ acre there : rent 4d. The said Robert similarly 1 acre at la Yoldelane : rent 8d.
John Curteys 5 acres of arable and ½ acre of meadow in Gostelond : rent 11d.
Robert Martyn 5 acres of arable and ½ acre of meadow :rent 11d. and to plough 1 perch of the lord's land every other year in the fields which were formerly of ancient demesne, and reap 1 perch of wheat or oats every year. Total 48s.9d.
John le Bole one piece of land of the highway for life by livery of Sir Philip de Odyham steward : rent 6d, and has raised a house thereon.
John Faber one daywork of land of the highway for the lives of himself and his wife by livery of Sir Philip : rent 6d, and has raised a smithy thereon. Total 50s.9d.
MSS Wells Liber Albus II Folios 50 –52

Other entries concerning the tenants of Newport are as follows:

1339
Acknowledgement by Ralph de Middelnye that whereas he has made a bridge over the bounds between the lordship of Dean and Chapter of Wells and himself, and over it has driven his cattle upon the common this has been done by permission of the dean and chapter and not as of right.
MSS Wells Liber Albus II Folio 214d

1349
Grant by Walter Pontefer (Pontefer could be translated as bridge keeper) *to John atte Sloo, Margery his wife, and John, their son, and the heirs and assigns of John atte Sloo, of a burgage and a half at Nywportes, in the Hundred of Northcory. Witnesses: Thomas de Somerton, Thomas de Knapp, William Hacc. Dated La Nywportes AD 1350*
MSS Wells Charter 304.

1372
Richard Craddoc, parson of Cory Malet Church, and Nicholas Mancel, chaplain to Margery atte Sloo, grant to Margery at Sloo the burgage (dwelling house) in Newport given to them by Walter Portyfer (the present Brook House could be on the site of this dwelling).
MSS Wells Liber Albus II Folio 222d.

Another reference to Newport in 1618, at a Court Sessions of Sewers held at Bridgwater, reports fines imposed on some of the inhabitants of the *Burrow of Newporte* for not clearing rhines, and for not raising a wall in *Currimoor*. As time went on each tithing was made responsible for repairing the highways and in 1680 the appointment of a Waywarden for Newport was recorded in the North Curry Churchwardens' Accounts. In 1695 there is an entry in the Chapter of Wells accounts for a payment of £7 made by the Dean and Chapter for re-building a new stone arch bridge at Newport.

The Newport Borough staff of office or mace is held in the Somerset County Museum. The staff of oak of which half a metre remains is surmounted by a bronze mace-head and was perhaps carried before the Portreeve by the Constable. In 1909 the Foster family of North Curry donated it to the museum (see Plate i) and in 1901 Hugh Olivey recorded that Ambrose Millett Foster had written:

> *I have the old staff that my uncle called the Newport borough staff. The total length is now 2 ft. 8in., one end is much worm eaten, but from a four-sided tapering hole nearly in the centre I think it was never much longer, but ended in an iron ferrule or spike. The diameter of the wooden part is about 1¼ in., and fairly uniform throughout, but tapering a little towards the metal head. This is made of copper or bronze, first a shaft into which the wood fits, this is roughly octagonal and about 1⅜ in.long; then a twelve pointed knob, made apparently by filing a rough knob rather flat on the top, diagonally to right and left from four points, these deep valleys make the points stand out. It is rough work, and I should think old, but I can find no date. I should think it was a baton. The metal end would hit a man a murderous blow, but the shaft is too thick and not well enough balanced to be used as a weapon of offence. It could not be handled with any rapidity.*

In 1787 five houses in Newport are listed in the *Schedule of the Survey for Newport Borrough* and the copyholders are named as Philip Foster, Kewer and William Weaver. In the 1851 *Census Return* for North Curry there were ten households living in the Newport area. Susanna Foster, a landed proprietor, who was 74 years of age, inhabited Newport House, later Newport Manor. She lived there with her daughter Sarah aged 34 and her unmarried son Philip aged 38. He is listed as a farmer of 230 acres employing 14 labourers and 2 servants in the house. There are four other farmers listed in the Return who held between six and nine acres together with two carpenters. In 1861 Philip Foster is recorded as living there with his sister Sarah and Aunt Sarah Millett aged 80, and farming 290 acres and employing 15 men. In 1881 Philip Foster was living alone with two servants and farming 160 acres and employing seven men. By 1891 he had retired and is listed as independent *living on his own means*. Newport House and Newport Farm, with other land, were sold in 1916 by the widow of Ambrose Millett Foster.

The earliest reference to Newport Mill was in the 1840 *Tithe Schedule* for North Curry when William Edwards is listed as the lessee and occupier of a millhouse and garden in Newport. In the 1851 *Census Return* for North Curry he and his son Samuel are listed as bakers living in *Green Way*. In the 1861 *Census Return* he is listed as a retired miller aged 70 and his son Samuel, aged 37, is listed as the miller in Newport.

In 1871 Thomas Bowyer is listed as the miller in Newport and in 1881 John Kinglake aged 29 is listed as a miller and farmer at Newport Mill. In the 1891 *Census Return* Isaac Hall aged 49 with his sons Herbert 20 and Edward 16 are all listed as millers at Newport Mill. In 1901 Charles Burrow aged 31 is listed as a farmer and corn miller. The mill is described as a corn mill in 1928 when it was re-geared and the wheel re-built and converted to steam power for use when the water was low.

HELLAND

References pertaining to Helland vary the spelling as *Hillend* and *Hillond*. Hillend is easily explained being the area at the bottom of the hill in North Curry that descends from White Street towards West Sedgemoor. The element of *Hel* or *hell* in the name points to the old English word *healh* meaning a 'corner, angle, secret or hidden place'. The old Cornish word hel means an arm of the sea or estuary as in Helford. Many explanations of *hel, hell* or *helle* connect the name with *Hel* - the mistress of the gloomy underworld. Many German place-names commence with *Hell* such as *Hellegat* meaning 'bright path, way or channel'. Professor Eilert Ekwall refers to the Welsh *Henllan* meaning 'old church'.

The *Calendar of the Manuscripts of the Dean and Chapter of Wells* refer to lands of *Hullendmede* and *Helledmede* and to the names Hugh de la Hele and Hugh atte Hele.

> *1280*
> *Hugh, son of Hugh atte Hele of Northcory, has been absent from the county of Somerset for some time, and the d/c have dealt with and cultivated his lands at Northcory as has seemed fit to them. He now yields to them all the fruits which they have received from the day of his departure until the day of execution of this deed.*
> *MSS Wells Liber Albus II Folio 210*

> *1289*
> *Grant by Edward Dean of Wells and the chapter to Hugh de la Hele and the heirs of his body, of a messuage and ferdel of land in North Curi, formerly held by his father Richard de la Hele, upon an annual payment of 11s.1d in lieu of all secular services, saving hundred and manor court dues and services due to the crown and a relief of 5 marcs; heirs minors to be wards of the dean and chapter. Tested Sir Walter de Loueny, Sir Baldric de Noneton, Geoffrey de la Slo, Thomas de Mere etc. AD 1289.*
> *MSS Wells Liber Albus I Folio 18d*

> *1294*
> *Gift by Walter de Kaam granting to Hugh de la Hele a tenement in Hountham.*
> *MSS Wells Liber Albus II Folio 220*

> *1296*
> *Gift by Mabel Rowles of North Cory, granting to Hugh de la Hele and Alice his wife, a messuage in consideration of 4 marks.*
> *MSS Wells Liber Albus II Folio 216*

> *1373*
> *Release granted to the Dean and Chapter by John Beauchamp, knight, and lord of Lillesdone, for all services due from the lands of the men of Hele.*
> *MSS Wells Liber Albus II Folio 336d*

In 1314 it was recorded that there were ten tenants of *Hillond* in the Manor of North Curry, and William atte Mere was to *mow the first swathe the length of the meadow and no more, and afterwards be overseer of the mowers.* In the 19th century Helland House was the home of J B Hellard, a farmer. It later became a school and is now a private house. Much of the land is farmland with a few working farms including Nythe Farm, Thong Farm and Bowldish Farm, although today the use of the name of Helland tends to be restricted to the northern part of the area.

2 - 2

THE MANORIAL SYSTEM, LAWS AND TAXES

The Manorial System

For many generations before the Norman Conquest of 1066 English society had been moving towards the evolution of a manorial economy. The background to manorial tenancy lies in the pre-medieval organisation of a mostly rural country, when all land belonged to the monarch and was *real* estate or royal estate. The great majority of people were peasants living and working their family holdings and owing rent to their local lord.

When the Norman commissioners undertook the Domesday Inquest they found that England during King Edward's time had been divided into estates which they described as *mansions,* and these were grouped into *maneria* from the Latin *manerium* or manors from the French *manoir.* These were governed by persons known as lords who were seen as superior to the mass of peasantry. The Lord of the Manor held the property from a superior lord in return for allegiance and service. The Lord of the Manor was not necessarily titled and his superior lord could have been the King. The estates of these lords were organised around their chief residence or *demesne* on which the peasantry worked on the lord's behalf. Many of these *manaria* covered an appreciable part of a county, and some included a large number of dependent villages, hamlets and farms. Hence the term *manor* meant a piece of landed property held by a Lord of the Manor with tenants.

William the Conqueror, on ascending the throne of England, kept some lands for himself and gave some to his major barons as a reward for supporting him. The gifts were not without obligation - the barons owed the King military service in time of war. Each baron was allocated estates which were not necessarily adjoining, and, after choosing one as his main seat he appointed Stewards and Bailiffs to run the others. The barons granted the smaller estates to their knights as a reward for their military support. This created a system of feudal relationships between greater and lesser lords, stretching from the King at its summit to the peasants at its base. The manor land was cultivated to provide food for the Lord of the Manor and the tenants or serfs who belonged to him.

These serfs were granted enough arable, meadow, pasture and woodland with which to support their own household, paying the lord money rent. Serfs were not allowed to escape or leave the manor unless they and their families, together with the land they worked, were sold to another lord. They were required to devote about a third of their time to the lord's *demesne* spread all through the year, including during the lord's harvest. They ploughed the lord's land as a priority over their own using the lord's plough and oxen overseen by the foreman or Reeve. The land was issued in thin strips of half an acre separated by baulks or narrow grass paths and allocated so that everyone had a share of good and bad land. The cultivable land of the manor was normally divided into three or four fields, and the whole of a field put down to one crop, either wheat, oats or rye, barley for beer, or beans as cattle fodder. When it ceased to produce well it was left fallow for one year and cattle grazed and fertilised it. The Lord of the Manor had the rights to all timber, the rights to all wild animals for hunting and shooting for sport, and the rights to minerals under the earth.

As time went on, and depending on the quality of their work, serfs were given extra land and privileges and were upgraded and described as *villeins, cottars* and *bordars.* The more prominent serfs were styled *villeins* and were given between 60 and 100 acres of land. The younger or lesser serfs or *cottars* were given between 4 and 10 acres and the *bordars* were those who lived on the waste of the cultivated manor and were granted land if they cleared it.

A clever *villein* could arrange to buy himself out of bondage. This gave him the right to educate his sons and marry off his daughters without paying the *merchet* fee or gaining permission from the lord. It also enabled him to move to another manor, and he was free from recovery if he found refuge for a year and a day.

When a serf tenant died a *heriot* tax became due. The word *heriot* meant 'army goods'. This stemmed from Saxon times when horses, weapons and shields and military apparel were returned to knights or Lords of the Manor on the death of a tenant on the premise that it was originally supplied by the lord. As time went on it became the custom when a serf tenant died for the land that he had worked to pass to his eldest son. Initially on taking over the tenancy the family's best beast, normally the plough-ox, was taken back by the lord, but later the equivalent goods or a money payment was substituted. This entry fine or heriot tax was usually two to ten times the annual rent of the land. The Church in turn took one tenth of his produce and shared in the death duties, often removing another beast.

In the early days of the manorial system tenants were secure with their tenure and paid minimal rents, enjoying many a perk as *customs of the manor.* These rights were called *botes* or *estovers.* The word *bote* stems from the Saxon word *botan* and the word *estover* from the French word *estouffer* meaning 'to furnish' and interpreted to mean the right of manorial tenants to take material from the commons for their own use. These rights included:

Cartbote	*The right to take living wood from the commons to make or repair fences*
Cattlegate/Beastgate	*The right to graze animals on the pasture or waste and benefit from the produce*
Common in the Soil	*The right to take sand, gravel, and minerals for use on the commoner's holding*
Common of Pasture	*The right to graze stock on the common*
Common of Vicinage	*Permits a man's cattle to stray onto adjoining land without molestation*
Firebote/Fyrbote	*The right to gather dead wood for fires*
Foldbote	*The right to gather wood for houses, carts, ploughs or hurdles*
Hey–Hedgebote	*The right to gather living wood to make or repair fences*
Housebote	*The right to take wood from the commons to build or repair houses*
Husbote	*The right to obtain more substantial wood for house–building*
Pannage	*The right to take fodder to feed pigs in the manorial woods*
Piscary	*The right to fish from the manor's waters*
Ploughbote	*The right to take wood to make or repair ploughs*
Turbage	*The right to dig peat or turf for use as fuel in a commoner's dwelling*

The Lord of the Manor also had a *demesne* staff of men and women who lived at his castle or manor house and who worked for him full time. These were the slaves who appear in the *Domesday Book*. The lord, in addition to his domestic buildings, probably had barns and byres, a garden, an orchard, a corn mill, a fishpond, a warren (where rabbits and game birds were bred for hunting) and a dovecote. He also had private woodland which, in the centuries after 1086, he may well have converted into a deer park.

Manorial Courts of Justice

A court of justice, called the *Court Baron or Great Court*, was held every three weeks and the lord exercised jurisdiction over all that resided in his manor. It was there as an organ of local government and it had jurisdiction over disputes between individuals and dealt with transfers of land.

Most manors had a free tenant or freeman, called a *franklin*, sometimes a dispossessed former Saxon landowner, who paid rent and owed certain duties in exchange for military protection and a share of hunting. His sons were expected to serve as soldiers if called upon. The lord had a duty to provide the holding, to protect the tenant and to do him justice in his court. In return he had the right to expect the services attached to the holding, whether military or agricultural. In addition to services, the free tenant owed homage to the lord, had to swear an oath of allegiance to the Crown, and was required to attend this court. The tenants who attended the manor court were known as the *homage*. Villeins were also required to attend regularly. The court appointed some local officials, including the Reeve or Bailiff who collected the lord's dues.

Petty common law offences were dealt with in the *Court Leet* or *Little Court* that was held every six months. The Court inspected the working of the frankpledge, whereby each man over the age of 12 was made answerable for the life and conduct of others within a group of ten households, or the tithing. If they failed to report a crime, they could be punished for the crime themselves, so the incentive to snoop was strong. Cases of assault, bloodshed, false weights and measures, gossip, eavesdropping, fouling the waterways, and disputes involving sums of money of less than 40 shillings were tried, and penalties such as trial by ordeal, the pillory, stocks or small fines were imposed.

A Court Baron and a Court Leet, both dealing with local issues, were held in North Curry, probably in one of the more important houses, or possibly in an ecclesiastical building near the church. These courts were presided over by the Steward, one of the canons of the cathedral, who, with his servants, came from Wells for that purpose. Persons who failed to attend three consecutive courts without an excuse or proxy were fined.

In 1166 Henry II introduced a new procedure of trial by jury, denying the feudal courts most of their jurisdiction as to the title and possession of land. Circuit judges were introduced with judges travelling to preside over the County Courts which evolved into Assize Courts. Policing arrangements were aided by the continuing custom of frankpledge. A large part of the King's revenue came from fines imposed at the Assize.

The Tudor period saw the expansion of central government and the reorganisation of local administration when manor courts lost much of their earlier responsibility. In particular, the functions of the Court Leet were taken over by the Quarter and Petty Sessions with the Constable being appointed by the Parish Vestry. Quarter Sessions were held quarterly for the hearing of offences of a more serious nature and prison or death sentences were given if necessary. In Somerset in the medieval period the County Court became established at Ilchester, where a County Gaol was built, and it replaced Somerton as the county town. These courts were eventually held only in Taunton and Wells and lasted until 1971 when a new Crown Court system was introduced.

Tenancy Laws

From as early as the 12th century there is evidence that some lords found it to their advantage to commute labour services into a money rent when there was a scarcity of labour. This process was accelerated by the labour shortages caused by the Black Death or bubonic plague of 1348-1349, after which the commutation of these feudal liabilities to money payments created the custom of copyhold tenancies. The Wars of the Roses (1455-1487) impoverished many barons and knights. They had borrowed money from their *villeins* and *franklins* and they paid the loans back in the form of land, free of service obligations. These tenants became freeholders, and a yeoman land-owning class was born, which could sell, buy and mortgage land. This land or freehold property called a *fee* was subject to common law and could be inherited and passed to a lawful heir without restraint.

Other tenants had become entitled to perpetual tenancies from the Lords of the Manor. The conditions of tenancy varied from manor to manor according to custom. In most cases, on the death of the tenant the holding passed to his widow for her lifetime and then to those named on the Manor Court Roll as reversionary tenant, usually the children. Each time the holding passed to another a fine or *heriot* was paid. The named tenant had only to pay a yearly rent to the manorial lord with no labour services except work in various small ways such as ditch clearing and helping to repair roads. All tenants had the right to graze a fixed number of cows, sheep or draught horses on the pastures and wastes of the manor and to a share of hay mown from the meadows. They also enjoyed a feast at Christmas provided by the Reeve. The title to the holding was an entry in the Court Rolls, of which the tenant had a copy that was deemed to be a title deed. This became known as copyhold tenancy.

When the open fields of the manor were *enclosed* from the early-18th century onwards, much land was sold to speculators, and the smaller copyholders' suffered, emerging with less land and committed to expensive fencing costs. More land was leased, and more was changed from arable to pasture. The ties of villeinage were a thing of the past. New designations like gentleman, yeoman and husbandman emerged, as did a new kind of tenure. Copyhold tenure was abolished in 1922 with the Law of Property Act and many families who owned land were forced to leave it completely in 1930. In North Curry copyhold tenancies were held under reversionary grants and there were three sorts of holding as exemplified in various Wells documents:

> *The Old Auster copyhold applied to a dwelling and had the privilege of communing on the moors, but with an obligation of performing a certain amount of wall-work or the providing of walling or fencing. The right to a feast at Christmas was included. The term Old Auster applied either to an actual dwelling or to the site of the original tenement. The earliest Old Auster tenement found in North Curry was in 1343.*
> *The Stinted copyhold did not pass to the widow on the death of the copyholder, paid only a reduced or no heriot, and had no feast or rights on the commons, but usually included a dwelling.*
> *The Overland copyhold enjoyed neither widow's estate nor benefit of the commons, and paid no heriot.*

Various particulars of the Customs of North Curry were:

> *That the copyholder to take 3 bushels of wheat to the mill to be ground for the gestum* (feast) *at Christmas if he have a horse, and then certain demands associated with the feast.*
> *If he be ill he may send some one for the bread and the beef and the bacon raw* (feast food).
> *And he may come with one man on the 2nd day after Christmas, St Stephens day immediately after 9,* (3 o'clock in the afternoon,) *and he is to have his medale for the cutting of Brodemede until evening.*
> *And to have common of his beasts in all moors in the hundred.*
> *And to have his horse fed in the Lord's stables in winter and pasture in summer with the horses of the lord.*
> *For Heriot on his death the Lord to have his best ploughing ox, and if none the best acre he has sown, and if he have neither animal nor land sown, then no heriot.*
> *His wife to have his tenement while she is a widow and of good character, if she give security to the bailiffs of the Lord to keep up the tenements.*
> *And not to marry his daughter without license, or put his son to literature, or get him ordained without license.*
> *No one of them, unless he be free, to have more than one cotsetle,* (cottage), *or if he have, the Lord to have 6d each for the rest. Youngest son to succeed to the holding.*

40 tenants appear to have been held on the same tenure with small variations.

An example of the wording of a *Court Roll* is as follows:

> *Manor of Knapfee*
> *To this court came Robert Curry who by copy dated 25th April 1688 has and holds by his own payment for the lives of Elizabeth his wife, Robert son of Matthew Curry and Mary Pears the Reversion of one cottage with curtilage and 13 acres of land and meadow lying on the west side of the said cottage 3 acres in Binsbeare and I acre of meadow in Knapmeade of overland with the appurtenances in the said manor, now in the tenure of Joan wife of John Ceely and after her to default to Robert Curry. And the said Robert Curry has now in full Court on behalf of himself and the said Elizabeth his wife, Robert son of Matthew Curry and Mary Pears surrendered into the Lords hands the said Reversion of cottage and other premises and all right and title thereto, together with the copy for cancellation.*
> *Reverse 22nd August 1686 Robert Rowswell junior, Thomas Andrews and Martha Frances 5 acres of land and meadow of overland. Robert Rowswell purchaser.*
>
> *20th October 1697 Robert Rowswell junior takes a Reversion.*
>
> *13th October 1703 Surrendered with an after copy and then Robert Rowswell put in himself, Hannah and Richard in the copy and in the 2nd copy the same date put in Mary his wife and his first and second lawful born children.*
>
> *Addendum (in different hand) I find in North Curry Manor 26th April 1705. We present the custom of the said Manor that if the possessioner lives until the 26th day of March in one yeare there being customary ground and overland belonging there unto that the Executor and Executrix shall hold both the customary and overland until*

the 29th day of September thence after, except Stockmeade and Fellow Ground. The Overland tenants do not enjoy any common or widowhood or anything as the old auster tenants do, nor pay any herriot.

In 1189 North Curry Manor and Hundred passed into the hands of Bishop Reginald, Bishop of Bath, and to the canons of the Cathedral Church of St Andrew in Wells. In 1242 Bishop Jocelin made a gift of North Curry Manor to the Dean and Chapter of Wells and they became Lords of the Manor of North Curry and became responsible for the administration of the hundred. All property in North Curry was leased to tenants for their life and reverted to others at their death with the local court granting the new holding. The Dean and Chapter of Wells continued to be the administrators of North Curry until 1866 when all North Curry property was handed over to the Ecclesiastical Commissioners who then became Lords of the Manor of North Curry, and it was only then that the tenants were allowed to become possessors of freeholds. The manor included the present civil parishes of Stoke St Gregory and West Hatch, and the Dean and Chapter of Wells are still patrons of the living after more than 760 years. Some rulings, judgements and punishments given to North Curry inhabitants by the Dean and Chapter of Wells found in the *Calendar of the Manuscripts of the Dean and Chapter of Wells* follow:

May AD 1228. Charter of King Henry III to Joscelin, Bishop of Bath, the Dean and Chapter of Wells, granting them licence to disafforest the manor of Northcuri and enclose and make parks of the woods thereof and them dwelling there shall be free of forest dues.
Wells MSS Liber Albus I Folio 10

September AD 1264. Robert, son of William Gyan to have six wagonloads of brushwood for the repair of his dwelling and for the repair of fences annually to be fetched by him from Stathemore.
Wells MSS Liber Albus I Folio 62

AD 1335. Statement by William Parle, parishioner of the church of Northcuri, that he, assisted by William atte Rowe, had wickedly abstracted certain tithes of sheaves, belonging to the chapter of Wells as rectors of the said church, whereby he had incurred the sentence of greater excommunication, but on supplication for remission, and on surrender of the keys of certain houses wherein he and his companion above mentioned has stored the tithes, to the treasurer of Wells, he was to receive absolution.
Wells MSS Charter 247

July 5 AD 1337. Robert Gyan, a layman of Northcory, is summoned before the Dean and Chapter to answer the charge of having wrongfully caused to be cut down their timber and beaten their servants. He appears, has no defence to offer, and his offence having been notorious and of ill example he is excommunicated. But afterwards having made his submission and taken an oath to abstain from injury and to support the Dean and Chapter's rights, he is ordered to restore within two months the timber to the value of £10 publicly to the place whence he took it; he shall also three times on three Sundays within or during the aforesaid two months let him be whipped around the church of Northcory, and three times around the church of Wells on other three Sundays before the procession, naked except his trowsers, carrying in his hands one lighted candle of a pound in weight every day on which he undergoes the aforesaid penance, and hold in his hands in the naves of the churches aforesaid from the time of the processions until it is stated whether the offertory is celebrated, and then let him approach the high altar of the same churches and offer the wax candle humbly to the celebrant of the masses, and shall forthwith, celebrant as well as himself, penitently, publicly, distinctly, and suitably declare and explain in the mother tongue before clergy and people the reason of the penance.

The said Robert Gyan shall give satisfaction to Robert Coppe, the servant whom he assaulted, to the amount of forty shillings; and for the ecclesiastical offence, he shall again be whipped around the said churches other six Sundays, and make an offering of a wax candle as aforesaid.

For damages by poaching he is to pay eight marcs, and for the ecclesiastical offence go through the same course of discipline for another six Sundays. He is forbidden by himself or his agents to enter upon any of the properties of the Dean and Chapter without permission, or to aid or abet those who do so, etc. He is also to give a bond for £20. He shall also take oath to the observance of all these conditions, and shall appear in public in the cathedral, and shall pray that he may be bound to obey all these conditions, and shall give his consent that a sentence of excommunication shall be pronounced against him if he offend in the future, etc.
Wells MSS Liber Albus II Folio 212

July AD 1339. Robert Gyan of Bristol gave to his son and heir William Gyan of Northcory and to Cristina, his wife, a messuage, windmill, and all his lands in North Cory, a moor and tenements in Chereleyestath.
Wells MSS Liber Albus II Folio 204

August 1 AD 1377. A jury of 24 heard a case of a number of people illegally entering the lands of the Dean and Chapter of Wells. They had come in with swords, and bows and arrows, and had taken salmon, peel, pike, lampreys, lamprons, eels, and flounder 2,000 hares, 10,000 rabbits, 1,000 pheasants, 1,000 partridges, wood and corn, etc., together worth £240, and had pastured stock the imperilled their cattle, and beaten their servants, so that they dared not stay for fear of their lives. The names of eleven servants who had been beaten and maltreated were given, and six others who had to fly to save life or limb. They are ordered to pay damages.
Wells MSS Liber Albus II Folio 232

March 24 AD 1379. Inasmuch as certain persons unknown have taken many fish in the River commonly called Tone within the manor of North Cory, to the prejudice of the Chapter of Wells to whom it belongs, to the peril of their own souls, and to the encouragement of evil doers. Wherefore we command you as to all and singular daring persons of this kind, also those affording them assistance, that they incur the just sentence of the greater excommunication, and they have been and are bound by it in aforesaid monasteries, chapels, etc., on several Lord's days and festivals between the solemnities of mass when the most number of the clergy and people are present with cross erect in hand and bells ringing, candles lighted, and for censure of evil doers of this kind at last cast on the ground and extinguished, etc. They are to report what they have done, giving the names of the culprits if they can be found.
Wells MSS Liber Albus I Folio 277

LAW AND ORDER

The law that was dealt with through the manor courts in North Curry was administered by a Steward who was the representative of the Dean and Chapter of Wells. As time went by the conditions for the accommodation of the visiting Steward and his staff were set out in the *Calendar of the Manuscripts of the Dean and Chapter of Wells* in 1633 and are detailed in the extract given on page 129.

The following are typical examples of cases heard before the manor courts of North Curry:

27th October 1685: We present William Dummett to dick and scour his ditch from John Betteys garden till he come to Widdow Crutches ditch by the 5th November next ensueing making default to forfitt 10s.

On the following day at the same court is recorded:

We present that a sufficient gate at Overlonge Lane or Riefurlong goinge into Westfield maye bee made and gott up by the 8th November next to bee putt up by Andrew Wadham and John Tucker, and all thoase who have that waye to his field paye towards itt uppon paine of 2s a peace.

Also at the same court, a stark reference to the recent Monmouth rebellion:

We present that John Hucker was convected at Taunton Assizes last for being a rebell and was summarily executed there and that he died possessed of a copyhold estate within the Manor of North Curry.

Concern was expressed at a Court Leet on 23rd April 1685, regarding misuse of the moors

We present that there is a great nuicance and abuse to the commons by the multiplicity of geese kept in the commons and that no person whatsoever doo presume to keepe above six geese and one gander in any or either of our commons after Christmas next on paine of 10d each household for exceeding that number after the time for before commited.

The responsibility for the repair and maintenance of property under the Dean and Chapter of Wells rested with the tenant and this was confirmed in a presentment dated 15th April 1729:

We present Mr. John Wine to sufficiently repair his dwelling house commonly called or known by the White Hart lying and being in the middle of North Curry town. Time is given him to do the same by Michael Court next or to forfeitt £5.

The County Assize Court Quarter Sessions in Taunton heard the following cases:

1657: concerning the theft of twenty shillings from the home of Mrs. Abigail Symes of Hankridge in the Parish of West Monkton. Suspicion fell upon Susan Baker, servant of Mrs. Symes. Giving evidence Edward Pavy, tailor of North Curry, who was working at the house of Mrs. Symes at the time, stated that Susan Baker "being willing to have the truth discovered, or having a guilty conscience" asked him to go to Glastonbury to see a person named Bambury "to learn of him who had the 20s. and she would give him four pence for his pains" whereupon Pavy went to Glastonbury to see Banbury who told him "that it was a maid servant that waited upon Mrs. Symes that had the 20s. and that she had a wart behind her right ear, and another on her belly."

5th August 1688: concerning the burial of the child of Robert Stevens in North Curry Parish Churchyard. John Northam, rope maker, also of North Curry, gave evidence that "one Henry Guddridge of the same parish, being gotten into the belfry and tollinge the bell for the funeral, he (Northam), being Saxon (Sexton) *of the parish told him it was his duty to toll the bell, and laying his hand upon the rope to toll the bell, the said Henry Guddridge strook him with the end of the bell rope."*

During the service and whilst Mr. Lewes Parris, the minister, was attending the corpse to the grave, the said Henry Guddridge and William Guddridge his brother, interrupted the said Mr. Parris "in doeing of his duty and called him knave, and the said Henry Guddridge pushed him the said Mr. Parris aside from the end of the grave as he was going to read the service appointed for the burial of the dead."

John Northam also gave evidence that on the previous Wednesday in the evening, having been at John Lodwells house in North Curry "and goeing away, the said Henry Guddridge came out of the said Lodwells house after him and called to speake with him, whereupon, going back to him, the said Henry Guddridge assaulted him, and without any provocation strook him severel violent blows on the face in soe much that he lost a greate quantity of blood at the nose."

Another important office was that of Churchwarden, which dates from the early-14th century, and is the only office that survives in the parish to the present day (see page 181). From the middle of the 16th century the government made the parishes responsible for the relief of the poor, care of the roads and for the maintenance of law and order under Justices of the Peace. Ordinary parishioners were obliged to serve as Reeve, Churchwardens, Tythingmen, Waywardens, Overseers of the Poor and Constables.

THE PARISH CLERK

TAXATION

Taxes have been collected from early times on behalf of both the Church and the monarch or the state. Considering the Church first, from AD787 compulsory tithes (one-tenth of all produce) were exacted from the laity by the Church (see also page 202). Tithes were of three kinds, praedial (on income derived from agricultural crops), mixed (on the income from a combination of stock and labour - wood, pigs, milk etc.) and personal (from income derived from labour - mills, fisheries etc.) The greater part of these tithes remained in the hands of the local parish clergy. As farmers' improvements to their land and stock increased their tithe commitments increased and there was much resistance to and obstruction of their payment. A money rent from titheable lands was substituted for the more inconvenient payments in kind. In the 14th century a proportion of tithe income was used for the relief of the poor. In 1836 the Tithe Commutation Act resulted in rates of payment being reviewed. A new charge was made based on an annual assessment linked to agricultural prices. A tax known as the Church Rate was paid by parishioners to repair the parish church and pay all the other bills to defray the expenses of the church. Each man paid according to the size of his house and land. In boroughs, parishes and counties, from as early as the 14th century specific rates or taxes on the annual value of property financed such services as building and maintaining bridges, repairing highways and supplying drainage.

The taxation levied by the monarch, and later by the state, was collected by the Revenue Department or Exchequer of Government. Initially under the presidency of the monarch, it was founded in about 1110 during the reign of Henry I and met at Westminster. Its name - *eschequier* in French, *scaccarium* in Latin, came from the great chequered cloth on which the sums of money owed to the King from various sources were computed, using counters. This procedure was based on the principle of the abacus and was used initially to assist the officials from the department who had difficulty performing their calculations without the zero figure when they were required to use Roman rather than Arabic numerals. Tallies were used at the Lower Exchequer or Exchequer of Receipt as a record of payment of moneys. They were made from strips of wood into which notches were cut to signify the amount paid. The stick was then split lengthways and one section was kept by the person paying, the other by the Crown. The Exchequer was finally abolished in 1833, but the title lives on in the designation of Britain's minister of finance, the Chancellor of the Exchequer. Earlier exchequer records included the *Domesday Survey* that was used as a means of counting the population and eventually as a tool for collecting taxes. Records of taxation from the 12th century commence with the ancient levies known as *scutage* - a tax granting relief from military service; *tallage* - a tax required from urban communities and the King's *demesne*; and *hidage* and *carucage* - taxes levied from land.

Various medieval records give an insight into population estimates with the names of tax-paying inhabitants in the country. From 1155, Pipe Rolls, documents of parchment stitched together to form one continuous roll that looked like a pipe, gave written accounts of payments to the King and monies collected by the Sheriff of each county. Systems of indirect taxation were levied on imports and exports of merchandise according to rates determined by central government. From 1202 to 1206 King John imposed customs duties of one-fifteenth of their value on all imported and exported goods. In 1275 Edward I devised administrative means of raising money through duties on wools and hides, and local customs duties were levied at the ports on behalf of the monarch. In the 25th year of the reign of Edward I in 1297, it was reported that the collection of duties of one-tenth of the value of personal or moveable property due to the King in respect of the inhabitants of the Hundred of North Curry were misappropriated by the collectors. A translation follows:

> *Edward, by the grace of God King of England, lord of Ireland and duke of Aquitaine, to our beloved and faithful Gilbert de Bere greeting.* (Gilbertus de Bere was returned to Parliament for the County of Somerset in 1299) *Whereas there is owing to us £54.15s.10¾d of the arrearages of the tenth lately granted to us from the laity from the men of the hundred of North Cory in the county of Somerset, which Hugh de la Hele and John de Knappe, assessors and collectors of the said tenth in the said hundred raised and appropriated to themselves as we have heard by the assertion of our faithful Robert Guyan. We have assigned you that you make diligent inquiry into the matter by the oaths of honest and lawful men of the said hundred, and especially those who paid the said arrearages to the said collectors. Therefore we commend you that on certain days and at a certain place which you shall provide for the same, you shall take the inquisition in the most discreet and faithful manner that you can. We have also commanded the Sheriff of the said county he shall cause to come before you and the said Hugh and John to hear the said inquisition.......*

Between 1290 and 1334 the military campaigns of Edward I and Edward II required funding and a royal taxation was imposed on the laity or free householder's 'movable property', in other words their personal possessions. These levies were assessed on the value of such things as their animals, corn and trade equipment, as well as domestic articles such as silver spoons, bedding and cooking pots. This new system required tax collectors to record names of the taxpayers on parchment rolls, often 9 to 12 metres long, called Lay Subsidy Rolls. The rolls consisted of lists of names of inhabitants of each village with each name denoting either a person's abode (e.g. Willelmo atte Mere), his occupation (e.g. Johanne le Webbe - John the Dyer) or his relationship within a family. The tax assessment in Roman numerals followed each name and a total for each village was given. The tax was set in terms of fractions, which varied throughout the period, and between town and country dwellers. In 1327 one twentieth of the value of every taxpayer's possessions was demanded. By 1334 the rate was standardised at one-tenth or one-fifteenth and the taxes became universally known as the *Tenths* and *Fifteenths*. A transcript of the North Curry *Lay Subsidy Returns* for 1327 follows:

De Waltero Fairmay	ijs.	
Johanne Roley		xijd.
Richardo atte Chanbre	ijs.	
Thoma Coppe		viijd.
Richardo atte Pyrye		xviij.
Willelmo Dobyn	ijs.	
Roberto Preostes		xviijd.
Willelmo le Schippes	ijs.	
Willelmo Scarlette		xviijd.
Richardo Rugge		xijd.
Willelmo in therew		xijd.
Johanne le Webbe		xijd.
Nicholo Lacy		xijd.
Roberto Coterel	ijs.	
Willelmo Spryngod	iijs.	
Rogero Bat		xviijd.
Gilberto Portefer		xijd.
Thoma Chapeleyn	ijs.	vjd.
De Willelmo Edwyn	ijs.	vjd.
Willelmo atte Mere	ijs.	
Richardo Damolde	iijs.	
Richardo Gent	iiijs.	
Richardo Arthur	ijs.	vjd.
Roberto le Fisshher		xijd.
Waltero Smale	ijs.	vjd.
Alicia Dracote		xviijd.
Johanne Stytte		xijd.
Bartholomoeo Ganne	ijs.	vjd.
Summa xxe villate predicte	ls.	viijd.

The total of the above table translates into 50s.8d. There were separate lists for Knapp, Wrantage and Lillesdon. Knapp lists 12 householders paying in total 30s.6d, Wrantage lists 34 householders paying in total 52s.9d, and Lillesdon lists 21 householders paying in total 25s.

NOTE: Arabic numbers were not common in English documents until the late sixteenth century. Roman numerals being used, with pounds 'li, libri', shillings 's, solidi' and pence 'd, denarri' written after in superscript. A score is indicated by 'xx' in superscript above the appropriate number. Where numbers end in digits each is dotted and the final one 'j'.
Before the letter j emerged as a distinct letter, a series of letters i in Roman numerals was commonly ended with a flourish; hence they actually looked like ij, iij, iiij, etc. This proved useful in preventing fraud, as it was impossible, for example, to add another i to vij to get viij.

From the late-14th century a form of individual direct taxation was introduced and these taxes, described as Poll Taxes, provide one of the best sources for population estimates. In 1377 a tax of 4d per head was levied on all lay inhabitants aged 14 and over, except beggars. More Poll Taxes followed in 1379 and 1380 and again in 1513 and 1660, and these taxes were charged according to individual's rank and status. The tax was revived for a short period in 1990. Other income was obtained from ancient ecclesiastical taxes, rents and dues. In 1535 the Crown appropriated a tax amounting to one-tenth of the possessions of the church, levied by medieval Popes for the recovery of the Holy Land, and another tax called *Annates* which was revenue from ecclesiastical benefices, which was also paid to the Pope. *Peter's Pence* was a tax of a penny for each hearth or house, also imposed by the Pope in the 10th century, and finally abolished in 1534 with the revenues again being diverted to the Crown.

When in 1538 Thomas Cromwell ordered parish registers to be kept to record every marriage, christening and burial in a parish, many thought these registers would be used to levy taxation. Later in 1694 indeed a Registration Tax was levied to fund the war against France with a duty of 2s per birth, 2s.6d per marriage, and 4s per burial of all non-paupers. The higher echelons of society paid more i.e. £30 for the birth of the eldest son of a Duke, £50 for a Duke's marriage, and £50 for his burial. This was superseded by The Stamp Act of 1783 which granted the Crown a stamp duty of 3d upon every register entry of a burial, marriage, birth or christening, but this only remained in force until 1794 when it was repealed.

The Poor Law of 1563 enacted that Overseers of the Poor be appointed to collect and administer poor relief to provide food, clothing and shelter for the poor. From 1597 poorhouses were built and provision was made for poor children to be apprenticed. The Poor Law Act of 1601 clarified how the poor rate was spent and categorised who should receive it. Thereafter many different Acts were passed which set rules for such things as the care of lunatics and vagrants and the enabling of parishes to erect workhouses. Eventually boards were set up to control public health and provide social insurance.

The Hearth Tax, also known as Chimney Money, was a tax levied from 1662 to 1689, and provided an indication of the size of each assessed house. Most houseowners with property having a potential rental value of 20s a year or more were rated. They were liable to two half yearly payments of one shilling for every fireplace or stove in their houses, which were collected on Lady Day and Michaelmas. In 1670 there were 66 householders paying Hearth Tax in North Curry, 13 in Lillesdon, 19 in Knapp and 20 in Wrantage.

A Land Tax was first levied in 1692. Throughout the 18th century the rate of tax fluctuated between one and four shillings in the pound, based on the annual value, not the acreage, of land, but in 1798 the tax was fixed at a rate of four shillings in the pound. This land tax was used as a qualification to vote in parliamentary elections until 1832 when the Reform Act provided for a separate Register of Electors. The revised Land Tax of 1892 continued until 1949.

The Window Tax was imposed on house occupiers in 1696, replacing the Hearth Tax. Each household paid a basic 2s and those with between 10 and 20 windows paid a further 8s. In 1747 an extra 6d was required on each window for those with 10-14 windows. Those with 15-19 windows paid an extra 9d, and those houses with more paid an extra shilling. In 1825 those with fewer than eight windows were made exempt. The tax was abolished in 1851. In 1717 24 householders were paying Window Tax in North Curry (see illustration on next page). To save expense, windows in older buildings were blocked up, and when new houses were built the number of windows was reduced to a minimum. Wisteria Cottage in Church Road in North Curry shows evidence of this former practice. The Window Tax was replaced in 1851 by House Duty, which was levied on inhabited houses until 1924.

Income tax was implemented by William Pitt the younger in 1798 to pay for weapons and equipment in preparation for the Napoleonic Wars. Pitt's new graduated tax began at a levy of 2d in the pound on incomes over £60 and increased to a maximum of 2s on incomes over £200. Pitt hoped that the new income tax would raise £10 million, but actual receipts for 1799 totalled just over £6 million. It was abolished in 1802, and revived in 1803 at the rate of 2s in the pound. It was abolished again in 1816 but was restored in 1842 (at a rate of 7d in the pound on incomes over £150). At the end of the 19th century it rose to 14d in the pound, and early in the 20th century a new super tax was introduced, aimed at those with incomes of more than £3,000 a year. In return for these taxes the country would benefit from such things as old age pensions and labour exchanges. The Income Tax rate fluctuated for a number of years until in 1943 a scheme christened pay-as-you-earn (PAYE) was introduced whereby the government would take tax at source and the wage earner would have what was left.

Income Tax and National Insurance continue to contribute 45% of government income, although VAT, introduced in 1973, is now also a major contributor. UK Government Income in 2004/2005 was split approximately as follows:

Income Tax	28%
National Insurance	17%
VAT	16%
Excise Duties	9%
Corporation Tax	8%
Business Rates	4%
Council Tax	4%
Other	14%

Many other taxes were exacted during the 18th and 19th centuries. These included taxes on silver plate (1756-77), playing cards and dice, and on the employment of male servants (1777-1852). These taxes were originally conceived to finance the American War of Independence (1775-83) and were later extended to include the employment of gamekeepers (1784-1807) and female servants (1785-92), the possession of horses (1784-1874), coats of arms (1793-1882), hair powder (1795-98), dogs (1796-1882) and clocks and watches (1797-98).

When comparing historical taxes and incomes we need to be aware of the dramatic changes in values that have taken place over the centuries. According to equivalent contemporary values of the pound based on the Bank of England's statistical abstractions, £1 today would be the equivalent of approximately £460 in 1337. 1s (12d) or 5 pence today would be the equivalent of £23. However, there is no easy formula when comparing today's wage rates with earnings of the past. Money only has value in terms of what it can buy and when trying to measure buying strength with money incomes there is no simple or exact method. In 1450 it has been suggested that an agricultural labourer's wage was 4d a day and in 1592 the justices of the peace fixed the wage at 7d or 8d a day for labourers and 1s for master craftsmen, dependent on the economy in the area. It was assumed that the labouring man's meat and drink at home was valued at 4d a day, and women's and children's less.

At the time of William and Mary (1688) a gentleman would expect an income of £880 a year, a lord bishop £1,200 and a well-bred nobleman about £3,000 a year. Wages for ordinary workers in Somerset at the time were for a maid servant £1.10s a year; a dairymaid £2 a year; a labourer without meat and drink 7d a day; a mower or reaper 1s a day; a thatcher 1s.2d a day; a carpenter and a mason 1s a day. In 1995 the ordinary rate for an agricultural labourer was £149.44 for a 39 hour week, which implies £30 a day. A simple way to measure the value of 1s would be to find out how much bread could be bought at the earlier dates and what the same amount of bread would cost in modern times. Can a Middle Ages loaf of bread be compared precisely with its modern equivalent? This is probably an impossible comparison when the price of grain moved so erratically over the period. Money wages and personal incomes have altered quite differently for different people. In 1995 the Master of the Rolls was paid £109,435. His predecessor in 1636 was salaried at between £1,600 and £2,200 a year. So the money earned was some 50 to 70 times greater in 1995 than it had been 360 years earlier. By contrast the agricultural labourer in 1995 who earned £30 a day, received over 700 times the money of the labourer who earned 10d a day in 1636. In 1850 the labourer's average wage in the Taunton area was 7s a week with a daily allowance of three pints of cider. The standard of living in Somerset was not much above starvation level at that time. It has been estimated that the National Income of the United Kingdom rose 3.5 times between 1870 and 1938 and average income per head increased by 2.25 times during that period.

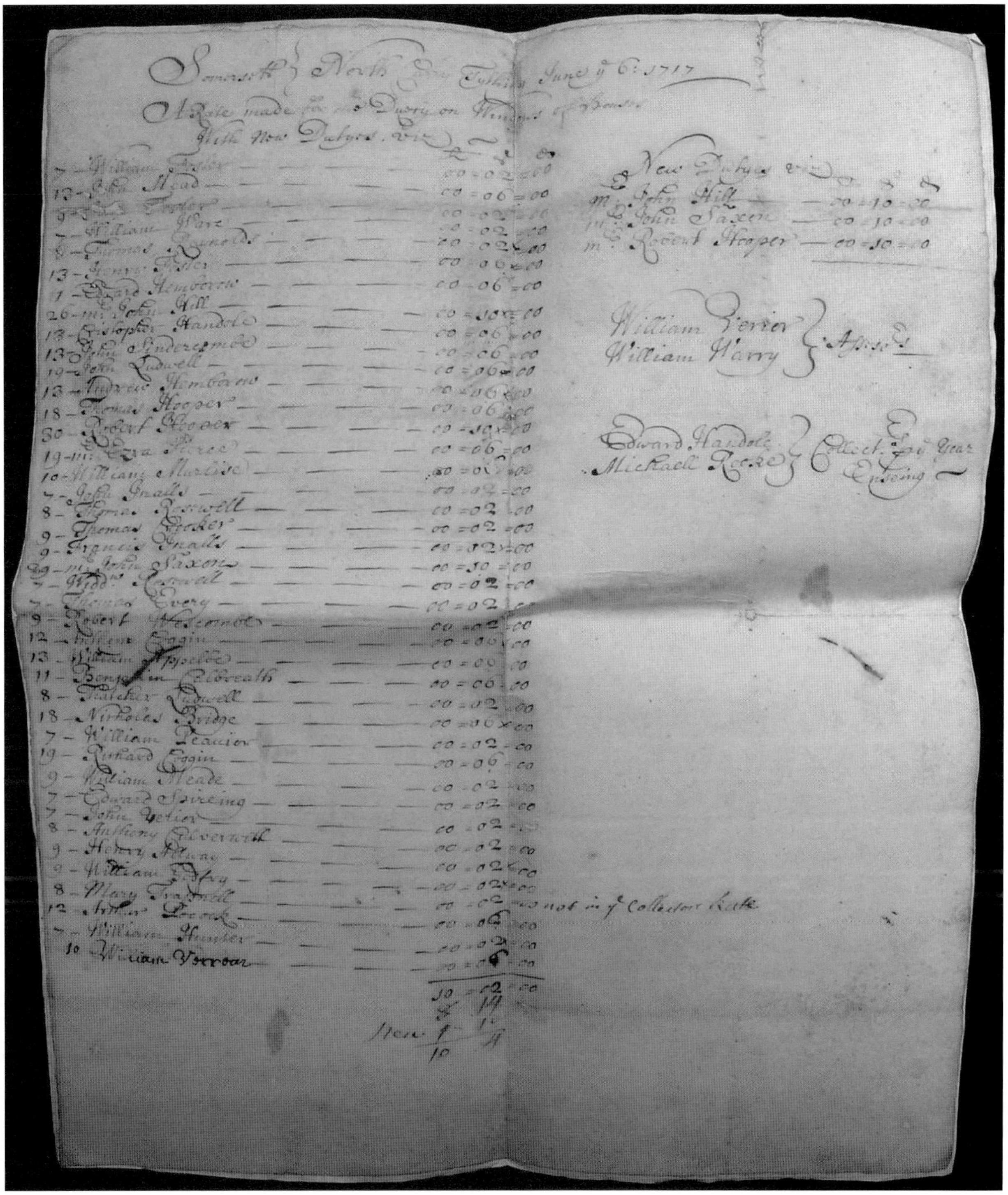

Somersett } North [illegible] Tything June ye 6: 1717

A Rate made for the Duty on Windows of Houses With New Dutyes, viz

		£	s	d
7	William [illegible]	00	02	00
13	John Mead	00	06	00
9	[illegible]	00	02	00
7	William Ware	00	02	00
8	Thomas Reynolds	00	02	00
13	Henry [illegible]	00	06	00
7	Edward Hemborow	00	06	00
26	Mr John Hill	00	10	00
13	Christopher Handole	00	06	00
13	John Sindercombe	00	06	00
19	John Ludwell	00	06	00
13	Andrew Hemborow	00	06	00
18	Thomas Hooper	00	06	00
30	Robert Hooper	00	10	00
19	Mr Ezra Pierce	00	06	00
10	William Marlise	00	0[illegible]	00
7	John Gnalls	00	02	00
8	Thomas Roswell	00	02	00
9	Thomas Crocker	00	02	00
9	Francis Gnalls	00	02	00
29	Mr John Saxon	00	10	00
7	Widow Roswell	00	02	00
7	Thomas Every	00	02	00
9	Robert [illegible]	00	02	00
12	[illegible] Coggin	00	06	00
13	William Appelbee	00	06	00
11	Benjamin Colbreath	00	06	00
8	Fletcher Ludwell	00	02	00
18	Nicholas Bridge	00	06	00
7	William Peacior	00	02	00
19	Richard Coggin	00	06	00
9	William Meade	00	02	00
7	Edward Spireing	00	02	00
7	John Vetier	00	02	00
8	Anthony Culverwell	00	02	00
9	Henry [illegible]	00	02	00
9	William [illegible]	00	02	00
8	Mary [illegible]	00	02	00
12	Arthur Brock	00	02	00 not in ye Collectors Book
7	William Hunter	00	06	00
10	William Verrear	00	02	00
		00	06	00
		10	02	00

8 14
New 1 10
10 4

New Dutyes viz

	£	s	d
Mr John Hill	00	10	00
Mr John Saxon	00	10	00
Mr Robert Hooper	00	10	00

William Verrier } Assessors
William Warry

Edward Handole } Collect. for ye Year Ensuing
Michaell Rooke

A SCHEDULE OF WINDOW TAX RATE PAYERS IN NORTH CURRY – 1717

2 - 3

THE REEVE'S FEAST

North Curry, with its neighbours West Hatch and Stoke St Gregory, maintained the custom of holding a feast at Christmas time. From early times up to the 19th century the *Reeve* was a man elected by his fellow tenants to act as intermediary with the Lords of the Manor and to undertake certain customary duties. Providing this feast on behalf of the Lords of the Manor for the customary tenants was one such duty.

Traditionally the belief was that the feast was held to commemorate King John who reigned from 1199-1216, but many people support the theory that the celebration originated in Anglo-Saxon times. It may have been connected with rights of pasturage and services within the ancient village community of North Curry. In early times in many Somerset manors the lord gave a *gestum* or feast in his hall on Christmas Day when all the free tenants and villeins had the right to be present. Their allowances of food and even their seats in the hall were minutely defined by custom.

The *Calendar of the Manuscripts of the Dean and Chapter of Wells* contains long accounts of the *Customs of the Manor for North Curry*. The following extracts describe the feast of 1314 and give instructions to the Reeve and the tenants on how they must conduct themselves.

> *1314 AD*
> *Customs of Tenants*
> *The tenant to bring to the gestum* (feast) *at Christmas his own mappa, ciphus and dish, and to sit at dinner with his two friends in the Hall of the Lord's court in a certain place assigned to his tenement, and to have for him and his friends two white loaves and one black and good ale to drink as much as he will while the day lasts, and the same allowance of meat as the Sacristan. If he was unable to come from ill health he was to have these things at his home. And to have fire and fuel, and when it is evening he and his friends are to have the two candles. And he may take home with him all the food that was on his napkin. If he be ill he may send some one for the bread and the beef and the bacon raw.*
> *MSS Wells Liber Albus II Folios 55-59*

> *1314 AD*
> *John de Cnappe, the King's bailiff* (Reeve) *in the hundred of Northcory, receives his gestum at Christmas with two others, namely two white loaves, as much beer as they will drink in the day, a mess of beef and of bacon with mustard, one of browis (broth) of hen, and a cheese, fuel to cook his food and that of the other tenants of the King's ancient demesne, and to burn from dinner time till even and afterwards, and two candles of assize to burn out while they sit and drink one after the other if they will sit so long, and if he come not he may send three men in his stead, or send for the bread, beef and bacon and two gallons of beer ; and the next day immediately after noon his medale (party with ale) with one man, as much beer as he will drink till even. And he may take home with him all the food that was on his napkin.*
> *MSS Wells Liber Albus II Folio 60*

Another tenant granted the feast was a W. Brygge who was ordered to bring his own napkin, cup and dish to the Christmas dinner, and he could *carry away in his napkin anything that is left. Moreover he shall have for himself and his neighbours one wastel divided into three parts to play with at the old Christmas games.* The *wastel* was a superior kind of bread or cake, and is mentioned in Chaucer in his *Canterbury Tales* where the Prioress fed her *small houndes* on *milke and wastel-brede.* Nothing is recorded of the game played with it. A Wiltshire medieval reference describes noblemen at Christmas-time eating with their followers in the great hall, where *mummings, cob-loaf stealing* and *great numbers of old Christmas plays* were performed. Maybe this was a similar activity.

An account of the feast is contained in a document of 1528 (source unknown), and this states:

> *The Lords of this manor have been anciently and are now charged with One Hundred Forty Six Feasts to be distributed at Christmas amongst severel tenants of the Manor of North Curry, East Curry, Wrantage and West Meare, each feast being of a dough 15 lbs weight, of strong beer one gallon, of small beer one gallon. In beef four pence half penny, in pork one penny half penny, towards disbursment the Reeves of the said manor of North Curry have yearly received from the severel tenants of this manor mentioned in our severel notes of copyhold lands thereof eighteen bushels of wheat, and from the parsonage of wheat thirty six bushels, and of oats forty eight bushels. Eight loads of wood from the Lord's wood in Wrantage, and the rest in money from the Lords of this Manor being the sum of £4.5s.0d.*

In 1791 the Reverend John Collinson in his *The History and Antiquities of the County of Somerset* states that West Hatch had a share in the feast as follows:

> *West Hatch, North Curry. The following ancient custom is still observed here. The Reeve, or Bailiff to the Manor, provides at the lord's expence a feast on Christmas-day; and distributes to each householder a loaf of bread, a pound and a half of beef, and the like quantity or pork, undressed, and the same evening treats them to a supper.*

It is widely assumed that these feasting customs form the basis of the North Curry Reeve's Feast, which was to become a well-known annual event in the village until the middle of the 19th century. Certain privileges, customs and rituals were performed and enacted and passed down through the centuries. It seems probable that the feast at Christmas became more elaborate and required that on the day before Christmas tenants called Jack of Knapp and Jack of Slough acted as masters of ceremonies. They had to distribute portions of three bullocks and some loaves of bread, provided by the Reeve, among the tenants according to their holdings. The remainder, after some portions had been reserved for the feast, was divided among the poor of the parish. On the day after Christmas the feast itself was held and liberty was given to continue drinking until two candles of one pound in weight were burnt out. During the feasting the custom of drinking a toast to King John may have started when he became honoured and revered for bestowing privileges on the Manor of North Curry such as granting the market in 1199 and later the fair.

At the beginning of the 19th century the feast was served to the seven holders of freehold manors in the Parish, 160 occupiers of tenements in the Manors of North Curry, Knapp, Wrantage and East Curry (Stoke St Gregory), the Reeve of West Hatch for the tenants of that manor, the Reeve of North Curry and two tenants who were elected to be the Jacks of Knapp and Slough.

The following is a transcript c.1820 (source unknown) of detailed arrangements, which adhere to the traditions of the Reeve's Feast. It refers to the two Jacks as the Lords of the Manors of Knapp and Slough but there is no evidence that these had actual manorial status.

The Reeve provides the feast and in order to enable him to do so the Lords of the Manor allowing the Lords rent of the Feast Tenement in respect of which he is appointed to the office, an annual allowance of two pounds by the name of Leaze Fees a payment of two pounds under the name of Cane Wood and four pounds and five shillings under the name of Beef and Pork.

The Reeve is also allowed by the occupier of the Lay Rectory now held by Mr. Charles Holcombe Dare for Lives under the Dean and Chapter of Wells thirty six bushels of good marketable Wheat and forty eight shillings in money to be rendered on demand at any time within a month before Christmas annually and likewise by the holders of the undermentioned Estates the quantity of Wheat set opposite the names of their Tenements respectively to be rendered within the like period.

Names of Manors	*Tenements*	*Present Owners*	*Wheat they contribute*
North Curry	*Moredon*	*R.Hooper Scott*	*2 bushels*
North Curry	*Late Halls*	*William Long*	*2 bushels*
North Curry	*Late Collins'*	*Samuel Bucknole*	*2 bushels*
Wrantage	*Late Morris*	*James Mead*	*2 bushels*
Wrantage	*Listoke*	*Representatives of the late Samuel L. Crossman*	*2 bushels*
Wrantage	*Stones*	*James Faun*	*2 bushels*
Wrantage	*Late Hills*	*Charles Spiller*	*2 bushels*
Wrantage	*Burrows*	*John Ludwell*	*2 bushels*
Wrantage	*Late Smiths*	*Philip Foster*	*1 bushels 1½ pecks*
Wrantage	*Late Ludwells*	*John Ludwell*	*2½ pecks*
Wrantage	*Late Elsons*	*William Potter*	*1 bushel 2 pecks*

The custom of preparing and holding the Feast is for the Reeve to provide three fat Heifers and put them in the Manor Pound adjoining the North Curry Churchyard the Sunday before Christmas Day, if Christmas happen to be on any other day than Monday or Tuesday but if it falls on Monday and Tuesday then the Sunday week before Christmas Day for the inspection of the persons entitled to the Feast who may insist on having them changed if good ones are not provided, then these are killed by a butcher appointed by the Reeve and the day before Christmas Day delivered with a good half Pig to two tenants of the Manor of North Curry called Dealers who continue for many years but are annually summoned to their duty by the Reeve and have their vacancies filled up by him.

The Dealers are to attend the day before Christmas Day except that day be on a Sunday and then the day preceding at the Reeves with a clerk to cut or deal or dole out the Beef and Pork to the persons entitled to receive it and they have provided for them by the Reeve, Beef Stakes and Onions for Breakfast top but of Beef and three marrow Bones boiled with the marrow taken out and spread on toasted Bread for Dinner and a feast each of two loaves of Bread eight pennyworth of Beef and 2d. in money and 1lb. of Beef Suet to be sent home to their houses for their trouble. The Dealers serve out two ribs of Beef, two ribs of Pork, two loaves of Bread and 2d. in money to each of the holders of the following Freehold Manors.

Manors	*Tenements*	*Present Owners*
North Curry	*Moredon late Ceeley's*	*Robert H. Scott*
Curry Vowells	*Moredon late Ceeley's*	*Edward Berkely Portman*
North Curry	*Calmadys*	*John Hopkins Foster*
Knapp	*Jack of Knapp*	*Francis Richardson*
East Curry	*Slough Farm*	*Henry Powell Collins*
East Curry	*Huntham Farm*	*Robert Hooper Scott*
Curry Cumwell	*Bridges*	*John Perratt*

They also serve out to the occupiers of each of the two following Tenements namely William Hembury's Tenement in the Manor of East Curry now belonging to Robert Hooper Scott and Murless' Tenement in the Manor of North Curry and belonging to William Payne a Feast and half namely three loaves of Bread one shilling worth of Beef and 3d in money. They also serve to the occupiers of the following Tenements two loaves of Bread and 8 pennyworth of Beef and 2d in money.

Manor of North Curry

Tenements	*Present Owners*	*Tenements*	*Present Owners*	*Tenements*	*Present Owners*
Late Collins' (2)	*John Bucknole*	*Cornelius' (2)*	*William Burnell*	*Late Hembrows*	*Sarah Burge*
Late Wares	*John Bucknole*	*Dennis'*	*William Burnell*	*Shoemakes*	*John Bobbet*
Late Alloways' (3)	*William Burnell*	*Late Whatleys*	*Sarah Burge*	*Dibbins and*	*James Crease*

Tenements	Present Owners
Brewers	
Parks'	*Rachel Crease*
Late Coombs'	*Martha Coombes*
Ludridges	*William Comer*
Late Seymours or Barringtons	*Charles H. Dare*
Prowses	*Charles H. Dare*
Parish Plot late Richards	*Charles H. Dare*
Late Perhams	*Lawrence Dare*
Late Stones	*Lawrence Dare*
Late Meads or Baskets	*Henry Foster*
Late Cadburys	*Bernard Murless*
Late Hillards	*Samuel Foster*
Late Derhams	*William Derham Foster*
Late Battens	*William Haddon*
Late Jennings	*William Lea*
Late Pophams	*Robert Ludwell Long*
Late Ludwells	*Robert Ludwell Long*
Late Houses	*Robert Ludwell Long*
Late Lowshay	*Robert Ludwell Long*
Late Verrier	*Robert Ludwell Long*

Tenements	Present Owners
Late Birds	*Robert Ludwell Long*
Late Halls	*William Long*
Late Gales	*William Long*
Late Virgins	*Martha Miller*
Late Whatleys or Gudridges	*James Mead*
Late Morris	*James Mead*
Late Manifies	*James Mead*
Late Robinsons	*James Mead*
Late David Coombes	*Mary Priddle*
Moredon (2)	*Robert Hooper Scott*
Dobles	*Robert Hooper Scott*
Hurtons	*Robert Hooper Scott*
Milliners	*Robert Hooper Scott*
Morrises	*Robert Hooper Scott*
Tarrs	*Robert Hooper Scott*
Spearings	*Robert Hooper Scott*
Rowsells	*Robert Hooper Scott*
Hammonds	*Robert Hooper Scott*
Handoles	*Robert Hooper Scott*
Bowers or William Payns	*Robert Hooper Scott*
Goodwyns	*Robert Hooper Scott*

Tenements	Present Owners
Mewses	*Robert Hooper Scott*
Late Lloyds	*Widow Bridge*
Late Sandfords	*H.F. Sandford, Esq*
Late Bayhams	*William Wescombe*
Half Feast Tenements	Present Owners
Late Alloways	*William Burnell (one loaf of bread four pennyworth of beef and one penny in money)*
Late Goddards	*Richard Bridge (allowance as above)*
Late Mary Pococks	*Richard Crease (allowance as above)*
Late Parkers or Dummetts	*Charles Holcombe Dare (allowance as above)*
Late John Juxons	*John Hopkins Foster (allowance as above)*
Late Nash's	*Robert Ludwell Long (allowance as above)*
Late Coggans	*William Potter (allowance as above)*

Knapp in North Curry

Tenements	Present Owners
Cornishes late Sealy	*John Bird*
Late Juxons	*Betty Derham*
Hoars	*William House*

Tenements	Present Owners
Late Hurstons	*Philip Foster*
Cornishes	*Josias Rowsell*
Wadhams	*Francis Southwood*
Crossmans	*Charles Barrington*

Tenements	Present Owners
Sellicks	*Charles Barrington*
Evans	*Charles Barrington*

Manor of Wrantage

Tenements	Present Owners
Late Smiths (4)	*Philip Foster*
Gudridges	*Philip Foster*
Late Ludwells (2)	*John Ludwell*
Burrows	*John Ludwell*
Strangeways	*John Ludwell*
Late Samuel Stones	*William Adams*
Late Hurstons (2)	*John Sweeting*
Stones	*Representatives of late John Weaver*
Late Crimps	*Representatives of late John Weaver*
Late Weavers	*Representatives of late John Weaver*
Moorend	*Bernard Murless*
Late Hurstons	*Bernard Murless*
Late Hurstons (2)	*Christopher Spiller*

Tenements	Present Owners
Widow Hurstons or Brownswords (2)	*John or Mrs. Ludwell*
Burtons	*Isaac Smith*
Late Locks	*William Goodland*
Late Potters	*William Potter*
Late William Elsons	*William Potter*
Late Yards	*Representatives of the late Samuel Crossman*
Late Lloyds	*Widow Bridges*
Late Stones	*James Faun and William Barrington*
Late Cousins or part of Stones	*James Faun and William Barrington*
Late Currys	*Thomas Linton and John Keats*

Tenements	Present Owners
Late Widow Keats	*Henry Pocock*
Late Totterdells	*Charles Totterdell*
Late Hancocks	*Charles Hurman*
Late Collins	*Charles Howe*
Late Sisters or Sisters	*John Chambers*
Tices	*John Sweeting*
Nutts	*William Nutt*
Half Feast Tenement	Present Owner
Tarrs	*John Ludwell (one loaf of bread, four pennyworth of beef and one penny in money)*

Manor of East Curry (Stoke St. Gregory)

Tenement	Present Owners
Late Collings	*James Brewer*
Late Wrights (2)	*Francis Richardson*
Late Palmers (2)	*Clement Bargery*
Late Bartletts	*William Morrish*
Late Collings	*Thomas Hurman*
Peddles and Sellicks	*Richard Peddle*
Lockets	*James House*
Lockets	*Joshua Brewer*

Tenement	Present Owners
Late Peddles	*Joshua Brewer*
Quicks	*Laurence Dare*
Churley or late Rowsells	*Richard Weaver*
Late Warrs	*John Verrier*
Collickshire	*William Sawtell*
Boyers	*William Barrington*
Late Powells	*Thomas Morrish*
Hancocks	*Robert Barrington*
Late Seymours	*John House*

Tenement	Present Owners
Late John Hoopers	*John Hooper Scott*
Late Derhams	*John Hooper Scott*
Late Kinglakes	*Widow Kinglake*
Andrews	*John Leaky*
Late Hoyals	*George Hearne*
Carkes or Powells	*Thomas Morrish*
Andrews	*Richard Franklin*

Tenement	Present Owners
Riches or Sticklands	*Charles Holcombe Dare*
Trotts	*Joan Richards*
Pykes	*Thomas Dyer*
Beddles	*William Barrington*
Late John Brewers or Curtis	*Thomas Bond*
Lane End	*John Barrington*
Taylors	*Arthur Bobbett*
Late Smiths	*Widow Bridge*
Late Dr. Taylors	*Mary Dare*

Two Thirdingale Tenement	Present Owners
Late Samuel Powells	*Mary Dare (a loaf and one third of bread and two thirds of eight pennyworth of beef and two pence in money)*
Late Thomas Powells	*Mary Dare (half of the above allowance)*

Half Feast Tenements	Present Owners
Palmers or Minifies	*John Palmers (one loaf of bread four pennyworth of beef and one penny in money*
Widow Smiths	*William Sawtell (allowance as above)*
Poor House	*Overseers of Poor (allowance as above*
Poor House	*Widow Bridge (allowance as above)*
Healy's	*William Barrington (allowance as above)*
Tuckers	*John Meade (allowance as above)*

Each of which loaves of Bread is to be made of good white flour. To be baked and to weigh after baking five pounds and the Beef is to be valued at the price for which Beef of the like quality is then currently selling.

To the Reeve of West Hatch within the said Manor the Dealers serve half a Bullock and the hind quarter of half a Pig for the use of the tenants of that Manor on his paying five shillings for it to the Reeve of North Curry. But before he is allowed to enter the Reeve's house he is to sing the following song:

"King John he was a noble knight

I'm come to demand my right

Open the door and let me in

Else I'll carry away my money again."

The Dealers serve out these feasts to the persons entitled to them, who are to send for them between sunrise and sunset on the day before Christmas Day, unless it happen to be on a Sunday and then the day preceding and the Dealers also serve out for the Reeve a Chine, Round and Rump of Beef for mince meat and the belly part of the fore quarter of the half of Pig for a feast to be provided the day after Christmas Day except it be a Sunday and then the day following by the Reeve for the Lords of the Manor of Knapp and Slough, who are called the "Jacks of Knapp and Slough" and have the feast for themselves and their attendants after mentioned. Besides the chief Feasts of Beef etc. in common with the holders of the other five Freehold Manors they or their deputies arrive at the Reeves house the Feast day about one o'clock. The Jack of Knapp or his Deputy attended by three men and a boy. And the Jack of Slough or his deputy by two men and a boy.

When the Jack of Knapp or his Deputy arrives the key of the Reeve's cellar in which there is to be provided a half hogshead (a large cask, a measure – 52 gallons) at least of good Ale for the feast is given to one of his attendants. The Jack or Deputy proceeds to divide the Offal or inferior parts of the Bullocks and half Pig, not distributed by the Dealers to the holders of Tenements, into portions to be given away in the afternoon to the 'Second Poor'.

The Jack of Slough, or his Deputy, divides six dozen of Bread weighing five pounds each Loaf when well baked provided by the Reeve for the like purpose.

The Jacks and their attendants then sit down to a dinner provided by the Reeve consisting of the Chine of Beef roasted, and the Rump and Round boiled, the Belly piece of the forequarter of a half Pig rolled up and made into a collar of Brawn scalded and served up with a sprig of Rosemary and powdered with Flour, a Hen with the head and tail on, but the rest of the feathers except the tail plucked off a little boiled and served up on sops of Bread, proper Vegetables, a large Mince Pie with an effigy of King John in paste properly painted to represent a King stuck up in the middle of it. Bread and Ale and Cheese after. When they sit down to Dinner two candles weighing a pound each are lighted and until they are burnt out the Jacks and their attendants have a right to sit drinking ale. After dinner the regular toasts are:

"To the immortal memory of King John.
The real Jack of Knapp.
The Real Jack of Slough"

Afterwards other toasts are given. The Jacks give away the Bread and the Offal Beef and Pork to the Second Poor.

When they have drunk as much as they like they depart. The Jack of Slough or Deputy holding the stirrup of the Jack of Knapp or Deputy for him to mount, and receiving a shilling as his fee.

The undersigned declare the above to be the Immemorial Customs of the Feast held annually in the Manor of North Curry and as contributors thereto or partakers thereof they make this recognition for better preserving and keeping up the same.

Charles Holcombe Dare admits his liability as Lessee of the Parsonage to contribute 36 bushels of Wheat and forty eight shillings annually towards the Feast above mentioned but he admits nothing further in regard to the above statements.

Robert Hooper Scott	*William Goodland*	*E B Portman, Esq. by John Perratt*	*Isaac Smith*
William Long	*Josias Rowsell*	*John Perratt*	*Henry Foster*
John Bucknole in the right of my father Samuel Bucknole	*Henry Lea*	*Robert L. Long*	*Thomas Linton*
James Meade	*Rachel Crease*	*James Crease*	*John Keats*
Francis Richardson	*Martha Miller*	*John Barrington*	*William Comer*
Jack of Knapp	*James Yard*	*Richard Weaver*	*Sally Burge*
	John Mead	*James Brewer*	*William Nutt*
	William House		*Philip Dare*

The above is the list of signatories

In 1850 the custom was in danger of dying out, and in order to restore its observance, Mr Henry Powell Collins of Hatch Beauchamp, being the owner of Slough Farm in Stoke St Gregory, provided a marble tablet inscribed with instructions for the feast (see illustration on page 99). This hangs in the vestry of the Parish Church of St Peter and St Paul in North Curry, and a copy can be seen at the west end of the nave.

The following is from the book *North Curry – The Ancient Hundred and Manor* by Hugh P Olivey and reports on the last two feasts.

> *"The Reeve for the year 1865 which was the last feast to be observed was Mr. Robert Bobbett. I (Olivey) was present at the feast of 1864, when the late Mr. William Hurman, then living at White Street Farm, held the office and at whose house the feast was held. For the year 1863 Mr. James Temlett was reeve. I have the accounts of the two latter, and it may be of interest if I give copies of them. They show that the office, when properly carried out, was by no means a lucrative one.*

Mr. James Temlett's Account December 1863

Receipts	£	s	d
From the Dean and Chapter of Wells	14	10	0
Mrs. Scott Gould for 4 bushels of wheat	1	2	0
Mr. Cousins for 2 bushels of wheat at 5/6d	0	11	0
Mr. William Hurman for 2 bushels of wheat	0	11	0
Mr. Derrick for 1 peck of wheat	0	1	4½
C.H. Dare, Esq. for beer	2	8	0
Mr. Phocion Foster for meat sold	7	1	0½
Mr. Jones for 9½lbs beef	0	4	9
Mr. Batten for 10¼lbs suet at 6d	0	5	1½
J.H. Nicholls for 13½lbs beef at 6d	0	6	9
Anthony Poundsberry for 18lbs beef at 5d	0	7	6
Mr. J. Collier for 33lbs at 5d	0	13	9
Mr. J. Collier for 16 bushels wheat at 5/3d	4	4	0
Mr. Cousins for the hides	2	9	2
Rough fat	1	11	0
By Beef sent to London	4	11	3
3 bellys	0	10	6
Bran	0	13	0
½ sack flour left over	0	15	0
Due to Reeve	0	10	1½
Total Receipts	43	6	4

Payments	£	s	d
To bought one bullock at Langport	13	0	0
To two bullocks at Combe St. Nicholas	26	5	0
To half pig	0	13	0
Mr. John Collier for making the flour	0	15	0
Mr. Edward White for baking 19 dozen and 9 loaves of bread	0	13	2
Mr. Anthony Poundsberry (same as above)	0	13	2
Mrs. Wilding for cooking the dinner	0	6	0
Mr. Henry Foster for killing 3 beasts	1	1	0
Total Payments	43	6	4

Mr Hurman's account for 1864 is similar and included 4s.6d for spices for the mince pie and 2s for candles, and Mrs Wilding was paid 7s.6d for cooking the dinner. The whole account amounted to £48.11s.3d.

> *The Jack of Knapp was Mr. Charles Barrington, by virtue of his being the owner of a piece of land situated at Knapp, near the River at Haymoor's End and behind the Royal Oak Inn, called Parkers Mead and which was formerly and for many years in the possession of the Richardson family, late of Langford House, Fivehead. No finer specimen of the British yeoman could be found than Mr. Barrington, more the figure of King Harry than King John. The dinner was served in conformity with the statute, and afterwards the toasts were given, and others of a loyal and patriotic character; and interspersed with songs which included one by the Jack of Knapp "The Roast Beef of Hold Hingland", "O for the Hold Hinglish Roast Beef". Among the company were Mr. George Crease, Mr. James Temlett, Mr. Reed of Fullands, Mr. William Hellard of Taunton. His agent represented the Jack of Slough, who was then Mr. Gore-Langton. The minutiae of the feast were duly observed, besides other unwritten laws. The toasts were drunk in bumpers, and if the glass was not emptied (no heeltaps were allowed) the offender was fined by having it over again (high beer glasses were then used). I do not think the company remained sufficiently long to see the two candles burnt down, but although the genuine hospitality of the reeve did not limit us to the conventional "beer" I do not think any went away incapable. A law usually observed was that the servant who brought in the mince pie with effigy of King John (which was somewhat grotesque) should receive a shilling if she did so with due sedateness; this she did and received her reward. The servant on that occasion was the wife of the butcher Mrs. John Stone.*

In 1868 Mr Gore-Langton, then Member of Parliament for West Somerset, together with Robert Bobbett, the Reeve of North Curry, George Mitchum, the Reeve of Stoke St Gregory and Charles Cousins, Reeve of West Hatch, 22 inhabitants of North Curry and the Ecclesiastical Commissioners submitted an application to the The Board of Charity Commissioners of England and Wales to convert the funds of the Reeve's Feast to a parish charity for the poor. This appeal was successful and the Reeve's Feast Charity was instigated for the benefit of the poor of the three parishes of North Curry, Stoke St Gregory and West Hatch, all three places having formerly been included in the original and undivided Parish of North Curry. The Board considered that the gross annual income of the feast charity did not amount to £50 and because all were desirous that the funds should be converted, thereby approved and established the scheme.

The copyholders and leaseholders of the Manor of North Curry relinquished their rights and dues and a yearly income of £33.13s.9½d was secured as a charity for ever, divided between the three parishes. They made an order that trustees were appointed and they were to be the Vicar, Churchwardens and Guardians of the Poor. They were to administer to the most deserving inhabitants of the parish items such as clothes, bedding, fuel, medical or other aid in sickness, food or other articles in kind as should be considered to be most advantageous to them. In 1896 it was decided to elect two persons in the position of Churchwarden who were to be elected every three years. Records in 1901 show the income was used to provide every poor person in North Curry, Stoke St Gregory and West Hatch with 76 kilograms of coal at Christmas, and in 1930, 154 poor people received enough fuel to cook their Christmas dinner.

In an earlier century there was another fund, amounting in 1643 to £75, to which wealthy people of the Parish voluntarily contributed for the assistance of parishioners in temporary financial difficulty. Various sums were lent to them according to their need, on security and on easy terms, the capital being repayable and the interest used in direct relief of the very poor. Amongst the donors to this fund were Mrs Johan Connock, whose name is on the altar frontal of 1633, and the Reverend J Gibbes who was Vicar from 1588.

Bequests were made by others in the community of North Curry to support the poor and needy in the Parish and these were described in the early-20th century as follows:

The Charity of an Unknown Donor
Described on a painted board in the vestry "A sum of fifty pounds left by an unknown benefactor is in the hands of the Churchwardens, and the interest thereof is applied from time to time for the benefit of the second poor of the parish May 1845". The Charity Commissioners' Reports 1819-1837 state "the sum of forty pounds appears to have been given to this parish many years ago, the donor of which is wholly unknown. The money is secured by mortgage on the property of Josias Rowsell, of this parish, and the interest is regularly received by the churchwardens, who distribute it only once in five or six years, as the sum, if annually given away, would be too inconsiderable to be of any benefit in so large a parish."

The Charity of Sophia Gould
This is also described on a painted board in the vestry, as being "the interest of a sum of £200, bequeathed by Mrs. Scott Gould, of Moredon, January 9th 1869, to be given yearly in bread on October 14th, amongst the deserving poor, by the vicar and churchwardens."

The Charity of Charlotte Burge Robbs
A bequest made in 1892 of the interest of £250, to be given annually in clothing to the poor by the vicar and churchwardens. There is also a sum of £50 given by the same, the interest to be employed for keeping the churchyard in order.

The Charity of Mary Ann Crease
A bequest made in 1895 of the interest of £200, to be given in coal by the vicar and churchwardens in January in each year. The whole of the principal relating to all these charities is invested in Consuls through the Charity Commissioners.

In 1932 the Charity Commission for England and Wales restructured all of these charities, including the Reeve's Feast Charity, and established a new scheme for the regulation of the Charities. The Reeve's Feast Charity was divided into three separate charities, The North Curry Reeve's Feast Charity, West Hatch Charity and the Stoke St Gregory Charity. The endowments of these charities were to be administered and managed by a body of trustees of six persons as follows:

One ex-officio Trustee – The Vicar of North Curry
Three Representative Trustees to be appointed by the Parish Council for a term of three years
Two Cooptative Trustees appointed by the Trustees themselves for a period of five years
A Clerk to hold office during their pleasure

The annual income of the Trustees was made up of cash payments, made in lieu of contributions in kind to the former Reeve's Feast, by persons occupying certain lands. The interest on the capital endowments of the respective charities was to be invested in 2½ per cent Consolidated Stock. The total income from all the charities available for distribution each year amounted to a little under £50. The recipients were to be persons of pensionable age resident in the Parish and widows under that age. The disbursement of the income was to be made in the form of vouchers to be exchanged at local shops. In 1973 the funds were transferred from Consolidated Stock to the Charities Official Investment Fund because the Charities Act of 1962 allowed funds to be re-invested. This enabled the North Curry Trustees to sell their gilt-edged securities, the value of which had dwindled, producing an income of decreasing purchasing power, and reinvest the capital realised in a wider range of securities. The long-term prospect of this decision would increase the sum of money available for distribution to the community.

At the present time the Trustees meet twice a year in March and November to decide which worthy pensionable-age people in North Curry will receive vouchers. In 2001 vouchers were distributed in early December. There were five recipients of £8 vouchers and fifteen recipients of £5 vouchers resulting in a total distribution of £115. On average 25 persons benefit annually.

In 1904 a subsidised savings society in the form of a Coal Club existed in North Curry to enable the poor to purchase winter fuel. Club members - the poor members of the parish - would pay money into the funds as and when they could afford, throughout the year. Wealthier members of the congregation also paid money into the club. Coal was bought at wholesale price and the poor savers in the club would then receive coal in proportion to the amount they had managed to save during the year. Mrs Maud Berthon started and became the Treasurer of this Parish Coal Club.

Re-enactments of the Reeve's Feast as fund-raising events have taken place in North Curry in 1986, 1993, 1995 and 2002, with the residents of the village acting the roles of the various characters. On 11th December 1993, the Reeve's Feast was organised by The Friends of North Curry Parish Church and took place in North Curry Village Hall, where 120 residents were involved, either as organisers, actors or participants in the feast. A meal of beef stew with vegetables, bread, fruit, cake, mince tarts, apple juice and lots of cider was served by wenches to the accompaniment of taped medieval music with a lutist and recorder player providing live entertainment. Interspersed throughout the eating of the meal a Master of Ceremonies introduced the various actors in the roles of the original Reeve's Feast characters performing the re-enactment. A boar's head, candles, an effigy of King John, a horse costume and pouches containing *tuppences* were props which added to the entertaining staging of this ancient historical event. Profits from the sale of beer, wine, entrance and raffle tickets provided a large sum of money, which was donated towards a new heating system. The feast re-enacted in North Curry Village Hall on 14th December 2002 once again entertained many villagers, old and new, some taking the parts of the historic characters. The audience dressed and participated in the medieval fashion and antics of the time, and a sum of £275 was raised and donated to a children's hospice charity.

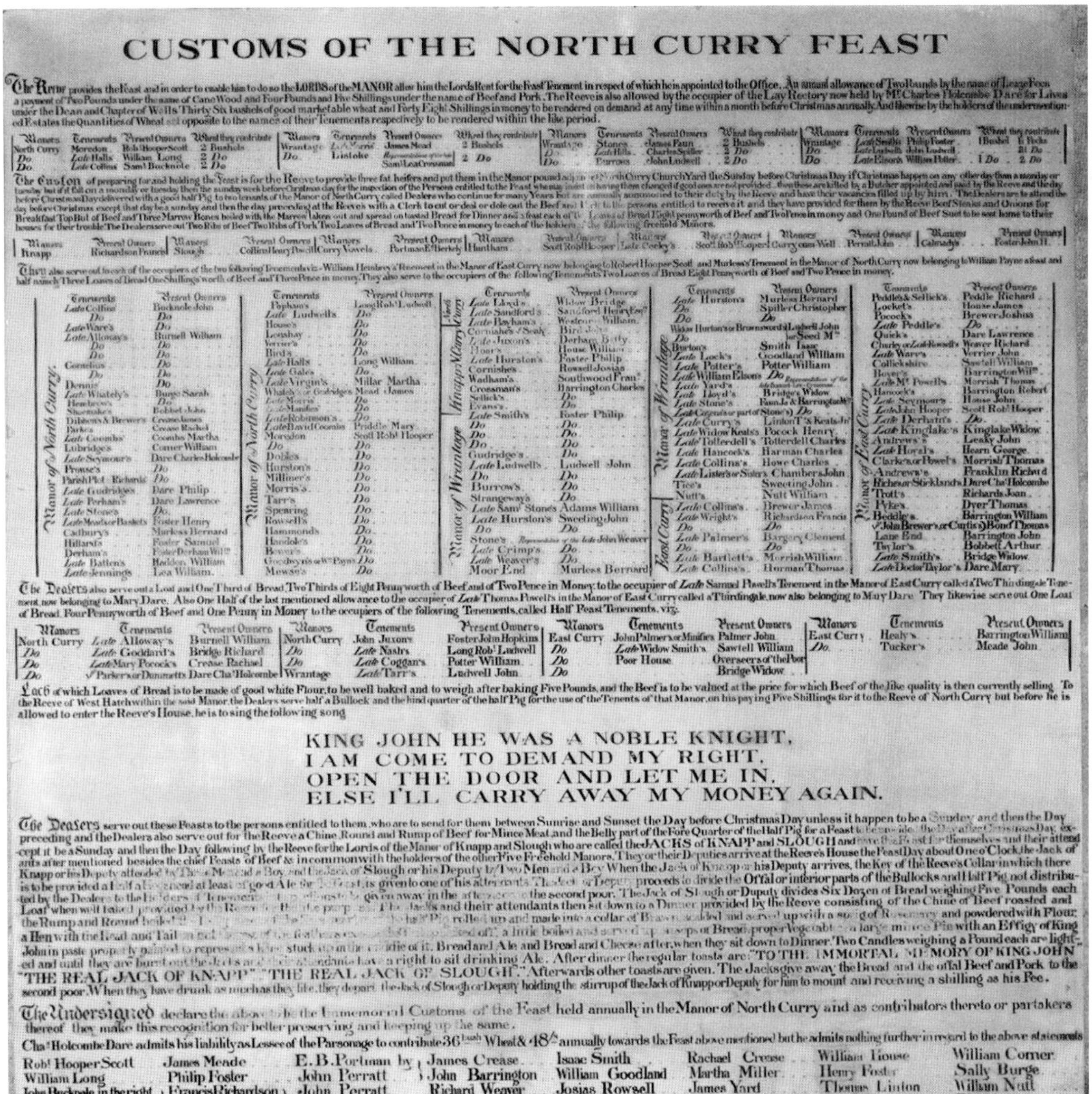

MARBLE TABLET IN NORTH CURRY CHURCH RECORDING REEVE'S FEAST CUSTOMS

2 - 4

THE CHURCHES

THE HISTORY AND STRUCTURE OF THE PARISH CHURCH

The Church of St Peter and St Paul is the Parish Church of North Curry. From the earliest records the Parish of North Curry was divided into four tithings - North Curry, Lillesdon, Wrantage and Knapp. The hamlets of Broad Lane and Newport were included, and until 1846 Stoke St Gregory and West Hatch were also part of the parish.

The church stands on the northern slope of a long ridge of high ground, originally a promontory between marshes on either side, which extended from West Hatch to Athelney. The view from the north side of the church encompasses the vale of Taunton Deane and the southern slopes of the Quantock Hills, whilst from the top of the tower views of the Blackdown Hills, the Brendon Hills, Exmoor, the Poldens and the Mendip Hills expand into a magnificent panorama. It is said that on a clear day looking across this vast expanse of flat country one can see the towers of seven other churches.

The church has been described as one of the finest in the West of England. Being a handsome and substantial building that might be considered large for a village, it is frequently referred to as *The Cathedral of the Moors* and has for centuries been a very important part of the Diocese of Bath and Wells (see Chapter 1-5).

The building is of cruciform shape, having chancel, nave, north and south aisles and transepts. It has a prominent south porch and central octagonal tower, which has a clock and a peal of eight bells. The tower is almost entirely built of grey sandstone raised from the neighbourhood; the rest of the building being chiefly of Blue Lias stone mixed occasionally with Hamstone and sandstone. All the windows and arches are of Hamstone.

The present church was built about 1300 in the period of the *Decorated Gothic* style of English architecture, which lasted between 1272 and 1377, and some architectural detail together with some window tracery date from that period. The church was substantially altered about 100 years later when extensive re-modelling took place. The architecture of the church as we see it today is of the *Perpendicular Gothic* style period from 1377 to 1530.

However, because the Manor of North Curry (Curig) was a royal settlement in Saxon times as defined in a Saxon Charter of AD854 (see Chapter 2-1) it was more than likely that a church existed on the site during the Saxon period.

Earlier in AD705 the Saxon King Ine divided Wessex into two. The eastern part fell under the bishop in Winchester and the western part became the diocese of Sherborne with its own bishop. In AD909 this latter diocese was divided into four new ones and one of these became the Bishopric of Wells, which included the whole of Somerset. The 10th century was a period of great reform in the Church and most of the parishes in the county had been established, each with its own church.

In AD888 King Alfred founded the monastic house at Athelney, which is only three miles from North Curry. The influence of this monastery would have seen a development in church life in the surrounding neighbourhood when the clergy there acted as parish priests and maybe, bearing in mind that North Curry was a royal manor, they founded a centre in North Curry. Such a church built on the edge of the marsh would have been a small, simple and primitive structure consisting of a single aisle and constructed of wood as was typical in Saxon times. In choosing this commanding site overlooking the waters of the marsh in the early days before the land was reclaimed by drainage prominence would have been ensured.

In Norman times during the reign of William the Conqueror between 1066 and 1145, a more substantial stone building would have replaced any Saxon building on the site, and would have recognised the importance of the Manor of North Curry in those times. Whilst there is no proof of a Saxon place of worship in North Curry - indeed very few features of these early Saxon churches have survived anywhere in the country - a Norman church was definitely built on the current church site in North Curry. This could indicate that the Normans, as was their custom, had adopted an earlier Saxon location.

The Parish Church of North Curry is one of the few churches in Somerset that shows evidence of Norman architecture. The door arch in the north wall of the present church is of Norman construction with a segmental arch with dogtooth ornamentation, and is almost all that remains of the Norman structure (see Plate ii). It may well have had a stepped approach from the water's edge through a porch-way on the north side. The church would have been of a simple rectangular plan with a semi-circular apse at the east end where the clergy would sit. Suggestion of a keystone to a chancel arch of this building is to be found at the east end of the north aisle. There is also, in part of this wall, a sill and one jamb of a filled-in window. Again the building was considerably smaller than the present church. Evidence of early wall work suggesting the south wall of this Norman church was uncovered during the installation of heating apparatus during 1992.

The Manor of North Curry remained in the possession of the Crown until 1189 when Richard I, wishing to raise money for a crusade, sold it to Reginald Bishop of Bath (see Chapter 1-5). In 1242 these lands were given to the canons of the Cathedral of Wells and in 1245 a new bishop was elected, having for the first time the title of the Bishop of Bath and Wells.

The population of the manor had increased over this period, possibly partially as a result of the large influx of people from Witham, near Bruton, who were transferred to Knapp as described on page 77. With this large influx of new worshippers, a chaplain, Geoffrey, was allocated to the church at North Curry. Between 1145 and 1272 a new church in the *Early English* style of building may have been built, or the original one adapted. In 1234 the first Vicar, Richard de Treigoz, was appointed to North Curry. The Chapter of Bath and Wells and possibly other benefactors provided the money to alter and enlarge the church. A possible reason why so spacious a church should have been built is that a larger church was needed to cope with an enlarged population in the Parish. It may also have been considered that the Manor of North Curry, being a very valuable property, justified a larger church for the glory of God.

By c.1300 the new building was in the shape of a Latin cross, i.e. a cross with one limb much larger than the other three. It consisted of a chancel and nave, having a low tower with a square base between projecting north and south transepts. The tower may have carried a spire. The nave and chancel would have featured the *Decorated Gothic* style of architecture being covered with a high, pointed, steeply sloping roof, descending to low walls. The lines of the old high-pitched roof of this early church are clearly visible over the western arch of the crossing between the nave and tower base. There were probably no aisles at this time. This appears to be confirmed by the absence of the bottom stringcourse, which is carried round the chancel and nave, but is not continued round the walls of the aisles. Also the buttresses supporting the transepts are of a different and older type than those against the aisles. The length of the church from east to west through the chancel, tower and nave, and the two fine windows of the south transept are the only two features that remain of this early building.

After a few years the church underwent further alterations and two aisles were added. These had low sloping roofs; the line can be seen clearly at the entrance of the north transept. At the same time the walls of the nave were pierced for arches and raised, to sufficient height to permit the insertion of *clerestory* (clear storey) windows to give light in the enclosed nave. The sites of these early windows can be seen, although all but two have been blocked up. Other early features belonging to this period include part of a springer of a small arch incorporated into the wall, and a filled-in rectangular shape at window height, both at the east end of the north aisle. The entrance arch of the south porch being also in the *Decorated Gothic* architectural style, leads us to assume there was an entrance into the church there.

About 100 years later the church was re-modelled and further rebuilding took place between 1377 and 1460 in the early *Perpendicular Gothic* style of architecture. At this time the walls of the aisles and nave were raised and the roof was raised to it present elevation. The new aisle roof obstructed the light through the original clerestory windows, which as a consequence were blocked up and new clerestory windows were opened up above them. The roof of the porch was raised at this time with fan vaulting of Hamstone.

The octagonal tower was also raised to its present height at this time when it became dwarfed by the heightened roofs of the other parts of the church. Evidence for this appears in the stone staircase in the south turret leading to the belfry, which ends a little above the level of the chancel arch. The steps above this point are of wood. The stone used in the whole of the upper part of the tower is grey sandstone, and that within the ringers' chamber shows signs of having been long exposed to the weather. There is a story in the village that the stones for the tower were passed from hand to hand, along a line of men, from the quarry at Knapp to the church.

Parapets were added around the nave, chancel and aisle roofs and at the top of the tower. In 1824 a weather vane was erected on the tower. The tower parapet, which is of a different building style, was replaced in 1837 when part of it fell on the roof of the church causing considerable damage. Finial crosses were placed on the parapets of the transepts and chancel. There are two turrets on the outside of the church, one on the south-east corner and the other on the north-east corner of the tower between the transepts and chancel. Stone figures of *Hunky Punks* (derived from words *hunker* and *punchy* and meaning squatting and short-legged creatures) of pagan or superstitious origin, unique to Somerset, and many grotesque gargoyles were added to the gutters and corners of the roofs. One represents the devil in chains, struggling to get away from the north-west corner of the church and he is depicted being driven away into the darkness (see Plate ii).

In 1502 the chancel was reported as having become *wholly ruinous* and was rebuilt under the supervision of Master Thomas Harries, Surveyor of the Fabric of Wells Cathedral. This was recorded in the *Calendar of the Manuscripts of the Dean and Chapter of Wells* as follows:

> *1503 December 21*
> *Ordered that a certain bill made contracted with the consent of the canons as to the new building of the chancel of the Parish Church of North Cory, to be done by Master Thomas Harreis. He was requested by the Chapter to undertake this work. Expenses to be paid at the rate of 20s. a year. The total cost came to £52.13.8d.*
> *MSS Wells Liber Ruber II Folio 99*
>
> *1505-1506 January 29*
> *Ordered that every canon residentiary for the year ending Michaelmas last shall out of his portion of great commons pay to Master Thomas Harryes 20s., in part payment of what is due to him for rebuilding of the chancel of the Parish Church of Northcory.*
> *MSS Wells Liber Ruber II Folio 123*

1506 July 18
Grant of 40 days of grace to Canon Peter Carslegh, he having promised to build the battlement of the chancel of Northcory at his own expense.
MSS Wells Liber Ruber II

The massive piers that support the tower are not of uniform appearance. Those to the east at the entrance to the chancel are finely moulded, while those to the west are plain, and may have been cased up when the chancel was re-built. The piers are built of a mixture of sandstone, Blue Lias stone and Hamstone.

In 1832, as in many churches throughout the country, much restoration was begun, and to accommodate an increasing population further seating was built. Much of the old oak was cleared away and square box pews were installed to replace the older open seating. Many walls were plastered and whitewashed to protect them from erosion.

NORTH CURRY PARISH CHURCH

A restoration was carried out from 1875 to 1882 initiated by the Reverend Christopher Harrison and brought to a conclusion by the Reverend R C Lathom Browne. The architect was Sir Gilbert Scott who died before it was completed but his son, Mr Oldred Scott, carried on his work. Some £8,000 was spent on this restoration, a vast amount in those days. It is thanks to the Scott family and the Barrett family (see Chapter 2-6), that the Parish Church was restored sympathetically. The floor for the nave that was previously at the present porch level was excavated, and the bases of the tower piers remodelled. The outer wall on the north side of the church was rebuilt, the door was replaced, and the Norman doorway may have been re-sited. The whole of the nave was panelled in oak and the interior of the church was greatly changed in appearance. A gallery at the west end of the church where the orchestra played and the choir sang, was removed. The remains of a fireplace were discovered in the wall of the north-west corner of the nave at the time of this restoration. A chimney passed up through the wall at this point and it is said the panelling is removable revealing evidence of a priest's hiding chamber. The porch door was replaced but the older ironwork on it was reinstated. The plaster was removed from the walls at this time and the box pews were also removed and a completely new seating arrangement for the entire church was installed.

The following is an extract of the plans from the faculty papers that record the works of restoration to North Curry Parish Church carried out in 1880.

To take down and remove the reading desks, clerks desk, font and the whole of the pews and seats, the organ, the west gallery and staircase thereto.
Take up and remove wood and stone floors throughout the church and chancel, carefully removing any memorial inscriptions now lying on such floors and replacing them in their present position or as near as possible thereto as may be.
Remove fireplace and flue from east wall of vestry.
To remove all plaster from internal walls of church.
Take off roof and re-roof with proper materials.
To point all external walls.
To excavate such portions of the ground inside the church as may be necessary for laying the new floors, and to spread the earth removed over some portion of the churchyard.

The original heating apparatus was installed in the church in 1881, to be renewed by Messrs Hadon and Sons of Trowbridge in 1922. After many estimates and deliberations it was decided in 1925 to adopt the system known as *silverlite* as one of the best methods of lighting the church. However in 1926 the adoption of that method was substituted for electric light and the Taunton Electric Light Works installed this. It cost £270, but that figure did not include a shed to house the engine and batteries.

The Lady Chapel in the north transept, which may have been in the area once used as a chantry chapel, was restored between 1931 and 1936 when Canon A G Robinson was Vicar. Death Watch Beetle was found in the roof of the chancel in 1930, and in 1939 it was found in the church roof and panelling, and remedies were put in hand. Some church doors were also replaced in 1939.

The Chapel of St Michael and the Holy Souls in the south transept was restored in the 1960s during the incumbency of the Reverend Michael Lewis. At that time pews were removed from under the tower and replaced with an altar.

Major work was undertaken between 1967 and 1968 when the chancel roof was renewed. In 1998 much of the outside stonework of the church was repaired. Wind, rain and frost had taken their toll on the soft sandstone and Hamstone, especially in the tower, on the parapets and around the windows. Following experts' advice the church decided to invest in preserving and protecting this stone. A financial contribution from the Diocese of Bath and Wells was matched by funds raised by the parishioners. Three stages of this renovation work have been completed.

Between May and July 2000 an internal lavatory and kitchenette were installed at the west end of the south aisle of the church. In 2003 donations and legacies from parishioners helped towards the cost of installing an induction loop hearing system. This assists the hard of hearing during services and other events held in the church.

Architectural Details and Furniture within North Curry Parish Church (see Plate iii)

Altar Frontals

Hanging on the wall at the western end of the north aisle is a glass case that contains an altar frontal. This was a gift given in memory of a gentlewoman of the Parish named Johan Connock, who died aged 91 at Lillesdon Court in North Curry in 1633. Towards the end of her life John Gibbes, Vicar of North Curry at that time, gave licence to her to eat flesh during Lent to sustain and nourish her in her weakened state. This was recorded in the *Parish Register of North Curry for 1539–1720* as follows:

> *I John Gibbes Vicar of Northcorri gave Licence (as much as in me lieth) to Mrs. Johan Conock widow of North Currie aforesaid, a Gentelwoman of about 90 years of age, of much weaknes and greate infirmitie, continuallie keepinge her bedd, to eat fleshe this Lente such a lawes doe pmitt, to sustaine and nourishe nature in her. For witness whereof I have hereunto sett my hande the 6th daie of March 1632. By me John Gibbes.*
>
> *The above said Licence I John Gibbes have given and continued unto the same Mrs. Johan Conocke in the same maner and forme. In witnes whereof I have subscribed my name the 14th day of March 1632. John Gibbes.*
>
> *The same Licence I the said John Gibbes have given and continued unto the same Mrs. Johan Conocke in witnes whereof I have subscribed my name the 22nd March. John Gibbes.*
>
> *The same above written Licence I the said John Gibbes have given and continued to the same Mrs. Conocke. In witnes whereof I have subscribed my name the 30th March.*

Sadly she did not survive the Lenten season. She was buried in Devon but left various local bequests in her will including £10 to the poor of the parish, £50 for repairing and beautifying the Parish Church of North Curry, and her brown-stone cup, with a foot and a covering in silver, to the Vicar, John Gibbes.

Johan Connock's father was Thomas Williams of Stoford, who was speaker to the House of Commons in the reign of Queen Elizabeth I. Johan was married four times, and her second husband was John Buller of Lillesdon, whom she married in 1596. The only memorial to her in North Curry is the altar frontal that is made of green velvet and embroidered with silver wire on which is embroidered her paternal coat of arms of a shield with three snipes or curlew heads, and the inscription *Johan Connock 1633.* When the altar frontal was restored about 100 years ago the crest on the cloth for many years posed a puzzle to those interested in heraldry because it represented three cock's feet, one on top and two below. It is customary for heralds, when designing arms, to place the two chief images on top and one base image below. The puzzle was solved when it was it was discovered that the coat of arms had been sewn back upside down, i.e. representing feet rather than heads! Today only two of these feet remain.

In c.1890 two sisters of the Vicar, the Reverend William Buller, gave a new white altar frontal, the appliqué work of which was transferred onto new silk brocade by Mrs Stobart, a parishioner, in the 1950s. In the 1960s a new altar together with an altar cloth, was given to the church by King's College, Taunton. There are a number of other altar frontals in use today including a new stitched frontal for the altar that stands under the tower and has recently been made and hand embroidered by supporters of the church.

Aumbry

An aumbry is a small cupboard for storing the vessels containing the three holy oils used for baptism, confirmation and for anointing the sick, or for bread, whether for use at the Eucharist, or distribution to the poor. The ancient aumbry in North Curry Parish Church in the south wall of the south transept, beneath the large window, has been restored, but is no longer used for its original purpose. More recently a new aumbry was installed in the Lady Chapel for the storing of the sacramental vessels.

Bells

Bells were introduced into churches in AD676, and in the 11th century a curfew bell was rung by the *Beddman* by order of William the Conqueror to put out all fires and lights by 8 pm at night. From 1662 the *passing bell* was rung to call the people to pray for the departing souls of the dead. This was substituted for the *death bell* when the bell was rung at the conclusion of the burial service. Nine strokes were rung for a man, seven strokes for a woman, five for a boy and three for a girl. This was followed by ringing strokes to denote the age of the person in series' of twenty, with an interval between each score. Another custom was the ringing of the bells to call the congregations to church services on Sundays at 8.00 am and at 1.00 pm. Bells were always rung on Coronation Day and royal birthdays, for sea and land victories and numerous other important occasions, but in 1868 these ringing days were discontinued by a resolution of the vestry.

The tower of North Curry Parish Church now carries a peal of eight bells, the total weight of which is a little over four tons. The age of the six original bells is unknown but references were made frequently to the bells in the church records of the 16th century. A good deal of money was spent on mending *baldricks* and *clappers*, on new ropes and wheels, and frequent oiling and renewing of the timbers took place. The six earliest bells were re-cast in 1811 by Thomas Mears at the Whitechapel Bell Foundry, London, which had been established in 1570. The heaviest is the Tenor 'E' and weighs 896 kilograms, and is inscribed *Six Bells were cast 1811. R M Whatley, W House, Churchwardens; T Mears, Founder. May all whom I shall summon to the grave, the blessing of a well spent life receive.* The two lightest, the Treble 'E' and Second (II) 'D' were given to the church in 1894 by the Reverend Prebendary Buller, who was Vicar at that time. On the Treble 'E', which is the lightest and weighs 308 kilograms, is inscribed *Praise Him upon the well-tuned cymbals.* On the Second (II) 'D' is the inscription *Praise Him upon the loud cymbals.* Both are engraved *William Edmund Buller, M.A. Vicar, gave me, AD 1894.* In 1953 these two bells were re-cast again by Messrs Mears & Stainbank, Whitechapel Road, London at a cost of £150 and impressed with a Crown surmounting the royal cypher, *E II R.*

In 1898 the end of the supporting beams of the old bell cage had become decayed and it was felt that the vibration this caused would loosen the mortices and cause the tower stonework to become damaged. Four iron girders were securely bolted to the beams and cage assuring that the belfry was secure. The peal was re-hung again in 1902 and soundproofing to the belfry floor was added. In 1915 the clappers of the bells were again found to be in need of attention and were repaired again at the suggestion of Mr T Doble, church bellhanger of Taunton.

Originally the bells were hung in what is now the ringing chamber of the tower, the storey below the present bell chamber, and until 1833 they were rung from the floor of the church. The turret staircase into the tower was entered through a door at the east-end of the south transept within the church, but in 1833 an opening into this turret was made on the outside to provide an entrance to the belfry without going through the church. The cost of *fetching the stone from Ham Hill for the belfry doorway* as described in a book of church accounts (1819-1875), *with four horses and waggon and 3 turnpikes* amounted to £1.10s.0d (see Chapter 3-1).

Brasses

North Curry Parish Church possesses only two ancient memorial brasses - two small brass plates that can be found on the floor of the north aisle, one by the pillar of the crossing, and the other beside a pew. These are inscribed respectively as follows:

> *Here lyethe the bodye of Elizabethe Bullor, late the wife of John Bullor the elder of Lillesdon, Esquier, who deceased the 12th March 1588.*
>
> *Heere lyethe the bodye of John Bullor the younger, of Lillesdon, Esquier, who was buried the 29th of Februarie, 1598.*

Bronzes

Fifteen small bronzes representing the *Stations of the Cross* hang from the panelling around the nave. They were hung during the incumbency of the Reverend Michael Lewis, c.1970.

Candelabrum

The brass candelabrum hanging from the roof in the middle of the nave bears the inscription *John Pocock and Charles How, Churchwardens, 1809.* When electricity was installed in the remainder of the church in 1926 it was decided not to adapt this fitting.

Chancel Screen

In medieval times the chancel, the eastern part of which was known as the sanctuary and contained the high altar, was reserved for the priest, and the nave was reserved for the congregation. The screen, with locked doors, was used to keep the people and dogs from the chancel. Over the screen was the rood beam on which was fixed the *rood* - an image of Christ on the Cross, and on top of the screen was a loft for the organ, choir or soloist which was approached by a staircase and door in the wall. The chancel or rood screen in North Curry Parish Church that spanned the chancel arch was probably removed during the days of the Puritan destruction, and the marks where it was attached to the walls of the chancel and to the pillars of the chancel arch are still visible. In the south wall of the chancel is a blocked up doorway that gave access to a staircase to the rood loft and belfry. Above this doorway at the back of the chancel arch is a little *squint* or *hagioscope*, a hole in the wall intended to enable the Sexton to look down on the altar from the belfry staircase.

Clock

The Reverend Prebendary Buller, who was a great benefactor of the church and was Vicar of North Curry from 1891 to 1900, gave the clock in the tower of North Curry Parish Church in 1895. This clock replaced earlier ones to which several references are made in the Churchwardens' Accounts. 1586 - *for oylle for the clock and for the bells, 2s. and to the smith for the mendynge of the hammer of the clocke, 2s.* 1685 - *for new making the clock £2.10s.* The clock was restored most recently in 1994. For years it had required winding at regular intervals by hand, but in 2000 an automatic winding mechanism was installed with money from a millennium fund-raising project in North Curry.

Chests

On either side of the west door stand two wooden chests; the one on the right bears a brass plate with the names of the Churchwardens and the date 1790.

The other chest or coffer, referred to on page 21, is considered by most to be the most interesting object in the church, being a lot older than the building. Experts have dated it as being made well before 1200. For many years the coffer remained below the bell pit of the tower in the ringing chamber of the church, unseen and unheeded except for being used as a seat. How it could have been lifted into the ringing chamber of the tower is a mystery. It was too large and heavy to have been moved there by means of the narrow staircase. The Reverend A Kirke, Vicar of North Curry from 1828 to 1931, had the chest moved into the main body of the church by lowering it through the floor in the ringing chamber. There is a hole large enough to let up and down the largest of the church bells, and the weighty chest was thus manoeuvred by a very arduous process down into the church where it could be properly seen and examined.

The coffer, measuring 178 centimetres long by 61 centimetres wide by 66 centimetres deep, weighs 300 kilograms and is constructed of thick slabs of elm butted together and reinforced with iron studs with wrought iron bands that clamp the body together. The planked lid, which is 10 centimetres thick, fits into the top of the coffer, and not on to it, and three knuckle hinges and two pin hinges secure the lid. Signs of other fastenings are evident, suggesting looting of the contents at various times. The lock plate resembles the boss of a Viking's shield with the keyhole pierced diagonally through the metal. The Reverend A Kirke suggested this chest might have been used at the time of King Alfred's conflict with the Danes. It may have been made by Saxon craftsmen to hold captured treasures or have been secured as a trophy during the famous victory over the Danes. North Curry Parish Church, being only three miles from Athelney, may have been a safe haven for it when Athelney Abbey was destroyed in 1539.

In the early-20th century Mrs Stobart, a parishioner, purchased an oak music chest that stands in the chancel in front of the organ. It was carved and made by Mr Hunt of Henlade, who carved it to match the linenfold panelling surrounding the chancel.

Corbels

The stone corbels supporting the roof under the tower and in the transepts show features of human faces and probably represent royal and other personages of the time. One corbel under the tower is of wood and may have been replaced at a later date. There are many others in the chancel, nave and aisles all showing human figures.

Effigies

The church contains two stone effigies, the Effigy of Thoma atte Sloo and the Cadaver Tomb.

Within the sanctuary, and close to the door leading into the vestry, is a tomb resting upon which lies a stone effigy, dating from 1360. The figure has been identified as Thoma atte Sloo or Thomas of Slough Court, a layman who was a great benefactor to the church and neighbourhood, and who led a pious life. Most effigies found represent ecclesiastics but because this figure is wearing a lay gown rather than a cassock it seems likely that it is of a franklin or freeholder. The long tight fitting cote, which was a garment in vogue at that time, falls in folds from the neck. The gown has tight sleeves coming to the wrist, with other sleeves ending just below the elbow. A combined cape or hood covers the neck, and part of the breast. The effigy has pointed shoes that rest on a moulded bracket, and hands, which are now damaged, are raised in prayer. The head, showing a high forehead and long hair to the neck, beard and moustaches, rests on a large tasselled cushion, which at one time probably had the figure of an angel supporting it on either side. This has been chiselled away and all that remains is one hand supporting the head and the other resting on the shoulder. On a fold of the cote are incised the words, *Thoma atte Sloo,* facing the wall and hence possibly proving that the monument does not occupy its original position. The inscription shows the effigy was of a member of the ancient family of *de la Sloo,* who continued to be the owners of the Manor of Slough in the Parish of Stoke St Gregory until the reign of Richard II, when the Montagues of Sutton Montis acquired it.

In a document of 1337, Bishop Ralph of Shrewsbury *gave two licences to John of Slough, of North Curry, to have divine service celebrated in his oratory at Slough for a year.* A portion of carved stonework, which was considered to have been part of this ancient oratory, was discovered in a wall at Slough Court, Stoke St Gregory during some repairs early in the 20th century.

In the north aisle at the entrance to the chapel is a chest tomb known as the Cadaver Tomb. Hearsay suggests this came from Athelney Abbey and that it is an amalgamation of various parts from different ages. Resting on top of this table tomb is a *cadaver* or a stone effigy of an emaciated body in death, although the head, which is of a later date, represents a rough-haired and bearded man in life. In earlier times it was customary for effigies sometimes to represent persons lying in tombs as bodies rather than as skeletons. The tomb is adorned with *heater* or *flatiron* shaped shields, and a series of *weepers* or images of mourners in canopied niches. Underneath the effigy are figures dressed as friars telling their rosary beads. It is uncertain when this monument was placed in its present position, but from Collinson's description in *The History and Antiquities of the County of Somerset* in 1791 it appears to have been there in his time.

Epitaph

When North Curry Parish Church was undergoing restoration in 1882 the following inscription was found on a stone tablet which had been covered up by the flooring of the chancel. It is to the memory of the first wife of a man named Perret, who was formerly a Lay Impropriator and so claimed burial in the chancel. The flooring of the chancel stalls now covers this stone.

In the flower of my age
In the year of twenty-nine loth to die;
Before that I was taken hence
To live for ever in God's presence
In love I liv'd, in peace I died,
Life was disir'd but God denied.
Tho' death have parted you and me,
My body to dust must turn,
I hope that we shall meet again,
You have no cause to morn.

Font

The font, of Hamstone, is octagonal in shape, matching the tower of the church and the original plinth of the churchyard cross. It probably belongs to the early *Perpendicular Gothic* architectural period of 1377-1460. The faces of the bowl are panelled alternately with a shield and the conventional Tudor Rose. The inside bowl is circular and lead-lined with vertical sides. It is surmounted by a particularly elegant and well-designed font-cover that is coloured and gilded in medieval style and dates from 1881. There is a handsome brass ewer, which is probably of the same period.

Lectern

Major William Barrett Jnr of Moredon presented the fine eagle lectern of brass on the coming of age of his eldest son Colonel Barrett in 1884.

Model of Church

At the west end of the north aisle is a model of North Curry Parish Church, made in the early 1950s by Mr Dredge, a parishioner.

Oil Painting

At the back of the nave resting on the ancient coffer is an antiquated painting in oils, of a style both quaint and crude. It represents a King, possibly King David, playing a harp, the crown lying on the ground, while an angel in flight is depicted as sounding a trumpet towards the royal harpist. The origin of this picture is obscure, but it is said to have adorned the old choir gallery at the west end of the church, when a *serpent*, an obsolete wind musical instrument, and bassoon performed the functions of an organ.

Organ

The organ was built in the 19th century, but contains some pipes from an earlier 18th century organ. The organ, given by Mr J Scott Gould of Moredon in 1837, was altered and enlarged by the Reverend Prebendary Buller, and in 1882 was removed from below the west window where it obstructed the light and moved to its present position. A few surviving fragments of the rood screen were built into the organ case that was designed by Oldred Scott. In the early-20th century the Vicar, the Reverend Daniel Pring and the Organ Committee started a fund-raising scheme to raise £600 for a new organ. However in 1911 a second-hand organ, which was described in the *Parish Magazine* of the time as *built at the order of King Edward VII for use in Sandringham Church and is of the best workmanship,* was offered to North Curry Parish Church for £400. A sum of £200 was in hand at that time so plans went ahead to raise the required amount from the parishioners. Unfortunately the First World War intervened and the money already raised was invested in the War Loan instead. By 1921 repairs to the organ were urgently needed, when amongst other defects the leather of the bellows perished as a consequence of heat and drought and the organ collapsed. Money became available from the previous organ fund and restoration work commenced. The bellows were renewed and the keyboard, pedals and couplings were repaired, and in March 1922 the organ was re-commisioned when the Bishop of the Diocese preached at a special service. The organ has been in constant use ever since, with repairs undertaken when the need arises.

Piscina

In the Lady Chapel in the north transept is a piscina that has been restored, and its position may be where there was an altar in earlier times. Above it are two plain corbels upon one of which stands the figure of the Virgin Mary.

Plate

Early vessels were made of silver, and reference in the Churchwardens' Accounts of 1653 lists *one Sillver Challis, one sillver cover thereunto belonging, and one sillver plate.* In 1664 the Churchwardens' Accounts tell of the pawning of the chalice to meet a hospital maintenance charge, but in 1665 it was redeemed. No further reference is made to the silver vessels. Thereafter the church plate was pewter. Pewter was said to have been introduced into churches by the Puritans to show their disregard for the sacredness of material things when pewter flagons were in use in public houses at the time of the Commonwealth period c.1530. It is stated that in 1930 the aumbry cupboard contained two pewter flagons and five pewter plates. The church now possesses modern plate - two large chalices and patens, and a large flagon. Each of these carries the Sheffield date letter for 1830 and is inscribed with a shield bearing the inscription *Presented by Mrs. Mary Scott of Moredon to the Parish of North Curry 1831.* The silver-gilt Communion Service in general use was presented by the Bishop of Taunton in 1916. There are two candlesticks and an ornamental double inkstand of solid silver, which were given to Dr Hugh Olivey in 1899 to mark his leaving the Parish, and in recognition of his many years' service as Churchwarden. They were returned to the church at his death and the inkstand is now used during marriage services. During the 20th century a chalice was given in memory of Annie Liddon, a former Churchwarden.

Pulpit

The pulpit is of Hamstone, dating from the last restoration of the church in 1881. It is accessed by stone steps with a brass handrail and replaced one of painted wood that stood on a high stone pedestal and was made in 1832. The former pulpit was built with the wood of an old pew, and incorporated some surviving fragments of the wooden chancel screen with ornamentation representing a vine and grapes' which has been imitated in the present pulpit.

South Porch

There is a wooden board inside the porch that shows the names of all the Vicars of North Curry from 1234 as follows:

1234	*Richard de Treigoz*
1256	*Simon Guyan*
1325	*Richard de Baac (Baaker)*
1328	*John de Taunton*
1348	*John Seyat (Seyac) de Harewell*
1349	*Thomas Sanywere*
1350	*John Purie de Trowbrugge*
	John Mulewarde
1410	*John Crass*
1433	*Thomas Pay*
1437	*Henry Wegge*
1441	*Hugo Peret*
1442	*John Heeth*
	John Moreton
	William North
1452	*Richard Whyte*
1457	*Thomas Combe alias Baker*
1474	*John Ryche*
	Robert Gentt
1488	*John Stephyns*
1504	*Roger Churche*
	William Capron
1529	*Richard Austyn*
1554	*John Seyman*
1569	*Ralph Dele*
1588	*John Gibbes A.M.*

1638	*Sebastian Smith, S.T.B.*
1661	*Henry Griffeth (Griffith), alias H. Owen*
1686	*Ludovicus (Lewis) Parris, A.M.*
1693	*John Chester, A.M.*
1697	*Ezra Pierce, A.B.*
1732	*Stephenus (Stephen) Hunt*
1739	*Thomas Farewell*
1746	*John Woodford*
1760	*Robert Wilson, B.A.*
1791	*John Turner, M.A.*
1817	*James John Talman, M.A.*
1820	*Walter King Coker, M.A.*
1845	*John Castle Burnett, M.A.*
1857	*William Graeme Gibson, M.A.*
1866	*Carter Hall, M.A.*
1867	*Christopher Robert Harrison, B.C.L.*
1877	*Robert Charles Lathom Browne, M.A.*
1890	*William Edmund Buller, M.A.*
1901	*Daniel James Pring, M.A.*
1928	*Albion Kirke*
1931	*Augustus Gossage Robinson, M.A.*
1936	*Herbert Jocelyn Davies, M.A.*
1948	*Martin Charles Browning, B.A.*
1956	*George Thomas Rogers, M.A.*
1965	*Michael Douglas Lewis, M.A.*
1987	*Bernard Shackleton, B.A., B.D.*
1994	*Charles Townshend, M.A.*

On the right of the inner doorway of the porch is a holy water stoup, which is a recessed basin built into the stonework and contained holy water that was blessed every Sunday. All entering church dipped their fingers into the water and made the sign of the cross on their forehead and breast to remind them of their baptismal vows. This was badly mutilated in the 16th century. The stone figures in the niches above the outer and inner doors were destroyed and were replaced at the time of the restoration of the church in 1881 with statues of Jesus Christ, Mary with the Holy Child and St Peter and St Paul carved by Mr Harry Hems of Exeter. Faint but certain lines of a *mass scratch dial* may still be traced on the soft sandstone on the left of the entrance. A drawing of the porch of 1850 shows a sundial mounted at the centre of the parapet, but it is not there today. A cross now stands above that position and this may have been moved more recently from the parapet on the north transept. The iron gates at the entrance to the porch were given c.1895 by the Vicar, the Reverend Prebendary Buller.

Statue

The south Chapel of St Michael and the Holy Souls contains a fine modern statue of St Michael, Guide of Departing Souls, by Francis Stephens. Mrs Prowse, a parishioner, gave it in memory of her husband.

Tablets

There are 27 brass, wooden or stone memorial tablets affixed to the walls around the church. They are dedicated to members of the families of Barrett, Berthon, Butt, Coker, Gould, Hellard, Hooper, King, Kirke, Long, Ludwell, Meade, Morris, Peard, Plowman, Pring, Ryall, Ryan and Selfe. A brass tablet that marks the restoration of the fabric of the church in 1881 is affixed to the north wall of the north aisle near the entrance into the north transept.

In the vestry is a marble tablet giving details of the customs of the ancient Reeve's Feast. There is a written explanation of the feast hanging at the west end of the church. Also displayed is a copy of the document issued by the Charity Commissioners when the funds of the feast were converted to a Charity in 1868. The history of the Reeve's Feast is discussed in Chapter 2-3.

Vestry

The vestry was not part of the early church and there are no records indicating when it was built. In 1912 an idea was put forward, but later rejected, to erect a choir vestry by enclosing and roofing over the paved area adjacent to the present vestry to provide a practice room. In addition to the items described elsewhere, there is also a set of eight handbells presented to the church by Mrs Sharman, a parishioner, in the hope that the ringers would use them to learn the art of change ringing. Also housed in the vestry is a Donyatt pottery porringer of the 18th century, which was found in a crevice inside the north wall of the belfry during restoration of the stonework in 1998 (see Plate i). It was probably misplaced by a painter, since inspection revealed traces of a mixture of red lead and olive oil that may well have been used for painting the metal fittings of the bell-hanging beam.

Windows

The 19 windows are fine features of the church and all display the *Decorated Gothic* style of architectural tracery. There is no ancient glass except perhaps a fragment or two in the upper lights of the east window. The window tracery in the south transept is the oldest and dates from c.1300. There are five windows with clear glass and 13 of them have been filled with stained glass within the last 100 years.

The west window represents the hymn *Ten thousand times ten thousand* written by H Alford in 1867 and was placed by subscription in memory of the Reverend Christopher Harrison, Vicar of North Curry 1867–1877. He was one of the principal compilers of *Hymns Ancient and Modern*, and the window contains his portrait and also that of his son, who fell at Majuba Hill, Pretoria at the hands of the Boers in 1881. They are both represented as the figures without haloes in the fifth panel of the window.

A window over the north door was placed by Hugh Olivey in memory of his wife Harriet and represents the Raising of Dorcas. These together with a small window in the south aisle placed by Mrs Robbs in memory of her mother Mrs Derham, are the work of Messrs Heaton, Butler and Bayne.

The window in the north aisle, inserted to the memory of Captain Charles Barrett by his widow, appropriately depicts three soldier saints. The large north window in the north transept, representing the Ascension, is to the memory of Major William Barrett, who died in 1914, and his son Charles, killed at the battle of Ypres. It is the work of Messrs Burlesson and Grylls, and was dedicated by the late Canon Holmes, Chancellor of Wells Cathedral, in 1916.

The east window in the north transept is to the memory of Lieutenant George Macdonald Barrett, who drowned when fishing in the River Dee, near Ballater in Scotland, when his duties included the guarding of Queen Victoria. A wreath sent by Queen Victoria at the time is preserved and rests under the north window in the north transept.

The north window in the chancel is in memory of the late Mr Philip Foster, who was a Churchwarden and was placed by his nephew the Reverend A M Foster.

The magnificent east window in the chancel is dedicated to the Reverend R C Lathom Browne who was Vicar from 1877. One panel depicts Christ's sufferings on the Cross and shows eight angels holding the symbols of passion; 30 pieces of silver, the crown of thorns, scourging whips, cross with a shroud, a hammer and pincers, a sword and staff, three nails and crossed lances. Other panels depict St Peter with crossed keys, St Mary with lilies, the crucified Lord with a lamb, St John with a chalice and dragon and St Paul with crossed swords. One of two windows on the south wall of the chancel represents the two gardens, Eden and Gethsemane and is dedicated to C M Foster, whilst the other is dedicated to Albion Kirke.

The two windows in the south transept are dedicated to members of the Barrett family and in the south aisle a window is dedicated to John Hopkins Foster, the founder of the Sunday School.

WOODWORK

The woodwork is a notable feature of the church. The carved *reredos*, behind the high altar, designed by Mr Bligh Bond, and executed by Messrs Boulton & Sons of Cheltenham, was inserted by the Barrett Family in 1916, in memory of Captain Charles Barrett, who fell in the first Battle of Ypres. The central panel represents the appearance of Jesus Christ to His Disciples on the evening of Easter Day; the right-hand panel the Empty Tomb, and that on the left the Walk to Emmaus. The altar with its vesting was given at the same time.

It is said that the gallery, which was removed from the west end of the church at the time of the last restoration in 1875, may have been built out of the materials of the ancient rood screen when that was removed. A few surviving small fragments of the mouldings of this chancel screen have been preserved in the vestry, and some have been built into the organ case. Others are incorporated into the panelling in the door arch in front and above the chancel door in the south wall.

The nave had been re-panelled in oak at the time of the 1881 church restoration, and new oak panelling was added to the chancel walls in 1929. This was designed in 1929 by W E Pennington on behalf of the Ecclesiastical Commissioners and incorporated a wealth of carving by W D Caroe, FSA. Further woodcarving was the work of Mrs Maud Berthon, a life-long parishioner, who received her training at South Kensington and who ran woodcarving classes in the village. The whole work was finished in 1931 and dedicated on Armistice Day as a War Memorial to those who died in the First World War with their names inscribed onto the panelling as follows:

To the Glory of God
And In Honoured memory
Of the Men of this Parish Who
Fell in the Great War 1914–1918

SOMERSET LIGHT INFANTRY

Alec Ashman	*Private*
Alfred H. Bale	*Private*
Marcel Bellringer	*Private*
Joseph Bowey	*Private*
Frederick Duke	*Private*
Clifford Hayes	*Private*
James Staple	*Private*

DORSET REGIMENT

Charles C. Adams	*Private*

DEVONSHIRE REGIMENT

Henry Gannett	*Private*
Charles Stevens	*Private*

ROYAL SCOTS FUSILIERS

Charles J.C. Barrett	*Captain*

WEST SOMERSET YEOMANRY

John Batstone	*L/Corporal*

A.C.C.

Cecil Dennis	*Private*

K.R.R.C.

Bedford Dare	*Rifleman*
Percy Duke	*Rifleman*
Charles Staple	*Rifleman*

GLOUCESTERSHIRE REGIMENT

Frank Grinter	*Private*
Stephen Slade	*Private*

M.C.C.

Edwin J. Hucker	*Private*

R.F.C.

Thomas T. House	*Corporal*

NORFOLK REGIMENT

Charles E. Luard	*Major DSO*

LANCASHIRE FUSILIERS

Hubert C. May	*Private*
Charles Wembridge	*Corporal*

NORTH STAFFORDSHIRE REGIMENT

H. Ronald Selfe	*Captain*

ROYAL ENGINEERS

William Squire	*Sapper*

R.F.A.

William Wakeley	*Driver*

SOUTH WALES BORDERERS

Frederick E. Andrews	*Private*

A further inscription was incorporated into the panelling and serves as a memorial to those who fell in the Second World War (1939–1945). The names of North Curry men who died were inscribed onto this panelling by Mr W F Underhill, of Holcombe Rogus as follows:

Royal Navy		Army		Royal Air Force	
Francis W. Denman	*A.B*	*Peter J Carr*	*Lieutenant*	*Charles Edwards*	*Flying Officer*
		Francis J Garwell	*Private*	*John B Hebditch*	*Sergeant*
		William May	*Private*		

In 1903 a Glastonbury church chair that was carved by members of the North Curry Carving Class was added to the furniture of the church. The wooden parish bier on iron rimmed wheels stands at the west end of the church and is inscribed *To North Curry in memory of his sister Florence, by W.W. Buller, Vicar, 4 Dec. 1891.*

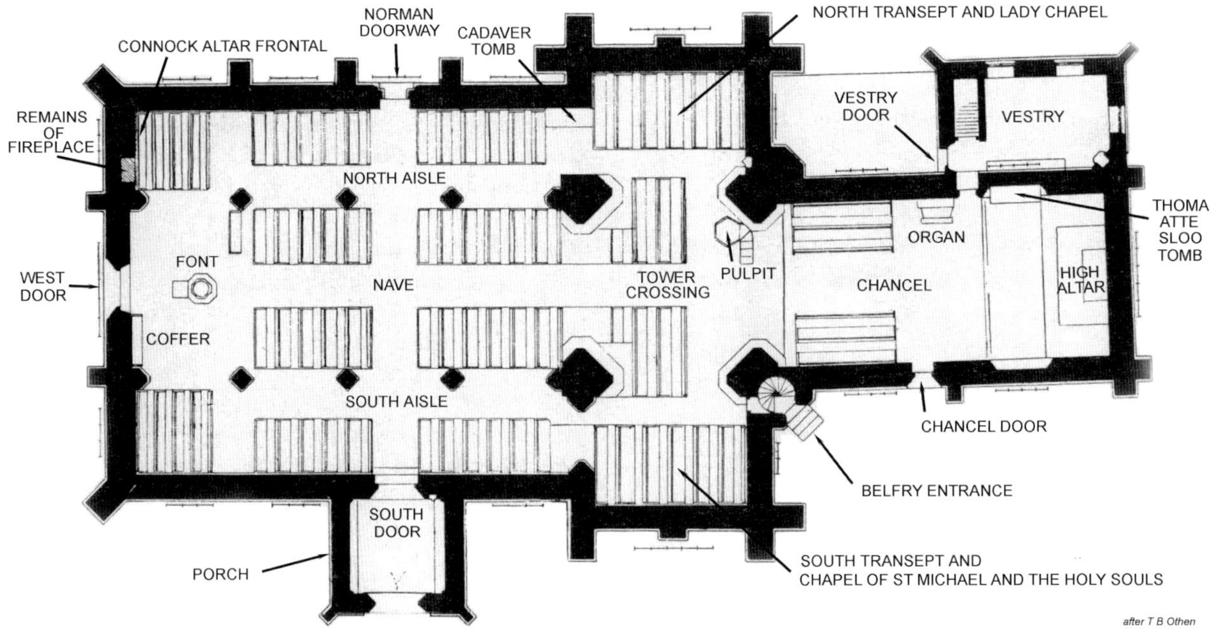

NORTH CURRY PARISH CHURCH GROUND PLAN – 1901

NORTH CURRY PARISH CHURCHYARD

The churchyard is probably older than the present church. Measuring about two acres, it is entered from the four cardinal points, the main entrance being in the south. Until 1930 this entrance was through a common farm gate. This was then replaced by a lych-gate (see Plate ii). *Lych* was the old English word for a dead body. At the lych-gate or corpse gate the coffin was rested on a wooden or stone table while the priest said part of the burial service. Only rich people were buried in coffins in medieval days; the poor were brought in a parish coffin, usually carried on the parish bier, then taken out and wrapped in a sheet for burial directly in the ground.

In the reign of Edward IV in 1442 laws were in operation that stipulated that all corpses should be buried in woollen cloth to encourage the industry of woollen manufacture. In 1679 an Act was passed, the wording of which is as follows:

> *.... no corpse of any person (except those that die of the plague), shall be buried in any shirt, shift, sheet, or shroud, or anything whatever made or mingled with flax, hemp, silk, hair, gold or silver, or any stuff or thing other than what is made of sheep's wool only, or to be put into any coffin lined or faced with any sort of cloth or stuff, or any other thing whatever that is made of any material but sheep's wool only....*

Ministers were to keep an exact account of all burials in a register. If these conditions were not complied with, the goods and chattels of the deceased were liable to forfeiture of £5, half of which was to be given to the poor and the other, after costs to the justices, to the informer. This Act was repealed in 1814.

The North Curry lych-gate was built thanks to the generosity of Mrs Charlotte Barrett of Moredon in memory of a grandson, Mr C W H Luard, who died in 1928. It was designed by Mr W D Caroe, FSA, and constructed by Mr John Merrick of Glastonbury. It is built of stone from a quarry on the Moredon estate, and the roof is of English oak and covered with Cotswold stone tiles.

Carved in the stonework of the south-west side are crossed keys and crossed swords. The sword is the emblem of St Paul, the weapon with which he was martyred. The keys are the emblems of St Peter in reference to Jesus Christ's words to him *I will give unto thee the keys of the kingdom of heaven.* The Lord Bishop of the Diocese, the Right Reverend St J Basil Wynne Willson, dedicated the gate in June 1930, with the donor in her 91st year being present at the dedication.

On the crossbeam above the entrance in shining gold letters is the text *Enter into His gates with thanksgiving.* The inscription in gilded letters on a central cross-beam reads: *In loving memory of Charles William Hartley Luard, born Whitsun, 31st May 1914 died Sunday 18th March 1928 in his 14th year, only child of Major Charles Elmhirst Luard, DSO Norfolk Regiment, killed in action at Missy-sur-Aisne, 19th September, 1914, and Dorothy Frances, his wife.* On the reverse side is the following: *This memorial was erected in 1930 by his grandmother, Charlotte M.H.Barrett, wife of William Barrett, of Moredon, who died 10th October 1914. The Lord gave and the Lord taketh away, blessed be the name of the Lord.*

In 1246 there is a reference in the *Wells Manuscripts* to a chantry chapel located in the cemetery of North Curry (see Chapter 1-5). Chantry chapels were destroyed in 1545 soon after the Dissolution of the Monasteries in England and no evidence remains of the location of this one.

The churchyard Memorial Cross (see Plate ii) was re-erected during the incumbency of the Reverend Prebendary Buller between 1890 and 1901; only the socket of the original survives and dates back to the 14th century. This was incorporated into a design by Mr Edmund Buckle, the diocesan architect, and built at the expense of the Reverend Prebendary Buller, then Vicar of the Parish, in memory of his sister, Miss Florence Buller in 1891. The following description before the Cross was rebuilt is by Charles Pooley in his book *Old Crosses of Somerset*:

> *The beautiful socket and the stump of the shaft of this Cross remain. The socket is much weather worn and partially sunk in the soil. Its upper bed is octagonal, the alternate angles being worked into pilasters with trefoil-niched facings. Each of the four sides is ornamental with a quatrefoil, in the centre of which a Greek cross is carved. The stump of the shaft has a dowel-hole for the insertion of a pin, used to support the stone above, and has also quatrefoils on each side of its base, 14th century.*

The Saxon coin which is referred to in Chapter 1-3 was found at the time of the re-erection. The site of the original cross was at the point where the pathways intersect in the centre of the churchyard.

In 1714 Ezra Pierce who was Vicar of North Curry Parish Church between 1697 and 1732 planted an avenue of elms. In 1910 they suffered damage after the great gale of 20th February, and they were eventually removed in 1914 when they succumbed to Dutch elm disease. There are some old yew trees in the churchyard and from early times these were looked upon as the emblem of immortality. Traditionally from the time of Edward I (AD802) they were planted in churchyards to protect the church against high winds and storms because of their close growth. Twigs and boughs were used to decorate the churches at Easter and were used as a substitute for the palm on Palm Sunday.

In 1908 the main churchyard path was drained and newly gravelled at a cost of £12 and in 1929 was re-made and put in good condition at great expense according to a report of the time. It has since been edged and finished with tarmac. The lamp-post that originally stood near the lych-gate was moved in 2001 and a new lamp-post erected to light the crossing point of the church path. This was funded by gifts made to the church by and in memory of several parish residents.

Forming part of a threshold to a pathway on the southern boundary of the churchyard beyond the lych-gate is a plain stone slab. This formed the hard and cold seat for those delinquents whose fate it was to have their feet made fast in the stocks. The woodwork of the stocks has disappeared.

The rare blue *Mountain Anemone (A.Apennina)* has established itself and grows freely in the south-east corner of the churchyard in early spring. The churchyard walls were repaired in 1941.

The oldest graves are south of the church because people wished to avoid the shadow of the church falling on their graves, and the north side was often associated with the devil. Most churchyards on the south side are higher than the road outside. This is due to the medieval custom of burying people on top of others, and so gradually raising the level of the ground. In the 17th century the first gravestones were erected to mark individual burials. Some of the early ones carved on soft sandstone are illegible but there are many with interesting information on the early North Curry families.

In 1988 a survey of gravestones in the churchyard was compiled. It listed 316 graves in the old churchyard. A further survey of gravestones including those in the new part of the churchyard has recently been completed and a gravestone location map now hangs in the church porch.

A box tomb on the south side of the churchyard bears the inscription *My good lads, do not sit on this stone on account you do disfigure it with your heels, lean on it if you please - Yours etc. Robt.Pocock.* He was born in 1749 and died in 1830. The grave of Harry Barnard near to the lych-gate bears the words *Harry, An English Gentleman.*

There are also graves for cremated remains in North Curry Parish churchyard, some being marked with inscribed plaques. Cremations were carried out at Bristol Crematorium until the Taunton Deane Crematorium was opened in 1963.

Nonconformist Worship

As far back as the 14th century, when John Wyclif questioned both papal authority and the clergy's right to property, and argued that the only certain source of authority was the word of God as revealed in the Bible, religious nonconformity was born. As time went on many Protestant Christians who did not belong to the Church of England became known as nonconformists. In 1377 Pope Gregory XI condemned the views of Wyclif who became known as the first Protestant. His followers were termed *Lollards* and they denied the validity of infant baptism. In c.1390, inspired by Wyclif, they made a translation of the Bible from Latin into English, which was subsequently banned.

John Calvin (1509–1564) was a French born Protestant theologian who came to dominate the reformation, and who believed in the predestination of souls either to salvation or damnation. He also argued that Church government should be performed by *Presbyterianism*, or in other words government by ministers of equal status who made decisions together in council presbyteries.

From early times *Baptists*, who were Protestant Christians, wished to be free from the Church of Rome. They also believed that Christ was the head of the Church and they wished to be independent and free from the control of the King and of Parliament. They believed that infants were not fit subjects for baptism and that baptism of adults by immersion should follow a declaration of personal faith. In 1538 groups of Dutch and Flemish believers in re-baptism were burnt at the stake as heretics and became martyrs known as *Anabaptists*. John Smith (1570–1612), a Church of England minister, re-baptised himself and then members of an English congregation in Amsterdam. The Baptist movement grew in England and from 1589 Baptist churches were established. In Somerset Joseph Alleine was known to have held Baptist meetings in Neroche Forest using a stream for baptism, and in 1653 an Association of Baptist Congregations was formed for Somerset. As time went on divisions occurred between different factions creating *Particular Baptists* and *General Baptists* and in the 18th century some general congregations became *Unitarian Baptists*. The first congregation of Particular Baptists can be traced to between 1633 and 1638 with John Spilsbury (1593–1668) as the pastor. In 1813 the Baptist Union of Great Britain and Ireland was formed.

After the Restoration many Presbyterian congregations became *Dissenters*, or those Protestants who refused to accept the Prayer Book in the Church of England, becoming *Unitarians* in the 18th century. Unitarians were Christian groups who denied the Trinity or one God in three persons - The Father, The Son and The Holy Spirit. The Presbyterian Church of England that united with the *Congregationalists*, or those Protestant separatists who reject all Church hierarchy, became the United Reformed Church in 1972.

George Fox founded the *Quakers* in 1650. Followers adopted the name of *Religious Society of Friends* and their code was to shun liturgical and sacramental worship, rejecting a professional ministry and worshipping as individuals. The name of this religious group arose as a nickname when Fox told a judge to tremble at the name of the Lord. They refused to swear oaths and to pay tithes to the established Church, and in 1682 after much persecution, William Penn founded Pennsylvania in the New World as a refuge.

In 1720 a group of Oxford undergraduates established a *Holy Club*, an evangelical movement led by Charles and John Wesley. The term *Methodism* seems to have been used first in the 17th century and was the term given to those leading a highly structured devotional life. In time offshoot bodies of devotees were formed with Wesleyism the dominant group, forming a Free Church Movement. They eventually accepted permanent separation from the Anglican Church and joined Protestant Methodists to form the United Methodist Free Church Movement in 1857.

The year 1537 had seen the dawn of the Protestant Reformation in England. During the reign of Queen Elizabeth I from 1558–1603 some Presbyterian members of the Church of England and some Calvinists adopted a plain style of dress and pursued lives of strict morality becoming known as *Puritans.* Oliver Cromwell (1599–1658) became a Puritan in c.1630 and most places in England had Puritan ministers during his time in power. Charles II was restored to the English throne in 1661 and the fight for religious liberty began. The King wanted to achieve religious tolerance in England and offered to ordain some of the Puritan leaders as bishops. However, the Cavalier parliament of the day, led by the Lord Chancellor, the Earl of Clarendon, was intolerant of this idea and a number of acts were adopted which were called the Clarendon Code. Among them the Act of Uniformity reinstated the Book of Common Prayer and required all clergy to be ordained by an Anglican bishop, and the Five-Mile Act of 1665 obstructed the worship and residence of dissenting clergy. Nearly 2,000 clergy in England and Wales lost their livings because they refused to conform to all the requirements of the Act of Uniformity. In Somerset many of those ejected clergy, who continued to preach illegally, were imprisoned at Ilchester.

It is known that nonconformists held meetings in houses in North Curry, and one meeting was held in 1669 in Fivehead in the house of Nathaniel Barnard. The 'teachers' at that meeting were John Baker, George Pierce and John Bush, who had been ejected as ministers from the established Church of England from Curry Mallet, North Curry and Langport respectively, together with Thomas Marshall, the minister of the Ilminster nonconformists. It is recorded that c.1650 The Society of Friends or *Quaker* teacher Jasper Batt held a meeting in North Curry with the congregation of 340 'hearers'. He remained a leading light in Quaker life and centred his activities on Ilchester for some two decades. In 1672 it was required that houses used for nonconformist worship be registered with the Bishop. Several houses were registered as meeting-houses in Isle Abbots, Curry Mallet, Isle Brewers and Fivehead and many different nonconformist groups or dissenters used them as places of worship.

THE METHODIST CHURCH IN NORTH CURRY

The Methodist preacher John Wesley was reported to have visited the area from 1778 and in 1785 he is known to have preached in the *great hall at Cathangar*. It is also reported that he visited North Curry and that he baptised infants in Knapp. During the 40 years following his death a number of applications by Methodists to register houses for worship in North Curry were made to the Bishop of Bath and Wells or his representative. Among those recorded applications were one at the house of John Gridley in 1799 and another at the house of Elizabeth Husen in 1807 as follows:

> *This is to certify to the Worshipful John Turner, Master of Arts, Archdeacon of the Archdeaconry of Taunton in the County of Somerset and Diocese of Bath and Wells.*
>
> *We whose names are underwritten desire that the house of John Gridley in the Parish of North Curry in the County of Somerset and Diocese of Bath and Wells may be registered among the records of this county, as a House set apart for the worship of God and religious exercises, for Protestant Dissenters.*

Peter House	*Lawrence Dare*
John Andrews	*Phocion Mitchell Snr.*
Samuel Foster	*William Edwardes*
Jacob Kewer	*A. Stone*
John Ford	*Poshton Machel*
Samuel Gridley	*John Gridley*

> *To the Right Reverend Father in God Richard Lord Bishop of the Diocese of Bath and Wells or his Registerer.*
> *We whose names are here unto Subscribed do certify that the House of Elizabeth Husen in the Parish of North Curry in the County of Somerset is set apart for the Public Worship of Almighty God by a Congregation of Protestant Dissenters of the Methodist Denomination. And we require that this our Certificate be registered according to the Statute in that case made and provided.*
> *Witness our hands this Day 16 of October 1807.*
> *Elizabeth Husen, William Adams, Anna Foster, Mary How, Sarah Adams, Samuel Barrington, John Hardwick, Henry Dinham.*
> *Certificate granted hereon 19th October 1807*

A further two applications to register houses in Knapp were made by Phocion Mitchell and John Lockyer in 1812. Phocion Mitchell had been converted to Methodism c.1798 when Methodist preachers visited Knapp. An obituary in the *Wesleyan Methodist Magazine* of 1823 states *He had sweetness of temper, agreeable conversation and was upright of conduct. He felt deeply for the distressed, and to the utmost of his power, relieved them.* For many years he was afflicted with asthma and was paralysed for the last fifteen months of his life. He died aged 63, on March 7th, 1823, at Knapp. His wife Mary Mitchell was also a devout Methodist and held weekly prayer meetings at 5 am in her house. An extract from her obituary, published in *The Wesleyan Magazine* of 1828 states *her attachments to the ministers of the Gospel was undiminished and that she would rather sacrifice her own food than give up the receiving of the preachers in her house.* She died at Knapp in 1828 aged 60.

The entry extracted from the *Registry of the Consistorial Episcopal Court of Wells* that applied to the house of Phocion Mitchell now known as Manor Farm, and formerly as Lower Knapp Farm, is as follows:

> *To the Right Reverend Father in God Lord Bishop of Bath and Wells.*
> *This is to acquaint you that We the Inhabitants of Knapp in the Parish of North Curry have set apart the house of Phocion Mitchell for worship of Almighty God and we desire that it may be recorded in the records of the Lord Bishop of Bath and Wells according to the Act made and provided in favour of Protestant Decenters Witness whereof we set our hands this the 15th day of January 1812.*
> *Phocion Mitchell, John Gridley, William Mitchell, John Lockyer, Samuel Waterman, S, Lockyer, Samuel Gridley, Jacob Kewer.*
> *As witness my hand Edward Parfitt, Deputy Registrar*

In 1819, and again in 1827, John Foster applied to use a room adjoining a house in North Curry as a Methodist Sunday School. In 1833 an agreement to purchase land, previously used as an allotment, was made by Mr Peter Smith with the intention of building a Methodist Church. Lawrence Dare, gentleman, John Lockyer and William Mitchell, yeomen, William Edwards, miller and John Edwards, cabinetmaker, signed the agreement. The sum of £40 was paid for the land on which a building with an outside measurement of 12.2 metres long by 11.6 metres wide was to be erected. The Account Book shows that the actual cost of building the church was £380.11s.0d. Subscriptions and collections from local people amounted to £293.1s.3½d. Mr Andrews gave £25, presented the plans for the building and superintended the building work, and Mr Lawrence Dare gave £100. The trustees borrowed a further £70 from him and when he died during the same year he bequeathed £60 to the church. This enabled the debt to be cleared by the end of the first year.

METHODIST CHURCH

The church is situated opposite the junction of Windmill Hill and Greenway, North Curry, and the rectangular two-storey building of three bays was built of red brick with Flemish bond with a hipped and pyramid slate roof. When first built the church had round-headed four by three paned moulded mullion windows and vestry rooms attached at the west corner. The large windows provide much light to the lofty church, which has pew seating for a congregation of c.170. A gallery supported by two pillars and reached by a staircase stretches along the back of the church and provides additional seating.

A Hamstone tablet inscribed *Wesleyan Chapel 1833* is displayed above the original church entrance. In 1901 an extension was built to the original church building that included a vestry, kitchen and schoolroom with matching mullioned windows. This was built in memory of Ann Mitchell Morris whose grandfather was Phocion Mitchell. She was married to Cuthbert Rodham Morris who served for many years as Trust Secretary and Treasurer of the Methodist Church and who died in 1923. A marble tablet affixed to the outer wall of the extended building bears her name and the date of her death in 1900. A graveyard extends to the east of the church and cast iron railings on a dwarf wall divide it from the road leading into the village of North Curry. Gravestones are inscribed with the names of many Methodist worshippers of North Curry including Foster, Brewer, May, Duke and Peard.

Memorial tablets are displayed in the church and include one to James Peard of Lillesdon Court who died in 1885, and his wife Anne, whose son John Grigg Peard later built Highcroft House in North Curry. Another tablet in the church is dedicated to the memory of Elizabeth Morris who died in 1831 and to Richard Morris her husband and Susanna Joan her eldest daughter. The altar cross was made from the wood of a pew from the Parish Church of St Peter and St Paul, and until 1991 a pump organ provided the music for services. The vestry is furnished with a portable wooden pulpit desk, reputed to have been used by John Wesley at the beginning of the 19th century.

Rose Cottage, in Queen Square, North Curry, where Ann Mitchell Spearing was born, was acquired in 1929 using money from the estate of Cuthbert Rodham Morris, and it is stated in the house deeds that the building was for the use of Ministers, Supernumeraries and Evangelists of the Methodist Church.

A Wesleyan Sunday School was started in 1827 and a centenary celebration took place at the Methodist Church between the 16th and 19th June 1927. A 150th anniversary celebration was held on 24th and 25th September 1983, which included a Flower and Harvest Festival with floral arrangements in the church, a concert, a coffee morning, and afternoon teas with special services being held.

Approval was given on the 26th March, 1845 for the building of a Methodist Church on a plot of land in Wrantage. This church was to fulfil the religious needs of the Methodist residents of that area in the Parish of North Curry to worship, until the building was de-consecrated in c.1975 when it was converted to a private house.

The Baptist Church in North Curry

The Baptist Chapel in North Curry today is an independent church originating from the Taunton Baptist Church in Silver Street, Taunton, with which it was united at the beginning of the 19th century.

Early North Curry Baptist believers held services in a cottage near Borough Post occupied by Mr I Lawrence, and the principal preacher was Mr B Cox. A need for a chapel for worship by the Baptist members of North Curry was fulfilled in 1825 when John Bobbett, a miller residing in Windmill Hill, agreed to sell land to a body of trustees for the purpose of building a Baptist Chapel. The parcel of land, 27.4 metres from east to west and 17.4 metres north to south, was bounded to the south by the road leading to the village of North Curry. The land was on a slope to the north that fulfilled the earlier custom of building Baptist chapels into hillsides to provide protection from persecution. The Trustees were as follows:

John Bobbett, miller of North Curry
Philip Dare, baker of North Curry
Ezra Dare, servant of North Curry
John Burrows, cordwainer of North Curry
Samuel Hellard, farmer of Stoke St Gregory
Thomas Clatworthy, ironmonger of Taunton
James Blatch Cox, ironmonger of Taunton
Philip Foster, gentleman of Newport, North Curry
John Bult, farmer of Kingston
Henry Richardson, farmer of Taunton
Richard Maynard, chandler of Kingston
James Flower, farmer of North Curry

They were .....*to permit and suffer a Chapel or Meeting House with offices and suitable conveniences for the worship of God to be erected thereon for the use of a church of Society of Protestant Dissenters called Particular or Calvinistic and Baptistic baptising adult believers by immersion maintaining the important doctrines of three equal persons in the Godhead.....*

Baptist Chapel

The chapel was duly erected by the efforts of many that gave their money, labour and skills, who lent horses and wagons and who brought stone, lime and many other materials. Mr Foster of Newport House was instrumental in helping to finance the project and in April 1825 a stone was placed above the entrance doorway that bore the inscription *1 SAM.VII : XII EBENEZER CHAPEL 1825*. The Reverend G Clark, who was the first minister, conducted the first service. Early deacons of the Baptist

Chapel were Messrs Foster, Day, Bobbett, Garland, F Wilcox, John and Robert Dare, Charles Gillard, Charles Winter John Bradbeer and James Burrows.

The two-storey chapel was built of Knapp Lias stone with a pyramid slate roof and pointed arched windows. The chapel was entered under a gallery enclosing three sides, and had a vestry and a reading room at the rear. A tank that was filled with water for the immersion of candidates for baptism was provided underneath the floorboards at the site of the communion table. In April 1826 a schoolroom was added to the building and a Sunday School was established. Very soon the scholars numbered 170, and the teachers 32, and in 1827 the first tea party was given. Later ministers were the Reverends Richardson, Perratt, Gibson, Humphrey and May. Land adjacent to the chapel was used as a burial ground and among the gravestones is one erected in memory of William Serle who was the Baptist Minister in c.1850. There are 60 memorial gravestones and tablets in the churchyard, the earliest dating from 1835. In earlier days those that were erected in memory of chapel *members* faced towards the chapel, and others faced away from the chapel.

During the ministry of the Reverend W Gabriel, who succeeded the Reverend May, a cottage or manse was built, attached at the rear eastern side of the chapel building, as the residence for the minister. The cottage contained two bedrooms, a large kitchen and a study over the schoolroom. The stipend of the minister at the time was £20 a year. A flute, cornet and bass viola, together with a choir led by Mr Joshua Corpe played music at the services at that time. Ministers Richard Serle, B W Osler, and J Sprague followed and during the pastorate of Benjamin Osler in 1870 a dwelling house at 2 Victoria Terrace, Windmill Hill (now named The Old Manse) was purchased by the Baptist Chapel for the sum of £242.5s to become the new Baptist manse. At about this time an account for expenditure of £290 was presented for re-seating the chapel, providing an iron railing for the burial ground and building a school and seven classrooms. It is possible the old manse building attached to the chapel was refurbished to provide more accommodation for the Sunday School.

The Reverend W Fry held the pastorate for 20 years, and it was during his time at the Baptist Chapel in 1891 that many additions and improvements were made to the building. These included a new roof, new drainage, renewal of much of the woodwork and a new ceiling. The gallery was lowered with book rest boards supported by iron standards, new brass lamps were suspended from the ceiling and a new organ was purchased. The erection of a screen partition to provide a vestibule inside the front door was erected with new steps to the gallery, and a hatch for the entry of coffins was installed through the screen. Thirteen new windows of tinted glass were installed and a front porch on pillars erected. Mr T Penny was the surveyor who prepared the specifications, and Mr Handford of Taunton carried out the works costing £280. Financial contributions and subscriptions were received from Mr W Foster, Mr T Penny, Mr John Thorne, Major Barrett, Mr Gibson, Lady Peto, Mr F Thompson, Mr Buller, Messrs Sommerville, Summerfield and Sully. Further contributions came from the members of the church, from collections made and the proceeds of a bazaar that had been held in the Morris Memorial Hall.

In 1894 Mr B W Osler became the pastor of the Baptist Chapel for the second time. Soon afterwards there was a proposal to build a new Baptist Chapel in Stoke St Gregory, to serve the needs of over 40 Baptist members who resided there, and to become a united Pastorate with North Curry. The building costs were estimated at £1,150 for a new chapel building, school and classrooms, a horse and trap shed and a stable. At the same time it was proposed to enlarge the burial ground in North Curry and to erect a horse and trap shed and a stable and to renovate the Baptist manse in Windmill Hill. The cost of the latter works was estimated to be £200, and the financial outlay was to be met by donations and subscriptions from church members.

In 1899 William Price became the pastor followed in 1905 by G J Whiting, and then by D J Howell and C Carter. G R Cole was pastor in 1925 when celebrations to mark the centenary of the chapel took place. These included special services, a public tea, and a concert of sacred music given by a choir, string orchestra and organ.

In 1930 Pastor J Stark was installed as the minister. He was followed by the Reverends H Wyatt, D Russell Smith, E R Fowles, C E Lawrence, W W Burch, M Taylor and in 1971 by D K West. In 1968 the old minister's house that was attached to the chapel building was demolished, a new kitchen was built, and refurbishment of the Sunday School room above was undertaken. In 1969 the Baptist manse in Windmill Hill was sold and the proceeds went towards the erection of a new bungalow for the pastor which was built on land adjacent to the Baptist burial ground. In 1975 the 150th anniversary of the building of the Baptist Chapel was celebrated and in 1978 a service was held to welcome and recognise Mr Anthony Smith as lay pastor of the Chapel. He was followed in 1997 by Colin Waltham who remained until 2005.

2 - 5

THE DWELLINGS

THE NATION'S BUILDINGS EVOLVE

Our earliest ancestors were nomadic hunters and did not build houses of a permanent nature. Seeking shelter from rain, snow and wind they initially built crude tent-shaped huts constructed of a circle of wooden poles tied together at the top with withies, and covered with brushwood or reeds, weighted down by stones. Later, in order to achieve more space and headroom, they developed an oblong shaped shelter set over a pit with two timber uprights supporting a ridge pole with earth piled up around the feet of the poles. With the domestication of animals and crop cultivation, people built farmstead dwellings to shelter more permanently. They were built in groups for protection against wild animals and enemies and were defended with earth banks, timber palisades and ditches. An Iron Age settlement found near Glastonbury shows evidence of round hut-like shelters with an outer ring of timber uprights having wickerwork plaited between them and daubed with mud, clay, straw, animal hair and blood. A central post took the weight of a thatched roof with a gap to let the smoke out. Tools became more sophisticated and the shaping of timber-framed walls and partitions and the tenon and mortice method of jointing became more widely used. Evidence of elongated wooden buildings with walls of vertical timber has been discovered on other Iron Age sites in the country.

After the Roman invasion of Britain dwellings in planned communities were built of rectangular shape using Roman building techniques in timber and later in stone. The timber buildings developed as time went on when vertical timbers were jointed into a horizontal timber ground-sill bedded on stone walls to keep the wood from rotting, and with full height end gable walls filled with panels of wattle and daub. These villas were often built with surrounding verandahs, many with two storeys, and stone and tiles replaced thatch on roofs.

After the end of Roman rule in the early-5th century much destruction of Roman dwellings took place and as the Anglo-Saxon civilisation emerged the vast majority of houses were constructed of timber with a few stone houses built for the more wealthy and privileged. Although many poorer people lived in crude mud hut hovels, the more important farmers built timber rectangular barn-like dwellings. The whole family lived, ate, slept and died around an open hearth in the centre of an earthen floor, with the smoke from the fire escaping through a hole in the roof. To resist the force of the wind the upright timber posts were set into pits in the ground, but were inevitably subject to rotting.

The earliest timber-framed buildings had a ridge pole supported at each end by a pair of poles leaning against each other, and tied together at the top. Naturally bent timbers superseded these straight poles, each pair formed from the split halves of the same tree trunk. Placed in reverse they formed an arch, or a *cruck* opening up the interior of the house. The space between the two pairs of crucks was known as the bay, open to the rafters, and placed five metres apart. Animals were the most prized possession of the Saxon farmer and this space was the exact size for the early farmers to house two oxen side by side when they shared their dwelling with their animals. This measurement in time became the standard for all buildings and the overall size of a man's dwelling was dictated by the amount of land he held. Typically a man who held 30 acres had a house of five bays in length while a man with only six acres lived in a building of one bay.

As centuries passed these simple timber dwellings developed with box frame construction into a rectangular box of timbers, comprising horizontal and vertical posts jointed to form walls. The open panels were infilled with wattle and daub, bricks or clay blocks. The rafters leant on this box which rested on a ground-sill. The roofs were protected by wooden shingles, which were also sometimes used to provide additional outer protection to the walls. They were between 9 and 12 metres in length and about half as wide, and inside wooden pillars divided the living space into aisles with a central hearth. One bay was for the animals and their keepers, another for the grain and hay, and another for the farmer and his family. In cruck construction pairs of curved timbers or angled timber cruck blades were spaced at intervals along the building to support the roof by means of ridge beams, purlins and wall plates to transmit the loads to the ground. The wealthy occupied more elaborate aisled halls and although the family, friends, relatives, chaplains and servants shared the communal living room around a central hearth, a raised upper end or dais with partitions provided a more private sleeping area away from draughts for the lord and his immediate family.

By the 10th century the Saxon timber-framed house displayed much skilled workmanship and comfort to rival any in Europe, but when the Normans came to England in 1066 they brought new methods and ideas. They erected moated and walled castles, and built houses with defences not only of timber, but also of stone. Some houses were built with the hall standing above a ground floor undercroft, with a surrounding moat, palisade and ditch. The living accommodation was on the upper floor, known as the solar, supported on vaulting from the floor below, and reached by an outside flight of steps. The vault below was used for storage and only accessible by an internal staircase.

By the 11th and 12th centuries the hall houses were extended to encompass storerooms at the lower end. These included the pantry (from the Latin *panis*) for bread and the buttery *(wine and ale in butts)* for drink. In some houses the kitchen was installed outside reached by a passageway. The addition of a two-storeyed cross wing at the upper end may have contained a first floor private apartment for the master of the house and this storey might protrude (jetty) outwards to overhang the courtyard. By the 14th century halls developed with a cross wing at each end. The lower one served as a dairy, pantry and buttery with a storeroom above, and the upper one accommodated the living and sleeping rooms. By the 15th century the heart of the house shrank from prominence between the gabled jettied wings. Smoke bays, smokehoods, and later fireplaces with chimneys were inserted. The central hall area was floored over with a staircase inserted to access the upper storey and windows replaced the mullions.

Stone buildings were erected at all social levels in areas of readily available building stone. Material was found in rock strewn areas or from nearby quarries, or was provided by re-using stone from demolished buildings or abbeys. Buildings with walls of cob and clay survive from the 16th century. Cob is one of the names given to the material that resulted when earth and clay were trodden to a certain consistency and mixed with stones, sand and chopped straw. The walls were raised in layers of cob and wood or wattle on a stone plinth, with a limewash to provide a weatherproof skin. Alternatively clay and straw was fashioned into rectangular blocks, dried in the sun, and used in courses cemented together with mud and dung. There are many stone and cob walled houses in North Curry.

During the 13th century Anglo-Saxon and Norman builders scavenged Roman sites for bricks and tiles to incorporate into buildings for the wealthier people. In the 15th and 16th centuries brick-making became a skilled art and bricks were used for the building of chimneys, in-filling timber frames and for gable walls. The first houses predominantly to use brick were built from the middle of the 17th century. At first the style of housing or vernacular architecture was dictated by the locally available materials, and houses were built by country craftsmen, provincial masons and carpenters with no academic training who were bound by tradition and worked to methods and patterns learned through long apprenticeship and practical experience. Later, in periods of prosperity, new houses were built or older houses remodelled by professional architects working to a style and plan, using fashionable materials of the day.

North Curry Buildings

North Curry's earliest record is probably its place-name that arose when the original tribal settlements gave way to the establishment of territorial divisions of shire and diocese (see page 75). From the 8th century Anglo-Saxon land charters record North Curry as an established area with boundaries and it is likely that there were many dwellings of Saxon date built in North Curry. The Domesday record in the 11th century further confirms it as being an important village. After the Manor of North Curry passed into the hands of the Dean and Chapter of Wells Cathedral (referred to within this text as DCW) in 1242, documents refer to the many facets of their rule and management of the village. All the land in the Parish was divided into plots that were given names, and although there are many references to these apportionments, there are few references to individual buildings. Information about land and property exchanges can be found from the Manor Court Rolls, but in the case of North Curry only locations are given and the names of the buildings, if any, are only rarely recorded. None of the very early timber houses of these times have survived due to the fragility and rapid disintegration of wood, and many buildings were constantly re-built, often lasting for a single lifetime.

Probably the house of most importance that still survives in the village is Lillesdon Court. The house has undergone remodelling over the centuries and today shows little evidence of its early-14th century origins. In 1311 John de Bello Campo *(Beauchamp)* is recorded as the owner, followed in 1317 by Hugh de Bello Campo who in 1355 was granted a chantry chapel at Lillesdon. This dwelling had close connections with Slough Court in Stoke St Gregory when in 1369 William de Monte-Acuto *(Montacute)*, Earl of Salisbury acquired both estates from Hugh de Bello Campo. It is recorded that in c.1377 John Beauchamp, who was a knight of Richard II, had possession. The Buller family inherited the house through marriage in 1633.

Recent research into buildings in North Curry has identified a number of houses in the Parish that show evidence of being built in the 15th and 16th centuries. Many of these houses hide their origins behind outside rendering, modernisation, remodelling and extension, and much new evidence of earlier building techniques and knowledge of the earlier tenants of the village is often uncovered when new building work is undertaken. Manor Farm, off Stoke Road, a substantial house of Blue Lias stone, was built c.1570 and has connections with the Sealy family whose arms are represented over a doorway. Fosse Cottage with Blue Lias stone and Hamstone walls was possibly the *Church House* in the 16th century. Substantial part-timber-framed buildings are scattered throughout the Parish and include The Old Vicarage in Church Road, Fosse End in Stoke Road, Thatcher's in White Street, Flagstones in Queen Square, Payne's Farmhouse in Moor Lane, Pury House in Stoke Road, 1 Greenway, Greenway Farmhouse in Greenway, Weaver's Farmhouse in Wrantage and Lower Knapp Farm, The Rising Sun, Bird's Farm and Knapp Farmhouse in Knapp. In the 17th century much more building took place when houses of brick or stone replaced earlier dwellings such as many of the terraced houses in Queen Square, The Warren in Stoke Road, The Old Brewery in Queen Square, Angel House in Stoke Road, and Long's House in White Street. In the 18th and early 19th centuries as the village became more prosperous, larger houses such as Whatley House, Calmady House, Greenway House and 2 Queen Square were built in the contemporary Georgian style, and many houses were built with the newly fashionable Bridgwater brick. The 19th and early-20th centuries brought much speculative building and a lot of infilling occurred as demand for housing increased. A number of the houses mentioned above are described in greater detail later.

Accurate dating of houses can be made difficult when later alterations to the basic structure have affected the outer walls or reshaped a roof, or when chimneys were inserted into houses. Internal inspection of a roof can usually indicate the development of the buildings over the years, even when they have been enlarged or altered at a later date. For example, evidence can sometimes be quite clearly seen of early sooting of roof timbers. Structural and cosmetic changes to a building are most likely to affect the outer walls, and very few early houses survive today in the form in which they were first built.

As the centuries passed and more houses were built, property deeds became necessary, but even as late as the 18th and 19th century house names were not given and properties were referred to only by the householder's name. A written schedule giving names of owners, lessees and occupiers of land together with the description and acreage of all plots in the Parish of North Curry accompanied the 1787 DCW *Survey Map of the Manor of North Curry* (Plate xiv) and the 1840 *Tithe Map of North Curry* (Plate xv). These are the first reliable sources for historians in establishing locations of house sites. This information has been used in conjunction with other research in the detailed descriptions of North Curry dwellings later in this Chapter.

In 1947 an inventory of the more important buildings and structures in England was started, compiled and published by the Secretary of State for the Environment, and is known as the *Statutory List of Buildings of Special Architectural or Historic Interest*. In 1962 the first survey of Somerset was completed, and in 2005 Taunton Deane had approximately 2,000 Listed Buildings with 67 buildings and structures listed for North Curry. The list is updated from time to time, and buildings are included that are considered to be of special or exceptional interest, which warrants every effort being made to preserve them as significant elements of our culture and heritage. The buildings are grouped according to their importance: *Grade I* are buildings of exceptional interest, *Grade II** are particularly important buildings of more than special interest and *Grade II* are buildings of special interest. To safeguard their character, listed buildings cannot be altered inside or outside, extended or demolished, unless Listed Building Consent has first been obtained through the local council. A full *Statutory List of Buildings and Structures of Special Architectural or Historic Interest* for North Curry in 2005 is at the end of this Chapter, some being identified in the more detailed descriptions of buildings that precede that list.

Local authorities have a duty to designate conservation areas in England in any area of special architectural or historic interest whose character or appearance is worth preserving or enhancing. These may cover a whole village, part of a town or a single street. There are now nearly 9,000 conservation areas in England, with 69 in Somerset, and in January 1970 the main part of the village of North Curry was designated the first conservation area in Taunton Deane. Planning has been controlled ever since to retain the general character of the village where possible. Conservation tries to ensure, by education, persuasion and statute, that the essential character of an area is appreciated and respected in the activities of the present and future generations for the benefit of both. All of the buildings, listed or otherwise, within a Conservation Area are recognised as contributing to its special character. Planning applications are needed for changes that might affect the character of a Conservation Area. Trees are also given protection in that proposals affecting them require notification. Legislation gives control over the demolition of most buildings in Conservation Areas. Today there are some 650 houses in Wrantage, Lillesdon, Knapp and the village of North Curry. The earliest houses date from the 15th century with the newest currently nearing completion.

A Brief Introduction to Vernacular Architecture Terminology

To aid those unfamiliar with the subject we give below a few diagrams to try and explain a selection of the technical terms used in the ensuing text.

Roof Types

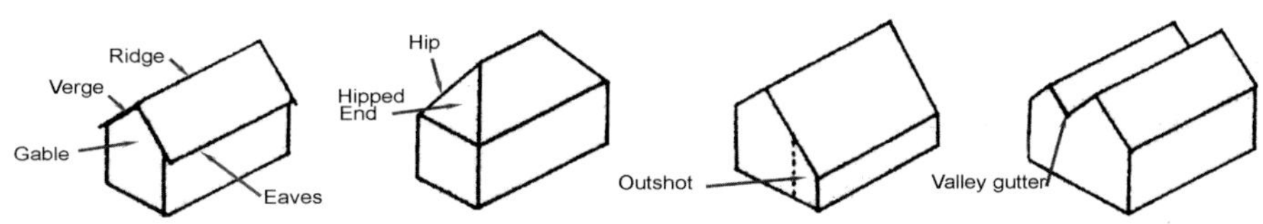

Gabled Hipped Catslide Double Pile

Evolution of the Chimney

"F" denotes location of fire hearth

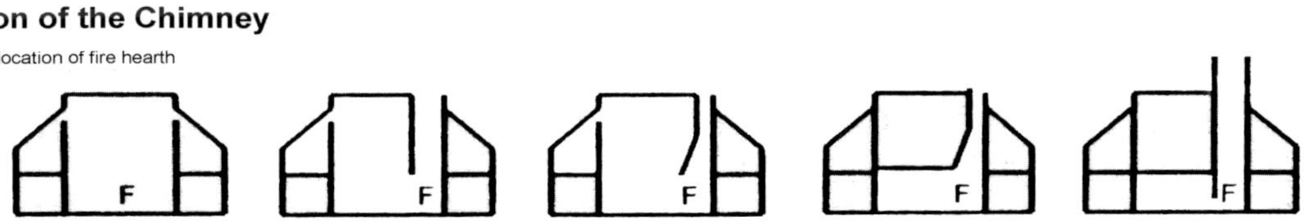

Open Hall | Open Hall with Smoke Bay | Open Hall with Smoke Hood | Open Hall with Floor and Smoke Hood | Chimney House

Typical Ground Floor Plans

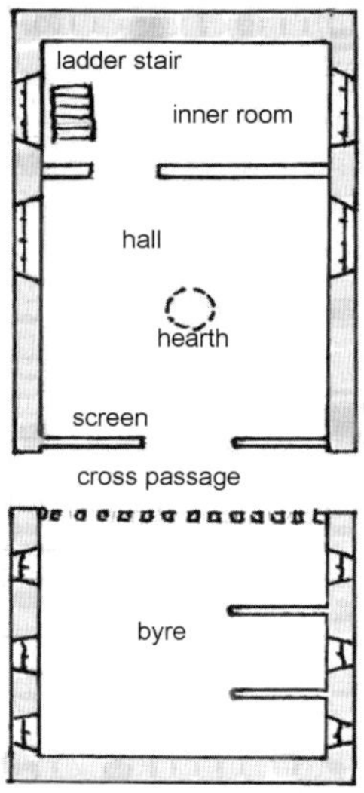

Traditional Longhouse

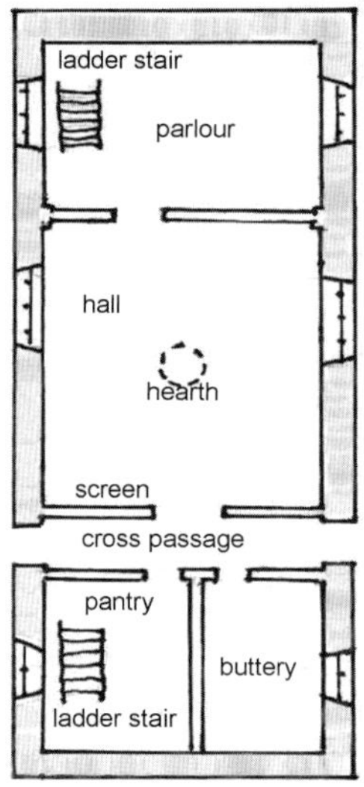

Medieval Open Hall House

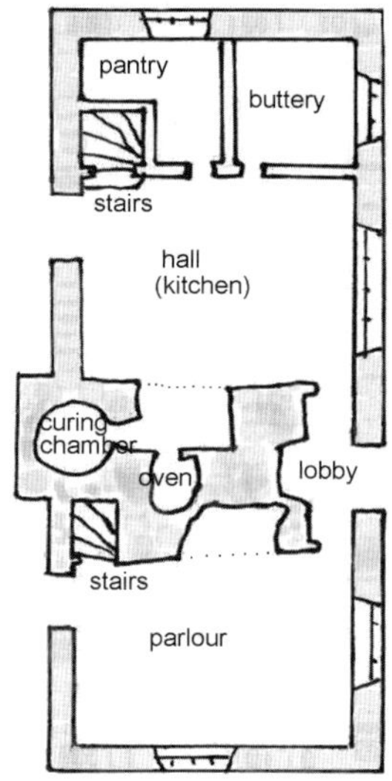

17C Chimney House

Frame and Roof Construction

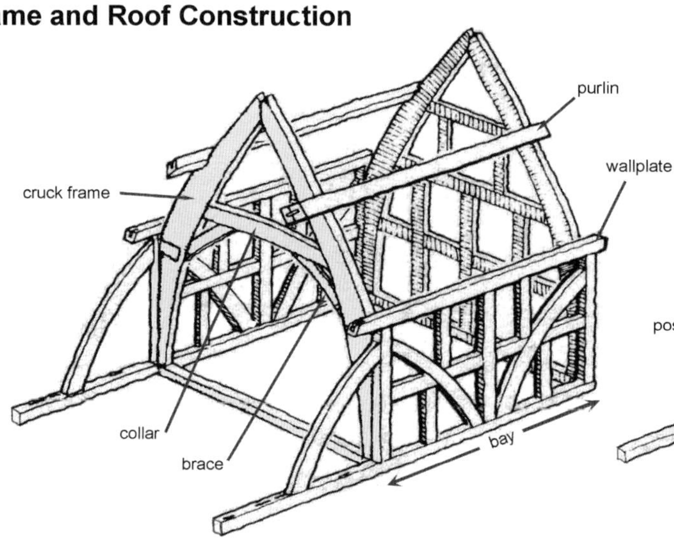

Cruck Frame

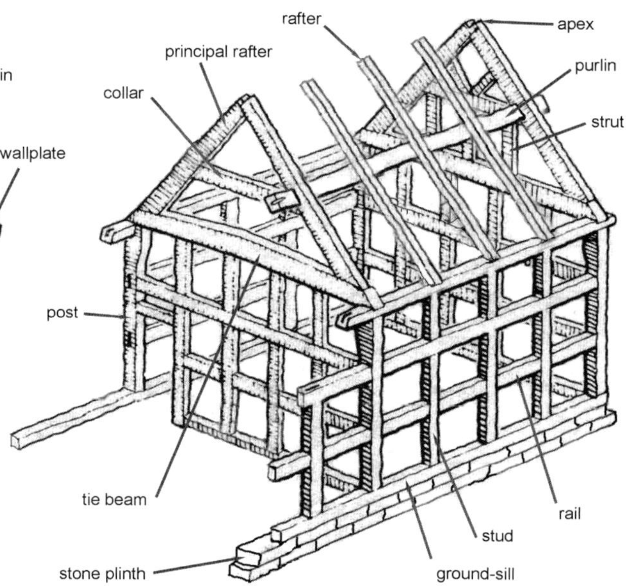

Box Frame

External Features

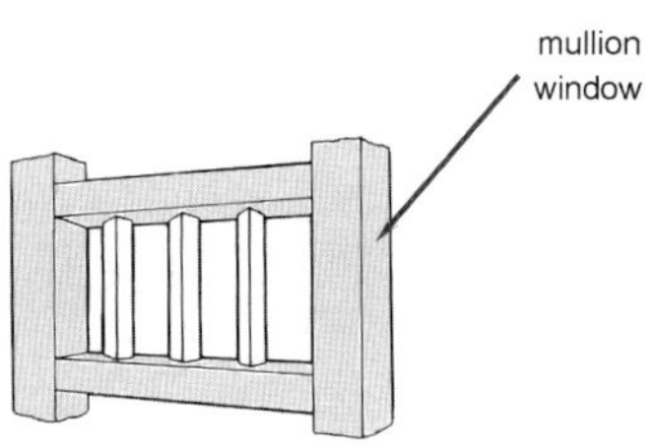

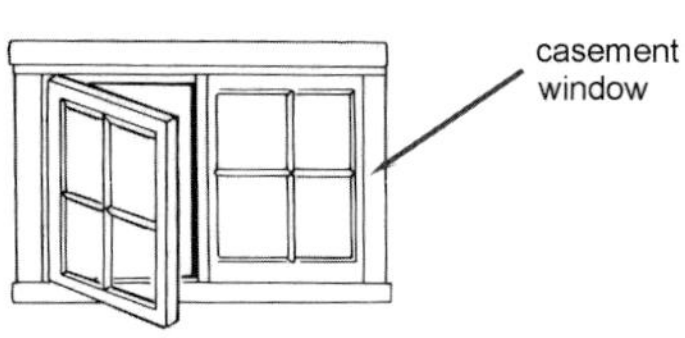

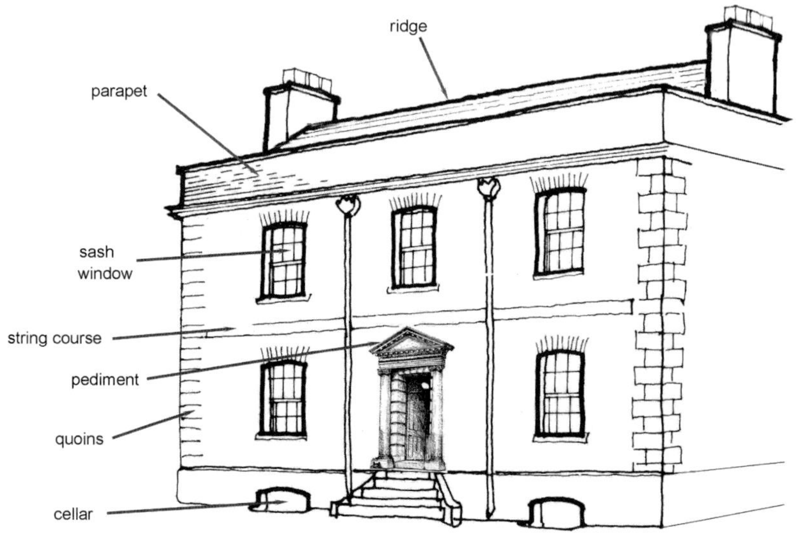

Some of the Notable North Curry Houses

A number of the houses in the Parish of North Curry which are either *Listed Buildings* or have interesting historic details and have been the subject of reports and surveys by architectural historians have been selected for detailed commentary below. Extracts from the reports, particularly those by the Somerset Vernacular Building Research Group, together with research notes of ownership and land acreage from early maps and other parish documents are included. These house descriptions are presented in a logical geographical sequence within the Parish and are followed by a location map to assist in their identification. Also see Plate v. This selection is not exhaustive.

1. The Post Office Stores, 4 Queen Square
2. The Old Bakery, 5 Queen Square
3. Manchester House and 6 Queen Square

These houses form part of the island of dwellings in Queen Square that were originally part of The Shambles or market area of the village. They were all built and continued until recently as shops or workshops of trade. Now only The Post Office Stores continues as a trading establishment.

The Old Bakery is a *Grade II Listed Building* and was built c.1700 to a double-pile four-bay plan with a cross-passage and central doorway. In c.1851 it was expanded to include a bakery and subsidiary buildings at the rear. In c.1894 two downstairs rooms together with part of a staircase and upper room became part of the building now called The Post Office Stores. The building was possibly re-roofed with slate and a chimney removed at that time. The house has been remodelled and now has a central front doorway with a room to either side leading to a back kitchen area and a well-preserved baker's oven exposed. The walls are roughcast over rubble and evidence of the shape of the original central front door opening can be seen around the window to the left of the present front door. A water well opening located in the present kitchen has been covered. The 12-pane sash windows are of a Georgian style. The building fronting The Shambles, which is now semi-detached from The Old Bakery, may well have been part of the original curtilage. It was probably used for other trades during the 19th century and is now in separate ownership.

Court Rolls give the names of copyhold tenants as Robert Ceely in 1763, Mary Taylor, John Burd and James Body in 1778, and James House in 1803. The tenement is described as *one Cottage with a Workhouse or Shop standing in the Shamble Row of North Curry and also one parcell of vacant ground lying on the South and West part of the said Cottage containing 40 feet in length and 30 feet in breadth.* This vacant ground later became part of the site of the present Post Office Stores.

In c.1787 the house was occupied by James Body, whose occupation is unknown, but in 1841 the house was occupied by William Perratt, a linen draper, who probably used the small separate shop as a trading place.

The building marked in the position of the present house on the 1840 *Tithe Map of North Curry* is numbered 1543 and is described in the *Schedule* as follows:

1543 House with 15 perch of land

Landowner	*James House of Hatch Beauchamp*	*Lessee of the DCW*
Occupier	*William Perratt*	

In the 1863 *Rate Schedule* for North Curry Robert Marchant was the Landowner (DCW) with Edward White as the Occupier. Edward White, a baker, probably remodelled the house and outbuildings, sharing them with Henry Goodland, a plumber/glazier and Eli Edwards, a mason who were trading within the curtilage. Edward White also became the Postmaster c.1866, and we can therefore assume the house which included part of The Post Office Stores at that time served as the Post Office. It is said to have been one of the first Post Offices in the country to open for public service.

The *Census Returns* list William Richards in 1871 and Thomas Jordan in 1881 and 1891 as bakers occupying the premises. In the *Trade Directories* for North Curry Mary Jordan was listed as the baker c.1910-1914, and c.1900-1902 James and John Bradbeer are listed as bakers and confectioners in residence there. Later residents of The Old Bakery were Nurse Rich and Miss Burrows c.1948 who later moved to a semi-detached building in The Shambles, and it is recorded a dentist had a practice at The Old Bakery and called once a fortnight.

A small 17th century cottage sited on the corner of the present Stoke Road and The Shambles is now part of The Post Office Stores storage area. Together with a plot of vacant land that is now the shop area of The Post Office Stores it is mentioned as part of the curtilage of a building in The Shamble Row belonging to Robert Ceely (1763) and later to James Body (1778) now called The Old Bakery as mentioned above. In 1787 this cottage was tenanted by Robert Farnham (occupation unknown), and later c.1840 this building as mentioned above was possibly used as the shop premises of William Perratt, a linen draper, whose residence was The Old Bakery.

In c.1851 John Knight, a grocer, possibly expanded the shop premises and provided living accommodation above the shop. In c.1860 until c.1880 Joseph Foster, a draper and grocer, became the proprietor of the shop. He possibly enlarged the shop premises and living accommodation to include the corner of Queen Square and Stoke Road.

James Elihu Beel, a painter and glazier, was resident there in 1881. His mother-in-law Elizabeth Foster, widow of Joseph Foster, was also living there. The dwelling became the Post Office c.1894 and James Elihu Beel became the Postmaster and proprietor of a grocery and draper's shop. He remained there until c.1914. When the shop became the Post Office in the late 1800s, part of The Old Bakery building was possibly incorporated to provide larger living accommodation and outbuildings.

Entries in the *North Curry Trade Directory* of the time state that the Post Office was an establishment dealing with Post, Telegraph and Money Orders, and was a Savings Bank and an Annuity and Insurance Office. Letters arrived from Taunton at 6.35 am, and the box closed for dispatch at 7.20 pm. It is also recorded that it was the first place in North Curry to be connected with a telephone and became the telephone exchange for the very few in the village who were connected. The Post Office had the telephone number 1, the doctor's surgery number 2 and the Police Station number 3.

In c.1914 Mrs Henrietta Edwards became the postmistress and David Edwards ran The Post Office Stores trading as a grocer, draper and general outfitter. They remained there until 1928. In 1928 Kenelm Kennedy became the Postmaster and proprietor and expanded the store, selling groceries, confectionery, tobacco, ironmongery, earthenware, outfitting and haberdashery.

From 1930 to 1947 Harold Cuthbert Turner became the Postmaster and proprietor of a large general store selling a range of groceries and provisions, ironmongery, glass, china, mats and rugs, coats, frocks, millinery, shoes, ladies and children's underwear, hosiery, tobacco and stationery.

In 1947 Austin Tarrant became the Postmaster and proprietor of the shop selling all household requirements. Later Postmasters and owners were Frederick Simmonds in 1968 to 1972, and Charles Daniel Willson in 1972 to 1976, followed by June and Donald Chandler between 1976 and 1993, when the shop became a *Spar* mini-market, advertised as your *local SPAR shop for everything from stamps to shoelaces – with a smile!!*

Manchester House and 6 Queen Square were built as shop or workshop premises c.1700. There is a building marked in the position of these dwellings on the 1787 DCW *Survey Map of the Manor of North Curry* and numbered 62. In the *Schedule* William Creese (sic) is listed as the Copyholder of a house with 7 perch of land.

The building marked in the position of the present house on the 1840 *Tithe Map of North Curry* is numbered 1540 and is described in *the Schedule* as follows:

1540 House, Court and Stable with 13 perch of land

Landowner	*James Crease*	*Lessee of the DCW*
Occupier	*William Spearing*	

The *Census Return* of 1841 lists James Crease as a glazier and William Spearing as a shopkeeper.

In the 1863 *Rate Schedule* for North Curry the Landowner is Maria Crease who had acquired the freehold and the premises were described as a House, Shop and Stable. The Occupier was William Crease who was listed as a grocer and draper in the 1861 *Census Return*.

In 1881 the Crease family held the positions of postal and telegraph Clerks and the building was possibly used as the Post Office. This may have continued until 1894 when the Post Office moved to its present site.

The Hutchings family (George and sons Mike and Ken) ran their business of newspaper shop and delivery service, stationery, tobacco, sweets and confectionery, plants etc. there from the 1930s. It is also recorded that the building once housed a school and a bank. In January 2003 the premises ceased trading and became a private residence of two dwellings.

4. Flagstones, 23 Queen Square

This is a *Grade II Listed Building*. The original house was a timber-framed cob walled thatched house of two bays with a cross-passage possibly built in the 16th century. It is now part of a row of houses and was refronted in the late-18th/early-19th century. The front is of stone and the back is brick and is rendered. There are sash windows with keystones to the lintels. An early fireplace is on the north end wall and a later fireplace is on the south wall. In 1900 a steeply pitched clay-tiled roof replaced the thatched roof and a large addition was built on the south end which was used as a shop, with a door inserted by the fireplace. Earlier this century it was called Sheffield House. The property was sold at auction in 1900. It is described in the sale particulars as *Dwelling House with workshop, stable, sheds, loft, piggery, enclosed yard and garden, altogether ½ acre. House contains entrance passage, sitting room, front kitchen and back kitchen, larder, five bedrooms and box room. At the rear are wash house, carpenters shop and W.C. There is also a pump and well of good water.*

A Parliamentary Survey dated 1st July 1637 describes a holding of a cottage by Lawrence Chislett as *one Cottage with a Garden standing on the further side of the Dinney, formerly in the tenure of Eleanor Kingman.* Later *Court Rolls* list copyhold reversions with tenants Lawrence Stacey, William Larkham, Gabriel and John Morlesse, John and Mary Stephens, William and Anthony Culverwell, John Fry Reeves and Henry Denman giving Flagstones a long history of tenants.

There is a building marked in the position of Flagstones on the 1787 DCW *Survey Map of the Manor of North Curry*, numbered 86. In the *Schedule* Anthony Culverwell is listed as the Copyholder of a Garden and Cote with 1 rood and 16 perch of land.

The building marked in the position of the present house on the 1840 *Tithe Map of North Curry* is numbered 1529 and is described in the *Schedule* as follows:

1529 House and Garden with 1 rood and 25 perch of land

Landowner and Occupier	*William Elson Wescombe*	*Lessee of the DCW*

In the 1863 *Rate Schedule* for North Curry Samuel William Wescombe is listed as the Landowner (DCW) with John Jones listed as the Occupier.

The Gillard family used part of the premises for their saddlers and harness-makers business and enlarged the premises c.1906 to incorporate an ironmonger's shop which was sold in 1956 and continued trading until 1979 as Webb's ironmongery.

The building has recently been split into two properties, now known as Flagstones and Sheffield House.

5. Auster Cottage, 1 Church Road and Linden Cottage, 20 Queen Square

Auster Cottage was originally a two-bay dwelling with a cross-passage, possibly built in the 17th century. An outshut was added at the back later. An addition (now Linden Cottage, which is a *Grade II Listed Building*) was built later in the 19th century adjacent to and behind the right-hand bay when the house became a saddlery shop and workshop. The house was sold in 1888 and possibly at that time the premises were divided into two separate dwellings. There is a blocked doorway on the first floor between the two buildings. Linden Cottage has a steeply pitched double Roman tiled roof with a brick and random rubble façade, slightly forward of Auster Cottage which also has a brick façade that has been rebuilt. Both cottages share a brick stack. A fire insurance plaque engraved with the date 1714 is displayed on the front of the house, which could be the date of an earlier rebuild. There is a clay tiled roof over the original building with pantiles over the rear outshut.

The Gillard families were saddlers, harnessmakers and ironmongers and owned various business premises in North Curry in the 19th century. When they moved from Auster/Linden Cottage in 1888 they moved to Sheffield House (now Flagstones), which they also owned, probably to enlarge their business. On 12th December 1752, the property was transferred to Sarah Alloway widow of William Alloway and Henry her son. On 30th September 1818 the property was transferred to William Burnell.

There is a building marked in the position of Auster Cottage on the 1787 DCW *Survey Map of the Manor of North Curry,* numbered 2. In the *Schedule* Henry and William Alloway are listed as the Copyholders of a House etc. with 10 perch of land.

The building and plot marked in the position of the present houses on the 1840 *Tithe Map of North Curry* are numbered 1525 and 1525a and described in the *Schedule* as follows:

1525 House and Garden with 5 perch of land
1525a Plot with 2 perch of land

Landowner	*William Burnell*	*Trustee of the late Lessees of DCW*
Occupier	*John Bucknole*	

In the 1863 *Rate Schedule* for North Curry Charles Millett Foster, Gentleman of Newport House, is listed as the Landowner (DCW) with George Gillard listed as the Occupier. When Charles Millett Foster died Charles Salway Gillard continued to pay rent for the cottage to Charles Millett Foster's widow Helen until she died in 1887.

On 3rd May 1888 the House, Garden and Plot of 7 perches were sold at auction to Charles Gillard who took out a mortgage for £200 on the property with Cuthbert Rodham Morris. The description of the dwelling in the sale particulars was *This shop comprises a good Front Shop, with Workshop at the rear, and a Dwelling-House adjoining, in which the business of a harness maker has been successfully carried on for some years. The House contains 2 front Sitting-rooms, Kitchen and 4 Bedrooms, with a Pump and Well, Furnace, and detached W.C. Brick built and tiled.* Charles Gillard paid off this mortgage in 1906 and became the sole owner.

6. The Old Brewery, 19 Queen Square

This *Grade II Listed Building* was originally built in the late-17th century as a two-storey, two-bay, cross-passage house with leaded windows, with an attached single-storey three-bay outbuilding with a cross wing at the rear. In the 18th century the outbuilding was raised to two storeys, and an outshut with a slate roof was added to the other end of the house. The walls are of red brick with a rubble plinth, and there are a number of iron cross ties, a moulded cornice and brick stacks. The house has a double Roman tiled roof and the outbuilding has a plain clay-tiled roof. On the front of the façade below the eaves of the house is one of the original insurance plaques - two hands crossed - the sign of the Union Assurance Society, one of the oldest companies. These signs were for identification by fire engines because companies ran their own brigades and only dealt with fires on premises insured with them. Buildings within the present garden of The Old Brewery which runs along Church Road, one of which is now demolished, were possibly part of The Old Brewery complex. Research has shown that a malt kiln was housed in the outbuilding which is attached to the house together with accommodation for horses and drays and possible living quarters for the men employed.

There is a building marked in the position of The Old Brewery on the 1787 DCW *Survey Map of the Manor of North Curry,* numbered 382. In the *Schedule* William and Henry Alloway are listed as the Leaseholders of a House etc. with 1 acre and 31 perch of land. A bill of sale of 1827 describes the house as follows:

> *A brick Dwelling House and Malt-house comprising 2 good Sitting-Rooms, 7 Bedrooms, a large Hall, Kitchen, Brew-House, Cellar, Milk-House, and many other Conveniences. The Malt-house adjoins the Dwelling-House and contains 2 lime and sand Working Floors, 3 good Store-Rooms, an excellent Kiln, Couch and Cistern, with a good Pump annexed, and every other Convenience requisite for manufacturing 5 to 6,000 bushels of Malt in a season. They are well adapted for a Brewery, or any other extensive concern, and may be easily converted into comfortable Residences for more than one respectable family, North Curry possesses the advantage of a Weekly Market, and a daily post from Taunton. Proprietor - Mr. J Foster.*

The building marked in the position of the present house on the 1840 *Tithe Map of North Curry* is numbered 1611 and is described in the *Schedule* as follows:

1611 House and Garden of 1 rood and 30 perch of land		
Landowner	*William Burnell*	*Trustee of the late Lessees of the DCW*
Occupier	*William Crabb*	

There is evidence to suggest that a maltster running a malting house in Stoke Road moved his business here after 1840 (see The Old Malthouse below). A property auction offered a dwelling house and malthouse tenanted by James Temlett for sale in 1849.

In the 1863 *Rate Schedule* for North Curry John Radford is listed as the Landowner (DCW) of a House, Garden, Malthouse, etc. with 1 acre and 8 perch of land. James Temlett, a maltster, is listed as the Occupier. He remained there until 1910 when his son Walter Temlett took over the brewery business until the 1920s. He employed several men and the barrels of *excellent beer* were delivered to public houses in the village and beyond in drays drawn by cart horses. When the business premises became a private dwelling in 1980 the house was named Selwood and the malthouse attached to it became a garage. The house was re-named The Old Brewery in recent times.

7. The Old Vicarage, 5 Church Road

This is a *Grade II Listed Building* with evidence suggesting that the house was built in the early-16th century and was originally of three bays with a cross-passage and a smoke bay or smoke hood at the south-west gable end. A jointed cruck in the roof with wattle and daub infilling to the apex has smoke blackening on the south-west side, indicating an early smoke bay.

A chimney stack and fireplace with oven and possibly a bacon curing chamber was inserted into the smoke bay at a later date and together with the third bay became a kitchen. In the 19th century an additional bay which then became the kitchen was built beyond the original south-west gable wall. A brick fireplace was built with stone access arches to the existing oven and bacon chamber from the earlier fireplace behind. A front wing was also constructed at this time. A large brick arched fireplace was built in the former kitchen and this room was upgraded to become a parlour. Another jointed cruck, again filled with wattle and daub to the apex of the roof, is at the position of the cross-passage partition.

At the other side of the original cross-passage an arch braced jointed cruck in the roof indicates the position of the south-east end of the original principal room or hall. The passageway of the present house is narrower than the original cross-passage, which is now partly inside the hall room. Evidence of two further jointed cruck trusses remains in the roof where purlins have slots for missing windbraces matching the other remaining crucks. A beam at collar level between the original hall end trusses suggests the position of a ceiling above the original hall where a chamber over the hall would have been. A brick fireplace on the south-east outside wall is of a later date. Transverse and axial chamfered beams divide the ceiling into three long panels. A room beyond the hall to the north-east was presumably an original chamber within the hall, although no early features remain in the re-built roof space.

A single-roomed wing at the north-west end was an early addition. A single-storey corridor was added to the centre linking the two wings. The walls are roughcast with exposed red brick on the north-east gable end, the roof has plain clay tiles and the stacks are brick. The house has leaded casement windows with gabled dormer windows rising through the eaves at the rear of the house.

It seems likely that the house was used as the vicarage to the church from early times. A *terrier* (a survey of church possessions) of North Curry dated 1613 states *First there belongeth to it a vicarage house with a garden a dove house and church yard ...*

In the list of copyholders that appear in the 1787 DCW *Survey of the Manor of North Curry*, the Reverend Robert Wilson, Vicar of North Curry held lands and buildings amounting to 4 acres, 3 roods and 27 perch of land numbered 369 to 380. We may assume this allocation to be the same as above and therefore he probably resided at The Old Vicarage at that time. Collinson, in 1791, writes *The vicarage was rated in 1292 at twenty marks. It lies in the deanery of Taunton. The Rev. Canon Wilson is the present incumbant.*

The building marked in the position of The Old Vicarage on the 1840 *Tithe Map of North Curry* is numbered 1521 and in the *Schedule* is described as follows:

1521 Vicarage House with 1 rood and 3 perch of land		
Landowner and Occupier	*The Reverend Walter King Coker*	*Lessee under DCW (Glebe)*

The next Vicar, the Reverend John Castle Burnett, lived at The Old Vicarage until 1857. In the 1863 *Rate Schedule* for North Curry the Reverend William Graeme Gibson is listed as the Landowner (DCW) and Occupier. He held various plots, namely the Church, Churchyard, Vicarage House (The Old Vicarage) and various other buildings amounting to 4 acres and 24 perch of land. The Reverend Gibson lived there until 1867 when the Reverend Robert Harrison became the Vicar of North Curry. In 1871 he moved into the new vicarage (see The Manor House) and the house ceased to be the vicarage.

Residents of The Old Vicarage that followed were William Frederick Liddon Green until 1910, Mrs Mary Cartwright until 1923 and Daniel A Vere-Smith until 1931. In 1931 Colonel John James Aitken, CMG, DSO, OBE, MRCVS, and his wife moved to The Old Vicarage on his retirement from the Army. He had qualified as a veterinary surgeon at Glasgow Veterinary College at the end of the 19th century and went to South Africa. He served firstly as a civilian attached to the Army and in

1901 was granted a commission and was awarded the Queen's South Africa Medal and the King's South Africa Medal. He went to India and Tibet with a military column of 20,000 transport and riding animals. He returned to South Africa and then served in the First World War in France with the 1st Division BEF with responsibility for sustaining 500,000 animals, and in 1916 was awarded the DSO. In 1917 he was despatched to the United States to assist in the formation of the American Veterinary Corps. Subsequently he was Commandant of the RAVC School at Aldershot and he retired to The Old Vicarage in North Curry in 1932. At the outbreak of the Second World War he raised the 8th (Home Guard) Battalion Somerset Light Infantry and commanded it throughout the War. He died in 1946 and Mrs Aitken remained at the Old Vicarage until her death in 1967.

8. Calmady House, 6 Church Road

This house is a *Grade II Listed Building*. The main part of Calmady House was built in c.1783 and styled in the architectural fashion of the day *(late Georgian)*. It is a symmetrical building with a central entrance opening into a hall with stairway, the hall giving access to the main rooms. The house is built of red Bridgwater brick in Flemish bond, with Hamstone dressings. The roof is of slate with coped verges behind a parapet with brick stacks to the gable ends. Below the parapet there is a moulded ashlar cornice. The house was enlarged in the early-19th century with an addition to the south end, which has a separate lower slate roof. There is a long service wing to the rear (east) a portion of which may form part of an older building, again with a lower slate roof. The main house is of two storeys with the attic rooms forming a third under the low-pitched Welsh slate roof. A blocked stepped external access at the rear of the house at sub-basement level suggests that the cellars may originally have housed service rooms. The Georgian sash windows are of 12 and 16 panes. Their frames are set back 10 centimetres into the brickwork and the sash boxes are concealed as was dictated by fire regulations of that period. The rear wing has mainly casement windows. The original block six-panel door with ashlar open pedimented doorcase, together with a fanlight and Tuscan columns and brass door furniture remains.

The house is named after a medieval Devonshire family. John Calmady is the earliest recorded and lived around 1460 on family estates at Langdon, Devonshire. Through marriage, lands were acquired in Cornwall and Somerset. Josias Calmady, grandson of John was a ship's chandler and in 1584 equipped ships leaving Plymouth for the Americas. He married the wealthy Catherine Courtenay who was heiress to the Courtenays of Powderham, the Earls of Devon. In 1618 their son Shilston was knighted by King James I, but died in battle supporting the parliamentary side in the Civil War. His son Josias II again made an attractive marriage extending the Calmady lands and his nephew Josias III was successful as a Member of Parliament and also was appointed by William of Orange as Lieutenant Colonel with the Devon Militia. His son Francis Vincent married Elizabeth, heiress to John Pollexfen and they in turn had one son, Francis John and two daughters, Pollexfen and Elizabeth. By 1782 when Francis John Calmady died the family had added land in North Curry to their property. His sister Pollexfen inherited the North Curry lands, and after an unpopular second marriage when her husband Charles Holmes Everitt, Admiral of the Red, assumed the name Calmady, her family disputed her right to the Devon estates. She was alienated from the rest of the Calmady family. In 1781 the property in North Curry was called *Savery's tenement* and was occupied by John Pocock.

Pollexfen and her husband built Calmady House between 1783 and 1785 on the current site and decided to live in Somerset. However they lived in Calmady House for only a short time and played no recorded part in parish administration. In 1791 John Collinson states in *The History and Antiquities of the County of Somerset* that *There is also a manor here belonging to Warwick Colmady, esquire.* The house and four plots of land was sold in 1798 and referred to as *lately Calmadys*. It was bought by John Sperring who qualified as a juror in 1819 on the basis of ownership of *Calmadys*. John Hopkins Foster became the owner between 1825 and 1840. His son Charles Millett Foster, a solicitor who made substantial alterations to the house in the mid-19th century, succeeded him. After 1881 it remained empty for some time when it was owned by John Erskine Grant Sandford, the solicitor and clerk to the West Sedgemoor and Stanmoor Drainage Boards. William Winter Goode, of the same occupation, owned it in 1897, then Thomas Plowman, a physician, in 1906, who then sold it to the Barretts of Moredon. In 1914 the owner was Major Arthur Platt, in 1923 a Mrs Protheroe, and in 1939 the Reverend George Edmund Warlow, who died in 1948. Stanley Talbot who then bought Calmady sold the orchard, which was part of the original Calmady land, and in the 1950s a contemporary house was built on the orchard site.

The building marked in the position of Calmady House on the 1840 *Tithe Map of North Curry* is numbered 1520 and 1520a and is described in the *Schedule* and in the 1863 *Rate Schedule* for North Curry as follows:

1520 House, Garden etc. 1 rood and 12 perch of land
1520a Stable and Yard with 8 perch of land

Landowner and Occupier	*Charles Millett Foster*	*Freehold*

9. Gwyon House, 8 Church Road

This *Grade II Listed Building* faces east and is rendered to imitate stucco. At present it is of an 'L'-plan of two storeys plus attics and a service wing to the west. A decorative cast iron verandah along the side of the house fronts the garden to the south. The house has a shallow pitched hipped slate roof and sash windows. A Hamstone pilaster doorcase has a moulded cornice and fanlight.

The house may incorporate parts of earlier thatched cottages that were demolished when the house was built on the site. In 1256 Simon Guyan was invested as Vicar of

North Curry. In 1264 the Lords of the Manor of North Curry granted William Gyan a house, outbuildings and land amounting to 45 acres. In 1321 his widow, Alice Gyan, was granted custody of all of his lands. His son Robert with his wife Matilda is recorded as being given rights of timber to repair a house. If we assume the above to have been of the same family it is likely that Gwyon House was the site of this early dwelling close to the Parish Church in North Curry.

There is a building marked in the position of Gwyon House on the 1787 DCW *Survey Map of the Manor of North Curry,* numbered 274. In the *Schedule* William Paine is listed as the copyholder of a House etc. with 1 rood and 30 perch of land.

There are three separate dwellings marked in the position of Gwyon House on the 1840 *Tithe Map of North Curry* numbered 1615, 1615a and 1616 and they are described in the *Schedule* as follows:

1615 House and Garden with 7 perch of land

Landowner	*William Paine*	*Lessee of the DCW*
Occupier	*Thomas Smith*	

1615a House and Garden with 5 perch of land

Landowner	*William Paine*	*Lessee of the DCW*
Occupier	*William Wood*	

1616 and 1616a House and Garden and Orchard with 1 rood and 35 perch of land

Landowner	*William Paine*	*Lessee of the DCW*
Occupier	*James Durham*	

In 1858 the properties were auctioned at The Bird in Hand public house, and Charles Millett Foster on behalf of Cuthbert Rodham Morris took the reversion of the copyholdings from the Lords of the Manor of North Curry for £195.

In the 1863 *Rate Schedule* for North Curry Cuthbert Rodham Morris who had acquired all the above plots appears to have rebuilt the house or incorporated the three separate dwellings into one house. This new house was built in an *Italianate* architectural style. He is listed as the Landowner (DCW) and Occupier of a House, Garden and Lands amounting to 3 acres 1 rood and 39 perch. Sketches by a member of the Morris family of early photographs of the site show the older cottages as thatched c.1850 and by 1865 show a more substantial re-roofed house of two storeys with a verandah on the south side.

In 1871 Cuthbert Rodham Morris purchased several properties from the Ecclesiastical Commissioners, the new Lords of the Manor of North Curry at that time, including the property known as Gwyon together with 14 acres of land in the parish for £665. In 1873 he purchased a parcel of land from James Temlett, the brewer at The Old Brewery for £61.5s.0d and formed a walled garden for his property. By 1880 Gwyon House was further enlarged by adding another floor, which entailed raising the roof and adding dormer windows, and enlarged the rear of the premises to form another bedroom, a billiard room, a wash-house and storeroom. He also built an office building, now known as Gwyon Cottage, where the firm of C R Morris, Sons and Peard, Auctioneers and Estate Agents, began business, later moving to Melbourne House in Queen Square.

10. 1 & 2 Church Cottages, off Moor Lane

A *Grade II Listed Building* of 18th century build with map evidence suggesting possibly a dwelling of much older date stood on the site. The house of two storeys, three bays of double pile has an addition at the end of the right hand cottage. It is constructed of Blue Lias random rubble stone with rendered returns, a slate roof with a catslide roof over the addition, coped verges and brick stacks. In the 19th century modifications took place to form a pair of semi-detached cottages.

There is a building marked in the position of Church Cottages on the 1787 DCW *Survey Map of the Manor of North Curry,* numbered 58. In the *Schedule* William Comer is listed as the Copyholder of a House and Cote with 35 perch of land.

On 30th March 1836 the owners of the land, the Dean and Chapter of Wells, executed a reversionary grant of the cottage and garden to Joseph Foster, tailor, of North Curry in the names of Penelope Foster his daughter and Samuel Talbot of North Curry. It was described as *one cottage with a curtillage of Old Auster,* which allowed rights of common on the moors and commons belonging to the Lords of the Manor. A condition of the grant was that there was to be no way to the premises for carts, carriages or vehicles, or horses or cattle through or across the churchyard.

The building marked in the position of the present houses on the 1840 *Tithe Map of North Curry* is numbered 1618 and is described in the *Schedule* and in the 1863 *Rate Schedule* for North Curry as follows:

1618 House, Garden with 22 perch of land

Landowner and Occupier	*Joseph Foster*	*Lessee of the DCW*

In 1875 the copyhold was reversed to Samuel Talbot, and on his death in the same year the Talbot family sold the premises known as *Churchyard Cottage* by auction at The Bird in Hand inn. In the sale particulars it is described as *a cottage residence with lawn in front and kitchen garden and orchard behind and occupied by Mr. O.P. Derrick as tenant at an annual rent of £13. It is conveniently arranged, and contains four bedrooms, dressing room, parlour, sitting room and best and secondary kitchens. There is also a detached washhouse, pump house, two W.C.s with piggery etc. Also a small tenement adjoining. The whole is stone-built and slated.*
In 1884 the property was sold to Cuthbert Rodham Morris and was then divided into a pair of semi-detached cottages to provide accommodation for his outdoor staff of a groom and a gardener. They became known as 1 and 2 Church Cottages. On the death of Mr C R Morris in 1915 his son Cuthbert William Morris inherited the

premises. After his death the cottage became the property of his daughter Marguerite Sherlock who gave it to her unmarried aunts Ada Susan Morris and Ethel Louise Morris. In 1939 it became the property of Morris Williams who was their nephew. One cottage was wired for electricity in 1939, and both cottages were improved in 1969 and 1973 by providing modern drainage, a bathroom and a modern kitchen.

11. Payne's Farmhouse, 4 Moor Lane

This *Grade II Listed Building* was built c.1605 and has random rubble local Lias stone walls and a double Roman tiled roof. Originally the house was a two-storey, three-bay with cross-passage structure with the outer and inner rooms of less width than the hall and having outshuts unusually beyond the house wall, forming two rooms on either side. There are several early features: chamfered Hamstone mullioned windows, a refronted 17th century door and a moulded lintel in the kitchen with evidence of a bread oven and curing chamber. The hall has a six-panel chamfered compartment ceiling, a chamfered lintel on stone sides to the fireplace with dogleg stairs with turned balusters. The outer room has unstopped plain chamfered ceiling beams and a four-foot-deep hearth with evidence of an early bread oven. Three original trusses survive in the roof giving evidence of an early jointed cruck roof, with tenoned collars and trenched purlins. The house is no longer a farmhouse and the barns and outbuildings now form numerous new dwellings.

There is a building marked in the position of Payne's Farmhouse on the 1787 DCW *Survey Map of the Manor of North Curry,* numbered 518. In the *Schedule* Robert Hooper Scott is listed as the Leaseholder with 1 acre, 3 roods and 12 perch of land.

The building marked in the position of the present house on the 1840 *Tithe Map of North Curry* is numbered 1629 and in the *Schedule* it is described as follows:

1629 House and Garden with 3 rood and 32 perch of land

Landowner	*Charles Holcombe Dare*	*Lessee under the DCW*
Occupier	*John Kinglake*	

In the 1863 *Rate Schedule* for North Curry Charles William Dare is listed as the Landowner (DCW) with Elizabeth Kinglake as the Occupier.

12. Manor Lodge, The Fosse

This house is also a *Grade II Listed Building* that was built as the Lodge to the Manor House c.1815 on the site of the earlier village animal pound. The original plan was probably of two storeys of two rooms with an outshut at the rear. It has a hipped slate roof and a brick stack. The walls are of squared and coursed Blue Lias stone, with brick voussoirs to window openings. There are two pointed arch leaded casement windows on each floor, and a ground floor oriel window.

The building marked in the position of the present house on the 1840 *Tithe Map of North Curry* is numbered 1706 and is described in the *Schedule* as follows:

1706 Cottage and Garden with 26 perch of land

Landowner	*Charles Holcombe Dare*	*Lessee of the DCW*
Occupier	*Robert Andrews*	

13. The Manor House, The Fosse

This *Grade II Listed Building* was built in 1815 by Charles Holcombe Dare who was the Lay Impropriator and later in the 19th century it became the North Curry Parsonage. The double pile, two-storey house has three bays with the central bay projecting into a semi-circular porch. The house has a shallow-pitched hipped roof with overhanging eaves and brick stacks and the walls are roughcast. There are numerous sash windows, some converted to casements.

The back entrance of the house is at a lower level to the front entrance and this floor forms a large semi-basement and cellar area with an underground passage running around two sides and the front of the dwelling. This underground area has evidence suggesting that the present house used the foundations of a much older dwelling and stone mullion window openings in this area may have been part of an earlier house.

Details in a Court Roll dated 13th April 1714 may well refer to this building. Elizabeth Brewer is named as the Copyholder *...of the west part of a tenement containing one hall, cellar, shop with small garden adjoining, two chambers, court and great garden, one barn, stable and carthouse, orchard by the footpath leading out of the King's Highway called the Foss.* James Dibben and Sarah and Mary who were his sisters were the Copyholders *...of the eastern part of the same house containing one kitchen and beer cellar, two chambers, two stables, one wellhouse, one pig sty, one ox stall, orchard and shared court situated at the back of the mansion house.*

Later Charles Holcombe Dare seems to have been an interested party in a property possibly relating to this one when, in a *Court Roll* of 1792, he is mentioned as the eight-year-old recipient of the copyhold reversion from William Weaver. It is suggested that when he came of age at 21 years he inherited the property and in 1815 he proceeded to rebuild the house.

There is a building marked in the position of The Manor House on the 1787 DCW *Survey Map of the Manor of North Curry,* numbered 531 and 532. In the *Schedule* the Leaseholder of the Parsonage House, Offices and Home Ground with 8 acres and 7 perch of land is listed as Seymour.

The building marked in the position of the present house on the 1840 *Tithe Map of North Curry* is numbered 1705 and is described in the *Schedule* as follows:

1705 House, Premises etc. with 1 acre 3 rood and 24 perch of land

Landowner	*Charles Holcombe Dare*	*Lessee of the DCW*
Occupier	*James Holcombe Dare*	

In the 1863 *Rate Schedule* for North Curry Mary Frances Dare was listed as the Landowner (DCW) of a House, Cottage, Garden and Premises amounting to 2 acres and 10 perch of land which included Plot 1706 (now Manor Lodge). Lieutenant Colonel Molyneaux was listed as the Occupier.

The house became the property of Charles William Dare, son of Charles Holcombe Dare, and in 1866 when a re-arrangement of tithes and glebe was made by the Ecclesiastical Commissioners the vicarage was relocated from The Old Vicarage (see above) to Parsonage House. In 1871 the Reverend Christopher Robert Harrison moved into Parsonage House and in 1875 he borrowed the sum of £697 to enlarge and alter the house and built a new wing to house servants. The house continued as the parsonage until 1939 when it was acquired by Mrs Stobart and re-named The Manor House. Later owners during the 1950s were said to have housed a night club in the cellar area.

14. Manor End, The Fosse

This semi-detached wing to the right of the Manor House (see above) is also a *Grade II Listed Building*. It was built as the service wing and integrated into the parsonage house to accommodate the servants who worked for the Reverend Robert Harrison from 1875. This part of the building imitates the period of the Manor House with similar features and a hipped slate roof. The wing was altered to form a separate house in the middle of the 20th century.

15. The Warren, 19 Stoke Road

This *Grade II Listed Building* was built as a farmhouse in the 17th century and enlarged to form a brewery and larger dwelling in the 18th century. The original farmhouse fronts the road and a two-bay wing was added at the north-east end in the early-19th century with sash windows and panelled reveals. The house is built of Blue Lias random rubble stone, with a brick parapet and brick surrounds to window openings with a slate roof and brick stacks at the gable ends. The brewery is of random rubble and brick with four bays and three storeys diminishing to two and one-and-a-half storeys at the west end, with mixed fenestration including small round or oeil-de-boeuf style windows under the roof in the gable end. The original kitchen of the house has a wealth of early features: a stick stair, plank doors with early hinges and a fireplace with large chamfered lintel with a small cupboard set in the south wall.

The building marked in the position of the present house on the 1840 *Tithe Map of North Curry* is numbered 1710, and is described in the *Schedule* as follows:

1710 House, Garden, Bartons with 3 rood and 32 perch of land

Landowner	*John Andrews*	*Lessee of the DCW*
Occupier	*Eli Bellringer*	

In the 1863 *Rate Schedule* for North Curry John Read is listed as the Landowner (DCW) and Occupier.

It has been suggested that the building housing the brewery was altered and later used in connection with corn milling. The 1861 *Census Return* lists John Read, aged 50 and residing in Stoke Road, as a miller and farmer. The 1861 *Kelly's Trade Directory* lists Andrews and Read as corn millers of North Curry Steam Mills. The building housed a school at the beginning of the 20th century.

16. Pury House, 24 Stoke Road

This former farmhouse was probably built in the late-16th century or early-17th century and had originally three bays and a cross-passage with rubble walls. In the 18th century alterations were made to the early house. Evidence suggests that a fireplace was removed from the hall and a passage inserted to access the inner room. In line with this presumed fireplace are mural cupboards with raised panel doors of 18th century date, possibly in the position of an earlier stair. Additions were made at the north-east end and at the front. The inner room has an inserted fireplace. The third room was a kitchen with a cross-passage; the partition has been removed. A cross beam with deep chamfers and step and runout stops is possibly of late medieval date, and a hearth shows a blocked cloam or clay oven together with a brick-lined oven with a tunnel beneath, showing that it was inserted into a former curing chamber. Most windows are modern but there is a wooden mullioned window at the rear. The roof has four trusses with mortice and tenon apex joints, the collars halved and nailed and the purlins trenched. The roof is of double Roman tiles.

Outside there are a number of former farm buildings, one of which is a barn with evidence of a throughway for wagons and a wooden threshing floor. Although the walls are rebuilt there is evidence of a cruck post and truss structure typical of medieval barns of the local area. A sunken animal watering pond has been uncovered in the farmyard with sloped, stepped access. There is also evidence of a stone foundation wall and post holes of another dwelling or barn fronting the road to the north, which may have been part of this large, busy former farm.

There is a building marked in the position of Pury House on the 1787 DCW *Survey Map of the Manor of North Curry*, numbered 14. In the *Schedule* John Baynham is listed as the Copyholder of a house with 2 acres 1 rood and 33 perch of land.

William Wescombe, yeoman of North Curry, attended a Court Baron on 23rd July 1828, and was awarded the copyhold tenancy of one dwelling house, outhouses, garden, pastures and meadows amounting to 15 acres of land. A reversionary grant was made for a sum of money for the term of the lives of three of his children - Robert, Mary and Louisa - and his wife Sarah. He was to pay a yearly rent of four shillings and was subject to a heriot fine or a money payment of up to £3.0s.0d with the lords retaining the mineral and timber rights of the land.

The building marked in the position of the present house on the 1840 *Tithe Map of North Curry* is numbered 1727 and is described in the *Schedule* as follows:

1727 House, Garden, Barton, Outbuildings with 1 acre and 6 perch of land

Landowner and Occupier	*William Wescombe*	*Lessee of the DCW*

In the 1863 *Rate Schedule* for North Curry Sarah Wescombe is listed as the Landowner (DCW) with William Elson Wescombe listed as the Occupier.

17. Moredon, off Stoke Road

As mentioned on page 16 the name Moredon can be linked to a Roman origin when it could possibly have been the site of a Roman camp called *Moridunum.* The field-name of a meadow near to Moredon called *Casters or Castor Mead* has a connection with the Roman word *castra* meaning a camp or fortified place. The driveways to Moredon are very deep with high banks on both sides, and it is imagined that heavy Roman chariots helped to create the depth as they trundled to their camp at the top of the promontory where Moredon now stands. It has also been suggested that Edward the Confessor and later King John established a hunting lodge on the hill overlooking the moorland at Moredon when they were hunting visitors to the local royal forests of Neroche, North Petherton, Selwood, Mendip and Exmoor. After the Bishop of Bath and the Church of St Andrew in Wells acquired the Manor of North Curry the lands of Moredon were often mentioned in Wells charters and manuscripts.

In 1247 Adam and Robert de Meridon were mentioned in connection with land called Meridon. In 1233 it is recorded that *Ascelina late wife of Adam de Meridon* held land in *Meridone.* In 1263 a land exchange agreement mentions a meadow called *Meridonesmede.* In the list of *Customs of the Manor* for tenants of North Curry in 1314 *Muriden* is a large separate area with its tenants allowed certain privileges with *John de Muridene* instructed to serve as Reeve.

The description given by Ekwall for *Morden* is *hill in the fens* and Dr Michael Costen of Bristol University gives the meaning for *Meridonesmede* as merry, cheerful hill.

The following extract from the *Calendar of the Manuscripts of the Dean and Chapter of Wells* in 1633 leads us to question whether this lease refers to Moredon.

1633 October 23
Lease to Sir William Portman of Orchard, c. Somerset, for three lives of the capital mansion house of the manor of North Curry, and the barns called North Curry Barns, and all tithes of "sheffe corne" and grain within the Parish of North Curry, certain lands "the herbadge", mastadge and pannadge" of Knapp Wood, and a culverhowse" there and a barn and the tithes of "sheffe corne" and grain in Westhatch; excepted and reserved all perquisites of courts, fines, heriots etc., and the advowson of the vicarage of North Curry; rent £48.19s.10d. Lessee covenants to deliver yearly to the reeve of North Curry so much wheat and other corn for the feast of Christmas as the said Sir William Portman or Sir John Portman, his father, or any farmers of the said barns have used to deliver, and any wheat and other corn not used at the feast is to be handed to the d/c and their servant; to find yearly for the officers of the d/c sufficient bread, meat and drink, for two visitations, two law-days and one quarter court, "tarryeing at every of the said visitacions and lawdaies the space of fower daies, and at the said quarter court by the space of three daies, that is to say, two honest and sufficient messes of meate for the said officers and their servauntes and retinew at every meale during the dayes aforesaid, and alsoe honest and sufficient lodginges for the steward of the said d/c, and six other persons, and also to finde unto the grand jury sufficient meate and drinke for one dynner onely; and to give in reward amongst the servauntes of the steward yearly at every of the said lawdaies and court 2s.; and alsoe to find sufficient stable roome, hay, litter and provinder for seaven horses, or more not to exceede the number of tenn horses". On default of such entertainment and provision for the officers, the lessee shall forfeit £6.13s.4d; also to repair all buildings, etc. and the chancel of the parish church of Northcurry, for which he may cut "grosse timber" and take sufficient frith, hedgeboote and gateboote, and the he shall be allowed an annuity of £6.13s.4d.
MSS Wells Liber Ruber II Folio 151d

In 1666 a *Land Tax Return* states that Robert Hill was the Copyholder of the Moredon building and farm and that Sir William Portman held the surrounding land, but in 1674 there is another reference in the *Calendar of the Manuscripts of the Dean and Chapter of Wells* as follows:

1674 January 19
Lease to William Portman of Orchard, knight and bart., for three lives, of the capital messuage or mansion house of Northcurry, etc. rent £48.19s.10d.
MSS Wells Liber Ruber II

Robert Hooper is listed as leasing the property in 1708 and 1710 and Henry Portman is listed as holding the land from 1710 and William Portman until c.1782.

A stone set into the south wall of Moredon bears the date 1697, and it could be assumed that this is the date of the building of the house in its present form, which may have replaced a much older one. The lands of Moredon have been cultivated for generations, certainly from c.1200, and the vineyard mentioned in the *Domesday Survey* of 1066 has lately been attributed to a site on a western slope within the Moredon boundary. Also on the western side of Moredon was a site where sandstone was quarried in early days and much of this North Curry sandstone was used in the building of North Curry Parish Church and other buildings in the parish.

According to John Collinson writing in his *The History and Antiquities of the County of Somerset* in 1791, Moredon is a separate tithing or hamlet, and he refers to *Moordon* or *Moordown* as the property of Henry William Portman.

There are buildings marked in the position of Moredon on the 1787 DCW *Survey Map of the Manor of North Curry* and the plot is numbered 468. In the *Schedule* it is described as a House etc. with 3 acres, 3 rood and 1 perch of land with Henry Hooper listed as the Leaseholder. However two other houses are listed in the same area also leased to Henry Hooper. One is described as *Old House* with 1 acre, 3 rood and 17 perch of land and the other house described as *Moordon* with 2 acres and 1 rood of land.

In 1810 Robert Hooper Scott is described as the owner and occupier of Moredon and Fields. When he died in 1829 his nephew John Scott Gould became the owner and occupied the house from 1831.

The building marked in the position of the present house on the 1840 *Tithe Map of North Curry* is numbered 1686 and is described in the *Schedule* as follows:

1686 Moredon House, Garden, Buildings etc. with 2 acres and 17 perch of land

Landowner and Occupier	*John Scott Gould*	*Lessee of the DCW*

In the 1863 *Rate Schedule* for North Curry Sophia Gould is listed as the Landowner (DCW) and Occupier of a House, Garden, Lawn, Outbuildings etc. amounting to 4 acres and 6 perch. Sophia Gould née Barrett was John Scott Gould's wife and when he died in 1846 she continued to live at Moredon until her death.

Major William Barrett was the nephew of Sophia Gould and the son of her younger brother George Barrett, and he moved into Moredon in 1871 on the death of his aunt. He made additions and alterations to the house, adding a conservatory and billiard room, a 'tin house with a stage' and an east wing among others.

Donald Phillips, who was the great grandson of George Barrett, lived at Moredon until 1985. He described the house as having had 16 bedrooms and nursery, drawing room, hall, butler's pantry, kitchen behind green baize door, game larder, ordinary pantry, scullery, flower arranging room, washing room, shoe cleaning and lamp room. There was no electricity in the house until the 1960s and acetylene gas and candles supplied lighting. However the greenhouses were heated by coke boilers and ran continuously. In 1972 a fire caused substantial damage to the coach house, stables and some other outbuildings. The back drive to Moredon was improved when it was used to drive to the railway at Durston Station. Life at Moredon c.1890 is shown in Plate xvi.

18. Thatcher's, White Street

This *Grade II Listed Building* was originally built in the early-16th century as a jointed cruck frame three-bay house with an end smoke bay. There are two trusses of a jointed cruck frame and large rectangular panels of wattle and daub in the roof at the south-east end of 16th century date. A large beam flush to the south-east gable end spanned a large deep hearth indicating that this was the position of a smoke bay. In the 17th century the house was rebuilt to form three rooms with a cross-passage. A central fireplace was inserted and the smoke bay blocked. In the mid-17th century the central fireplace was removed and gable-end fireplaces were inserted into the gable ends, the date 1637 is marked on the south-east end fireplace confirming this. Also at this time the walls were raised, and lean-tos inserted along the back with stairs inserted to an upper floor. 17th century axial ceiling beams with scroll stops to plain chamfers are evidence of the insertion of this upper floor. The front wall was rebuilt with large squared blocks of Blue Lias stone to form two storeys. A two-bay brick cottage was attached at the rear. The thatched roof with brick stacks was extended in a long catslide over the one-and-a-half storey lean-tos at the back. The walls are a mixture of squared Blue Lias stone and red sandstone random rubble with a cob wall in one outshut. The windows are 18th century style iron casement with some re-used fittings. In the 20th century further rebuilding was undertaken with gable ends renewed and some roof trusses replaced, and two buttresses were built to contain outer walls. There is much evidence of other early features: chamfered beams with step and run-out stops, tenoned collars, trenched purlins in the roof and chamfered cambered doorways with planked doors. Formerly known as Clarke's Farm there is a barn incorporating a loading bay and cart shed with a double Roman tiled roof near to the farmhouse probably built in the late-18th century.

During the period from 1700 to 1711 Richard White together with Ann White and John Wyn are all listed in the *List of North Curry Tennants* paying land tax. In 1712 Mr John Wyn is listed paying tax of £1.1s.2d for *Whites*. In 1766 Samson Derham is listed as the occupier and between 1781 and 1793 Sarah Derham is listed as the copyholder with Hugh Foster as the occupier paying tax of £1.10s.10d.

There is a building marked in the position of Thatcher's on the 1787 DCW *Survey Map of the Manor of North Curry*, numbered 112. In the *Schedule* Sarah Derham is listed as the Copyholder of a cottage with 1 acre and 1 rood of land.

The building marked in the position of the present house on the 1840 *Tithe Map of North Curry* is numbered 1735 and is described in the 1840 *Schedule* and in the 1863 *Rate Schedule* for North Curry as follows:

1735 House, Garden, Barton & Outbuildings with 3 rood and 5 perch of land

Landowner	*Anna Long*	*Lessee of the DCW*
Occupier	*William Hurman*	

19. Manor Farm, off Stoke Road

This farmhouse, a *Grade II* Listed Building*, is one of the oldest substantial buildings in North Curry and its construction can be fairly accurately dated to 1570. Part of the left gable end and adjoining left-hand bay on the façade was possibly rebuilt when the house was re-roofed c.1840. It is built of coursed Blue Lias stone, partially rendered, with Hamstone dressings and a shallow-pitched slate roof. There are overhanging eaves with a soffit board on the façade, and coped verges on the left gable end. It has brick stacks at the gable ends and to the right of the cross-passage.

The original plan of the house is of three cells and a cross-passage having a corridor running along the back. This corridor is an unusual early feature. There is an attached agricultural wing to the rear. The present house is of two storeys with five bays. On the front elevation are a number of original ovulu moulded mullion windows which are mostly painted and all under hoodmoulds, one of which is dated 1570. If this date is correct this is a very early example in Somerset. There are relieving arches over the three of the ground-floor windows. In the right gable-end wall there is a small stair window.

The front entrance is through an early door surrounded by a moulded Tudor arch head doorway with moulded jambs and a hoodmould. There is also a relieving arch above this doorway together with a tablet with an unidentified coat of arms bearing the initials *W.V.* It has been suggested that this coat of arms belongs to the Sealy family.

On the rear elevation there is an unpainted stone ovulu moulded window under a hoodmould. This is flanked on the right by a moulded Tudor arch head doorway with moulded jambs to the rear of the cross-passage. To the left is a chamfered stone Tudor arch head doorway with an early door to the hall corridor. Internally a chamfered depressed Tudor arch head wooden doorframe leads to the hall. The inner room (kitchen) has a large chamfered lintel to the fireplace. At the lower end is a fine Hamstone moulded Tudor arch head chimney piece with spandrels.

A watercolour of 1850 by William Walter Wheatley (1811-1885) in the Somerset Archaeological and Natural History Society's Braikenridge Collection, shows different fenestration with the 19th century roof in situ.

A barn and cartshed about 10 metres west of the farmhouse is also a *Grade II Listed Building*. This threshing barn was built of Blue Lias stone with a hipped double Roman clay tiled roof. The plan is 'L'-shaped with three bays and the date was probably late-18th century.

There is a building marked in the position of Manor Farm on the 1787 DCW *Survey Map of the Manor of North Curry*, numbered 232. In the *Schedule* Jonathan Loscombe is listed as the Copyholder with 1 acre and 9 perch of land.

The building marked in the position of the present house on the 1840 *Tithe Map of North Curry* is numbered 1487 and is described in the *Schedule* as follows:

1487 House, Garden, Buildings etc. with 3 rood and 31 perch of land

Landowner and Occupier	*Simon Meade*	*Lessee under the DCW*

In the 1863 *Rate Schedule* for North Curry Simon Meade is listed as the Landowner (DCW), with George Crease listed as the Occupier. From the early-20th century the Coate family has occupied the farm.

20. Fosse End and Hayes Cottage, 14 & 15 Stoke Road

This building has been extensively rebuilt and is now divided into two dwellings. The original house has a jointed cruck structure, now much altered with the upper part of the house totally removed. There are insufficient remains of the structure to be certain of the exact date, but it was probably built as a yeoman's house in 16th century as a two-bay cruck frame open hall house. It was originally built with cob walls, which have been partly replaced with brick. The roof is thatched and the windows modern although there remains one window with mullion bars. The fireplace and chimney were inserted into the open hall later and this room also has a six-panel framed ceiling. The large fireplace has a small brick oven to one side. Behind the fireplace two half beams show this area to have been a cross-passage. The room to the south-west of this is totally rebuilt with no evidence of the original structure remaining, but bay lengths suggest the original house could have extended this far. Three crucks survive in part, one of which is visible in the middle truss of the house. The house north-east of the hall is re-fronted in brick and divided into three rooms. The end room was made into a kitchen in late-16th century or 17th century with a fireplace at the gable end. At one side of this was a dog-leg stairway and on the other the remains of a curing chamber which at one time had an oven inserted into it. Part of the masonry of this chamber is re-used moulded stone, its origin unknown. The rooms between the hall and the old kitchen may have been a buttery. The house may also have extended beyond the old kitchen. Over the centuries the house has undergone many alterations and has often been divided to form two dwellings, as is the case at the present time.

The *Rent Rolls* for the Manor of North Curry for the period 1528 to 1771 list taxpayers for the house as follows:

1528 - Leonard Crease,
1714-1733 - J. Crease (John)
1733 - Henry Crease
1771 - William Crease.

The *Court Rolls* from 1714 to 1810 list tenants in the east part of the house (Fosse End) as James Dibben and his sisters Sarah and Mary in 1714, reverting to Sarah Dibben in 1778, to William Crease in 1799, and to James Crease in 1810. It is described as *....containing one kitchen and Beer* *cellar, two chambers over the kitchen, two stables and wellhouse, one pigstye, one ox stall and orchard….*

There is a building marked in the position of Fosse End and Hayes Cottage on the 1787 DCW *Survey Map of the Manor of North Curry,* numbered 64 and 65. In the *Schedule* William Creese (sic) is listed as the Copyholder of two half-houses etc. with 1 rood and 24 perch and 1 rood 39 perch of land each.

The building marked in the position of Fosse End on the 1840 *Tithe Map of North Curry* is numbered 1515 and is described in *the Schedule* as follows:

1515 House and Garden, Barton etc. with 1 rood and 17 perch of land

Landowner	*Alexander Crease*	*Lessee of the DCW*
Occupier	*James Willicombe*	

In the 1863 *Rate Schedule* for North Curry John Horsey Nicholls is listed as the Landowner, with George Dinham listed as the Occupier.

The building marked in the position of Hayes Cottage on the 1840 *Tithe Map of North Curry* is numbered 1532 and is described in the *Schedule* as follows:

1532 House and Garden with 1 rood of land

Landowner and Occupier	*James Crease*	*Lessee of the DCW*

In the 1863 *Rate Schedule* for North Curry William Crease is listed as the Landowner (DCW), with Avice Crease listed as the Occupier.

21. Angel House, Stoke Road

This is an 18th century house built in brick, which may have replaced a much earlier 16th or 17th century house. The evidence of earlier brickwork at the back of the house suggests an earlier date. The plan of the house has a three-room cross-passage front, which is repeated in a one-and-a-half storey lean-to along the back. The front wall of the house is red brick in Flemish bond, but the west gable is one metre thick and roughcast. The front wall is bonded with the adjoining house and has a stone plinth. The tiled roof is tusk tenoned and the west gable is coped. The stack is of cob. Much internal re-modelling has been done to the house. Passage walls were removed, which facilitated a bar area when the building was used as an inn, and only plastered beams remain. Stairs rise in the lean-to but the position of the original stairway is unclear. Many early features remain: ceiling beams have narrow chamfers and scroll stops and the hall has a plain chamfered wooden lintel to the fireplace. Another fireplace has a depressed four-centred wooden lintel on stone sides with moulded ovolo and scroll stops.

The dwelling was formerly a Commercial Inn and Posting House and was mentioned as *a common ale house* in 1736. It appears on the Map and Survey of 1773 of the estates of Henry William Portman (see page 204) where it is described as *The Angel Inn.* It remained a public house until 1985.

There is a building marked in the position of Angel House on the 1787 DCW *Survey Map of the Manor of North Curry,* numbered 264. In the *Schedule* Thomas Nash is listed as the Copyholder of a House etc. with 3 rood and 35 perch of land.

The building marked in the position of the present house on the 1840 *Tithe Map of North Curry* is numbered 1506 and is described in the *Schedule* as follows:

1506 Angel Inn, Garden, Outbuildings etc. with 38 perch of land

Landowner	*Sarah Millett Foster*	*Freehold*
Occupier	*David Richards*	

In the 1863 *Rate Schedule* for North Curry Sarah Millett Foster is listed as the Landowner with 1 acre 1 rood and 6 perch of land, with Alice Dyer listed as the Occupier.

The Angel Inn was occupied by various landlords from 1840 - Jacob Foster (1850), James Hugh Foster (1861), William Layland (1866), James French Edwards (1872), Frances Georgiana Edwards (1897), Frederick Edwards (1902), Priscilla Durman (1914), Archibald Duke (1923), Leonard Edwards (1935), Mr Smitheram (c.1936), Harry Trim Snr (1937), Harry Trim Jnr and Freda Trim (1953-1979). Between 1979 and 1985 The Angel Inn was run as a free house by various owners until it became a private house in 1985.

22. The Old Malthouse, 3 Stoke Road

The building known as The Old Malthouse comprises a house, probably formerly a farmhouse together with another building believed to be a former malthouse. The house was possibly originally built in the late-17th century as a thatched farmhouse mainly in brick and cob with a central chimney, and a service lean-to or outshut at the back. It is probably one of the oldest houses in North Curry that was built using brick.

In the principal room there is a large inglenook fireplace with very little evidence to date it. Stairs may well have risen beside this where the ceiling timbers show an opening. A large lamb's tongue stop chamfered elm beam rests on the window lintel in this room. These features are consistent with a 17th century dwelling. It is said that the bow window was inserted into this room in Victorian times. The original outshut has been rebuilt to extend the house along the back.

There are the remains of a bread oven on the back wall of the original house in the extension to the side of the inglenook, which has a small brick arch with a Hamstone opening to the 'oven'. This could have been converted from the original smoking chamber accessed from the main fireplace. The back of this secondary fireplace shows slate and brick in a herringbone pattern. It is possible this oven was used for drying corn and used to supplement part of the malting process, which would account for the position of such a large oven with an opening possibly out into the yard. Lime putty and ash were found during previous building work, as was a lime and reed ceiling in the main room of the house.

In 1720 the combined dwelling was listed as a malthouse. It is possible that at that time the malting house with a number of bays was added to the original farmhouse. This was built of cut Blue Lias stone with massive timber beams across at wall plate height, but they have no stops. The truss at the original house end of the building is possibly of 17th century origin with a number of original posts with principal beams cut to accommodate the 'new' building. A previous occupier reports the building to have been of three floors, and describes evidence of an early stone kiln floor with later 19th century clay kiln base tiles. This building was later converted to house a wheelwright and carriage works, at which time a larger opening was made out to the road to allow access for vehicles into the old malthouse building. It is known that wedding and funeral cars were kept there at one time.

Another outbuilding or stabling was also possibly built opposite the side of the malting house at the back to form a 'U' shape building around a courtyard. The 1787 DCW *Survey Map of the Manor of North Curry* shows the shape of this building. This building was later demolished with only a small outbuilding remaining now within the neighbouring curtilage.

The house and malthouse are covered with clay pantiles, the malthouse tiles are possibly the original ones, but the tiles on the main house are more recent and possibly replaced a thatched roof and incorporated the outshut into the main house. The gable end wall is painted and is mainly brick with some cut Blue Lias stone protruding, under which is a rubble plinth. The front elevation of the house shows a string course in the brickwork at the bottom of the window level. The brickwork has been painted. The windows have been replaced in recent years and it can be assumed they replaced casement windows and the already mentioned Victorian bow window of the main bay.

Research using *Court Rolls* and other early documents shows that Anthony Coggan was the occupier when the house was listed as a malthouse in 1720, with the title transferring to Thomas Nash later. In 1787 Richard Franklyn is mentioned as a Copyholder with his wife Hannah. In 1800 James Body and in 1807 William Brewere were both listed as maltsters living there. They were succeeded by Richard Ludwell Long followed in 1820 by M. Perratt. It is known the maltster at The Old Brewery in North Curry after 1840 was named Perratt. This could indicate that the malthouse moved from this location to The Old Brewery site at that time.

There is a building marked in the position of The Old Malthouse on the 1787 DCW Survey *Map of the Manor of North Curry,* numbered 152. In the *Schedule* Richard Franklyn is listed as the Copyholder with 3 rood and 36 perch of land.

The building marked in the position of The Old Malthouse on the 1840 *Tithe Map of North Curry* is numbered 1505a and in the *Schedule* it is described as follows:

1505a House, Garden, Malthouse etc. with 1 rood and 5 perch of land
Landowner *Anna Long* *Lessee of the DCW*
Occupier *James Andrews*

In the 1863 *Rate Schedule* for North Curry Charles Stacey is listed as the Landowner (DCW) and Occupier of a House, Garden and Orchard with land amounting to 2 rood and 21 perch.

23. Greenway Farmhouse, 27 Greenway

This *Grade II Listed Building* was originally a two-roomed one-and-a-half storeyed cottage built c.1600 of cob with a thatched roof. The larger room at the north-west end was heated by a gable fireplace. In the 18th century a brick-walled third room was added at the south end together with a rear wing kitchen with a gable fireplace to form an L-plan. Three lean-tos were added - one in the angle of the 'L'-plan, one behind the original fireplace and one beside the kitchen wing. The original cob walls were refaced in brick and they sit on a low Lias rubble plinth. There are eyebrow dormer windows with their sills at eaves level, and ground floor casement windows with tapered keystones in the lintels. The original site of entry and stairs is uncertain and a possible cider cellar is in one of the lean-tos. The interior shows a wide chamfered axial beam in the original larger room with deep step and run-out stops. The thatched roof is hipped on the south side and the rear wing has a roof of pantiles. Brick stacks mark the end of the original building and there is dogtooth moulding in the brickwork of one gable.

The building marked in the position of Greenway Farmhouse on the 1840 *Tithe Map of North Curry* is numbered 1322 and is described in the *Schedule* as follows:

1322 House and Orchard with 1 rood 3 perch of land
Landowner *Thomas Plowman* *Freehold*
Occupier *Ezra Dare*

In the 1863 *Rate Schedule* for North Curry Thomas Plowman is listed as the Landowner (Freehold) with William Dare listed as the Occupier.

24. Thong Farmhouse, West Sedgemoor Road

The house sits centrally upon a slightly elevated island of land on the west edge of West Sedgemoor. The name *thong* appears to have first been used in Saxon times when ownership of land was acquired by enclosing it with strips or thongs cut from a bull's hide. In c. AD450 the British King Vortigern allotted the Isle of Thanet to the brothers Horsa and Hengist who were mercenaries. They built Thong Castle on the site and the name is probably derived from this Saxon custom. Thong Farm with its circular formation could possibly have been named following this theory (see also page 77).

This *Grade II Listed Building* is a two-storey, three-room, cross-passage house with a roof of clay tiles with gabled ends with chimneystacks and a single-storey lean-to range of buildings with a catslide roof along the northern rear side. The building is of stone and has Blue Lias stone horizontal banding to the south front with four window openings on that side. There are plank and muntin screen partitions and Tudor arch door frames, remains of ovolo timber moulded mullion windows and many features suggesting a very early house.

It was originally a 15th century open hall house, open from ground floor to ridge with jointed cruck trusses, although because of the limited amount of smoke blackening there may have been a smoke bay or large smoke hood. Evidence suggests the house had a floored wing and a stair turret and was built entirely of cob.

From c.1600 the house was completely re-built with banded stonework, and the inner room or hall was extended to form a large parlour with a framed ceiling and chamber above, and fireplaces, a stairway and a stack were built. Another fireplace was built with an oven in a room at the other end of the house, which became the kitchen. A corn-drying kiln was built behind this fireplace in a chamber that had stairs to another chamber above.

In the 18th century the house was remodelled to form three rooms with a cross-passage, and re-roofed with tenoned purlins but leaving the jointed crucks and thatch. The single-storey lean-tos and the catslide roof were added when a dairy replaced the original wing, and the attics were made habitable. In the 19th century the parlour and chamber were converted to a cider-house and loft. In the 20th century the south and east front were refenestrated and the walls rendered. The thatch was replaced with double Roman clay tiles.

There is a circular plot shape marked in the position of Thong *Island* on the 1787 DCW *Survey Map of the Manor of North Curry* and the plots are numbered 497 to 501. In the *Schedule* John Pine is listed as the Leaseholder of Thong Farmhouse, orchard and various lands etc. with the house allocated 2 acres 1 rood and 29 perch of land.

The building marked in the position of the present house on the 1840 *Tithe Map of North Curry* is numbered 1404 in the *Schedule* and described as follows:

1404 House, Garden, Barton etc. with 1 acre and 37 perch of land

Landowner	*Charles Howe*	*Lessee under the DCW*
Occupier	*George Marsh*	

In the 1863 *Rate Schedule* for North Curry the Landowner (DCW) is listed as Henry House and the Occupier is listed as Henry Coate. Other members of the Coate family continued to occupy the farm until the beginning of the 20th century when John Henry Kinglake farmed there from 1906 to 1939, followed by Frank Coate.

25. Oldways, Oldway Lane, Wrantage

This is a *Grade II Listed Building* which at the time of a recorded survey in 1992 was a two-storey house of five rooms in line with a thatched roof and roughcast over rubble walls. A catslide roof covered most of the back of the house. The original cottage was of a two room plan with a fireplace and a bread oven, one-and-a-half storeys high, with a catslide roof over an outshut, and was built in the early-17th century. A third room, again with a catslide roof over an outshut at the back, incorporated a fireplace with a stair beside and a scroll-stopped ceiling beam, dating this addition to the 17th century. Further undatable additions provided a fourth room with another fireplace and subsequently a fifth room. There are plain chamfered axial beams with square cut stops in the two original rooms and a fireplace at the east end has a plain chamfered wooden lintel and an oven, while narrow steep stairs replace spiral ones. There are three dormer windows set below eaves level.

The building marked in the position of the present house on the 1840 *Tithe Map of North Curry* is numbered 822a and is described in the *Schedule* as follows:

822a House of two dwellings and garden with 1 rood and 6 perch of land

Landowner	*Thomas Parsons*	*Freehold*
Occupier	*Thomas Parsons and John Murless*	

In the 1863 *Rate Schedule* for North Curry Thomas Parsons is listed as the Landowner and Occupier.

26. Lillesdon Court, Lillesdon

This house is a *Grade II Listed building* which is one of the oldest substantial houses in North Curry. As mentioned earlier in the Chapter evidence suggests there has been a dwelling on the site from the 14th century, and it has been suggested it was the site of the manor court in North Curry. It is recorded that in 1311 Hugh de Bello Campo (Beauchamp) had possession of a seat in Lillesdon and was later granted a chantry chapel building in 1327 (see page 78).

The present house was built in the 16th century and altered in the 18th and 19th centuries. It is constructed of Blue Lias stone with some brick at the south gable end. The four-bay house which stands on the site today is of an F-plan with wings at the rear. The end bay has a stepped buttress. The house has two storeys with attics. The south gable end abuts farm buildings and there is a later kitchen adjoining the south-east corner. The roof is slate with overhanging eaves with decorative bargeboards to the north gable end and has a rebuilt 19th century stack at the south gable end rising from the eaves at the junction with a wing. There are a number of hollow chamfered Hamstone mullioned windows under hoodmoulds, with three in the north gable wall. The house is entered through an open pedimented doorcase with Ionic columns into an entrance hall with a staircase dividing in the first flight giving access to both wings of the house.

In 1790 John Collins of Hatch Court in Hatch Beauchamp was the reputed owner of Lillesdon Court which passed to his second son Henry at his death. It subsequently passed through the family to the Gore-Langtons of Newton Park. Both families were prominent landowners in the area and benefactors to the church in Hatch Beauchamp.

The building marked in the position of the present house on the 1840 *Tithe Map of North Curry* is numbered 482 and is described in the *Schedule* as follows:

482 House, Garden, Barton, Outbuildings etc. with 2 acres 1 rood and 25 perch of Land

Landowner	*Henry Powell Collins, Esq*	*Freehold*
Occupier	*Robert Trent*	

In the 1863 Rate Schedule for North Curry Robert Trent remains as the Occupier but the Landowner is now listed as William Henry Powell Gore-Langton, Esq, MP, who leased it to a series of tenant farmers as follows:

1851 William Dobin farming 365 acres employing 10 labourers
1861 George Coate farming 333 acres employing 9 men and 3 boys
1871 John Day farming 335 acres employing 9 men and 3 boys
1881 John G. Peard farming 328 acres employing 7 men and 3 boys
1891 and 1901 William Hancock is listed as the farmer.

In 1928 the Lillesdon Court Estate, which comprised Lillesdon Court, Lillesdon Green Farm, and Hammonds Farm, together with nine cottages and 175 acres of feeding pastures in West Moor, Curry Moor, Stanmoor and grazing in Sedgemoor extending in total to over 818 acres, was sold as 35 lots. Lillesdon Court with numerous other farm buildings and over 309 acres of land was at that time the residence of Mr B S Hebditch and the family have continued to live and farm there to the present day.

27. Lower Knapp Farm, Knapp

This is a *Grade II* Listed Building* recently re-named Manor Farm. The present house of four bays, with a cross-passage with an outshut to the rear has a long façade of one-and-a-half storeys with wooden casement windows. The upper windows are eyebrow dormers under a thatched roof. This house was originally possibly a 15th century open hall house with yoked apex crucks. These crucks were extended due to the lack of adequately long timbers, and were the forerunners of later jointed crucks. In the 16th century the hall was ceiled and an unusually large fire-hood was inserted. The house was modified in the 17th century to form a typical three bay cross-passage dwelling. A fireplace with a large chamfered bressumer with the date 1636 inscribed, together with a curing chamber, were added to the east gable and the roof was rebuilt at that end. The west gable was demolished and a fourth bay added, and possibly at that time the hall fire-hood was replaced with a fireplace and stack, and the ceiling modified. An outshut or lean-to with a fireplace at the east end was added at the back later.

There is evidence of a full cruck and jointed cruck truss roof with soot blackening on the timbers and the remains of wattle and daub infilling. All thatch, including under-thatch, has been renewed but it is laid on blackened laths. Above the curing chamber there would probably have been a separate outlet for the smoke to escape in the form of a louvre directed by sacking or woven straw matting.

The walls are of squared and coursed local grey sandstone with the west gable wall of thick cob and the stacks of brick. There are cambered moulded framed ceilings, stud and plank screens and the remains of scroll plaster friezes, a fielded panel spice cupboard, and moulded head four-centred arch doorframes, which all indicate a house of significant status in its time.

The house was for many years the farmhouse of a farm of 200 acres. To the west of the house are farm buildings including stables built in the 17th century for up to ten working horses. The house and farm buildings have been extensively restored in recent years.

There is a building marked in the position of Lower Knapp Farm on the 1787 DCW *Survey Map of the Manor of Knap-Fee* and is numbered 146. In the *Schedule* Samuel Foster is listed as the copyholder of a House etc. with 1 acre and 27 perch of land.

There is evidence to suggest that Lower Knapp Farm was the meeting place for Methodists before the Wesleyan Chapel was built in North Curry (see page 113).

The building marked in the position of the present house on the 1840 *Tithe Map of North Curry* is numbered 172 and is described in the *Schedule* and in the 1863 *Rate Schedule* for North Curry as follows:

172 House, Garden, Barton etc. with 2 rood and 28 perch of land
Landowner and Occupier *John Lockyer* *Lessee under the DCW*

During the first half of the 20th century the Mitchem family followed later in the 1950s by the Foster family resided and farmed at Lower Knapp Farm.

28. The Rising Sun, Haymoor End, Knapp

This is a *Grade II Listed Building* with evidence to suggest that its origins are c.1500. It was originally possibly a longhouse with animal byre or built as an open hall house. It was rebuilt in the 16th century when a fireplace was inserted, with a further re-build in the 17th century. This building stands at the foot of a steep hill high above the road at the north end. It has a typical plan of three bays and a cross-passage with various later additions at the back and south end, and has a raking buttress to the façade. The present two-storey house has a double Roman tiled roof and coursed rubble walls which were raised in brick when it was re-roofed with substantial trusses with tusk-tenoned purlins, possibly in the mid-18th century. A date stone of 1746 is set high in the north gable. The wooden doors and casement windows are late replacements. The north gable end, the front wall as far as the entrance of the cross-passage, and the back of the hall stack are set unusually on a plinth.

Between the north outer room and the cross-passage is a stud and panel screen, which has plain chamfered mason-mitred studs with a sill-beam on a stone base. This room was possibly rebuilt in the 17th century as a kitchen, before which it might have been the animal byre of a long house. The hearth in this outer room has a blocked hearth tunnel indicating a former curing chamber, now a plain recess. There is also a brick-lined oven with an iron door on the right. Stairs in this room are of a later date. The hall fireplace backing onto the cross-passage and the 12-panel compartment ceiling have moulded chamfers of high quality that suggest a date of early-16th century. The date of the fireplace is uncertain due to the loss of the original roof, but the hall was evidently open, its ceiling inserted. There is evidence of two doors in the stud and plank screen in the inner room south of the hall, one of which would once have given access to stairs to an overhead solar, the other through to the hall. Although this room has been much altered the walls are very thick, and together with the plain chamfered studs, flat stops of the screen and the remains of a sill-beam indicate a very early building not later than c.1500.

In contrast to the high quality of the ceiling and fireplace in the hall, the very narrow small steep spiral stairs that rise to the left of the fireplace in the hall, and not as is more usual beside the cross-passage door, are a puzzle. These stairs are now blocked. The door between the cross-passage and the hall is plain chamfered and mason mitred to a shallow peaked head and indicates a later date. The house, which was used as a beerhouse or inn from c.1850, was later converted to a fully licensed public house from 1965. It has recently reverted to a private dwelling.

The building marked in the position of the present house on the 1840 *Tithe Map of North Curry* is numbered 136 and is described in the *Schedule* as follows:

136 House, Garden, Buildings etc with 3 rood and 37 perch of land.
Landowner and Occupier *John Smith* *Lessee under the DCW*

In the 1863 *Rate Schedule* for North Curry Hugh Foster, who was a farmer and beer retailer, is listed as the Landowner (DCW) and Occupier. He was followed by John Woodman, a withy merchant and beer retailer in 1875 and later by others who were listed as innkeepers in the North Curry *Census Returns.*

29. Knapp Farm, Knapp

This *Grade II Listed Building,* originally a medieval hall house, retains no early external features but has many exceptionally high-quality internal carpentry details and the use of much Hamstone. It stands close to an equally superior house, Bird's Farm (see below), probably built at about the same time. Knapp Farm lies 30 metres above sea level on a spur of higher ground overlooking the lower reaches of the River Tone. Before modern drainage this would have been subject to flooding, but the siting of the house on this spot would have provided good arable land and pasture on the high ground in winter, and summer pasture on the lower ground in the summer.

The plan of the present house is of two rooms separated by a cross-passage with an added wing to the rear at the north end. The room south of the passage is the hall of a medieval house built possibly in the late-15th century, and entered through an elliptical-headed stone doorway with double ogee moulding. The pattern of this moulding is seen on the wooden lintel of the fireplace in this room. On a stone beside the door is a deeply cut cross which if seen on a church wall would be regarded as a Consecration Cross. Maybe this house was built on the site of an early chantry chapel and the doorway originates from that time. This room has a six-panel hollow chamfered and cambered ceiling. The west wall has been rebuilt and the boundary beam is about one foot clear of the wall suggesting a third room has been demolished; this would have been an unusual pattern in medieval times suggesting an important house. In the passage is a plain chamfered half beam against the hall stack with step and run-out stops, and a stud and panel screen to the north side has 12 panels. The doorway into the outer room has been re-sited to accommodate a later stairway.

This outer room has a nine-panel framed ceiling although slots for joists in the head beam show there was an earlier ceiling. On the east side the boundary beam is missing indicating a rebuild. The framed ceiling and the addition of the wing are alterations to an earlier room of which the gable fireplace is an integral part. The hearth has been reduced in width and the lintel extends through the wall.

The back of the lintel is deeply cut back indicating the presence of a curing chamber before the wing was added. To the right of the hearth is an oven of brick with an iron door. Below this supposed bread oven is another chamber, possibly for the use of drying corn.

The present house is roughcast over rubble and has a double Roman tiled roof. Most of the roof has been rebuilt but there is one surviving early truss. There is evidence of a second early truss now removed. The in-line tenoned purlins are 17th century. There is no evidence of an earlier roof over the hall, leading us to suppose that after early neglect it was repaired and rehabilitated in the 17th century using materials of lesser quality than the original 15th/16th century timber.

In 1733 Benjamin Luxton is listed as the Copyholder with 15 acres of meadow and pasture. There is a building marked in the position of Knapp Farm on the 1787 DCW *Survey Map of the Manor of Knap-Fee,* numbered 27. In the *Schedule* Henry Derham is listed as the Copyholder of a House, Orchard etc. with 2 acres and 19 perch. In a document of 1827 the property was known as *Luxxon's Tenement.*

The building marked in the position of the present house on the 1840 *Tithe Map of North Curry* is numbered 93 and is described in the *Schedule* as follows:

93 House, Garden, Barn, Barton etc. with 1 acre and 6 perch of land.

Landowner and Occupier	*John Durham (sic)*	*Lessee under the DCW*

In the 1863 *Rate Schedule* for North Curry Cuthbert Rodham Morris is listed as the Landowner (DCW) of a House, Garden and Mow Barton, with James Tattle listed as the Occupier. In 1916 *Knapp Farmhouse, Outbuildings, Garden, Orchard, Meadow and Arable lands, occupied by Douglas W. Day,* were sold at auction according to sale particulars.

30. Bird's Farm, Knapp

This *Grade II Listed Building* is a 16th century house, incorporating part of a medieval hall house. The original hall house of unusual tapered plan was built no later than the early-16th century and the east wall and part of an early cruck survive. During the 16th century the hall was ceiled with a chamber above. There has been much rebuilding at different times as evidenced by the varying wall thickness. One wall of cob was replaced later with stone and brick and largely refaced with stone.

To the south is a cross wing of two rooms giving the house an 'L'-shape, and is probably a 16th/17th century remodelling of an earlier upper end of the hall. The larger west room has been divided to make a passage and an extra room. The width of this room is equal to a missing pair of panels of the framed ceiling in the main room, which is now an entrance lobby with modern stairs. A fireplace on the west wall may have been lost with this remodelling when a wall was re-built. An early stair may have been in the angle of the 'L'-Plan indicating the house had an original cross wing. The east room, with a plain chamfered six-panel framed ceiling, has a gable fireplace. To the north is an outer room, which was possibly part of an 18th century phase of re-building and could have been larger than now. There are also lean-tos on the east and north sides of this room.

The six-panel moulded framed ceiling in the hall has tapered side panels to fit the varying width, and the fireplace has a moulded wooden lintel set on moulded timber side posts with a moulded shelf. In the east wall in line with the front of the stack is an upright timber on a horizontal baulk 1.4 metres above the floor, possibly the post of a cruck truss. No roof structure is visible higher up. The door beside the fireplace is in a moulded four-centred wooden frame.

Externally all details are recent, the south and east sides of the wing on the first floor are tile hung, a rare feature in Somerset, otherwise walls are rendered over rubble and cob. The house has a hipped roof of triple Roman tiles and a brick stack, and the windows are casement with an angular oriel dormer extending above eaves level. In the yard is a cob-walled barn 43 centimetres wide internally of five 3.65 metre bays; the six trusses are tenoned jointed crucks with tenoned collars, three rows of trenched purlins and tenoned apex, with some crucks missing. There was also a large wagon shelter, possibly built in the 19th century, with cow stalls to one side and a machinery store to the other. These external buildings have recently been the converted to dwellings.

In the *Court Roll* William Cornish is listed as the Copyholder of 30 acres in 1761. In 1779 the holding reverted to John Sealey, in 1801 to John Bird and Robert Mead, and in 1812 John Bird is listed as the sole Copyholder.

There is a building marked in the position of Bird's Farm on the 1787 DCW *Survey Map of the Manor of North Curry,* numbered 321. In the *Schedule* John Sealy is listed as the Copyholder of a House etc. with 1 acre and 10 perch of land.

The building marked in the position of the present house on the 1840 *Tithe Map of North Curry* is numbered 8 and is described in the *Schedule* as follows:

8 House, Garden, Outbuildings with 3 rood and 31 perch of land.

Landowner	*John Bird*	*Lessee under the DCW*
Occupier	*Samuel Foster*	

In the 1863 *Rate Schedule* for North Curry Mrs Sophia Gould is listed as the Landowner (DCW), with Phocion Edwards listed as the Occupier. In 1919 Bird's Farm was occupied by W D Hembrow and was part of an auction sale of 455 acres sold in 57 lots.

Locations of Notable Houses in North Curry Described in This Chapter

Houses in village centre (map below)

1 The Post Office Stores, 4 Queen Square
2 The Old Bakery, 5 Queen Square
3 Manchester House and 6 Queen Square
4 Flagstones, 23 Queen Square
5 Auster Cottage, 1 Church Road and Linden Cottage, 20 Queen Square
6 The Old Brewery, 19 Queen Square
7 The Old Vicarage, 5 Church Road
8 Calmady House, 6 Church Road
9 Gwyon House, 8 Church Road
10 1 & 2 Church Cottages, off Moor Lane
11 Payne's Farmhouse, 4 Moor Lane
12 Manor Lodge, The Fosse
13 The Manor House, The Fosse
14 Manor End, The Fosse
15 The Warren, 19 Stoke Road
16 Pury House, 24 Stoke Road
18 Thatcher's, White Street
19 Manor Farm, off Stoke Road
20 Fosse End/Hayes Cottage, 14 & 15 Stoke Road
21 Angel House, Stoke Road
22 The Old Malthouse, 3 Stoke Road

Houses on parish outskirts (map opposite)

North Curry
17 Moredon, off Stoke Road
23 Greenway Farmhouse, 27 Greenway

Sedgemoor
24 Thong Farmhouse, West Sedgemoor Road

Wrantage
25 Oldways, Oldway Lane

Lillesdon
26 Lillesdon Court

Knapp
27 Manor Farm (formerly Lower Knapp Farm)
28 The Rising Sun, Haymoor End
29 Knapp Farm
30 Bird's Farm

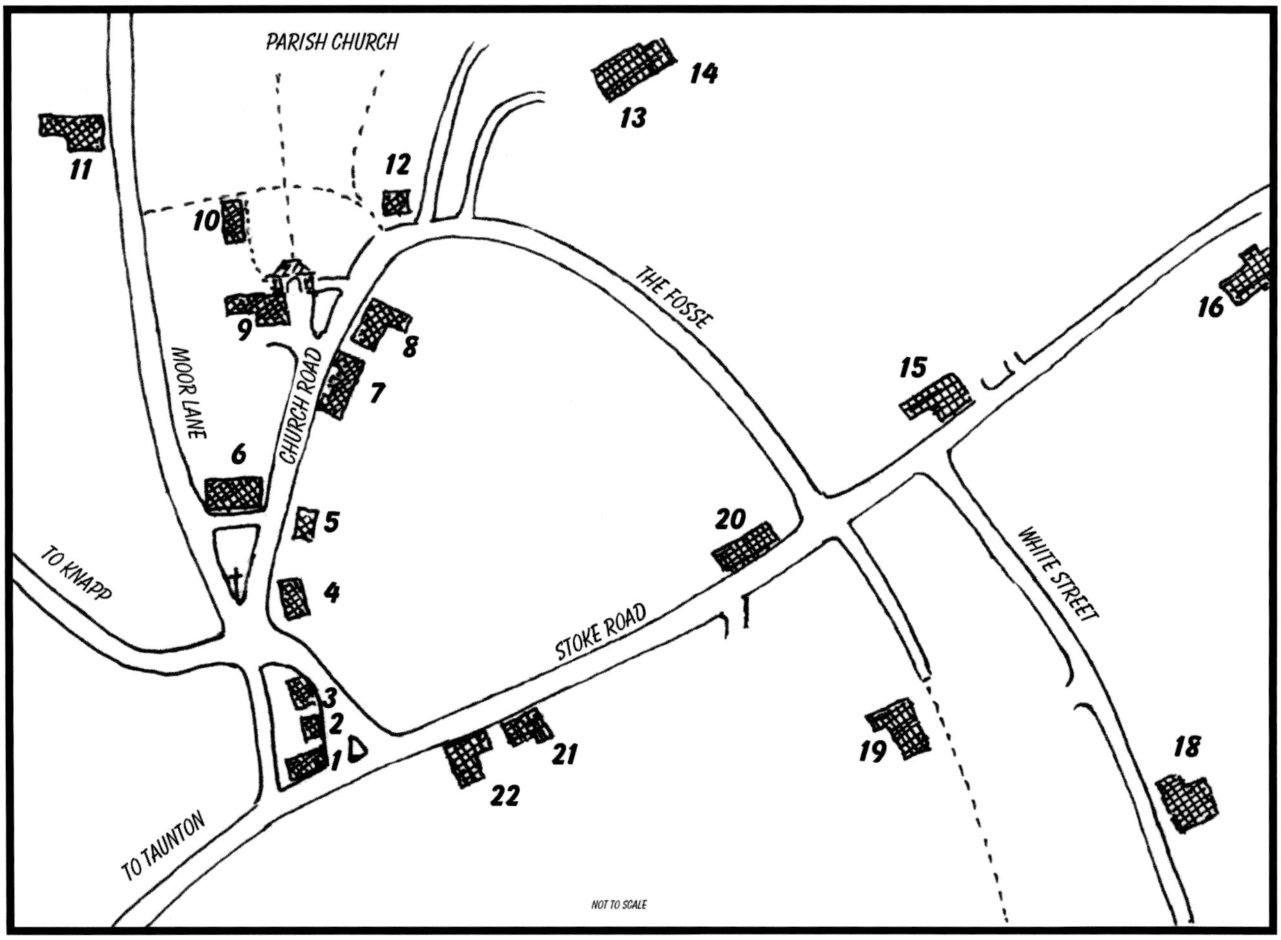

LOCATIONS OF NOTABLE HOUSES IN NORTH CURRY DESCRIBED IN THIS CHAPTER

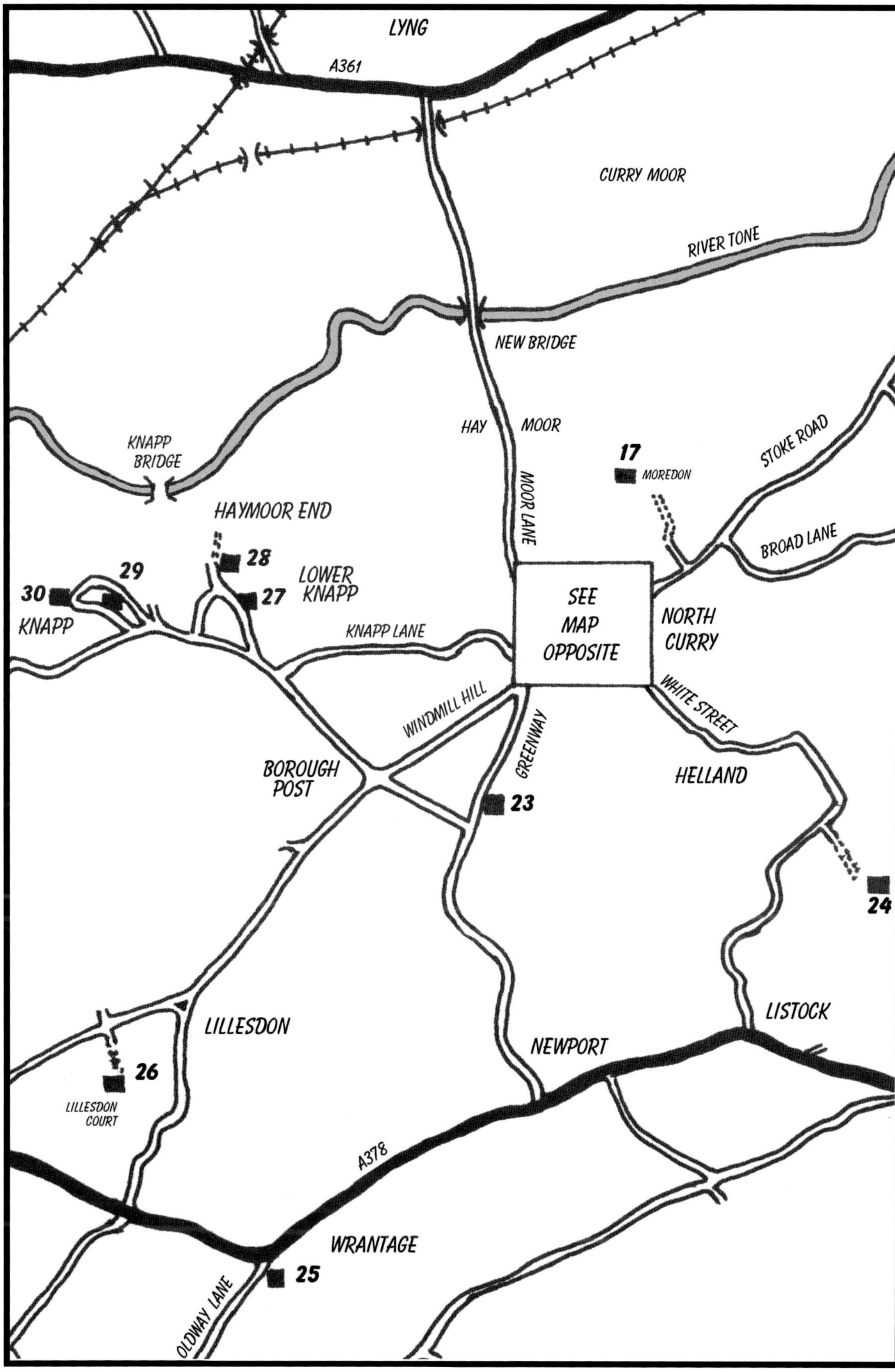

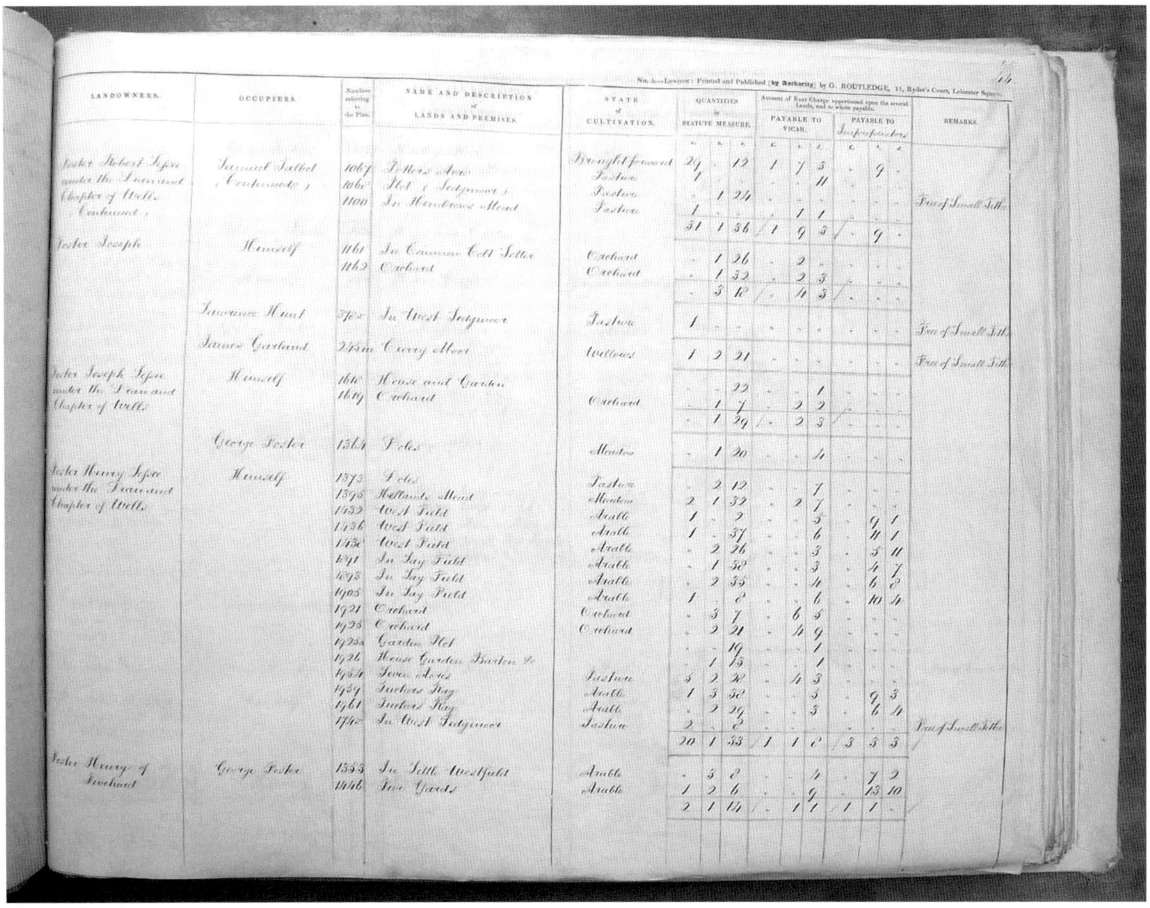

NORTH CURRY TITHE SCHEDULE – PAGE 44 – 1840

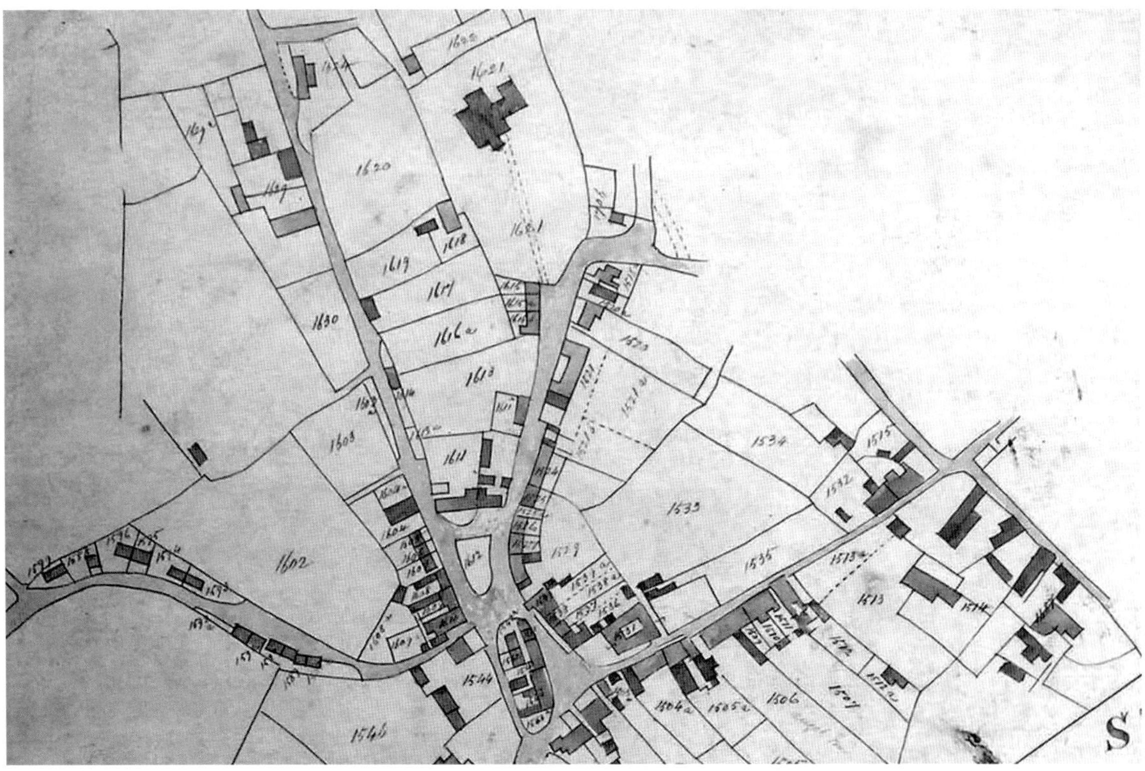

SECTION OF NORTH CURRY TITHE MAP INSET – 1843

Listed Buildings in North Curry

The 67 buildings, structures and monuments in North Curry which are included in the *Statutory List of Buildings of Special Architectural or Historic Interest* for Taunton Deane in the year 2005 are set out below either with a summarised description of their features or reference to a fuller description detailed earlier in the Chapter.

Building	Date of Build	Description	Grade
Broad Lane Farm, Broad Lane	16C	L-Plan Farmhouse. Roughcast over Lias rubble and cob with some Lias exposed. SE gable end rebuilt in brick. Thatched roof with 2 eyebrow dormers. Double Roman tiled NE front. Roof structure possibly original.	II
Church of Saint Peter and Saint Paul	Norman c.1300 c.1400 c.1500	Parish Church of Norman origins, built with local sandstone, Blue Lias, Hamstone dressings, slate roofs. Stained glass windows. c.1300 chancel and nave with steeply sloping roof, transepts and lower stages of tower built. c.1400 upper stage of tower, porch and aisles added and nave walls raised. c.1500 chancel rebuilt, aisles, nave and porch walls raised with new roofs. Octagonal tower raised with parapets added to tower, chancel, nave and aisles. Much renovation and re-modelling in 1881 and many 20C modifications.	I
Churchyard Cross 80m south of chancel	15C& 1891	15C socket and rebuilt in original style later by Edmund Buckle with Buller family names.	II*
Lych-Gate at south entrance to churchyard	1930	Built by W D Caroe in memory of husband and son of Mrs Dorothy Luard, later Phillips. Dressed local sandstone, stone slates to gambrel roof with pierced wooden infill to gable ends. 2 bay roof, north front looking onto churchyard. South front set back buttresses with offsets reaching to eaves, flat wooden lintel on corbelled out wooden uprights. Low wooden double gates with wrought iron cresting. Inscription on tie beam.	II
Crease family monument 27m south of chancel	Early-19C	Crease family monument. Blue Lias, square in plan, ledger topped altar tomb with family inscriptions.	II
Pocock family chest tomb 12m south of transept	Late-18C Early-19C	Family chest tomb. Hamstone, ledger topped, moulded cornice and plinth, raised and fielded panels, pilasters flanking sides divided into 3 panels. Inscription on south side.	II
Unidentified chest tomb in church 30m south of chancel	Late-18C Early-19C	Hamstone, ledger topped moulded cornice and plinth, raised and fielded panels, pilasters flanking sides divided into 3 panels. Top damaged. Illegible inscription.	II
2 Church Road (Greenhaze Cottage) 3 Church Road 4 Church Road (Barham Cottage)		Originally one house and divided later to form terrace of three dwellings of 2 storeys. Original house red brick with steeply pitched slate roof with projecting hipped centre. Overhanging eaves and sash windows. Adjoining cottage to north incorporated with north end of original house to form Barham Cottage which is rendered and has double Roman tiled roof and casement windows.	II
5 Church Road (The Old Vicarage)	16C	Detailed description in main text	II
Stables and wall adjoining 5 Church Road		Blue Lias squared and coursed, wall roughcast. 4 bays. Triple Roman tiled roof.	II
6 Church Road (Calmady House)	Late-18C	Detailed description in main text	II
8 Church Road (Gwyon House)	1858	Detailed description in main text	II

BUILDING	DATE OF BUILD	DESCRIPTION	GRADE
FOSSE COTTAGE, THE FOSSE	16C Mid-19C	Altered and enlarged from original. L-Plan, 2 storeys. Hamstone and Blue Lias, with randomly placed rubble. Tile hung east side, slate roofs, overhanging eaves. Some Tudor arched head mullion windows. Possible site of early church house and village poorhouse.	II
THE MANOR HOUSE, THE FOSSE	15C Early-19C Mid-20C	Detailed description in main text	II
MANOR END, THE FOSSE	Early-19C	Detailed description in main text	II
MANOR LODGE, THE FOSSE	c.1800	Detailed description in main text	II
25 GREENWAY (GREENWAY HOUSE)	E19C	Rendered probably over brick, shallow pitch slate roof, coped verges, moulded cornice. 2 storeys, 3 bays, sash windows. Porch flush with façade with Doric columns.	II
27 GREENWAY (GREENWAY FARMHOUSE)	Late-16C Early-17C Early-18C	Detailed description in main text	II
THONG FARMHOUSE, HELLAND	15C	Detailed description in main text	II
HIGHER HUNTHAM FARMHOUSE, HUNTHAM	16C Early-18C	Farmhouse. Lias rubble, possibly cob faced with brick. Hamstone dressings and thatched roof. Original 3 cell and cross-passage much altered. 2 storeys. Internal large chamfered bressumer to east gable end, possible smoke bay with inserted dogleg stair. Exposed chamfered curved truss, steeply chamfered beams with stops.	II
BARN 40M SW OF HIGHER HUNTHAM FARMHOUSE, HUNTHAM	17C	4 bay threshing barn. North gable end wall rebuilt 1883, south end altered c.1930. Squared and coursed Blue Lias, partially rendered, south end weather boarded. Jambs to double doors formed of lower section of jointed cruck. Interior thought to contain 3 pairs of arch braced trusses with wind bracing.	II
BIRD'S FARMHOUSE, KNAPP	16C	Detailed description in main text	II
KNAPP BRIDGE, KNAPP	c.1820	Road bridge over River Tone. Squared and coursed Blue Lias, Hamstone coping and voussoirs. Single span, semi-circular arch, string course, end pilasters, hump- backed bridge, probably to a design of James Hollinsworth.	II
KNAPP FARMHOUSE, KNAPP	Late-15C 16C	Detailed description in main text	II
LOWER KNAPP FARM (MANOR FARMHOUSE), KNAPP	15C	Detailed description in main text	II*
RISING SUN INN, KNAPP	1500 16C 17C	Detailed description in main text	II
SNELLGROVES, KNAPP	Early-17C Late-18C	Farmhouse. L plan 3 cell and cross-passage with addition covered with slate roof. Red sandstone rubble plinth, cob and rubble faced with brick late-8C. Roof and outshut raised, house re-roofed and doorway inserted mid-19C. 2 storeys with casement windows. Doorcase reputed to have come from secular building. Interior with chamfered lintel to right gable end fireplace with bread oven, remains of scratch moulded screen to cross-passage, exposed joists.	II

BUILDING	DATE OF BUILD	DESCRIPTION	GRADE
LILLESDON COURT, LILLESDON	16C	Possible manor house altered 18C and 19C. Blue Lias rubble, Hamstone dressings, some brick south gable end, slate roofs, overhanging eaves, decorative bargeboards north gable end. F-Plan with wings at rear. 2 storeys with attic, 4 bays. Hollow chamfer Hamstone mullioned windows under hoodmoulds. Open pedimented doorcase with Ionic column. End bay with stepped buttress.	II
LILLESDON FARMHOUSE, LILLESDON	16C 17C	Farmhouse. Original plan 3 cell and cross-passage with cross wing. Local sandstone with thatched roof. Farmhouse. Squared and coursed local grey sandstone, thatched roof hipped to left. Triple Roman tiled outshut addition adjoining slate roofed cross wing. Original possible 3 cell and cross-passage. 15C re-used arched entrance doorway. Interior chamfered lintel to right gable end fireplace with bread oven, remains of scratch moulded screen to cross-passage, exposed joists.	II
METHODIST CHURCH AND RAILINGS, WINDMILL HILL	1833	Rectangular chapel with set back vestry rooms attached. 2 storeys, red brick, hipped and pyramid slate roofs. Extended c.1900 in memory of Ann Mitchell Morris. Cast iron railings fronting graveyard.	II
1 CHURCH COTTAGES, MOOR LANE	Late-18C Early-19C	Detailed description in main text	II
2 CHURCH COTTAGES, MOOR LANE	Late-18C Early-19C	Detailed description in main text	II
4 MOOR LANE (PAYNE'S FARMHOUSE)	Early-17C	Detailed description in main text	II
5 MOOR LANE (THE VICARAGE)	Early-18C	House previously known as Moorland Cottage. Red brick on Lias plinth and Hamstone dressings. 4 bay house subsequently altered and rebuilt to left of butt-joint down centre of façade providing possible new entrance into extended passageway with outshut. Single storey addition on left. Slate roof, coped verges, brick stacks, sash windows.	II
NEWBRIDGE, NEW ROAD	Early-19C	House. Roughcast over rubble, double Roman tiled roof, coped verges. 2 storeys, double pile, 3 bays. Listed primarily for historic interest for its association with the reclamation of the flood plain of the River Tone.	II
NEWPORT COTTAGE , NEWPORT	Late-18C	Small house. Coursed grey limestone rubble, right gable wall rebuilt. Thatch roof, half hipped to right with brick end stack. 2-room plan, 2 storeys. Original plank door, timber lintels over casements. Interior with stop-chamfered 17C reused bressummer over open fireplace with bread oven. Collar truss roof. Original plank door.	II
THE QUEEN'S JUBILEE MEMORIAL	1897	Memorial to Queen Victoria's Diamond Jubilee designed by Edmund Buckle. Hamstone on Blue Lias steps, triangular in plan. Three arched openings with carved Dutch gables with inscriptions, topped by spire. The original railings have been replaced.	II
2 QUEEN SQUARE (BOURNSTREAM) AND OUTBUILDING	Early-19C	House and attached coach house. Roughcast over rubble with hipped slate roof, overhanging eaves. Double pile, 2 storeys, 3 bays, adjoining coach house projecting forward. Sash windows.	II

BUILDING	DATE OF BUILD	DESCRIPTION	GRADE
5 QUEEN SQUARE (THE OLD BAKERY)	Early-19C	Detailed description in main text	II
7 QUEEN SQUARE	17C	Semi-detached cottage. 2 single-cell dwellings or shop with dwelling right. Rendered over rubble, pantile roof, triple Roman tiles at rear. Roof raised and refenestrated early-19C. Possible site of medieval prison or lock-up.	II
10 QUEEN SQUARE (WHATLEY HOUSE)	Early-19C	House. Brick, rubble plinth, roof of Bridgwater tiles and pantiles. Double pile, 3 bays, 2 storeys over basement. Sash windows. Entrance by brick stairway to original door and furniture in pedimented doorcase.	II
19 QUEEN SQUARE (THE OLD BREWERY) AND OUTBUILDINGS	Late-17C	Detailed description in main text	II
20 QUEEN SQUARE (LINDEN COTTAGE)	Early-19C	Detailed description in main text	II
21 QUEEN SQUARE (GRIDLEY COTTAGE)	18C	Semi-detached brick cottage possibly coach-house to No 22. Original 2-cell with cross-passage. Altered 19C to 2 storeys, 2 bays with paned casement windows. Red brick, with 20C brick work below eaves. Double Roman tiled roof originally thatched. 2 brick stacks.	II
22 QUEEN SQUARE (WISTERIA COTTAGE)	18C	House in row altered Early-19C. Brick, random rubble plinth, shallow pitch clay tiled roof with coped verges. Brick stack gable end. Double pile plan. 2 storeys, 3 bays. Window openings with keystones, sash windows with central first floor blind painted window.	II
23 QUEEN SQUARE (FLAGSTONES)	16C	Detailed description in main text	II
UPPER LODGE, MOREDON, OFF STOKE ROAD	c.1860	Snecked squared and coursed local grey sandstone with Hamstone quoins and lintels. Decorative patterned tiles, overhanging eaves, decorative pierced bargeboards. 1½ storeys with single storey cross wing south. Central brick stack with Tudor style pots.	II
RAILINGS ENCLOSING UPPER LODGE, MOREDON, OFF STOKE ROAD	c.1860	Cast iron crested with 'C' scroll supports on east, south and north sides.	II
7 & 8 STOKE ROAD	Early-19C	Pair of brick cottages in a row. Red brick, Blue Lias rubble plinth with clay tile roofs and brick stacks. 2-cell cross-passage with rear projection. 2 storeys with sash windows.	II
9 STOKE ROAD AND WALL	Late-18C	House altered Early-20C. Painted brick, painted ashlar cornice, slate roof, coped verges, brick stacks to gable ends. Double pile, 2 storeys, 3 bays, sash windows. Interior with stone flagged through passage, early-19C stick stair. Boundary wall to west 2 metres in length, painted brick on random rubble, with chamfered saddle back brick coping and ball finial.	II
STABLES AT 9 STOKE ROAD	Late-18C Early-19C	Outbuildings comprising former basket maker's workshop with room over, stables and coach house. Painted brick walls, hipped slate roofs. Loft over stables and coach house. Sash windows.	II
MANOR FARMHOUSE, OFF STOKE ROAD	1570	Detailed description in main text	II*

BUILDING	DATE OF BUILD	DESCRIPTION	GRADE
Barn & cartshed 10m west of Manor Farmhouse, off Stoke Road	Late-18C	Detailed description in main text	II
19 and 20 Stoke Road (The Warren)	17C	Detailed description in main text	II
Long's House and outbuilding, White Street	17C	Farmhouse and workshop linked and enlarged 18C and E19C to form dwelling with outbuilding. Workshop dated 1762. Probably original L-Plan set gable end to road. 2 storey SW wing addition. Squared and coursed local limestone and Hamstone ashlar, coped verges south gable end, decorative ridge tiles, pyramid roof to 2 storey porch addition. Slate roofs. Decorative wrought iron lamp standard.	II
Thatcher's and cottage, White Street	16C	Detailed description in main text	II
Ebenezer Chapel, Windmill Hill	1825	Nonconformist Baptist Chapel altered mid-19C. Rendered façade, Knapp stone Lias rubble with slate roof. 2 storeys, single cell chapel, entered under gallery, vestry and reading room and upper schoolroom at rear.	II
3 Windmill Hill (Victoria Cottage)	Late-17C Early-18C	Semi-detached cottage in terrace, altered early in 19C. Façade painted over red brick. Red sandstone rubble left return, double span clay tile roof altered to single span, coped verges, brick tack. Double pile. 2 storeys, 3 bays, sash windows. Blocked door and window openings on left return.	II
4 Windmill Hill (The Old Manse)	Early-19C	House in terrace. Formerly the Baptist manse. Red brick butt jointed with No.5 Windmill Hill over which the plain clay tiled roof extends. Double pile, 2 storeys, 3 bays, sash windows.	II
5 Windmill Hill (Middle House)	Early-19C	House in terrace. Altered 1985. Red brick, butt jointed with No.4 Windmill Hill over which plain clay tiled roof extends. Coped verges, brick stack double pile, 2 storeys and 3 bays.	II
6 Windmill Hill	Early-19C	Semi-detached cottage in terrace, altered subsequently when bay windows inserted on ground floor. Sash windows on first floor. Painted brick with clay tiled roof and brick stack. 2 cell with cross-passage.	II
Oldways, Wrantage	17C	Detailed description in main text	II
Weaver's Farmhouse, Wrantage	Late-15C	Farmhouse. Originally a hall house ceiled and fireplace inserted 16C. Walls raised and re-roofed 17C to form 3 cell cross-passage plan. Random rubble, Hamstone and local grey sandstone, double Roman tiled roof, brick stacks. Interior shows a 16 panel moulded compartment ceiling with evidence of a spiral stair. Deeply moulded lintel to fireplace and remains of bread oven and curing chamber. An early jointed cruck roof still in evidence. Restored and refenestrated 20C.	II

2 - 6

SOME FOUNDING FAMILIES

Many families living in the parish of North Curry today can trace their roots in the locality back for several centuries. Manuscripts from the Wells Cathedral Archive from as early as 1200 mention areas in the parish familiar in the village today and many family names are derived from these areas.

There are eight main derivation categories for surnames: personal name, nickname, patronymic (derived from the father's name), physical characteristics, moral attributes, place-name, location, occupation and status. In the period before hereditary surnames came into use a son William of a man named John might be referred to as either William the son of John, William John or Williamson. It is only in recent centuries that surnames have achieved the status of stabilised family names and have tended to become hereditary. They started off as bynames or nicknames to distinguish two people in the same locality with the same name. At the highest level we recognise Alfred the Great and Richard Coeur de Lion, and for common people, Thomas the Shepherd and Maude the Widow. After the Conquest surnames began to emerge, many to Domesday tenants-in-chief who used the names of their place of origin, large numbers of which were French. As time went by many bynames became surnames, but were often changed when individuals changed location.

Many surnames were derived from topographical features - wood, hill, brook, field, bridge, lake, etc., with the origins of present day surnames such as Attwood, Byfield, Townsend, Mead and Pitt being obvious. Sometimes personal names such as Richard led to surnames such as Rich, Hicks, Hitchcock and Dicks, and many names stem from occupations such as Fowler, Weaver, Miller, Carpenter and Cooper. Typical examples of early local names following some of the above patterns are Willelmo atte (*at*) Mere, Thomas de (*of*) Cnapp, Rogero le Towker (*the fuller*) and Johanne filio (*son of*) Osberti.

The early *Parish Registers* of North Curry that started in 1539 list many North Curry surnames that continued to have a prominent role in the life of the village for the next 400 years. The names Andrews, Barrington, Bellringer, Bridge, Bulpin, Currie, Dare, Duke, Derham, Foster, Gente, Guddridge, Handole, Hemborow, Hooper, Hurston, Lockier, Kewer, Meade, Nurton, Pocock, Rowswell, Sperring, Verrier and Webber were listed among others. Some gave their names to farm settlements, and appeared in the various early manorial documents and church manuscripts.

ANDREWS

Andrews was a widely known family name in North Curry in the 19th century and early-20th century and can with certainty be traced back to John Andrews who was born to John and Ursula Andrews on 12th October 1727. John married Rachel Coggan in 1755 and they had nine children between 1755 and 1776. One of these children, Robert, was born in 1773 and was their eighth child, marrying Jane Hewlett in 1803 and becoming a blacksmith. He died in 1840, but in the *Tithe Schedule* for North Curry in that year he is listed as landowner and occupier of a house and shop, with 3 perch of land, in the position of the present day house called Lantern Cottage in Moor Lane. Robert and Jane had ten children between 1804 and 1826. Two of their children, John and James, who were born in 1808 and 1815 respectively, were transported to Australia for life for the crime of highway robbery. They were sentenced at Somerset Assizes on 4th August 1838 and were taken to New South Wales, Australia, on the prison ship *Parkfields*. James received a conditional pardon in 1847 and married Catherine White in 1853. They had nine children. The Australian branch of the Andrews family thrives, and one of the descendants has visited North Curry in recent years. One of the other children of Robert and Jane Andrews, Robert, who was born in 1815, married twice, first to Mary Ann Bell and then to Alice Dyer, and went on to take his father's place as a blacksmith in the village until c.1891. Among numerous other children, his sons Bradon, Robert, Hiram and Josiah, are all listed as blacksmiths in the North Curry *Census Returns* from 1851. Josiah married Elizabeth Parrett in 1875 and their sons Hiram and Christopher also became blacksmiths. Josiah Andrews continued the business in the premises in Moor Lane until at least 1931, when he was listed in *Kelly's Trade Directory* as a blacksmith.

BARRETT

The Barretts were a leading family in North Curry during the 19th century and early-20th century, living in the prominent and important house of Moredon. They became great benefactors to the Parish Church and other good causes in North Curry. They sponsored many improvements and embellishments to the church, such as stained glass windows, furniture and artefacts. They were heavily involved with the restoration programme of the church in 1881, and served the village by hosting many fund-raising events, annual fairs and fetes in the fields below Moredon. The Barrett family inherited Moredon through marriage. In 1810 Robert Hooper Scott was the owner and occupier of Moredon. When he died in 1829 his nephew John Scott Gould, who was married to Sophia née Barrett, became the owner. He died in 1846 and she continued to live in the house until her death in 1871. Under her will she set up the Sophia Gould Charity in North Curry, which received £200 to provide for annual distribution of bread to the poor. As John and Sophia Scott Gould were childless, Moredon passed to Sophia's nephew, Major William Barrett, son of her brother George.

Major William Barrett married Charlotte Maria Herring Chard (see **CHARD** below) from Othery. She was a watercolour artist, and sister of John Rouse Merriott

Chard who won the Victoria Cross in a renowned military action at Rorke's Drift in South Africa in 1879. William and Charlotte had seven children. These included William, who became Colonel of the Somerset Yeomanry and married Gwerfyl Lloyd, and George Macdonald, known as Donald, who was commissioned into the 1st Battalion Royal Scots Fusiliers and served Queen Victoria as guard of honour at Balleter in Scotland. George Macdonald drowned while fishing in the River Dee when off duty, and the Queen sent a wreath of dried flowers to his funeral in North Curry. This wreath is preserved and can be seen in the Parish Church. Another son, Alexander, known as Alec, served as Major in the Somerset Infantry, and inherited Burrow Mump, the mound at Burrowbridge crowned by the ruins of the Chapel of St Michael which he gave to the National Trust in 1946. He died in a car crash at the age of 87. Two daughters, Charlotte, who was known as Elizabeth and Florence, lived into their 80s and 90s, whilst Charles was killed in action during the First World War while serving as Captain in the Royal Scots Fusiliers. The seventh child was Dorothy who laid the foundation stone of The Queen's Jubilee Memorial in Queen Square in 1897 when she was 12. She married Charles Elmhirst Luard, an officer in the Royal Norfolk Regiment in 1913, who died in military action in 1914. A son Charles died of pneumonia at the age of 14. She was re-married in 1919 to Frank Roff Phillips, a Lieutenant Colonel in the Royal Artillery, and their son Donald eventually came to live at Moredon in 1974, remaining there until 1985. Mrs Charlotte Barrett arranged for the lych-gate to be built at the entrance to the Parish Church of St Peter and St Paul as a memorial to both her son-in-law Charles Elmhirst Luard and to her grandson, Charles. Barrett family life at Moredon c.1890 is shown in Plate xvi.

Bellringer

There are many references to the Bellringer family in North Curry. The earliest descendants appear in the North Curry *Baptisms Register* of 1640 when William, a son of John and Catheren Belringer (sic) was baptised on 26th March. Later registers c.1670 list William and Joane Bellringer and William and Jane Bellringer having numerous children baptised. During the 18th century the branches of the Bellringer family grew, each generation spawning large families, and by 1840 the family had firmly established roots in North Curry, living in eight or so different dwellings in the village.

The 1840 *Tithe Schedule* for North Curry lists five members of the Bellringer family as landowners and householders, and in the 1863 *Rate Schedule* for North Curry three members of the family are houseowners. Their occupations in 1851 and 1861 were varied with the men employed as farmers, agricultural labourers, stonemasons, shoemakers or cordwainers and servants, and the women as laundresses, dressmakers and dairywomen. From 1771 James Bellringer was an agricultural machine proprietor, Robert Bellringer was the sub Postmaster in Wrantage, and Charles Bellringer was the Bailiff to Philip Foster, Esquire. During the early-20th century James and later Ernest Bellringer continued their steam threshing machine business, Robert William Bellringer was an assistant overseer, while another in the family was a tailor and another an insurance agent.

Chard

The Chard surname, although not strictly a North Curry family name, has links with the village through the Barrett family as mentioned previously. The Chard family appears to have descended from Cerdic, King of the West Saxons, and by the time of the *Domesday Survey* it had been corrupted to Chard. The line includes Thomas Chard, the last abbot of Forde Abbey in South Somerset. John Chard (1736-1812) was born in Pathe House in Othery, near North Curry. He married Honor Merriott, who died in 1783 aged 37, and they had a son William, who in turn in 1818 had a son William Wheaton, who married Jane Brimacombe of Cornwall. William Wheaton and Jane Chard lived for a time in Othery, before moving to Mount Tamar, Plymouth. They had three sons. The first, William, was born in 1841 and became a Colonel in the Royal Fusiliers serving in India and Egypt; the second, John Rouse Merriott, was born in Plymouth in 1847 and became a Colonel in the Royal Engineers; and the third, Charles Edward, became the Rector of St John the Baptist, Hatch Beauchamp, near North Curry. In addition five daughters were born, one of them being Charlotte Maria Herring who married Major William Barrett of Moredon, North Curry. Another daughter, Florence, married a Vicar of North Curry, the Reverend R C Lathom Browne.

It was, however, the fame of John Rouse Merriott Chard, which had the biggest impact on the residents of North Curry. In 1868 he was commissioned as a Lieutenant in the Royal Engineers and sent to Bermuda and Malta, to Aldershot, Chatham and Devonport and in 1878 to South Africa. It was there whilst defending Rorke's Drift against between 3,000 and 4,000 Zulus in the South Africa War that he was awarded the Victoria Cross for the gallantry he displayed on 22nd and 23rd January 1879. Zulu warriors were posing an increasing threat to the British colony of Natal in South Africa, and when the British presented the Zulu King, Cetewayo, with an ultimatum that the Zulu army be disbanded the Zulus declared war. An Irishman, Jim Rorke, had established a trading station that went on to become a mission-station, becoming known as Rorke's Drift. The British Army under the command of Lord Chelmsford had commandeered this station as a hospital and from which point it was intended to cross the Buffalo River and lead the initial thrust into Zululand. Lieutenant Chard, with a few sappers, was detached from No. 5 Field Company and proceeded to Rorke's Drift to organise a pont system or bridge of boats across the river. Meanwhile a Zulu attack annihilated a large part of the British Army at Isandlhwana ten miles away and Chard, who was in charge of only 100 men, made ready for an attack at Rorke's Drift by making defence walls of mealy bags and biscuit tins. The roof of the hospital was set alight and, with their water supply cut off, this exhausted band of men continued to fight up to 4,000 Zulus. After 20,000 rounds of ammunition had been fired and 1,000 Zulus killed the rest retreated and the battle was won, with 17 of the defenders killed and seven wounded. Lieutenant Chard later wrote *In wrecking the stores in my wagon, the Zulus had brought to light a forgotten bottle of beer, and Bromhead* (his second in command) *and I drank it with mutual congratulations on having come safely out of so much danger.* Chard and ten others were awarded the Victoria Cross for this last stand and he was promoted to the rank of Brevet-Major. Soon after this he was struck down with enteric fever whilst rebuilding the defences at the mission station at Rorke's Drift, but recovered and took part in the final defeat of the Zulu's at Ulundi on 4th July 1879. Interestingly, the Republic of South Africa created the John Chard decoration and John Chard medal as long service awards for their Citizen Force.

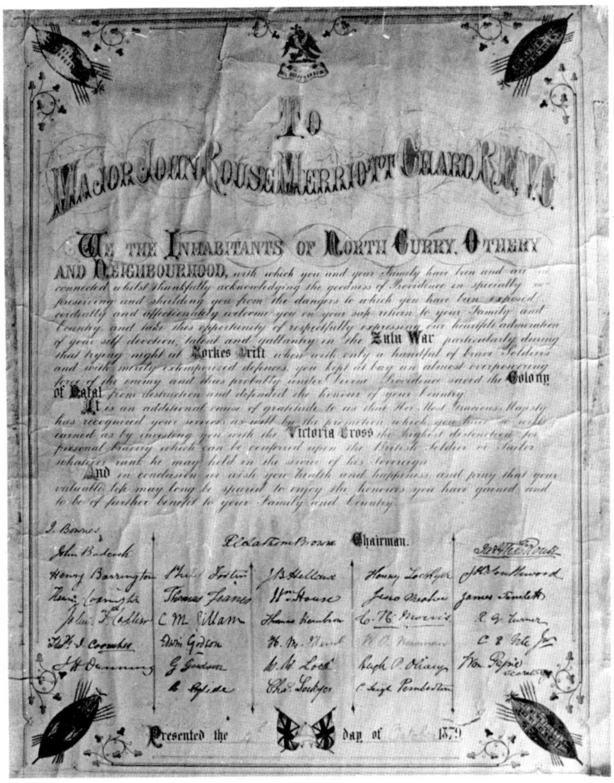
To Major John Rouse Merriott Chard R.E., V.C.

We the Inhabitants of North Curry, Othery and Neighbourhood, with which you and your Family have been and are connected, whilst thankfully acknowledging the goodness of Providence in specially preserving and shielding you from the dangers to which you have been exposed, cordially and affectionately welcome you on your safe return to your Family and Country, and take this opportunity of respectfully expressing our heartfelt admiration of your self devotion, talent and gallantry in the Zulu War particularly during that trying night at Rorkes Drift when with only a handful of brave Soldiers and with merely extemporized defences you kept at bay an almost overpowering force of the enemy and thus probably under Divine Providence saved the Colony of Natal from destruction and defended the honour of your Country.

It is an additional cause of gratitude to us that Her Most Gracious Majesty has recognized your services as well by the promotion which you have so well earned as by investing you with the Victoria Cross the highest distinction for personal bravery which can be conferred upon the British Soldier or Sailor whatever rank he may hold in the service of his Sovereign.

And in conclusion we wish you health and happiness and pray that your valuable life may long be spared to enjoy the honours you have gained and to be of further benefit to your Family and Country.

R C Lathom Browne Chairman.

Presented the day of 1879

CHARD CITATION FROM NORTH CURRY PARISH COUNCIL

Major Chard returned to Portsmouth, England aboard the steamship *Egypt* in October 1879, and made his way to North Curry, via Bristol and Taunton to visit his brother-in-law Major William Barrett and his sister Charlotte. When his train arrived in Taunton on 3rd October 1879 a large crowd of townspeople, relatives and friends afforded him an official welcome in recognition of his courage at Rorke's Drift. A procession took place through the streets of Taunton led by the Mayor's carriage, after which Major Chard was driven to North Curry. The village was extensively decorated with flags, flowers, banners and a series of decorative arches from Borough Post to Queen Square. The banners were inscribed with words such as *Honour to the Brave, Joy to the Defenders of Rorke's Drift and Long Life to Major Chard.* At Moredon, the Barrett's home, an archway carried the words *Welcome to Moredon* and a representation of the Victoria Cross. An estimated 3,000 people were to witness the reception at the homecoming by carriage, horseback and on foot, not only from North Curry parish but also from Othery and neighbouring parishes. As soon as Major Chard's carriage was sighted at Borough Post the band of the 3rd Somerset Rifle Volunteers played, followed by hearty and prolonged cheers. The Vicar, the Reverend R C Lathom Browne, a relative of Major Chard, read an address on behalf of the inhabitants of North Curry. Major Chard made a speech in reply and, cheered by the crowd, he proceeded to Moredon in a carriage fastened with ropes pulled by volunteers. There his mother met him, with more speeches following and everyone flocking to large marquees erected in a field nearby for beer, tea and sandwiches. A pyrotechnic display was staged in the evening. A few days later he was to attend Balmoral for an audience with Queen Victoria, during which he related the story of the defence of Rorke's Drift. He resumed duty firstly in Devonport, then in Cyprus, Preston and Singapore, returning to England in 1896 to assume his final post as Colonel and Chief Royal Engineer at Perth, Scotland. He became ill with cancer and died aged 49 on 1st November 1897 at Hatch Beauchamp Rectory, where his brother was Rector. He was buried at the Parish Church of St John the Baptist, Hatch Beauchamp, and among many messages of condolence was a wreath from Queen Victoria.

COATE

Many of the Coate family came originally from Stoke St Gregory in the middle of the 19th century. George Coate was the first to arrive and farmed in Helland in 1851. Daniel Coate, another Stoke St Gregory born farmer, lived in Helland from 1860 with his wife Lavinia. Their son Henry Langford born in 1879 continued to farm and in 1913 his son, also Henry Langford, was born in Helland House. The family moved to Manor Farm in 1916, and father and son established the largest apple orchards in the village, and went on to supply cider-making factories in Nailsea and Taunton and members of the Coate family still continue farming there today. In 1939 Henry Coate married Marjorie Dare from Knapp in the Baptist Chapel. From 1861 to 1871 George Coate from Drayton with his wife Elizabeth were farming 333 acres and employing 9 men and 3 boys at Lillesdon Court Farm. Henry Coate from Stoke St Gregory married Emma Webber Tattle who was born in North Curry and they farmed at Thong Farm from 1861, later moving to Wrantage, with other members of the Coate family continuing to farm Thong Farm. Emma Coate was acclaimed as the oldest woman in England dying on 18th November 1939 when she was reputedly 108 years old.

The Willows and Wetlands Visitor Centre in Meare Green, Stoke St Gregory, is the home of the company P H Coate & Son, founded by willow grower and merchant Robert Coate in 1819, and still run by the Coate family today. When Kathleen Boobyer, daughter of the well-known willow grower and furniture maker Edmund

Boobyer, married Percy Coate in 1940, the joining of the two families created the present company.

CREASE

The earliest record in the *Parish Registers* of entries for members of the Crease family is of John and Elizabeth Crease whose first-born son John was baptised on 6th February 1694. John married Elizabeth Owen in Moorlinch on 31st May 1694. *(Note: May 1694 came before February 1694 in the years prior to 1752 when the year began on 25th March - Gregorian Calendar)* They went on to add a further five sons and three daughters to their family. Their fourth son, Henry, married Rachel Hooper in 1736 and they in turn had seven children. The next Crease family to emerge from the *Parish Registers* was William and Rachel (née Hooper) who had eight children between 1771 and 1789. The Crease family appears regularly in the *Rent Rolls* as taxpayers in North Curry during the 17th and 18th centuries. In 1787 William Crease is listed as the copyholder of two half houses in North Curry, with 1 rood and 24 perch of land, identified and described on page 131 as the houses Fosse End and Hayes Cottage, a 16th century building in Stoke Road. In 1801 James Crease, a glazier, son of William and Rachel, married Avice Pocock, and in the 1851 *Census Return* he is listed as a landed proprietor, aged 79. They had numerous children who firmly established themselves in the village together with other members of the Crease families as glaziers, plumbers, curriers, bakers, farmers and butchers, and in 1881 and 1891 as grocers and drapers residing in Manchester House, Queen Square. However according to the *Census Return* there were no members of the Crease family residing in North Curry in 1901.

DARE

There have been members of the Dare family residing in North Curry from at least the early 1700s. In the various parish documents of the 19th century they are described as landowners and farmers in the parish, and one branch of the family continues to farm today. Charles Dare, who was born in Stoke St Gregory and aged 59 in 1861, farmed at Nythe Farm in Sedgemoor, living there with his wife Hannah and two sons and four daughters. His second son Robert Henry with his wife Elizabeth continued to farm there until c.1914, passing it on to son Douglas. Another Charles Dare farmed in Higher Knapp from early in the 20th century and the farm became known as Bulpin's Farm in 1939 and later as Higher Knapp Farm where the Dare family farm today. Other members of the Dare family are listed in the various *Trade Directories* and *Census Returns*. Edwin Gilbert Dare was the Sexton and verger in North Curry in 1914 and is also listed as a miller in Newport in 1910, and a baker, grocer, draper and confectioner at London House in 1931. Another Charles Dare and later his son John are listed as withy growers and merchants from 1889 living in Broad Lane. Beer retailers, carpenters, shoemakers, willow basket and chair makers are all occupations attributed to members of the Dare family during the 19th and early-20th centuries.

On 9th April 1820 Charles Holcombe Dare and his wife Mary Frances, who had moved to North Curry from the Isle of Wight, had a son Charles William baptised in North Curry Parish Church. There followed two other sons, Walter John in 1821 and Edmund Holcombe in 1828, together with a daughter Frances Emma Coker in 1825. Charles Holcombe Dare is listed in the 1840 *Tithe Schedule* for North Curry as a landowner and he lived for a time in The Manor House. He was a farmer, and became a lay rector c.1861 when he was 75. His brother, Walter King Coker, was Vicar in North Curry between 1820 and 1845. Charles William Dare was a barrister and lived in Fosse Cottage in North Curry. His son, Edmund Coker Dare, was a planter in India before contracting malaria and returning to live with his parents where he became a prominent figure in the life of the village. He served as a Churchwarden from 1902 to 1914, a Parish Councillor, Secretary of the North Curry Flower Show and the Cricket Club, and a member of the school Management Committee for many years.

DERHAM

Other ways of spelling the surname Derham have been Dearham, Deram, Dirrham, and Durham and the earliest reference appears in the *Marriage Register* of 1561 when John Dirrham married Johan Hurston. There were 42 male Dirrham/Derham marriages in North Curry between 1561 and the early-19th century, resulting in many children. Many had moved away by the time of the first Census in 1841 when only one Derham family is listed. However by the beginning of the 20th century there were six Derham families living in North Curry, the largest being the family of Thomas Derham. In 1901 he was a farmer and innkeeper of the Royal Oak Inn, Haymoor End, and he lived there with his wife Mary and their nine children. During the first half of the 20th century a Derham family ran a thriving withy yard in Knapp, which is still used by the family today.

FOSTER

The Fosters were one of the largest and oldest established families in North Curry. They feature frequently in the early *Parish Registers* with no fewer than 155 children baptised in North Curry between 1666 and 1841. Many Foster families gave birth to up to ten children. The *Census Returns* from 1841 to 1901 are filled with the Foster name, covering occupations and trades ranging from agricultural labourers to farmers, cordwainers, butchers, bakers, tailors, dressmakers, glovemakers, pig dealers and hay merchants, innkeepers and maltsters, grocers and drapers, independent landed proprietors, annuitants and a solicitor.

Charles Millett Foster was a practising solicitor in North Curry from 1841 to 1872. He lived in Calmady House with his wife Eliza and children Charles, Arthur and Harriet in 1851. By 1861 he was a widower living with five children, a governess, housekeeper and servant. By 1871 he had re-married and lived there with his new wife Helen Jane, two of his children from his first marriage and two additional children, Theodore aged six and

Ernest aged three, together with a cook and a housekeeper. By 1881 the family had left North Curry. According to the North Curry *Census Returns,* between 1841 and 1901 there were five innkeepers in North Curry with the Foster name - Richard Foster in 1841 in Greenway and Jacob Foster in 1851 in Knapp Lane. Hugh Foster was at the Angel Inn in Stoke Road in 1861, and was an innkeeper at Haymoor End in 1871. George Foster was keeping the Halfway House, New Bridge in 1871, 1881 and 1891, and in 1901 Sarah Foster had taken over this inn now named New Bridge Inn.

HANDOLE

Handoll, Handall, Handol, Handdoll and Handole are the different spellings of the name of this family that appear in the North Curry *Parish Registers.* The earliest is a record of the death of John Handoll in 1583, and by 1666 several branches of the family had established themselves in the village. The last entry of the Handole name in the North Curry *Baptism Register* is William Handole; son of John and Jane baptised 12th January 1783. In 1649 a John Handoll was granted the copyhold of land at Poundhill, Knapp. This had an area of two acres paying a rate of 14s.6d per annum, and in 1685 John Handoll is listed as a tithing officer. In the 1787 DCW *Survey of the Manor of North Curry* Widow Handole is listed as the copyholder of 1 acre 2 roods and 16 perch of land in Knapp called Binsborow. A cottage in Sedgemoor now called Sedgemoor Cottage was formerly known as Handoles, and is mentioned as a tenement in the record of the Reeve's Feast, and was possibly the home of Christopher Handoll who was Churchwarden in North Curry in 1718.

HEMBROW

This surname has one of the most varied spellings of all the North Curry early names. Hembry, Hembery, Hembury, Hembrey, Hembrew, Hemborow, Hemborough, Hembrough, Henbury, Henborow, Henboroughe, Henboroe, and most commonly Hembrow, which is the way it is spelt today. The earliest spelling of the name that occurs in the *Marriage Register* was Henboroughe when John married Edith Hoote in 1545. With so many derivatives there is a certain amount of guesswork in trying to establish whether they were all of the same early family. However, very few with this name remained in North Curry and by the end of the 19th century most had gone from the village. The name is held by one North Curry resident today, and still survives in the adjacent village of Stoke St Gregory.

KEWER

The surname Kewer was alternatively spelt Kew or Keur in the early *Parish Registers* of North Curry. The earliest marriage was of William Kewer who married Edith Ceelie in 1609 followed by that of Robert Kewer to Agnes Combes in 1664. Jacob Kewer was one of the witnesses to the application in 1812 for a nonconformist licence for a house in Knapp for Methodist worship. James and Elizabeth Kewer were worshippers at the Baptist Chapel in North Curry during the 19th century and they, together with three of their children, are buried in the graveyard there. By 1900 the name had ceased to be present in the village.

PORTMAN

The Portmans have been among the leading merchant families in Somerset since the 14th century. In the 15th century they acquired the estate of Orchard through marriage, and that became their main Somerset home. Sir John Portman was a London lawyer in the early-16th century and his son William was responsible for valuing the possession of Taunton Priory during the Dissolution in 1536. In 1599 the Dean and Chapter of Wells granted Hugh Portman a lease for 21 years for fowling in the Manor of North Curry. There is an entry in the *Marriage Register* of Ladie (sic) Ann Portman marrying Edward Popham, Esquire in 1618. The Portmans went on to acquire many monastic lands and in 1633 and 1674 there is reference to Sir William Portman acquiring leases of a mansion house and land in North Curry, possibly Moredon, from the Dean and Chapter of Wells. It is improbable that he lived in North Curry but he was certainly a lessee of land. An estate map of 1773 is shown on page 204. Records in 1883 showed that 108 landowners owned 43 per cent of the area of the county of Somerset, the greatest of them, Viscount Portman, having a Somerset estate of more than 24,000 acres.

PRIDDLE

Research into the origins of the Priddle name by John Priddle of the Somerset Family History Society identifies Raoul Priddle, as armourer to William the Conqueror, who was granted land in the West Country following the Norman invasion. Thomas Hardy chose to characterise Retty Priddle in one of his books as *one of the Paridelles.* Sir Paridell also featured in Edmund Spenser's *Faerie Queene.* Priddle's Hill lies 10 miles north-east of Yeovil. Interestingly in the 1881 *Census Return* there were only 490 Priddles in the United Kingdom and 267 were in Somerset. These Priddles were almost all concentrated in the west and 30 per cent of those were found around Curry Mallet and North Curry. Study of the North Curry parish documents shows two Priddle marriages, those of William Priddle to Mary Jennings in 1789, and George Priddle to Elizabeth Ceeley in 1803. The first baptisms of Priddle children in North Curry were of three born to George and Elizabeth from 1804 to 1815. Other early residents were Emmanuel and Charlotte Priddle from Curry Mallet who, together with the other Priddle families contributed to the growth of this name in the area. Their occupations, according to the *Census Returns,* were mainly in agriculture with many of the women working as needlewomen.

TOTTERDELL

Early entries in the North Curry *Baptism Registers* and *Marriage Registers* list Matthew Totterdale marrying Joan Wadham in 1696 and having a son Matthew baptised in 1705, and George Totterdall marrying Jane Verryor in 1726 and having a son Matthew baptised in 1730. The Totterdell name does not re-appear in the registers until the early-19th century when two families are prominent. Twins of Charles and Elizabeth Totterdell, Hannah and

William, were baptised on 19th December 1804, and John Totterdell, a yeoman and Miriam his wife had their six children baptised between 1815 and 1827. John Totterdell is listed in the 1840 *Tithe Schedule* for North Curry as occupying Sunny Farm and leasing much pasture and meadowland. In the *Census Returns* of 1851 and 1861 he is listed as a widower and farming 120 acres in Lillesdon, and the 1871 *Census Return* suggests his son John continued to farm 140 acres in Lillesdon. In 1871 Henry Totterdell, an agricultural labourer, aged 36, with his wife Sarah and four young children, together with his mother, were living in Wrantage. He is listed in 1901 as a widower aged 60 years.

VERRIER

Verrier, Verriar, Verryer, Verryor, Verier are the various spellings of the name that appear in the North Curry parish documents. The *Baptism Registers* list 122 Verrier baptisms from 1665 to 1841. The earliest Veriar marriage in the Marriage Register is one John Veriar on 24th November 1541. In the *Census Returns* from 1841 a number of Verrier families lived in the hamlet of Knapp with the majority of menfolk occupied as agricultural labourers. James Verrier, who lived in North Curry in the 18th century, was a clockmaker, and a letter to the editor of the newspaper the *Western Flying Post* in 1755 describes a clock that he had invented as follows:

> *Sir,*
> *I flatter myself the following description of a new invented clock which I have seen at North Curry, made by James Verrier of that Place,......this clock I take to be the nearest to Perpetual Motion of anything yet discovered as it requires no manual assistance whatever, either to wind it up or to keep it in motion, though it sometimes descends, and sometimes ascends according to the different direction of the barrel, without any rachet or click, the first wheel being fixt to the barrell, it shows apparent time. W B Bridgwater July 26 1755.*

WARBURTON /WARBUTTON/WALLBUTTON

The name is first found in a North Curry *Baptism Register* with an entry of a son John born to William and Sarah Warbutton in September 1798. The name seems to have been spelt differently by the various scribes of the registers in North Curry and as time went on the spelling Walbutton or Wallbutton is the one most widely used. As well as William and Sarah, James and Mary and Robert and Mary continued to have there children baptised in North Curry Parish Church during the early-19th century. The *Census Returns* from 1841 to 1901 give the main occupations of the Wallbutton families as carpenters. They handed down there knowledge and skills to their sons who continued in the family tradition, and the name Wallbutton became synonymous with carpentry in the village. A descendant of the North Curry Wallbutton family from Australia has been engaged in extensive research into the origin of the Wallbutton name and attributes a link to the town of Warburton in Cheshire named after the Saxon princess and martyr St Werburghe. William and Sarah Warbutton mentioned above had a son William who married Harriet Spicer. Their daughter Mary Anne Emma, born in 1835, suffered a weak chest (possibly tuberculosis), and was advised by a doctor to move to a warmer climate for her health. Family stories suggest arrangements were being made to send her to a family in the South of France - perhaps as a servant or companion - but Mary replied, *I might as well move to New South Wales*, which she did. She emigrated to New South Wales in Australia on *The Victory*, arriving in Sydney in May 1855 at the age of 19. Life was dangerous and hard and when she married she set up a store for gold miners.

WESCOMBE

The first recording of the name was when Robert Wescombe married Elizabeth Collins in North Curry on 31st May 1708. It is probable they lived in Ruishton and it was not until 1780 that a Robert Wescombe married Ann Elson and the family settled in North Curry. Their son William married Sarah Howe in 1805 and they lived and farmed at Pury Farm, now Pury House, naming their son William Elson. William and Sarah were early members of the Baptist Chapel in Windmill Hill, and two daughters Louisa and Mary Aquila, aged 19 and 29 were buried in the graveyard. William Elson Wescombe continued to farm at Pury Farm, and in 1861 he was listed as a farmer of 80 acres employing four men and one boy. His son Samuel who resided there with his wife Sarah maintained the farm until his death in 1913.

BRIDGE/GARNSEY/COZENS/NOBLE

The Bridge family name has been prominent in North Curry since 1564 when Robert Bridge married Johan Shephearde. In 1697 a Nicholas Bridge is recorded as being a Churchwarden and in 1712 pew rents are recorded for the Bridge family. A village story tells of a Mary Bridge at the time of the Battle of Sedgemoor when some of Feversham's soldiers were billeted in North Curry. One of them insulted the lady of the house and her daughter, Mary Bridge, drew the man's sword and plunged it through his heart. Only 12 years old, she came for trial before Colonel Kirke, but he so liked the girl's spirit that he pardoned her and gave her the sword to be handed down through her family. It can be seen in the Somerset County Museum in Taunton.

Robert Garnsey of Uffculme married Mary Bridge, who was the granddaughter of Nicholas Bridge, and the Garnsey name first appears in the *Parish Registers* in 1753 when their eldest son, Robert Wescombe Garnsey, was baptised in North Curry. He grew up to be apprenticed to his uncle, Josiah Crocker Bridge, who was a surgeon in London. When free of his apprenticeship he was allowed to take a wife, and he went on to marry Mary Apperly in 1778. He was of a jealous disposition and made his pretty wife wear two veils when she went out following an advance by a fellow student Sir Joseph Banks, who later went on to finance Captain Cook's Pacific voyage. Robert and Mary moved back to North Curry where he worked as the surgeon in the parish and held the office of Churchwarden and Overseer of the Poor. His father died in 1760 and Robert Wescombe Garnsey inherited much landed property in the parish and often waived the medical fees when he attended to the poor. A farmhouse in Knapp, now divided to form Garnsey Farm and Garnsey Cottage, may have been one of his properties.

Robert Wescombe and Mary Garnsey had ten children; the youngest of whom, Josiah Bridge Garnsey, was born in 1801 and emigrated to Australia in 1835. Their eldest child Robert was born in 1781 and followed his father into the medical profession to serve as an Army surgeon. Their second child, Joanna, born in 1785, married Henry White Meade of Bishops Lydeard, who worked as a solicitor and District Registrar in North Curry. His brother Robert Meade was a surgeon who practised in North Curry and it is possible they met as a consequence of a medical connection with Joanna's father. Their sixth child, Thomas Rock, born in 1792, followed an evangelical life and became a missionary in Sierra Leone. The next son William was born in 1794 and became the 'black sheep' of the family having been found guilty at the age of 28 of deserting his wife and children for three weeks and leaving them chargeable to the Parish of St James Taunton. He was sentenced to three months hard labour at Wilton Prison in Taunton. He was a currier by trade and it seems he returned to North Curry where he is listed in the *Census Return* of 1841 living with his wife Sarah and a son Robert, who was an apprentice harness maker. It is interesting to note that the enumerator of this Census was Robert Garnsey Meade, and that the District Registrar at the time was his brother-in-law Henry White Meade. William Garnsey and his family moved away from North Curry soon after this, and no other Garnsey name appears in any parish documents thereafter.

Mary Bridge married William Cozens of St Mary le Bow, London in North Curry in November 1785. Their daughter Martha, born in 1798, went on to marry firstly Captain Ware Adamson of Jersey, who died in 1823, and secondly Lieutenant Francis Noble RN of Ireland. Noble was invalided out of the Royal Navy and they moved back to live in North Curry in the house formerly called Mount Pleasant and now known as Yew Tree Cottage. In the 1841 *Census Return* they are listed living there with their ten children, but in 1843 Francis Noble died at the age of 60. Mary Cozens, the mother of Martha, died in North Curry in 1842 at the age of 83.

JEANES/BARRINGTON/LOCKYER

The Jeanes family originated in Long Sutton and the earliest reference is in the *Court Rolls* dated 1651. Members of the family moved to Othery and Stoke St Gregory and in c.1841 a Thomas Jeanes aged 37 years took a lease on a property in Higher Knapp and farmed 110 acres, employing three men. He was first married to Rachel Hembrow having three children, and later to Hannah who died at the age of 88 years. The eldest son, Thomas, married Sarah Hembrow in 1866 and farmed at Frog Lane Farm, Stoke St Gregory, and his son John George Jeanes who married Sophia Lockyer moved to Town Farm in North Curry which had been farmed by the Lockyer family for many years. From the mid-18th century the Barrington family of Stoke St Gregory were linked by marriage to the Lockyer family with John Barrington marrying Ann Lockyer in 1775. Various other marriages took place linking all three families and they continue to farm in North Curry to the present day.

MORRIS/SPEARING/MITCHELL/PEARD

Richard Morris, a yeoman farmer, auctioneer and land agent, and his wife Elizabeth moved to Stoke St Gregory and later to North Curry from Bampton. Two sons were born in North Curry - Robert Smith in 1828, who became an accountant, and Cuthbert Rodham in 1831 who became an attorney's copying clerk. Richard Morris died in 1852 and Cuthbert Rodham, following in his father's footsteps, became an auctioneer and surveyor. He built up a thriving business handling the sale of estates for some of the leading families in Somerset, Devon and Cornwall, including dealings with the royal estate of the Prince of Wales.

Phocion Mitchell, a yeoman of Knapp, and his wife Sarah had their daughter Ann baptised in 1801 in North Curry. Sarah Mitchell died and Phocion married Mary Edwards in 1807. Ann Mitchell married William Spearing whose family name had been in North Curry for a century. Their daughter, Ann Mitchell Spearing, was born in 1838, and she married Cuthbert Rodham Morris in 1857. They lived in Gwyon House in North Curry, and were married for 42 years until Ann died in 1900. They had a family of eight daughters and two sons, Cuthbert William and Richard Spearing. A daughter, Anne Elizabeth Morris, married John Grigg Peard from Devon, who in 1881 farmed 328 acres at Lillesdon Court Farm, and later became a land agent, surveyor and auctioneer living in 1901 in Whatley House, Queen Square. He later built and lived in Highcroft House. In 1812 Phocion Mitchell had been one of the first to seek nonconformist registration for his house in Knapp to become a Methodist meeting place, the forerunner to the Methodist Chapel in Windmill Hill. The schoolroom extension to the chapel, which was built in 1900, was dedicated to his granddaughter Ann Mitchell Morris. The Peard family were also worshippers at the Methodist Chapel in North Curry and many members of the family are buried in the graveyard there (see page 113).

Cuthbert Rodham Morris proceeded to take his two sons and son-in-law John Peard into partnership and the firm Messrs C R Morris, Sons and Peard became firmly established in North Curry. Cuthbert William Morris built Fosse House in 1895 and on his marriage he enlarged and improved the house and lived there with his wife Florence and young son. Unfortunately, a fire broke out in the roof of the house soon after this. Although the villagers made great efforts, with Mr Alec Barrett and his hand-pumped fire engine from Moredon together with the Taunton Corporation Fire Brigade using water from surrounding ponds, the fire was not extinguished for some hours. Much furniture was salvaged but the damage to the house was severe with only the outside walls remaining, although the outbuildings were saved. Cuthbert William Morris died in 1922 and left the sum of £500 to be used for improvements in the village for the benefit of the inhabitants. A public hall to be used by the community was favoured, and Richard Spearing Morris, the brother of the late Cuthbert William, gave the Parish Council a gift of the Assembly Rooms in Greenway. This building had been in the Morris family for some years, and he suggested his brother's bequest of £500 be spent on additions and improvements to enable the hall to be used for the benefit of all or anybody in connection with the parish. It became known as The Morris Memorial Hall. Richard Spearing Morris lived from 1897 in Long's House, White Street, where he made substantial alterations, and in 1912 it was the first house in the area to be connected with electric light. In 1929 the house passed to his son Richard Rodham Morris who continued at the family's estate agency. In 1938 he married Kathleen Tacchi Stagg who had been born in Johannesburg in 1899 and whose family returned to England shortly afterwards.

Kathleen Tacchi Morris became internationally well known as a peace campaigner. When she was ten she was expelled from school for leading a strike against excessive caning. Her father, the inventor Percy Tacchi, took her as a child to Freethought Society Meetings where she met and was influenced by Annie Besant, H G Wells and George Bernard Shaw. She became interested in dance and studied the holistic philosophy of dance with Jacques Dalcroze in the 1920s. She created her *Tacchomo* School which taught a radical educational philosophy to arts students in 1931 at Long's House. She appeared in several silent movies, including *Men are Not Gods* in 1937 with Gertrude Lawrence and Sebastian Shaw. She met and formed a close friendship with the Duke of Windsor and Mrs Simpson and also Pablo Picasso whose influence directed her towards her mission for peace. At the 1950 Peace Conference in Sheffield she became aware of the lack of women delegates. Soon after this Picasso asked her to represent him at the Peace Conference in Warsaw. She was moved on seeing the ruins of Warsaw and hearing the stories of suffering under Nazi occupation and vowed to devote the rest of her life to the struggle for peace. Kathleen Tacchi Morris took in the children of black American servicemen during the Second World War and because of her peace-making activities with contacts in the Soviet Union was wrongly suspected of spying. She was responsible for inspiring friendship between people of many different races and cultures, culminating in her foundation of the organisation *Women for World Disarmament* to pursue global peace. Her legacy of drama teaching remains in the Tacchi Morris Arts Centre at Monkton Heathfield today.

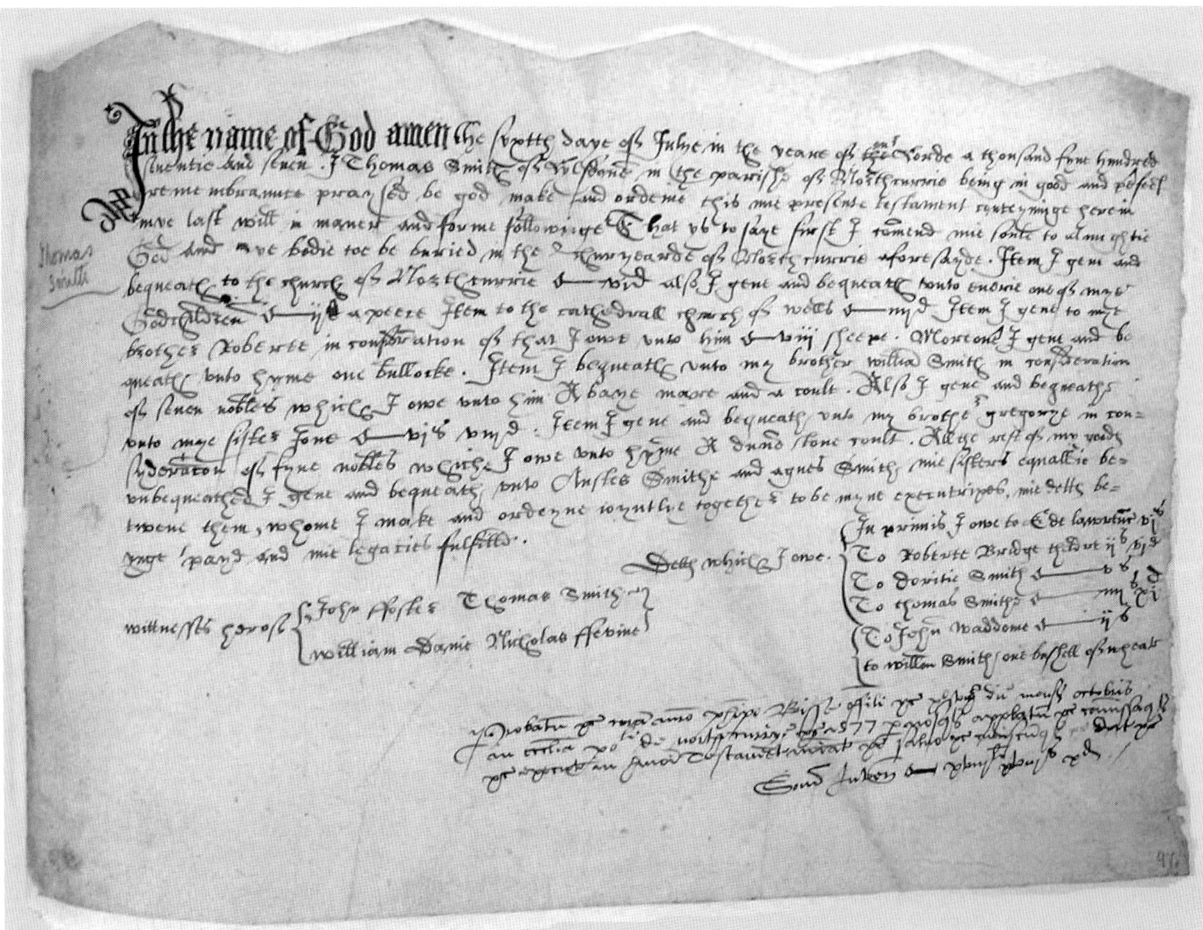
In the name of God amen

WILL OF THOMAS SMITH OF LILSDON – 1577.

The Medical Families of North Curry

The surgeons and medical practitioners who served in North Curry who can be traced through the parish documents are detailed below.

Robert Wescombe Garnsey, whose details appear earlier in this Chapter, was the first surgeon recorded and was practising from the end of the 18th century in North Curry. The next surgeon was James Rich who was listed in the North Curry Baptism Registers as the father of two children in 1813 and 1816, but it is not clear how long he practised in the village.

A surgeon named Robert Meade from Bishops Lydeard followed Rich. Robert Exford, the son of Robert Meade and his wife Harriett, was baptised in 1820. Robert Exford died in 1825, aged five, and Harriet died in 1835 aged 45. Robert married again to Elizabeth and another son was baptised Robert in 1838. Robert Meade, Snr was a member of the Royal College of Surgeons and was the general practitioner to North Curry until at least 1861. In the 1851 *Census Return* he is listed as living in Greenway, aged 59, with his wife Elizabeth aged 47, and three servants, a cook, housekeeper and stableboy. By 1861 he is listed as living in Taunton Road with his wife and son Robert, now a land proprietor, together with his servants.

Another member of the Royal College of Surgeons who came to practise in North Curry in 1823 as a general practitioner, and later as a consulting surgeon, was Robert Marchant. He was born in Kensington, London, and his name first occurs in the North Curry *Baptism Register* when his son William Robert Faun was baptised in 1830. He had his consulting rooms at 2 Queen Square where he lived with his wife Sarah, two daughters and two servants until his death in 1874.

Thomas Plowman came to North Curry from Dorset c.1841 and lived in Greenway House. He was a member of the Royal College of Surgeons and in the 1861 Census Return he is listed as a general practitioner and landowner, aged 55, living there with his second wife Sarah and three children under five. By 1881 he had retired and was listed as deaf and farming 17 acres. Also at that time he was sharing Greenway House, not only with his wife and three daughters, but also with two boarders, one of whom was a lunatic, a nurse and two servants.

Hugh Pengelly Olivey was resident and practised his medical profession in North Curry for over 40 years from c.1860. He was a member of the Royal College of Surgeons but found time to study the history of the village, which culminated in his definitive work *North Curry - The Ancient Hundred and Manor*, published in 1901. He was born in Mylor, Cornwall and married Harriett Ann also from Cornwall; he lived and practised at 4 Victoria Terrace before building Trevarrick House in 1887. He established a medical practice there that was to survive for 90 years. Other doctors followed him at Trevarrick House. First was William Frederick Liddon Green, MRCS, LRCP in 1902, Dr Fisher in 1906, and then John Grandisson Watkins, MRCS, LRCP from 1910 until 1917.

The year 1917 saw the beginning of the era of the Satchwell family of doctors who served North Curry until the late-20th century, all living and practising in Trevarrick House. Hubert John Satchwell from Ireland lived there from 1917 until 1928, handing over the practice to his son Richard Eric Satchwell, who was the doctor in the village until 1967. Eric Satchwell was a much-loved and well-remembered doctor, a man of immense stamina, charm and kindness and reportedly had excellent medical skills. By 1954 he had built the service in North Curry into the largest single practice in Somerset. In 1926 he looked after 726 patients as a single-handed doctor, and was visiting up to 30 patients each day, delivering babies, undertaking night and weekend visiting, and leaving prescriptions for patients to collect from his doorstep. The Reverend M D Lewis conducted his funeral in 1986, giving an address that included the following words. *I witnessed his work, and observed the respect he enjoyed and the confidence he inspired. How many times I have visited sick rooms and been told "Doctor have been", and the tone of voice and the expression on the face showed that anxiety had been lifted as well as treatment prescribed. Eric Satchwell embodied a style of medical practice that has now almost vanished - the single-handed doctor, who lived among and knew his patients - and their parents, and their children. He would say general practice is one part medicine and three parts common sense, and on being told he looked well he would reply that he never took his own medicine!* When he retired his son George Satchwell followed him in the practice, and many times Eric was referred to as *old doctor*. George Satchwell altered the premises at Trevarrick House to accommodate larger consulting, treatment and waiting areas and in 1980 a separate Health Centre with in-house auxiliary facilities was built nearby in North Curry. Since the Satchwell era another father and son team, Philip and James Hickman, have continued the tradition of family succession in medical service to the village and beyond.

Further Research

Many of the families who have made a contribution to, and influenced the life of North Curry from early times are recorded above. Numerous marriages between them took place, resulting in the children having large extended families within the village with whom they shared skills and gained employment. This led to a harmonious and friendly community, with close family bonds forming the backbone of life in North Curry.

Should you wish to undertake further research on your own family a great deal of information is available in the Somerset County Record Office, or you may wish to join the Somerset & Dorset Family History Society, which has a branch in Taunton.

Arithmetic
45 ÷ 9
15 + 19
1 × 9
2 × 9
3 × 9
4 × 9
5 × 9
6 × 9
7 × 9
8 × 9
10 × 9
11 × 9
12 × 9

2 - 7

EDUCATION AND SCHOOLS

The Broader Picture

During the Middle Ages the education given to the people, if they had any at all, had been training suited to their class and to the activities they would undertake in later life. The sons of gentlemen were trained in chivalry, fighting and hunting, together with music and manners. Reading and writing were not essential, but the ability to decipher heraldic bearings and coats of arms was desirable. Their sisters were trained in housekeeping, the management of servants, needlework and to be accomplished in singing and dancing. The section of the community who were to earn their living as craftsmen or merchants was trained as apprentices to their chosen trade. If necessary for their job, they were also taught to write and cast accounts. Others who were to pursue a monastic life entered schools for novices attached to a monastery or convent and trained for holy orders. As time went on more occupations demanded the ability to read, write and keep accounts, and by 1500, when books became more widely available, the gentry and the governing classes, who were to give orders and make regulations, were compelled to go to school. Schools such as Winchester, St Paul's, Shrewsbury, Westminster, Eton and Harrow taught Greek and Latin. Children from the age of three or four were expected to learn the alphabet and figures, to suffer whipping with good grace, and to call their father and mother *sir* and *madam*. Grammar schools, supported by wealthy noblemen or merchants, opened in towns and attracted children of yeoman, tradesmen and merchants as well as the gentry, but many wealthy families preferred to educate their children by tutors at home. Children toiled from 6 am to 5.30 pm at Latin and Greek, mathematics, rhetoric and logic, and by the age of 13 they were considered old enough to attend university. In the 17th century the two great universities, Oxford and Cambridge, were largely theological colleges and finishing schools for gentlemen. Only male members of the Church of England had the right to a university education and teaching standards were often haphazard. In the 19th century however, other university colleges were opened, written examinations were introduced and many new subjects were available for study. Some boys were encouraged to travel or to pursue a legal education at the Inns of Court.

Schooling in Taunton

There were many fee-paying schools founded in Taunton and the surrounding area from early times. The Saxon Manor of Taunton Deane belonged to the Bishops of Winchester, and Richard Fox, Bishop of Winchester from 1501 to 1528, built a Grammar School at Taunton in 1521, later to be known as the College School. The structure survives today as the Municipal Buildings, and there may have been a school on the site from as early as 1286. In the 18th century the Master, James Upton, had made it one of the largest and most respected of England's provincial schools, providing an education based on the study of Greek and Latin. By the 19th century problems occurred due to lack of space, and eventually in 1870 the school moved to a new site at South Road. Funding however became inadequate, and when the sons of dissenters were allowed entry to the school earning the enmity of the established Church, numbers declined and in 1880 College School was forced to move back to its original site in central Taunton. Eventually in 1885 the Taunton College School Company was wound up. In 1879 Canon Woodward bought the buildings in South Road that had been built for the new College School and in 1880 founded King Alfred's College, now called King's College.

In 1843 a school called the Wesleyan Collegiate Institution was established on Wesleyan principles, firstly at Taunton Castle, and then in 1847 at new premises at Haines Hill in Taunton. This school was renamed Queen's College in 1888.

A school called the West of England Dissenters Proprietary School, which became known as the Independent College, had a congregational foundation and was established in its first home in Wellington Road in 1847. In 1870 extensive new buildings were erected in Staplegrove Road and it became known as Taunton School. Taunton School admitted only boys until the early 1970s when the sixth form merged with Weirfield Girl's School sixth form. Eventually in 1976 all Weirfield Girl's School day pupils merged with boys of Taunton School, and in 1979 a girl's boarding house brought all Taunton School's pupils together on one campus. Taunton School, Queen's College and King's College are now all co-educational establishments.

Schools such as Mary Street, a young ladies' academy, and George Roger's Fullands School, together with other small private schools, provided secondary education for the prosperous middle class in the later part of the 19th century.

In 1871 the Endowed School Commission proposed forming two non-sectarian middle class schools that would be open to nonconformists and well as children of Church of England parents. Having rebuilt the almshouses in Taunton in 1867, Richard Huish's Charity used surplus funds to support this initiative. However there was considerable opposition to the establishment of these schools, and in 1872 Herbert Rogers, the son of the founder of Fullands School, set up a competing school in the buildings recently vacated by College School in the middle of Taunton, now the Municipal Buildings. In 1875 the two foundations were amalgamated under the name Huish with the school under the leadership of Fullands' headmaster. In 1877 the return of the College School from South Road into its former buildings forced Huish Boys'

School into other premises in East Street where it was rebuilt in 1892. The College School was finally wound up in 1885.

The setting up of the Huish Girls' School was delayed until 1876 through lack of premises, and its development continued erratically for several years with further changes of premises. In 1890 the endowment of the former College School was transferred to this school following which, in 1891, it was renamed Bishop Fox's Girls' School and became Taunton's one and only grammar school for girls.

The names Richard Huish and Bishop Fox survive today as the Richard Huish Sixth Form College, and Bishop Fox's Community School in the South Road area of Taunton.

Today Taunton School, Queen's College and King's College remain as independent schools providing education in the Taunton area. There is also a range of state-maintained community comprehensive secondary schools in Taunton that provide education of specialist status. The Castle School specialises in sport, Ladymead School in technology, Heathfield School in performing arts and Bishop Fox's School in business and enterprise. St Augustine of Canterbury School specialises in science. These schools, together with Richard Huish Sixth Form College and the many primary and preparatory schools in the town and surrounding villages, provide a diverse range of educational opportunities for the children of Taunton today.

Somerset College of Art and Technology (SCAT) in partnership with the University of Plymouth, provides post-16-year-old student education in vocational and academic subjects. This establishment also has part-time and evening courses for people of all ages.

PRIMARY EDUCATION

Provision for a lower level of primary or elementary education in the 18th century and 19th century included charity schools, Sunday Schools, private schools of one sort or another, the voluntary church or chapel schools, 'ragged' schools, poor-law or workhouse schools and factory schools. In 1698 charity schools were started to educate the poor by the *Society for Promoting Christian Knowledge* (SPCK). No fees were paid and grants and voluntary contributions supported these schools. The masters were required to be members of the Church, and the curriculum included religious instruction such as learning the catechism and reading the Bible together with some arithmetic and a few craft skills such as spinning, gardening and ploughing.

Another contribution to the elementary education of the poor was made by the Sunday Schools. Factory work left one day in the week free, and this made possible the Sunday School movement. In 1785 the *Sunday School Society* was established to support and encourage Sunday Schools in the different counties of England. It provided local committees whose aim was to offer religious and social education rather than intellectual learning, with their main activity being to teach the uneducated masses to read the Bible. In 1787 there were 250,000 pupils attending Sunday Schools in Great Britain. Attending a school on a Sunday did not interfere with labour in the mills and factories.

Other types of school included the dame school for younger children. An elderly woman, whose weekly fee for each pupil was a few pence, usually ran these for child minding and a very rudimentary education, with some children only just managing to learn to read and write. To quote from a poem *The Schoolmistress* by William Shenstone in 1742:

In ev'ry village mark'd with little spire,
Embow'r'd in trees and hardly known to fame,
There dwells, in lowly shed, and mean attire,
A matron old, whom we Schoolmistress name;
Who boasts unruly brats with birch to tame;
They grieven sore, in piteous durance pent,
Aw'd by the pow'r of this relentless dame;
For unkempt hair, or task unconn'd, are sorely shent.
And oft-times, on vagaries idly bent,
For unkempt hair, or task unconn'd, are sorely shent.

Seventy years later in 1812 the poet George Crabbe describes a dame school:

Yet one there is, that small regard to rule
Or study pays, and still is deemed a school;
That where a deaf, poor, patient widow sits
And awes some thirty infants as she knits –
Infants of humble, busy wives, who pay
Some trifling price for freedom through the day

An institution which gave some kind of elementary education to rather older children was the common day school, or private day school, which charged a small weekly fee. These schools, which the state did not aid or control, were run by private individuals who were often cruel and ignorant. Most girls from the upper and middle classes who were not educated at home by a governess attended private schools of a more genteel type where they were taught not only to read and write, but also the domestic skills needed to help them in their married lives. Some competency in painting, embroidery, singing and instrumental music, together with some French and Italian were considered important.

An organisation called the *Society for Bettering the Condition and Increasing Comfort of the Poor* was founded in 1796 and sought to remove pauper children and children of the very poor from the workhouse and send them to schools of industry. Children were admitted at an early age and they were taught to spin, wind, plait, sew and cobble shoes. The sale of the resulting products paid the expenses of the schools and provided the children with meals. Provision was made for religious instruction and reading. However, employers tended to object to these schools because they diminished the supply of labour and parents were denied their children's earnings from the mills and other industries.

PLAN of a SOCIETY

Eſtabliſhed in LONDON, for the Support and Encouragement of

SUNDAY-SCHOOLS

In the different Counties of England, 1785.

NOTWITHSTANDING the numerous Inſtitutions of Charity which are extant in this nation, there are many diſtreſſes which are ſtill unrelieved, and many wants which are ſtill unſupplied. It is not to be expected that any proviſion of human policy can wholly extirpate wretchedneſs and ignorance; and while that inequality of condition, which ariſes from the nature and conſtitution of things, prevails in the world, the poor muſt be allowed their humble claim on the generoſity of the rich.

The ſame providential Hand that has permitted the exiſtence of evil, has implanted and encouraged in the human breaſt, a principle of benevolence to reſtrain and alleviate it. The precepts of Chriſtianity are, perhaps, in no inſtances, better exemplified, than in attempts to comfort the afflicted, to aſſiſt the induſtrious, and to inſtruct the ignorant.

For this purpoſe more particularly, Charity-Schools are maintained in many parts of the country, and eſpecially in the metropolis: of the utility of which, there can be no doubt.

In places where extenſive manufactories are eſtabliſhed, the children are taught to be of uſe to their parents and maſters in their childhood; and their time is ſo wholly engroſſed in their occupation, that few opportunities remain of their gaining even the loweſt degree of learning: when they grow up, they are therefore found in the groſſeſt ignorance with reſpect to religion and morality; and, as what they poſſeſs not themſelves, they cannot communicate to others, it becomes the inheritance of their poſterity, and is entailed from generation to generation. The conſequence too frequently is, a total thoughtleſſneſs about their moral duties, and the important concerns of a future ſtate.

To remedy this evil, the Inſtitution of Sunday-Schools has been ſuggeſted, and, in ſeveral parts of the country, has happily produced the moſt ſalutary effects. Very reſpectable authorities have teſtified to the pleaſing alteration which has been derived from them, in the behaviour, language, and manners of the children.

The benevolent mind that has beheld the Anniverſary-Meeting of the Charity-Schools of this City, and compares the preſent comfortable ſituation of the children with the filthineſs, rags, and vicious ignorance, in which they muſt have otherwiſe been left, will ſcarcely forbear wiſhing that ſuch benefits may be extended, and the example followed, wherever, and as far, as it may be practicable.

To promote the extenſive influence and advantage of ſuch Schools; to give the children an opportunity of knowing what the ſacred oracles contain; and, above all, to reſcue them from low habits of vice and idleneſs, and to initiate them into a moral and religious courſe of life, are the ends propoſed in the preſent Deſign.

The influence of it may indeed be felt comparatively leſs in London, where numerous Schools already exiſt; but will, it is reaſonable to hope, produce the moſt beneficial conſequences in the country manufacturing towns and villages; where inſtitutions of this kind are ſeldom eſtabliſhed, and are of more difficult acceſs.

It is matter of congratulation to the preſent age, that the mutual animoſities which have in former times diſunited the profeſſors of the Chriſtian Faith, have now given way to a more liberal conſtruction of each other's motives; and while every man enjoys with freedom the rights of private judgment, all denominations can concur in promoting the common intereſts, and, by cheriſhing genuine Chriſtian principles in the minds of children, prevent the deſolation of morals, and advance the peace and felicity of their country.

PRESIDENT.

The Right Hon. JAMES, Earl of SALISBURY.

VICE-PRESIDENTS.

THOMAS BODDINGTON, Eſq.
JOHN HARMAN, Eſq.
JAMES MARTIN, Eſq. M. P.
BROOK WATSON, Eſq. M. P. Ald. & Sheriff.

TREASURER.

HENRY THORNTON, Eſq. M. P.

COMMITTEE.

JOHN BACON, Eſq.
THOMAS DORRIEN, Eſq.
Mr. SAMUEL FAVELL,
THOMAS FLIGHT, Eſq.
Mr. WILLIAM FOX,
Mr. JOSEPH GUTTERIDGE,
SAMUEL HOARE, jun. Eſq.
Mr. THOMAS HUNT,
HENRY KEENE, Eſq.
DAVID PARKER, Eſq.
THOMAS PLUMMER, Eſq.
THOMAS RAIKES, Eſq.
JAMES SANDERSON, Eſq. Ald. & Sheriff.
PHILIP SANSOM, Eſq.
Mr. RICHARD SHARP,
Mr. THOMAS STIFF,
Mr. JOSEPH STONARD,
SAMUEL THORNTON, Eſq. M. P.
Mr. THOMAS VALLANCE,
JAMES WARD, Eſq.
Mr. JAMES WEBBER.

RULES AND REGULATIONS

FOR THE

SUNDAY-SCHOOL SOCIETY,

Eſtabliſhed in LONDON.

I. THIS Society ſhall conſiſt of a Preſident, four Vice-Preſidents, a Treaſurer, and all the Governors.

II. A ſubſcription of one guinea per annum ſhall conſtitute the ſubſcriber a Governor, during the continuance of his ſubſcription.

III. A donation of ten guineas or upwards at one time, or within the year, ſhall conſtitute the donor a Governor for life; and all contributions, however ſmall, will be gratefully accepted.

IV. A General Meeting ſhall be held on the ſecond Wedneſday in January, April, July, and October; at which Meetings ſeven Governors ſhall conſtitute a Board.

V. The Preſident, Vice-Preſidents, or Treaſurer, or any ſeven of the Committee, ſhall have power to call a General Meeting, giving one week's notice in the public papers.

VI. A Committee of twenty-four, to conſiſt equally of members of the Church of England and Proteſtant Diſſenters, ſhall be annually choſen from among the Governors, at the General Meeting in January, who, ſhall meet the laſt Wedneſday in every month, for conducting the affairs of the Society. The Preſident, Vice-Preſidents, and Treaſurer, ſhall be members of all Committees, and five members ſhall be a quorum.

VII. A Preſident, Vice-Preſident, Treaſurer, or Secretary, when a vacancy happens by death or reſignation, ſhall be propoſed by the Committee, for the approbation of the General Meeting.

VIII. No Governor ſhall vote at a General Meeting for any appointment to this Charity, after the firſt year, who has not been a Governor for twelve calendar months.

IX. The Treaſurer ſhall not pay any bills on account of this Charity, without an order ſigned by three of the Committee.

X. Five Auditors ſhall be appointed annually by the General Meeting, to examine the bills and accounts of the Treaſurer.

XI. An Account of the receipts and diſburſements of this Charity, ſhall be annually printed, for the inſpection of the Governors.

XII. The Secretary ſhall perſonally attend all the Meetings of this Charity, unleſs prevented by indiſpoſition; in which caſe he is to ſend a deputy. He ſhall keep an accurate and methodical account of the proceedings, and do all the incidental buſineſs of this Charity. He ſhall apply for the annual ſubſcriptions in London and its vicinity; and produce two or more ſecurities, to be approved of by the Monthly-Committee, who ſhall be bound with him in the amount of £500 in one or more bonds. He ſhall pay all the ſubſcriptions to the Treaſurer or Banker, and produce his account to the Committee every month, and not retain the amount of £100 at any time in his poſſeſſion.

XIII. In all places where the Schools of this Society may be eſtabliſhed, gentlemen of reſpectable character in the neighbourhood, ſhall be requeſted to viſit them every Sunday, receive ſubſcriptions, correſpond with the Society, and ſuggeſt any improvement in the Plan they may think neceſſary.

XIV. The Society ſhall provide Bibles, Teſtaments, and Spelling-Books, for the uſe of the ſcholars.

XV. The Committee ſhall be at liberty to order leſſons on working days, where they ſhall think neceſſary.

XVI. All the ſcholars ſhall attend ſome place of public worſhip every Sunday; but ſuch as their parents may reſpectively approve.

RULES

FOR THE

SUNDAY-SCHOOLS.

I. THE objects of this Charity ſhall be poor perſons, of each ſex and of any age; who ſhall be taught to read, at ſuch times, and in ſuch places, as the Committee by themſelves or their Correſpondents ſhall appoint.

II. The Teachers, by direction of the Committee or their Correſpondents, ſhall take care that all who are committed to their charge, attend public worſhip every Sunday; unleſs prevented by illneſs, or any other ſufficient cauſe.

III. The Teachers ſhall take care that the ſcholars come clean to their reſpective Schools; and if any Scholars be guilty of lying, ſwearing, pilfering, talking in an indecent manner, or otherwiſe miſbehaving themſelves, the Teacher ſhall point out the evil of ſuch conduct; and if, after repeated Reproof, the ſcholar ſhall not be reformed, he or ſhe, ſhall be excluded the School.

IV. The religious obſervation of the Chriſtian Sabbath being an eſſential object with the Society for the ſupport and encouragement of Sunday-Schools, the exerciſes of the ſcholars on that day, ſhall be reſtricted to reading in the Old and New Teſtament, and to ſpelling, as a preparative for it.

V. A printed copy of the above rules ſhall be put up in the School-Room, and read by the Teacher to the ſcholars, the firſt Sunday in every month.

SUBSCRIPTIONS for this CHARITY

Will be received by

Meſſrs. BLAND, BARNETT, HOARE, and HILL, *Lombard-Street.*
Meſſrs. DORRIEN, MELLO, and MARTIN, *Finch-Lane.*
Meſſrs. DOWN, THORNTON, and FREE, *Bartholomew-Lane.*
Meſſrs. DRUMMONDS, *Charing-Croſs.*
Meſſrs. FULLER, SON, and Co. *Lombard-Street.*
Sir HERBERT MACKWORTH, DORSET, and Co. *Bond-Street.*

AND

Meſſrs. MARTIN, STONE, and Co. *Lombard-Street.*

PLAN FOR THE ESTABLISHMENT OF THE SUNDAY SCHOOL SOCIETY

A *Government Return* of 1804 showed that there were 188,794 children aged five to fourteen in receipt of parish relief, but only 20,336 were in schools of industry and receiving education.

Robert Owen started one of the most important educational movements of the early-19th century. He was a factory owner who fixed a minimum age for employment in his factory at ten years and provided free schools for his workers' children between the ages of five and ten. Lessons were given in the three R's, together with geography, history, nature study, dancing, singing and drill. In 1816 he opened an infant school, the forerunner of the modern nursery school. He became one of the founders of the English Elementary education system. In 1811 the *National Society for Promoting the Education of the Poor in the Principles of the Established Church throughout England and Wales*, which had taken over the charity schools which had been sponsored by the *Society for Promoting Christian Knowledge* (SPCK), sponsored elementary education in church schools, relying on private financial support.

Many child victims of the Industrial Revolution, who were ill-fed and housed in insanitary conditions and whose hours of employment were excessive, were helped by the introduction of various Factory Acts. In 1820 the Parish Schools Bill was passed which provided for the better education of the poor in England and Wales, and more schools were erected. The cost of the maintenance of these schools was recovered from ratepayers, but fees of twopence to fourpence a week were to be paid by parents who could afford them. Schoolmasters were to be members of the Church of England and appointed by the Parish Vestry. Lessons were largely confined to basic arithmetic and writing, and a monitorial system was introduced where teachers trained older pupils who themselves taught younger ones, whilst the teacher kept an overall eye on what was happening.

The earliest state intervention in education occurred in 1833, requiring the provision of half-time education for employees aged less than 13 years. Owing to the poor conditions of many schools at the time, the government made its first educational grant to supply half the cost of building new school premises. The other half was to be supplied by voluntary contributions. Out of every ten children of school age four went to no school at all, three to Sunday Schools only, two to inefficient dame schools or private day schools, and only one received a satisfactory education.

The Church of England claimed a traditional right to dominate public education. However there was a demand for a state system of education with less emphasis on religious teaching, but the great weakness of the system was the early leaving age due to the demand for child labour. The moral tone of the schools was said to be improving, but the education given was elementary and superficial with a tendency for teachers to neglect the younger children and hand them over to pupil-teachers. Several parliamentary bills floundered owing to the Church of England's domination of public education. In 1843 a Bill was passed which allowed children between the ages of eight and thirteen in mills and workhouses to have at least three hours instruction a day. Schools were to be maintained out of the poor rate and government loans were to be available for the erection of schools. The schoolmaster was to be a member of the Established Church and trustees themselves were to include the parish clergyman and the Churchwardens. The religious instruction was to be that of the Church of England, and the children were to attend the parish church on Sunday. However there were many dissenters to this rate-aided educational scheme - which put the education of the poor under the control of the Church of England - and it failed. The proposed state system of education was postponed for nearly 30 years.

By the 1850s the state's contribution to education as well as voluntary grants was growing, and the Commissioners recommended an assessment by inspectors of examination achievements, which led to payment by results. This was not wholly successful, causing anxiety and pressure on the children and resulting in a temptation to falsify registers and to teach children to learn their reading books by heart.

In 1868 the Reform Bill gave the vote to householders who paid rates, and more people expressed an interest in improving the education system. In 1870 under Gladstone, William Edward Forster introduced a new Education Act, the purpose of which was to provide more schools, good and active schools inspectors, grants to church schools, and to establish non-denominational schools. The Act provided that England should be divided into districts and that elementary schools be established in areas where schooling was insufficient. About 2,000 School Boards were set up to manage these districts. These Boards, supported by local rates, were given powers to enforce attendance of children to the age of 13, and 5,000 new schools had been founded by 1874. For the first time children would not be denied an elementary education because they came from impoverished families. This led to a national system of primary schools. An Education Act of 1880 made school attendance compulsory to the age of ten, and at that age children could obtain a certificate and leave; however, if their record of attendance did not meet a standard they were required to stay on at school longer.

In 1891 a special fee-grant of ten shillings per head was introduced and this made elementary education virtually free. However, with no government watchdog to set standards, elementary education only concerned itself with overcoming illiteracy, and children's education was poor in quality, limited in range, and far from stimulating. In the late 1880s conditions in school buildings were reported to be dismal and very squalid. Attendance was very poor due to bad weather, lack of boots, epidemics, stone picking (from fields), potato planting, harvesting, helping with the washing, market days, tea treats and fairs, and as a consequence many punishments were inflicted on the children.

By 1889 the County Councils were to provide technical education maintained by a government grant, and new subjects such as history, geography, drawing, physical education, algebra, geometry, domestic science and craft became more common. In 1891 all elementary education was to be provided free. The school leaving age was raised to 11 in 1893, and then to 12 by 1899.

With Balfour's Education Act of 1902 local authorities were empowered to provide elementary and secondary education, thereby superseding the old School Boards. The Act transferred control of education to 140 new Local Education Authorities (LEAs). The Act also provided for the support of voluntarily schools from the local rates. Usually the secondary education was not co-educational - the boys went to state Grammar Schools and the girls to High Schools. In 1902, 55 per cent of teachers had no college training, but after 1905 new regulations improved the situation. In 1906 cheap school meals were provided and in 1907 medical examination of children in elementary schools became compulsory.

The Education Act of 1918 abolished any remaining fees for elementary education, and made compulsory attendance universal until the age of 14, but as late as the 1920s 80 per cent of pupils did not advance past the top class of elementary school. In 1921 free milk supplies were given to children in need, and from 1946 to 1971 milk was free to all. In 1936 an Act made provision for the school-leaving age to be raised to 15.

In the Education Act of 1944 primary and secondary schools were divided at the age of 'eleven plus', and elementary education was re-organised into infant and junior schools, with secondary education being graded into modern, grammar and technical schools. Powers were created to raise the school-leaving age to 15, and fees in state secondary schools were abolished. Universal education from five to 15 was achieved in 1947 and from five to 16 in 1972, these being the years when the school-leaving age was actually raised. In 1974 comprehensive education was introduced, and in 1976 the direct grant system was phased out, but most schools that were affected went independent. In 1980 an Education Act established an assisted-places scheme to provide financial support for some students in independent education.

EDUCATION IN NORTH CURRY

The education of the children of North Curry began in the early-19th century. The Sunday School for the tithing of North Curry was founded in 1809 by Mr John Hooper Scott of Moredon and Mr John Hopkins Foster, and was aided by the church and from subscriptions from parish residents. The Sunday School, for the instruction of boys and girls, opened on 11th February 1809, and had a voluntary attendance of 24 boys and 34 girls. A master and mistress whose joint salary amounted to £4.3s.0d were appointed, with the boys instructed in the vestry room of the church, and the girls at the house of the mistress. The education was very rudimentary, comprising the alphabet and words of one syllable, spelling and Bible reading of the Old and New Testaments. The hours of attendance were from 9.00 am until morning service and 2.30 pm until 5.00 pm, and if the church service was in the afternoon, from 9.00 am until 12 noon and from 2.00 pm until afternoon service and one hour afterwards each Sunday. Rules had been laid down in 1785 by *The Sunday School Society* and included the following:

> *...that the teachers shall take care that the scholars come clean to their respective school, and if any of them be guilty of lying, swearing, pilfering, talking in an indecent manner, or otherwise misbehaving themselves, the teacher shall point out the evil of such conduct, and if after repeated reproof, the scholar shall not be reformed, he or she, shall be excluded from the school.*

At the end of the first year, John Hopkins Foster, who was the first superintendent, was able to report: *Since the establishment of this Society, one hundred and forty-four children have been admitted into the school, some of whom have made considerable progress in reading etc. and we flatter ourselves the moral instruction they have received will not wholly prove ineffectual in their future conduct.* It was noted that many parents and their children, who before had habitually devoted the Sabbath to idleness or drunkenness, were now attending church worship and establishing morality, warranting the cost to the subscribers of the Sunday School as being fully beneficial to the community.

An Improved Day School was established in North Curry on 1st May 1820. It was conducted on the principles of the Church of England in association with the Sunday School, as laid down in a plan instituted by the Reverend J Poole of Enmore, Somerset. The boys were taught reading, writing and the common rules of arithmetic. The girls were instructed in the same, together with needlework, knitting and other handicrafts. Payment was to be made on Monday mornings of two pence a week, with an extra halfpenny for the use of books and slates and an additional halfpenny for the use of pens and ink. The rules of misbehaviour followed at Sunday School were to apply.

In 1830 there was need for dedicated school premises in the village, and a parcel of land was given by Robert Hooper Scott's sisters Sarah Gould and Mary Scott. This parcel of land amounting to 35 perch was situated on what is known today as Moor Lane, and a small schoolhouse and garden was built.

In 1846, following government Bills granting aid for the erection of school houses for the education of the children of the poorer classes, it was decided to build additional school premises. The Dean and Chapter of Wells and Mrs Sarah Gould conveyed a further plot of land, adjacent to the existing site in Moor Lane, amounting to 1 rood and 21 perch to the Vicar, the Reverend John Castle Burnett, and the Churchwardens to enable a new facility for the children of poor persons of the Parish of North Curry to be provided. Alterations and additions to the existing schoolhouse took place, based on plans drawn up by Carver and Giles of Taunton in 1846, and the new North Curry Parochial School was opened in 1848. The new school consisted of a single classroom and a small house that was to be used as the residence for the school master and his family. Boys and girls were taught separately, and usually the wife of the master took charge of the girls. The first teachers appointed to the school, who started on the 19th June 1848, were Mr Henry Suddaby and his wife Charlotte, who were appointed at a salary of £12.10s, to be paid quarterly.

When the Education Act of 1870 came into force, alternative systems of administration, either as a Board School or a Voluntary School, were established. North Curry School adopted a Voluntary School status by calling for voluntary subscriptions from parishioners, and continued to collect the *School Pence* paid by the children: a number of benefactors paid for the schooling of certain pupils, but most parents were required to pay one penny a week for each child's instruction. The school became known as North Curry National School and received a government grant of £45.17s.10d for reaching a standard of efficiency recognised by government inspectors.

In 1870 the number of children attending North Curry School was 156 with 33 infants under six years old, and a new classroom was built to accommodate the growing number of pupils. The teachers were helped with the instruction and control of the large number of pupils by monitors and pupil teachers. The unpaid monitors were senior pupils who taught the younger children to form letters of the alphabet and undertake simple sums. The paid pupil teachers, who were training to become teachers themselves, were instructed by the master before each day's lessons began. The curriculum in the early days consisted of the three R's together with religious instruction.

From 1862, when the *Revised Code for Education* was introduced, the curriculum for elementary schools included geography, grammar, arithmetic, spelling, writing, ciphering, dictation, multiplication, division, sewing, needlework and singing. The code enabled schools to claim four shillings a year for each pupil with a satisfactory attendance record. An additional eight shillings was paid if the pupil passed examinations in reading, writing and arithmetic. The Vicar, a frequent visitor to the school, undertook the religious instruction, reading prayers in the morning, teaching the catechism and sacraments and arranging for the children to attend church services in the nearby church.

Many children were absent from school due to diseases such as mumps, measles and scarlet fever and from many illnesses caused by their poor hygiene in the overcrowded classroom where all pupils were taught. Others were kept from school when required to help work the land and provide greater manpower at times of harvest, apple picking, potato digging, withy stripping and cider making at home and on the farms in this agricultural area. Sometimes children were kept at home when bad weather made the journey impossible. Leave of absence was not always obtained for outings to Bridgwater and North Curry Fair days, or to watch the visiting circus or a military display. Hardship was all too evident in the lack of suitable shoes and clothing. Many walked long distances to school without warm clothing or shoes, and clothing and shoe clubs operated by charities in the village attempted to provide for these basic needs.

A night school had been started in 1865 at the school's premises in Moor Lane, and was attended by adults and children who had left full-time education. In 1919 a Young Men's Instruction Class was held every Wednesday evening at the school. Instruction was given in *practical arithmetic, book-keeping, composition, varied by lectures on general information, historical, geographical and biographical*. Members paid twopence a night, and brought their own materials.

In 1879 the Ecclesiastical Commissioners granted land in Wrantage on Tithe Plots 811, 812 and 813 for the building of a school there. John Blackmore built it, with the architect Shrobrooke, at a cost of £308.4s.7d for the school building and £327.0s.9d for internal fitments. The building was provided by voluntary subscriptions from parishioners, and the Vicar of North Curry the Reverend R C Lathom Browne, and the Churchwardens oversaw the collecting. The school, under the control of the North Curry School Managers, educated almost 50 children from the Wrantage area, rising to almost 80 children in the early 1900s. Two teachers were employed, with one, the headmistress, teaching the juniors and seniors, and the other the infants.

From 1929 children over the age of 11 were transferred to North Curry School, and Wrantage School only taught children from 5 years old to 11. On the night of 27th and 28th June 1940 Wrantage School sustained bomb damage by enemy action and was destroyed. The damage was reported to the County Council and the War Damage Commission, with a request to use a nearby building that was called *The Hut* as a temporary school. Compensation was also applied for and a request made to re-build the school as a Voluntary School. These requests were not fulfilled and the schoolchildren of Wrantage were eventually sent, from 1948, to school in North Curry.

In 1891 an average of 140 children were attending North Curry School; this increased year by year until in 1905 there were 190 children on the roll. Harvest holidays ran from mid-August for three weeks, with a Whitsuntide holiday of one week, and Christmas holidays of one week. In 1902 an Act was passed whereby the cost of running the schools was levied by a Public Rate. However, this only paid for running the school and for a school caretaker, and did not cover the costs of the repair and upkeep of the school buildings, for which the private

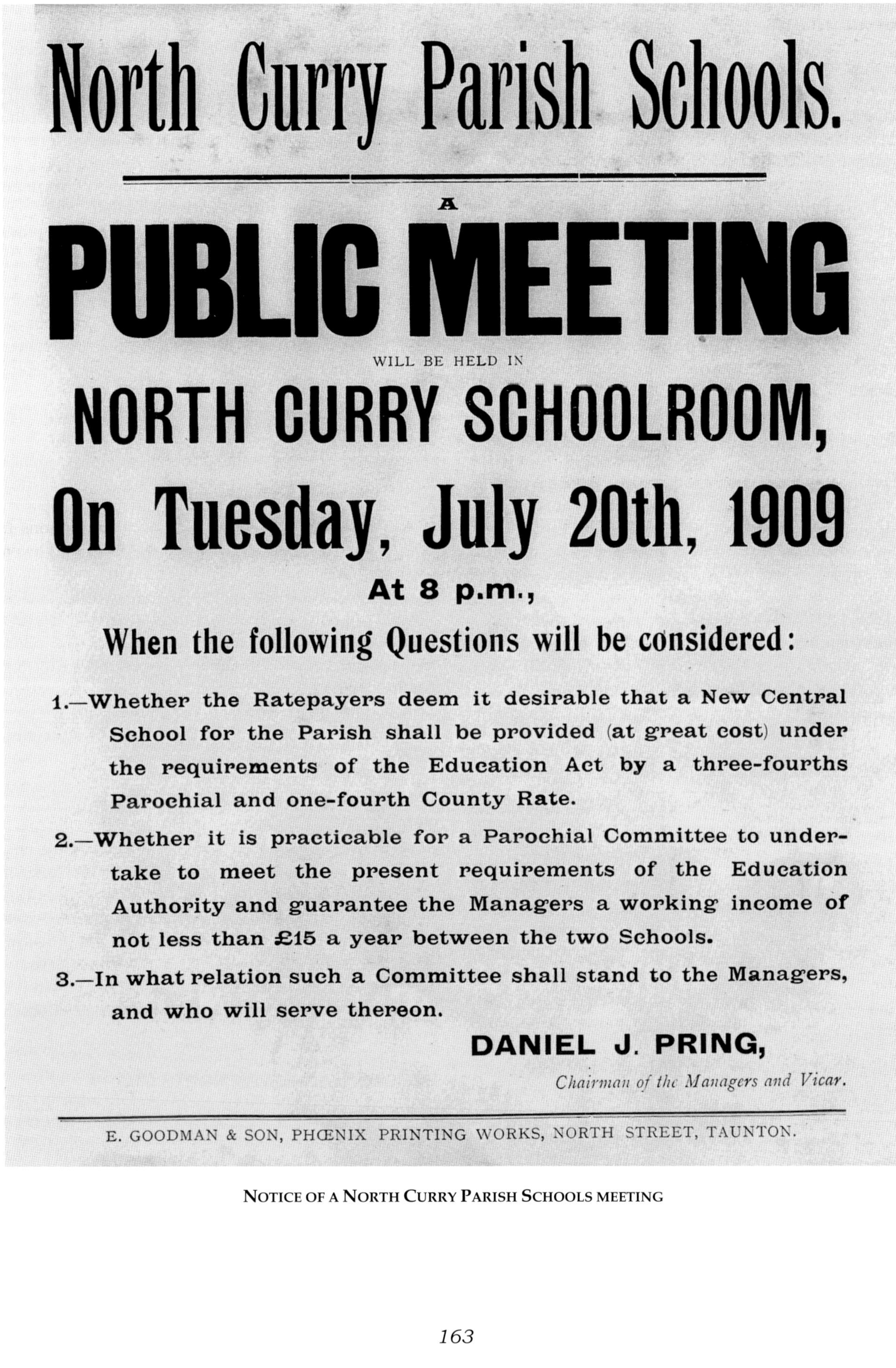

North Curry Parish Schools.

A

PUBLIC MEETING

WILL BE HELD IN

NORTH CURRY SCHOOLROOM,

On Tuesday, July 20th, 1909

At 8 p.m.,

When the following Questions will be considered:

1.—Whether the Ratepayers deem it desirable that a New Central School for the Parish shall be provided (at great cost) under the requirements of the Education Act by a three-fourths Parochial and one-fourth County Rate.

2.—Whether it is practicable for a Parochial Committee to undertake to meet the present requirements of the Education Authority and guarantee the Managers a working income of not less than £15 a year between the two Schools.

3.—In what relation such a Committee shall stand to the Managers, and who will serve thereon.

DANIEL J. PRING,

Chairman of the Managers and Vicar.

E. GOODMAN & SON, PHŒNIX PRINTING WORKS, NORTH STREET, TAUNTON.

NOTICE OF A NORTH CURRY PARISH SCHOOLS MEETING

school managers shouldered the burden. In 1903 the school's water closets were pronounced by the sanitary inspectors as totally insanitary, and a system of flushing was recommended, adding to the costs. Once again voluntary contributions from parishioners in the form of subscriptions, donations or funds raised by sales of work, concerts or other public entertainment, helped towards these costs. The alternative would have been for North Curry School and Wrantage School to become Council Schools, possibly moving to a new site to include both schools in a new building. The cost of this move would inevitably have fallen upon the ratepayers.

In 1907 the feeling in the village was for North Curry School to continue to be maintained by voluntary contributions from parishioners, and many appeals were made to retain this independence. The Vicar, the Reverend Daniel Pring, was instrumental in the ratepayers being asked to pay a minimum subscription of 2s.6d in order to retain the church's influence over the school in North Curry. The years that followed saw much deterioration of the school buildings and the school struggled to educate and support a rising population of children comfortably.

An enlargement of the school became necessary and in 1911 the Vicar again called successfully for more financial help from parishioners. The sum of £244.8s.9d was raised and one of the classrooms was enlarged. The master's house on the school site was made available for the caretaker, with the headmaster moving to a house in Windmill Hill. The larger of the classrooms was fitted with movable partitions to allow for better division of the classes of children. The dimensions of the two schoolrooms were as follows:

	Length	*Breadth*	*Height*
School Room	*15.35 metres*	*5.6 metres*	*4.3 metres*
Infant School Room	*10.5 metres*	*5.6 metres*	*4.3 metres*

The curriculum was broadened to include scientific subjects, nature study, cookery and a wider appreciation of singing and music. Outdoor activities such as physical exercise were included and gardening was taught with great success when a piece of ground was acquired for the purpose. The First World War brought much change as many pupils were required to leave early and take the place of men called for active service. After the War numbers of pupils started to rise again and in 1933 there were 147 on the roll. More subjects were introduced, such as biology and beekeeping for the boys, and laundry and housekeeping for the girls. The Second World War saw the arrival of evacuees from London and south-east England, and school life was adapted to accommodate them. In 1944 the school premises were wired for electric light and the playground was levelled and re-surfaced.

The 1944 Education Act required the educational system in the country to be reorganised to provide separate primary, secondary and further education. Children remained at North Curry School until they were 14 years old, with the most gifted gaining entrance to grammar schools in Taunton.

The school building continued to deteriorate, and there were many costs due to repairs and updating. In 1947, due to the heavy financial burden of maintaining the building, the Managers of North Curry School could no longer continue to run it as a Voluntary School. With this status it had been funded by the Church, assisted by the National Society and by voluntary subscriptions. The Managers applied to the Local Education Authority (LEA) for Controlled Status and asked for them to take financial control of all aspects of the school's affairs. The school became known as North Curry VC (Voluntary Controlled) School and retains that name today.

In 1960 the school became a primary school, educating children from 5 to 11 years old only. Pupils were required to leave the elementary or primary school at 'eleven plus' years and enter grammar, secondary modern or technical schools in the area. North Curry children left and entered either Huish's or Bishop Fox's in Taunton or went to West Monkton Secondary Modern School. The latter later became Heathfield Community School.

During the 1950s a kitchen was built at the school for the preparation of school dinners, in 1965 a swimming pool was built in the playground, and soon afterwards central heating was installed to replace the very inadequate stoves. In 1970 a new lavatory block was built. However, the ageing buildings were by this time in need of replacement, and North Curry was earmarked for one of the Somerset LEA's model new primary school buildings. A new site in Greenway was chosen and the school building, which cost £277,000, was eventually constructed.

In 1987 the school was moved to these new premises, and the following year, after the 1988 Education Reform Act, the governing body at the school was given more control and financial responsibility, and the National Curriculum was introduced, with Standard Assessment Tests (SATs) for all pupils being instigated. Today the new school buildings include a large carpeted hall for PE, drama, music and assemblies, and an attractive library area. The grounds are well landscaped and include a playing field, playground and an environmental pond area. The school now has over 140 pupils in five classes.

School teachers in North Curry

The *Census Returns* for North Curry between 1841 and 1901, together with information from *Trade Directories* and school records, provide the names of many school masters and school mistresses in both the National Schools and the private teaching establishments within North Curry.

1841 Census Return

NAME	AGE	POSITION	ADDRESS	SCHOOL
John Bucknole	*55*	*Schoolmaster*	*North Curry*	*Private*
Mary Salway	*35*	*Schoolmistress*	*North Curry*	*Private*
Mary Parks	*35*	*Schoolmistress*	*North Curry*	*Private*
Sarah Smith	*40*	*Schoolmistress*	*North Curry*	*Private*

1851 Census Return

NAME	AGE	POSITION	ADDRESS	SCHOOL
Henry Suddaby	*30*	*Master*	*Moor Lane*	*National*
Charlotte Suddaby	*23*	*Mistress*	*Moor Lane*	*National*
Louisa Edwards	*17*	*Pupil Teacher*	*Moor Lane*	*National*
John Paddock	*14*	*Teacher*	*Greenway*	*National*
John Bird	*44*	*Schoolmaster*	*Shambles*	*Private*
Eliza Bird	*33*	*Schoolmistress*	*Shambes*	*Private*
Sarah Paddock	*65*	*Schoolmistress*	*Greenway*	*Private*

John and Eliza Bird possibly ran a small school on the site of 6 Queen Square and had three children living with them called Sarah, Thomas and Elizabeth Lloyd aged 9, 7 and 5 who were presumably their pupils. There were 174 children listed as scholars receiving education in North Curry in the 1851 *Census Return*.

1861 Census Return

NAME	AGE	POSITION	ADDRESS	SCHOOL
James Wilkins Sheppard	*44*	*Certificated Schoolmaster*	*Moor Lane*	*National*
Phibi Shepherd	*56*	*Schoolmistress*	*Moor Lane*	*National*
John Dinham	*18*	*Pupil Teacher*	*Stoke Road*	*National*
Jane Priddle	*17*	*Pupil Teacher*	*Paynes Farm*	*National*
Eliza Liddon	*50*	*Schoolmistresses*	*Angel Row*	*Private*
Maria Crease	*32*	*Schoolmistress*	*Stoke Road*	*Private*
John Jones	*36*	*Principal*	*Queen Square*	*Private*
Anne Jones	*37*	*Principal*	*Queen Square*	*Private*

John and Anne Jones are listed as principals of a Young Gentlemen's and Ladies' School Establishment in Queen Square. This school was probably on the site of Melbourne House and they lived there with their two children, Ellen and Owen Jones aged 10 and 8, one governess Sacha Morris, aged 19, and five boarders, aged 9 to 16. It is listed as a seminary in *Kelly's Trade Directory* of 1861. There were 327 children listed as scholars receiving education in North Curry in the 1861 *Census Return*.

1871 Census Return

NAME	AGE	POSITION	ADDRESS	SCHOOL
Josiah Warry	*39*	*Schoolmaster Certified*	*Moor Lane*	*N.C.National*
Julia Warry	*44*	*Schoolmistress*	*Moor Lane*	*N.C.National*
Harriett Warry	*16*	*Assistant teacher*	*Moor Lane*	*N.C.National*
Henry Warry	*14*	*Pupil Teacher*	*Moor Lane*	*N.C.National*
Thomas Dyer	*17*	*Pupil Teacher*	*Moor Lane*	*N.C.National*
Gilbert Dudeney	*46*	*Schoolmaster*	*19 Knapp Lane*	*Private*
Lucy Dudeney	*39*	*Schoolmistress*	*19 Knapp Lane*	*Private*
John Dudeney	*16*	*Private Tutor*	*19 Knapp Lane*	*Private*
Louise Lock	*57*	*Schoolmistress*	*Wrantage*	*Wrantage National*
Louisa Pearce	*24*	*Schoolteacher*	*Greenway*	
Emilie Keales	*26*	*Schoolmistress*	*Village*	

Lucy and John Dudeney are listed with their five other children, aged 6 to 13, and nine boarders, and we may assume this to be the same teaching establishment previously listed as Melbourne House, a private boarding and day school. There were 324 children listed as scholars in North Curry in the 1871 *Census Return*.

1881 Census Return

NAME	AGE	POSITION	ADDRESS	SCHOOL
Josiah Warry	*49*	*Schoolmaster (Certified)*	*Moor Lane*	*N.C.Parochial (National)*
Julia Warry	*55*	*Schoolmistress*	*Moor Lane*	*N.C.Parochial (National)*
Harriett Warry	*25*	*Teacher*	*Moor Lane*	*N.C.Parochial (National)*
Anne Sanderson	*37*	*Schoolmistress*	*Melbourne House*	*Private*
Alice Shepperd	*19*	*Schoolmistress*	*Wrantage*	*Wrantage Parochial (National)*
Annie Baker	*24*	*Schoolmistress*	*Wrantage*	*Wrantage Parochial (National)*

NAME	AGE	POSITION	ADDRESS	SCHOOL
Emilie Adams	36	*Schoolmistress*	*Greenway*	*Private*
William Derrick	26	*Schoolmaster*	*Queen Square*	*Private*

Melbourne House has only one teacher and no boarding children recorded and may have ceased to be a boarding school. There were 459 children listed as scholars in North Curry in the 1881 *Census Return*.

1891 Census Return

NAME	AGE	POSITION	ADDRESS	SCHOOL
Josiah Warry	59	*Certified Teacher Public Elementary*	*Moor Lane*	*N.C.National*
Julia Warry	65	*Assistant Certified Teacher*	*Moor Lane*	*N.C.National*
Harriet Warry	36	*Assistant Certified Teacher*	*Moor Lane*	*N.C.National*
Sarah Wallbutton	25	*Teacher*	*Stoke Road*	*N.C.National*
Florence Spearing	11	*Monitress Infant Department*	*Windmill Hill*	*N.C.National*
Rose Dunster	14	*Schoolteacher*	*Lillesdon*	
William Derrick	28	*Schoolmaster*	*Queen Square*	*Boys Private*
Amy Hamilton	28	*Schoolmistress*	*Queen Square*	
Louisa Wolfe	26	*Schoolmistress*	*White Street*	*Private*
Alfred Wolfe	23	*Schoolmaster*	*White Street*	*Private*
Albert Wolfe	19	*Schoolmaster*	*White Street*	*Private*

The private schools listed were possibly on the site of Manchester House and Long's House. There were 300 children listed as scholars in North Curry in the 1891 *Census Return*.

1901 Census Return

NAME	AGE	POSITION	ADDRESS	SCHOOL
Sydney C Coombes	40	*Head teacher and organist*	*1 Victoria Terrace*	*N.C.National*
Harriett Warry	46	*Assistant schoolmistress*	*Queen Square*	*N.C.National*
Alice Dinham	28	*Assistant Schoolteacher*	*Greenway*	*N.C.National*
Ellen Stone	24	*Schoolteacher*	*Greenway*	
Edith Bellringer	19	*Schoolteacher*	*Greenway*	*N.C.National*
Frances L Peters	34	*Schoolmistress*	*Wrantage*	*Wrantage National*
Hilda B Warry	15	*Schoolteacher*	*Queen Square*	*N.C.National*
Annie Marshall	45	*Private Schoolmistress*	*Queen Square*	*Private*
Albert R Wolfe	29	*Private Schoolmaster*	*Helland House*	*Private*
Louisa C S Wolfe	34	*Music Mistress*	*Helland House*	*Private*

The private school in Long's House had moved into Helland House. In the 19th century Helland House had been the home of farmer Samuel Hellard and in the early-20th century became a private school. There were only 21 children listed in North Curry as scholars in the 1901 *Census Return*, but only probably because of the enumerator's system of mostly only listing the occupations of adults.

The *Trade Directories* of North Curry list headteachers at the school at Wrantage as follows:

1881–1883	*Mrs A Baker*	*Parochial Mixed School*
1889–1894	*Miss Fay*	*Parochial Mixed School*
1894–1902	*Miss F L Peters*	*Parochial Mixed School*
1906–1927	*Miss Beatrice Coombs*	*Public Elementary Mixed School*

The *Trade Directories* list head teachers at the National School in North Curry as follows:

1861	*John Wilkins Sheppard and Miss Phoebe Sheppard*
1866	*Stephen Smith and Mrs Martha Smith*
1872–1896	*Josiah Warry (master for 29 years) and Julia Warry, Henry Warry*
1896–1902	*Sydney Charles Coombs*
1906–1926	*James Alexander Williams*

The *Trade Directories* list Private Schools in North Curry as follows:

1861	*Mrs Eliza Liddon*	*Girls Day School*
1861	*John Jones*	*Boys Boarding School*
1866	*Gilbert Dudeney*	*Boarding and Day School for young gentlemen*
1872–1889	*Mrs Emily Adams*	*Ladies School*
1889	*Miss Emma Hamilton*	*Ladies School*
1889–1894	*Alfred Wolfe*	*Helland House*
1902	*Mrs Ann Marshall*	*Melbourne House*
1906	*Mrs Mary Bates*	*Melbourne House*
1910	*Mrs Mary Bates*	*Knapp Lane*
1914	*Mrs Mary Bates*	*Whatley House*
1919	*Mrs Mary Bates*	*The Grange*
1923	*Celia Wontner*	*Newport House*
		(moved to Poltimore Park, near Exeter later in 1923)

More recent Headteachers of North Curry School

1926–1929	*Edward Fletcher*
1929–1931	*William J Allen*
1931–1941	*Alfred E Willcox*
1942–1952	*E A John*
1952–1957	*W S Grainger*
1959–1984	*Geoffrey Harper*
1985–1995	*Graham Linacre*
1996–2000	*Mustafa Sheikh*
2001–2002	*Alan Sullivan*
2003	*Elsa Hedges*

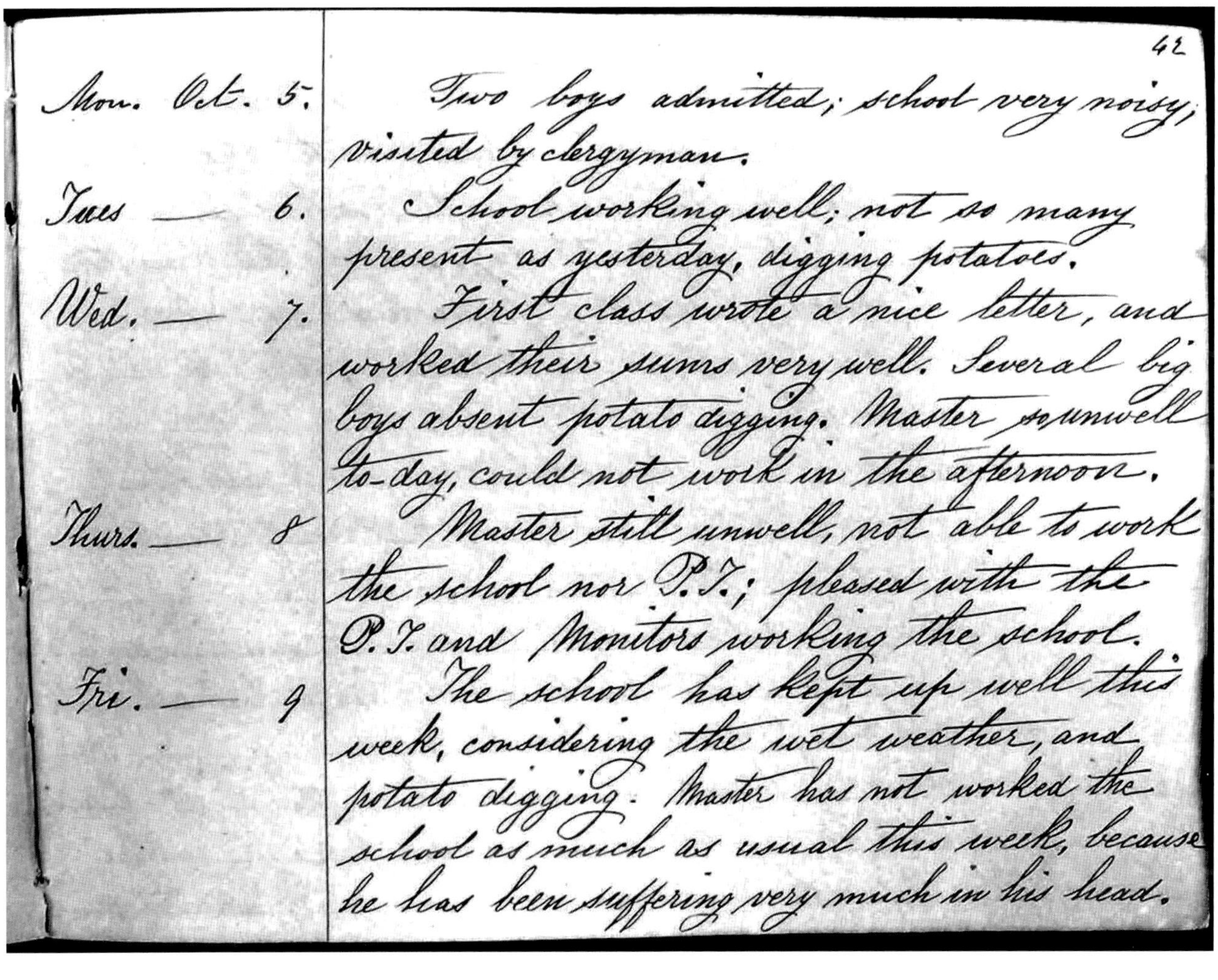
42

Mon. Oct. 5. Two boys admitted; school very noisy; visited by clergyman.

Tues — 6. School working well; not so many present as yesterday, digging potatoes.

Wed. — 7. First class wrote a nice letter, and worked their sums very well. Several big boys absent potato digging. Master so unwell to-day, could not work in the afternoon.

Thurs. — 8 Master still unwell, not able to work the school nor P.T.; pleased with the P.T. and Monitors working the school.

Fri. — 9 The school has kept up well this week, considering the wet weather, and potato digging. Master has not worked the school as much as usual this week, because he has been suffering very much in his head.

EXTRACT FROM NORTH CURRY SCHOOL LOG BOOK – **1863** TO **1870**

2 - 8

ROADWAYS, WATERWAYS AND RAILWAYS

ROADWAYS

From prehistoric times when man roamed the land hunting for food and looking for suitable materials to make his tools and weapons, he used trackways that avoided densely wooded or marshy areas for his journeying. These tried and tested routes, together with ridgeways over the hills, provided important lines of communication between settlements as man evolved and communities were established. In Somerset early man cleverly constructed trackways built of logs covered with brushwood that provided dry and flat crossings over the swampy ground of the Somerset Levels.

When the Romans arrived in Britain they built stone-surfaced roads with good foundations and drainage which were able to sustain heavy military use between their chosen centres of population and their fort sites. During the Saxon period many of these roads had only limited use and were allowed to deteriorate, as most of their villages were self-supporting. By the Middle Ages most heavy loads were carried by sea and river and unloaded onto horse-drawn carts and packhorses, with many of the older trackways and ridgeways, droveways or green roads being resurrected for the movement of animals and for everyday foot traffic. Journeys using horses were limited to about 20 miles a day.

As time went on and individual loads became heavier, drawn by larger horse-drawn wagons, the lanes became eroded by deep hollows and ruts. In the 16th century, wheeled horse-drawn traffic of all types became common, and maintaining the roads became necessary. In 1555 an Act of Parliament gave the parishes the responsibility of maintaining the roads that passed through them under the stewardship of two unpaid surveyors elected annually. All householders were obliged to give four days labour, and later six days, to keep the roads in repair, with farmers providing horses and carts to help with this operation. The main roads that passed through many parishes deteriorated owing to lack of maintenance direction, and travellers were diverted to better paths when some roads became impassable.

New road-making techniques were gradually introduced by people such as Jack Metcalf and Thomas Telford and later by John Macadam, whose name became part of the English language to describe his road surfacing process. New roads were laid as demand by mail coaches and passenger coaching for fast and speedy routes became pressing. Turnpike Trusts were set up by Acts of Parliament in the 18th century. These empowered local people to raise money by public loans to build and repair roads and to levy tolls to repay them. The tolls varied with different loads and sizes of carriage, wagon or wheel trim and were collected at gates or turnpikes at intervals along the road.

With the introduction of the railways in the early 1840s roads became even busier, with traffic to the new stations increasing. However, as new branch rail lines were built much of this road traffic was diverted onto the railways. The Turnpike Trusts were eventually dissolved. Parishes were grouped together into highway districts to be maintained by borough councils and county councils and the new trunk roads came under the control of central government.

As discussed in previous chapters archaeological evidence dating from the Iron Age and Roman times is spread over a large area of the parish, indicating a mainly agricultural community that established itself along trackways, near water and centred on sites giving easy access to the open field system of farming. When in 1242 Bishop Jocelin of Bath gave North Curry Manor to the Dean and Chapter of Wells Cathedral, as Lords of the Manor they became responsible for the administration of the parish and the village took on a more structured form. The trackways became more established with the need to link the various outlying communities with the centre of the village of North Curry. The roads today probably follow the same course as in those early days, extending from the Square or the Shambles to the hamlets of Knapp, Lillesdon, Wrantage, Newport, Helland, Broad Lane and Moredon.

An ancient watercourse, referred to as the *Dinney*, followed Greenway and The Pavement to Queen Square and continued its course at the rear of the cottages in Church Road, crossing The Fosse into the old Village Pound (Manor Lodge) and finally discharging into the moor. In early times this provided a ready-made sewer, and houses were built along its bank. In fact it probably determined the layout of the centre of North Curry, deciding the positioning of dwellings on roadways that followed its course. Reference is made to it as a stream in a *Presentment* at a Court Baron held on 27th April 1726:

> *We present the Supervisors of the High Ways to erect a bridge in the body of North Curry Town by Wm. Godfrey's house* (near the junction of Stoke Road and Queen Square) *over the water course by Lammas Day next or to forfitt 20s.*

The court made a similar order on 12th October 1726:

> *We present the Supervisor of the Highways for the Tything of North Curry to make a sufficient bridge over a water course commonly called The Dinney. We also present all those persons that have any closure against the said water course or Dinney from the above said bridge home to the pound to make sufficient closure against the said water course of Dinney by 20th November next.*

Nothing is now visible of this stream, a closed sewer having taken its place.

Stage and mail coaches passing through North Curry gave the residents improved communication from afar and the facility to make extended journeys. The stopping place on the stage-coach route from London, where horses were changed, was reputedly at the Rock Inn at Curry Mallet.

The Angel Inn in Stoke Road, North Curry, was a coaching inn, and would have been where the shorter-distance coach horses were watered and changed and where passengers could receive hospitality.

In the 19th century North Curry supported a number of road makers and workers, together with a tollgate keeper as listed in the North Curry *Census Returns* as follows:

1871	*Edward Tucker of Hellend*	*Road Contractor*
1871	*Ruth Humphry of Turnpike Gate, Wrantage Road*	*Collector of Turnpike Tolls*
1881	*James Bellringer of Clarkes Hill*	*Road Contractor*
1891	*Solomon Hooper of Knapp Road*	*Road Stone Cracker*
1891	*Philip Bowey of Sedgemoor Drove*	*Road Contractor*

The roads and pathways through North Curry in those days were not up to modern-day standards, being very rough and full of potholes. Both children and grown-up pedestrians were required to wear heavy boots when walking. To walk to church or chapel they wore pattens, an overshoe worn to raise ordinary shoes out of the mud or water and consisting of a wooden sole mounted on to an iron oval ring. It is recorded that the first pavement in Church Road was laid in readiness for the wedding of Mrs C R Morris in 1857 so that she could walk dry footed from her home at Gwyon House to the Methodist Chapel. North Curry farmers' wives often had to walk to Taunton with their butter and eggs, and they delivered the milk round the district by means of a shoulder carrier bearing two buckets.

Horse-drawn vehicles such as donkey carts were used increasingly to make local deliveries. These, together with ponies and traps or more elaborate horse-drawn carriages for the wealthier people, were used to make a journey to town and market a real outing, taking the best part of the day to get there and back. At the beginning of the 20th century the carrier's van served as a conveyance for parcels and produce as well as passengers.

Within the first decade of the 20th century the internal combustion engine established itself for both private and public transport in the form of car, bus, lorry and coach. Eighty years had seen the means of travel pass from the age of the horse, though the age of steam into the age of petrol. Roads were improved, straightened and widened; crossroads, roundabouts, by-passes and eventually motorways provided easy long-distance travelling; and today every mile of road whether minor or major is kept to a suitable standard for both comfort and safety.

WATERWAYS

In relative terms Somerset's main rivers can be considered new, for at one time the plain from the Quantock Hills to the Mendip Hills and from Bridgwater Bay to North Dorset was a shallow sea with low islands rising from it. Before the religious communities began their work of cutting ditches and drains, the rivers distributed their waters over a large tract. Now the swamps are rich green pasture and the rivers flow between willows.

The River Tone, which rises in the Brendon Hills and joins the River Parrett at Burrowbridge, passes through the Parish of North Curry and is important in assisting the drainage of the area. Much of the land through which these rivers flowed had for generations been under the control of the ecclesiastical foundations of Muchelney, Glastonbury, Athelney and Wells Cathedral. The rivers had been used for fishing since very early times and the *Domesday Survey* for North Curry mentions an important fishery (see page 26).

The River Tone has also been an important commercial waterway used for generations for the transportation of fuel, agricultural products and raw materials, and later for manufactured goods. Ham in particular was an important inland port supplying a large district. Subsequently the Dean and Chapter of Wells, who were the Lords of the Manor of North Curry since 1242, derived much income from fishing weirs and water mills located on the River Tone and other smaller waterways. The water mills located on rivers or streams at Newport, Ham and Knapp were used for many centuries for the grinding of their tenant farmers' grain.

The following reference in the *Calendar of the Manuscripts of the Dean and Chapter of Wells* is one of many giving details of licence being sought by the Dean and Chapter to make new watercourses for mills.

> *AD 1316*
> *The precentor and the succentor to go as quickly as possible to Montacute Priory to seek licence to make a new watercourse for Knappe Mill.*
> *Wells MSS Liber Albus I Folio 148*

On 15th January 1489 there is mention in the Wells Manuscripts of a controversy between the Dean and Chapter of Wells, the Prior of Montacute and the Bishop of Winchester concerning a mill built in the Ham area of North Curry and the course of the waters of the River Tone. (The Bishop of Winchester held the lands above Ham Mills, and from the time of Domesday held the large Manor of Taunton.) The building of the mill by the Chapter of Wells had caused the waters of the Tone to flood surrounding lands inhabited by both the tenants of Taunton and the tenants of other land near to the River Tone in Ham and Knapp, both in the Manor of North Curry. These tenants made complaints and in due course the King commanded the destruction of the mill. Entries in *the Calendar of the Manuscripts of the Dean and Chapter of Wells Liber Ruber II* give the following references to this dispute:

1489 January 15
Mr. William Bocat, steward of the church, to ride to the manor of Northcory to confer with the counsel of the prior of Monte Acuto as to the controversies between them concerning the newly-built mill, the fishery of the waters there, and other matters.

1504 May 5
Master William Cousyn, dean and others were deputed to ride to the manor of Northcory, to treat and communicate with the counsel of Lord Richard Fox bishop of Winchester as to the course of the water of the Tone and the mill lately built near the same within the said manor.

This visit was followed with a letter to the Bishop of Winchester from the Chapter of Wells disputing the mill to be the cause of any problems and pleading with him to ignore complaints:

1505 November 4
A letter missyve sent to my lord of Wynchester by the brethren of Chapitre. Right reverend fader in God and to us moste singular gode lord in our mooste humble wyse we recommende us. Please it the same to understande howe that dyverse of the Bretheren of our Chapitre were with your officers at our myll of Northcory and ther hard the gretes and complayntes which your tennants made, and wher as it is thought by theym that our said myll shulde be the occasion of the grete floods and drowning of the medews which in our mynde was not thought possible to be. Nevertheless to have you good lord unto us as ye have ever been and also to cesse theyr clamours we shal be contented to lose a quarter Rent. And for that time to cause the floodgats of our said myll to be pulled up, so that the water shall have his full course, whereby it shal appere hereafter whether that our myll be the occasion of eny suche floods and drownynge of the medews. And as for bote passage your said officers knowe right well that in all the said season the water was so lowe and so many shelpes and bayes in the ryver betweene our myll and Taunton that it was not possible to convery eny bote that way. And in the wynter season the medewes be so filled and replenyshed with water that the boots may go over at every place so that they shal not be lett by the myll. My lord these things considered we trust that ye wull contynue as good lord nowe unto us as ye have been by former tyme. And thus the holy Trinite contynue you accordying to your noble desires.
By your dayly oratours the bretheren of Chapitre of Wells.
MSS Wells Liber Ruber II Folio 114d

However, William Cousyn, the Dean of Wells, wrote secretly to the chapter as follows:

1505 November 13
A letter from the dean William Cousyn to the chapter.
Right honourable bretheren I recommende me unto you certifying you that according to your mynds concluded in the Chapitre I have spoken with my Lord of Winchester for our myll and have moved hym both with resons and prayers to be good lord unto us for the said myll by in noo wyse I can not have his lordshipp at no conclusion but that he will have downe the bay of stone made by the prior. And at one season he said he would be content to remytt his action but he wold have a commission of shewyers by the reason whereof he said he was sure to have his mynde. And after my porre mynde it were better to putt the matter into gentilmens hands than to laborying men of the cuntrey for they do speke upon will and make a grete clamour without reason as we may knowe opynly by the copy of a bill the which I send you be my servant, and which my lord the Winchester toke me to rede and I in the moste haste I cowde make caused it to be wrytten and gave xxxd[??] therfor to th'entent ye shuld knowe thas complaynte, and also the doblenesse of the prior of Mountacu or elles of his tenants. Wherfor after this my writyng with the copy of the complaynte I pray you send me your mynde howe ye wold I shuld doo and whedder I shuld conclude uppon a commission of the sheywers or upon gentilmen of the cuntry to the which I thynk it wil be hard to be brought. And as towchyng the openyng of the floode gats as yet I cannot bryng his lordshipp to apply therto for he seith that he will not beleve his trusty counsell in saying nay, and me nor none of us in saying soo. Wherfor in this matter I pray you send me your mynds and the best I can doo possible I shal do. And if I may I shal cause hym to bee content to prove the experyence of the plukking up of the floodegats, but as yet I can not have hym at no conclusion nor I thynk shal not tyll the season mayster ffroste be come to London. The which was not come as this day at nyght at the which season I spake with my lord Wynchester as God knoweth who preserve you. Wrytten at London the xiiijth day of November with the hand of your brothre William Cousyn deane of Wells. I pray you kepe the copy of these complaynts as secretely as ye can for if it were knowen that I did copy theym it mygte pereventure turne to my rebuke.
MSS Wells Liber Ruber II Folio 116d

The following letter to the Chapter of Wells was sent by tenants near the mill complaining of flooding caused by the presence of the mill and the resulting hindrance to navigation on the river.

1505 November
The piteous complaint of the tenants near the mill:
Pytuously complayneth unto you maysterships the poore men duellyng nygh adjoyaunt to Hammyll, that where we be sore greved by reson of the same mylle, that it to say, our medewes, called Newe Medewes and Nate Medewes, and other pastures, certayn grene corn, our hay, ofttymes drowned, our highways foundered, wherby we have been grevously amerced in the shire and soore troubled; the fordes depe worne, wherthoroughe we be sore charged to make a brigge for weynes and horses every twoo or thre yere to be newe mended and made ; oure bestes standyng in water, without mete; our corne and hay to stand long afeld, till it be almoste lost by cause we can have no good cariage home. And we have paied to moste parte of oure goodes for oure places, and nowe we can take but litel profite therof. And oftentymes we have spoken therof in our courts. And can have no remedy. And we understand your maystership, have auctorite to enquere of all maner hurtes and greves done by occasion of the same mylle. Wherfor we beseche your maistership, in the way of charite, to have pite upon us, and be our socour for reformation herof, orelles we must medes forsake our places, to our uttre undoynge. And we shall pray to God to send you long life after his pleasure.
MSS Wells Liber Ruber II Folio 119d

The Chapter of Wells were reluctant to acknowledge these complaints:

1505 November 18
The chapter answer that if their proposal for pulling up the floodgates is not accepted, that they are willing that the bishop may at his own will decide whether that matter be settled by shewyers or by certain gentilmen of the country. There have been great floods as there have been time out of mind but no drowning of the country.
MSS Wells Liber Ruber II

A meeting to discuss events was arranged after it was learned that a judgement had been made that the common passage of boats on the King's stream (River Tone) had been affected. The Chapter did not attend.

> *1507 April*
> *Letter from John Prior for Montague to the chapter. The archdeacon and steward of Wells had been to "our pore place" to have friendly communication about the mill* (Ham). *The prior had made no direct answer then because he had not taken advice but had sent answer shortly afterwards by the prior of Kerswell. And appointment had been made for a meeting at Cory, "and thidder I came, but the chapter did not keep the appointment, and the matter was put off until May 1st, in order that Mr. Mylles might look into it. He desires to know what they think best to be done."*
> *MSS Wells Liber Ruber II Folio 143*

> *1507 May 2*
> *The Chapter's answer to the last. "They intend to remove suche beldynges as we hadd made in the water of Tone in the lordship of Northcory as we be commanded to doo by the Kyng's commaundment."*
> *MSS Wells Liber Ruber II Folio 143d*

The following entry was thus made:

> *1507*
> *The Chapter to Richard Philips under Shereffe of Somerset. Given at Wells on Wytsonday in haste. "They have obeyed the writ to remove the building made in the water of the Tone, and beg him to come and inspect the place."*
> *MSS Wells Liber Ruber II Folio 144*

Reference is made some 150 years later in 1671 to a lease granted to Francis, Lord Hawley of Buckland Sororum (Durston) of a newly erected mill at Ham. Remains of an early millhouse and waterwheel are evident on the site of Ham Mills, a listed house in the Parish of Creech St Michael on the River Tone.

The important activity of land drainage and reclaiming the flooded land of the Levels within the Parish of North Curry was taking place during the 13th century, producing easily worked fertile soil for farming activity. The Dean and Chapter of Wells engaged in this reclamation activity to define and consolidate their estates in the area. An impressive series of embankments and walls was built to surround the moors and exclude the floodwaters. The reclamation that centred on the Tone valley contained Hay, Boterlake and Curry Moors, Stan and Stathe Moor together with the area north of the River Tone and the Isle of Athelney and west of the River Parrett, Salt Moor and North Moor. Land was exchanged between owners and compensation was sometimes paid. Many references to these deals and to claims of wrongful enclosure appear in the Wells Manuscripts. In 1233, John and Agnes de Aure were accused by the Dean of setting up a dyke in Salt Moor, and of enclosing Stathe Grove. After a counter-claim both parties reached agreement, exchanging land and rights of way.

However, the reclamation of the area of the Tone Valley was not successful and flooding became a serious concern, caused mainly by the overflow of the River Parrett. The Tone at this time divided at East Lyng before entering the Parrett at two different places. One branch passed through the Lyng/Athelney gap and flowed over North Moor, and the other ran close to the modern course south of the island known as Athelney. In 1374–5 the Abbot of Athelney and other landowners diverted the River Tone into a new embanked channel, three-quarters-of-a-mile long, which today is still called *Cuts*. To protect further the area of Saltmoor from flooding from the Tone, the Balt Moor Wall was built; this also serving as a causeway. As a result of this illegal diversion Stathe Moor was more likely to be affected by flooding. The uniting of the two channels of the Tone meant there was more pressure on the river banks at flood time, and the River Tone entered the River Parrett further upstream where it was too narrow to cope with the flood discharge. Many of these problems are still unresolved today.

In the 16th and 17th centuries many goods were hauled by river up the tidal waters of the Parrett from Bridgwater to Langport, and by the River Tone from Burrowbridge to Ham Mill. From early days Ham and Knapp were used as loading and unloading places for goods being carried by water from Bridgwater to Taunton. In 1624 the Dean and Chapter of Wells fined one Thomas Hancock, described as *a gent from Gregorystoke*, the sum of ten pounds with a future yearly rent of ten shillings for unauthorised use of their landing stage near Ham Mills. In the *Calendar of the Manuscripts of the Dean and Chapter of Wells* an entry in that year referring to a deed poll states:

> *1624*
> *Foreasmuch as divers persons of late have incroched and usurped on our rights, priviledges and possessions therre scituate and being, in briginge upp iron, sea coles, pitt coles and other marchandize from Bridgewater by water, and landinge the same on our soile neere unto Ham Mills, without our leave and consent. In consideration of £10 fine and 10s. yearly rent, of Thomas Hancock of Gregorystoke, gent., as deputy and assignee, with full power to contract and compound for royalties for the landing of merchandize on the dean and chapter lands, all moneys so taken by him to be for his own use, without rendering any account. For the lives of Paul, Robert and William Hancock, his sons.*
> *MSS Wells Liber Ruber II*

There is uncertainty about the construction date of the first Knapp Bridge. Wells manuscripts referring to the Tone at Knapp in 1324 state Hugh de Bello Campo *shall make and maintain two bridges over the new watercourse aforesaid* (see page 77). In 1629 three men were bound over at Quarter Sessions following a dispute concerning transportation of goods from a bridge called *newe bridge in North Currie*. A bridge on the site of the current New Bridge in North Curry was not built until 1815 (see page 176), and this dispute almost certainly refers to Knapp Bridge. The Bridge was re-sited c.1703 when the River Tone was straightened from a course about 100 metres from its present position as part of the work of the Conservators of the River Tone (see next paragraph). Collinson mentions Knapp Bridge in 1790 (see page 51). The current Knapp Bridge is believed to be the result of further rebuilds in 1766 and again in 1821.

Barges were sometimes unable to reach Taunton from Bridgwater because of the tide variations and the winding and narrow nature of the river towards Taunton. Some stretches of the river were difficult to navigate without the help of towing horses, and often at certain times of the year goods were transferred to packhorses to reach inaccessible parts. The person responsible for making the River Tone navigable was John Malet of Enmore, who commenced the scheme in 1638 at his own expense. He and his successors were granted the letters patent for sole navigation of the river as far as Ham Mills. In 1698 a group of 30 gentlemen completed the navigation towards Taunton at a cost of £330 and in 1699 they were appointed Conservators of the River Tone. Unfortunately this work was not entirely successful owing to the lack of locks and the formation of a sand shoal by Knapp Bridge, which caused the river to be non-navigable in winter. In 1708 an Act of Parliament was passed which enabled the Conservators to increase the tolls and carry out further improvements They were granted powers to improve the passage and to remove obstructions, build bridges, wharves and locks, and to make pathways alongside the river. These further improvements included the construction of half-locks at Ham, Knapp and Curry Moor.

Any profits, after repair costs and the Conservators' own personal costs, were to be used for the building of a hospital for the poor of Taunton to be governed by them. Daniel Defoe, writing in 1724, comments that *the River Tone is made navigable up to Taunton, by a very fine new channel, cut at the expence of the people of Taunton, and which by the navigation of it, is infinitely advantageous to that town, and well worth all their expence.*

Coal was the main cargo carried at the time and in 1684 the Bobbett family had set up premises at Ham Mills as *dealers in sea coles* bringing the coal by barge from Wales and distributing it to merchants by packhorse from Taunton, North Curry, Langport and Wellington. Tolls were levied *at fourpence on three tons of coal and two pennies for every ton of other goods to be paid and received at Knapbridge* for goods from Bridgwater to Ham Mills. From Ham Mills to Taunton a further toll of *four shillings for every three tons of coal and a further two shillings for every ton of other goods* was levied and collected at Coal Harbour, near Ham. Other goods carried down river were timber, lime, stone and bricks, grain, apples and cider, cloths and basketwork and other agricultural produce. By 1768 wharves in Bridgwater were receiving coal from Swansea and in 1823 28,000 tons of coal was brought to Taunton from Bridgwater by river.

During the 1960s evidence of an old ford spanning the river bed was uncovered at Coal Harbour, and in 1968 a private suspension bridge was designed and built by Royal Marine Engineers linking a building on an island to the road.

During the 18th century canals were being constructed, offering a more convenient means of water transport without obstructions from weirs and mills and affording a consistent depth of water. In 1811 the Conservators of the River Tone objected to the newly formed Bristol and Taunton Canal Company's proposals to provide a better means of water transport between the ports of London, Bristol, Bridgwater and Exeter. They feared that their monopoly of water trade would be lost. However the plan proved to be too ambitious and costly and a revised plan of a shorter canal between Huntworth, just north of Bridgwater, to Firepool in Taunton received support. This Bridgwater and Taunton Canal was authorised in 1824 to link Taunton directly to Bridgwater, by-passing the Rivers Tone and Parrett. Although the canal was channelled through fairly flat terrain, unforeseen tasks connected with re-routing streams and installing side drains added to the costs, but eventually work was completed in 1827 and a little later the Conservators of the River Tone sold their rights of the river to the Bridgwater and Taunton Canal Company and were reimbursed the money they had subscribed, together with a sum of £2,000. In 1838 they built a new wing to the Taunton and Somerset Hospital becoming known as the Conservators' Ward - a name retained today at the Musgrove Park Hospital in Taunton. Although they were relieved of their responsibilities towards the upkeep of the River Tone in 1832, they were given the duty of inspecting the canals once a year, ensuring the Canal Company maintained the new waterway.

At about the same time a scheme was envisaged for a canal linking Seaton and Bridgwater Bay through Chard and crossing the River Tone about half a mile below Ham Mills at Creech St Michael joining into the Bridgwater and Taunton Canal. The cut of this canal included mechanical lifts and inclines to traverse the many differences in land height. Projected costs escalated and the scheme was abandoned. However in 1834 a 13.5 mile length of canal with three tunnels and four inclined planes was begun from Creech St Michael to Chard to use tub-boats rather than larger barges. This section of canal passed through Lillesdon, where there was a bridge and a tunnel, and Wrantage where an aqueduct carried the canal over a road, leading to a short incline and the entrance to the 1,660-metre-long Crimson Hill Tunnel. During its construction the population increased dramatically in the Parish of North Curry due to the influx of canal workers. A story is told that the canal workers were housed in dormitories in the building that became the Canal Inn, which was located next to the construction work. The canal was opened in 1841, but because of the narrowness of the waterway, the long tunnels and the difficulties of working the inclined planes, its operational life was only 20 years and there was a proposal to replace it with a railway. The decline of the River Tone navigation started with the opening of the Bridgwater to Taunton Canal in 1827, but it continued to be used until 1929 when the last barge reached Ham Mills.

In the 1851 *Census Return* for North Curry a family is listed as living in the area of Crimson Hill and working on the canal as follows:

Samuel Vincent of Crimson Hill – Incline Plane Worker, his sons John aged 18 are listed as a Boatman on Incline, and William and Samuel aged 16 and 15 as Assistant Boatmen on Incline Plane.

Also in the 1851 *Census Return* James Jenkins of New Bridge is listed as a *Waterman*, and three *Boatmen* are listed as living at Ham.

In 1842 Brunel's Bristol and Exeter Railway for passengers reached Taunton, and in 1866 a line was opened from Taunton to Chard. In the same year the Railway Company purchased the Bristol and Taunton Canal and thereafter river transport began to decline steadily. The inadequacy of the water supply had been one of the River Tone Conservators' main concerns regarding the Bristol and Taunton Canal. Confrontations between the Canal Company and the River Tone Conservators had been rife during the construction of the canal, as water from certain stretches of the River Tone was needed to feed the canal. With the prospect of a railway in the area making further demands on the limited water supply the Conservators became concerned once more.

By 1874 the tolls charged for using the canal were not enough to maintain it and the competition for freight with the Bristol and Exeter Railway became too great. The canal became choked with weed and began to be a health hazard. After an amalgamation in 1877 of the Bristol and Exeter Railway and the Great Western Railway, it was decided the canal would be maintained primarily as a source of water for the railway.

Annual inspections of the canal by the Conservators continued, and 30 years after the canal had been closed to navigation the lock gates and sluices were still in good working condition. The Railway Company was obliged to ensure it remained free flowing, as it became an important land-drainage channel. During the Second World War both the Chard and the Bridgwater and Taunton canals formed part of an anti-tank barrier which became known as the Taunton Stop Line. The whole line of 44 miles contained over 350 inland defence pillboxes that were to be used to accommodate soldiers with Lewis guns and rifles to quell an enemy invasion force. Scattered over the area of Lillesdon and Wrantage in the Parish of North Curry are the remains of a number of these pillboxes.

After the 1947 Transport Act the Western Region of British Railways assumed responsibility for the upkeep of the Bridgwater and Taunton Canal and it came under public ownership. During the war swing bridges had been adapted to low-level fixed bridges which did not allow the canal to be used for navigation, making any sort of maintenance and weed control impossible. In 1952 the canal had been without traffic for 50 years and the Association of Inland Waterways started to promote the canal as a possible recreational asset. The British Transport Commission resisted the efforts to make it navigable by adapting the bridges; traffic was barred and the locks were padlocked. In 1955 the Ministry of Transport Bowes Committee considered the Bridgwater and Taunton Canal to be of value only for drainage water supply, recreation or amenity. At the end of the 1960s the British Waterways Board was relieved of its responsibilities for the canal. Somerset County Council considered recreational uses of the canal and in 1975 the Somerset County Council, the councils of Sedgemoor and Taunton Deane and the Wessex Water Authority agreed a joint financial input, and work on the canal as a recreational waterway commenced. The process of restoration is now complete.

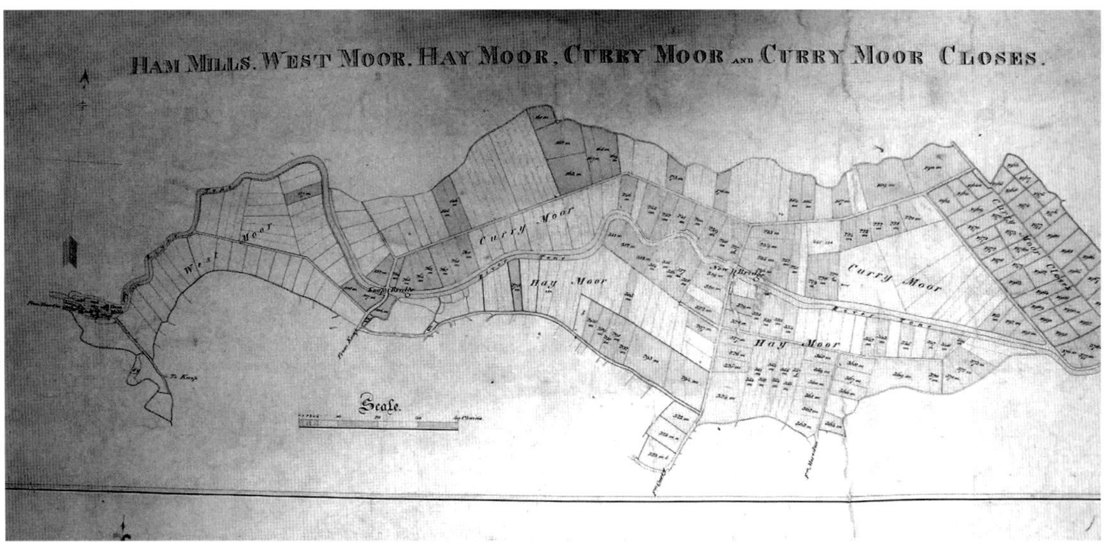

SECTION OF INSET FROM MAP OF CURRY TITHING – 1840 SHOWING RIVER TONE

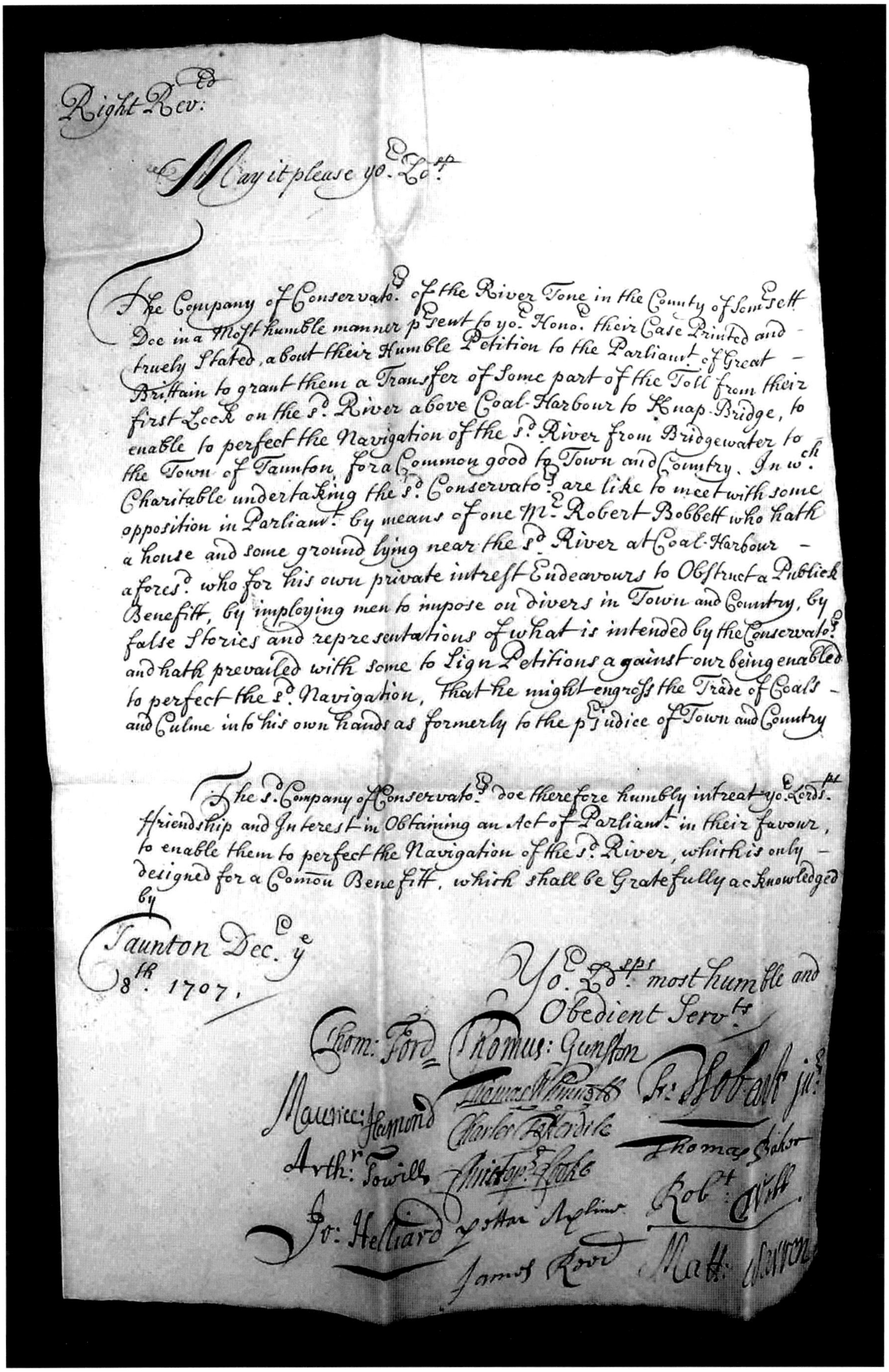

Right Revd:

May it please yo. Lordp.

The Company of Conservators of the River Tone in the County of Somersett Doe in a most humble manner present to yo. Hono. their Case Printed and truely Stated, about their Humble Petition to the Parliamt. of Great Brittain to grant them a Transfer of some part of the Toll from their first Lock on the sd. River above Coal-Harbour to Knap-Bridge, to enable to perfect the Navigation of the sd. River from Bridgewater to the Town of Taunton, for a Common good to Town and Country. In wch. Charitable undertaking the sd. Conservators are like to meet with some opposition in Parliamt. by means of one Mr. Robert Bobbett who hath a house and some ground lying near the sd. River at Coal-Harbour aforesd. who for his own private intrest Endeavours to Obstruct a Publick Benefitt, by imploying men to impose on divers in Town and Country, by false Stories and representations of what is intended by the Conservators and hath prevailed with some to Sign Petitions against our being enabled to perfect the sd. Navigation, that he might engross the Trade of Coals and Culme into his own hands as formerly to the prejudice of Town and Country

The sd. Company of Conservators doe therefore humbly intreat yo. Lordspt. friendship and Interest in Obtaining an Act of Parliamt. in their favour, to enable them to perfect the Navigation of the sd. River, which is only designed for a Comon Benefitt, which shall be Gratefully acknowledged by

Taunton Decr. ye 8th. 1707.

Yo. Lordsps most humble and Obedient Servts

Thom: Ford
Thomas: Gunston
Maurice: Hamond
Arthr: Powill
Jo: Helliard
Thomas Baker
Robt: Will
Matt: Warren
James Rood

Petition from Conservators of River Tone regarding Knapp Bridge – 1707

Railways

The world's first commercial railway was opened in Britain in 1825 between Stockton and Darlington beginning the age of cheap and rapid communication and giving a new mobility to rural society for both work and pleasure. During the latter half of the 19th century the railways enabled people to leave the country villages, some to emigrate or seek work in the towns and some to marry partners who lived much further afield. The railways had a major impact on the industries of Somerset, not only in terms of quicker transportation of coal, but also in terms of accessing wider markets. Major industries affected included bricks and tiles from Bridgwater, glass from Nailsea, stone from the quarries of Bath and lead and iron from the mines of the Mendips and Brendons. Many smaller industries such as market gardening, basket making, and manufacturing of woollen and leather goods also found great benefit in sending their produce to larger markets, and this led to the decline in many weekly markets in the small towns.

In c.1815 a bridge was built over the River Tone at North Curry, subsequently to become known as New Bridge. Some claim it to have replaced an older one built in 1680 upstream of the half-locks or *half hatches* which we know to have existed near its site in 1787. The Great Western Railway built a station at Durston in 1853 to serve the Yeovil Branch Line and this benefited the residents of North Curry for many years, giving them rail access to the whole country. The New Bridge was replaced with the present more substantial one when the road, renamed New Road, was built alongside a drove to link the village of North Curry with Durston Station in c.1870. At first it was difficult to hire a conveyance to the station with only a stonebreaker's donkey cart available. Later, Mr Bown of the White Hart Inn ran a thriving business with horses and carriages taking the more affluent passengers to and from the station. The first train to pass through caused a sensation, with many people assembled to see the marvellous carriages that were drawn along without horses. Some people in the village today can remember older people's stories of helping to build the road, indicating that local labour was used. Large stones were brought and dumped on the grass verges and then cracked smaller with heavy stone hammers by the older men, sitting all day at the job.

In September 1906 the Vicar, writing in the North Curry *Parish Magazine*, reported a trip to Burnham by rail from Durston station for the children of the Sunday School as follows:

> *The Sunday School Treat was to Burnham and Major Barrett kindly gave £5 to assist taking the children to the sea, instead of having them as usual at Moredon. For many of the children, never having seen the sea before, it was a special treat. A railway journey too, is not without its delights to the juvenile mind. Our party, which comprised children, parents, teachers and friends, in all 127, was conveyed to and from Durston Station in vehicles. The Railway Company reserved compartments, and the carriages were shunted at Highbridge, thus avoiding the difficulties of a change. On reaching Burnham our young folks rushed off to the sands, where donkey rides, cocoanut shies, sand-castles, and paddling were all soon in full swing. Unfortunately a storm broke during the afternoon but the children's enjoyment was not diminished. Tea was served in the Lifeboat Pavilion and the tide came up high in the latter part of the afternoon, and paddling was freely indulged in. Alas the rain came down in earnest during the journey home, and as we drove across the Moor many children sought refuge under the seats of the conveyances.*

Another trip, this time to Weston-super-Mare for the Vicar's Bible Class was as follows:

> *September 1912*
> *The Lads of the Vicar's Bible Class went on their Outing to Weston by train from Durston. A swim in the Knightstone Bath for those who cared to indulge in the exercise occupied part of the morning. Lunch was partaken of at the Tea Shanty followed by a visit to the Old Pier, where special delights in the shape of the Water Chute and Cake Walk were enjoyed. A corridor carriage, allowing communication between the compartments, lent an additional charm to the return train journey.*

Another treat, this time for the children of the school in North Curry, also ended with rain, but the journey did not necessitate a station change.

> *September 1924*
> *The weather prophets had promised some improvement after a damp and showery July and August. Seldom do we remember such a succession of wet days in the holiday months. However, fortune favoured us greatly with the School Treat to Burnham. It was not only fine, but gloriously bright and sunny. The party numbered 71 children and 34 adults. The G.W.R. reserved carriages which were shunted at Highbridge, saving trouble and confusion of a change. An excellent Tea was provided in the afternoon at Mr. Ilett's "Beach Cafe". When it was time to go to the station a useful storm of rain, without which the day would have been incomplete, served to round people up by driving them to shelter, and all at last got safely into the train in their proper compartments, and in due course disembarked at Durston.*

The railway age reached its climax after the First World War and in 1923 the railway companies were organised into new groups, with most of Somerset under the direction of the Great Western Railway. After nationalisation in 1948 the lines of Somerset were under the control of the Western Region of British Rail, but with increasing competition from motor vehicles many branch lines proved to be uneconomical and were closed. The Yeovil branch line was one of these, and Durston station closed in 1962.

Despite this closure North Curry still remains well served by the national railway system, with the journey from Taunton to London now taking a little over two hours.

1

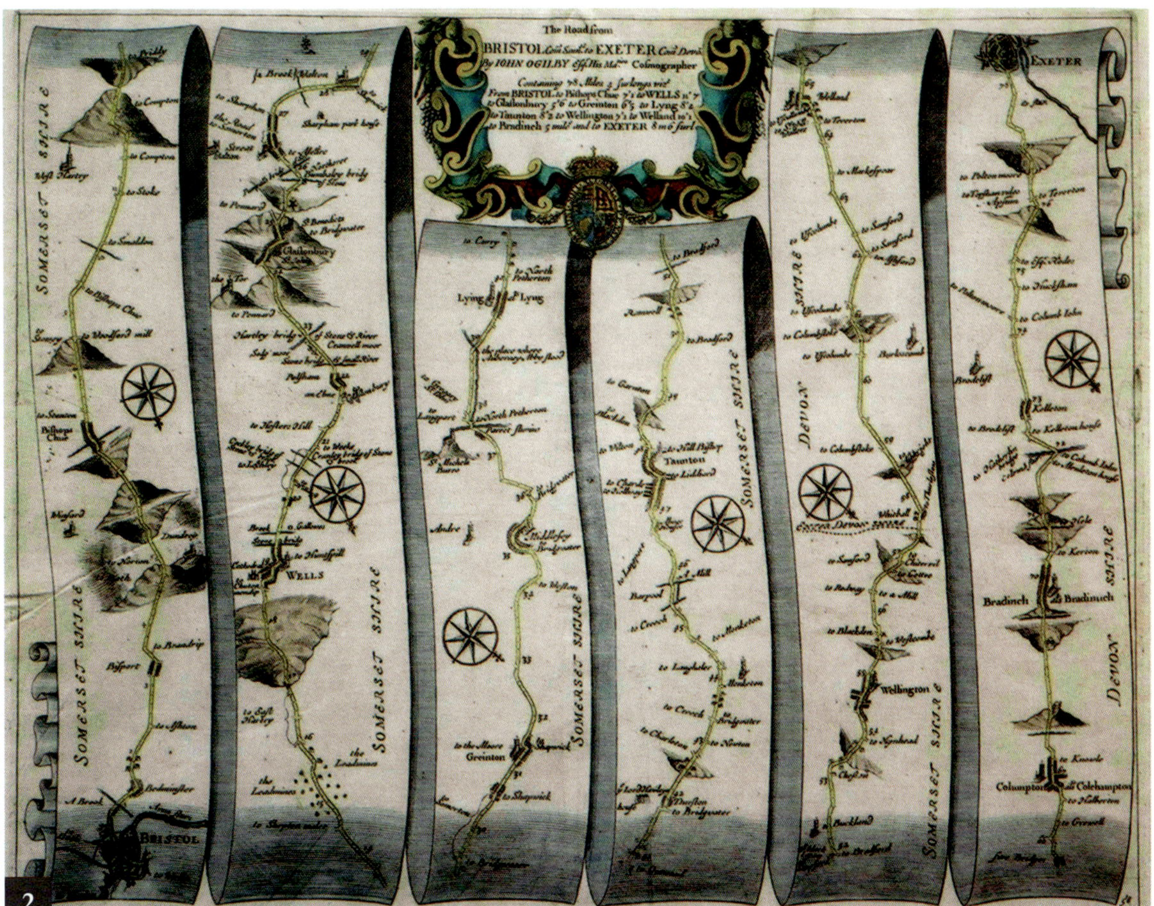

2

Early Somerset maps: 1. *Map of Somerset – published by Christopher Saxton – 1575,* ***2.*** *Strip map of road from Bristol to Exeter via (North) Curry – published by John Ogilby – 1675*

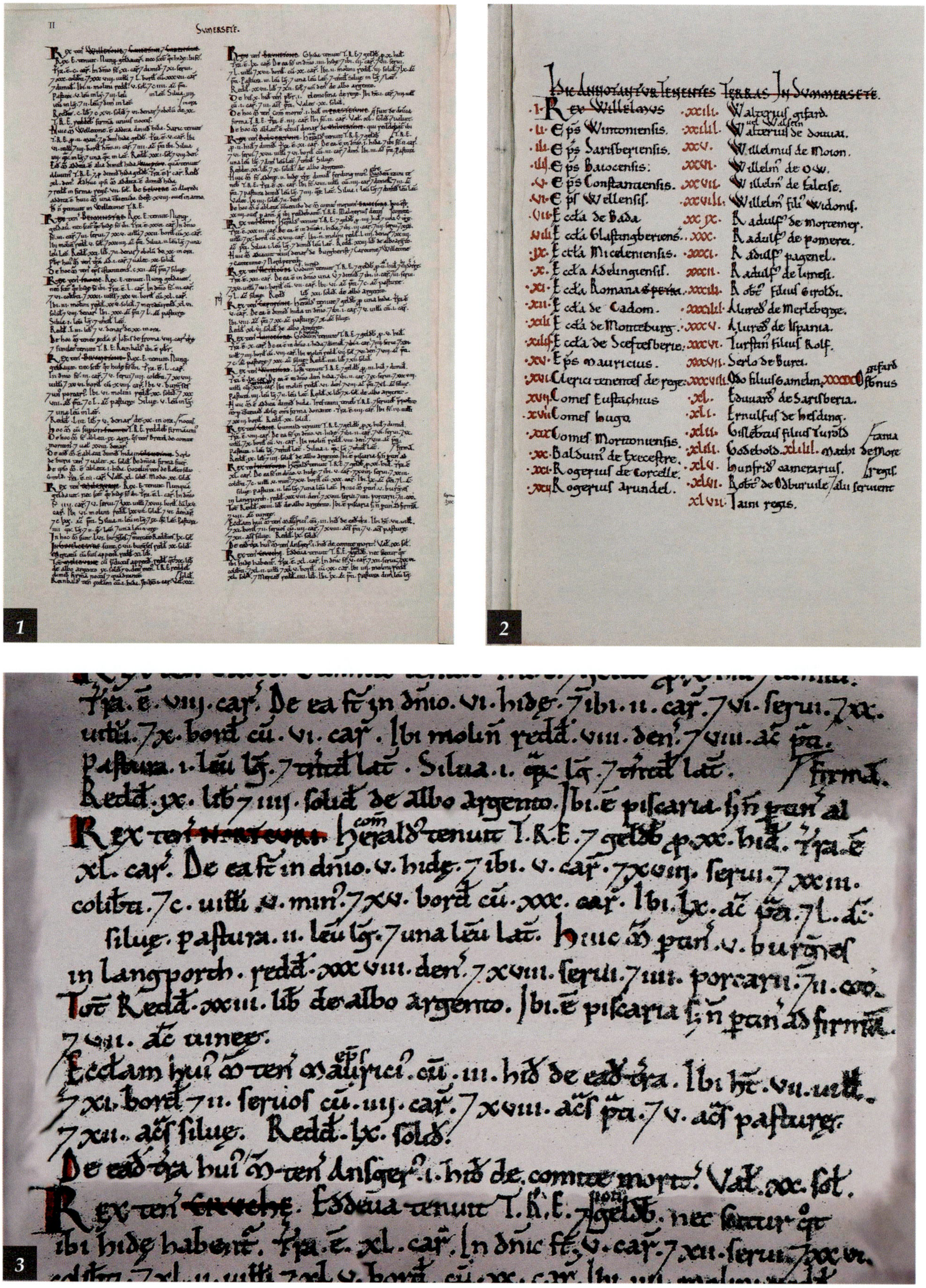

Facsimile of Domesday Book or Great Survey of England of William the Conqueror – AD MLXXXVI (1086):
1. *Some Somerset entries including North Curry,* **2.** *Somerset landholders,* **3.** *Detail of North Curry entry*

***North Curry Charter** – Charter 15 from the Wells Cathedral Archive – 1199*

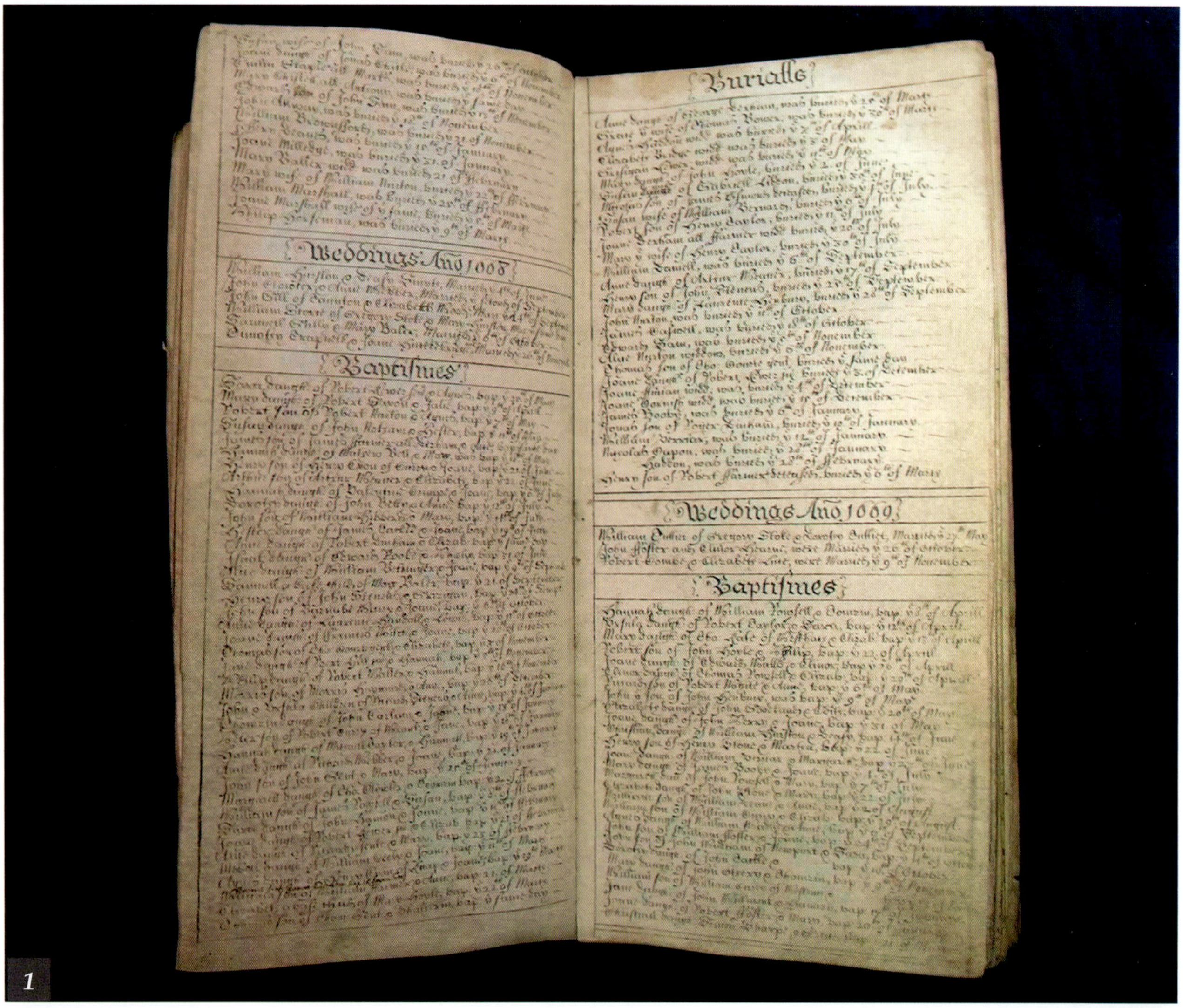

1

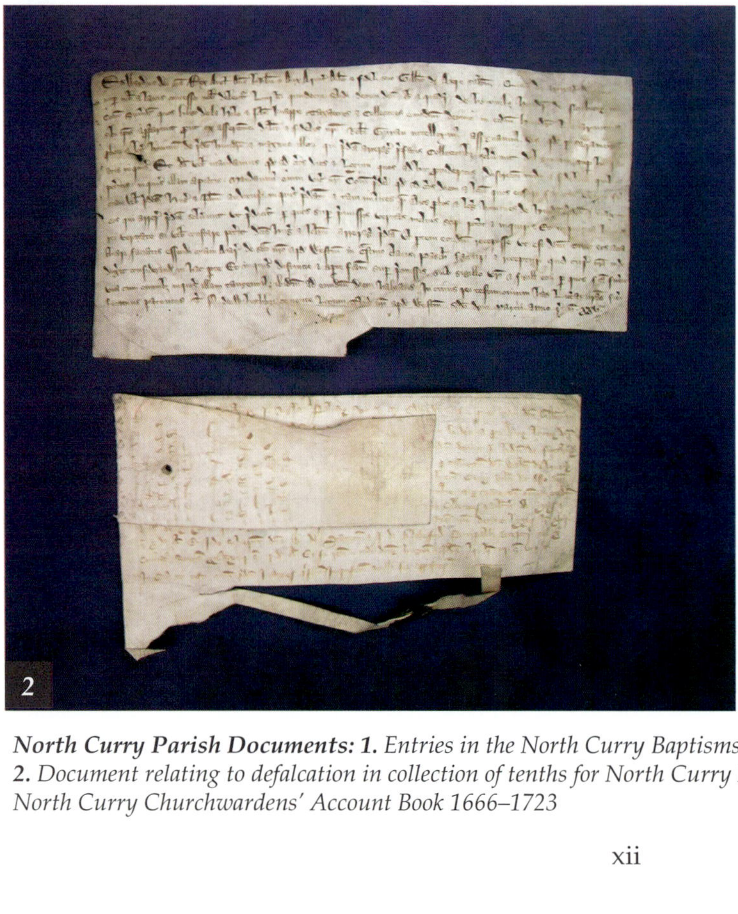

2

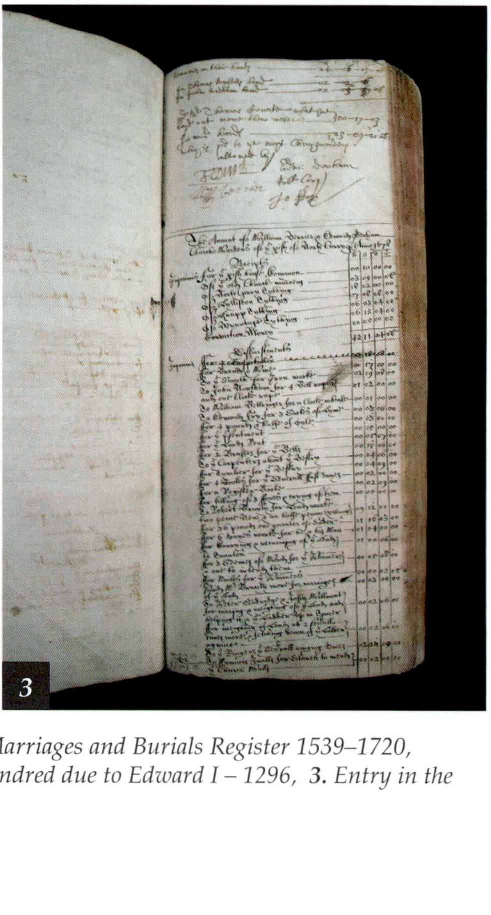

3

North Curry Parish Documents: ***1.*** *Entries in the North Curry Baptisms, Marriages and Burials Register 1539–1720,* ***2.*** *Document relating to defalcation in collection of tenths for North Curry Hundred due to Edward I – 1296,* ***3.*** *Entry in the North Curry Churchwardens' Account Book 1666–1723*

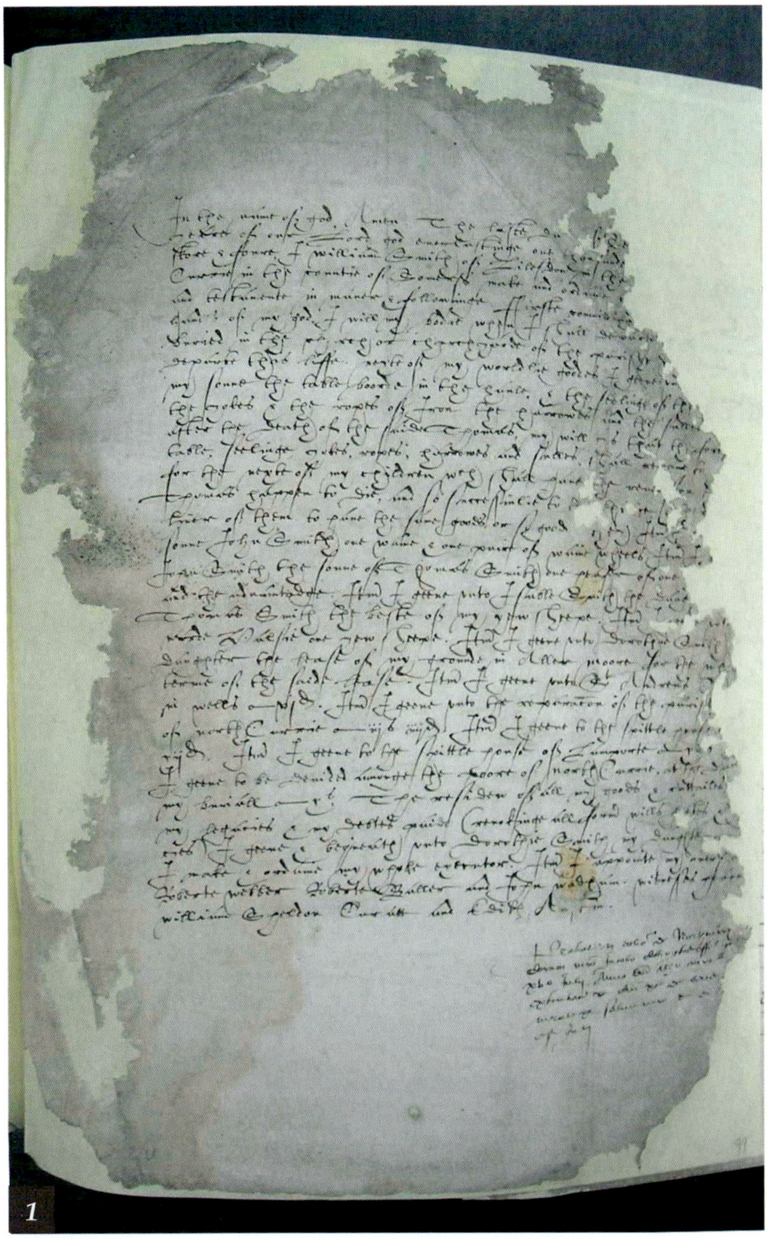

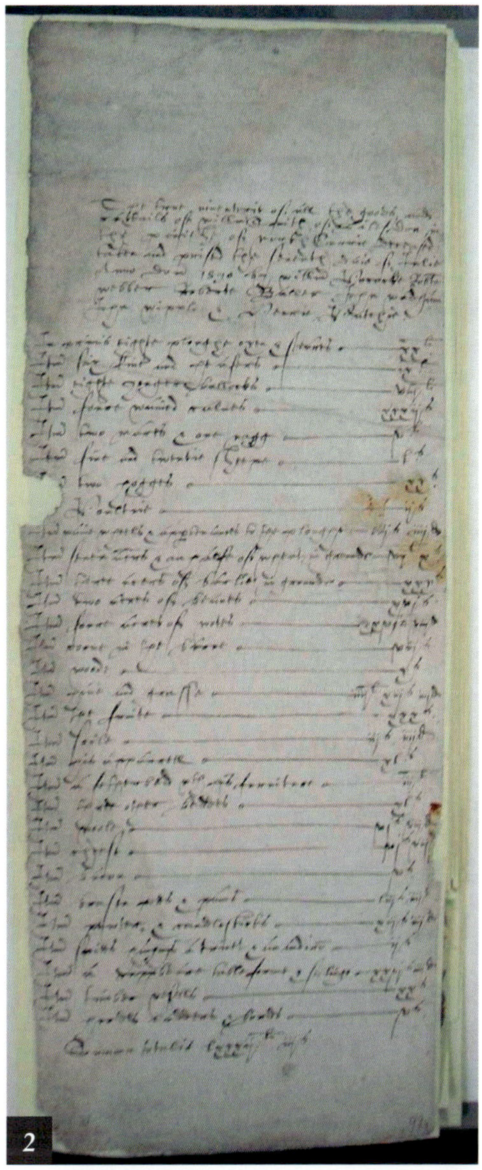

This is the last Will and Testament

[illegible] William Barrett [illegible] North Curry in the County of Somerset Gentleman [illegible] Officer in the fifth Regiment of the Bengal Light Cavalry – I give devise and bequeath all my real and personal estate whatsoever and wheresoever unto my sister Sophia Barrett To hold the same unto her the said Sophia Barrett her heirs executors administrators and assigns according to the nature thereof respectively for her own absolute use and benefit. And I appoint the said Sophia Barrett sole Executrix of this my Will [illegible] set my hand and seal this eighth day of July 1837 – Wm Barrett 5th Light Cav[illegible] –

Signed sealed published and declared by the said William Barrett the Testator as and for his last Will and Testament in the presence of us who in his presence have hereunto subscribed our names as Witnesses the words "and delivered by the" having been first struck out in this attestation

[illegible] – Abraham [illegible] – [illegible]

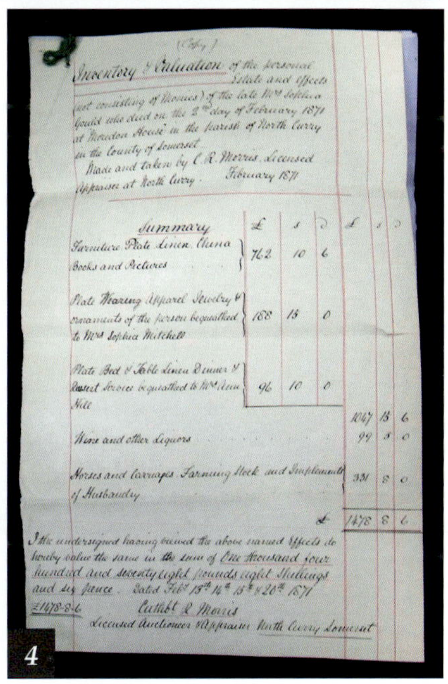

(Copy)

Inventory & Valuation of the personal Estate and Effects (not consisting of Monies) of the late Mrs Sophia Gould who died on the 2nd day of February 1871 at Moredon House in the parish of North Curry in the County of Somerset

Made and taken by C. R. Morris Licensed Appraiser at North Curry. February 1871

Summary	£	s	d	£	s	d
Furniture Plate Linen China Books and Pictures	762	10	6			
Plate Wearing Apparel Jewelry & ornaments of the person bequeathed to Mrs Sophia Mitchell	188	15	0			
Plate Bed & Table Linen Dinner & Dessert Service bequeathed to Mrs Ann Hill	96	10	0			
				1047	15	6
Wine and other Liquors				99	5	0
Horses and Carriages Farming Stock and Implements of Husbandry				331	8	0
£				1478	8	6

I the undersigned having viewed the above named Effects do hereby value the same in the sum of One thousand four hundred and seventy eight pounds eight Shillings and six pence. Dated Feby 13th 14th 15th & 20th 1871

£1478-8-6 Cuthbt R Morris

Licensed Auctioneer & Appraiser North Curry Somerset

North Curry wills and inventories: 1. *Will of William Smith of Lilsdon – 1584,* **2.** *Inventory of William Smith of Lilsdon – 1590,* **3.** *Will of William Barrett of Moredon – 1837,* **4.** *Inventory and valuation of Sophia Gould of Moredon – 1871*

The Dean and Chapter's Map of the Manors of North Curry, Wrantage, Knap-Fee and Newport Borough – 1787

Section of Tithe Map of Curry Tything – 1840

1

2

3

4

5

6

7

8

9

10

***Moredon and the Barrett family circa 1890**: **1.** Servants and estate workers, **2.** W W Barker – photographer, **3.** Younger members of the Barrett family, **4.** Village band, **5.** Drawing room, **6.** Tenant's Rent Day lunch, **7.** Major and Mrs Barrett with family and friends, **8.** Major John Chard VC, **9.** Mrs Dobson and Dobson, **10.** The High Sheriff's coach*

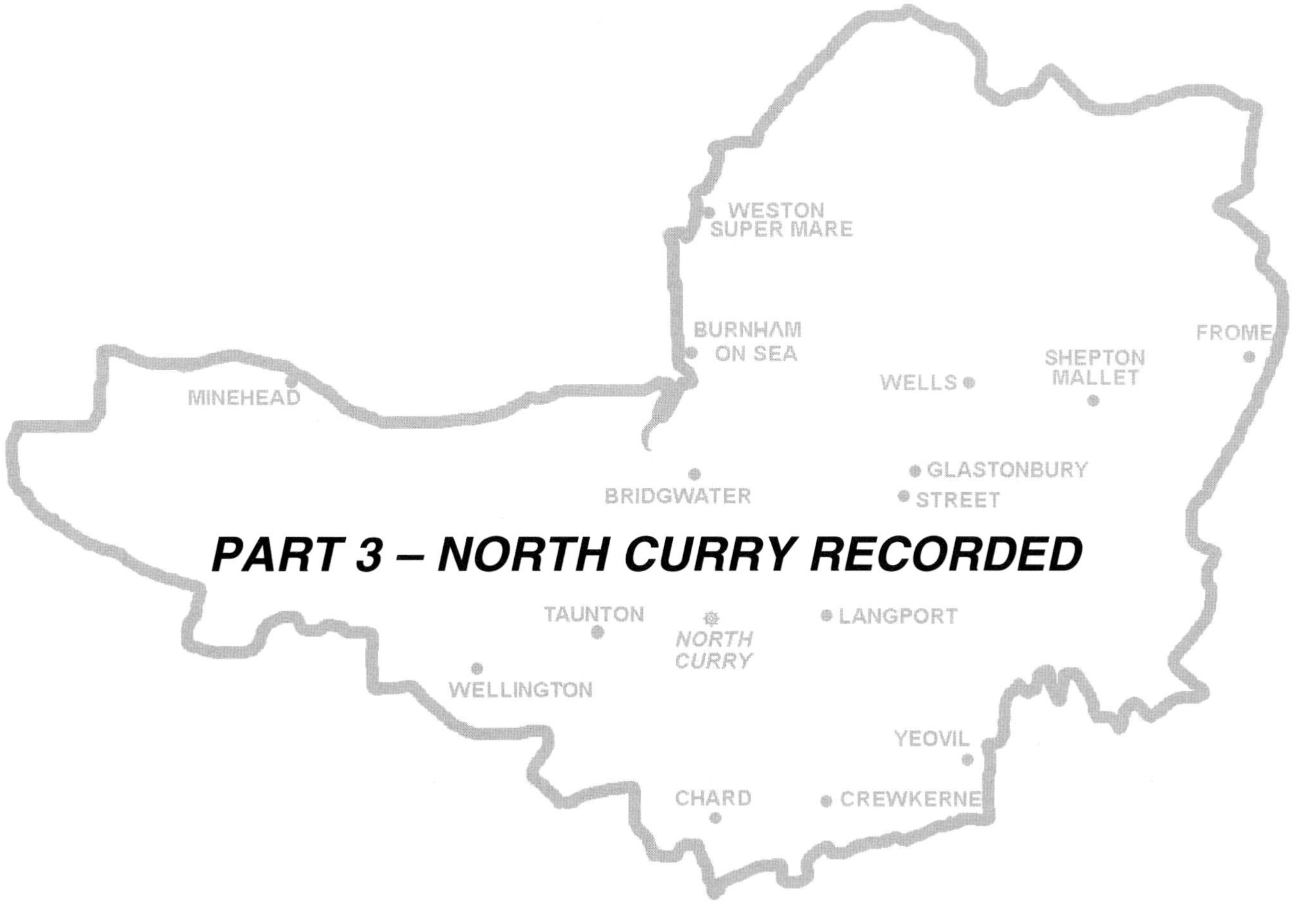

PART 3 – NORTH CURRY RECORDED

3 - 1

PARISH DOCUMENTS AND RECORDS

PARISH REGISTERS

Parish records in the form of hand-written parish registers of births and baptisms, marriages and burials, records of marriage banns, Churchwardens' Accounts, vestry minutes, poor relief accounts and other miscellaneous papers were originally held in the parish chest within the parish church.

In the 12th century parish priests began the custom of noting in an album or in the margins of the service books, the births and deaths of the leading local families. In the late-15th century proper registration of baptisms began in Western Europe. In England in about 1536 the first mandate for keeping parish registers was made in the time of Henry VIII. This was after the Dissolution of the Monasteries by Sir Thomas Cromwell, who was Vicar General. He ordered every parson, vicar or curate to enter in a book every wedding, christening and burial in his parish, with the names of the parties so that these events should be recorded to establish population statistics for poll tax purposes - *kepe one boke or registre wherein ye shall write the day and yere of every Weddynge Chrystenyng and Buryeng...and every persons name.* By the year 1538 a written record of every baptism, marriage and burial was made compulsory for each English parish. The entries were to be made each Sunday after service in the presence of one of the wardens, and the incumbents of churches with their Churchwardens were therefore appointed as local registrars.

Some early records were kept on loose sheets, and in 1597, during the reign of Elizabeth I, all existing parish registers were copied into bound parchment books. It follows that most entries before this date are not the original ones, having been copied by a later incumbent. In 1812, separate registers for baptisms, marriages and burials were stipulated. The Churchwardens' financial accounts specify outgoings and income, accounting for the spending of the church rate. The administration of the parish was directed by representative parishioners, known as the Vestry, assembled in the vestment room or sacristy of the church. Minutes and accounts, some commencing in the 14th century, record aspects of village life and communal affairs, together with the management of ecclesiastical affairs. These registers, accounts and minutes, together with Poor Law rate books and other church and parish documents provide an insight into the many aspects of the former social, religious, economic and administrative life of a parish from Tudor times.

Following Oliver Cromwell's mandate of 1538 each parish was to provide *a sure coffer of stoat oak with two weighty locks*, the parson having the custody of one key, and the Churchwardens the other, and this parish chest housed in the parish church served as the repository for valued records. The Poor Law of 1552 directed the parishioners in every parish to provide *a strong chest with a hole in the upper part thereof, and having three keys*, for holding the alms of the poor. An Act of 1812 demanded a dry well-painted iron chest, stamped with the date 1813, to hold church records and treasures. An entry in the North Curry Churchwardens' Accounts for the year 1845 records as follows:

> *April 26th Paid Mr. W.C. Cox of Taunton for an Iron safety chest for to keep the Register the one we had in use not large enough so there is two chestes now of Iron belong to the Parish.*

In 1978 parishes were required compulsorily to transfer these documents to the Somerset County Record Office. Many of the original documents for North Curry are in good order and are available to view on request, either in their original form or on microfilm or microfiche, at the Somerset County Record Office. Nonconformist and Free Church congregations also keep registers, and these can also be seen in the Public Record Offices.

When studying the older parish registers it can be seen that the early years do not begin with 1st January. During the 16th century a revised calendar - the *Gregorian Calendar* (from the time of Pope Gregory XIII) had been drawn up, with its system of leap years. Most countries in Western Europe had gradually adopted this system, and in 1752 Britain followed suit. The day after Wednesday September 2nd was called September 14th, this cancelling the eleven-day error that had accumulated over the years. The alteration caused some outcry *Give us back our eleven days* ran the slogan of those who thought that the government had cheated them out of several days of their life - and summer days too! At the same time as this major change the New Year was defined as beginning on January 1st, instead of on March 25th (Lady Day) as previously.

Since early times the church was the centre of life in the village with most people attending at least one service on Sundays. The parish registers listing baptisms, marriages and burials form the only record of the growth of families until the formalising of records began in 1830. They provide an invaluable insight into the family histories of the population of the country. Descendants of many of the earliest families recorded within the parish registers are living in the same parishes today, with some families known to have been in the same area as far back as the 12th century.

The North Curry *Parish Registers of Baptisms, Marriages and Burials* commence in 1539, the year after their introduction by Cromwell. They are written on parchment leaves, loosely stitched together and are practically complete. There is some discontinuity at the time of the Puritan domination, when the care of registers was commonly neglected and there were several instances of marriages being performed by laymen.

The first North Curry register covers the period 1539–1720 and begins with the words:

> *The beginning of this register was in the year 1539 being the same year the first English edition of the Bible was authorized, and five years after the Reformation under Henry VIII. John England.*

The entries start with 28 baptisms, followed by 4 weddings and then 10 burials for the year 1539. The entries give first name and then surname of each individual, with the date the ceremony was performed, but with no other details such as parents or occupation. From 1570 the father's name is given, and the word son or daughter is written in each baptism entry, and the women and children buried are entered with the name of their husband or father. From 1634 the names of both the father and mother are sometimes given in the entry of baptism, and from 1664 they are always given. From 1652 the title *marriages* is used instead of *weddings*. Throughout the registers the place where a family or individual lived, if outside the Parish of North Curry, is recorded and occasionally the abode of an important North Curry family or individual is given. The average number of events in each year throughout the registers is 36 baptisms, 36 burials and 7 weddings.

Large families were common, and from 1539 to 1841 there were 54 families in North Curry with 7 children, 24 with 8, 20 with 9, and 7 with 10. Anthony and Rachel Coggan (1748–1768), John and Joan Elson (1726–1752), Henry and Jane Fry (1768–1788) and Jacob and Grace Kewer (1802–1819) had families of 11 children.

Often a child is named with the same name as a child who died earlier, as the following list of the children of Henry and Jane Fry illustrates.

CHILD	PARENTS' NAMES	BAPTISM	BURIAL
William	*Henry & Jane Fry*	*13/03/1768*	–
Henry	*Henry & Jane Fry*	*13/08/1769*	
Mary	*Henry & Jane Fry*	*02/06/1771*	*13/10/1771*
Mary	*Henry & Jane Fry*	*31/05/1772*	
Jane	*Henry & Jane Fry*	*18/09/1774*	
John	*Henry & Jane Fry*	*16/06/1776*	
Thomas	*Henry & Jane Fry*	*20/09/1778*	
Betty	*Henry & Jane Fry*	*22/04/1781*	*12/1/1783*
Betty	*Henry & Jane Fry*	*23/02/1783*	
Sarah	*Henry & Jane Fry*	*25/09/1785*	
Ann	*Henry & Jane Fry*	*27/04/1788*	*5/4/1789*

The first register, as well as containing entries by numerous hands with varying degrees of handwriting expertise, legibility and tidiness, includes various notes throughout the book as follows:

> *1673*
> *Elm growing in middle of churchyard was planted by Mr. Owen.*
>
> *Memorandum in this present year viz 1709 was built at the expense of Ezra Pierce, then vicar, a pew in the north–east side of North Curry Church for the use of the vicar for ever.*
> *Ezra Pierce, Vicar*
> *Alexander Potenger and John Moor, Churchwardens*
>
> *1714*
> *A note by Ezra Pierce of his planting of the walk of elms in the churchyard.*
>
> *North Curry Procession for the viewing of the Bounds of the Parish was the 30th and 31st May 1717 by common guess 26 miles and a half round. Ezra Pierce, Vicar William Mead, John Hurston and Anthony Coggan, Churchwardens*

Written on the last page of this register:

> *This Register was 182 years filling up*

The register for the years 1721–1783 contains baptisms and burials for those years and marriages between 1721 and 1754, as well as notes as follows:

> *Note*
> *A baptism privately at the Rock in Curry Mallet Elizabeth d. of John Dornford and Elizabeth of Exeter, March 27th 1724. Born upon the road near Honiton, Devonshire.*
>
> *16th June 1749*
> *A very hard frost at Uphill in this county, the ice was as thick as a crown piece.*
>
> *North Curry Procession for viewing the bounds of the Parish was 24th May 1750*
> *John Woodforde, Vicar*
> *John Ludwell and John Pocock – Churchwardens*
>
> *The stile altered 1752. All the intermediate nominal days from the second of September to the fourteenth of the same month are omitted or rather annihilated this year.*
>
> *November 1st 1755*
> *A most dreadful earthquake happened at Lisbon in Portugal, which almost destroyed the whole city. By letters received from thence many thousand persons perished. The Jesuits account amounts to 90,000 killed in the whole, others reduce it to 50,000 and some 30,000. By accounts received from Africa in that part of Barbary on the opposite coast to Gibraltar they have suffered as much if not more than in Portugal. At Tetuan, Tangier, Sallee, Fez, Morocco and Meguinez it is said greater damage has been done in the heart of the country. God preserve us from such dreadful catastrophes, and comfort those who have suffered in them. By accounts received, it appears that the earthquakes have continued for the space of 61 days, that is from the 1st November to the 31st December inclusive, in which space of time they have been felt with more or less violence from the Eastern shores of the Atlantic Ocean to the heart of Germany and from the frozen climate of Iceland, almost to the Tropic of Cancer, taking a range of about 4,000 miles from West to East and about 2,000 from South to North. The 6th February 1756 was appointed for a General Fast and Humiliation to Humble ourselves before Almighty God in a deep sense of His late*

visitation by a most dreadful and extensive earthquake, in order to the obtaining the pardon of our crying sins, to the averting of His judgements and for the continuance of His mercy which Fast by accounts was strictly observed throughout these Kingdoms.

October 19th 1760 was buried Robert Roggers died in Mrs. Gales outhouse and buried by the charge of the parish died on his journey home to Crew Carne.

Sunday June 23rd 1771
A man a native of Taunton St Mary Magdelen was burried at North Curry August 5th 1771
Robert Dwelly

Every moment spent unto some usefull end.
Robert Dwelly his hand 1772

In 1754 it was required that marriage particulars were entered into a book of pre-printed lined sheets. Instructions were given as to how these sheets were to be completed. Banns of Marriage were also to be entered into a similar book.

There are separate registers for baptisms and burials for the years 1784–1812. The baptism entries are hand-written as in the earlier registers and the burials are hand-written onto pre-printed sheets. Notes written within the *Baptism Register* for 1784–1812 are as follows:

This Book was Bought by Robert Ludwell,
Churchwarden Anno Domini 1785
Joannes Anglia, Scribe
John England May 1796
Memorandum that in the 24th day of October 1796 that John Woodman was sworn into the office of Clerk of the Parish of North Curry in the County of Somerset before the Reverend John Turner Clerk Master of Arts Surrogate of the Reverend Charles Moss Clerk Master of Arts Official of the Dean and Chapter of the Cathedral Church of St Andrews in Wells in the County aforesaid lawfully constituted now void by the death of John England the last clerk thereof at the nomination of the said John Turner Vicar of the said Parish. (Written on last page of the register)

All the later *Parish Registers* of North Curry are in the style of printed forms with the incumbents required to fill in the prescribed details.

Churchwardens' Accounts and other Parish Books

Churchwardens are defined by ecclesiastical authorities as the proper guardians or keepers of the parish church and they had certain additional civil duties imposed upon them from time to time. They have been known by titles such as Stewards, Guardians of the Church, Wardens of Church Goods, Keepers of the Parish Church, or Church Reeves. The office of Churchwarden began in very early times and possibly the first was appointed as an officer of the church by the first Canon of the Council of London in 1127. The Churchwardens were annually elected officers in each parish representing the church or parish interests. From medieval times the administrative role of the Churchwarden increased, and, as well as becoming responsible for keeping parish registers and the church accounts, they administered charitable doles. They presented miscreants to Church Courts, if appropriate, and worked alongside Overseers of the Poor for the administration of poor relief before parishes were organised into Poor Law Unions in 1834 and the poor were accommodated into workhouses. The earliest paper book of North Curry Churchwardens' Accounts is for the year 1585–1586 and is written in Elizabethan handwriting. It has become known as the *Ould Rusty Booke* from words written on the outside of its paper cover by a 17th century hand.

It begins with an account of receipts that the Churchwardens Richard Newnam and John Wych received. Monies were received for the burial of the dead ranging from 12 pence for simple burials and more than 18 shillings from John Selye for the burial of his father and mother, seemingly for a burial within the Church. Money from the separate tithings of North Curry was collected and the wardens received 43s.4d from *Corrye tythynge*, 15s.3d from *Wrantage tythynge*, 19s.8d from *Knape tythynge*, and 7s.2d from *Lilsdon tythynge* on 6th September 1586. Receipts for the rental of the Parish House are shown together with receipts for the rental of seats in the church.

Money-raising efforts are featured in church accounts at this time, and one of the most profitable was the periodic festive meeting, wake or revel called the *Church Ale* when ale and food were sold. The wardens begged or bought the malt and food and brewed the liquor and cooked the provisions in the Church House (possibly Fosse Cottage) which was the equivalent of the village hall. The first account book of 1585 lists numerous payments. Some of the more interesting items of expenditure are as follows:

ITEM	S	D
Spent upon the plomers for worke about the church	4	12
Spent to helpe to drawe up the lead to the ruffe of the churche		3
To Richard Roweswell for bord, nayles and spikerdes	2	6
Wode for the plomer to mult his lead		22
Bread and wine to serve to wholle parishe the firste ester	12	8
Laid out at a visitation for the wardens and eight men to make them drinck	2	11
For the mending of the clock		2
To William Chick for leather to mend the bawdripte		6
For drinck when we gathered monye to send to London about our matter in lawe		4
Laid out at Wells about our matters in lawe for the serchinge of bookes	10	1
For sope to wayshe the serples and other clothes		4
To Michel for the mendynyg the bells	6	
For grasse to kepe his horse for 10 dayes		20
To John Spiring for mendynge the allehouse end		2

ITEM	S	D
For meat and drincke for the plomer and his companye		*20*
Spent at Tanton at the bysshope of canterburyes visitation		*8*
To Leonard Crosse for 700 of lead	*59*	
To Walter Noke for the carriage of the same	*4*	*4*
To Markes Stapell for the mendynge of the great bell clapper	*2*	*6*
For candells and drincke at the coronation daye		*6*
For the makinge of a steare in the parishe howse	*2*	
For bread and wine for Christmas Daye	*2*	*4*
For nailes and hoopes tohange up the spoutes in the church waulle		*10*
For meate and drincke for the wardens being about the churche to helpe the plomer		*12*
To John Foxe for setting up the vesterie		*3*
Paid to Guie Chicke for strapes and leather for the bawdript		*5*
Laid out to ride to Wells to the chapter about the parishe howse		*17*
Laid out for bread and wine when John Roger was married		*6½*
Laid out the plowmen drincke when they carried the bell to Ylmister		*2*
Laid out for our brekefaste at Ylmister	*2*	*6*
Laid out the same daye at night for our supper	*3*	*4*
For bread and wine when Lawrens Collens wife went to church with child		*4*
For Richard Newnams mares meat at Ylmister		*3*
To John Foxe for the makinge of a whealle for the litel bell	*4*	*4*
For the writinge of our account	*2*	
For paper spent about our account and other things		*2*
For the makyng of a stylle in the churche yeard		*10*
To Mr. Crosse for syxe hundred and halfe of leade	*52*	
To the smythe for towe showes set upon John Hurstons mare to feache the lead		*6*
To John Combe to goe to Grayenton to feache John Deram at the castynge of the bell		*6*
To Lawrens Foxe the baylyfe beyinge arrested at the sute of Nicholas Fennie	*2*	

Some of the largest expenditures were on candles, beeswax and tallow for lighting the church, the maintenance of the bells and clock, rushes for the floor and boughs and flowers for the decoration of the church. Bequests of items such as brass and silver to churches were frequent, with the Churchwardens selling them when the need arose to supplement the church income. Fees were levied for the font tapers at baptisms, and for services such as ringing of the passing bell and hiring of the pall, cross, cope and censer for burial in church. Interest on cash loans or stock money to help parishioners in temporary financial difficulty provided income, as did the profits from the church flock of sheep or hive of bees.

An extract from the North Curry Churchwardens' Accounts of 1644 details the administration of *stock money* as follows:

	£	S	D
Of the Lady Portman	*10*	*0*	*0*
Of Mrs. Johan Connocke	*20*	*0*	*0*
Of Mr. William Goodman	*10*	*0*	*0*
Of Mrs. Rachell Portman	*15*	*0*	*0*
Of John Smith	*1*	*0*	*0*
Of Mr. William Ceely	*2*	*0*	*0*
Of the widow Rogers	*2*	*0*	*0*
Of John Trapnell de Chard		*10*	*0*
Of Thomas Pococke	*5*	*0*	*0*
Of Mr. John Gibbes, late Vicar of the parish	*10*	*0*	*0*

The interest of which money is appointed by the donors thereof to be applied towards the clothing of the poore of the said parish. Layd out for woollen Cloth, buttons and makinge of 6 sutes of the sum of £3 5s.8d; for a payre of shooes for Walter Collens 3s.6d; a shirt for William Willmot 2s.0d.

The next book of accounts for North Curry that survives is dated 1642–1666 and deals with pew rents, church plate and books, with an entry in 1645 for the distribution of *The Dowlis,* which was a coarse linen worn chiefly by the lower classes. The renting of pews led eventually to buying of freehold pews, kept under lock and key for certain proprietors or landholders, and leaving the poorer parishioners to be crammed onto deal benches in odd corners. This custom continued until the 19th century when free seats became available to all.

The book of Churchwardens' Accounts and rates which dates from 1666 to 1724 is a bulky volume, about 6.5 centimetres thick, 38 centimetres long and 15 centimetres wide, strongly bound in leather. The rates are written at one end and the accounts at the other. The rates are made out under the headings for the four different tithings, North Curry, Knapp, Lillesdon and Wrantage, amounting to £10.16s.0d and involve 122 ratepayers.

Some of the names on the rate are Every, Ceely, Bowey, Dummet, Rowsell, Trapnell, Maurice, Staple, Foster, Knight, Webber, Balch, Dare, Meade, Tuttiett, Howse, White, Bridge, Guddridge, Smith, Andrews, Lea, Hearne, Palmer, Lokier, Verrier, Hembrow, Sir William Portman, Hill, Cote, Stacey, Derham, Belringer, Curry, Edwards, Dinham, Edward Courte, Esquire, Mr Thomas Courte of Lillesdon and John Pine, Esquire of Wrantage. The entries appear to have been made by a scribe other than a Churchwarden who was paid *For making ye rate and keeping ye account.*

A list of serving Churchwardens is given in this volume as follows:

1666	*John Nurton*
1667–1670	*Robert Shepperd and Henry Exon*
1671	*Giles Foster and Michael Potter*
1673	*Thomas Owen and Thomas Keegar*
1674	*Arthur Weaver and John Smith*
1675	*Robert Hill, Jnr. and John Derham*
1676	*Thomas Courte and Thomas Brayly*
1677	*Thomas Rowsell and John Wadham*
1678	*William Verrier and Edward Derham*
1679	*Henry Foster and William Brounsford*
1680	*Robert Handole, Snr. and Henry Nurton*
1681	*Lawrence Fox and John Nurton*
1682	*Amos Burd and William Smith*
1683	*Henry Steevens and John Hurston*
1684	*Richard Rowsell and Richard Jeanes*
1685	*Symond Sharpe and John Saxon*
1686, 1687	*Ralph Thring and John Goodland*
1688	*William Morris and Laurence Hurston*
1689	*Josia Crocker and Anthony Larcombe*
1690	*Samuell Powell and Edward Watts*
1691	*Robert Hill and Edward Derham*
1692	*William Hurston and Ralph Clothier*
1693	*Andrew Wadham and Henry Stone*
1694–1696	*Robert Fox and William Androse*
1697	*Richard Coggin and Nicholas Bridge*
1698	*Edward Sperring and William Hurston*
1699	*William Bower*
1700	*William Hunter and Henry Pococke*
1701	*William Tice and John Ludwell*
1702	*John Stevens and Robert Ceeley*
1703	*Thomas Rowswell and John Nurton*
1704	*Robert Hill and Charles Weaver*
1705, 1706	*Thomas Rowswell and Artear Weaver*
1707	*Robert Hooper and Thomas Edwards*
1708	*Alexander Potenger and John Moor*
1709	*Thomas Hooper and Thomas Edwards*
1710	*Robert Wescombe and William Brounsford*
1711, 1712	*William Foster and Thomas Wadham*
1713	*William Mead and John Foster*
1714, 1715	*Nicholas Bridge and Matthew Pileman*
1716	*Anthony Coggan and John Hurston*
1717	*John Saxon and Francis Derham*
1718, 1719	*Thomas Ware and Christopher Handoll*
1720	*Henry Foster and Edward Samme*
1721	*Malachi Stroud and John Facy*
1722	*Thomas Were and William Mead*
1723	*John Weaver and Richard Coggan*

Within this volume are many entries dealing with the expenses of the repairing and ringing of the church bells. These were rung for village burials and marriages and also to mark special days of rejoicing such as national events, royal birthdays and victorious battles. Other items included wages paid to artisans repairing church property, costs for bridge repairs and conveyance, and the payments of county poor rates to hospitals or poorhouses for paupers, maimed soldiers and travellers or tramps. Extracts from the account of Robert Shepperd and Henry Exon, Churchwardens for the years 1667, 1668 and 1669 follow:

ITEM	£	S	D
Payd forteen Hospitalls	14	10	3
Layd out about the bell	4	6	4
Payd Brayly for leed worke	28	3	0
Payd the glasiear	11	0	0
Payd for carring casting and setting in of the brasses of ye bell	0	19	6
Payd Andrew Olford ye mason	0	18	10
For carrige for Leede to Taunton	0	10	0
Payd for lime	4	16	7
Payd for rooting of trees	0	5	6
Payd sawinge of timber and making of a sawpitt	0	7	10
Payd for bindinge ye church Bible	0	14	0
Payd for wyer for ye clocke	0	1	4
Payd to the Crouneofice and about the Bridge	3	4	2
Payd for ringing the fift of November 1668	0	7	10
Layd out for bread and wine	2	8	6
Payd for ye rent of the Parish House for 4 yeares	0	6	4
Layd out for expenses for jurneyes to Wells, visittacons and other expences	3	15	0
For breaking the ground for Mr. Thomas Court's child	0	6	8
Payd to poore travelling people	1	0	0
To the ringers for several ringing days	1	2	6
At precescion (beating bounds)		15	6

Beating the Bounds or *Perambulation* was an old ritual carried out on Rogation Days which are the Monday, Tuesday and Wednesday before Ascension Day. The incumbent and officers of the vestry and other officials, accompanied by a number of inhabitants, walked round the boundary of the parish to ensure that boundary stones and other markers had not been removed and that no new buildings had been erected without their knowledge. They were armed with willow rods which were used to beat the bounds to keep fresh in the local memory the location of boundaries which may never have been recorded. This procession was usually accompanied by liberal quantities of food and drink. In 1717 an entry in a register book records:

> *North Curry procession for viewing the bounds of the Parish was the 30th and 31st May. By common guess 26 miles and half round. Ezra Pierce, Vicar.*

In the year 1676 details are given in the accounts of workers' wages. Mr Brayly, the plumber, was paid two shillings and sixpence a day with his man being paid two shillings. His apprentice son was paid one shilling and sixpence a day, and Edward Rowsell, a labourer, was paid one shilling a day. Legislation was passed that payment would be made to any person destroying vermin within a parish. A penny would be paid for every three heads or six unbroken eggs of crows and rooks, twelve heads of starlings, or one head of *woodwall* (woodpecker), *pye* (magpie), jay, raven or kite, bullfinch or kingsfisher. Twopence was paid for every head of a martin, hawk, buzzard, shag, cormorant and ringtail. Fourpence was paid for every head of an *iron* (heron) or osprey. One penny was paid for the heads of any polecat, weasel, stoat, badger or wild cat, or three heads of rats or mice. Twopence for every otter or hedgehog, and a halfpenny for every mole was paid together with fees for organised fox-hunts with dogs. All dead vermin was brought before a standing committee in each parish. Payments accounted for in the North Curry Churchwardens' Accounts were as follows:

ITEM	£	S	D
For killing of 3 Foxes and crying of them (1678)	0	5	0
For 5 hedggoges heades (1682)	0		10
For killing of 7 foxes (1683)	0	15	0
For killing of a hedgod (1683)	0		2
Paid for takeing of 4 polecats (1687)	0		8
For killing of all sorts of varmints (1694)	0	13	7
Paid for 38 hedgdogs and one field catt (1718)	0	6	8
Paid John Curry for taking a bitch fox (1721)	0	1	0
The decoy man for field cats and stoats (1721)	0	1	4
One hedgdog that I killed myself (John Hurston)	0	0	2

From 1669 there are many entries in the accounts for payments towards the upkeep and maintenance of the church fabric, especially the tower and bell cages. In 1680 there is mention of nine Waywardens or Highway Surveyors being elected for the separate tythings of North Curry, Knapp, Lillesdon, Wrantage and the Borough of Newport, with one of them required to sit on a Highway Board to represent North Curry's interests. The following are extracts of typical entries in the accounts for that time.

ITEM	£	S	D	YEAR
For making ye Wherlgog (turnstile)		6	0	1680
Went to South Petherton to agree with Purdue for casting of ye 2nd bell (the Purdues had a foundry at Closworth)	0	5	0	1681
To Edward Rowsell for mending the church walls and washing ye Lineinge skowring ye plate and clenisingwe ye leddes, for lime, oyle and leathar for ye bells	0	16	0	1682
To John Cornelius for glazing ye church windows	3	10	0	1683
For whiteinge ye church and culleringe ye pillers and painten ye pullpitt	4	0	0	1684
Sold to Emanuel Appelbee a seate in the fore seate next to the Clarks seat for	0	1	0	1684
To the ringers 26 June for the takeing of Monnmeth	0	12	8	1684
For new making the Clock	2	10	0	1684
To Mr. William Sealy for seting up a new Lion and two new Turkes and other crosspeaces (restoration of Royal Arms)	14	2	6	1686
Paid Mr. Collins towards Standmoors Bridge (NC contribution for repair)	6	0	0	1688
To the ringers for rejoycing for the birth of ye Prince of Wales	1	14	6	1688
Paid for mending the church walls and covering the graves in ye church	1	0	0	1690
For raising the ends of Knap and the wale at New Bridge	3	0	0	1696
For the quarters of prisner and his gard at Godfrays	0	3	6	1696
For cullor for the weather cock and post and oyle for same	0	2	0	1696
For 150 reed sheaves for ye church house (repair to house after great storm when Bishop Kidder and his wife were killed by fall of chimney at the Palace of Wells)	1	8	4	1704
Paid Tho. Thomas for laying reed sheaves and watering	0	11	4	1704
For 50 lidgers, 100 spars and 80 twigs	0	0	8	1704
Paid for making and coluering the Dial	0	14	0	1713
Paid for carrying of six load of Timber and Ledd from Knap Bridge	1	1	0	1715
Paid the workmen in beer whilst they were about the church	1	1	0	1715
Expended when Richard Webber sett in Stocks	0	1	0	1718
For a summons for persons keeping disorderly ale housen	0	2	0	1722
Gave the ringers in beer this year	1	2	6	1722

The book of North Curry Church accounts from 1724 is missing. Other books that are preserved and held in the Somerset Record Office are *Church Accounts and Vestry Minutes* from 1819–1875; an *Expense Book* of 1875–1897; the *North Curry Rate Book* of 1823; *The Parish Book* of 1823–1894; *The Parish Vestry Book* of 1834–1880 and *The Church Book* of 1875–1898.

Churchwardens are listed from 1821 as follows:

1821–1823	*Robert L.Long and James Faun*
1824	*Robert Ludwell Long and James Faun*
1825–1827	*Robert Ludwell Long and Charles Barrington*
1828–1834	*Robert L.Long and William House*
1835–1846	*John Scott Gould and Philip Foster*
1847–1851	*Philip Foster and William Hurman*
1852–1856	*Philip Foster and Charles Barrington Jnr.*
1857–1858	*Philip Foster and James Temlett*
1859–1862	*Philip Foster and William Hurman*
1863–1866	*Philip Foster and George Crease*
1867–1869	*William Barrett and Isaac Palmer Smith*
1870–1877	*Isaac Palmer Smith and William Barrett*
1878–1880	*William Barrett and James B. Hellard*
1881–1889	*William Barrett and Charles Lockyer*
1890–1898	*William Barrett and Hugh P. Olivey*
1899–1900	*William Barrett and W. Winter Goode*

The book of church accounts for 1819–1875 continues to itemise all church expenditure; some of the more interesting entries follow:

ITEM	£	S	D	YEAR
Pointing windows and tolling the bell on the death of Rev. Mr. Talman		*5*	*0*	*1820*
Binding the church Bible	*1*	*8*	*0*	*1820*
Tolling the bell for Queen Caroline wife of George IV		*2*	*6*	*1820*
Richard Foster for a gallon of cider when the Vane was put up		*1*	*4*	*1824*
Mr. Poole for Clarionet Reeds and Instruction book	*3*	*11*	*0*	*1828*
Mr. Bishop of 200 advertisements to discover who broke open the church		*8*	*6*	*1828*
Paid Mr. Howse for 349 dozen sparrows at 3d per dozen	*4*	*7*	*3*	*1829*
The ringers being the Coronation day of King William ye 4th and Queen Adelaide	*1*	*0*	*0*	*1831*
Form of prayer and thanksgiving for not being afflicted with the Cholera		*2*	*6*	*1833*
Journey to Ham Hill to bespeak the stone for Bellfry doorway.		*5*	*0*	*1834*
Journey to Ham Hill with four horses and waggon and 3 Turnpikes	*1*	*10*	*0*	*1834*
Paid Rev. W.D. Coker for copying the Register and Parchments 8 years	*8*	*8*	*0*	*1834*
Paid Wm. Laurence for Carpenter's work and timber for repairing the roof of the South aisle being broke in by the falling of the parapet wall of ye church	*4*	*7*	*5*	*1837*
Paid for Proclamation and prayer for the safe delivery of the Queen and the happy birth of the Prince of Wales		*2*	*6*	*1841*
Paid for a ribbon to put in the prayer book			*9*	*1846*
Paid Fuzzy for preventing the Rooks building in the church Yard (Fuzzy was an old Waterloo man)		*6*	*0*	*1858*
Dec. 31st. Paid for tolling the bell at the Death and Burial of the late Prince Consort		*7*	*6*	*1861*

The vestry, consisting of representative members of the parish, held meetings to manage various church administrative matters. The book of *Vestry Minutes* for 1819–1875 gives summaries of meetings and decisions. Some extracts follow:

15th April 1833
A meeting for inspecting Mr. Carver's plan and estimate for the new pewing and alterations and repairs of the church. The Rev. W.D. Coker produced a list of subscriptions amounting to £300.

24th April 1833
Mr. Carver's plan was adopted with slight alteration. Mr. Trump's tender (for executing the work) *being the lowest, it is therefore accepted at a total of £440.*

12th June 1833
It was moved that Mr. Carver be applied to for a design for a new pulpit to be made out of the Lillesdon Pew, with handrail, steps, painting etc.

17th July 1833
Mr. Trump is directed to erect a Pulpit accordingly.

10th January 1834
Meeting to consider the propriety of appointing the Pews. It was resolved that all those persons having seats before the new pewing in right of their dwelling houses, shall first have seats again, but a seat shall first of all be assigned to the vicar.

12th January 1860
Mr. Cuthbert Morris will only ask the consent of the Vicar for the key to enter the churchyard with a cart in dry weather and when he will undertake that no injury shall occur to the churchyeard, and this he would not do had he not built his coal house behind his house, which he would now have to remove at expense and inconvenience.

13th May 1860
The present practice of the sexton or clerk applying for any refreshment or gratuity during the time of digging the grave, and also after the funeral was discontinued.

18th June 1863
A very large and excited meeting for inspecting accounts and making a voluntary church rate of 1¼d in £ was proposed to be paid by parishioners. A poll to vote to abolish the rate was agreed, and there was 158–vote majority in favour of the rate. Two ratepayers, Mr Phocion Foster and Mr John Read, who refused to pay the rate were lodged in gaol for contempt of court after a lawsuit, and they eventually left the country for America. (Soon after this rates were abolished by statute).

25th June 1864
Miss Mary Marchant and Philip Foster presented three alms plates of walnut wood lined with crimson velvet to the parish church.

1866
It was agreed that the payment to the ringers for ringing on 29th May and 5th November shall be discontinued, but then if the conduct of the ringers is satisfactory a donation will be made to them of £1 at Christmas.

The *North Curry Parish Book* of 1823–1894 and *North Curry Rate Book* of 1823 include the minutes and accounts of those responsible for looking after the poor and the highways.

An Act of 1600 imposed on the parson of a parish the duty of exhorting his parishioners to show charity to their neighbours. After the Poor Law of 1601 the Churchwardens and two to four substantial householders, nominated each year as Overseers of the Poor, were given the duty of maintaining the poor and setting them to work. These Overseers of the Poor were the principal executive servants of the vestry, and they administered the funds towards the poor and sick, which were provided by taxation from every inhabitant of the parish. Their duties included the arrest of vagrants, superintending their whippings or escorting them to other parishes, the relief of licensed travellers, and care of the chronic sick and disabled. The overseer ensured none of the parish starved to death and the needy had somewhere to sleep. Overseers of the Poor for the parish in 1823 were William Wescombe and William Payne for North Curry, William Long and William House for Knapp, William Goodland and Joseph Wood for Lillesdon and Edward Trent and William Potter for Wrantage. John Bobbett was appointed assistant overseer, with a salary of £40 per annum, and he was responsible for collecting the poor rate of one shilling and eight-pence in the pound, for collecting the Highway Rate and for superintending the repairs of the highways in the parish. Thirteen payments and eight allowances to the poor, the overseer's and doctor's salary together with a wooden leg are itemised in the account book. Mr Robert Marchant was appointed to *take care of the Poor in the said Parrish in Surgery, in Occultation, Physic and Midwifery for the year ensuing for a sum of twenty pounds.* Extra voluntary subscriptions from parishioners were required from time to time to pay for certain road repairs and resurfacing, for drainage and sewer problems and requests for public amenities. The following meeting minutes report some of these requests:

> *10th July 1857*
> *A meeting to consider the repair of a public Footway leading from the Vicarage House* (The Old Vicarage) *to the upper part of Mr. Wescombe's premises* (Flagstones), *and to determine whether a good stone pavement shall be laid, provided a certain sum be guaranteed by subscription in aid of the Highway rate. The estimate was £65. It was resolved to lay the said pavement of Pibsbury Stone, 5ft. 2in. wide* (This was almost certainly the pavement in Church Road)

> *13th November 1868*
> *Meeting to consider notice served on the waywarden by Mr. Lovibond, Bridgwater, requiring the Drove, 2,848 yards in length,* (possibly New Road?) *commencing in Haymoor, at Lawn Moor Farm and ending at the archway in Curry Moor, near Streaky Lane should be stoned and put in repair forthwith, or that in default he was instructed to prefer a bill of indictment. It was moved that in preference to making the whole of the road as threatened with indictment, the vestry undertake to make a road according to the plans submitted to them for a certain distance on the present drove, provided that sufficient subscriptions be received.*

> *14th January 1869*
> *Another meeting held for considering means of raising the necessary funds. It was resolved that with the consent of the Highways Board, a sum of £1,000 be borrowed, to be paid off in fifteen years.*

> *9th April 1869*
> *It was agreed to raise the road two feet with earth and one foot with stone throughout. It was agreed to borrow a sum not exceeding £1,500, to be paid off in 15 years, and Captain Barrett reported that Mrs. Scott Gould had offered the required sum at 4½ per cent.*

> *20th January 1879*
> *A meeting to consider a communication from the Ecclesiastical Commissioners and final notice of a School Board issued by the Commissioners of Education. It was resolved that a voluntary rate of 5d in £ be collected at once. A Committee was formed and it was resolved that Mr. Dinham of Taunton be asked to prepare plans for the proposed school at Wrantage.*

> *25th March 1879*
> *A letter from the Bishop of the Diocese with reference to the Rural Dean's report that the south wall of North Curry Church is saturated with moisture, owing to defective drainage. It was resolved that the wet part be effectually drained so that water may not accumulate in any grave or vault. This was accomplished at a cost of £31.13s.11d and paid out of the Poor Rate.*

> *26th March 1886*
> *A subscription by the inhabitants of the parish was distributed to the people for a feast to commemorate the Jubilee year of her most gracious Majesty, Queen Victoria, and also that an Iron Lamp Post with an inscription was erected on the Village Green, and that a printed bill announcing the entertainment be deposited in the Vestry Chest.*

An 1834 Act amending the laws for the relief of the poor required parishes to elect a *Select Vestry*. This consisted of 20 householders to meet fortnightly to settle the monthly accounts. In 1836 Poor Law Unions were established and it was arranged to sell the parish house or poorhouse in North Curry in order to erect a new workhouse for the Taunton Union. The *Parish Vestry Book* of 1834–1880 contains entries of payments to poor people in North Curry with reports of administering their needs. Extracts from vestry meeting minutes for that period follow:

4th July 1834	£	S	D
Monthly disbursements	79	6	2
Mary Edward one hundred of cole			
William Collier in sickness			6
Sarah Andrews in sickness		1	0
To pay Mr. Standerd for attendance on Jane Waggott	2	2	0
William Smith for want of Labourer two loves of bread and one pound and a half of bacon and one shilling		1	0
Henry Kewer for want of Labourer two loves of Bread			
Mark Edwards in sickness two loves of breade and one pound of bacon and bag of potatoes			
George Bradbeer for want of Labourer 4 loves of bread two pound of Bacon and one bag of potatoes			
Robert Duke to have a pair of shoes			
Anne Slade to have a sheet			
Sarah Hayman a bandag for her leg			
A hatt for John Adams			
A smock fork for Robert Sweeting			
A pair of trowsers for William Totterdell			
Hannah Keen's maid five yards of calico and five yards of cotton			
George Daw is givd a flenell shirt in Distress			
Elizabeth Adams a pair of shoes and a pair of stockings and a sheft.			

31st March 1835
The Vestry agrees to rent of Anthony Pittard a cottage with two dwellings and gardens at Knapp, at one shilling and sixpence per week, for the use of the Poor.

Contract for medical attendance: "I agree to attend the sick and hurt poor (including midwifery of the Parish of North Curry (except women in labour with illegitimate children) and all Paupers residing within six miles of my residence for the sum of Twenty-five pounds for the year ending at Lady-day, 1836". Robert Marchant, Surgeon

8th May 1835
Moved that Elizabeth Ducke and Hannah Ducke be moved out of the workhouse within a week and go into the house belonging to the parish in Knapp Lane unless they procure a dwelling for themselves.

Moved that John Foster be moved out of the workhouse before this day week, Mr. Dare offers to employ him on Monday morning at four shillings per week.

21st August 1835
The assistant overseer has this day reported that John Foster, Hannah Duke and Elizabeth Duke positively refuse going out of the poorhouse, and states that they have declared in the poorhouse that they do not care for order of the parish.

Ordered that the Assistant Overseer prepares the situation in Knapp Lane forthwith, and apply to the magistrates for an authority to remove them by force, John Foster included.

4th September 1835
Mary Macey undertaken the office of Governess in the Workhouse. There are sixteen beades and beadsteads, bolsters, eight blankets, twenty-five sheets and eleven quilts left in her care. Betty Duke and Hannah Duke was aloude to take from the workhouse to the Parish House in Knapp Lane with William Davise and family a bead and beadstead, two blankets, one sheet and one quilt.

7th September 1835
It was resolved that all land be newly measured and map'd, and that a new valuation be made. Mr. Richard Hodges tender was accepted. The Churchwardens at that time were Philip Foster and William Hurman, and the Overseers of the Poor were George Crease, John Totterdell, Phocion Foster and Charles Dare. They accepted the tender to survey the lands of North Curry from Richard Hodges of North Petherton for the sum of £254. He surveyed and measured the lands, and in 1841 produced a complete map, a valuation, a poor rate and a schedule of reference. Property and land was awarded an annual rateable value and the resulting rates and taxes financed such services as bridges, poor relief, highways and drainage in the parish (see Chapter 3-3 for Tithe Map information).

The North Curry *Rate Schedule* for 1863 includes the four tithings of North Curry which were valued separately, and lists 428 parcels of land in North Curry, 661 in Wrantage, 377 in Lillesdon and 695 in Knapp, the rate being made at ten pence in the pound.

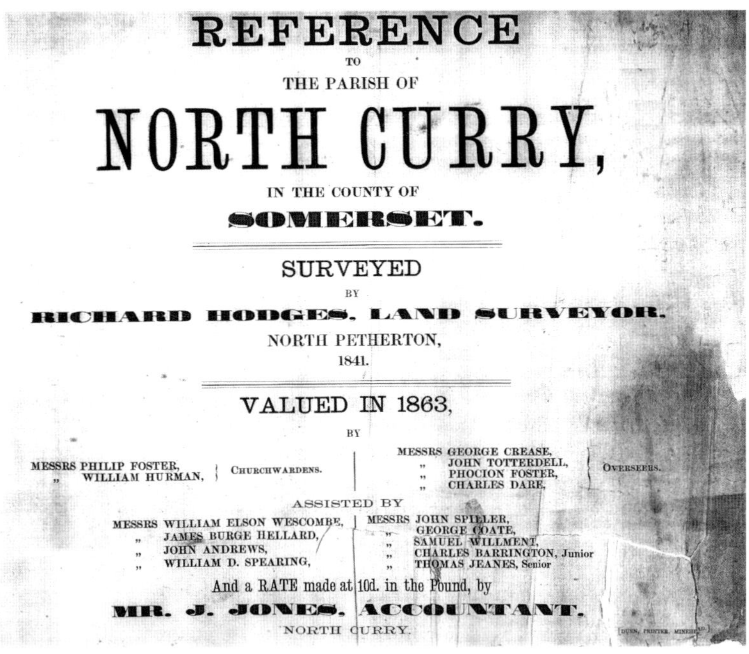
REFERENCE
TO
THE PARISH OF
NORTH CURRY,
IN THE COUNTY OF
SOMERSET.
SURVEYED
BY
RICHARD HODGES, LAND SURVEYOR.
NORTH PETHERTON,
1841.
VALUED IN 1863,
BY
MESSRS PHILIP FOSTER, „ WILLIAM HURMAN, } CHURCHWARDENS.
MESSRS GEORGE CREASE, „ JOHN TOTTERDELL, „ PHOCION FOSTER, „ CHARLES DARE, } OVERSEERS.
ASSISTED BY
MESSRS WILLIAM ELSON WESCOMBE, „ JAMES BURGE HELLARD, „ JOHN ANDREWS, „ WILLIAM D. SPEARING,
MESSRS JOHN SPILLER, „ GEORGE COATE, „ SAMUEL WILLMENT, „ CHARLES BARRINGTON, Junior „ THOMAS JEANES, Senior
And a RATE made at 10d. in the Pound, by
MR. J. JONES, ACCOUNTANT.
NORTH CURRY.

NORTH CURRY RATE SCHEDULE - 1863

The following is the summary of the valuation for the Parish of North Curry:

Tithing	*Quantities in Statute Measure*			*Gross Estimated Rental*			*Rateable Value*			*Rate at Ten Pence in the Pound*		
	A	*R*	*P*	*£*	*s*	*d*	*£*	*s*	*d*	*£*	*s*	*d*
Curry	*1,931*	*1*	*6*	*5,485*	*17*	*7*	*5,023*	*13*	*0*	*209*	*6*	*4½*
Knapp	*1,305*	*0*	*4*	*3,155*	*10*	*9*	*2,893*	*13*	*0*	*120*	*11*	*4½*
Lillesdon	*1,133*	*2*	*5*	*2,477*	*7*	*9*	*2,255*	*1*	*0*	*93*	*19*	*2½*
Wrantage	*1,202*	*0*	*3*	*1,543*	*1*	*11*	*2,328*	*4*	*0*	*97*	*0*	*2*
The Whole Parish	*5,571*	*3*	*18*	*12,661*	*18*	*0*	*12,500*	*11*	*0*	*520*	*17*	*1½*

Numerous references are made in the *Parish Vestry Book* to applications to send persons to America and Canada, under powers conferred by the emigration acts to Boards of Guardians of the Poor. An example is:

31st March 1843
John Murless applies for means for himself and family of six children to go to Canada. £52.16s.9d was paid towards the emigration of this family.

The *Church Book* of 1875–1898 contains details of notable events, gifts and bequests to the church including the following:

1887
The planting of the churchyard was finished this year, the Jubilee of our Most Gracious Majesty Queen Victoria.

1892
Entry relating to a bequest from the late Mrs. Robbs, and extract from her will bequeathing the sum of £250, the interest to be given annually to the poor in clothing; and also £50, the interest of which is to be applied for keeping the churchyard in order.

1894
A vote of thanks to Rev. Preb. W.E. Buller recording thanks on behalf of the parishioners for his munificent gift of two additional bells in the tower, making a total of eight, and also for the restoration of the old Parish Cross in the churchyard.

1896
Entry relating to a bequest by the late Miss M.A. Crease, of £200, the interest to be given in coal in the first week of January in each year.

This *Church Book* also contains details of the North Curry Parish Church restoration programme and other procedures as follows:

13th April 1875
A meeting held to consider the subject of the proposed church alteration. The following approximate estimate had been obtained from Sir Gilbert Scott.

Roofs, internal repairs and floors	*£1,385*
Fittings of Oak	*£980*
External repairs, excepting tower	*£620*
Tower, externally	*£520*
Vestry	*£135*
Spire, if erected	*£300*

It was agreed that a levy of five shillings in the pound be asked of owners, and two shillings in the pound of the tenants. It was also agreed that a subscription list be opened, to which Major Barrett offered £500 and the Rev. C.R. Harrison £500.

2nd April 1877
It was resolved that a voluntary subscription be opened for church expenses instead of a rate, and a quarterly collection be made in church.

25th May 1880
Major Barrett offered on certain conditions the sum of £2,000 for the church restoration.

It was decided that the cost of the church restoration and the restoration of the organ would be met by voluntary subscription by Major Barrett and other parishioners and that past resolutions would be rescinded. Mr. Oldred Scott, son of the famous Victorian architect Sir Gilbert Scott, was selected as architect, and his estimate of £3,300 was accepted. The tenders of Mr. Charles Trask of Ilminster to execute the works in the church, and of Mr. Clark of Bath for the organ restoration were accepted. The total cost of the restoration including the repairing of the organ was £4,501.17s.3d. The Ecclesiastical Commissioners spent £2,000 on the restoration of the chancel and on the stained glass windows.

In early times the Parish Clerk's duties were laid down by Canon Law, the chief of them being to keep the parish school, to read the Epistle at the Eucharist and to sing the Psalms at Divine Service. During the Middle Ages the clerk of a parish became a very important person, and many other tasks were laid upon him. He had to open the church at an early hour every morning and lock up again at night, to ring the bell for the various services as well as taking part in them, and to attend the priest when he visited the sick. He was responsible for providing oil for the lamps and rushes for the church floor, he also acted as handyman, and one of his duties was keeper of the keys to the parish chest.

In 1881 Mr G Oates was appointed as Caretaker to the Church and he was to perform the duties of the previous clerk and previous Sexton. A new scale of fees for burials was instigated as follows:

	£	S	D
For Graves (Class A – Poor Persons, Class B – Persons in better position)			
For infants under one year – Class A		*7*	*6*
For Infants under one year – Class B		*10*	*6*
For persons over one year – Class A		*10*	*6*
For persons over one year – Class B		*15*	*0*
For Adults – Class A		*12*	*6*
For Adults – Class B	*1*	*1*	*0*

All graves are to be dug six feet deep
Deeper graves will be charged five shillings per foot below this depth
Brick graves will be charged for digging double that of ordinary graves
For the minute bell for all persons ten shillings
Caretaker's fees for attendance on funerals Class A one shilling, Class B two shillings and sixpence including ordinary bell
Caretaker's fee for Weddings and Banns inclusive Class A one shilling Class B five shillings
Caretaker's fee for opening the church on any other occasion two shillings and sixpence

In 1913 Mr A W Colley, who was Caretaker and Verger of the Church, emigrated to the Colonies and a notice leading to the appointment of Mr Gilbert Dare as new Caretaker for North Curry Parish appeared as follows:

This is an annual post, which runs from Easter to Easter. The duties are those which formerly belonged to the Sexton. The Caretaker will also act as Verger and Deputy Clerk when required. He will be responsible for grave digging, grass cutting, general care of graves, paths, approaches, trees, shrubs, all attaching to the churchyard. The wages will be 16 shillings per week and a cottage. Applicants must have a fair education and be members of the Church of England.

EXAMPLES OF THE VARIETY OF FORMS OF LETTERS USED IN EARLY DOCUMENTS

3 - 2

POPULATION, CENSUSES AND OCCUPATIONS

EARLY SOURCES AND METHODOLOGY

Our knowledge of population changes and occupations relies on a variety of records, and very few were designed specifically to produce this information.

By the use of various lists from medieval times such as Subsidy Rolls, Hundred Rolls, Poll Tax Assessments, Local Tallage Lists and Manorial Extents detailing the notable taxpayers and possessors of property, the population of the land can only be guessed at because these lists only give a fraction of any village's total inhabitants. In 1980 Zvi Razi used a particular village's Court Rolls to measure population trends between 1270 and 1348, but this statistical sample of the manorial population accounted for no more that 60 per cent of the male population of a village and only 40 per cent of females, as many people fell into the category of lesser tenants and peasantry.

The parish registers of baptisms, marriages and burials dating from 1538 can also be used to estimate the population. Sometimes the entries in the parish registers mention an individual's place in society or occupation and, as discussed in Chapter 3-1 these registers exist for North Curry from 1539. *Gentlemen* and *yeomen* together with tradesmen such as carpenters, bakers, masons and farmers are often mentioned, but these entries are very random and certainly not consistent.

In 1676 the Archbishop of Canterbury, Gilbert Sheldon (1663-1678), gathered from his clergy parochial statistics of families, communicants, dissenters etc. From time to time various schemes have been proposed to work out the probable total population of a district from the average annual number of baptisms, marriages and burials in the area concerned. In early days these methods were rather crude. Methods used included multiplying by 30 the mean annual number of baptisms, multiplying by 125 the mean annual number of marriages, and multiplying by 31 the mean annual number of burials. However, making assessments using these methods is unreliable given economic cycles, the fluctuation of burial records because of the incidence of disease and epidemics, the distortion of marriage records by the varying popularity of different churches, and under-registration as a result of nonconformist views.

THE NATIONAL CENSUS

In the 18th century proposals for a full enumeration of the population were raised in Parliament. In 1801 John Rickman (1771-1840), who was a statistician and clerk assistant in the House of Commons, organised the first census of population in England and Wales to gauge manpower resources during the Napoleonic wars and to settle disputes over whether the population was expanding or contracting. He requested the clergy of every parish and Overseers of the Poor in England and Wales to count the entries in the registers for the baptisms and burials at ten-yearly intervals between 1700 and 1780, and then for every year from 1781 to 1800. Marriages were counted for every year from 1754. On the basis of the data collected he produced totals of the numbers of baptisms, marriages and burials for the whole of England and Wales for every tenth year, from 1700 to 1780, and thereafter, for every year up to 1800. They were also asked to answer questions with respect to the number of individuals or families working in agriculture and other basic economic categories. In 1821 a more detailed enumeration was made of ages, and in 1831 of occupations. Rickman prepared reports and published the results as parliamentary papers for these first four censuses up to 1831.

Since 1831 a census has been taken every ten years, except in 1941 when the country was at war. From 1841 an increasing amount of information was gathered and this is now available through the Office of National Statistics, the Returns for each Census becoming available for public inspection after a period of 100 years.

In 1836 Thomas Henry Lister became the first registrar general or head of the national system of civil registration. His task was to maintain a central register of births, marriages and deaths. Local officers were responsible for registers in their local areas. From 1838 William Farr was the Superintendent of Statistics at the General Register Office and wrote the Census Reports of 1851, 1861 and 1871. Much of the occupational data collected revealed the structure of the economy and was important for medical research. The administration was therefore in place for a more radical change in the organisation and collection of Census data.

In 1840 the responsibility for census-taking was transferred to the General Register Office, and the establishment of the means of enumerating the population, which eventually led to the current national system of civil registration, was begun. Each registration area was divided into enumeration districts of not more then 200 and not fewer than 25 inhabited houses. Enumerators visited each household in the district and collected details of each person residing in the house on the particular chosen Census Day, even if permanently resident elsewhere. The individual returns were copied by census enumerators into their books, and these records provide the basis for the public record.

The first modern Census was in 1841, when details were collected of such information as the address, name, age, rounded down to the nearest term of five years if over 14 years, sex, profession, trade, employment or of independent means for each person. The person's country of birth or whether they were born in the particular county of the Census was also recorded. In 1851 and thereafter the Censuses sought additional information on relationship to the head of a household, marital status, full ages, the parish and county of birth and details of medical disabilities.

The local registrars selected an enumerator for each enumeration district. They could appoint whoever they liked as long as they met the basic requirements:

> *He must be a person of intelligence and activity; he must read and write well, and have some knowledge of arithmetic; he must not be infirm or of such weak health as may render him unable to undergo the requisite exertion; he should not be younger than 18 years of age or older than 65; he must be temperate, orderly and respectable, and be such a person as is likely to conduct himself with strict propriety, and to deserve the goodwill of the inhabitants of his district.*

Each enumerator was allotted an area of a size to enable all information to be collected on the chosen day. Those covering scattered farms and cottages had fewer properties to visit than those in more densely occupied areas. Enumerators were paid a fixed fee of 23s.6d for every 100 persons in their districts above the first 400 enumerated and 6 pence for every mile above the first 5 covered in delivering the schedules and similar for collecting them. It was hoped men of local standing would undertake the work as a social duty. From 1891 women could be enumerators. Where they were able, householders filled out their own Census forms, but the enumerators were obliged to enter many details themselves and much time was spent visiting each household.

The information collected from each household by the enumerator was often inaccurate. In a period before systematic record-keeping many people were unsure about their precise date of birth. Many were ignorant or confused and made a round guess, some were reluctant to be honest, and the young sometimes exaggerated or falsified their age for employment reasons. People were required to indicate the county and the town or parish of their birth, or specify if they were born abroad. Many did not really know their birthplace if the family moved when they were very young. Rich people often gave London as a fashionable birthplace.

Understanding unfamiliar pronunciation or dialect was often the cause of misspelling or incorrect entries. There was confusion on what constituted an occupation, householders were not asked to indicate their paid occupation, and many interpreted the question to imply their social status. Enumerators were asked to complete this column using only broad occupational categories and inaccuracies occurred. There was often no distinction between employers, employees and the unemployed or retired; between masters of trades, journeymen, dealers and manufacturers. The work of women and children and the recording of seasonal and part-time labour were not recorded in any precise way. All children over the age of five were listed as scholars. All residents of the household were stated in order of status and age, combined with marital status (single, married, or widowed). Wives, sons, daughters, in-laws, servants, nurses, lodgers and visitors were all listed. Children born out of wedlock were sometimes concealed as the children of elderly parents or stepchildren, and the designation of housekeeper sometimes concealed unconventional relationships. People who were blind, deaf and dumb were mentioned, as were imbeciles, idiots and lunatics. Errors were inevitable due to the enumerators making errors when copying the household schedules into their books, and to local peculiarities and interpretation of information.

The Census Schedules or Returns are among the most useful printed sources for learning about population numbers and the residences and occupation of the population in any area. Records from 1841 to 1901 are at the present time available for the public to consult.

National Population

At the time of the Domesday Survey in 1086 the population of England and Wales was 1.25 million, as discussed in Chapter 1-4, and it has been suggested that the population in around 1200 was 2.5 million.

By 1700 the figure had risen to 5.5 million, and by 1750 to 6.25 million people. By the time of the first Census in 1801 a more accurate assessment was made giving a total of 9 million people. By 1831 the population of England and Wales had grown to just under 14 million and in 1851 to nearly 18 million. That of Scotland grew from 2.2 million to 2.8 million, whilst that of Ireland fell from 7.8 million to 6.6 million for the same period. Many people from the United Kingdom emigrated to the overseas territories of the British Empire, including large numbers from Ireland after the potato failure of 1846. By 1854 the annual emigration to North America, Canada, Australia, South Africa and the West Indies reached 325,000.

Between 1801 and 1901 the population of Somerset increased from 273,577 to 434,945. In 1961 the figure at 600,000, was not much more than double the 1801 figure, with the national increase being six times the original figure. Over the years population in some areas of Somerset has fluctuated significantly due to the presence of casual workers engaged in the construction of canals and railways. Somerset is the seventh largest county in England but only about one twentieth of the land is occupied by towns and villages. Agriculture was always the principal industry of Somerset and nearly three-quarters of the land is still used for that purpose. The cloth industry was closely connected with agriculture and depended on the wool from sheep from all parts of the county, with large numbers of workers being employed in Taunton and the outlying villages. When the cloth industry declined at the end of the 18th century there were no large or important industrial undertakings in Somerset to replace it.

The population in Great Britain in 1870 was 31.5 million and the two most common occupations were agricultural workers and domestic servants. By 1901 as the Victorian Age closed, the population given in the 1901 Census of England, Wales, Scotland and Ireland was 41 million with 6.5 million people living in London. By 2001 the population in the United Kingdom had risen to 59.2 million people, as published by the Office for National Statistics.

Trade Directories

Commercial or Trade Directories listing people of importance, including private residents and tradespeople, are another excellent written source for research into the social and occupational structure of a place. The first directory was one for London in 1671 that contained the names of gentry and local officials. From the 18th century until the 1930s numerous local directories were published periodically providing commercial, mercantile and political information, details of local offices and of the personages who held them, and of the occupants of major residences in towns and rural areas. As commercial markets widened they provided an accessory to trade, bringing manufacturers, retailers and customers together and making the distribution of goods and services easier.

From c.1820 publishers such as Pigot and Company and William White employed investigators and agents all over England to supply information for the compilation of directories. The most widely circulated were the *Kelly's Directories*, published in county and city volumes between 1799 and 1939. The publishers Kelly, Bragg and Morris distributed the directories for Taunton. Early directories contained brief lists of the chief inhabitants, and included the more substantial tradesmen and professional classes of all the villages and towns of a county, arranged alphabetically, giving each man's occupation. Details of inns, coaching services, arrivals of mails and stagecoaches and barge transport were given, as well as some historical detail about the particular place.

By the mid-19th century a pattern of presentation was established. Firstly, the position of the place in relation to neighbouring towns was given together with its distance from them, followed by architectural and historical detail about the church, its fabric, the living, and its glebe land and tithe-owners. The Lord of the Manor as well as the principal landowners and the chief industries that employed the inhabitants were named. Also included was the nature of the soil, its chief crops, details of geology and natural history, statistics of the area, rateable value and total population at the last Census. There was information on local officials and services with details of post offices, insurance agents, doctors and medical officers, veterinary surgeons, tax collectors and poor rate overseers. Details of national schools, school boards, church schools and private teaching establishments were followed by the list of chief inhabitants that began with private residents including gentry and clergy. The commercial classes were arranged alphabetically and divided into their trades, which provided valuable information for residents and visitors alike.

The North Curry Population and its Occupations

An interesting account of the village of North Curry can be obtained from the information available from the Census Returns and Trade Directories.

The information in the Census Returns included the names of the various areas of the village and some road names, but the names of the individual houses were only rarely given and the route of the enumerator's journey was not recorded. However, it is the most accurate record there is of the layout of the village, which appears much as it is today, and provides a fascinating picture of life in the 19th century.

Although 100 years must elapse before *Census Returns* are available for public scrutiny, various statistics are published giving general population information.

A summary giving information on the people living and working within the North Curry Ward of the Taunton Deane Local Authority District, which includes Durston, was published from the 2001 Census. The resident population of the North Curry Ward was recorded as 1,740, (1610 quoted in the chart overleaf excludes Durston) of whom 49 per cent were male and 51 per cent were female, with an average age of 43.1. There were 751 households, with an average size of 2.3 persons.

Henry White Meade, a solicitor living in The Shambles, was the Registrar for North Curry for the 1841 and 1851 *Census Return*. His son Robert Meade, a general practitioner living in Greenway, was engaged as one of the four enumerators in the five enumeration districts of North Curry for those years. John Horsey Nicholls, the North Curry Postmaster and Registrar of Births and Deaths was the Census Registrar for the years 1861 and 1871. William Pyne, Relieving Officer and Registrar of Births and Deaths, living in Victoria Terrace, was the Census Registrar in 1881 and 1891, whilst George Medway, also Registrar of Births and Deaths, was the Census Registrar in 1901. Prominent men in the village who had considerable local knowledge and whose occupations included farmers, schoolmasters, doctors and merchants, were engaged in North Curry as the enumerators between 1841 and 1891.

The published *Census Returns* for North Curry from 1841–1901 list all the households in the centre of the village and in the outlying hamlets including Knapp, Wrantage, Lillesdon, Broad Lane and Newport. The chart overleaf shows the population of North Curry detailed from 1801 to 2001.

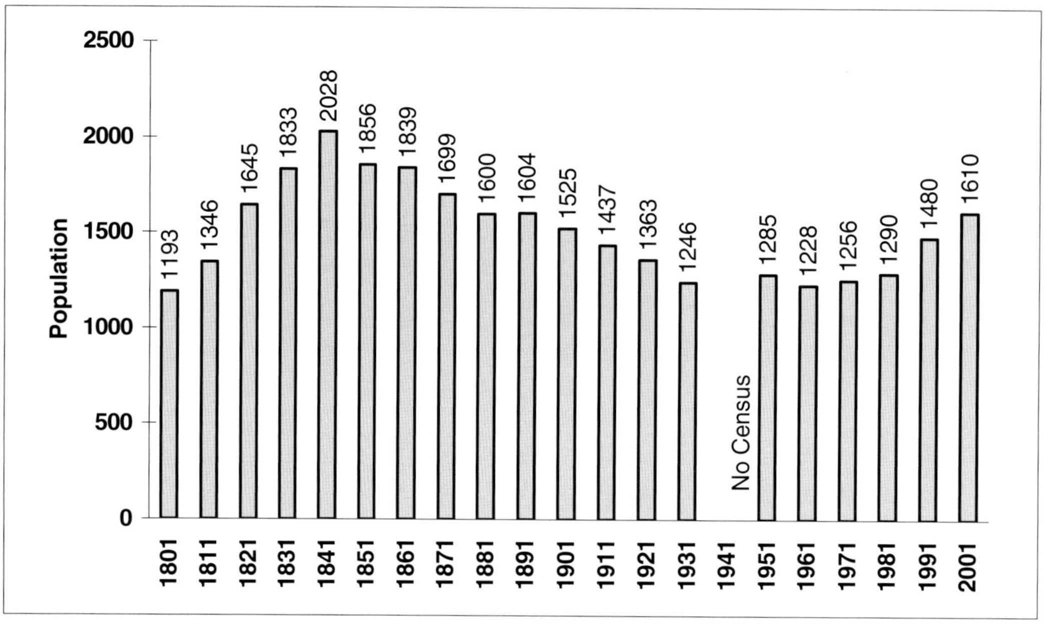

CENSUS POPULATION OF NORTH CURRY

There were over 250 separate occupations recorded in the *Census Returns* for North Curry between 1841 and 1901. These are listed in detail in Appendix 1 and summarised below.

OCCUPATION	1841	1851	1861	1871	1881	1891	1901
Agriculture, fishing, livestock and associated	319	373	349	387	276	271	215
Building and contracting	47	20	25	72	63	48	71
Conveyancing	3	18	7	24	4	5	9
Domestic service	105	122	123	143	97	136	153
Manufacturing and craft	114	141	165	250	124	123	110
Not employed and retired	49	114	67	92	67	71	70
Professional	20	31	32	73	20	35	37
Public service	4	5	8	36	9	11	13
Scholar		175	228	325	328	301	21
Trade	26	36	30	74	41	40	29
Unskilled				3		4	3

The names of roads and areas used in the *Census Returns* for North Curry throughout the Census period changed from time to time as follows:

1851	*1861*	*1871*	*1881*	*1891*	*1901*
Knapp Lane	*Knapp Lane*	*Knapp Lane*	*Knapp Lane*	*Knapp Road*	*Knapp Lane*
Chapel Hill	*Taunton Road*	*Windmill Hill*	*Windmill Hill*	*Windmill Hill*	*Windmill Hill*
Greenway	*Greenway*	*Greenway*	*Greenway*	*Greenway*	*Greenway*
	Queens Square	*Village*	*Village*	*Queen Square*	*Queens Square*
Shambles	*Shambles*	*Shambles/Road*		*Shambles*	
White Street	*White Street*	*White Street*	*White Street*	*White Street*	*White Street*
Helland	*Helland*	*Hellend*	*Helland*	*Helland*	*Helland*
Pury Street	*Stoke Road*	*Stoke Road*	*Stoke Road*	*Fore Street*	*Fore Street*
Moor Lane	*Moor Lane*	*Moor Lane*	*Moor Lane*	*Moor Lane*	*Moor Lane*
Ham	*Ham*	*Ham*	*Ham/Mills/ Road*	*Ham*	*Ham/Mills*
Moredon	*Moredon*	*Moredon*	*Moredon*	*Moredon*	*Moredon*
New Bridge	*Newbridge*	*New Bridge*	*Durston Road*	*New Road*	*Newbridge*
	Broad Lane	*Broad Lane*	*Broad Lane*	*Broad Lane*	*Broad Lane*
Huntham				*Huntham*	*Huntham*
Burrowpost	*Burrowpost Hill*	*Burrowpost Road*	*Burrow Post*	*Boro Post*	*Borough Post*
Knapp Street	*Knapp Street*	*Knapp Street*	*Knapp*	*Knapp*	*Knapp*
	Ford Lane	*Fords Lane*	*Coomb Lane*	*Knapp*	*Owls Lane*

1851	1861	1871	1881	1891	1901
Higher Knapp					*Higher Knapp*
	Haymoors End	*Haymoor End*	*Haymoors End*		*Lower Knapp*
Lillesdon	*Lillesdon Green*	*Lillesdon Green*	*Lillesdon Green*	*Lillesdon*	*Lillesdon/Road /Green/Higher*
	Stoneyhead	*Stoney Head*	*Stoney Head*	*Stoney Head*	*Stoneyhead*
Newport	*Newport/boro'*	*Newport/boro'*	*Newport/Hill*	*Newport/Road*	*Newport /Hill*
Wrantage	*Wrantage*	*Wrantage Road*	*Wrantage*	*Wrantage Road*	*Wrantage*
Crimson Hill	*Crimson Hill*	*Crimson Hill/ Spillers Lane*	*Crimson Hill*	*Crimson Hill*	*Crimson Hill*
Oldway	*Oldway*	*Oldway Road*		*Oldway Lane*	
Rock Hill	*Rock Hill*	*Rock Hill Road*	*Rock Hill*	*Rock Hill*	*Rock Hill*
Listoke Road	*Listoke*				*Listoke*
Sedgmoor	*Sedgmoor*	*Sedgmoor*	*Sedgemoor*	*Sedgemoor /Road/Drove*	*Sedgmoor*

North Curry is seven miles from the facilities of Taunton and as can be seen from the survey of occupations opposite it was totally self sufficient, and independent of other centres, supporting all the trades, occupations and needs to sustain a fairly large population. People were mostly occupied with agriculture and the trades that supported it, and the remainder in occupations that serviced the needs of the residents in order that they might live comfortably and be satisfied in their day-to-day domestic needs.

The occupation of the head of the household determined the lifestyle of the family, dictating how and where they lived. Sons followed their fathers' occupations or carried on the family business, while marriage strengthened ties between families already connected by trade or occupation. Although people designated their own occupations on the household schedules, the Census enumerators were given official guidelines to establish specific classifications. Tradesmen were defined in the *Census Returns* as master, journeyman or apprentice, and in the case of employers the number of employees was stated. Women and children were given their own occupations. Children at school or not employed were defined as scholars. Some occupations came and went, with many no longer existing having been overtaken by machinery and technological developments.

The *Census Returns* confirm the presence of a number of houses and premises used for professional and trade use. Professions represented included accountants, auctioneers, lawyers, medical practitioners, surgeons and surveyors.

There were mills at Ham, the building of which was mentioned in 1316 in the Dean and Chapter of Wells documents, and at Newport, which was converted to a steam mill and where the residents of North Curry went with their wheat to be ground into flour. There is also evidence to suggest that The Warren in Stoke Road was a mill in early times.

Brewing took place on the site of The Old Brewery in Queen Square for over 200 years until after the First World War. The Old Malthouse in Stoke Road was the site of a malting house in c.1720 and the malthouse was moved to The Old Brewery site in c.1840 to provide a larger establishment. Several men were employed and beer was supplied to the many inns and beerhouses in the village. There were numerous inns, beerhouses and cider houses in the village from early times. The Angel Inn, a former posting house, was first mentioned as a *common ale house* in 1736. The Bird in Hand in Queen Square was first licensed to sell beer in 1790. The Canal Inn at Wrantage was used by the workers on the Chard Canal, c.1840. The Rising Sun in Knapp, originally a cider house, became an inn in the 19th century. The Halfway House at New Bridge was used as a stopping place for people using Durston Station. Other inns included The Bell Inn and The White Hart in Knapp Lane, The Star Inn at Lillesdon, The Wrantage Inn, The Wheelwright's Arms, licensed in 1813 in Wrantage, and The Royal Oak at Haymoor End.

Somerset, a predominantly rural county, has had farming and its associated trades as the main source of employment for centuries and this is confirmed by the recorded information found in the *Census Returns.* By 1851 the number of landed proprietors in Somerset was 1,873, whilst there were 8,438 farmers. There were 8,500 farm servants living-in, and 37,000 agricultural labourers earning a weekly wage of between 8 and 10 shillings augmented by a cider allowance, with bonuses given at hay making and harvest. North Curry families reflected this pattern with one in six males engaged in agriculture and whole families including children as young as five working the land. The Somerset Levels has rich pastureland where in summer the cattle graze and grass is cut for hay and silage to feed animals who winter on higher land.

As can be noted from the *Census Returns* there were a number of people in North Curry engaged in the withy industry, which entails the growing and harvesting of the willow (Salix,) and the crafts which use the end product. Withy is the name for the young flexible branches of the willow tree. Willow weaving played a vital role in early societies and willows have been found in prehistoric woven hurdle trackways across the Somerset Levels. The use of willow can be traced back to two late Iron Age fragments of basket found on the site of the Glastonbury Lake Village, and a another piece found in a Roman salt making site on the River Huntspill.

Pollarded willows, a renewable source of withies, line ditches and rhines across the Somerset Levels, strengthening the banks and acting as markers in floods. The clay soils are well suited to willow cultivation because they retain the moisture so essential to growth. Until the beginning of the 19th century uncultivated withies were used. Not until some time after 1810 was the first withy bed planted on West Sedgemoor and subsequently the area was to provide three quarters of all England's output. Until the Second World War over 3,000 acres of willows were grown commercially in Somerset, but today this figure has declined. As withies are susceptible to frost damage, early premature growth in spring is controlled by grazing cattle. Constant care is needed in the growing season from mid-May to mid-August, spraying to control aphids and weeds. Early in September, sheep are used to graze the grass and weeds. The withies are cut from mid-November, when the leaves fall, right through the winter until April. They are bundled by size, boiled in large tanks, stripped of bark, and dried in upright bundles. They are then handcrafted into a variety of traditional Somerset baskets and other products.

Basket-making used to be a flourishing activity as baskets were used extensively in agriculture, industry and the home. Apples, potatoes, fish, glass, china and pottery were always carried in wicker baskets. Huge wickerwork skips were used in the wool and cotton mills of the industrial north of England. Eel traps, willow bee hives, furniture and hurdles for fencing all contributed to the domination of the Somerset Levels as a willow craft centre. Originally the harvesting, boiling, stripping and drying of the withies was a laborious process using only rudimentary machinery. Outworkers, mainly women and children, often stripped the rods of willow in their homes using a crude 'hand brake' device. A country dance which imitates the movement of the willows pulled to and fro in the willow stripping hand brake is known as 'Strip the Willow' and is still danced in schools and barn dances today. In more recent years limited mechanisation has been introduced. In many applications foreign baskets and plastic goods have replaced those made locally and today only a handful of withy yards operate in the area with only a few skilled basket makers weaving items mainly for domestic use. Today there are still some 300–400 acres of commercially grown willows in Somerset and this is used for willow sculpture, garden furniture, coffins and hurdles in addition to some of the traditional uses of the past. Today artist's charcoal made from willow has also found a worldwide market.

Another significant traditional Somerset occupation is cider-making. In the 18th and 19th centuries up to a gallon of cider a day was included as part of an agricultural labourer's wages. Evidence of the making of a cider-like beverage in Roman times has been found in Kent and later in the 13th century monasteries were making and selling cider. By the middle of the 19th century extensive and productive orchards of cider apples and pears stretched across the whole of Somerset. In North Curry many farmhouses had their own orchards and presses and there were a number of cider houses where locals would meet together. It takes 13 kilograms of apples to make 10 litres of cider. Two days of pressing, fermenting and adding yeast is followed by a ten-day wait before it is ready to drink. Today manufacture is concentrated in a few local firms who produce traditional flat cider, cider brandy, 'perry' and apple juice.

An occupation enjoyed more as a leisure activity by the inhabitants of North Curry was eel fishing. The rivers and ditches of the Levels make an ideal habitat for the young eels or elvers, which gather in estuaries in springtime and swim inland to feed off worms in the fresh-water streams. All along the banks of the Rivers Parrett and Tone fishermen have for centuries waited for the night tide in spring and caught vast quantities of tiny elvers - 4,000 of them weigh one pound. From October through the winter the elvers that survive the inward journey begin their swim back to the sea as mature eels and once again become prey for the local fishermen.

Before improved transport took the residents of North Curry further afield to service their needs, and before people experienced a wider choice of goods, there were numerous trades operating in the village. There were a number of bakeries, most of them in the village centre, and many people remember a baker in Queen Square who would cook customers' joints of meat in his ovens for a penny or two. There were smithies and blacksmiths, one beside The White Hart, one in Moor Lane and another opposite the entrance to White Street. There were also butchers and slaughterhouses, boot-makers, harness-makers and saddlers, wheelwrights, coach-builders and many other shops and small businesses which serviced day-to-day needs.

Included in the *General Directory for the County of Somerset* printed and published by William Bragg in 1841 is an entry for North Curry that seems to be the earliest available for this area. The entry begins with a description of the village as follows:

> *North Curry is a large village and parish in the Hundred of North Curry, situate 6½miles E. by N. from Taunton. In 1748, an urn containing Roman coins was found here. King John granted a Market, which has long been disused. Newport in this parish formerly had the privileges and officers of a corporate Town, and is yet called a Borough. The village is a very respectably inhabited, having many wealthy inhabitants. A curious custom of great antiquity, is still observed here, under the designation of the Reeve's Feast, in which certain characters figure, who take their titles from the tithings into which the parish is divided; certain quaint standing dishes form a part of this singular ceremonial, of which we have endeavoured, but in vain, to procure some authentic history. The church is dedicated to St Peter and St Paul; the living is a discharged vicarage, with the perpetual curacies of Stoke St Gregory and West Hatch annexed, in the peculiar jurisdiction of the Dean and Chapter of Wells; of the net annual value of £375. Population at the last census 1833. It is in the electoral division of West Somerset, and in 1839, contained 138 registered electors, of whom 83 were freeholders, 4*

leaseholders, 31 copyholders and 20 occupying tenants; polling place Taunton. It is in the Taunton Union, to which it sends 2 guardians; the annual amount of poor relief previous to the New Poor Law was 1356l. It is in the Magisterial division of Taunton. The area of this parish is 5,538 acres. Fair – the first Tuesday in September.

The schedule of the 105 persons listed is reproduced in Appendix 2, and it is interesting to compare these with the 169 people listed 98 years later in the 1939 edition of *Kelly's Directory of Somerset* reproduced in Appendix 3. The areas in the Parish of North Curry where the trades were offered and some particular residences are also mentioned. Among the public officers listed were the following:

Public Overseer, Bailiff of the Hundred of North Curry, Commissioner in Chancery, Commissioner for Taking Acknowledgments of Married Women, Commissioner for Administering Oaths, Clerk and Correspondent to the West Sedgmoor and Stanmoor Drainage Board, Agent to the Dean and Chapter of Wells, Clerk and Correspondent to Isle Abbotts School Board, Perpetual Commissioner for Somerset and Devon Affidavits, Registrar of Births and Deaths, Relieving Officer of North Curry District, and a Stamp Distributor.

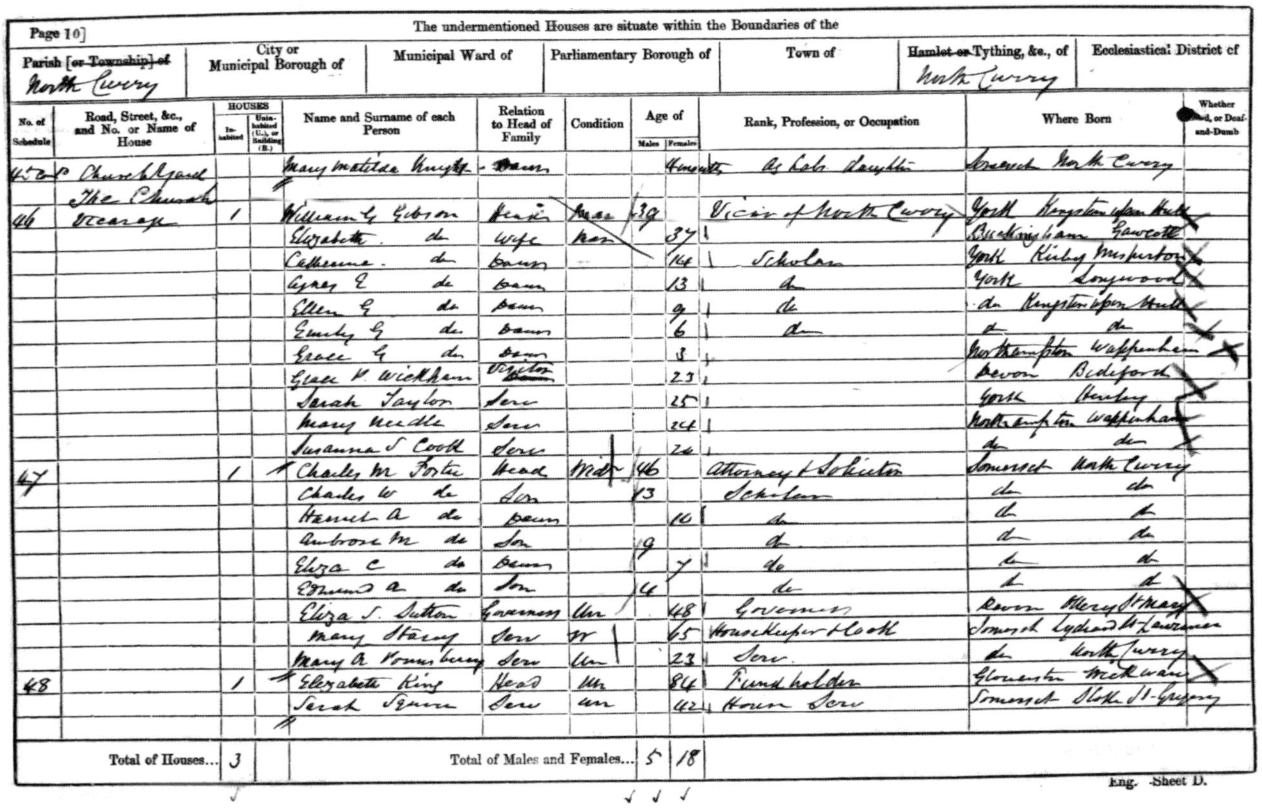

Page 10]

The undermentioned Houses are situate within the Boundaries of the

Parish [~~or Township~~] of	City or Municipal Borough of	Municipal Ward of	Parliamentary Borough of	Town of	~~Hamlet or~~ Tything, &c., of	Ecclesiastical District of
North Curry					North Curry	

No. of Schedule	Road, Street, &c., and No. or Name of House	HOUSES Inhabited	HOUSES Uninhabited (U.), or Building (B.)	Name and Surname of each Person	Relation to Head of Family	Condition	Age of Males	Age of Females	Rank, Profession, or Occupation	Where Born	Whether Blind, or Deaf-and-Dumb
45 cont	Churchyard			Mary Matilda Knight	Daur			4 months	Ag Lab Daughter	Somerset North Curry	
	The Church										
46	Vicarage	1		William G Gibson	Head	Mar	39		Vicar of North Curry	York Kingston upon Hull	
				Elizabeth do	Wife	Mar		37		Buckingham Gawcott	
				Catherine do	Daur			14	Scholar	York Kirby Misperton	
				Agnes E do	Daur			13	do	York Longwood	
				Ellen G do	Daur			9	do	do Kingston upon Hull	
				Emily G do	Daur			6	do	do do	
				Grace G do	Daur			3		Northampton Wappenham	
				Grace P. Wickham	Visitor			23		Devon Bideford	
				Sarah Taylor	Serv			25		York Helmsley	
				Mary Needle	Serv			24		Northampton Wappenham	
				Susanna S Cook	Serv			24		do do	
47		1		Charles M Foster	Head	Widr	46		Attorney & Solicitor	Somerset North Curry	
				Charles W do	Son		13		Scholar	do do	
				Harriet A do	Daur			10	do	do do	
				Ambrose M do	Son		9		do	do do	
				Eliza C do	Daur			7	do	do do	
				Edmund A do	Son		4		do	do do	
				Eliza S. Sutton	Governess	Un		48	Governess	Devon Ottery St Mary	
				Mary Stacey	Serv	W		65	Housekeeper & Cook	Somerset Lydeard St Lawrence	
				Mary A Pounsberry	Serv	Un		23	Serv	do North Curry	
48		1		Elizabeth King	Head	Un		84	Fundholder	Gloucester Wickwar	
				Sarah Squire	Serv	Un		42	House Serv	Somerset Stoke St Gregory	
	Total of Houses...	3		Total of Males and Females...			5	18			

Eng. Sheet D.

PRO RG9/1614

EXTRACT FROM CENSUS RETURN FOR NORTH CURRY – 1861

Most people were content if their occupations provided enough money for their basic needs and most accepted their position in society. As reflected in the Census Returns of the 19th century the occupations of the people of North Curry covered a broad spectrum from labourers to the professional classes. The following quotations encapsulate two views of society during that time.

O let us love our occupations,
Bless the squire and his relations,
Live upon our daily rations,
And always know our proper station.

(Charles Dickens, The Chimes, 1845)

All society would appear to arrange itself into four different classes
1. *Those that will work*
2. *Those that cannot work*
3. *Those that will not work*
4. *Those that need not work*

(Henry Mayhew, reporting in London Labour and the London Poor, 1861)

3 - 3

MAPS AND MAPMAKERS

The word map is derived from the Middle English *mapemounde*, from the Old French *mapemond*, and from the Medieval Latin *mappa (mundi)*, map (of the world). The Latin *mappa*, means napkin or cloth on which maps were drawn, perhaps of Punic origin.

The earliest maps of Britain were probably drawn in about AD150 by the Greek geographer and astronomer Claudius Ptolemy of Alexandria (AD90 to AD168) although none of his original maps have survived. He accepted from other Greek astronomers that the world was round and had a perception of a world held together by an astronomically determined mathematical grid, and he calculated a figure for its circumference. These scientific theories and co-ordinates were preserved and his maps of Great Britain were reconstructed during the Middle Ages with numerous versions printed from the 1470s onwards. The other early maps were sanctioned by the Church and constructed around the symbolic core of a 'T' (life) within an 'O' (eternity), the 'T' representing the Mediterranean with the Rivers Don in Russia and Nile in Egypt forming the cross piece and the 'O' representing the hemisphere. Religious attitudes to map-making were replaced by scientific principles, and mariners' charts were devised to aid navigation. Together with knowledge gained from the geographical discoveries of Vasco de Gama, Cabot and Columbus, improved world maps that delineated all the world's coastlines were produced by Juan de la Cosa (1500), Martin Waldseemuller (1507) and Diego Ribero (1529).

The earliest English school of cartography is characterised by the four maps of Great Britain by Matthew Paris, a monk working in St Albans in the middle of the 13th century. His maps are the first in northern Europe to have north at the top (early medieval mapmakers set east to the top in deference to the holy places of the Orient, hence the term orientation). Paris had a general idea of the shape of Britain, although Scotland is shown as an island. The maps are constructed around the pilgrim route from the north to Dover, and are drawn to a uniform scale naming over 250 places, as well as rivers and hills.

One of the finest world maps, called the *Mappa Mundi*, was made c.1290 by Richard of Haldingham and is preserved in Hereford Cathedral. Measuring over 1.5 metres in diameter, this circular map illustrates the Biblical world, centred on Jerusalem, with the figure of Christ presiding at the top or east. A particularly important medieval map of Britain is the anonymous map named after the antiquarian Richard Gough who first noted its existence in 1780. It is likely that it was compiled in about 1360 and is now housed in the Bodleian Library. It shows more than 600 settlements and the delineation of road distances is fairly accurate.

Before the invention of printing, maps were drawn on vellum, sheepskin or other suitable material, and could only be reproduced by laborious hand-copying. The advent of printing allowed the production of multiple copies by means of a print or impression taken from a wood block or from a copper or steel plate. The earliest printed maps were impressions taken from engravings on wood blocks. Engraving on sheets of copper allowed for more precision, and lettering and detail could be finer and neater. The first copper-engraved map of the British Isles appeared in 1546 and is attributed to George Lily, a Catholic refugee living in Rome. Steel engraving followed, which because of the hardness of the metal, allowed for more impressions to be taken before the plate was worn. Lithographic printing was introduced in the 19th century when greasy ink was applied to a specially prepared stone and impressions taken. Metal, plastic and paper plates superseded the stone, the image being transferred photographically on to the plate, from which copies were run off on offset litho printing machines.

These early cartographers endeavoured to make their work as accurate as possible, but crude equipment and limited background knowledge hampered them. It was not possible to establish longitude and there was no established unit of measurement. All these early maps have a pictorial element and are more like diagrams than 'true' maps. Early maps were invariably printed in black and white and to differentiate between sea and land the early engravers drew shaded hills, trees and fencing, house shapes and spires, and used wave patterns, drawings of sea monsters or sailing vessels to depict sea and land features. Colour printing only came into use in the late-19th century, but traditionally maps had been hand-coloured, map colouring being a specialised profession.

COUNTY MAPS

The study of maps obviously gives clues to earlier landscapes and helps to reconstruct the origins of an area, but maps of specific areas are only available from the 16th century when they were first drawn. Before the late-16th century Britain had been mapped as a single unit rather than on a regional basis, but from Elizabethan times until the early-19th century, with the advent of the Ordnance Survey, the counties of England were mapped by private surveyors.

The first known series of county maps was that of Laurence Nowell (1559-1576) though these remained unprinted. The first great English map-maker to emerge in the 16th century was Christopher Saxton, who was born near Wakefield, Yorkshire in 1542, and was named the *father of English cartography*. He was commissioned by a Suffolk gentleman, Thomas Seckford, to survey and map all the counties of England and Wales and produce the first complete set of county maps. Thirty-four maps were published in 1579 as *An Atlas of England and Wales*. They were published in black and white only and any colouring was added by hand later.

His method of surveying was to travel the countryside on horseback making compass sketches and to take bearings from a high position and then ask the locals to name sites and distances. Hills are shown using conical sugar loaf symbols, settlements are shown randomly with occasional symbols of church towers, rivers, bridges, woodland and parks, but roads are, surprisingly, omitted. A map by Saxton of the County of Somerset was published in 1575 (see Plate ix). He later produced a large-scale map of England and Wales on 21 sheets and with a scale of eight miles to the inch.

John Norden (1548–1626), a Somerset man, was an estate surveyor. He had an idea of a scheme of county histories with maps, entitled *Speculum Britanniae*, which he thought would be more useful to the general public, and included information on archaeology, industry, agriculture and history, also showing the road network. He provided a triangular table of distances between places, which is still used today. He also introduced a grid reference system, dividing the maps into squares, together with tables of conventional signs which included items such as houses of noblemen and gentlemen. However, he was plagued by financial difficulties and only a few surveys were published in his lifetime, a small number of his county maps being printed later, and much of his work copied thereafter.

William Smith (1550–1618) produced maps of 12 counties incorporating place-names, roads, hundred boundaries and a table of conventional signs based on Saxton's and Norden's work. He also published a series of plans and profiles of towns called *A Description of England*. An atlas called *Britannia*, including a set of county maps based on the work of Saxton and Norden, was published in 1607 by William Camden. In 1571 Leonard Digges published *Pantometria* in which he described his own surveying instrument, the forerunner of the theodolite.

From the early-17th century, mapmaking came under the dominance of publishers, rather than surveyors. The London publishers John Sudbury and George Humble launched a compilation of historical research and cartography called the *Theatre of the Empire of Great Britaine* by John Speed in 1611. John Speed (1552–1629) was born in Cheshire, the son of a tailor. His enthusiasms were drawing maps, writing religious works and studying antiquity. His maps issued after 1610 included county town plans that he borrowed freely from Saxton, Norden, Smith and others, and other elements copied from their work.

Speed's maps were themselves copied until about 1770 by such map producers as the Dutch firm of Blaeu. Willem Janszoon Blaeu (1571–1638) was a map engraver, who, in his youth was an assistant to the Danish astronomer, Tycho Brahe. He later set up a business in Amsterdam as a maker of mathematical instruments, a globe manufacturer, and an engraver and printer of maps. After his death the business passed to his two sons, John and Cornelius, and later to his grandson, Cornelius. In 1645 John Blaeu published an atlas of maps of English and Welsh counties as *Part IV of Theatrum Orbis Terrarum*. These maps were derived from the work of John Speed, and included the arms of the principal nobility and gentry of each county, who made financial contributions to the production costs. The quality of the engraving has rarely been surpassed, but the map adds little to our topographical knowledge as roads and town plans are not shown, and symbols are smaller. A county map of Somerset was published by Blaeu in 1648. Another Dutch publisher of maps was Joannes Jansson (1696–1664) who published an atlas containing county maps of the British Isles in 1646.

In 1675 the publication *Britannia* was produced by John Ogilby (1600–1676). After a period of misfortune when his printing and bookselling business was destroyed in the Great Fire of London in 1666, he was appointed to survey the devastated areas of London. Charles II later granted a royal warrant to him to improve the delineation of roads in England and Wales to satisfy travellers' needs. He invented a *wheel dimensurator* with which he measured each statute mile, and these measurements were used later to locate milestones on main roads. His surveys resulted in strip road maps. These were a series of maps on vertical strips of parchment showing roads between large towns represented as a continual scroll, with hills and landmarks annotated and compasses drawn to indicate direction to aid the traveller (see Plate ix).

Robert Morden, a bookseller, publisher and mapmaker, produced a series of county maps from 1695. They were corrected and updated revisions of earlier surveys and maps, and included a set of small county maps entitled *The New Description and State of England* which he published in 1701.

A number of cartographers such as John Senex in 1719 and Emanuel Bowen in 1720 produced smaller-scale maps based on Ogilby's *Britannia*. In 1724 Hermann Moll, a Dutch publisher and engraver, produced a set of county maps known as *A New Description of England and Wales* derived from earlier sources. Between 1749 and 1755 Emanuel Bowen and Thomas Kitchen produced many large-scale maps and atlases, and in 1762 issued *The Large English Atlas* that contained descriptive notes relating to the topography and history of each county.

In 1725 Henry Beighton (1687–1743) surveyed Warwickshire for a map with a scale of one inch to one mile, which was one of the first to be based on trigonometrical principles. Some of the finest maps of the 18th century came from the Huguenot immigrant surveyor John Rocque. He produced a number of county maps showing a distinctive engraving style for pasture, gardens, heath and cultivated land. He issued a set of small county maps in *The English Traveller* in 1746, in which county boundaries were shown by cross hatching.

John Cary (1754-1835), an engraver, produced a great number of maps including two sets of county maps published from 1789 that were beautifully engraved and accurately lettered. Roads appeared prominently on his maps for he was employed by the Postmaster-General to organise the survey of turnpike roads in Great Britain, which involved 9,000 miles of survey. In 1804 Charles Smith published a New English Atlas similar in style to Cary's.

William Day was a map surveyor who lived for some time in the Parish of Pitminster in Somerset. Charles Harcourt Masters was born in Bath in 1759 and was apprenticed to Day as a surveyor. They took seven years to complete the Survey of Somerset and it was finally published in 1782 (see front cover). A scale of one inch to one mile is used. The map is based on accurate triangulation rather than the sketch/traverse method, with accurate measurement of road distances. Triangulation is the use of triangles for surveying. To begin triangulation, a surveyor laid out an initial triangle by plotting three points: two at the ends of a base line and one at a distant landmark. Using a plane table or theodolite, the surveyor measured the angles towards the landmark at both ends of the base line. The baseline itself was measured by counting revolutions of a wheel or by using measuring chains or rods laid end to end. Once one triangle had been measured, further triangles could be constructed from its sides, producing chains of triangles that could accurately measure long distances. Day and Masters recorded the Somerset landscape after the disappearance of the open arable fields, but at a time when there were still vast areas of common grazing on the high ground. The state of enclosure can be reconstructed from the careful delineation of enclosed and open roads that indicates the spread of road improvements away from the major routes.

Christopher Greenwood was born in the West Riding of Yorkshire in 1786. After an apprenticeship with a local land surveyor he began by publishing a map of Yorkshire in 1817 and then went on to survey and publish a further 36 county maps over 15 years. The map of Somerset was published in 1822 as the eleventh county in the series and shows considerable topographical detail. His mapmaking company was known as C & J Greenwood, having his younger brother John as partner along with G Pringle and his son, G Pringle, Junior. After 1828, when the business was failing, he devised schemes to bolster his finances. One was for an atlas of county maps at a scale of three miles to one inch, but because he had to employ engravers his resources diminished, his company collapsed, and his plates were purchased by other publishers.

An index to the Somersetshire survey made in 1821 by Greenwood describes North Curry as follows:

Curry-North – a hundred, situated in the southern part of the county, east of Taunton; consisting of five parishes; viz. North-Curry, West-Hatch, Stoke-St Gregory, Thornefalcon, and Thurlbear; containing 713 inhabited houses, 728 families, 1,937 males, and 1,880 females. Total population – 3,817.

Curry-North – a parish in the hundred to which it gives name. It is situated 6 miles E. from Taunton, and contains 323 inhabited houses, and as many families, 228 of whom are employed in agriculture. This was formerly a place of considerable note, having had a weekly market, and a fair annually, the latter of which continues to be held on the first of August. The church is a large Gothic structure, dedicated to St Peter and St Paul, built in the form of a cross, with an hexagonal em-battled tower, containing a clock and five bells. The living is a vicarage (with Stoke-St Gregory and West-Hatch annexed,) in the deanery of Taunton, and a peculiar belonging to the Dean and Chapter of Wells; Rev. W.K. Coker, incumbent; instituted 1820. Population, 1801 – 1,194, 1811 – 1,344, 1821 – 1,645.

From 1823 Arthur Bryant produced maps that were more detailed than the Greenwood maps and at the larger scale of one-and-a-half inches to one mile. He only succeeded in mapping 13 counties.

During the 19th century county atlases continued to appear including Wallis's *New Pocket Edition of the English Counties* in 1810, a *British Atlas* from Pigot and Company in 1829, and in 1836 a set of county maps by Thomas Moule. He was born in Marylebone in 1794, and became an authority on the history of architecture. His county maps were engraved with illustrations of cathedrals, churches and country houses in gothic style. In 1837 these maps were published in atlas form by George Virtue and entitled the *English Counties Delineated*. It contained 57 maps of England and Wales, town plans and inland navigation. The map of Somersetshire is illustrated with the Glastonbury Cross and the Great Western Railway is shown from Exeter, together with a description of the county with Taunton, Glastonbury and the Mendip Hills featured. In 1837 J & C Walker published their *British Atlas* and this formed the basis for Hobson's *Fox-Hunting Atlas* published in 1850 which gave the areas and meeting places of hunts.

Ordnance Survey Maps

The origins of the Ordnance Survey go back to the military need for maps to be traced accurately in the second half of the 18th century. Britain was faced with the threat of invasion from France and the Army needed accurate maps of the south coast of England to provide information for the defence of the realm. General William Roy, who had produced military maps at the time of the Scottish rebellion in 1745, made surveys using compass traverses and field sketches, producing a survey of the south coast at a scale of one inch to one mile. In 1765 he was made Surveyor General of Coasts and Engineer for Making and Directing Military Surveys under the Board of Ordnance. In 1783 a French astronomer, Monsieur Cassini de Thury, promoted the advantages of linking the observatories of Paris and Greenwich by precisely surveyed triangulation, and Roy was placed in charge of operations on this side of the channel. After his death in 1790 the triangulation method was continued by the Duke of Richmond, Master of the Ordnance.

The Trigonometrical (later termed Ordnance) Survey was begun in 1791 with the aim of producing a military survey of the whole country, and the triangulation was completed by 1824. A first budget of £52,000 was given until 1811, and increased later, and the men responsible for the Survey from 1798–1847 were William Mudge and Captain Thomas Colby. The Ordnance Survey developed into a large publisher of maps with The Ordnance Survey Act of 1841 formally establishing the agency.

The original Ordnance series of 110 maps of the whole country at one inch to one mile, known as the Old Series, was published between 1801 and 1874, and revised and re-printed regularly without annotation of any changes. From 1863 six-inch to one mile and twenty-five-inch to one mile maps were also produced for some areas. Work on the New Series or Second Edition of maps began in 1840 and publication commenced in 1874. By 1901 work had started on a Second Revision (or Third Edition) and this was followed by numerous later editions.

By 1928 there were continuous revisions of areas which were rapidly changing. The largest scale published was the fifty inches to one mile plan. In 1935 the Davidson Committee was established under the directorship of Major-General Malcolm MacLeod who launched the retriangulation of Great Britain, and eventually the National Grid reference system was introduced. Retriangulation involved erecting concrete triangulation pillars (*trig points*) on prominent hilltops throughout Great Britain.

1969 saw the introduction of metric scales and the *Landranger Series* at a scale of 2cm to 1km, the *Explorer Series* at a scale of 4cm to 1km and historical maps including *Roman Britain* and *Ancient Britain* at a scale of 1cm to 6.25 km are now included in the Ordnance Survey portfolio. Today all information is stored in digital form on computer and may be used to draw out any part of a map required by a customer.

Tithe Maps

From medieval times the Church claimed one tenth *(tithe)* of the produce of all land, stock or industry as a contribution to support it (see also page 88). Tithes were taxes paid to each vicar or rector. Originally they were not paid in cash, but in animals, corn, hay, apples, honey, and many other items, including beer. These arrangements were probably made when the parish was first created, perhaps as long ago as the 10th century, at a time when money was scarce and farm produce was the only way a man could pay. Some landowners have, since early times, agreed informal arrangements to make a fixed cash payment, or modus, rather than payments in kind.

The Tithe Commutation Act of 1836 put an end to payments in kind, and in each parish a settlement was made whereby the owner of each property agreed to give the vicar money. In order to find out exactly what each should pay the Tithe Commissioners required a detailed map covering the whole parish to be drawn, stating which parishioners were subject to tithe payments. These Tithe Maps were produced between 1838 and 1854.

Commuted rent charges in North Curry for 1840 were:

For each Garden one penny
For every Hogshead of Cider one shilling
For Apples, Pears and Plums sold, the tenth of the money price thereof
For every acre of Potatoes ten shillings
For each Cow that is milked two pence
For each Heifer that is milked one penny half penny
For each winter Milch Cow one penny half penny
For every Calf fallen under seven two pence
For every Calf sold the tenth of the money paid
For every Calf killed in house the left shoulder
For every Tithe Calf eight shillings
For every Tithe Pig two shillings and six pence
For every Colt foaled two pence
For every sucking Colt sold the tenth of the money price
For every Tithe Colt one pound
For Sheep per score if shorn two shillings
For Lambs per score if shorn one shilling
For Sheep per score if not shorn one penny per week
For Lambs fallen under ten a halfpenny each
For every Tithe Lamb two shillings and six pence
For every acre of Flax five shillings
For every acre of Hemp five shillings
For every acre of Clover Seed five shillings
For every acre of Turnip Seed five shillings
For every acre of Fallow Turnips five shillings
For Oxen grazing on Summerlees one penny halfpenny each per week
For Heifers grazing on Summerlees one penny each per week
For every Tithe Gosling sixpence
For Goose Feathers and Quills sold the tenth of the money price
For Stock on the Moor
For Willow sold the tenth of the money price
For Honey and Wax sold the tenth of the money price
For Garden stuff growing in fields and orchards sold the tenth of the money price
For Turkeys, Ducks, Fowls and Eggs sold the tenth of the money price

The Tithe Maps were drawn by a surveyor to show every parcel of land, every house, road, outbuilding or stream and every acre of manorial waste or common pasture. This map was then used with a register, schedule or terrier, often known as an *apportionment*, to facilitate the collection of the tithes. Each parcel of land had a name (field name) or a description (house, premises, arable, meadow, pasture, orchard, etc.) and showed the names of the landowner and occupier, as well as the acreage of the land and the rent charge.

In 1840 an ink and watercolour *Tithe Map for North Curry* was drawn and surveyed by Richard Hodges of North Petherton with a scale of 26.6 inches to one mile (see Plate xv). The landowners shown in the *Tithe Schedule* (see page 140) were mostly lessees of the Dean and Chapter of Wells, and there were 2,719 separate plot entries with 439 dwellings listed. The only buildings listed by name were the Bell Inn, the Angel Inn, the School House, Moredon, the Vicarage House, a meeting house and the Malthouse. Smiths and blacksmiths shops, a coal yard and a windmill are also recorded, together with the field names.

Estate, Enclosure and Manorial Maps

Medieval land surveying meant valuation presented in written form derived from existing written documents, oral testimony, walking the boundaries and viewing the landmarks, and any map that was produced would be used merely as an illustration, with few actual measurements. However, from the 1570s mapping became part of estate surveying, encouraged by the growing complexity of landholding and agrarian advance. Although estate plans were private records of ownership, they entered the public domain as legal evidence concerning matters of trespass, disputed boundaries and contested wills.

In the 16th century demand grew from landowners for surveyors' maps to be drawn of their estates and landholdings to ensure effective rent fixing and collection, and for maps to be included when exchanges of land took place. They often delineated features of the manor, park, formal garden or farm. The best known of the early estate map-makers is Christopher Saxton who, after completing his county maps, became a professional estate surveyor. The practical aspects of surveying were published in books such as John Norden's *The Surveyors Dialogue* of 1607, and various instruments such as the theodolite, circumferentor and plane-table came into more general use following the publication of the rudiments of compass survey and basic triangulation.

In North Curry in 1773 a simple estate map and survey was drawn which shows a few properties such as *Moordon* Hill Farm and the Angel Inn, together with certain plots of land belonging to William Portman, squire of Orchard Portman (see page 204). Some 30 plots are listed with the names of 8 leaseholders.

When enclosure brought additional land into cultivation by dividing common land and rearranging existing cultivated strips, some of these changes were recorded on estate plans. From 1760 onwards enclosure of arable, common and waste lands by Acts of Parliament became common, and commissioners were appointed to re-allocate the landholdings of all landowners into coherent units, so that each landholder should have the same value of land as before. Surveyors were appointed to draw up a written survey and plan upon which the new layout would be based. Agreed changes were embodied into a large book or *Enclosure Award*. These awards depicted the new system of land ownership, indicating field boundaries and roads. Over 5,000 awards covered almost 7 million acres, of which two-thirds were open field arable land and one-third common and waste land. Twenty-one per cent of England was enclosed by Act of Parliament, which varied widely from place to place.

In 1787 the Lords of the Manor of North Curry, who were the Dean and Chapter of Wells, commissioned William White of Wedmore to draw a Manorial Map to a scale of 20 inches to one mile, with which was included a schedule of every plot. These plots had individual numbers with descriptions of the type of holding, together with the names of the leaseholders and copyholders to which these plots were allocated. The Manor of North Curry at that time included Stoke St Gregory, North Curry, *Knap-Fee* or Knapp, Newport *Borrough*, Wrantage, *West-Mear* and West Hatch. Very few of the houses and plots were named but Ham Mills and island, *Moordon*, Thong Farmhouse, Jackless Cross, a Poorhouse, the Parsonage House, the Bird in Hand and a meeting house, are mentioned in North Curry together with a *wrecked* mill in Knapp (see Plate xiv).

Below is a table indicating the number of landholdings and the number of buildings in the Parish of North Curry in 1787:

		Knapp	*Newport*	*North Curry*	*Wrantage*	*Total*
Land only	*Copyhold*	*177*	*16*	*354*	*298*	*845*
	Leasehold	*32*	*0*	*138*	*87*	*257*
	Waste	*2*	*0*	*6*	*0*	*8*
Land with buildings	*Copyhold*	*48*	*6*	*102*	*27*	*183*
	Leasehold	*4*	*0*	*53*	*3*	*60*
Total Land	*Copyhold*	*225*	*22*	*456*	*325*	*1,028*
	Leasehold	*36*	*0*	*191*	*90*	*317*
	Waste	*2*	*0*	*6*	*0*	*8*
Grand Total		*263*	*22*	*653*	*415*	*1,353*

Research using both the 1787 and the 1840 map schedules establishes that many of the houses, cottages and barns are still in the village today. Many of them have been altered, enlarged or converted and it is difficult to pinpoint the position of particular houses or to date them accurately by this method. Information about land and premises taken from maps and map schedules can indicate the residences of certain people and sometimes trade buildings are mentioned, but a certain amount of detective work is needed to establish where and which trades were pursued.

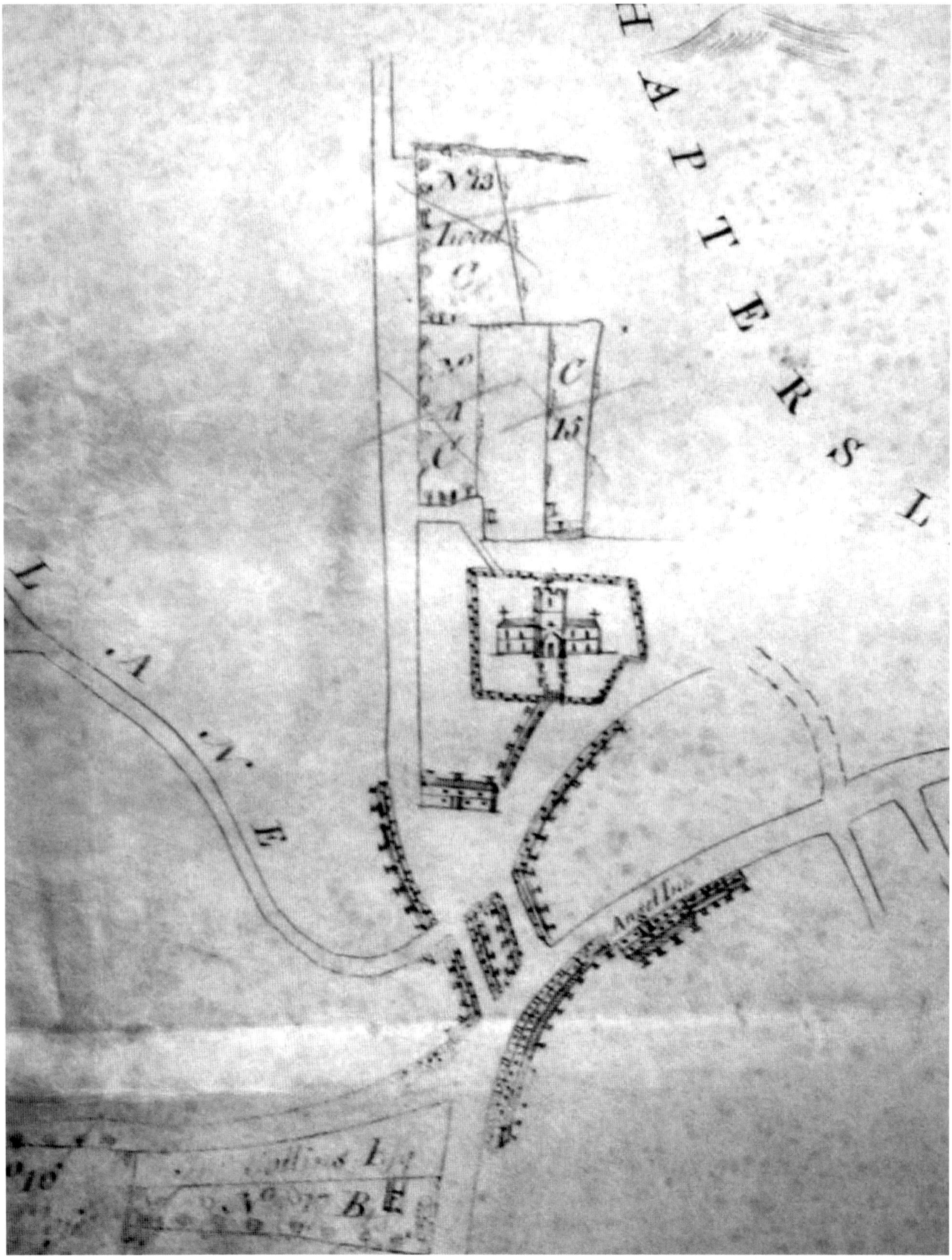

SECTION OF THE PORTMAN ESTATE MAP OF NORTH CURRY – 1773

APPENDIX 1

CENSUS OCCUPATIONS FOR NORTH CURRY – 1841 TO 1901

Accountant
Agricultural Engine Feeder
Agricultural Machine Proprietor
/ Agricultural Machine Labourer
Annuitant
Apple Seller
Apprentice
Architect Surveyor
Army Captain/ Captain Infantry
Assurance Agent
Attorney/ Attorney-Solicitor/ Attorney Clerk
/ Lawyer/ Lawyer-Innkeeper
Auctioneer/ Auctioneer Assistant
/ Auctioneer-Bill Poster/ Auctioneer-Estate Agent
/ Auctioneer-Land Agent
Baker/ Baker Apprentice/ Baker Assistant/ Baker Boy
/ Baker Journeyman/ Baker Junior/ Baker Labourer
/ Baker-Confectioner/ Baker-Grocer/ Baker-Grocer
/ Bread Boy
Barberess
Bargeman
Barmaid/ Barman
Barrister
Basketmaker/ Basket-Chairmaker
Beerhouse Keeper
Besum Seller
Bill Poster
Blacksmith Master/ Blacksmith-Farmer
/ Blacksmith/ Blacksmith Son/ Blacksmith Apprentice
/ Blacksmith Assistant/ Blacksmith Journeyman
/ Blacksmith Junior
Blousemaker
Boat Builder
Boatman/ Boatman-Canal
/ Boatman Assistant/ Boatman Boy
Book Keeper
Bookmaker
Bootmaker Master/ Bootmaker
/ Boot Manufacturer Master/ Bootcloser
/ Bootmaker Apprentice
/ Bootmaker-Shoemaker/ Master
/ Bootmaker-Shoemaker
/ Bootmaker-Shoemaker Apprentice
/ Bootmaker-Shoemaker Journeyman
/ Shoemaker Master/ Shoemaker
/ Shoebinder/ Shoemaker Apprentice
Botanist
Brewer/ Brewer-Maltster/ Brewer Labourer
/ Brewer Son/ Brewerman
Bricklayer/ Bricklayer Labourer
Brickmaker
Builder/ Builder Apprentice/ Builders Carrier
Butcher-Farmer/ Butcher Master/ Butcher
/ Butcher-Horse Breaker/ Butcher Apprentice
/ Butcher Assistant/ Butcher-Labourer
/ Butcher Journeyman/ Butcher Son
Cabinetmaker
Canal Worker
Caretaker/ Caretaker Canal Locks/ Caretaker Church
Carpenter Master/ Carpenter/ Carpenter Apprentice
/ Carpenter Journeyman/ Carpenter-Farmer
/ Carpenter Junior/ Carpenter Labourer
/ Carpenter Son/ Carpenter-Beerhouse Keeper
/ Carpenter-Church
Carrier/ Carrier Apprentice/ Carrier Letter
Carter
Carver
Cattle Dealer/ Cattle Driver/ Cattleman
Charwoman
Clergyman
Clerk/ Clerk Holy Orders/ Clerk of the Parish
/ Clerk of the Parish-Gardener/ Clerk of Works
/ Clerk Solicitor/ Clerk-Articled/ Clerk Auctioneer
/ Clerk Auctioneer Articled/ Clerk Postal
/ Clerk Postal-Drapers Assistant
/ Clerk Postal-Telegraph
/ Clerk Postal-Telegraph-Drapers Assistant
/ Clerk Telegraph Office/ Clerk Telegraph
Clockmaker
Coachbuilder/ Coachbuilder Apprentice
Coachman/ Coachman-Gardener
Coal Merchant/ Coal Merchant Son/ Coal Assistant
/ Coal Carrier/ Coal-Oil Merchant
Cooper Master/ Cooper/ Cooper Apprentice
Cordwainer/ Cordwainer Son
/ Cordwainer Apprentice/ Cordwainer Journeyman
/ Cordweaver
Corn Dealer
Coster/ Coster Agricultural
Currier/ Currier Junior
Cutter/ Spayer
Dairymaid/ Dairyman/ Dairywoman
Dealer Corn/ Dealer General/ Dealer General-Farmer
/ Dealer Poultry/ Dealer Withy-Fruit
Dentist/ Chemist

Draper/ Draper-Grocer/ Draper-Grocer Assistant
/ Draper-Grocer Apprentice/ Draper Apprentice
/ Draper Assistant
Dressmaker/ Dressmaker Apprentice
/ Dressmaker-Milliner/ Dressmaker Assistant
/ Blousemaker
Engine Cleaner/ Engine Driver
/ Engine Fitter's Apprentice
Engineer Civil
Errand Boy/ Errand Girl
Excise Man
Farm Bailiff/ Farmer/ Farmer Manager
/ Farm Assistant/ Farm Student/ Farmer Son
/ Farm Worker/ Farm Boy/ Farmer Nephew
/ Farmer-Builder/ Farmer-Butcher/ Farmer-Carter
/ Farmer-Grazier/ Farmer-Grocer/ Farmer-Innkeeper
/ Plough Boy
Farrier
Fewterer
Fisherman
Fundholder
Gamekeeper
Gardener/ Gardener-Groom
Glazier
Glover/ Glovemaker/ Glover-Grocer/ Glove Stretcher
/ Glover-Laundry/ Gloves Shop Girl
Governess
Graver
Grocer/ Grocer-Farmer/ Grocer-Draper
/ Grocer Assistant
Groom/ Groom Journeyman/ Groom-Gardener
/ Groom-Stable Boy
Hairdresser/ Hairdressers Apprentice
Harnessmaker/ Harnessmaker Apprentice
Haulier/ Haulier-Farmer
Hay Dealer/ Hay Merchant
Herdsman
Hotel Keeper
Housekeeper
Hurdle Maker
Independent/ Independent-Landowner
Inland Revenue Officer
Innkeeper/ Innkeeper Son/ Innkeeper-Farmer
/ Innkeeper-Saddler
Insurance Agent
Ironmonger
Joiner/ Joiner-Carpenter/ Joiner Apprentice
Labourer/ Labourer Agricultural
/ Labourer Agricultural-Carter
/ Labourer Agricultural-Coster
/ Labourer Agricultural-Groom
/ Labourer Agricultural-Plough Boy
/ Labourer Agricultural-Shepherd
/ Labourer Agricultural-Stone/ Labourer General
/ Labourer Maltster/ Labourer Mason
Lacemaker
Land Drainer
Land Surveyor-Auctioneer/ Land Surveyors Assistant
/ Land Agent
Landed Proprietor/ Landowner/ Landowner-Yeoman
Laundress
Lime Burner
Lock Keeper
Machine Labourer
Machinist
Magistrate
Maltster/ Maltster-Brewer/ Maltster Journeyman
Mason Master/ Mason/ Mason Journeyman
/ Mason Labourer/ Mason-Builder/ Mason-Church
/ Masons Boy/ Mason-Walling
Medical Student
Medical-Landowner
Merchant
Messenger
Miller Master/ Miller/ Miller-Farmer/ Millwright
/ Mill Worker/ Miller Apprentice/ Miller Labourer
Milliner/ Milliner-Dressmaker
Minister C of E /Minister-Baptist/ Minister-Methodist
/ Minister-Dissenting/ Minister-Lay
Molecatcher
Navy
Needlewoman/ Needleworker
Nurse/ Nurse-Seamstress/ Nursegirl
Ostler
Overseer Assistant
Painter/ Painter Apprentice/ Painter-Glazier
/ Painter-Plumber/ Painter-Plumber-Glazier
Parish Relief/ Pauper
Pedlar
Pensioner/ Pensioner Chelsea/ Pensioner Greenwich
/ Pensioner Marine
Photographic Artist
Pig Dealer
Pipe Manufacturer/ Pipemaker/ Pipe Maker Labourer
Plumber/ Plumber-Glazier
Police Sergeant/ Police Constable
Porter
Post Office Manager/ Post Office Assistant
/ Post Office Clerk
Postman
Postmaster-Registrar/ Postmaster-Farmer
/ Postmaster-Bellringer/ Postmaster-Grocer
Printer Apprentice
Publican

Quarryman
Railway Officer
Relieving Officer/ Registrar–Relieving Officer/ Registrar
Retired Agriculturist/ Retired Army/ Retired Baker
/ Retired Barber/ Retired Blacksmith/ Retired Builder
/ Retired Butcher/ Retired Carpenter/ Retired Carrier
/ Retired Cattle Dealer/ Retired Charwoman
/ Retired Chief Carpenter R.N./ Retired Civil Servant
/ Retired Coal Merchant/ Retired Dairywoman
/ Retired Draper/ Retired Dressmaker/ Retired Farmer
/ Retired Fisherman/ Retired Gamekeeper
/ Retired Grocer/ Retired Hay Dealer
/ Retired Housekeeper/ Retired Independent
/ Retired Inland Revenue Officer
/ Retired Innkeeper/ Retired Labourer
/ Retired Labourer Agricultural/ Retired Landlady
/ Retired Laundress/ Retired Medical Practitioner
/ Retired Miller/ Retired Navy
/ Retired Police Constable/ Retired Printer
/ Retired Relieving Officer/ Retired Schoolteacher
/ Retired Servant/ Retired Shepherd/ Retired Shoemaker
/ Retired Shopkeeper/ Retired Station Master
/ Retired Straw Hat Manufacturer/ Retired Tailor
/ Retired Toll Collector/ Retired Wine Merchant
/ Retired Withy Stripper
Road Contractor/ Road Labourer/ Road Stonecracker
Saddler/ Saddler–Harness Maker/ Saddler–Innkeeper
/ Saddler Apprentice/ Saddler Journeyman
/ Saddler Ironmonger
Sawyer/ Sawyer Assistant
Scaffolder/ Scaffolder–Church
Scholar
School Cleaner
Schoolteacher/ Schoolteacher Assistant
/ Schoolteacher Pupil/ Music Teacher/ Tutor
Sculptress
Seamstress
Servant/ Servant Bailiff/ Servant Butler
/ Servant Coachman/ Servant Coachman–Groom
/ Servant Cook/ Servant Cook–Housekeeper
/ Servant Cook–Dairymaid/ Servant Domestic
/ Servant Family/ Servant Domestic–Gardener
/ Servant Domestic–Groom
/ Servant Domestic–Stable Boy/ Servant Farm
/ Servant Farm–Carter
/ Servant Footman/ Servant Page
/ Servant Gardener/ Servant General/ Servant Vicar's
/ Servant Groom/ Servant House/ Servant Housemaid
/ Servant Kitchenmaid/ Servant Lady's Maid
/ Servant Parlourmaid/ Servant Miller/ Servant Nurse
/ Servant Nursemaid/ Servant Nurserymaid
/ Servant Ostler
Shepherd
Shirtmaker
Shopkeeper/ Shopkeeper–Huckster
/ Shopkeeper Apprentice/ Shop Assistant/ Shop Boy
Sievemaker
Smith/ Smith Apprentice
Solicitor/ Solicitor Clerk
Sparmaker
Stableman/ Stable Boy/ Stable Boy–Groom
Staymaker/ Staymaker–Quilter
Stock Dealer
Stocking Knitter
Stonemason/ Stonemason–Sexton/ Stonemaker
/ Stone Cracker/ Stone Cutter/ Stone Engraver
/ Stone Quarryman/ Stonecutter/ Stonebreaker
/ Stone Carrier
Straw Bonnetmaker
Strawjoiner
Subpostmaster
Surgeon/ Surgeon–General
/ Surgeon–General Practitioner–Landowner
Surveyor/ Surveyor–Land Agent–Auctioneer
/ Surveyor–Auctioneer/ Surveyor–Estate Agent
/ Surveyor Pupil
Tailor Master/ Tailor/ Tailor Apprentice
/ Tailor Journeyman/ Tailor Junior/ Tailor–Draper
/ Tailoress
Tallow Chandler
Teazle Dealer/ Teazle Grower/ Teazle Merchant
/ Teazle Worker
Telegraphist/ Telegraph Messenger
Thatcher/ Thatcher Helper/ Thatcher–Farmer
/ Thatcher–Hurdle Maker
Toll Collector/ Toll Gatekeeper/ Turnpike Toll Collector
Twine Manufacturer
Unemployed Labourer/ Unemployed Servant
Upholsteress
Washerwoman
Watchmaker/ Jeweller
Waterman
Wheelwright/ Wheelwright–Carpenter
Wicker Chair Maker/ Chair Makers Apprentice
Withy Farmer/ Willow Grower/ Withy Grower–Farmer
/ Withy Grower/ Withy Merchant/ Withy Worker
/ Withy Grower–Dealer/ Withy Dealer
Woodman/ Woodman–Cooper

APPENDIX 2

BRAGG'S DIRECTORY OF SOMERSET – ENTRY FOR NORTH CURRY – 1841

This is the entry for North Curry with present-day locations appended, based upon interpretation of the 1840 *Tithe Schedule* for North Curry.

DESCRIPTION OF RESIDENT	NAME OF RESIDENT	PRESENT–DAY HOUSE NAME OR LOCATION
Attornies	Bridge, Richard	The Grange, West Cottage & Barham Barns, Queen Square/Stoke Road
	Foster, Charles Millett	Calmady House, Church Road
	Meade, Henry White	Whatley House, Queen Square
	Rouse, James Alexander	Melbourne House, Queen Square
Auctioneers	Foster, John	1, 2, 3 The Pavement
	Morris, Richard	North Curry
Bakers	Crabb, William	The Old Brewery, Queen Square
	Foster, Francis	North Curry
	Poundsbury, Anthony	14 Queen Square
Boot & Shoemakers	Burrows, John	Rose Cottage, Borough Post
	Corner, Thomas	North Curry
	Edwards, George	North Curry
	Parks, John	15 Queen Square
	Parks, William	The White Hart, Knapp Lane
	Pinnow, John	North Curry
	Richards, David	4 Knapp Lane
	Shute, John	North Curry
Butchers	Andrews, James	1 Stoke Road
	Bobbett, Lawrence	North Curry
	Foster, Henry	Chestnut Farm, Helland
	Glyde, Jonas	Wrantage
	Spearing, William	Manchester House, Queen Square
Cabinetmaker	Linton, Arthur	16 Queen Square
Carpenters	Goodland, Charles	Greenway
	Wallbutton, Robert	Wisteria Cottage, Stoke Road
Cooper and Pattern Maker	Spearing, Eli	7 & 8 Windmill Hill
Currier	Crease, John	9 Stoke Road
Draper	Self, E	Queen Square
Farrier	Jennings, William	24 Queen Square
General Shopkeepers	Crease, Sarah	22 Queen Square
	Perratt, William	4, 5, 11 Queen Square
	Spearing, William	Manchester House, Queen Square
Gentry & Private Families	Andrews, John	Stoke Road
	Barrett, William	Moredon
	Budge, Mrs	North Curry
	Buncombe, Mrs	7 Stoke Road
	Dare, Charles Holcombe	Fosse Cottage, The Fosse
	Gould, John Scott	Moredon House
	Noble, Lieut Francis, RN	Yew Tree Cottage, Windmill Hill
Inns	Foster, Jacob	Angel House, Stoke Road
	Foster, Richard	Bird in Hand, Queen Square
	Richards, David	Bell Inn, 4 Knapp Lane
Ironmonger	Gibson, John	6 Stoke Road
Maltsters	Burnell, William Alloway	The Old Brewery, Queen Square
	Perrett, Matthew	The Old Malthouse, Stoke Road
	Spiller, Christopher	Rock Hill, Wrantage
Ministers of Religion	Coker, W H (Established Church)	The Old Vicarage, Church Road
	Humphrey, R (Baptist Minister)	Windmill Hill

Description of Resident	Name of Resident	Present-day house name or location
Painter/Decorator	Crease, James	14 Stoke Road
Pastry Cook/Confectioner	White, Edward	The Pavement
Post Office	Bucknole, John	Auster Cottage, Church Road
Registrar of Births/Deaths	Meade, Mr Henry White	Whatley House, Queen Square
Relieving Officer of NC	Morris, William	Queen Square
Saddler	Dinham, William	North Curry
Smiths	Andrews, Robert	The Old Smithy, Moor Lane
	Bobbett, John	17, 18, 18a Stoke Road
	Stevens, Thomas	2, 3, 4 Church Road
Stamp Distributor	Self, E	Queen Square
Surgeons	Marchant, Robert	2 Queen Square
	Mead, Robert	Trevarrick House, The Pavement
	Plowman, Thomas	Greenway House, Greenway
Tailors	Cross, Aaron	Pear Tree Cottage, Greenway
	Foster, Joseph	Church Cottages
	Jones, James	North Curry
	Jones, Rees	Queens House, Queen Square
	Spearing, Phocion	Spearings, Lillesdon
Wheelwrights	Dinham, James	Site of Gwyon House, Church Road
	Dinham, James, Jnr	Knapp
Yeomen	Bartlett, James	Huntham
	Bicknell, Edward	North Curry
	Bobbett, Arthur	Knapp
	Bulpin, Thomas	Higher Knapp Farm, Knapp
	Clarke, James	Lillesdon Green Farm, Lillesdon
	Coombes, David	Helland
	Derham, John	Knapp Farm, Knapp
	Dwelly, William	Knapp
	Dyer, William	Hammonds, Lillesdon
	Faun, James	Woodside, Newport
	Foster, Henry	Chestnut Farm, Helland
	Foster, Phillip	24 Queen Square
	Foster, Samuel	Borough Farm, Knapp
	Glide, Jonathan	Town Farm, The Pavement
	Hellard, Samuel	Helland House, Helland
	House, William	Orchard Farm, Knapp
	Hunt, John	12 Stoke Road
	Hurman, William	Huntham
	Jeanes, Thomas	Foster's Farm, Knapp
	Leakey, John	Nythe Farm, Sedgemoor
	Lockyer, John	Lower Knapp Farm, Knapp
	Marsh, George	Thong Farm, Sedgemoor
	Mead, Samuel	Manor Farm, off Stoke Road
	Mitchell, William	Garnsey Farm, Knapp
	Palmer, William	Higher Lillesdon Farm, Lillesdon
	Pocock, Robert	12 Queen Square
	Smith, John	The Rising Sun, Knapp
	Southwood, Francis	Knapp
	Spearing, John	25, 26 Stoke Road
	Sweeting, John Winsor	Wrantage
	Trent, Robert	Lillesdon Court, Lillesdon
	Virgin, Thomas	Lillesdon Farm, Lillesdon
	Wake, Francis	Honey Farm, Wrantage
	Weaver, John	Dawes Farmhouse, Broad Lane
	Wescombe, William	Pury House, Stoke Road

Appendix 3

Kelly's Directory of Somerset – entry for North Curry – 1939

The following is a list of 36 prominent residents and 106 members of trades, professions and public services in North Curry in 1939. These were published in *Kelly's Directory of Somerset*. The areas in the parish where the services were offered and some particular residences are also mentioned.

Description	Name	Address in Directory
Agricultural Machine Owner	Bellringer, Ernest	North Curry
Baker	Barrington, Wilfred	Newport
	Vaux, Harold	North Curry
Bank (sub branch)	Lloyds Bank Ltd. (Fri 10.30 - 1.30)	North Curry
	Westminster Bank Ltd (Fri 10.30 - 1.30)	North Curry
Blacksmith	Spiller, Edward	Wrantage
Boot & Shoe Repairer	Pester, Charles Edward	North Curry
Boot Repairer	Wembridge, Charles Henry	North Curry
Bootmaker	Brownsey, Harry Frost	North Curry
Butcher	Carter, Harold	North Curry
	Stone, Miss Annie Maria	Greenway
Carpenter	Denman, Dennis	North Curry
	May, Archibald William	North Curry
	Mills, Henry	Wrantage
Chairmaker (Wicker)	Tottle, Bertram Charles	North Curry
Clerk Drainage Board	Goode, William Winter	North Curry
Clerk Isle Abbots School Board	Goode, William Winter	North Curry
Coachbuilder	Baker, Frederick John	North Curry
Coal Merchant	Small, G & Sons Ltd	North Curry
Cowkeeper	Newis, Albert	Wrantage
District Nurse	Rich, Miss Alice, CMB	North Curry
Farmer (150 acres or over)	Diment, William	Lillesdon Farm
	Hebditch, Bernard	Lillesdon Court
	Hurford, Fred Ernest	Higher Lillesdon Farm
	Jeanes, John George	Town Farm
	Lane, James	Listock Farm
	Prew, Joseph Ernest & Son	Lillesdon Green
	Totterdell, John Christopher	Higher Wrantage Farm
	Whittle, Frederick William	Wrantage
Farmer	Baker, George Henry	Listock Farm
	Barrington, Robert James	The Laurels
	Brewer, Thomas John	Gould's Farm
	Brewer, William	Higher Huntham Farm
	Case, William Henry	Bird's Farm, Knapp
	Childs, Henry Robert	Moorland
	Coate, Charles Dare	Helland
	Coate, Frank	Thong Farm
	Coate, Henry Langford	Manor Farm
	Coate, Wilfred Daniel John	Borough Farm, Knapp
	Cox, Brian	Sunnyside, Lillesdon
	Cridge, Richard Metford	Pury Street Farm
	Dare, Brothers	Rose Farm, Knapp
	Dare, Charles	Bulpin's Farm, Higher Knapp
	Dare, Douglas Charles Robert	Nythe Farm
	Dare, John Robert	Helland
	Dare, Simeon Edmund	Clarke's Farm

Description	Name	Address in Directory
Farmer	David, Edwin	Lower Knapp Farm
	Derham, Charles B	Hillview, Wrantage
	Derham, Gilbert John	Lower Knapp
	Derham, Misses Florence & Bessie	Lower Knapp
	Duke, William	Greenway Farm
	Dunell, Robert John	Newport
	Hearn, George	Broad Lane Farm, Huntham
	Langford, William Henry (executors)	Lower Knapp
	Mitchem, Edgar	Lawnmoor
	Mitchem, Richard Welsh	Hill Farm, Knapp
	Moore, Samuel William	Hurman's Farm
	Palmer, Henry	Newbridge
	Pine, Albert	Payne's Farm
	Richards, George	Hammonds Farm, Lillesdon
	Sellick, Arthur George	Knapp
	Spearing, Frederick Francis	North Curry
	Stenson, John	White Street Farm
	Stone, Howard	Newport
	Upham, George Hooper	Ham
	Whittle, Herbert	Listock
Farmer Poultry	Derham, Miss Norah T	Lillesdon
Farrier	Loveridge, Arthur	White Street
Garage Proprietor	Foster, Eric Victor	North Curry
Grocer/Post Office	Goss, Wilfrid John	Hatch Beauchamp
Innkeeper	Baigent, George Thomas	Wrantage Inn
	Lock, Frederick	White Hart Inn
	Pipe, George Albert	Rising Sun Inn
	Staple, Frank	Canal Inn
	Tattle, George Henry	Bird in Hand
	Trim, Harry	Angel Inn
	Woodman, Charles John	Wheelwright's Arms, Stonyhead
Insurance Agent	Jones, Francis Llewellyn	North Curry
	Lunniss, Frederick Ernest	Knapp
Ironmonger	Gillard, Ewart Charles Wilkins	North Curry
Miller	Doble, Walter James	Hatch Beauchamp
Motor Engineer	Squire, Ottamere Rosewell	North Curry
Newsagent	Hutchings, George Henry	North Curry
Private Resident	Aitken, Col. John James, CMG DSO OBE	The Old Vicarage
	Baker, Cmdr Edmund H Buckingham, RN	The Cottage NC
	Barclay, Rev. Arthur Denny, BA	The Orchards
	Barrett, Mrs Gwerfyl	Moredon
	Barrington, Robert James	The Laurels
	Berthon, Mrs Alderson	The Thatch, Greenway
	Bodilly, Mrs	The Orchards, Greenway
	Burges, Misses	Moorlands
	Burgess, Charles	The Fosse
	Carr, David Leonard	Gables
	Chorley, John	Arden, Stoke Road
	Coates, Percy Brevitt	Hill Cottage
	Collis, Archibald William	3 Victoria Terrace
	Cookson, Mrs Violet E C	Jackless Cross
	Court, George Brabner	Oldways, Wrantage
	Cuvelier, Edward Augustus	Fosse Cottage
	Davies, Rev. Herbert Jocelyn, BA CF (TA)	The Vicarage

Description	Name	Address in Directory
Private Resident	Dove, Ernest Percy	Newport House
	Harding, Mrs John B	The Elms
	Hill, Major Hugh Tithe Copinger, MC	Knapp
	Lewis, Judge	Gordon House
	Lodge, Benjamin Ewart	North Curry
	Morris, Miss Ethel	Gwyon House
	Morris, Rodham Richard	1 Victoria Terrace
	Mould, Harry	North Curry
	Peard, Clifford James, DSO BA	The Croft
	Peard, John C N, MC BA	The Croft
	Preston, L H W	Hunts End
	Satchwell, Richard Eric, MB	Trevarrick House
	Starke, John	Collenette, Lillesdon
	Stobart, Mrs E F	North Curry Manor
	Tacchi, Miss	The Warren
	Warlow, Rev. George Edmund, MA	Calmady House
	Willcox, Alfred Edward	4 Victoria Terrace
	Wyatt, Rev Henry (Baptist)	2 Victoria Terrace
Saddler	Moulds, Henry Thomas	North Curry
Shopkeeper	Challenger, George Henry	London House
	Lunniss, Mrs Clara	Knapp
Shopkeeper/Post Office	Turner, Harold Cuthbert	North Curry
Smallholder	Derham, Mrs Laura	Ham
	Duke, George	Newport
	Duke, Thomas	Knapp Lane
	Duke, Thomas Edward	Knapp
	Dykes, Henry Philip	Lower Knapp
	Gridley, Mrs Elizabeth	Helland
	Lock, Howard H R	Underhill, Wrantage
	Norman, Herbert	Helland House
	Woodman, James	Knapp
Smith	Duke, Jesse	North Curry
Solicitor/Commissioner of Oaths	Winter Goode, William	North Curry
Stonemason	Duke, Edmund	Wrantage
Surgeon/Physician	Satchwell, Richard Eric, MB ChB (Public Vaccinator & Taunton Guardians Committee)	Trevarrick House
Surveyor/Auctioneer/Valuer /Land, House, Estate Agent	Morris, C R, Sons & Peard	North Curry
Tailor	Bellringer, Charles George	North Curry
Wheelwright	Hearle, Howard Edgar	North Curry
Willow Growers and Farmers	Derham, Stanley & Son	Foster's Farm, Knapp
Withy Grower	Denman, Charles	Sedgmoor
	Denman, John	Huntham
	Wembridge, Daniel	Listock

APPENDIX 4

HISTORIC ENVIRONMENT RECORD FOR NORTH CURRY – 2005

A Historic Environment Record (HER) is a regional record, generally county-based, of all known archaeological sites and events within that region. The list may also contain information on structures such as buildings, monuments, gravestones and bridges. Each site is given an individual entry on the record and is identified by a unique number.

There are currently 21,025 individual entries in the Somerset HER, and of those 6,530 relate to listed buildings whilst 592 are scheduled monuments. An online database gives detailed information of archaeological sites, events undertaken on them (excavations, surveys and watching briefs), scheduled monuments, listed buildings, registered landscapes and historic landscape character within the county of Somerset.

North Curry has 94 archaeological sites listed on the HER and a brief summary of those follows: North Curry Listed Buildings are dealt with in Chapter 2–5.

RECORD NUMBER	DESCRIPTION	HER NUMBER
1	Second World War stop line, The Taunton Stop Line	15410
2	Anti tank obstacles, Crimson Hill Tunnel	15411
3	Anti tank posts, SE of Wrantage	15412
4	Anti tank obstacles, Wrantage	15413
5	Canal aqueduct, N of Wrantage	15414
6	Anti tank obstacle, NW of Wrantage	15416
7	Concrete bases, East of Oakhill, Lillesdon	15417
8	Anti tank obstacles, S of Lillesdon	15418
9	Pillbox site, S of Lillesdon	15419
10	Vickers machine gun pillbox, W of Lillesdon Court, Lillesdon	15420
11	Road block site, W of Lillesdon Court	15421
12	Spoil heap, W of Lillesdon Court	15422
13	Anti tank obstacle, W of Lillesdon Court	15424
14	Evaluation (2002), Town Farm, North Curry	15613
15	Pillbox site, N of Weaver's Farm, Wrantage	15883
16	Pillbox site, Wrantage	15884
17	Pillbox site, Wrantage	15928
18	Farm site, Wrantage	15929
19	Anti tank ditch, N of Wrantage	15930
20	Musket ball and other finds, Stonyhead, Wrantage	15964
21	Cropmark ring ditch, S of New Barn , North Curry	16348
22	Second World War anti-tank island, Wrantage and Crimson Hill	16382
23	Pillbox site, NW of Lillesdon Court	16505
24	Watching brief (1988), North Curry Church	16710
25	Cropmark enclosures, S of New Barn, North Curry	16734
26	War Memorial, North Curry	16741
27	Resistivity Survey (2004), 260m south of New Barn Cottage, NC	16967
28	Pillbox, Hill View, Wrantage	18164
29	Watching brief (1999), 6 The Pavement, North Curry	35972
30	Deserted farm, NW of Frog Lane Farm, North Curry	43103
31	Flood bank, against Haymoor Old Rhyne, North Curry	43104
32	Duck Decoy, NNE of Moredon House, North Curry	43105
33	Deserted farm, SSW of Huntham, North Curry	43106
34	Trackway, West Sedgemoor, North Curry	43107
35	Enclosure on West Sedgemoor, North Curry	43108
36	Ridge and furrow, North Curry	43109
37	Church of St Peter and St Paul, churchyard and cross North Curry	43329
38	Roman coin hoard found 1798, Lillesdon	43330
39	Neolithic Flint implement find, North Curry	43331
40	Windmill site, S of Moredon North Curry	43332
41	Rod well, NE of Lillesdon	43333
42	Windmill site, NE of Lillesdon	43334
43	Corn mill, Newport	43335

Record Number	Description	HER Number
44	Duck decoy, N of Moredon House, North Curry	43336
45	Planned Borough of Newport	43337
46	Withy boiler, Knapp	43340
47	Pound, North Curry	43341
48	Cropmark enclosures, SW of New Barn, North Curry	43342
49	Landscape Park, Moredon House, North Curry	43344
50	Wind pump, NW of Frog Lane Farm, North Curry	43345
51	Engine or pump house, Moredon, North Curry	43346
52	Engine or pump house, Moredon, North Curry	43347
53	Palstave finds, North Curry	43348
54	Canal incline, SE of Higher Wrantage Farm, Wrantage	43836
55	Canal aqueduct, Higher Wrantage Farm, Wrantage	43837
56	Canal tunnel, W of Lillesdon Court, North Curry	43838
57	Cropmark features, New Barn	44190
58	Cropmarks, Lillesdon	44191
59	Beacon (field name), E of Rock	44253
60	Smithy, Wrantage	44254
61	Pillbox, NW of Lillesdon Court, Lillesdon	44303
62	Vickers machine gun pillbox, W of Lillesdon Court, Lillesdon	44305
63	Vickers machine gun pillbox, NW of Lillesdon Court, Lillesdon	44306
64	Vickers machine gun pillbox, NW of Lillesdon Court, Lillesdon	44320
65	Pillbox, NW of Lillesdon Court, Lillesdon	44325
66	Vickers machine gun pillbox, N of Honey Farm, Wrantage	44326
67	Vickers machine gun pillbox, N of Honey Farm, Wrantage	44327
68	Pillbox, N of Honey Farm, Wrantage	44328
69	Gun emplacement, N of Higher Wrantage Farm, Wrantage	44329
70	Pillbox, N of Higher Wrantage Farm, Wrantage	44330
71	Gun emplacement, E of Higher Wrantage Farm, Wrantage	44331
72	Pillbox, SE of Higher Wrantage Farm, Wrantage	44332
73	Pillbox, N of Crimson Hill Farm, Wrantage	44333
74	Pillbox, S of Ludwell's Farm, Wrantage	44334
75	Vickers machine gun pillbox, NE of Crimson Hill Farm, Wrantage	44335
76	Vickers machine gun pillbox, NE of Crimson Hill Farm, Wrantage	44336
77	Rectilinear cropmarks and rectangular enclosure, West Sedgemoor	44361
78	Anti tank obstacle, S of Lillesdon Court, Lillesdon	44545
79	Canal bridge and WW2 roadblock, N of Lillesdon Farm, Wrantage	44568
80	Post medieval building, Greenway, North Curry	44644
81	Flint finds, S of North Curry	44645
82	Flint tools and Bronze Age flint barbed and tanged arrowhead, S of NC	44646
83	ROC observation post site, S of Lillesdon	44669
84	ROC Orlit and underground monitoring posts, Crimson Hill, Wrantage	44670
85	Deserted settlement, S of Moredon House, North Curry	44691
86	Earthwork, Jackless Cross, North Curry	44693
87	Deserted settlement area, North Curry	44694
88	Cropmark boundaries, SE of Knapp	44695
89	Bronze-age pottery finds, SE of North Curry	44776
90	Chard Canal	53321
91	Pipeline watching brief (1991), North Curry to Stoke St Gregory	57107
92	Pipe trench watching brief (2000), North Curry Church	57168
93	Watching Brief (1992) Church of St Peter and St Paul, North Curry	90076
94	Pipeline watching brief (1997)	90089

APPENDIX 5

GLOSSARY

ACRE	From Anglo-Saxon *aecer*, meaning a piece of land of unspecified size. The term was originally used to imply a piece of land cleared for ploughing or grazing and later as a strip of open field, sufficiently large to be ploughed by a yoke of oxen in a day. Edward I standardised the acre as an area of land 40 rods long by four rods wide; a rod was five and a half yards. See also *Square Measure*.
ADVOWSON	The right to present a clergyman to a benefice, subject to the approval of a diocesan bishop. After 1164, a right of property.
AESTAL	It is believed that an *aestal* was some kind of special bookmark or pointer, and that the King Alfred Jewel is in fact one of these objects, missing the pointing part.
AISLE	From the Latin *ala* meaning wing; a lateral extension of a nave in a church. Part of a house separated from the main part by a row of posts.
ANNATES	A tax on the first year's income of a benefice which were paid to the Pope.
APEX	The top point of a roof truss.
APSE	A semicircular or polygonal shaped chapel extending anywhere beyond the walls of the main body of the church, usually at the eastern end.
ARCHBRACE	Curved bracing joining principal and collar of a truss to form an arch.
ASHLAR	Finely jointed smooth, square-hewn stone used to face rubble or bricks.
ASSIZE	The meeting of the King and his council. A national court sitting locally. Until 1972 a periodical county session for the administration of civil and criminal justice.
BAILIFF	The manorial lord's representative and estate manager, subordinate to the Steward.
BALDRIC(K)	Thick leather thong by which a clapper is attached to a bell.
BARTON	A farmyard.
BAY	A single structural unit or the space between roof trusses, usually 3.0 m; also a projecting window.
BEDDMAN	The west-country term for a Sexton.
BENEFICE	An ecclesiastical office or the income derived from it.
BIER	The movable stand on which a corpse is placed and carried to the grave before burial.
BLUE LIAS	Hard white/grey coloured liassic limestone.
BORDAR	A smallholding tenant with about ten acres of land and one of the lowest ranks of feudal society who was obliged to perform agricultural menial services for the lord free or for a fixed sum.
BOVATE	A variable measure normally considered to be one-eighth of a Hide. Alternatively called an *Oxgang*. See *Hide*.
BRESSUMER	A beam spanning an opening e.g. fireplace.
BURGAGE PLOTS	A tenure in an ancient borough which was held of the Crown or lords, and subject to customary rents or services.
BURGESS	Holder of land or house in a borough. A superior townsman paying rent for his property.
BUTTERY	Store for drink kept in butts; a general wet store.
BUTTRESS	Stone or brick support which gives additional strength to a wall and counteracts its outward thrust.
CALENDAR	An archival catalogue. A catalogue of documents with summaries of their contents.
CAMBER	Arching of a horizontal timber.
CANON	A member of a chapter of priests serving in a cathedral or collegiate church.
CARTULARY	A register of lands and privileges granted by charter, occasionally in rolls, but more often in book form.
CARUCA, CARUCATA	Latin term for a plough requiring a team of eight oxen.
CARUCAGE / HIDEAGE	A tax levied in 1194 on each carucate (hide) of land held, based on the information contained in the Domesday Book. In areas where Hide was used the tax was called Hideage. It was discontinued in 1224.
CARUCATE	See *Hide*.
CASEMENT	A side hung hinged window.
CATSLIDE	Sloping roof extended downwards to cover a ground floor extension or outshot.

CELL	One room in a plan.
CELLAR	Drink store, not necessarily underground.
CENSER OR THURIBLE	A metal vessel in which incense is burned. A thurible is usually suspended from chains by which it is swung.
CHAIN	A chain 22 yards long which was laid along the headland of a field to indicate the width of the area to be ploughed. From the headland the ploughman would plough furlongs of ten chains or 220 yards. See *Headland.*
CHAMBER	Any upper room.
CHAMFER	The small surface made by cutting away the angle of a timber along its length.
CHANCEL	Eastern continuation of the nave usually containing the altar and reserved for the clergy and the choir.
CHANCEL ARCH	Single span at the west end of the chancel, dividing it from the nave.
CHANTRY	An endowment for a priest ringing masses for the soul.
CHAPTER	The collective term for the body of canons. The word comes from the Latin *capitulum* and may have come into use because a chapter from a monastic rule was read daily to the assembled brethren.
CHARTER	A document recording a grant.
CHURCH ALE	A feast to commemorate the dedication of a church, at which ale was sold in aid of funds.
CHURCHWARDEN	A parish officer responsible for keeping the church and representing the people in parochial matters.
CIRCUMFERENTOR	A surveyor's angle-measuring compass instrument.
CLAPPER	The tongue of a bell.
CLOAM OVEN	An earthenware chamber set into hearth walls.
CLOSE	A hedged, fenced or walled enclosure.
COB	Walling material of compacted earth (mud), cow-muck, straw etc.
COLIBERT	A freed slave or freedman, usually given a small amount of land.
COLLAR (-BEAM)	Crossbeam linking opposite rafters. Horizontal beam connecting the mid-points of the sloping rafters of a pitched house. Horizontal member of A shaped truss.
COPE	A semi-circular cape worn over a cassock and surplice.
COPED VERGES	Covering stones over the edge of tiling above the end gable wall of a building.
COPYHOLD	Type of manorial tenure. Originally a tenure dependent upon custom and the lord's will, carrying obligations to perform certain services for the lord. These were later commuted to money payments. The tenant was protected by title written on the *Manor Court Rolls*, which he received a copy of. When transferring the property the tenant first surrendered it to the lord who held the fee-simple, and then the new tenant was admitted on payment of a fine.
CORBEL	A projection of stone, wood or brick supporting an arch, beam, parapet or moulding.
CORDWAINER	A leather worker or shoemaker.
CORNICE	A projecting decorative feature along the top of a wall. A plaster moulding round a ceiling.
COTE	An enclosure for sheep or cattle. A small cottage, isolated farmhouse or hut.
COTTAR	A cottager, the lowest of the main levels of peasant cultivators with five acres or less of land, and spending much of his time working for his lord either free or for a fixed sum.
COURT BARON	A manorial court which enforced the Customs of the Manor. It was the property of the lord and was a private jurisdiction. Originally the *Homage* or jury at meetings had to consist of at least two freeholders but later copyhold tenants formed the Homage.
COURT LEET	The term usually refers to a manorial court although it could also apply to a Hundred Court. It dealt with petty offences such as common nuisances or public affray, and with the maintenance of highways and ditches and the administration of communal agriculture. It was presided over by the lord. Each male over the age of 12 or 16 (depending upon local custom) was obliged to attend. The court met twice a year and appointed officials such as the Constable, Ale Tester and Pound Keeper. It was also responsible for the review of *Frankpledge.*
COURT ROLLS	Transfers or grants of land were recorded on the Rolls of the Court Baron.
CRANNOCK	An old English unit of volume for grain - roughly 10 bushels.
CROPMARKS	Differences in the growth and colour of a crop, observable sometimes from ground level and showing up more clearly in air photographs, which enable archaeological features to be traced.

CROSS-PASSAGE	Transverse passage with external door at front and back.
CROSS WING	A two-storied wing built at right angles to a hall.
CRUCKS	Curved or angled principal rafters from a single tree forming a structural frame extending from near ground level to apex.
CRUCKS (JOINTED)	Curved or angled principal rafters extending from near ground level to apex in two pieces.
CURING CHAMBER	An area or cupboard within the chimney where bacon is smoked.
CUSTOM(AL)	Traditional rules by which the manor was run, and the periodic reading of these rules as a reminder to the tenants.
CUSTOMARY TENANT	One whose tenure depended on the custom of the manor. When he died, his heir would be determined by this custom.
CUSTOMS OF THE MANOR	A set of locally established practices and rights in law which arise and are justified by their repeated operation rather than recorded as rights in written form.
DANEGELD	A tax raised prior to AD991, as tribute to the Danes to avert ravage of the land.
DCW	The Dean and Chapter of Wells. See *Landowner (DCW).*
DEAN	Presides over the Chapter of a cathedral From the Latin *decanus* meaning the chief of ten.
DEFALCATION	Misappropriation of money or funds held by an official, trustee, or other fiduciary.
DEMESNE	Land retained by the Lord of the Manor for his own use and upon which tenants gave free service according to the customs of the manor. Land which was part of the main farm of the manor.
DIOCESE	Territory of a bishop.
DOGLEG STAIR	A staircase with 180° turn and no central well.
DOLE	A share of a common meadow, distributed annually or periodically by lot or rotation, hence the phrase 'to dole out' or 'on the dole'.
DOMESDAY BOOK	A comprehensive record of property in England compiled in 1086 on the orders of William the Conqueror.
DORMER	A projection from the slope of a roof having its own roof, gabled, sloping or flat.
DORMER WINDOW	Window in a dormer.
DROVEWAY / DROVEROAD	A road of ancient origin not subject to toll and principally used for long-distance herding of cattle to market. Unenclosed road.
ECCLESIASTICAL COMMISSIONERS	The Ecclesiastical Commissioners were set up by Parliament in 1836 to reorganize dioceses, abolish surplus posts in cathedrals and take over both the responsibility for funding bishops and some cathedral costs, and the assets that had supported those responsibilities. In 1948 their work was taken over by the Church Commissioners.
ENCLOSURE	The conversion of landholding and agricultural practice from open field farming to compact holdings held by a single farmer.
ELEVATION	A façade; a drawing of a façade.
FANLIGHT	A window over a door.
FEE	Land or freehold property which could be inherited.
FEE SIMPLE	A freehold estate which passes without restriction to the lawful heir.
FEORM	A farm or holding that could provide one night's food and upkeep for the King's Court. By 1086 often commuted to cash.
FIELD NAME	A name given to a field. The practice originated in the early-13th century. In the 18th/19th century many fields were newly named and others were re-named.
FIELDWALKING	An activity when a group of people walk in a line across a tract of country searching for signs of ancient disturbance, scraps of worked flint, pottery, bone or metal.
FINIAL CROSS	A carved ornament on top of a pinnacle gable or spire.
FOSS(E)	A ditch or trench.
FRAMED CEILING	Panels formed of cross beams and edge beams etc.
FRANKLIN	A free tenant usually enjoying reasonable prosperity and often a Manorial Steward or Bailiff. The predecessor of the *Yeoman.*
FRANKPLEDGE	A system evolved in Anglo-Saxon times whereby each vill or area was divided into *tithings* of ten or twelve households which were held corporately responsible for each individual member's behaviour.
FREEHOLD	A tenure which was not subject to the customs of the manor or the will of the lord and which could be disposed of without restriction.
FREEMAN	A tenant who held land at a fixed rent and free of feudal service. Also known as *Sokeman.*

FURLONG	Originally the term meant the length of the furrow (furrow long) in the common field which was theoretically considered to be one side of a square of ten acres, i.e. 220 yards. The term was also applied to a rectangular block of parallel strips within an open field.
GABLE	A triangular end wall. The triangular upper part of a wall immediately beneath a ridge roof.
GENTLEMAN	A well-born man above the rank of yeoman, usually entitled to bear a coat of arms. It was assumed that a gentleman did not do manual work and the term gradually encompassed all those in the professions.
GLASTONBURY CHURCH CHAIR	A type of chair most commonly found in the chancels of parish churches, with the earliest examples from the mid-17th century. The components consist of shaped planks which are assembled by means of wooden pins.
GLEBE	Land held by a clergyman.
GREEN LANE / GREEN ROAD	A grassed right of way sometimes synonymous with a drove road.
GROUND-SILL / SILL-BEAM	The lowest member of a wall frame into which the posts and studs of the frame are tenoned.
GUARDIANS OF THE POOR	Members of a Board of Guardians established by the Poor Law Amendment Act 1834 to have charge of local administration of poor relief. See *Overseers of the Poor.*
HALL	All purpose room of a medieval house.
HATCHING	The drawing of parallel lines so as to produce the effect of shading.
HAM	A narrow strip of ground by the side of a river.
HAMMERSTONE	A stone or cobble used as a pounding or pecking tool.
HAMSTONE	A golden brown liassic limestone from Ham Hill in Somerset.
HEADLAND	A strip of land at the end of a ploughed field upon which the plough turned; the headland was then ploughed at right angles.
HIDE	This term originally signified the area of land that could be ploughed annually by a team of eight oxen, necessary to sustain a peasant household. Sometimes calculated to be 120 acres but in fact the hide varied according to locality, date, and government needs. This concept is discussed in some detail on page 21 of the main text. Alternatively called *Carucate, Husbandland, Ploughland, Ploughgate and Sulung.*
HIPPED ROOF	A pitched roof with sloped ends instead of vertical gables.
HOMAGE	The body of tenants acting as a jury at the manorial court.
HOODMOULD	Projecting moulding above an arch or lintel to throw off water.
HUNDRED	An administrative division of a shire, probably established in the 10th century, whose influence declined as parochial, manorial and judicial bodies became more important. It is thought to have originally contained a hundred families or ten tithings, or else a hundred taxable hides of land.
HUNDRED COURT	This Court, presided over by the Hundred Reeve, acted on behalf of the King and usually met monthly at an open place. It considered criminal offences, minor ecclesiastical matters and private pleas and also levied taxes. It first met in the 10th century.
HUNDREDMAN	The royal official in charge of a hundred.
HUNDRED ROLLS	County surveys or Crown rights and revenues.
IMPROPRIATOR	A lay person who received ecclesiastical benefices and the associated great or rectorial tithes.
INCLINED PLANE	A means of raising tub-boats from one level of a canal to another.
INGLENOOK	A bench or seat built within a large fireplace. Recess with seat beside fireplace.
INNER ROOM	Private room beyond the 'hall'.
INVENTORY	A detailed list of possessions, sometimes including a value of each.
JAMB	The side post of doorway, window or chimney-piece on which the lintel rests.
JETTY	Overhanging upper story of a house.
JOIST	A horizontal timber supporting floorboards.
KEYSTONE	The central tapering stone in an arch.
KNAP(P)	A hillock.
KNIGHT	The word derives from Old English *cniht* meaning servant. c. 1100 a knight became a lieutenant of the King or other superior, obliged to perform military service in exchange for lands granted to him, and evolving as lower nobility.

LANDOWNER (DCW)	Where specified in the1840 *Tithe Schedule* for North Curry and the 1863 *Rate Schedule* for North Curry, denotes a leaseholder or lessee under the Dean and Chapter of Wells.
LATH(ING)	Timber slats or reed; backing for plaster.
LEAN-TO ROOF	A roof with one slope only, built against a higher wall.
LEASEHOLD	Tenure held by lease, sometimes for a fixed number of years, or a number of 'lives' recorded in the original lease. When such a lease expired new terms or names could be added on payment of a fine.
LEAT / LEET	An artificial waterway to provide water for industrial and domestic purposes, e.g. for a mill wheel.
LEAZE / LEAS	Meadow land or a quantity of wheat from which impurities had been removed.
LIBER ALBUS	Latin for The White Book.
LIBER RUBER	Latin for The Red Book.
LIMEWASH	Mixture of quicklime, fat and water used as an external waterproof wall-covering.
LINCH / LINCHET	The turf between two strips of arable land in a common field.
LINENFOLD	Carving on early wooden panelling representing a piece of material folded vertically.
LINTEL	Timber or stone beam over an opening.
LONGHOUSE	A house with lower-end stalling for cattle.
LYNCHETS, STRIP	A series of low ridges or 'ledges' of earth formed by the continuous ploughing of a hillside and the gradual movement and accumulation of soil on the downward slope.
MANOR	An estate held by a landlord (not necessarily a titled person), who himself was a tenant of the Crown or a mesne lord. A manor could be part of a parish contiguous with its boundaries, or else be large enough to spread over more than one parish. The Lord of the Manor retained part of the land, called demesne, for his own use, while the rest was tenanted or else used for commons or waste.
MARK / MARC	A mark was 160 pennies, that is 13s.4d or two-thirds of a pound.
MEADE / MEAD	A meadow.
MERCHET	A payment from a tenant on the occasion of the marriage of his son or daughter.
MESSUAGE	A dwelling house with its outbuildings and land surrounding it. A capital messuage is a large dwelling house.
MINSTER	A religious community which served from the 7th century, prior to the development of ecclesiastical parishes, as a centre for conversion and administration.
MORTICE AND TENON	A carpentry joint with protruding male tenon fitting into a female mortice slot.
MOTTE AND BAILEY	A Norman castle. The motte was a mound upon which the lord's house or keep stood. The bailey was the forecourt surrounded by an earth wall.
MOULDING	A carved ornamental variety of contour.
MULLION	A vertical post or upright dividing a window into two or more lights.
MUNTIN	See *Plank and Muntin*.
NAVE	Main body or the western arm of the church in which the congregation is housed during services. Comprises the area between the chancel and the west end.
OEIL-DE-BOEUF OR OCULUS WINDOW	A round or oval window usually with radiating glazing bars.
OGEE	A moulding with 'S' shaped section.
OPEN FIREPLACE	Wide 16th-17th century fireplace opening; an inglenook if with seats.
OPEN HALL	Hall open from ground to roof, no first floor.
OPEN HEARTH	Fire base in the middle of a *hall* floor with no chimney.
ORDNANCE DATUM (O.D.)	The standard sea-level of the Ordnance Survey, now taken as mean sea-level at Newlyn, Cornwall.
ORIEL WINDOW	A curved or poly-sided window projecting from an upper floor.
OUTSHOT/OUTSHUT	An extension of the roof, at the same angle, to cover a service room. See also *lean-to*.
OVOLO	A rounded convex moulding, often a quarter section of a circle or an ellipse.
OVERLAND	A tenure which had no common rights attached to it.
OVERSEER OF THE POOR	An office established by the Poor Law Act 1597/8. Two persons were appointed yearly to levy a poor rate and supervise its distribution. See *Guardians of the Poor*.
OXGANG	A variable measure normally considered to be one-eighth of a Hide. Alternatively called a *Bovate*. See *Hide*.

PALL	A small linen cloth, from Latin *palla,* with which the chalice is covered at the Eucharist. A large cloth which is spread over a coffin during a funeral service. A pall-bearer was one of the mourners at a funeral who held the corners of the pall.
PANTILE	An 'S'-shaped roof tile with one curve larger then the other.
PANTRY	A general dry store.
PARAPET	A low wall erected above roof or eaves level of a tower or wall for reasons of safety or to conceal guttering.
PARISH	Originally a township or group of townships possessing its own church and parson, to whom it paid tithes and other ecclesiastical dues. A parish could contain one or several manors, and sometimes a manor was large enough to spread over more than one parish.
PARISH CLERK	A post originally appointed by the incumbent of the Church. Duties included arranging baptisms and communions, acting as Sexton, and ringing the church bell for service.
PARISH COUNCILS	Authorities established by the Local Government Act 1894. The Act specified that such bodies should be elected in rural areas with a population of over 300.
PEDIMENT	A gable above a classical portico.
PERCH	See Rod, Pole or Perch.
PETER'S PENCE	A tax of a penny for each hearth or house payable on Lammas Day or St Peter's Day (August 1st), imposed by the Pope in the 10th century.
PILASTER	A decorative column slightly projecting from a wall.
PILE	A building; single pile when one room deep; double pile when two rooms deep.
PISCINA	A basin, with a drain leading to the consecrated ground of the churchyard, used for washing sacred vessels. Some have a shelf called a credence. A piscina may be set into a wall, sill or floor, usually denoting that an altar stood there at some time.
PLANK AND MUNTIN	A type of non-structural timber partition which separated private rooms from the main living room. It consisted of alternate thick and thin planks, the latter set in grooves running vertically along the edges of the former.
PLINTH	Projecting stone/brick courses at foot of a wall.
PLOUGHLAND	See Hide.
POLE	See Rod, Pole or Perch.
PORTREEVE	The Reeve of a port (borough or town) - see Reeve.
POST AND TRUSS (BOX FRAME)	Timber-framing comprising wall posts, wall frames and roof trusses - not cruck construction.
POUND	An enclosure maintained either by the manor or vestry to confine stray animals.
PRESENTMENT	A jury's statement to a court on matters within its knowledge, or the report of the homage of a manorial court concerning alienations of land.
PRIESTS' HOLES	Secret hiding-places incorporated into the houses of Roman Catholic families in anticipation of religious persecution.
PURLIN	A horizontal beam running parallel to the ridge of a roof and carrying the common rafters. Trenched, tusk-tenoned, butt and clasped are forms of joint between purlin and truss.
QUERN	A stone device for milling by hand.
QUOIN	Dressed corner stone.
RAFTER	Timbers which run up the roof from wall plate to apex or ridge supported on the wall plate and purlins.
RENT ROLLS	A register of rents; includes the names of tenants and the amount of rent they paid.
REEVE	Usually a man of villein status elected by fellow tenants to organise the daily business of the manor.
RELIEVING ARCH	An arch incorporated in a wall to relieve superimposed weight.
RENDERING	Weatherproof skin for exterior wall.
REREDOS	A decorative stone or wood screen, usually supported on a shelf (predella) and covering the wall behind and above an altar, or filling the space between piers to the east of a sanctuary.
RHINE / RHYNE	Artificial drainage ditch from the Old English word *ryne* meaning water channel.
RIDGE BEAM / RIDGE PIECE	A horizontal timber at the roof apex, supporting the top ends of the rafters.
RIDGEWAY	A path along a ridge of land.
ROD, POLE OR PERCH	Originally a variable linear measure - of between 9 and 26 feet, but when standardised measured 16.5 feet.

ROLL	A document consisting of a number of single sheets (membranes) sewn end to end.
ROOD	When standardised an area measure of 40 square rods. An acre consisted of 4 roods. (A rood is different from a *rod* which is a measure of length). Also see *Square Measure*.
ROOD SCREEN	A decorative carved wooden or stone screen which divides the nave from the choir and chancel in medieval churches. The screen supported a rood loft above which was the rood beam upon which was supported the Great Rood or carved image of Christ crucified. The word Rood derives from the Old English *rod* meaning cross.
ROUGHCAST	Exterior wall coating of cement mixed with gravel.
RUBBLE / RANDOM RUBBLE	Unshaped stone. Walls built of stones of differing sizes, bound with mortar, sometimes laid in courses. Random rubble is arranged without any particular coursing or design.
RUMP	Members of the Commons of the Long Parliament who voted in 1648 to try Charles I and who declared the Commonwealth.
SASH WINDOW	Sliding window frame.
SCRATCH DIAL (MASS)	A medieval sundial which was lightly incised at eye level into the exterior south wall of a church. It was used to indicate the time for masses before mechanical clocks were used in the 15th century.
SECOND POOR	Poor people not in receipt of parish poor relief.
SEE	The official 'seat' of a bishop, hence the rank or position symbolised by a throne.
SEISIN	A feudal term denoting possession, rather than ownership, of a freehold estate in land.
SELION	A cultivated strip in an open field. It was ploughed in such a manner that the strip became a ridge with furrows on either side acting as drains.
SERF	An inhabitant with a status lower than that of a villein, who was annexed to the lord's person and could be sold to another person.
SERVICE ROOM	The domestic store room at the lower end of a medieval hall traditionally called the buttery or pantry.
SEXTON	An official paid by the parish responsible for grave digging, bell-ringing and odd jobs around the church.
SHERIFF	A Shire-reeve. He was the Crown's deputy and until the 14th century the main agent of the courts, responsible for royal revenues in the shire and for the county militia.
SHINGLE	A flat, wooden tile.
SHIRE / COUNTY COURT	A court consisting of freemen of the county, presided over by an earldorman in Saxon and early Norman times.
SLAVE	A class of bonded unfree tenant who was the property of the Lord of the Manor and absorbed into the serf class after the Norman Conquest. See *Serf*.
SMOKE BAY	A specially constructed timber-framed bay in a medieval hall house to channel smoke from open fires.
SMOKE HOOD	A plastered timber-framed hood or chimney with sloping front above the hearth in a medieval house to control smoke from an open fire.
SNECKED RUBBLE	Rubble walling construction which contains small stone blocks (snecks) which are laid to interrupt long vertical joints.
SOFFIT	The under-surface of a beam, arch or staircase.
SOKEMAN	See Freeman.
SOLAR	The private upper living room in a medieval house.
SPANDREL	The triangular space between the outer curve of an arch and a rectangular enclosure.
SPRINGER	A horizontal block on either side of an opening from which an arch rises.
SQUARE MEASURE (AREA)	The square measures of acres, roods and square perches translate to modern measurements as follows: 1 square perch =30.25 square yards or 272.25 square feet or 25.29 square metres 1 rood = 40 square perch (this is different from a *rod* which is a measure of length) 4 roods = 4840 sq. yards = 1 acre; 640 acres = 1 square mile In the 1840 *Tithe Schedule* a square perch is generally referred to as a perch (p), which is somewhat confusing.
STATIONS OF THE CROSS	The 14 incidents which occurred on Christ's last journey from Pilate's house to his Entombment.
STEWARD	The chief agent of the lord for the management of the manor.

STINTED COPYHOLD	A manorial tenure in which the cattle which a holder is allowed to pasture are limited to a specific number.
STOCK MONEY	Interest on rent received from land or interest from cash loans was used by the Churchwardens to distribute to the poor in the form of cash or cloth.
STOP	The decorative finish at the end of a chamfer or moulding. A variant is a step and runout stop.
STRING COURSE	A projecting horizontal stone/brick course along an exterior wall.
STUCCO	A plaster used for coating wall surfaces for moulding into architectural decoration or sculpture.
STUD	A non-structural vertical timber in the wall of a half timbered building.
TENEMENT	Any land or dwelling. Originally limited to land or dwellings held by a superior lord.
TENON	See Mortice and Tenon.
TERRACE (HOUSE)	Three or more houses linked in a row.
THEGN	Pre- Norman Conquest nobles below the level of an earl being local estate owners with at least five hides of land and a residence. Richer ones had grand halls behind large defences and were the backbone of the royal army.
TIEBEAM	A transverse timber linking the feet of paired rafters to prevent the roof from spreading.
TIMBER-FRAMED	A load bearing framework of timbers with the spaces in the framework filled with other materials.
TITHE	A tax of one-tenth, specifically a tenth part of the annual produce of land and labour. Formerly levied upon parishioners to support the clergy and the Church.
TITHING (TYTHING)	A land division once regarded as a tenth of a hundred. See *Hundred* and *Frankpledge*.
TORY	The word was first used as a nickname to dintinguish a group of aristocratic politicians from their Whig opponents in the late 17th century.
TRACERY	Openwork pattern of masonry or timber in an opening.
TRANSEPT	One arm of the crossing in a cruciform church.
TRUSS	The framing across a house from one wall post to another, usually spaced 3.0 m. apart. This framing extended from ground-sill to apex of roof.
TUN	An enclosure in Anglo-Saxon England. Later an isolated farm or village.
UNDERCROFT	A basement used for storage.
VERNACULAR	Traditional native style.
VERGE	The edge of the tiling projecting beyond the gable of a roof.
VESTRY	The governing body of a parish. The vestry appointed a Sexton, Churchwardens, Overseers of the Poor, Surveyors of Highways and Constables. This could be an Open Vestry, at which, in most cases, all male ratepayers spoke and voted, or a Select Vestry, at which members were nominated or co-opted.
VILLEIN	The highest class of dependent peasantry, often holding between 30 and 100 acres of land, who had rights to graze cattle and take hay on the commons, and to gather firewood cut timber to repair buildings, implements and fences. This involved working on the lord's demesne for one or more days a week. Neither he nor his daughter could marry without the lord's permission. Upon his death a heriot or fine was paid by his heirs.
VIRGATE	A variable measure normally considered to be a quarter of a Hide. Alternatively called a *yardland*. See *Hide*.
VOUSSOIR	A wedge-shaped stone in an arch.
WALL PLATE	Longitudinal timber along wall top to receive roof loads.
WATTLE AND DAUB	Walling of woven laths plastered with mud or dung.
WHIG	A nickname of uncertain origin applied to the aristocratic political party that was formed after 1688 to keep a check on royal power.
WINDBRACE	A brace, usually curved, running from the principal rafter to a purlin to stiffen the roof structure.
YARDLAND	A variable measure normally considered to be a quarter of a Hide. Alternatively called a *virgate*. See *Hide*.
YEOMAN	A free tenant, usually a prominent farmer. As he worked with his hands he could not be styled a gentleman but his status was above that of most other copyhold tenants.

Bibliography, Sources and References

Adkins, Lesley and Roy, *The Handbook of British Archaeology,* (Constable 1998), ISBN 0 09 478330 6
Alcock, N W, *Old Title Deeds,* (Phillimore 1986), ISBN 0 85033 593 0
Ashley, Mike, *British Monarchs,* (Robinson Publishing 1998), ISBN 1 84119 096 9
Aston, Michael & Burrow, Ian, *The Archaeology of Somerset,* (Somerset County Council 1982), ISBN 0 86183 028 8
Aston, Michael (ed), *Aspects of the Medieval Landscape of Somerset,* (Somerset County Council 1988), ISBN 0 86183 129 2
Aston, Michael, *Interpreting the Landscape,* (B T Batsford 1985), ISBN 0 415 15140 6
Barker, Ernest, *The Character of England,* (Oxford University Press 1950)
Barnard H C, *A Short History of English Education,* (University of London Press Ltd 1947)
Body, Geoffrey & Gallop, Roy, *The Parrett Navigation,* (Fiducia Press 2002), ISBN 0 946217 12 2
Bragg, William, *General Directory for the County of Somerset* (1840)
Breckon, Bill & Parker, Jeffrey, *Tracing the History of Houses,* (Countryside Books 1991), ISBN 1 85306 128 X
Bristow, Joy, *The Local Historian's Glossary of Words and Phrases,* (Countryside Books 2001), ISBN 1 85306 707 5
Brown, John, *Independent Witness,* (Taunton School 1997), ISBN 0 9530925 0 X
Brown, R J, *Timber-Framed Buildings of England,* (Robert Hale 1986), ISBN 0 7090 2591 2
Brunskill, R W, *Illustrated Handbook of Vernacular Architecture,* (Faber 1971), ISBN 0 571 11244 7
Brunskill, R W, *Brick Building in Britain,* (Victor Gollancz 1990), ISBN 0 575 06535 4
Brunskill, R W, *Traditional Buildings of Britain,* (Victor Gollancz Ltd 1981), ISBN 0 575 03616 8
Buchanan, C A, *The Bridgwater and Taunton Canal,* (Somerset Industrial Archaeological Society 1994)
Bulleid, Arthur, *The Lake Villages of Somerset,* (Glastonbury Antiquarian Society 1924)
Bush, Robin, *Jeboult's Taunton,* (Barracuda Books 1983), ISBN 0 86023 186 0
Bushell, H W D, *The Lamps of North Curry,* (Taunton Deane Borough Council 2001)
Calendar of the Manuscripts of the Dean and Chapter of Wells, (Historical Manuscripts Commission 1907)
Chapman, Colin R, *How Heavy, How Much and How Long?* (Lochin Publishing 1995), ISBN 1 873686 09 9
Clark, Sir George, *The Oxford History of England Vols I-XV,* (Oxford University Press 1971), ISBN 0 19 821716 1
Coleman-Smith, R & Pearson, T, *Excavations in the Donyatt Potteries,* (Phillimore 1988), ISBN 0 85033 502 7
Coles, Bryony and John, *Sweet Track to Glastonbury,* (Thames and Hudson 1986), ISBN 0 500 39022 3
Coles, J M & Orme, B J, *Prehistory of the Somerset Levels,* (Somerset Levels Project 1980), ISBN 0 9507122 0 5
Coles, J, Goodall A & Minnitt S, *Arthur Bulleid and the Glastonbury Lake Village,* (Somerset Levels Project 1992), ISBN 0 9507122 1 3
Collinson, John, *The History and Antiquities of the County of Somerset,* (1791)
Costen, Michael, *The Origins of Somerset,* (Manchester University Press 1992), ISBN 0 7190 3675 5
Cunnington, Pamela, *How Old is Your House,* (Alphabooks, 1980), ISBN 0 9506171 8 0
Davies, Norman, *The Isles – A History,* (Macmillan 1999), ISBN 0 333 69283 7
Dobson, D P, *The Archaeology of Somerset,* (Methuen 1931)
Domesday Book or Great Survey of England Facsimile of the part relating to Somerset, (Southampton O.S. 1862)
Domestic Buildings Research Group (Surrey), *Building Terms*
Dunning, R W (ed), *The Victoria History of the County of Somerset,* (1974–2004)
Dunning, Robert, *A History of Somerset,* (Phillimore 1983), ISBN 0 85033 461 6
Dunning, Robert, *Somerset in Domesday,* (Somerset County Council 1986), ISBN 0 86183 112 8
Dyer, James, *Discovering Archaeology in England and Wales,* (Shire 1997), ISBN 0 7478 0333 1
Ekwall, Eilert, *The Concise Dictionary of English Place-names,* (Oxford University Press 1959), ISBN 0 19 869103 3
Farrington, Susan Maria, *Wiveliscombe – A History,* (Colden Publications 2005), ISBN 0 9540992 1 4
Feiling, Keith, *A History of England,* (1973)
Fletcher, Ken, *The Somerset Levels and Moors,* (Somerset County Council 1991), ISBN 0 86183 195 0
Fraser, Antonia (ed), *The Lives of the Kings & Queens of England,* (Weidenfeld & Nicolson 1998)
Friar, Stephen, *The Local History Companion,* (Sutton Publishing 2001), ISBN 0 7509 2722 4
Gardiner, Juliet & Wenborn, Neil (eds), *The History Today Companion to British History,* (Collins & Brown 1995), ISBN 1 85585 1784
Gardiner, Juliet (ed), *Who's Who in British History,* (Collins & Brown 2000), ISBN 1 85585 882 7
Gathercole, Clare, *An archaeological assessment of Newport,* (Somerset County Council 2002)
Gentleman's Magazine Volume xviii, (1748)
Green, John Richard, *A Short History of the English People,* (Macmillan 1926)
Greenwood, C & J, *Somerset Delineated,* (Alan Sutton 1980), ISBN 0 904387 53 4
Hamlin J I & Whitby A J, *Baptists in Bridgwater,* (1937)
Harding, Joan M, *Four Centuries of Charlwood Houses,* (Charlwood Society 1976)

Harris, Richard, *Discovering Timber-Framed Buildings,* (Shire 1978), ISBN 0 85263 481 1
Haskell, Tony, *By Waterway to Taunton,* (Somerset Books 1994), ISBN 0 86183 260 4
Hey, David (ed), *The Oxford Companion to Local and Family History,* (Oxford University Press 1998), ISBN 0 19 860215 4
Hey, David, *Family Names and Family History,* (Hambledon & London 2000), ISBN 1 85285 255 0
Hickman, Philip, *North Curry Jubilee Photographic Albums* (1977)
Higgs, Edward, *A Clearer Sense of the Census,* (London: HMSO 1996), ISBN 0 11 440257 4
Hindle, Paul, *Maps for Historians,* (Phillimore 1998), ISBN 0 85033 934 0
Hodgkiss, A G, *Discovering Antique Maps,* (Shire 1983), ISBN 0 85263 581 8
Howat, G M D, *From Chatham to Churchill – British History 1760–1965,* (Nelson 1966)
Hunt T J & R R Sellman, *Aspects of Somerset History,* (Somerset County Council 1973)
Iredale, David & Barrett, John, *Discovering Your Old House,* (Shire 1994), ISBN 0 7478 0143 6
Iredale, David, *Enjoying Archives,* (Phillimore 1973), ISBN 0 85033 561 2
Kelly, *Directory of Somerset*, (Various editions between 1861 and 1939)
Kenworthy, J C, *The South Africa Wars, 1877 to 1879* (Research Paper)
Kirke, Albion, *North Curry,* (Sawtell, Sherborne 1932)
Leach, Peter, *Roman Somerset,* (The Dovecote Press 2001), ISBN 1 874336 93 8
Lee, Christopher, *This Sceptred Isle,* (Penguin Books/BBC Books 1997), ISBN 0 140 26133 8
List of Buildings of Special Architectural or Historic Interest, (Department of the Environment 1975)
Lunn, Chris, *The Ancient Borough of Newport, North Curry,* (Research Paper)
Malden, Richard H, *The Story of Wells Cathedral,* (Raphael Tuck & Sons 1947)
Mayberry, Tom & Binding, Hilary (eds), *Somerset – The Millennium Book,* (Somerset Books 1999), ISBN 0 86183 485 2
Mayberry, Tom, *The Vale of Taunton Past,* (Phillimore 1998), ISBN 1 86077 044 4
McCann, John, *Clay and Cob Buildings,* (Shire 2004), ISBN 0 7478 0579 2
McClure & Collins (eds), *Bede – Ecclesiastical History of the English People,* (Oxford University Press 1969), ISBN 0 19 283866 0
McGarvie, Michael, *Witham Friary,* (Frome Society for Local Study 1989)
Mee, Arthur (ed), *Somerset,* (Hodder & Stoughton, 1956)
Miles, Iain, *Bogs and Inundations…,* (Somerset Industrial Archaeological Society), ISBN 0 950977 667
Minnitt, Stephen & Coles, John, *The Lake Villages of Somerset,* (Glastonbury Antiquarian Society 1996), ISBN 0 9507122 3 X
Mitchell & Leys, *A History of the English People,* (Longmans, Green & Co 1950)
Morpurgo, J E (ed), *The Pelican History of England Nos. 1–9,* (Penguin Books from 1950)
Morris, *Directory of Somerset & Bristol* (1872)
Morris, John (ed), *Domesday Book – Somerset,* (Phillimore 1980), ISBN 0 85033 368 7
Moule, Thomas, *The County Maps of Old England,* (Studio Editions Ltd 1990), ISBN 1 85170 403 5
Munby, Lionel, *How Much is that Worth?,* (Phillimore 1989), ISBN 0 85033 741 0
North Curry Parish Magazines, (1903–2005)
North Curry Records including: Parish, Diocesan, Manorial, Estate, Quarter and Petty Session, Education, Water Transport Documents, North Curry Census Returns, Map and Schedules (Somerset County Record Office)
Olivey, Hugh P, *North Curry: Ancient Manor and Hundred,* (Barnicott & Pearce 1901)
Page, William (ed), The Victoria History of the County of Somerset, (1906, 1911)
Penoyre, Jane, *Traditional Houses of Somerset,* (Somerset Books 2005), ISBN 0 86183 407 0
Pevsner, Nikolaus, *Buildings of England, South and West Somerset,* (Penguin Books 1958), ISBN 0 14 071014 0
Phillips, Donald, *Private Collection of Photographs of Moredon and the Barrett family*
Powell, Christopher, *Discovering Cottage Architecture,* (Shire 1984), ISBN 0 85263 673 3
Preest, David (Trans), *William of Malmesbury – The Deeds of the Bishops of England,* (The Boydell Press 2002), ISBN 0 85115 884 6
Price, Mary & Mather C E L, *A Portrait of Britain 1485–1688,* (Oxford University Press 1954),
Pring, The Reverend Daniel J, *Early Christianity in Somerset,* (Research Paper)
Pring, The Reverend Daniel J, *The Cathedral of the Moors,* (The Phoenix Press 1930)
Proceedings of the Somerset Archaeological and Natural History Society, (SANHS – 1851 to 2005)
Quennell, Marjorie and C H B, *A History of Everyday Things in England Vols I–V,* (B T Batsford Ltd 1960),
Ransome, Cyril, *An Advanced History of England,* (Rivingtons 1913)
Richards, Denis, *Britain under the Tudors and Stuarts,* (Longman 1958), ISBN 0 582 31484 4
Richards, Denis & Quick, Anthony, *Britain 1714–1851,* (Longman 1961)
Richardson, John, *The Local Historians' Encyclopaedia,* (Historical Publications 1999), ISBN 0 9503656 7 X
Ridgway, Heather, *Langport – The Heart of Somerset,* (Wessex House Press 1994), ISBN 0 9524730 0 3
Roots, Ivan (ed), *The Monmouth Rising,* (Devon Books 1986), ISBN 0 86114 779 0
Smith, David, *Maps and Plans,* (B T Batsford Ltd 1988), ISBN 0 7134 5191 2
Somerset County Gazette

Somerset County Herald
Somerset Historic Environment Record (HER), (Somerset County Council)
Somerset Notes and Queries Volume XX, (1931)
Somerset Vernacular Building Research Group, *Reports, in particular those by E H D Williams and R G Gilson*
Somerset Vernacular Building Research Group, *Glossary of Architectural Terms*
Stuart, Denis, *Manorial Records,* (Phillimore 1992), ISBN 0 85033 821 2
Sutherland, Patrick & Nicolson, Adam, *Wetland – Life in the Somerset Levels,* (Mermaid Books 1986), ISBN 0 7181 2897 4
Tate, W E, *The Parish Chest,* (Phillimore 1983), ISBN 0 85033 507 8
Taylor, Richard, *How to Read a Church,* (Rider 2003), ISBN 1 8441 3238 2
The Connoisseur Magazine,(1930)
Trevelyan, G M, *A Shortened History of England,* (Penguin Books 1959), ISBN 0 14020443 1
Trevelyan, G M, *English Social History,* (Penguin Books 1967)
Waters, Colin, *A Dictionary of Old Trades, Titles and Occupations,* (Countryside Books 1999), ISBN 1 85306 601 X
West, John, *Village Records,* (Phillimore 1997), ISBN 1 86077 040 1
West, Trudy, *The Timber-frame House in England,* (David and Charles 1971), ISBN 0 7153 4979 1
Williams, Michael, *The Draining of the Somerset Levels,* (Cambridge University Press 1970), ISBN 521 07486 X
Williams, Robin and Romey, *The Somerset Levels,* (Ex Libris Press 1992), ISBN 0 948578 38 6
Williams-Ellis, Amabel & Fisher F J, *A History of English Life,* (Methuen 1936)
Wood, Eric S, *Field Guide to Archaeology in Britain,* (Collins 1963), ISBN 0 00 219235 7
Wood, Michael, *Domesday – A Search for the Roots of England,* (BBC 1987)
www.northcurry.com
www.somerset.gov.uk/heritage
www.tauntondeane.gov.uk
Yorke, Trevor, *Tracing the History of Villages,* (Countryside Books 2001), ISBN 1 85306 712 1

Documents, Maps and Objects photographed by courtesy of Somerset County Record Office (SCRO), Somerset County Museum (SCM), Somerset Studies Library (SSL) and Wells Cathedral Library and Archives (Wells)

Description	*Source/Reference*	*Page*
1717 North Curry Window Tax Ratepayers	*SCRO DD/SF (3114) H/145*	90
1840 North Curry Tithe Apportionment – page 44	*SCRO D/D/Rt 365*	139
1843 North Curry Tithe Map (Inset of centre of village)	*SCRO DD/CC/T/10865B*	139
1577 Will of Thomas Smith of Lilsdon	*SCRO D/D/Ct-Sp*	153
1863-1870 Log Book of North Curry School – page 42	*SCRO D/P/Cur.n 18/11/1*	166
1840 North Curry Map of Curry Tithing (Top Inset of River Tone)	*SCRO D/P/Cur.n 3/2/5*	173
1709 Petition from Conservators of River Tone regarding Knapp Bridge	*SCRO DD/MK/49*	174
1773 Portman Estate map of North Curry (section)	*SCRO DD/PR 58*	203
Athelred II coin, George III gold half-guinea, Roman coins, flint arrowhead, flint blades, Bronze palstave, Newport mace	*SCM*	i
1575 Saxton's Map of Somerset	*SSL*	ix
Domesday Book in Facsimile (extracts)	*SSL*	x
North Curry Charter 1199	*Wells*	xi
1539-1720 North Curry Baptisms, Marriage, Burials Register – 1668, 1669 entries	*SCRO D/P/Cur.n 2/1/1*	xii
1666-1723 North Curry Churchwardens' Account Book – 1678 Rates entry	*SCRO D/P/Cur.n 4/1/3*	xii
1296 Document relating to defalcation in collection of tenths for North Curry Hundred due to Edward I	*SCRO DD/X/RY1 C/955*	xii
1584 Will of William Smith of Lilsdon	*SCRO D/D/Ct-Sp*	xiii
1590 Inventory of William Smith of Lilsdon	*SCRO D/D/Ct-Sp*	xiii
1837 Will of William Barrett of Moredon	*SCRO DD/AY 104 1-11*	xiii
1871 Inventory and valuation of Sophia Gould of Moredon	*SCRO DD/AY 104 1-11*	xiii
1787 Survey Map of the Manors of North Curry, Wrantage, Knap-fee and Newport Borough	*SCRO DD/CC/T/10867*	xiv
1840 Tithe Map of Curry Tything (section of village centre)	*SCRO D/P/Cur.n 3/2/5*	xv
1782 Day and Masters Map of Somerset	*SSL*	Cover

GENERAL INDEX

(FOR SOMERSET SURNAME INDEX SEE PAGE 235)

A

B

C

D

T

U

V

W

Y

Z

ACKNOWLEDGEMENTS

In writing this book it has been necessary to research a vast range of material for details that have been recorded and written about the village. Many people have provided me with their own personal research data and I have called upon others to recall past incidents and happenings when written documentation has not been available. Inevitably it has been necessary to seek the assistance of some professionals engaged in history and associated fields and their help has been invaluable. Firstly my thanks go to all of the staff at the Somerset County Record Office, especially to Tom Mayberry, County Archivist and County Heritage Officer, Somerset County Council, who I mentioned in my Introduction. I thank David Bromwich, Somerset Studies Librarian and Honorary Librarian of the Somerset Archaeological and Natural History Society for allowing me to call upon his encyclopaedic knowledge of Somerset history and also for his meticulous reading of my early text. I also thank David Dawson, former Somerset County Museums Officer; Steve Minnitt, Head of Museums, Somerset County Museums; Bob Croft, County Archaeologist for Somerset and Richard Coleman-Smith who all helped me to understand the rudiments of archaeology in the early days of my research.

I am grateful to Mark Crouch, Short Run Press; John Dallimore, Somerset Vernacular Buildings Research Group (SVBRG); David Greenfield; Di Hartnell, Conservation Officer, Taunton Deane Borough Council; George Howard, Domestic Buildings Research Group - Surrey (DBRG); Iain and Mary Miles; Frances Neale, former Archivist, Wells Cathedral Library and Chris Webster, Somerset Historic Environment Record Manager; who have all contributed to my understanding and knowledge from their particular fields of expertise.

Many people in or associated with the parish of North Curry have provided a wealth of information. The Reverend Charles Townshend, Colin Waltham, and the late Peter Matthews all contributed enormously to my understanding of church matters here in the village. The owners of many of the houses described in the text have been kind enough to allow me access to their properties in the course of my research and I hope they will find my observations of interest. Donald Phillips, formerly of Moredon and a Barrett descendant, has helped me considerably with the story of the Barrett family. Marigold de Winton has assisted me with the dwellings maps. Eleanor Greeves has provided chapel sketches. Yvette Bennett, Stanley Derham, Geoffrey Durrant, Tom Jeanes, Betty Koppa, David Ryan, George Satchwell, Elizabeth Smith, Tina Stodgell, John Treble, the late John Webb and many more have all provided valuable input. I extend my heartfelt thanks to all of these contributors and the many others I have not mentioned. I hope they will gain some satisfaction from finding much of the information they imparted has been documented for posterity.

The majority of the photographs in this book were taken by Julian Comrie who I thanked in my Introduction. I must also thank Brian Dix, Tim Hale, Philip Hickman, Antonia Keith-Welsh, Richard Neale and Donald Phillips for the additional photographs provided by them.

Angela Dix

North Curry
October 2006